S0-FUF-504

THE POST
VICTORIANS

THE POST VICTORIANS

WITH AN INTRODUCTION
BY
THE VERY REVEREND W. R. INGE

Essay Index Reprint Series

 BOOKS FOR LIBRARIES PRESS
FREEPORT, NEW YORK

Framingham State College
Framingham, Massachusetts

First Published 1933
Reprinted 1972

Library of Congress Cataloging in Publication Data
Main entry under title:

The post Victorians.

   (Essay index reprint series)
   Reprint of the 1933 ed.
   1. Gt. Brit.--Biography.
CT783.P6   1972   942.08'0922   77-37791
ISBN 0-8369-2618-8

PRINTED IN THE UNITED STATES OF AMERICA
BY
NEW WORLD BOOK MANUFACTURING CO., INC.
HALLANDALE, FLORIDA 33009

CONTENTS

SUBJECT	AUTHOR	
INTRODUCTION . .	The Very Reverend W. R. Inge	vii
LORD BALFOUR . .	The Earl of Midleton . .	1
CANON BARNETT . .	Sir Reginald Kennedy-Cox .	21
WILLIAM BATESON .	J. H. Priestley . . .	37
GERTRUDE BELL . .	Sir E. Denison Ross . .	57
ARNOLD BENNETT .	Robert Lynd . . .	69
LORD BIRKENHEAD .	Sir Claud Schuster . .	83
JOSEPH CHAMBERLAIN .	Sir Fabian Ware . .	101
JOSEPH CONRAD . .	F. Tennyson Jesse . .	117
LORD CURZON OF KEDLESTON . . .	Sir Ian Malcolm . .	129
RANDALL THOMAS DAVIDSON	Sidney Dark . . .	141
LORD FISHER . .	Herbert Sidebotham . .	155
JOHN GALSWORTHY .	Hugh Walpole . . .	173
EARL HAIG . .	Henry W. Nevinson . .	187
LORD HALDANE . .	Shane Leslie . . .	203
KEIR HARDIE . .	James Maxton . . .	225
OLIVER HEAVISIDE .	Richard Whiddington .	241
W. H. HUDSON . .	H. J. Massingham . .	255
LORD KITCHENER .	Sir Ian Hamilton . .	273
ANDREW BONAR LAW .	Quintin Hogg . . .	295
DAVID HERBERT LAWRENCE . . .	R. L. Mégroz . . .	315
SIR THOMAS LIPTON .	William Blackwood . .	329
MARIE LLOYD . .	James Agate . . .	343

v

CONTENTS

SUBJECT	AUTHOR	
SIR EDWARD MARSHALL-HALL	Raglan Somerset	361
MARGARET MCMILLAN	Margaret G. Bondfield	375
LORD MILNER	Sir Edward Grigg	391
GEORGE MOORE	Humbert Wolfe	411
LORD NORTHCLIFFE	R. D. Blumenfeld	425
SIR WILLIAM ORPEN	C. R. W. Nevinson	443
LORD OXFORD AND ASQUITH	Rosslyn Mitchell	463
MRS. PANKHURST	Rebecca West	477
SIR CHARLES PARSONS	E. Kitson Clark	501
EARL ROBERTS	Sir John Fortescue	519
SCOTT OF THE ANTARCTIC	R. C. Sherriff	535
C. P. SCOTT	Ivor Brown	549
SIR HENRY SEGRAVE	J. Wentworth Day	563
LYTTON STRACHEY	Bonamy Dobrée	575
ELLEN TERRY	Marguerite Steen	591
SIR HERBERT BEERBOHM TREE	George Burns	605
ARTHUR BINGHAM WALKLEY	Harold Child	619
JAMES WHITE	Alan Bott	633

INTRODUCTION

By THE VERY REVEREND W. R. INGE

THE criticism will certainly be made that these " Post-Victorians " belong to three generations. The oldest of them might well be the grandfathers of the youngest. Those who were born between 1850 and 1870 were no more Post-Victorians than I am. They were, as I am, entirely unrepentant Victorians, thankful to have seen the light in one of the great eras of English history.

We all enjoy putting the household gods of our parents into a cupboard, or setting them up as an Aunt Sally. Our forefathers did the same. " I fear," wrote Renan shortly before his death, " that the work of the twentieth century will consist in taking out of the waste-paper basket a multitude of excellent ideas which the nineteenth century has heedlessly thrown into it." For a whole generation there has been an ungracious fashion to use " Victorian " as a term of abuse or contempt; though as the old Queen reigned for more than sixty years, and as those years were years of rapid change, it might be worth while for these Post-Victorians to explain whether it is the generation of Melbourne and Palmerston or that of Gladstone and Disraeli which moves their scorn. But the Victorians are already becoming too remote in time to arouse violent emotions. The young are beginning to see merits in Tennyson, Anthony Trollope, and William Morris just because they heard their parents disparage them. We shall soon see rooms decorated in the early Victorian style. The time may even come when the nineteenth century will be called, not disrespectfully, the middle age of modern history, to distinguish it from the meddle and muddle age which followed it.

The habit of dividing history into epochs, each with its label, is convenient but misleading. The business of the historian is to carve the past at the joints. But what if there are no joints? " The timid man," says Anatole France,

" dreads as a future cataclysm a change which began before his birth, which is going on under his eyes, though he does not see it, and which will become apparent a century hence." This is eminently true of English history. "We live in an age of transition." This sapient remark, I believe, was first made by Adam to Eve as they walked out of Paradise. "How wise you always are, Adam," said his wife, who did not wish to talk about apples and serpents.

Still, the river of history has rapids, pools, and shallows. In our period we may pick out two dates which really indicate considerable changes. The first is either 1897, the year of the second Jubilee, or 1901, the year of the old Queen's death. The second is 1914, which saw the beginning of the Great War. The Great War gave civilisation a severe shake, and generated revolutions almost everywhere. We are in the middle of ours. We do not shoot or guillotine people, or proclaim a "Year One"; but we do things pretty thoroughly in our own way.

But what on earth am I to make of this queer list of names? I have never been set a more difficult task. Am I to say that these men and women were, in their different ways, typical of the time in which they lived? But I have already objected that some of them were bald or grey-haired before others were born. Or shall I say that they were typical of their country? But they were totally unlike each other. Perhaps this makes them typical Britons; for really it is difficult to say what the national character is. The Englishman not only lives on an island, he is an island. I do not think that there is any quality, good or bad, that I have not heard attributed to my countrymen, except perhaps meekness and loquacity.

Lastly, were they, all or any of them, really great? Carlyle's "heroes" are out of fashion. H. G. Wells and Lytton Strachey will not let us burn incense before any great men. They take a vicious pleasure in knocking them off their pedestals. What was Alexander the Great but a petulant schoolboy, who, as was said by an unsuccessful imitator, invaded the women's quarters in Asia, and prudently left the virile West alone? And what was Napoleon but a *condottiere* thrown up by the French Revolution, a cad always and at last a madman? The world, we are told, knows nothing of its greatest men, and it is true that by the

INTRODUCTION

time the world hears of them they have often ceased to be great. The world itself takes care of that. If a man does anything very well, there is a general conspiracy to prevent him from doing it again. As for public recognition, no one can pretend that the garlands are placed on the right brows. As Sir William Harcourt remarked: " Some men deserve honours and do not get them, and others get them without deserving them; so that [as he added] on the whole justice is done." Sometimes the next generation redresses the undeserved neglect suffered by the great man in his lifetime. More often it throws mud upon those who really deserved their reputation. For a great man is always linked to his age by the weakest part of his mind, and where the next generation revolts against the prejudices of its parents, it takes its revenge upon the most conspicuous names which are popularly associated with these discarded beliefs.

Are the Post-Victorians, taking them at their best, as great as the eminent Victorians? I think, on the whole, that they are not. Carlyle used to place before him a portrait of the man whom he was describing, and I suspect that Ludwig makes use of photographs in composing his biographies. Well, the Victorian worthies seem to me finer-looking men than their successors. It would be difficult to match such heads as Tennyson, Darwin, Lord Lawrence, Leighton, Manning, Martineau, Bishop Selwyn, Gladstone, and others whom one might name. No doubt the greater crowd of respectable mediocrities seems to depress the stature of our modern giants, if we have any giants. But it seems to me that it is only in natural science that we continue to produce minds indisputably of the first rank.

Samuel Butler (of *Hudibras*, not *Erewhon*) said: " This age will make a very pretty farce for the next, if it have wit enough to make use of it." This is a remark which might be made about any age; and it does not require much wit in an historian to scold the men of the past for not foreseeing and averting consequences which were often both unpredictable and inevitable. But those who were responsible for the Great War brewed a broth which few were prepared for. Victorian Liberalism and Democracy have been discredited and almost destroyed. Popular government is falling into contempt. Who now reads the parliamentary debates which every Victorian *pater familias* devoured religiously with his breakfast? As an able writer predicted ten years ago:

> "We may be moving to an organisation of the world under a power which combines the characteristics of a political despotism and a great commercial trust. Everything which tends to make life disorderly and miserable makes such a consummation more possible; for if the choice is between chaos and despotism, most men in the long run prefer despotism. The one hope for the world seems to be that we should not pass into the state of violent struggle, whether war between nations or class war" (*Times Literary Supplement*, March 29, 1923).

The plain fact surely is that popular government is impossible unless there is a fundamental unity, a deep loyalty, underlying legitimate political differences. Sectional treasons, implacable feuds, crack-brained fads, are fatal to democracy. These descriptive tendencies became apparent in England in the reign of Edward VII, a feverish and unwholesome time when we were drifting unconsciously towards the abyss which yawned before us. As Burke said: "It is ordained in the eternal constitution of things that men of intemperate minds cannot be free." It is better for men of intemperate minds not to be free; but unfortunately they destroy the freedom of their fellow-citizens. Tyranny is the Nemesis of lawlessness, Fascism is a shield against the ruin of civilisation by the submen of the great towns and a few misguided intellectuals.

It is a race between peaceable emergence of a new order and violent revolution. I have not much doubt that we shall escape the latter disaster, since applied science has already put into our hands the means of material comfort for all. But prophecy is not my business in this introduction. "The future being not yet born, we will abstain from baptising it."

Among all short biographies none pleases me so much as Mr. Walpole's "John Galsworthy," perhaps partly because Galsworthy is a bridge between the pre-War and the post-War worlds. It is the fashion for the newest critics, who, fortified by their mutual admiration, are astonishingly rude to their seniors, to sneer at Galsworthy in the intervals

INTRODUCTION

of babbling in chorus about the " genius " of some salacious *détraqué*. That Galsworthy's novels are cold, without spiritual life or religious faith, cannot be denied; nor can it be disputed that his fastidious isolation kept him outside the interests of the younger generation. The very slang talked by his characters is fifteen years out of date. But his reputation on the Continent, much higher than at home, will be enduring, because he gives an admirable picture of the English business man and his circle in the opening years of the century. Future ages will find a sort of grim, Assyrian beauty in that tall-hatted, frock-coated figure, which dominated society when Edward was king. Now he is gone; old Jolyon Forsyte no longer " has a way with him " at board meetings, and Soames has probably lost his money. What is interesting from our present point of view is that Galsworthy begins by hating Soames, and apparently means us to sympathise with the bounder Bosinney and the " female cad " (an excellent characterisation, this by Mr. Walpole) Irene. But when Soames is no longer top-dog, his creator begins to like him, as his readers have done all through. The prosaic, honourable bourgeois is odious only when he sets the tone of society. The Forsytes were not a bad lot, after all.

It was a mistake to leave out Sam Butler, and I should have found room for Conan Doyle and Bishop Gore. But the list is a representative one, though it contains one name which the next generation may be glad to forget. There are of course many others who ought to be included, but for the fact that they happen to be still alive. This restriction rather spoils the portrait gallery; and the chivalrous maxim *de mortuis nil nisi bonum* has made some of the pictures not quite lifelike. But it is a very interesting collection, and it gave me pleasure to see justice done to more than one of my personal friends.

W. R. INGE.

THE DEANERY,
   ST. PAUL'S.
July 1933.

LORD BALFOUR
1848-1930

By
THE EARL OF MIDLETON

LORD BALFOUR

by THE EARL OF MIDLETON

TO exclude a statesman from a place among Victorian notabilities who in 1901 had been twenty-seven years in Parliament and a leader of the House of Commons for ten years is at first sight strange. If Lord Balfour, who had done some of his finest work for the country before he was fifty, had fared like his contemporary Lord Rosebery, he must have figured under Queen Victoria, or not at all; for despite the splendid early promise of Lord Rosebery's remarkable career, there was no return from the Elba of 1897. The fates were kinder to the one than to the other.

Apart from chronology, by no stretch of the imagination could Arthur Balfour be ranked among Victorians. The whole habit of his mind was alien to the rigidity of the nineteenth century. Society had reacted to dullness from the dissoluteness of the Regency, and Arthur Balfour was as far from being dull as he was from being dissolute.

Politics after Waterloo had fallen from great foreign problems to domestic economy; Arthur Balfour, who was at home in the fate of nations, had no head for figures, national or domestic; indeed, his personal fortune was seriously reduced during his long tenure of his estates. The literary controversies of the Victorian age no doubt attracted a man of his philosophic temperament, but surely after fifty years' immersion in politics the aphorism that, despite an intensive study of philosophy, " cheerfulness will come breaking in " is not inapplicable in his case.

In truth Arthur Balfour was a striking example, and might even be regarded as the protagonist, of the post-Victorian mind. Personally a man of correct principle and with high standards of life, he had not a trace of Puritanism in his composition. Lax views did not repel him. In matters of conduct every man and woman must be a law unto themselves. Indeed, though he knew clearly what he believed to be right, he was not prepared to denounce the opposite as wrong for others. Cast in such a mould, he was amused by the haphazard frankness of the twentieth century, and wasted neither time nor thought on the abandoned tenets of the society in which he had been brought up.

This detachment made itself felt at every stage of his life. If it is true to say of a statesman that *nascitur non fit*, it is interesting to consider whether any other modern Prime Minister, after neglecting the obvious path to fame, found himself shepherded into it by events. Disraeli, though not born to the purple, risked all that he had, and a good deal of money which he had not, to obtain a political opening. Gladstone marked himself out for statesmanship from his earliest days at the Oxford Union. Lord Salisbury graduated in the same sphere. Lord Hartington, bored as he was with his own speeches, listened to others when he would rather have been at Newmarket or Bolton.

But these were of the older school. The younger men followed their example. Lord Rosebery and Lord Lansdowne, both contemporaries of Balfour, lost not a moment in the pursuit of public life, and the Midlothian Campaign had made Lord Rosebery a power before Balfour's name was known to the political world. Balfour's story, as told by himself in his—alas, unfinished—memoirs, gives a happiness and fullness to his early life, but is from the public standpoint jejune. Apparently he had in early days neither interest nor ambition in regard to serving his country. His grandfather and his father had sat for Scotch seats; his mother had hereditary political interests; he had means, leisure, and ability; but the "books and good company, games, scenery, and music, which with philosophy filled his time and thoughts at Cambridge" seemed to have satisfied his energies for five years afterwards. He possessed large estates both in the Highlands and Lowlands, but we do not hear that he undertook any local duties. Instead he writes of this period as one " of no dominant occupations, unless that of ' the meditations intermittently pursued though never abandoned on the best way of giving effect to my philosophic ambitions.' "

There was a moment in Chatham's life when his only outlook was that of a "Cornet of Horse"; Talleyrand narrowly missed the seclusion of the cowl; Wellington, before the Peninsular Campaign, seemed fated to be buried in the oblivion which is the natural fate of Irish Chief Secretaries. Apparently at the moment when, as Balfour tells us, his " political ambitions were so cool " that he was well content to let things slide, fate in the shape of a family pocket borough took a hand.

The episode in itself was humorous enough. Lord Salisbury, an uncle with whom Balfour was on intimate and affectionate terms, figured in 1874 among the most prominent politicians of the day. His antipathy to Gladstone, whose great Ministry of 1868 was drawing to a close, was almost an obsession, believing as he did that Gladstone's policy, both at home and abroad, would bring the country to ruin. But Lord Salisbury, according to the narrator, as many of us afterwards learned, never gave advice unasked. It had apparently never occurred to Balfour that he might " seriously discuss with him either his political opinions or his political future," and unless Hertford had happened at this time to require a member, it seems likely that Balfour would for another six years have resumed his philosophic studies and country enjoyments. Indeed, his name meant so little to the Conservative Whips that when later in 1875 they were discussing with Lady Salisbury the names of new M.P.s to be included in the magnificent hospitalities of Arlington Street, they cut out her nephew's name, as being that of an untried local man, who was unlikely to take politics seriously. From their standpoint they were at the moment not far wrong.

To read Balfour's own account of his first Parliament, 1874–1880, the effect, viewed from the experience of his later life, is one of broad farce. The Conservative Party had a majority for the first time for many years, normally only about 40, but still a majority. How was it composed? It was not necessary for a member of the " stupid party " to be an orator, or even to go through the ordeal of public meetings. Lord Wemyss who, as Lord Elcho, sat in the House of Commons 1843–1883, and who not infrequently spoke half a dozen times in the same evening in Parliament, left it on record as a striking instance of self-denial that he had only made nineteen political speeches outside Parliament in forty years! Nine out of ten of the double-member seats which formed the mass of the constituencies were filled by stout country gentlemen, with a sprinkling of successful business men, who had no gift of speech of any description.

In this milieu the young gifted scion of a political family might have been expected to fill the too patent gap. Not at all. In his first two sessions he was writing *Philosophic Doubt*. Before the end of his second, he had given Parliament the go-by in order to visit Canada and Australia, a trip undertaken at a time of great personal sadness and preoccupation, of which his chief reminiscence in after life was the *mal de mer* which accompanied it. He strolled back to England to join the House of Commons when it was a third of the way through his third session. Different indeed this leisurely acquittance of Parliamentary calls from the rebuke he addressed to the writer seventeen years later. In 1893, after six years in office, and the daily attendance upon Parliament enforced upon Ministers, the culprit, having visited Australia and India, returned a few days late for the first session of the Second Home Rule Government: " Did you and Curzon tell your constituents last year that you were not going to attend Parliament? " was the somewhat caustic greeting of the leader. Had his own early misdemeanours been then public, even the worm would have turned.

In 1876 Balfour felt forced to get a move on. He determined to speak; he selected Indian silver currency as a sufficiently dull subject; an empty House of Commons in Committee; the emptiest moment of the dinner hour; and in this cherished seclusion the career of one of the first Parliamentarians of his time came to birth.

Fate was shortly to rescue the neophyte from the uninspiring discussions of Housing and Industrial Topics which had waited for forty years after the publication of Disraeli's *Sybil* for treatment by the Conservative Party. From 1876 the Eastern question dominated all others throughout Europe. It is not necessary, in a review of Balfour's career, to trace the stages by which the revolt of Turkish provinces against ruthless misgovernment gradually drew nearly the whole of Europe into consultations not far removed from war. So far as England was concerned, the main weight fell on Lord Salisbury, who, in place of a Foreign Secretary with failing nerve, represented England at the Constantinople Conference when Turkey was at Russia's feet. He also steered Lord Beaconsfield, who was terribly handicapped by infirmity and ignorance of French, through the Berlin Congress, when war and peace hung daily in the balance; a notable feat indeed to have established an equilibrium in Europe which endured for thirty years. Balfour, having, in 1878, become Parliamentary Private Secretary to Lord Salisbury, was behind the scenes at a moment when congresses and conferences had not lost caste by their frequency, or been vulgarised by premature disclosures. At Berlin he got to know first-hand all the leading statesmen of Europe. Characteristically he writes of this period in his fragmentary memoirs dictated when his active life was failing. " These great events supplied little material for reminiscences. I appear to have written no letters, and can find no more significant record of my impressions than the card of invitation to a State banquet and a photograph of Lord Salisbury's Staff."

He notes the kindness of Lord Odo Russell—our Ambassador—but strangely enough ignores two contributions of that astute diplomatist to the success of Great Britain at the Congress, with which Germany was still ringing when the writer visited Berlin the following year. Though already known they are perhaps worth recalling. Lord Odo, invoked by Lord Rowton to prevent Lord Beaconsfield opening the British case to the Congress in French, in which language he had no facility whatever, invaded the great statesman's bedroom soon after his arrival at the Embassy, and found him posturing before a pier-glass, and emitting sounds resembling French.

" My dear Lord, a terrible rumour has reached me that you intend to address the Congress to-morrow in French."

" And why not ? " said Lord Beaconsfield.

" Do you not know that the statesmen of Europe have come here in hopes of hearing English spoken by the greatest master of the language? Are you going to disappoint them ? "

" I had not considered that," said Lord Beaconsfield, and he spoke in English.

Again, at the moment of the greatest tension, when the Russians had definitely declined the Balkan frontier, Lord Odo arranged an early morning meeting between Bismarck and the British statesmen at the Embassy.

" The Russians will not give way," said Bismarck.

" In that case," said Lord Beaconsfield to Lord Odo,

"would you ring the bell? Order a special train; I shall leave Berlin to-night."

The Congress that day came to an agreement which England recognised as "Peace with Honour."

Are we to debit this lack of enthusiasm to the expiring embers of philosophic detachment, or to a still unawakened interest in material problems? Certain it is that after 1880, whether it was a question of high statesmanship, or Parliamentary swordplay, or even of party advantage, there was no one who threw himself into the fray with more skill and resource, or with more boyish enjoyment than Arthur Balfour.

There is another side to the picture. The ten years' period of gestation and leisure which terminated in 1880 was perhaps the most fruitful source of his great Parliamentary success. The lot of the youth who enters Parliament fresh from the University is often a chequered one. He cannot have made any question his own, and the demands upon him preclude his training himself in any wide sense. Bishop Creighton, on accepting the See of London, said: "I shall never have time to learn anything more." The young M.P. has to give out at every moment, and takes in very little except the questions on which Parliament concentrates. The strain on health in the 'eighties before the closure shortened debates was prodigious. To a delicate man, sittings up to 4 or 5 a.m. in the dog-days involved weeks of recuperation. Men like Balfour, whose mind was richly stored before he took up the routine of Parliament, or like Curzon, who did so after travels which placed him in the first rank of Eastern authorities, or like Joseph Chamberlain, with a great municipal career behind him, owed much of their Parliamentary success to the strength gained in other spheres. The House of Commons, it is true, will not accept outside prominence at its face value; it tries everyone anew by its own standards—but it has a genuine appreciation of merit and knowledge.

The year 1880 was the pivot of Balfour's life. During the General Election of that year he acted as interpreter, Lord Salisbury being at the moment abroad, of his views to Lord Beaconsfield, on the critical question of the resignation of the Government. Immediately afterwards the Fourth Party, generously advertised by sympathisers and detractors alike, burst into fame. It is difficult to add anything to the oft-told story of the havoc wrought by these four associates in Parliamentary forms and methods; but it may be safely averred that not even Randolph Churchill himself enjoyed the upheaval more than Balfour. He was not at the time a good speaker, his thoughts running far ahead of his vocabulary; but by incessant practice he became an excellent debater. He would speak at any moment to fill a gap. The heart-searchings of 1876 were replaced by intrepidity. On one occasion, in 1881, he rose in the momentary absence of his cherished colleague, Churchill, to move an amendment on the Irish Land Bill, which he confessed he had not read, and which, as he read it to the House, he admitted he did not understand; but which he commended as being worthy of attention as coming from such a quarter. Even Gladstone in replying could not withhold a compliment from such self-sacrificing fidelity.

A few nights later, the four conspirators having got the Government into a tangle, Balfour, about 1 a.m., a full hour before the Gladstonian " curfew," encouraged a respectable member sitting near him to move the Adjournment of the Debate. The Irish Attorney-General anticipated him in the Motion, saying the Government required time, whereupon Balfour promptly rose and initiated a spirited protest against this obstruction to progress, with the desired result that after two hours' discussion, the already shaken back-benchers on the Liberal side retired to bed, convinced that the Government conduct of the Bill was utterly futile.

When, however, the surrender of the Government to Irish intimidation by the Kilmainham Treaty was sprung upon an astonished House of Commons, the genuine indignation which caused Balfour to denounce it as an " infamy "— severing by that one word relations with Mr. Gladstone of many years' standing—showed the House that, whatever the trend of his colleagues in the Fourth Party, one member at least, like Cromwell's Ironsides, " had some conscience in what he did."

From 1885 onwards, Balfour's position in the Conservative Party rose by leaps and bounds. The abuse which had been showered on the guerilla warfare of the Fourth Party had shown the country his absolute indifference to obloquy; his association with Lord Salisbury gave him a special status in the political world, his ability and personal charm gave him a hold on the most truculent opponents.

He was now to face a staggering ordeal. After fifteen hectic months in 1885 and 1886—when Home Rule had been refused by the Liberal Party adopted by Gladstone, rejected by the House of Commons, and vetoed by Great Britain at a General Election—the Irish outlook was graver than at any time in the century. One main difference between 1886 and 1921 was that in 1886 the agitation against rent had gone so far that no Irish Government could have secured the most elementary rights as between landlord and tenant, whereas Wyndham's Land Purchase Bill had largely relieved Ireland of this time-worn sore before 1921. The Irish in 1886 had no experience of Local Government, and except the severance of the " last link," Parnell had no constructive policy. To this chaotic situation Gladstone's Home Rule Bill would have added financial arrangements doomed to failure.

To enforce the law, restore order, and create confidence appeared in 1887 an insuperable task. The Government recently called to office had already lost Randolph Churchill, after four months' unhappy leadership of the House of Commons; Lord Iddesleigh by death; and Sir Michael Hicks Beach, the Irish Secretary, by threatened blindness. Balfour's friends were amazed to hear that he had accepted the vacant post, the most strenuous in the Government, from which six men had retired, broken in health or reputation, in seven years. But within six months his determined assertion of the law, his acceptance of responsibility for the strongest measures, his rigid impartiality and unparalleled Parliamentary sword-play, had won him a great name.

It had also won him the chance of carrying remedial measures which appealed to a generation to which *laissez-faire* had become an odious anachronism. This is not the place to detail the steps by which Southern Ireland, under the Unionist policy of which Balfour was the protagonist, became possessed of its own land, made reasonably solvent the 500,000 cottiers of the West, increased its agricultural products and its exports by 25 per cent., and brought its total trade to £28 per head as compared to £20 per head in Great Britain. It is sufficient to quote Lord Bryce's tribute when he took the Chief Secretary's office in 1906, that " Ireland was more quiet than she had been for six hundred years."

Balfour had long before this been called to wider responsibilities. At the end of 1891, W. H. Smith, inarticulate in speech but great in heart, had died and the leadership fell to the man who, by his reluctance to enter Parliament sixteen years before, had done his best to justify Mr. Disraeli's aphorism that " the first requisite for success in the House of Commons is to be there." The five years' march to official prominence was over; ten years as second-in-command to Lord Salisbury were to ensue. Both these trials promised great things for his success as Prime Minister, which, however, must be accounted the most disappointing period of Balfour's career. He had long won the complete confidence of the House of Commons; he was second to no one as a debater; he was beloved by his party. As Lord Salisbury's representative, when that untiring and gifted worker held the Foreign Office as well as the Premiership, he composed difficulties of every description, he more than once replaced him at the Foreign Office during his brief absences, and deputised for him at the social functions which Lord Salisbury regarded as a mere disturbance of his labours. He was, in military parlance, a great Chief of the Staff. Moreover, his rapidity of thought enabled him to face the most startling transitions. He would leave a colleague in the House of Commons with a watching brief in a debate on which he was to reply; would hold a Cabinet Meeting on some urgent subject in his room; and would perhaps be called into the adjoining room to interview some important personage, without losing the control of either discussion. When face to face with anyone, Balfour showed almost unique insight into his thoughts; but in writing, his letters being mainly dictated, he neither conveyed his own feelings nor realised those of his correspondents. The recently published letters which passed between him and Lord Birkenhead are an instance of the misinterpretation to which he laid himself open at times.

Balfour throughout his life owed much to his interest in games and his power of laying business aside. He played golf and tennis assiduously, and his remark in a speech at St. Andrews that " even games are not to be regarded as wholly serious " was characteristic.

When rallied by his intimates for learning to play bridge during this period, he excused himself by assuring them that he got up later than any of them; but having to talk for two hours before lunch, again at lunch, in Parliament more than anyone else from 3 to 8, and again at dinner, his power of output was at an end by ten o'clock on a non-Parliamentary night. Like Asquith, who, despite his exceptional power of brain and concentration, was also a bridge enthusiast, he never became an expert at cards. But it would be difficult to imagine anyone, who had neither business habits, statistical training, a good memory, nor the most elementary system for the preparation of speeches, who managed to carry out so varied a programme in each week, and to clear away so many difficulties as was Balfour's lot at the time.

These years took toll of Balfour to a degree which largely accounts for his failure to achieve all that was expected of him as Prime Minister. Until the Great War there was never a period of greater political stress than 1895–1902. Ireland had usurped the centre of the stage so long that British calls were largely in arrear; foreign affairs, especially in regard to France, were so threatening that the defensive forces had to be strengthened against acute Parliamentary opposition. The Egyptian problem and the reconquest of the Soudan, which brought us to the very verge of war with France, were followed by the Boer War, which for two and a half years caused us as a nation to strain every nerve, apart from accentuating Parliamentary difficulties.

What England then accomplished has been forgotten, while the length to which an unequal struggle was protracted has barbed much criticism. Even in the Great War, no Power had to maintain 300,000 men, equipped and provided with every necessary, including 10,000 horses per month, at a distance of 6,000 miles from their base; and in German quarters, most critical of our strategy, this achievement was the subject of envious study.

Amidst all the troubles and vicissitudes of the war, and the early reverses in Natal, Balfour was the mainstay of the Ministry in Parliament and its life and soul behind the scenes. For months together he rarely left London. In the continued duel between the War Minister and a Chancellor of the Exchequer whose aversion to timely expenditure greatly lengthened the war, he was the recognised umpire, and early realised the effort necessary to cope with a mobile enemy over an area as big as France and Spain. Again in 1902, when the Government was faced with a serious difference between Lord Kitchener and Lord Milner as to the best method of bringing the still combatant Boers to terms, Balfour, who insisted on treating all opponents as reasonable, urged that our terms of peace should be stated to the Boers at Vereeniging; that they should be made aware of the full liberties they would enjoy under the British Crown, and that if they refused the terms, they would at least not continue to fight as men without hope.

His strategy, in which Chamberlain concurred, proved effective. The Boers, after refusing to make peace, came to an agreement within a few weeks.

But Balfour's great services in these difficult days were not appreciated by the public and his party. He was terribly sensitive as to the want of confidence shown in many quarters, and in some speeches, notably after the Colenso reverse, he failed to display the deep feeling or to convey the splendid resource which animated him when the call of country had replaced that of party. To the day of his death there were some of his supporters who most unfairly resented his attitude during the dark days of 1899.

It was unlucky that close on the heels of the war, and of his appointment as Prime Minister, came the Tariff issue, on which probably no man alive but Balfour could have kept his party from falling completely asunder. To reverse a doctrine under which England had flourished for sixty years was difficult enough, but to keep two contending parties, each of whom thought its case as clear as daylight, from wreckage, was almost beyond human power. The Boer War had robbed Lord Salisbury's closing years of a brilliant sunset; the Tariff struggle filched from Balfour's leadership what might have been a splendid dawn.

To the Tariff imbroglio was added a most unfortunate episode in Ireland. George Wyndham had been Balfour's private secretary, and was an intimate friend. His successful Land Bill in 1903 had encouraged the Nationalists to sound him on further measures. Wyndham's enthusiasm, coupled with the leanings of Sir Anthony MacDonell, recently appointed Under Secretary, towards Home Rule, caused general alarm to the loyalists. Balfour, only partially informed of the steps taken, threw his ægis over Wyndham, and even threatened resignation if his Chief Secretary was not trusted. But true to his nature, and averse like Lord Salisbury from giving unsought advice, he did not couple this with serious warning or restriction of Wyndham's future action. A few weeks later, a Parliamentary debate made it clear that Wyndham's position was incompatible with the temper of Conservative supporters, but Balfour's phenomenal loyalty did not save him from the double suspicion, on the one side that he had encouraged Wyndham's indiscretion, and on the other that he had thrown him over.

Thus from 1902–1905 rifts developed in his conduct of public affairs. In the press of great events he gave the go-by to smaller issues. The fusillade of a disappointed House of Commons naturally centres on any vulnerable point, small or great. In a war the equilibrium can be maintained by concentrating on the essential, but in the ordinary course of events, vital questions are not those on which Governments are most vulnerable. When Balfour became Prime Minister he carried the war procedure into ordinary Parliamentary life, and for the first time he lost his hold upon the House of Commons. He believed that the divergent elements in his party could be best kept together by making the whole case of the Government on Tariffs clear in a set debate and declining to be drawn into guerilla warfare. He consequently allowed hostile motions by private members to be ignored and even passed against the Government. Unfortunately, this procedure coincided with the necessity of retaining office until the " entente " with France and Japan, to which leading members of the Opposition were resolutely opposed, and which was of high import, had been carried through. In appearance, though not in fact, Balfour was clinging to office, and feared to face a General Election. The murmurs on his own side were deep.

Simultaneously, as will always happen, at the close of a long period of office, there were plenty of able Conservatives who had good Parliamentary standing, but from lack of space could not be included in the Government. Criticism was inevitable; but Balfour, who regarded censure by the Opposition as normal and acceptable, resented attacks from his own side. Indeed, when his defensive spirit seemed to be lacking in fire, it was not unusual for a colleague surreptitiously to incite a " back-bencher " to stimulate him by a few critical remarks; and this little strategy seldom failed to elicit the necessary response in his best style. The long strain had undoubtedly told upon his speaking power, and his exercise of patronage was much questioned. These were the first mutterings of the storm which caused his resignation of the leadership some years later.

Strangely enough, his unconcealed enjoyment of games,

by THE EARL OF MIDLETON

which should have appealed to the British public, added impetus to the charge of frivolity. It appeared as if a generation accustomed to Disraeli, Gladstone, and Lord Salisbury could hardly understand a Minister not sleeping in a frock-coat. The fact that Balfour's car was to be seen on a Saturday afternoon leaving Downing Street with a bag of golf-clubs was quoted by the Opposition press as showing his indifference to the Boer War. He would have felt it hypocritical to camouflage the necessity of exercise. Indeed, he had been known to walk down to the House of Commons for a Saturday sitting in a Homburg hat with a frock-coat hastily thrown over a golf costume, to the delight of his detractors, who apparently ignored the staleness which besets small and great alike when the body no longer feeds the brain. No doubt more acute criticism would have been evoked if it had been realised that he occasionally stole an hour to listen to music, which was a notable solace to him throughout his life.

One great service, however, was rendered by him to the country in the two and a half years as Prime Minister before the crash came. The Committee of National Defence, established in 1902, not merely brought order into our war machine, but went far to enable us to do our share in saving Europe in 1914. It is difficult in 1933 to remember that fifty years ago the military authorities concerned themselves exclusively with drill and discipline; they had no Intelligence Department, and waited for the outbreak of hostilities to estimate numbers, supplies, or the clothing requisite to the particular climate or seat of war. Under Lords Wolseley and Roberts this had been completely remedied, and by 1902 we had plenty of Intelligence, but no co-ordination. In consequence every year there was a scramble between the Army and Navy for funds; and while under Liberal Ministers these had been perilously clipped, under all administrations the tendency to economise had been reinforced by the absence of a definite plan of action, any departure from which might well be shown to be a national danger.

As soon as Balfour took the helm, the heads of the Army and Navy called upon him to bring the two services together under the chairmanship of a Cabinet Minister. Reluctant at first, he yielded to pressure, and from the first meeting, over which he presided himself, the questions raised appealed to his imagination, and he rarely missed a " Defence Committee." The problems of Asia and Africa; the Atlantic and Pacific; the Mediterranean and the Baltic, all came under review. The force for service abroad, already fixed at 120,000 men, could for the first time depend upon the necessary stores and equipment. The difficulties, from the point of view of high politics and the relative responsibilities of the Army and Navy in each sphere, were frankly debated, and the results recorded with great advantage to both parties.

Balfour, even on military matters, had in some respects more foresight than his soldier colleagues. The Germans, as we had learned through an indiscretion in high quarters, following Frederick the Great, had started a mobile siege artillery. We had found heavy mobile guns of service even in South Africa, and three mobile siege companies had been added to the force available for foreign service. Balfour's dictum was prophetic. "We are a rich nation with a small army; artillery cannot be improvised, and we ought to have gun power in advance of our infantry." Before 1905 we had added 75 batteries of field artillery to the 47 field and horse batteries previously existing. Between 1905 and 1914, despite Haldane's boasted "clear thinking," not a single additional heavy gun had been put upon wheels, and the Allies had only 15,000 machine guns against 50,000 of the Central Powers. It was alleged that at Maubeuge alone the total French loss, largely owing to the German heavy guns, approached 100,000.

As an example of one most important decision, which could never have been obtained except from this authoritative body, it was agreed that once the fleet was mobilised the whole of the Expeditionary Force could leave the country. It is true that in the face of this, Lord Kitchener, who, from continued employment abroad, had never attended a Defence Committee and had never seen a Territorial Battalion before 1914, relying on his own opinion, retained 2 out of the 6 Divisions at the outset of the struggle in France; but he was overborne by this high authority just in time to save Paris. Balfour's return to the Defence Committee in 1914 appropriately marked perhaps his greatest permanent service to the country.

The General Election of January 1906 was a debacle, headed by himself and his Manchester colleagues, who were rejected in a body. The Conservatives, consisting of 370 members with the Liberal Unionists, were reduced to 157, little more than one-fourth of the new House of Commons; indeed, in the early days of the new House, there was a disposition to treat the minority and its leader as a negligible factor, but Balfour's personal prestige was soon re-asserted.

The year 1906 was far more than a Conservative reverse. It opened a new era, in which social legislation pushed the ordinary functions of Government into the background. The Conservatives, after twenty years of predominance, did not yield readily to the newfangled and in some cases crude measures which were proposed. With the House of Lords at their back, they were unduly masters of the situation. Balfour was between two fires. Realising that after so complete a trial the country wanted a good run for Liberal money, he was never unreasonable; but his hot-headed supporters forced the pace. In 1910 it was assumed that if after four years' hard fighting, the Lords did not throw out Lloyd George's Budget the party would break up. Unfortunately the Bill, with its absurd Land Taxes, was intentionally punitive, and the Lords could not amend it. Balfour yielded most unwillingly, and the Conservative defeats at two elections in 1910 brought the Liberals and Irish together and revived Home Rule. Balfour's words in abandoning the leadership were weary: " I have only had one real holiday in twenty-six years; they say I am not leading well. Why should I abandon every pursuit I value to politics, unless to serve the country to the best advantage? "

Whatever the merits of the decision which threw the Conservative Party into the hands of a popular and eloquent but untried politician, it left Balfour, with nearly twenty years of service, destined, except in one remarkable case, to add very little to his fame. A man who has held supreme power is always in a difficult position under a new Prime Minister. To put a General in the field under one who was previously his subordinate is to court disaster. Dethroned kings never remain in their own dominions. The correlation of Russell and Palmerston was a warning. Balfour's fastidious taste cleared him from the ordinary pit-falls, but he was over-sedulous in avoiding even the appearance of control. By nature he was many-sided but indifferent to many issues. Sitting in a Cabinet as a subordinate, he held himself free from the responsibility of directing policy unless he was specially concerned.

Strangely enough his original indifference to office had entirely disappeared. In 1895 it was common talk in the House of Commons that he did not want to expedite the fall of the tottering Rosebery Government.

"I have been lying about you all Sunday," said a colleague to him after a June week-end in 1895. "In what respect?" said Balfour. "You were being abused for your slackness," was the reply, "and I assured them of the reverse, but I knew I was lying." "Tell me how to get the Government out and I will back you," said Balfour. "Stop their supply, as in 1885," said his mentor; and the train was shortly laid.

From 1915 when the first Coalition began, Balfour was in office for practically the remainder of his life. He took the Admiralty in 1915 and was responsible for the much-regretted Jutland *communiqué*. He held the Foreign Office till 1919, and represented England at the Peace Conference. He was subsequently Lord President for seven years. He thus shared in all the ups and downs of four years of war and seven years of reconstruction.

The position was not easy. He was sitting with men many of whom had been schoolboys when he was a Cabinet Minister. He had foreseen the danger of 1914 eighteen months before Sir Edward Grey took his belated action, and had probably forgotten more about Ireland than any of his colleagues ever knew. Under such conditions he appeared to have thought it pardonable or even necessary to circumscribe his efforts. At the Foreign Office he notoriously centred his mind on a few vital points, and left nine questions out of ten to permanent officials. In Paris, at the Peace Conference, he conceded to Lloyd George a degree of independent initiative which Lord Beaconsfield would never have claimed of Lord Salisbury at Berlin. But his visit as Foreign Minister to Washington was a veritable triumph, his fine manners and conciliatory mind appealing to a community with whom rarity is the measure of price.

Unfortunately, during many of these long years of office, Ireland was continuously to the fore, and his brilliant Irish record with his special knowledge gave some measure of confidence to the distracted loyalists, despite all the shifts and turns of the unlucky Coalition Government before 1921. He was often called in, but there was no "touch of the vanished hand" to allay the drift to disaster; none of

by THE EARL OF MIDLETON

the firm action of 1887 or the resolute marshalling of the country's forces as in 1900. He was Foreign Secretary; Ireland was not in his purview.

And yet to the end of his life he cut a great figure in the country. Few men have combined great experience with so well-stored a mind, so much social charm, so much power of getting the best out of others. Although he never married, he was on intimate terms with young and old of both sexes for two generations, and was *persona grata* in the most varied circles. Indeed, when approaching his eightieth year, he happened to be at a country-house party for a neighbouring ball, and was persuaded by the younger members to join them. His car broke down at the gate of General Higginson—then approaching his hundredth year. " Better ask him to join in," said Balfour. " He is of the age they seem to prefer for this festivity."

To estimate his actual influence in the Society of which he was perhaps the most acceptable unit for two generations is not easy. It was foreign to his nature to assume that he had any cause to exercise influence at all. When off duty he eschewed serious topics unless they emerged readily from lighter issues. He consequently resented the tendency of certain colleagues to " charge " the conversation at week-end parties. Teachers like Carlyle or table orators like Macaulay did not appeal to a man who had a genius for " trifling without being silly." As an ardent Etonian he humorously gibed at Harrow, as a Cantab at Oxford, as a bachelor at matrimony, and hurt nobody's feelings. The idea of setting a standard was foreign to him. Of devout mind, he was a regular attendant at divine service at his home in Scotland, but very rarely in England, and would have been surprised to learn that anyone was influenced by his example. Always *æquus in arduis*, he was capable of genuine indignation more rarely than of resolute action.

It could hardly be said of him, as was said of that prince of enthusiasts Albert Grey, that he " lit many fires in dark rooms," but it would be difficult to name any man whose presence during more than half a century so unconsciously gave a sense of uplift apart from social distinction to any gathering as Arthur Balfour.

CANON BARNETT
1844-1913

By
SIR REGINALD KENNEDY-COX

CANON BARNETT

by SIR REGINALD KENNEDY-COX

ONE day I was piloting a party of East-End youths round Westminster Abbey, and whilst they were scurrying off to find the tomb of the "Unknown Warrior," I happened to drift into the north aisle of the Choir; there—on the wall—one particular tablet caught my eye. It was an obviously post-Victorian tablet—a trifle ornate, but modest in comparison with its neighbours, and it bore these words:

"IN GRATITUDE TO GOD AND IN MEMORY OF
SAMUEL AUGUSTUS BARNETT
FEB. 8TH 1844–JUNE 17TH 1913.
CANON OF WESTMINSTER ABBEY 1906–1913 AND SUB-DEAN DESIGNATE, FOUNDER AND WARDEN OF THE FIRST UNIVERSITY SETTLEMENT TOYNBEE HALL, WHITECHAPEL 1884–1906, CANON OF BRISTOL CATHEDRAL 1892–1906, VICAR OF ST. JUDE'S, WHITECHAPEL 1872–1893"

I paused in my reading; so that was Barnett, the father of our modern "social work"; the founder of English "slum settlements"; the champion of once lost causes, which to-day, through his burning zeal, have become for many, indeed, triumphant causes; but these cold, official words—they told me, not of the Barnett of Whitechapel whom men loved, but in pompous measure—proclaimed "the Canon of Bristol," "the Canon of Westminster," "the Sub-Dean Designate," commonplace ecclesiastical titles which many men have won; a wave of disappointment swept over me; surely this was not the man of my dreams—

the quaint, lovable, unconventional being whom I had longed to know.

Before entering the Abbey I had been reading in the 'bus a collection of Bernard Shaw's old dramatic criticisms. In contrasting a hero of real life with the corresponding puppet of the stage he wrote:

> "All the movements for the realisation of religion in social reform have been largely the work of men of heroic devotion and sometimes of extraordinary eloquence. They present to the dramatist's study temperaments rich in the passionate qualities, and personal histories rich in the struggles and braveries which are the material of tragedy; whilst their characters positively sparkle with the incongruities and ironies and contradictions, which are the life of comedy."

Comedy and Tragedy—that was Barnett's life. If Shaw had written this obituary, how different it would have read!

My eye passed on; unwittingly I had done the unknown writer a wrong, I had paused too soon—the words upon the tablet now took different shape—I read:

> "Believing that we are all members one of another he laboured unceasingly to unite men in the service of God, and by his counsel and example inspired many to seek for themselves and for the nation the things that are eternal."

Now here was the real Barnett, the man whose driving force is still felt behind all our social work, the man who "inspired many to seek for themselves," and seeking, to "find the things that are eternal." What an impossible task for anyone to attempt to compress within a few pages of printed paper all those crowded years of rich vivid life. And what is more, not just the record of one life, but of two, for Samuel Barnett and Henrietta, his wife, were one in their work, if ever two lives can be one; they shone in the grey twilight of Whitechapel like two flaming spirits bound into one fierce blazing torch. I have taken a special interest in the joint life of those two triumphant pioneers, because in themselves they have exemplified and proved certain pet theories of mine. My main contention has always been that Happiness should be, and can be, the most powerful factor for unselfishness in workaday life. Happiness should be the handmaiden of Pity and Understanding; now both these persons came from essentially happy homes. Samuel Barnett was the elder of two sons born to Francis Augustus Barnett, a successful ironfounder of Bristol. The boy's whole childhood was passed in one of those completely happy Victorian homes which combine comfort with common sense. Another contention of mine is that a man more often inherits his characteristics from his grandparents than from his father or mother. Young Barnett seems to have inherited his inner vivid personality from his maternal grandfather, John Gilmore, a whimsical, kindly old ship-owner, who, having settled down at Clifton at the end of a successful active career, and having acquired considerable house property there, revealed his unusual personality by returning to his tenants all sums of money above and beyond the 5 per cent. profit on the property which he felt that he was entitled to, and so we may consider that Samuel Barnett, by heredity, was closely connected with one of the first schemes of profit sharing and co-partnership.

In those early days the boy was in grave danger of being spoilt; he was privately educated and sheltered in a comfortable—even luxurious home. It was not until he was sixteen that he had his first encounter with life in the raw when he went for a brief and miserable spell as a boarder to a crammer, where a definite percentage of his fellow pupils had been expelled from their public schools. Young Barnett, who was fundamentally shy and sensitive, suffered intensely from their uncongenial society, and was glad to pass his entrance exam. for the Varsity, and, having matriculated, to go up to Oxford for the October term of 1862. His father, after much heart-searching, had selected Wadham as his college, because the then Warden of that college, Dr. Simmonds, had the reputation of being an unbending Tory and a rigid evangelical—this reputation Barnett senior hoped would protect his son from the horrors of free thinking, which he had heard vaguely were beginning to be rife at Oxford. The years at Wadham were entirely happy ones for young Barnett, but he said in after life, " I made a mistake of using my time at Oxford to grind at books rather than to know men "; this failing he certainly remedied in the years to come. In 1865 he took his degree and obtained a second-class Honours in law and history. The following year was spent at Winchester, as a master, where he gained useful knowledge of boy life and the public school system, which is apt either to strangle or to sustain character.

From early boyhood he had consistently made up his mind to be ordained, no other profession offering him any attraction: the temptation to enter his father's prosperous business seems to have been non-existent. But before ordination he had a great desire to see the world, and so during his year of schoolmastering he saved sufficient money to pay for a full, even exhaustive, tour of the United States of America. This tour was in 1867, and the Civil War being but recently over, he encountered much strong feeling during his visits to such cities as Boston and New Orleans. His comment upon this first American visit was, " What I saw and heard there knocked all the Toryism out of me."

In December of that same year he was ordained Deacon and went to his first curacy at St. Mary's, Bryanston Square. Dean Freemantle, his first rector, in writing of young Barnett's initial spiritual work, uses the words, " Barnett took much pains in his Church work, though he was not a great preacher. I remember in a conversation which we had about preaching, an expression of his that the ordinary religious teaching was too much a ' religion of death' and that what was needed was ' a religion of life!' "

So far this record has been but the bare bones of a placid fortunate life, but now the strong outside influences, which were to mould and make the burning social reformer of the coming years, enter upon the scene. Samuel Barnett was shaped by two women, Octavia Hill, and her young friend Henrietta Rowland, the girl who later became his wife. He seems always to have been powerfully influenced by good women, but these two, each of outstanding character, took him into their hands and fashioned definitely the man that was to be. Octavia Hill soon fades out of the picture, but from now onwards it is almost impossible to separate the careers of husband and wife. Miss Rowland, then only eighteen, having once been swept into the social schemes which Octavia Hill was vigorously organising for the parish, naturally came into contact with the curate, who eagerly seconded all these new and exciting ventures. Apparently Samuel Barnett fell in love with her at first sight, but it seems to have been quite the reverse with Miss Rowland, and as this union meant so much in the years to come, to countless people who fell under the magnetic influence of this unique pair, it is worth while giving, in Dame Henrietta's own words, her first impression of her future husband:

" On February 4, 1892, Mr. Barnett wrote to ask me to marry him. The letter surprised me very much, as I had taken his many communications as representing his anxiety for the success of Miss Hill's social experiment and the consequent frequent supervision of one of her young workers. Moreover he looked so very much older than his age—twenty-seven—that I had accepted his interest as that of a kindly elderly gentleman, with small sensitive hands, a bald head, and shaggy beard. Indeed, both in appearance and manner, he was far removed from a girlish idea of a lover. He dressed very badly, generally obtaining his clothes by employing out-of-work tailors in the district. He always wore a tall silk hat which, as he had purchased it by post, never fitted. He was entirely different from any of the men I had ever known, and in the plans I had formed of spending my life at Bethnal Green I could see no place for marriage with its obedience and its ties. My inclination was to give a decisive ' No ' to his beautiful letter, but I knew that, if I did so, either he or I would have to give up Miss Octavia's work; and to injure her schemes at this juncture was an impossible conception. I therefore wrote to him and suggested that we should go on with our work for six months and not refer to the matter during that period."

At the end of the period Miss Rowland made the decision which fortunately she never had reason to regret, and the young couple, brimming over with ideas, looked round for a suitable battle ground upon which to commence their social campaign. A living at Oxford had been offered Mr. Barnett, but this offer was turned down—then Miss Octavia took a hand in the matter, and having duly pulled the right strings, the then Bishop of London, Dr. Jackson, offered Mr. Barnett the living of St. Jude's, Whitechapel. This slum parish boasted a population of over 6,000 souls, mostly men, the majority of whom lived in " common lodging-houses."

The Vicarage was small, dark, and stood close to the road—parish organisation was non-existent, having been allowed to drop into ruin during the long illness of the late Vicar. On March 6, 1873, the newly married couple entered upon their twenty-one years' work at St. Jude's, Whitechapel. Dame Henrietta gives us a vivid picture of the environment in which she and her husband worked:

> " Its area was but a few acres and the whole parish was covered with a network of courts and alleys. In some of these the houses were three storeys high and hardly six feet apart, the sanitary accommodation being pits in the cellars; a standpipe at the end of the court providing the only water. Each room was the home of a family, but in most cases the rooms were let out 'furnished' for eightpence a night. In these homes people lived in whom it was hard to see the likeness of the Divine. If the men worked at all it was as casual dock labourers, but usually they did not work; they stole or received stolen goods, they hawked, begged, cadged, drank, gambled, fought, and when they became too well known to the police, moved on to another neighbourhood—and then came back again!"

Naturally the work in such a neighbourhood was difficult and hard, progress was slow—the young couple had to feel their way.

Here are two extracts taken from a long letter of Canon Barnett's:

> " By those who, knowing something of the life of Christ, know what human life ought to be, the state of the people is hardly to be borne. Why must their sympathies remain torpid, while questions affecting thousands of their fellows are burning for solution? Why must existence be so dull, when in every soul a fight is raging over which God and the Angels watch and all around us are such lives being led by men and women whose homes are places for sleep and not for recreation, who go wearily to work, or as wearily to watch till some street entertainment stirs their worn-out senses."

And then:

> "If one sentence could explain the principle of our work, it is that we aim at decreasing, not suffering, but sin. Sin in the sense of missing the best."

It is intensely difficult to select extracts from the numerous writings of Canon Barnett and his wife which may best convey the dominating thought in their minds. For many people Barnett lives as a social reformer, or as an active Poor Law administrator; for others he lives as an ardent educationalist, but he was all these things and many more, because his one never sleeping desire was to help people to live their lives in relation to God. In his years of struggle he naturally caused much offence; this confusion of his aims for the people with his methods to obtain them, grieved him much, and though he never replied to attacks in the Press, he took pains to explain his position to those who entrusted him with money or who joined in the work.

In getting to grips with his people Canon Barnett had many things to say about going to church, and about staying away. He never asked people to come to St. Jude's; to teach people that to worship was a privilege, and that prayers and praises were personal actions for which men were only responsible to their Maker was, in his eyes, the first step towards reality in religious life, but, unfortunately, when his parishioners understood that they were not expected to go to church to please the parson, they followed their inclinations and stayed away. This form of misunderstanding was often the sequel to many of Canon Barnett's "revolutionary ideas," but over all his work brooded an almost divine patience. After five years' work he writes: "We must wait and watch with open eyes and open ears for the coming of the Spirit which will guide us to new ways."

New Ways—how revolutionary these seemed to our Victorian grandparents! It is almost impossible for us in these modern days of over-organised relief to visualise the chaotic conditions under which "relief" was administered to the poor when Canon Barnett first fought his fight against waste and moral deterioration. In the following few words he explains his principles:

"The relief of the poor is a matter which I hold to be of greatest importance. Indiscriminate charity is among the curses of London. To put the result of our observations in the strongest form I would say, 'The poor starve because of the alms they receive.' The people of this parish live in rooms, the state of which is a disgrace to us as a nation. Alms are given them—a shilling by one, a sixpence by another; the gift is not sufficient if they are really struggling, the care is not sufficient if they are thriftless or wicked. The effect of this charity is that a state of things to make one's heart bleed is perpetuated."

Canon Barnett did not rest in merely diagnosing the disease, he at once sped to effect a remedy. The C.O.S. came into existence, "after care" at the schools and systematic visiting were organised—then came the question of tackling the housing problem.

In 1875 the Guardians had sent a petition to Parliament showing that the death-rate in that portion of Whitechapel was 40 in 1,000, and that 80 per cent. of the paupers came from condemned houses. The problem was a threefold one. First, to get the houses condemned by the medical officer; secondly, to induce the authorities to demolish them once they were condemned; thirdly, to find wealthy philanthropists or building companies who would buy the land and erect decent dwellings. Authority was slow to move—so slow that even the patience of a Barnett was strained to breaking-point. At last he and his wife decided to build themselves. Mrs. Barnett sold her jewels, and Mr. Edward Bond was persuaded to pay half the cost of the purchase of the alley which it had been decided to demolish.

In 1876 Canon Barnett writes: "Our new tenements will be ready in June, and will accommodate about 50 families at an average rent of 2*s*. 6*d*. a room. They will be under careful supervision, and we may expect that 50 families being respectable will have a great missionary power in the neighbourhood." And then *ten years afterwards*, we read: "The rebuilding of the houses of the poor has been going on apace. In the broad streets with their clean, tall dwellings, it is almost impossible to recall the net of squalid courts and filthy passages which went by the name of streets. After nine years' waiting the improvement has been completed";

and a year after: " All the spaces—cleared in the parish for artisan dwellings—have now been covered. The buildings have been built with some regard for beauty. It is, I believe, false economy, as it is false benevolence, which provides for fellow creatures things acknowledged to be ugly. In the long run such things will be rejected."

It is difficult, in this era of wide social interests, to realise how odd appeared the actions of this strange vital East-End clergyman, and how many kindly but unintelligent Victorians were shocked and hurt by his non-parochial activities. We have to remember that side by side with his multitudinous wide interests Barnett was organising his difficult parish, and building up that vital side of all parish life— a live staff.

Mrs. Barnett herself writes of these days, referring to the ordinary " Church worker ": " the parish difficulties were being dealt with mainly by good women, generally elderly; few men, with the exception of the clergy and noted philanthropists, as Lord Shaftesbury, were interested in the welfare of the poor." The Barnetts were not only practical, they were wise—they realised that there must be spells of relaxation, and they combine with those holidays that which can only be described by a modern phrase, " propaganda work." Their happiest holidays were spent at Oxford, Balliol being their most fruitful place of rest—certainly in the famous Jowett they found a stimulating and attentive host.

As a result of these visits the inspiration came to Barnett to create Toynbee Hall, but as the history of its creation and progress is already recorded in a bulky volume, it is sufficient to record here that the germ of the idea first appeared in the rooms of a certain Oxford undergraduate named Cosmo Lang—now Archbishop of Canterbury; a group of undergraduates met together in his rooms with the firm intention of founding a Settlement to " enable men to live with the poor," but the great difficulty confronting these enthusiasts was, where to find a Head with the qualities necessary to bring the scheme to success. Mr. Barnett had written an article in the *Nineteenth-Century Review* of February 1884 picturing the man necessary for such a work, but such men were obviously not met with every day.

Again we must quote Dame Henrietta's words as they are found in her book, *The Beginnings of Toynbee Hall*:

"Mr. Barnett and I had spent eleven years of life and work in Whitechapel. We were weary. My health stores were limited, and often exhausted. We were therefore desirous to turn our backs on the poverty and passion of East London, at least for a year, and take repose after work which had aged and weakened us. But no other man was to be found who would do the work; and if this child-thought was not to die, we must undertake to try and rear it—solemnly on a Sunday morning we made our decision. 'God help us,' we said to each other, and then wired to obtain the refusal of the big empty Industrial School next to St. Jude's Vicarage, which we thought to be a good site for the first Settlement."

From that day and hour Toynbee became the rolling stone which set into motion an avalanche of productive idealistic ideas. One turns over the pages of Barnett's diary and reads such entries as these:

"After Toynbee Hall was built the simple literature of the parish bookshelves was insufficient, and the nucleus of a Student's Library was got together. It is proposed therefore to build a reading room adjoining Toynbee Hall. The cost of this building will be £1,100. If it is remembered how much books increase the joy of life to a man's self, and its value to others; and if then it is realised that for the mass of Londoners the best books are rare, and the means of quiet reading even more rare, there will not be much difficulty in raising the necessary sum."

This Library soon developed into the first Whitechapel Public Library, thanks to a cheque for £6,545 from Mr. J. Passmore Edwards, which Barnett found one morning on his plate amongst his breakfast post. The Library was soon followed by the institution of what is known to-day, as then, as the "Poor Man's Lawyer." We turn over a few more pages and come to the following extract: "*April* 4, 1897.— I am launched on the permanent Picture Gallery scheme. After long bargaining I have the offer of the land I want for £6,000 and now I have to raise it. Oh, dear!" Of course it came. Passmore Edwards sent a further £5,000 for this special venture, and so the Whitechapel Art Gallery rose up

—on yet another waste piece of ground adjoining the Public Library. Again we pass to another entry: " We felt very strongly that the advantages of travel should not be limited to any class, and therefore in December 1902 the ' Toynbee Workmen's Travelling Club' was founded."

But the magnitude of the various responsibilities were beginning to tell upon the strength of the man who had so eagerly shouldered them. The work involved by the series of Art Exhibitions, his position as a Guardian in the Poor Law administration, the Children's Country Holiday Fund, and housing reform, as well as the ever ramifying machinery of the parish, made him feel, not only its weight, but his inability to do justice to all the branches of the work. In the last report that Barnett wrote as Warden of Toynbee Hall he restates his opinion that the social problem is a religious one:

> " Every age is, I believe, inspired by the spirit in the age. The older generation may offer guidance, but the driving force comes from the young. I trust therefore that, driven on by younger men, Toynbee Hall may approach nearer and nearer to the solution of the great social problems of the time. My hope reached farther. The problem of Society seems to be at root a religious problem. Nothing lasting can be done to raise the poor above the cares of this world and the rich above the deceitfulness of riches, till all alike live to do the will of God. For the moment men seem to have lost their touch with God as they clamour over religious difficulties."

During the early days of his life in Whitechapel Canon Barnett was often ill and still more often depressed. That his plans for the public good should be misunderstood by his brother clergy and his more educated neighbours, gave him acute, surprised pain—he would question his fitness for the work. As the years passed by ill health increased—over-work began to take its toll. In 1892 he caught diphtheria whilst on a visit to Oxford—this was before the days of antitoxin—it was touch and go; later, convalescence in East London was very hard work.

The last time the Master of Balliol visited the Barnetts in Whitechapel he was much concerned by the obvious signs of their fatigue. They had then been twenty years there, and the work had grown to such proportions that it was almost beyond their strength. Jowett was not only a loyal friend, he was also a very discerning one; and he saw that the best form of relief would be to relinquish the duties connected with St. Jude's. Not long after this, Lord Herschell—then Lord Chancellor—was visiting Balliol, and closely following that visit the Lord Chancellor offered a Canonry of Bristol to Mr. Barnett. Its glad acceptance was soon decided upon, for it was a great joy to Barnett to return to the home of his youth. In his letter of acceptance he intimated, however, that he would have to refuse the Canonry if it meant relinquishing the Wardenship of Toynbee Hall. Matters were arranged upon a satisfactory basis, and on August 9, 1893, he was duly installed in Bristol Cathedral. For thirteen years Barnett was Canon of Bristol; gradually his health seemed to be restored; he preached upon many subjects—strikes, trade unionism, white slavery, socialism, class divisions, each and all were fearlessly handled. "We come to church to be comforted," was the complaint of one angry Christian, "whereas you seem to think it proper to make us uncomfortable."

In the spring of 1906 influenza gripped him; just as he was recovering Sir Henry-Campbell Bannerman wrote him a charming note offering him a Deanery. But to uproot himself from his London work seemed unwise. Mrs. Barnett had only just started the Garden Suburb, and Toynbee still needed the stimulus of its Founder Warden. The deanery was refused. "If you won't have this, what will you have?" asked Sir Henry. Then Canon Barnett had the courage to say that his heart's desire was to have a place in Westminster Abbey, where he could speak of his religious faith and turn men's thoughts to the condition of East London.

On August 9, 1906, he was inducted to a stall in the ancient Abbey. Unfortunately, the new Canon was too unwell to rejoice. The life of the Abbey was very different from that of Whitechapel, and Barnett missed sadly the contact with young vivid life. He conscientiously avoided frequenting his beloved East London, though all the men came individually to see him. But, by way of recompense, his new work seemed to open to him new opportunities; in special services he had great faith, and was anxious to use the Abbey, not only for functions, for prayer, and thanksgiving, or events of national importance, but as a sanctified place in which people, bound together by trade interests, educational aims, or any other common pursuit, could come together, and in its holy atmosphere test the standard of their intentions. On Bank Holidays, when the great building was thronged with people, Canon Barnett would stand on the Chancel steps and would tell the people something about the history of the Abbey.

In 1911, the year of the Coronation, Canon Barnett played his part in the great ceremony, and to him fell the duty of carrying the Orb. The same year he experienced intense pleasure by the conferring of the D.C.L. degree upon him by his Mother University. Two years later he was appointed Sub-Dean. Imperceptibly but surely the active life was drawing to its close. Just before the Coronation he had suffered from several violent heart attacks. In April 1913 he was again taken seriously ill, the end seemed very near, but he rallied, and then the terrible malady of insomnia supervened. The active brain refused to rest. For nights and days he lay completely sleepless—at last, on a Sunday afternoon, he fell asleep—ten minutes passed, half an hour, every minute of sleep meant reserves of restored strength; suddenly the tramp of a Salvation Army unit marching to its pitch was heard, the band crashed out just as they were passing the house, the sick man woke with a start. "How sorry they would be if they knew," was all he said. Slowly the strong brain lost its power, the fight for breath became less fierce, and at last, after a long unconsciousness, in the afternoon of June 17, 1913, Samuel Barnett passed to his well-earned rest.

I had paused in that quiet corner of the Abbey longer than I had intended—my young Docklanders returned from their quest, a little subdued, but impatiently ready for what might come next. Soon our luxurious motor-bus was bearing us swiftly from West London to the much-loved East. As we sped through the spacious, well-lit modern streets of Whitechapel, I had a vision of an alert little man, wearing a much too large top hat, and a shabby suit of badly made clerical clothes, flitting eagerly across the crowded street. The vision vanished, but to my mind there came the words I had but just now read: "Unceasingly he laboured to unite men in the service of God—believing that we are all one of another —by his counsel and example he inspired many to seek for themselves, and for the nation, the things that are eternal."

WILLIAM BATESON
1861-1926

By
J. H. PRIESTLEY

WILLIAM BATESON

by J. H. PRIESTLEY

IN estimating the value of a man to his day and generation every possible standard of comparison is available to the student of human endeavour. Some men are naturally measured against events, whilst others, as is the case with William Bateson, are remembered in connection with those movements of thought which provided the main incentive to endeavour in their lifetime.

One difficulty presents itself when the attempt is made to present an estimate of Bateson's contribution to science. Although his main interest was in problems of evolution which make a wide appeal, as was shown by the rapid and phenomenal circulation of the *Origin of Species*, his approach was by a close and detailed examination of the results of breeding experiments with animals and plants, and it would still be unwise to assume that the layman has followed the remarkable developments in this field sufficiently closely to find intelligible any detailed analysis of Bateson's share in work which has given a new direction to biological research since the beginning of the century. The general attitude to such a problem is well represented by some sentences used by Bateson in his Presidential Address upon "Heredity," delivered to the British Association at its 1914 meeting in Australia.

> "Recognition of the significance of heredity is modern. The term itself in its scientific sense is no older than Herbert Spencer. Animals and plants are formed as pieces of living material split from the body of the parent organisms. Their powers and faculties are fixed in their physiological origin. They are the consequences of a genetic process, and yet it is only lately that this genetic process has become the subject

of systematic research and experiment. The curiosity of naturalists has of course always been attracted to such problems; but that accurate knowledge of genetics is of paramount importance in any attempt to understand the nature of living things has only been realised quite lately even by naturalists, and with casual exceptions the laity still know nothing of the matter. Historians debate the past of the human species, and statesmen order its present or profess to guide its future as if the animal Man, the unit of their calculations, with his vast diversity of powers, were a homogeneous material, which can be multiplied like shot.

"The reason for this neglect lies in ignorance and misunderstanding of the nature of Variation; for not until the fact of congenital diversity is grasped, with all that it imports, does knowledge of the system of hereditary transmission stand out as a primary necessity in the construction of any theory of Evolution, or any scheme of human polity."

To appreciate the character of Bateson's contribution we must follow him into this relatively unfamiliar field, and he would be the last to complain if the result is a certain subordination of our interest in the individual in view of the magnitude of the problems which take shape before our minds.

Bateson was born at Whitby in 1861, two years after the publication of the *Origin*. He went to school at Rugby and then entered St. John's College, Cambridge, of which his father, the Rev. W. H. Bateson, D.D., had been Master. Here he received his early training in biology at a time when discussion of evolutionary problems was stifled under the "apathy characteristic of an age of faith."

In his first independent work—upon the anatomy and development of a worm-like sea-shore organism, *Balanoglossus*—he found himself required by convention to suggest its probable descent on the assumption that it had evolved from hypothetical ancestors, probably under the selective influence of its environment. He will probably be remembered when his contemporaries are forgotten, because from the outset he questioned the validity of the criteria to which he was thus introduced.

Bateson illustrates in himself the action of the hereditary

principles he was to spend his life in studying, for he was certainly that rare type, the " born " biologist. This is shown by his appreciation of the significance of " species "— of the grouping and arrangement of living organisms carried out by the systematist—for such appreciation is not the product of the formal discipline of the laboratory. Laboratory courses of instruction probably only began with Bateson's generation of biologists, and we have still to learn how to combine the earlier introduction to biological methods of enquiry, thus made possible, with that freedom to observe and speculate which is the birthright of every potential biologist.

In Bateson's case it is abundantly clear that any profit derived from instruction was without loss of individual judgment. At the same time his recognition of the real affinity between the organisms grouped together by the systematist, coupled with his appreciation of the variation that might be present amongst the individuals in such a natural group, put him at once into close sympathetic relationship with two groups of workers who are too often remote from the councils of biology, the naturalists who like to find and name plants and animals, and the breeders interested in developing new races of animals and plants.

On the other hand, he challenged from the outset the two main occupations of the academic biologist since the publication of the *Origin*—the construction of hypothetical schemes of descent, which can never be proved right or wrong, and an explanation of existing forms and structures in terms of a fitness for function which is presumed to have " survival value."

Bateson was convinced of the fact of specific diversity, but could not see that the varied specific forms necessarily had any immediate biological usefulness. Evolution was in progress, but natural selection did not seem an adequate mechanism for the production of such species. Naturally therefore the young worker to whom a species was real had an interest in the origin of species which transcended that of many of his contemporaries to whom the phenomenon appeared as a *chose jugée*. Undeterred by a friendly warning from a senior that " Darwin had swept the field," his first big piece of work is an attack upon this problem, which remains a major interest to the close of his life.

His demand was for facts, not for theories—" the great

corpus of knowledge grows by solid increments, definite, predicable discoveries of fact"—and he decided that the most hopeful line of attack was to study the variation shown in organisms, as any mechanism for creating species must be built upon this phenomenon of variation. " In Variation we look to see Evolution rolling out before our eyes." Organisms were therefore studied in the field, laboratory, and museum, and as Balfour Student of the University of Cambridge, Bateson travelled in the western parts of Central Asia and Siberia. The results were published in 1894 under the unpretentious title of *Materials for the Study of Variation*, the author attributing most importance to the facts therein collected, though the student of biology may still gain inspiration from the preface and introductory discussion of those facts.

In the preface a point is raised which becomes of even graver concern to biology with the passage of time. Biology or natural history gains a firmer footing every year as part of the school curriculum. This may be good for the future citizen, whose sympathies are readily enlisted for other living organisms, but it may easily be bad for biology, and ultimately bad biology will not make a fruitful contribution to Education.

Perhaps the most valuable discipline to be readily learnt from biology is the training in accurate description of form, structure, and event. Bateson points out that no two animals are more frequently dissected and described in the zoological laboratory than the cockroach and the crayfish. Each of these animals frequently presents a striking departure from the normal in external characters, but these variations, though described and published long ago, are unheeded by student and demonstrator.

Every honest teacher of biology will admit the temptation that exists in the class-room to gloss over the abnormality and persuade the class to observe only the phenomena of accepted significance, so that the generalisations that are standard in our day may the more readily be arrived at. But the gallant effort thus made to teach to a syllabus may be at the cost of discouragement of those powers of faithful observation and accurate description which are of great value in everyday life and vital to the future biologist.

Bateson reached the conclusion that the systematists' species were frequently definite and natural, because though they differed in degree in respect to a diversity of characters, there was sharp discontinuity between the extent to which particular characters were developed in different species. He thus had a vision of a vast assemblage of species, discontinuous in their diversity, and developed in an environment in which change had apparently been continuous over long periods of time, and was sometimes continuous over wide tracts of the earth's surface. Darwin had contemplated the possibility of either continuous or discontinuous variation, but since 1859 the emphasis upon natural selection had led to a tendency to stress the probability of the accumulation of continuous variations in directions that had survival value.

Bateson's own observations led him directly to the view that discontinuous variation must be part of the fabric of change leading to the production of species, whilst his study of structure and development led immediately to a further conclusion. Pattern, based upon repetition, is of the very essence of animate form and structure, and often causes it to stand out from the inanimate background. Repetition makes symmetry possible, and a change in the number of repetitions may often involve a remarkable change in symmetry. Bateson pointed to the frequency in nature of such variation in symmetry, in the number of petals in a flower, of joints in a limb, etc. In such cases the variation does not arise in a series of slow continuous stages, during which the additional part gradually emerges or an existing structure gradually diminishes in size. Apparently the conditions governing development lead sometimes to the emergence of the constituent part as a whole; in other cases it is absent, and we must assume the material that would have gone to its construction to have been used instead in the fabrication of its fellows. Bateson realised that the nature of the variation in this case was bound up with the process of development. He isolated this type of variation by giving it a name, and such " meristic " variation, while clear evidence of the discontinuity of diversity in species, became at the same time a line of argument and investigation, through which further enlightenment might be obtained upon the nature of the living organism.

Meristic variation is the natural outcome of an organic development which is based upon the repeated growth and division of the unit of construction, and Bateson, while primarily interested in the great pageant of evolution, realised that its elucidation must wait upon the study of that minute cosmos, the living cell. As a student Bateson would have received but little training with the microscope. He says on one occasion "neither my revered master, the professor of zoology of that time at Cambridge—a man of great learning and distinguished gifts—nor his colleague, the professor of botany, could use a microscope to any purpose: and I doubt if either of them would have seen much in a section of anything." Bateson thus makes acquaintance with the phenomena revealed by the microscope when he has already a wide knowledge of the complexities of the living organism and of the tremendous fact involved in the maintenance of species through heredity. As a result, he retains through life a vivid appreciation of the marvellous nature of the process of cell growth and division, while later generations of biologists, who make acquaintance with the details of the process before their minds are mature enough to grasp its implications, may fail in vision through a familiarity which breeds superficiality.

Bateson says in one of his later books (*Problems of Genetics*) : "When I look at a dividing cell I feel as an astronomer might do if he beheld the formation of a double star: that an original act of creation is taking place before me." And again: "I am sanguine enough to think that a comprehensive study of the geometrical phenomena of differentiation will suggest to a penetrative mind that critical experiment which may one day reveal the meaning of spontaneous division, the mystery through which lies the road, perhaps the most hopeful, to a knowledge of the nature of life."

These cell divisions, themselves rhythmic processes, he sees swept up into major rhythms which can be looked upon as "the immediate source of those geometrically ordered repetitions universally characteristic of organic life." Bateson's familiarity with the growth processes of both animals and plants enables him to see that the rhythms of development in the animal, radiating as it were from a centre of development, reach throughout its tissues to the surface in repetitive patterns carried through different structures. On the other hand, in the plant two growing centres are found, one at either extremity of the organism, which are carried farther apart during life. At these apical centres rhythms of development succeed one another to become visible in the orderly succession of leaves and floral parts

LIFE CYCLE OF SELF POLLINATING TALL PEA.

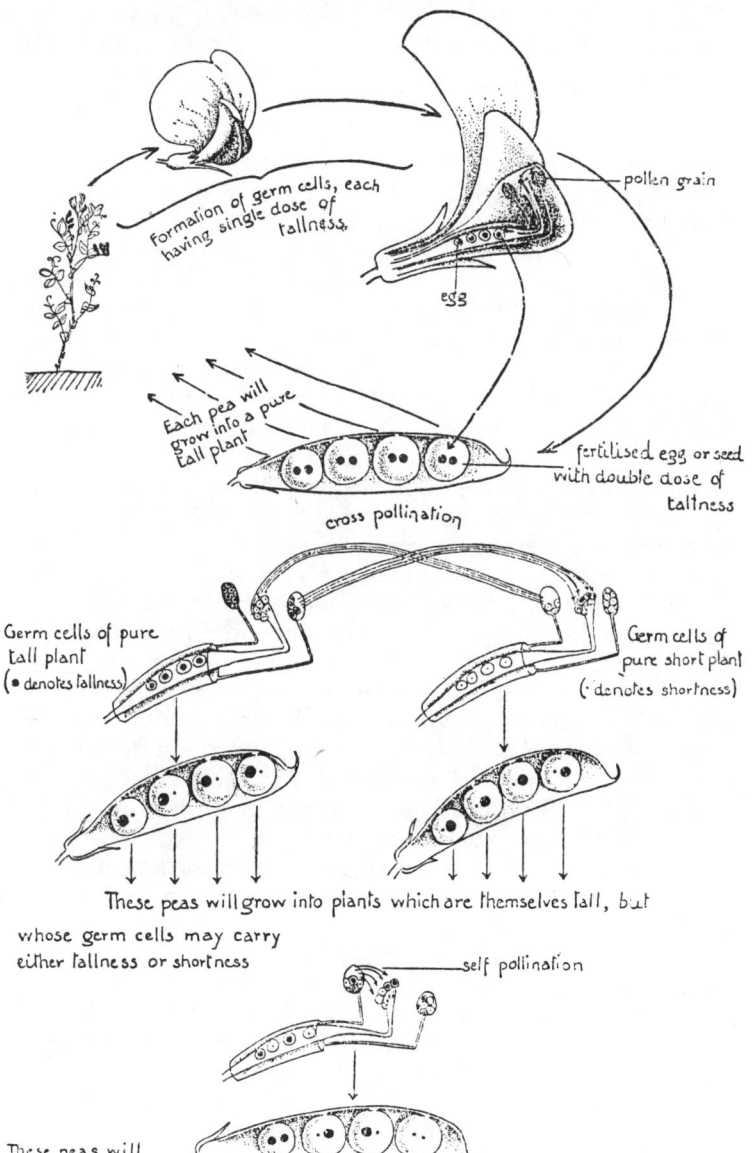

upon the shoot and of lateral branches upon the root. In his last published paper Bateson is still using his experience of the geometrical organisation of animal and plant to elucidate the way in which variations, originating during development, may be represented in the adult organism.

In the *Materials for the Study of Variation*, Bateson had assembled the known facts as to the nature of variation. The next essential was to learn whether such variations were handed on from one generation to the next. There followed some very fruitful years at Cambridge when, with the aid of a devoted group of collaborators, he initiated the long series of breeding experiments which led naturally to the creation of a Chair of Biology for him at Cambridge in 1908, and subsequently to the invitation to direct the activities of the new Institution for Horticultural Research established at Merton in 1910 under the John Innes bequest. During the Cambridge days a pilgrimage to Bateson's garden at Grantchester was always worth making; in the phrase of a contemporary there was " always something new to be seen, whether chickens or primulas, old drawings or Japanese prints," and in 1899 Bateson was able to report to the Hybrid Conference held in London that discontinuity was hereditarily transmissible. He was emphasising in this preliminary statement of aims and results, that the only practical way to follow the fate of an individual variation was to follow its distribution statistically amongst the descendants of a cross. It followed inevitably that the rediscovery in 1900 of Mendel's earlier experiments, published in 1866, inspired the Cambridge workers with a deeper conviction of the importance of their task and the soundness of their methods, though these now naturally underwent modifications in detail.

Gregor Johann Mendel, a priest of the Augustinian house of St. Thomas in Brünn, was sent by the cloister to study at the University of Vienna, subsequently returning to Brünn as a teacher until he was elected Prälat in 1868. In the large garden of the cloister he carried out the experiments which were to make him famous throughout the world, but of which an account, published by the Brünn Society of Natural Science in 1868, remained completely ignored until attention was directed to it in 1900 by three different investigators, who were able to confirm some of Mendel's conclusions from their own experience.

When Mendel's papers were thus brought to Bateson's notice he became the great protagonist of the new method of genetical study, and the Cambridge experiments were immediately directed along lines intended to confirm and extend the Mendelian hypothesis. This work was described in a series of reports to the Evolution Committee of the Royal Society 1905-1909, the first report containing an introductory statement of the essentials of the Mendelian discovery and their significance in connection with experimental breeding.

It is of the essence of Mendel's work that he carefully selected his original material, using mainly different races of the garden pea which he had first cultivated for several generations and found to breed quite true because of their habit of constant self-pollination. Selecting then certain characters of these different races of peas, which differed markedly and constantly, he hybridised forms bearing these characteristic differences, and examined the subsequent occurrence of these characters in succeeding generations resulting from the cross. The immediate result was to show order where no order had before been recognised, the achievement which gives most appeasement to the scientific spirit. Thus if a pea of a tall strain is crossed with one of a short strain, all the offspring from the seeds are tall, but if these plants are allowed to self-pollinate, 75 per cent. of the seeds give tall plants, 25 per cent. short. But while the short plants would continue to give rise only to short plants so long as they are selfed, being evidently " pure " for this character, one-third of the tall plants—or 25 per cent. of all the plants obtained on selfing the tall plants arising from the cross—are similarly " pure " for tallness; the remaining two-thirds of the tall plants—half the original progeny—continue on selfing to throw tall and short plants in the same 3 : 1 proportion.

These results, extended by the results of crossing the hybrid plants and their offspring, and holding for numerous pairs of characters, meant that for the future the phenomena of heredity must be regarded from an entirely different standpoint. Evidently each parent contributes to the offspring, not varying amounts of the infinite and mysterious complex of characters which constitute its individuality, but an assortment of definite " unitary " characters.

Some of the characters may not be able to show themselves

in the new individual as it develops from the fertilised egg; such a character we speak of as "recessive" to another "dominant" character which it has met in the fertilising process which initiates the new organism. Thus in the example quoted tallness is dominant to shortness, but in many cases, in the first hybrid generation both characters may find some expression, with the result that this generation is different from and possibly intermediate between its parents in respect to this character. The essential fact is that the characters of both parents, however blended in the hybrid, reappear in all their sharpness and permanence in one-quarter of the offspring from the selfed plants of the first hybrid generation. We thus learn that these characters were not indefinite in amount as originally received, and have not lost their identity in the hybrid, but have segregated sharply and at their original strength in its germ cells, so that in the chance matings of male and female sex cells, pollen with one character has met egg with similar character as often as it has met egg with opposite character and reciprocally, so that one-quarter of the offspring arising from the union of two germs bearing similar characters are pure for that dominant character, one-quarter are pure for the recessive character, and one-half still contain both characters. In this case the dominant is expressed in the plant, but upon selfing its seeds continue to give individuals in the proportions 1 pure dominant : 2 impure dominants : 1 pure recessive.

The essential point of this story is the "unit" nature of the contribution received in respect of a character from each parent, its retention of this unitary or discontinuous nature in the hybrid, and its segregation as a separate unit into half the germ cells of either sex formed at the reproductive stage. Mendel showed that seven characters of his peas behaved in this manner, and we can see how Bateson, conscious of the discontinuous nature of many of the variations, particularly the meristic variations he had been studying, would appreciate the magnitude of the vista thus opened to genetical experiment, and how at once he would see the appropriateness of the genetic mechanism thus laid bare, to the perpetuation of an organic mechanism in which symmetry was based upon the repetition of like parts and founded ultimately upon growing, dividing cells.

For the moment attention was withdrawn from the

evolutionary problem on the horizon and concentrated upon the behaviour of existing species upon hybridisation. One immediate result of Mendel's work is to necessitate a redefinition both of species and of variation. How do we know now, when we see an individual differing from its parents, that this is not the result of the reappearance of unitary characters, present as recessives in its parents, which are no longer masked in the new combination of characters provided by the union of the germ cells? Most of the range of variation to be seen within a typical species proves to be due to the appearance and disappearance of such hereditary characters in individuals of successive generations as new combinations of characters alternatively permit or prevent their expression. Furthermore, in the case of the plant, where individuals can often be regularly self-fertilised, it has been possible to show, as was first done by Jordan, that the species of the systematist can be resolved under continuous self-fertilisation into a number of practically invariable sub-species, now termed Jordanons, which breed true but which immediately provide the whole diversity of character present in the species when they hybridise freely with one another.

Every species would thus seem to be a group of organisms with a fairly wide range of characters which are continually interchanged and regrouped when the individuals breed freely amongst each other. But can such combinations and recombinations provide anything really new? Can they, possibly through a wider combination than usual, by the mating of more distant individuals or of individuals of more remote descent, provide the basis of a new species? Bateson discusses this problem in the Australian address already referred to. He expresses some sympathy with the views of the Dutch biologist, J. P. Lotsy, who had concluded that nothing new emerged in the organic world, except through the new combinations thus made possible by hybridisation between organisms as remote from one another in descent as possible.

Bateson was not yet prepared to think that we had exhausted the possibility of an actual change in the genetic complement of a living cell. Experience gained on the breeding grounds of Messrs. Sutton at Reading had shown him cases where a new character appears occasionally, even in pure self-fertilised material. Such cases are rarely recorded, but they provided evidence that convinced him that new characters might appear which behaved as recessives to other characters previously present, or which carried only part of the characteristics originally present in some unitary character of the organism. He was thus led to think that the evidence as yet available only demonstrated the appearance of characters which were now visible because of the loss of some genetic influence that previously repressed them or which now showed only in a fractional manner because a part of the original genetic character had disappeared, but that there was no evidence of anything new being added to the potential heritage of the race. With characteristic audacity Bateson followed this argument to its logical conclusion, and discussed the possibility of the whole great procession of organic evolution thus arising by the gradual loss, along different lines of descent, of various heritable characters carried in the primeval germ of life. Such an argument was probably only meant to force his hearers to visualise the full consequences of the theories which might emerge when the minutiæ of breeding data were passed in review. He would not regard it too seriously, as throughout his life Bateson held that we were not yet in a position to consider profitably the *causes* of variation. To quote from this Australian address once more, " we must confess also to a deep but irksome humility in presence of great vital problems."

The Mendelian work has accentuated the significance of that process of cell division to which Bateson had early drawn attention. The germ cells of the parent form but one term in a long series of such divisions, and evidently, in some division prior to their formation, the unit characters of the parent, which are a double set derived from the fusion of the sex cells that went to its formation, must be again segregated into two groups, each group the complete complement necessary to the genetic constitution of an individual. But such a group may contain almost any new combination of the unitary characters present in the parent. In Mendel's experiments, if one of the pea plants arose from a cross between a tall plant with round seeds with a short plant with wrinkled seeds, then into each germ cell of this plant must go one factor of the pair controlling length and one of the pair controlling the type of seed coat, but any combination of these characters is equally possible. It has been one of the great triumphs of biology in the early part of this century that the student of cell structure, the cytologist, has been able to show in the details of the process of division of the nucleus —a central structure of the living cell whose presence was only discovered by Robert Brown about one hundred years ago—that a procedure is followed which provides an effective machinery for this purpose. In fertilisation the male nucleus fuses with the nucleus of the egg, and in all subsequent cell divisions as the fertilised egg develops into the new individual, the nucleus separates before division into a number of fragments, of which not only the number but even the size and shape seem characteristic of the species. Each of these fragments, or chromosomes, then divides into two and the pair thus formed separate to opposite ends of the dividing cell where they enter into the formation of the two daughter nuclei, so that each nucleus contains a complete set of the original chromosomes, thus multiplied by division.

But prior to the formation of the germ cells a division occurs in which the original group of chromosomes, into which the nucleus resolves itself, separates into two groups, evidently the two original sets of chromosomes, maternal and paternal, very much as we might divide the chessmen in the full box into complete sets of white and black. But it would appear that in the successive combinations and separations which occur to our living chessmen, the chromosomes, as they meet in fertilisation and separate before the germ cells are formed, it must be as if when we swept the chessmen off the board and into the box any part whatever of a corresponding white or black chessman might exchange its position with the equivalent bit of the same chessman of opposite colour (the eight pawn and paired pieces being assumed to be individually distinct and paired in each set), so that whilst a full double set of pieces are always drawn again from the box in every case, equivalent fragments of the pieces have been exchanged as they lay side by side.

It is exceedingly difficult at present, however, to reconcile the structure of the cell, even of the nucleus and its constituent chromosomes, giving indication of complexities of structure of still finer texture, with the genetic requirements of almost innumerable hereditary factors or "genes," handed on through the germ cells from generation to generation. A gene within the growing dividing cell must itself be capable of growth and division; it represents apparently a concrete something which must always occupy its appropriate place in cell organisation. The Mendelian analysis has firmly established the fact that in any germ cell each individual gene may be represented in the organisation by one of at least a pair of possible genes, and that according to which of the pair is present will be the contribution in respect to certain hereditary characters that this germ cell makes to a new individual. Within the race or species it is now clear that it may be one of more than a pair of genes that is able to take this place in the organisation of the germ cell, and with our present knowledge of the gamut of change thus made possible through inheritance—in particular in the fly *Drosophila* studied in America by T. H. Morgan and his collaborators—it seems likely that Bateson's first attempt to define the relation between a dominant and recessive pair of characters, as due to the presence or absence of something in the chromosome, will have outlived its usefulness. There is as yet no certainty in this field, but the facts seem best fitted by the conception of a range of " genic structure " fitted to hold just this place and no other in the organisation of the germ, and finding expression always in reference to the same specific character or set of characters when that germ contributes to the production of an individual. Such a genic structure must apparently be so organised that, to use a phrase of Bateson's, only certain positions and arrangements are equilibrium positions, and can be maintained, so that there is not a continuous range of genic structure and similarly no continuity of range of expression of a character in a series of individuals possessing this gene.

The discontinuities of differences of form and structure found within the species are thus beginning to appear the natural outcome of the hereditary mechanism. The causes of the variations that will multiply this diversity and lead in the end to the production of new species still remain obscure, but the conception of a genic structure, precariously building itself up from one equilibrium position to another during the growth of the complex organisation of the cell, seems to make the appearance of new genic structures and new variations more intelligible.

And now new instruments of investigation are being fashioned in other laboratories. Under the penetrating analysis of the X-rays it has become evident that the linked carbon chains that provide the basal fabric of living protoplasm, while built up out of innumerable labile molecules, as resourceful in their variety as the life they nourish, attain a solidity and permanence as the chains increase in length that make them a suitable fibre out of which to weave the pattern that persists, more durable than the rocks, maintained in the delicate organisation of a succession of germ cells. The constituent units of such chains may only occupy certain spatial positions, and if more atoms are linked up to the chain these may only be added in suitable numbers and within certain equilibrium positions of spatial configuration: discontinuity of variation would be the necessary concomitant of a genetic mechanism in which fibres built up of such chains of atoms are woven into the living fabric.

At the same time the biologist has found that under the influence of the X-rays the rate at which variations appear during breeding experiments is remarkably enhanced; a fact which is made all the more suggestive by the discovery of the universal distribution of cosmic radiation as part of the environment in which organic evolution is proceeding.

Bateson turned to the study of variation because there he could grapple with facts: he left severely alone the interpretation of the adaptive character of the organism as an argument in support of the efficacy of natural selection, because there was no possibility of assessing quantitatively the value of various biologic structures to the race and thus putting speculation to the test of measurement. In the light of the genetic machinery which he took so large a part in revealing, the method of working of Natural Selection now seems to become faintly visible. On the one hand the complex developmental machinery linking the gene with the characters of the adult individual makes it more than possible that the specific characters, constant and reliable for the systematist, but remote from functional significance, may be linked in expression with other attributes derived from the same genes that are physiologically important and have survival value. On the other the continued study of Mendelian factors has brought to light groups of genes which modify the same character in different quantitative degrees, and which thus provide material on which selection would build up a character of biologic value in such small steps, that, in effect, we should be dealing with an accumulation of small variation in Darwin's sense, though the small steps are taken through a large number of discrete transitions governed by Mendelian laws.

In this brief retrospect of the field of biological enquiry in which Bateson was particularly interested, we have kept so closely to our main theme that we have neglected to chronicle the triumphs of achievement. Armed with the new methods of analysis the breeder has been able to identify qualities in his material which behave as Mendelian units, and which he may then either eliminate or combine with other desirable features. Thus valuable qualities of yield may be linked with resistance to disease, strains of wheat may be produced suitable for a more northerly latitude or for a belt of lower rainfall, and all over the world, since 1900, the breeder has advanced to new triumphs with confidence; yet at the same time with a most valuable appreciation of his limitations. From this standpoint it is difficult to overestimate the importance of Bateson's work to the community and its promise for the future. " In the mysterious properties of the living bodies of plants and animals there is an engine capable of wonders scarcely yet suspected, waiting only for the constructive government of the human mind."

But Bateson's mind never lingered for long upon the practical achievement attained in his chosen field of work. He was always distrustful of the claims of practice upon science, though sympathetic with the aims and interests of grower and breeder. " Alliances between pure and applied science are as dangerous as those of spiders in which the fertilising partner is apt to be destroyed "—and during his last years in the direction of the John Innes Institution he was not content to apply the now accepted Mendelian methods to the production of new and desirable horticultural novelties. " Treasure your exceptions " was still the watchword, and the attack was directed upon puzzling phenomena where Mendelian ratios did not seem to hold good, and to the analysis of material which seemed to hold out hope of showing more clearly the relation between variation and the progressive unfolding of the genetic constitution during development. Although the practice of the breeder and the outlook of the scientist upon genetic problems had been revolutionised within a generation, from Bateson's standpoint the foothills alone had been scaled from which the great problems of biology could be visualised on the horizon, clearer perhaps, but appearing more remote than before.

"If the naturalist is to succeed he must go very slowly, making good each step. He must be content to work with the simplest cases, getting from them such truths as he can, learning to value partial truth though he cheat no one into mistaking it for absolute or universal truth; remembering the greatness of his calling, and taking heed that after him will come Time, that 'author of authors,' whose inseparable property it is ever more and more to discover the truth, who will not be deprived of his due."

GERTRUDE BELL
1868-1926

By
SIR E. DENISON ROSS

GERTRUDE BELL

by SIR E. DENISON ROSS

IT is always profitable to examine and if possible discover the particular causes which lead to public fame; especially when such fame survives the death of the individual. The fame of the living is well described in modern parlance by the expression "to be in the news," while a successful undertaking is said to have " a good press." It is quite evident that Gertrude Bell would never have attained fame when living by reason of her books, or posthumous fame by her letters alone. Some outward happening was required to bring her special gifts into public prominence. Had there been no Great War her books might have been known only to the narrow circle of archæologists; her letters might have appealed only to her friends; her knowledge of the life of the Bedouins have been the wonder only of Arabs ; and her physical courage and endurance the cause of admiration only to her Swiss mountaineering guides. It was in fact the Great War which made a public figure of this remarkable Englishwoman and brought her a fame more lasting perhaps than that of any of the many devoted Englishwomen who served their country during that world crisis, although it must be remembered that her work did not end with the Armistice, but continued for many years after. The work she did was actually a man's work, and instead of comparing her work with that of other women, it would perhaps be fairer to rank her among the men who served their country best.

There was nothing in Gertrude Bell's family traditions nor in her upbringing to account for the devotion she was ultimately to give to the history and peoples of the Near East. It was indeed the merest accident that revealed in her this latent taste. She was in other respects a typical English girl of the well-to-do classes, indulging and excelling in all the delights of town and country. She enjoyed " roughing it " as much as she enjoyed a London season;

she cared as much for horses as she did for books; devoted as she was to music, she probably preferred a stiff climb in the Alps to a concert. She had one great friendship for a man whose untimely death in 1908 was one of the great sorrows of her life, but romance otherwise seemed to play but little part in her life.

There were several careers open to one possessing her rare gifts, but the task which fell to her lot during the last years of her life was not one for which a woman was really suited, though she lacked none of the necessary qualifications. It was indeed a strange fatality that placed a woman in responsible office in a land where women only go out in carriages and then closely veiled. To this day in Iraq no self-respecting Arab woman dares to walk in the street, however closely she may be veiled; yet it was in this land that Gertrude Bell, by reason of her exceptional knowledge, was destined to work for her country, and to mix with tribal chieftains of the Muslim faith whose knowledge of women was limited to their own households. We may never know what such men felt about it all in their innermost thoughts; all we know is that they accepted the situation with their inborn breeding, and that Gertrude Bell, by her natural sympathy, her understanding of the people, and her knowledge of their language and traditions, successfully performed the tasks allotted to her by her colleagues, who were indeed as unaccustomed to doing business with a woman as the Arabs themselves.

Gertrude Bell was born at Washington Hall, Durham, on July 14, 1868. Her father, Sir Hugh Bell, was a son of Isaac Lowthian Bell, F.R.S., an iron-master, colliery owner, and distinguished man of science. Her mother was Mary Shield, daughter of John Shield, of Newcastle-on-Tyne. Gertrude was thus a true North-countrywoman. When she was three years old her mother died after giving birth to Gertrude's brother Maurice. In 1876 her father married Florence Eveleen Eleanore Oliffe, and never was there a better understanding between a daughter and mother than between Gertrude and her stepmother, though the great friend of her life was her father, who was utterly devoted to his gifted daughter.

In 1886 Gertrude went to Lady Margaret Hall, Oxford, and before she was twenty she took a brilliant First Class in Modern History. Her examiners were enormously impressed by her answers, and some years later, when it was reported to her that York Powell, one of these examiners, had said she was the only girl he had ever examined who had read outside the prescribed course, Gertrude's only comment was: "What a little daring it takes to deceive this misguided sex!"

When I first met Gertrude Bell she was nearly thirty years of age. She was somewhat above medium height; her figure was slim for those days; her head set well on her shoulders; her hair fair and wavy; her face, with its somewhat irregular nose and rather severe mouth, was illuminated by steady steel-blue eyes, which often contained a merry twinkle. She always took trouble with her clothes and was always smartly dressed wherever she happened to be. She was intensely keen as a student, and I soon realised during the short time she was my pupil, that my stock-in-trade of learning, while good enough for beginners, was not of the quality she required, though I must confess that I resented this at the time, being then very young. She was indeed a really gifted linguist, speaking faultless German and French, and her Arabic in later days must have been equally fluent. Above all things she was thorough in everything she undertook. She was certainly one of the most blessed of mortals, for in addition to her intellectual gifts and her robust constitution, she was always in sufficiently easy circumstances to be able to indulge all her tastes, and down to the outbreak of the War she had as full and as interesting a life as could well be imagined. With her keen wits and her ease of manner she attracted all whom she met, and had the privilege of close acquaintance with many of the leading men of her day. She thus enjoyed every moment of her life, and if during the last ten years she was deprived of most of her favourite recreations, she had the enormous compensation of knowing that she was turning to good account in the service of her country the chief of her hobbies: the study of Arab life and literature.

Gertrude was an indefatigable letter-writer, and it is worthy of note that when her stepmother published Gertrude's letters in two large volumes, she was able to confine them to those addressed to Sir Hugh and herself and still leave very few blanks in her life record. No letters addressed to friends, however intimate, could have given us so clear a picture of Gertrude's real nature as these written to her parents, to whom she writes exactly as she would have spoken to them—using language which, though always clear, bears no traces of literary self-consciousness: if a slang expression occurred to her she used it. The letters are full of quiet fun, as for example in connection with a statement made by her servants to the effect that they had heard two bullets whizz past their ears while they were riding up to a Sasanian palace she was about to explore, when she writes: "There was no doubt about the bullets, and it is almost as annoying to be shot by accident as on purpose." In another letter she writes: "We motored that day to Birs Nimrud, which is supposed to be the Tower of Babel, and I need not say isn't, because, partly, there wasn't one, and partly because the one there wasn't in that place."

How Gertrude Bell was first drawn to the East history does not relate, but her interest in Persia was probably first aroused with the appointment of her uncle, Sir Frank Lascelles, to Teheran, for in February 1892 she writes that she is looking for a Persian teacher. In the spring of that year she accompanied her aunt, Lady Lascelles, to Persia. Unfortunately her letters to her family from Persia were lost, but her general impressions of this country are contained in a delightful little book entitled *Safar Nameh: Persian Pictures, a Book of Travel*, published anonymously by Bentley in 1894. Although favourably received it was quickly forgotten, and when in 1928 it was reprinted by Ernest Benn, it was with some difficulty that a copy for the printer could be found.

Gertrude thought very little of her first but excellent excursion into public letters, and it was only due to the urgent wishes of her father and mother that she allowed the book to appear, and then without the author's name. Many delightful books of a similar character on Persia have been published in English, but Miss Bell was, I believe, the first traveller to write on Persia from the purely belle-lettristic point of view. Previous travellers had concerned themselves with geography or antiquarian research, unless we are to except Morier and his immortal *Haji Baba*. All her subsequent publications were to be of a scholarly character, written as they were after she had definitely thrown in her lot with the Orientalists; and while recognising the permanent value of her archæological work, we should be grateful for her *Persian Pictures*, in which she tells us how she was first bewitched by this romantic country. For Persia is on the whole a wild and bare country, and its monuments—mostly in ruins—are few and far between: the spell it works on the receptive traveller is due to quite other causes than scenery or architecture. It is the result of some subtle magic in the air which all feel and no man can define. In one of her letters Miss Bell compares most aptly in a single phrase the scenery of Mesopotamia and Persia when she says that in the former the wilderness is laid flat, and in the latter is set upright.

Not until 1899 did Gertrude Bell again visit the East, but she had devoted much time during the interval to the further study of Arabic and Persian. The first serious result of these studies was a collection of translations into English verse from Hafiz, which were published by Heinemann in 1897. The renderings, though free, are perhaps the best ever made into English, and in some verses she reached a really high level of lyric beauty which showed real poetic genius. I cannot refrain from quoting here a few lines in support of this high praise:

> "*I cease not from desire till my desire*
> *Is satisfied; or let my mouth attain*
> *My love's red mouth, or let my soul expire,*
> *Sighed from those lips that sought her lips in vain.*
> *Others may find another love as fair;*
> *Upon her threshold I have laid my head,*
> *The dust shall cover me, still lying there,*
> *When from my body life and love have fled.*
>
> "*Each curling lock of thy luxuriant hair*
> *Breaks into barbèd hooks to catch my heart,*
> *My broken heart is wounded everywhere*
> *With countless wounds from which the red drops start.*
> *Yet when sad lovers meet and tell their sighs,*
> *Not without praise shall Hafiz' name be said,*
> *Not without tears, in those pale companies*
> *Where joy has been forgot and hope has fled.*"

But if Persia, with its gardens and its poetry, was Gertrude's first Eastern love, it was destined to be supplanted in her affections by the desert with its Bedouins and its camels; and from the time of her first excursion into the Syrian Desert in 1900, Arabic and the Arabs held complete sway over her affections. She did not, however, like Lady Hester Stanhope, turn Oriental, or show any inclination to adopt Eastern dress, though there were moments in her life in Baghdad when she confessed she was overcome with the sense of being as much an Asiatic as a European in her sympathies, and this feeling, combined with an unswerving loyalty to her own country, fitted her admirably for dealing with the Arab chiefs of Mesopotamia. It is an only too common experience to find English men and women whose enthusiasm for the Orient leads them into a state of antagonism towards their own fellow countrymen and their own national traditions. Miss Bell was not one of those European students, who, having contributed to the bridging of the gap between East and West, proceed to establish themselves on the other side and abuse their own; and although she hated home politics, and in referring to tariff reform could write with feeling that she valued one couplet of Imrul Kais (the ancient Bedouin poet) above all the fiscal pamphlets in the world, she was a firm believer in England's mission in the East, and realised how difficult it would be for Iraq to stand alone.

Gertrude Bell always remained typically Western in her tastes and recreations. The same qualities of endurance and daring required for her adventurous journeys in the desert were shown in her mountain-climbing in the Alps, in which she excelled as in all else she undertook. An episode on the Finsteraarhorn in 1902, where she and her two guides were obliged to remain roped for fifty hours on end, is related with great vividness and equal modesty in a remarkable letter from which I extract the following passage:

> "We thought the worst was over, but there was a more dangerous place to come. It was a place that had been pretty difficult to go up, a steep but short slope of iced rock by which we had turned the base of a tower. The slope was now covered with about 4 inches of avalanche snow and the rocks were quite hidden. It was on the edge of a big couloir down which raced a snow river. We managed badly somehow; at any rate Ulrich and I found ourselves on a place where there was not room for us both to stand, at the end of the extra rope. He was very insecure and could not hold me; Heinrich was below on the edge of the couloir, also very insecure. And here I had to refix the extra rope on a rock a little below me so that it was practically no good to me. But it was the only possible plan. The rock was too difficult for me, the stretches too big, I couldn't reach them: I

handed my axe down to Heinrich and told him I could do nothing but fall, but he couldn't, or at any rate, didn't secure himself, and in a second we were both tumbling head over heels down the couloir, which was, you understand, as steep as snow could lie. How Ulrich held us I don't know. He said himself he would not have believed it possible, but hearing me say I was going to fall he had stuck the pointed end of the ice axe into a crack above and on this alone we all three held. I got on to my feet in the snow directly I came to the end of my leash of rope and held Heinrich and caught his ice axe and mine, and we slowly cut ourselves back up the couloir to the foot of the rock. But it was a near thing, and I felt rather ashamed of my part in it. This was the time when I thought it on the cards we should not get down alive. Rather a comforting example, however, of how little can hold a party up."

In 1905 Gertrude Bell was back again in Syria and Asia Minor, and in 1907 she produced her second book of travels under the title of *The Desert and the Sown*. While in Asia Minor she had worked with Sir William Ramsay, and with him she wrote *The Thousand and One Churches*, published in 1909, in which were described, with plans and measurements, the more important churches and architectural remains of Bingbirklisse, at the foot of Mount Qara Dagh. But the greatest achievement of her life was her journey across the uncharted desert from Damascus to Hayil. As a result of this journey, which was full of exciting adventures, she put on the map a line of wells hitherto unplaced or unknown, and collected a mass of information regarding the tribal elements ranging between the Hejaz Railway on the one flank and the Sirhan and Nefud on the other, of which Colonel Lawrence made signal use in the Arab campaigns of 1917 and 1918. It was of course the political information which she accumulated at this time that led to her employment during the Great War at Cairo, Basra, and Baghdad. It is characteristic of her pluck that, writing from Baghdad after her long desert journey, she speaks of her projected journey across the Syrian Desert to Damascus as " quite safe and easy." To any other woman, before the desert motor service had been thought of, such a journey would have seemed adventurous enough.

Except for three short holidays in England and a visit in 1920 with Sir Percy Cox to Cairo to confer with Winston Churchill, who had just taken over the Colonial Office, Gertrude Bell was continuously in Baghdad from 1917 to 1926. Never was a more complex task set for British officials than that of adjusting the affairs of Iraq after the withdrawal of the whole Turkish personnel, together with the Turkish Army. Nothing was left behind in the shape of records, and the whole administration had to be organised afresh. No sooner had the British occupied Baghdad than the notables of Baghdad and the tribal sheikhs from near and far began to pour into the city to call on the Chief Political Officer, Sir Percy Cox, and one of the most important matters was to determine and record whence these visitors came, what their relations were to one another, and what was their relative importance among themselves. Gertrude Bell it was who first interviewed all these men before passing them on to Sir Percy Cox with a brief note on the tribe, the home, and the needs of each. The most thrilling interview for Gertrude Bell was her meeting with King Ibn Saud, who had accepted an invitation to Baghdad. We can imagine what it meant to her to be brought face to face with the greatest ruler in Arabia, from whom she might with luck receive permission to visit his capital when the clouds of war had dispersed. As for Ibn Saud he had never before come in contact with any European woman, but when the interview took place, "he met Miss Bell," as Sir Percy Cox tells us, "with complete frankness and sangfroid, as if he had been associated with European ladies all his life."

There was one side to Miss Bell's activities during her last years to which special reference must be made, namely, her establishment of a museum of antiquities in Baghdad. She had for some time past taken a lively interest in Sumerian and Babylonian archæology, and had paid several visits to Ur. It was with Mr. Woolley's help that she began to collect and arrange the various finds which had become the property of the Iraq Government. In March 1923 she writes: "I went to Ur with Major Wilson [the architect]. They are closing down for the season, and we had to go in person and divide the finds between the diggers and the Iraq [Government]. . . . It took us the whole day to do the division. . . ." On June 16, 1926, King Feisal opened the first room of the Museum, which had been built at her suggestion. How much she had the success of this museum at heart is shown by the fact that in her will she left £6,000 in trust with the British Museum for the furtherance of archæological research in Iraq.

It was no doubt the strenuous self-imposed work in the museum in the terrible heat of the Baghdad summer, in addition to the long hours of routine in her office, which finally overtaxed her already waning energies. When she went home in 1925 she was in very poor health, and although four months in England seemed to restore her to her wonted strength, she had a bad illness shortly after her return to Baghdad, from which she never quite recovered. She was destined to spend the last nine years of her life in Baghdad; and it was only her intense enthusiasm for the Arabs and their history that prevented her regarding this as a form of exile. But it required far more than enthusiasm to be able to face cheerfully those long years in the trying climate of Iraq: it required that single devotion to duty and patriotic optimism which are reflected in all her letters from Baghdad. Although she had hitherto possessed a physique which seemed to defy all climatic conditions and all manner of privation, since her illness the lack of fresh food, combined with the attacks of sand-flies, in addition to her work, was too much even for Gertrude Bell, and her energy and vitality were more than once reduced almost to vanishing point long before she finally rendered up her strong soul in sleep in July 1926. Her grave lies in the Christian burial-ground on a hill outside Baghdad, and is surmounted by a simple white tomb bearing her name in Arabic and in English. In the church of her village home in Yorkshire there is a beautiful memorial window round which is cut in deep letters one of her favourite quotations from the Persian poets, and her English adaptation of the verses:

" *Qazā dastīst panj angusht dārad*
Chi khwāhad az kasī kāmī bar āyad
Du bar chasmash nihad dīgar du bar gūsh
Yekī bar lab nihad gūyad ki khāmūsh."

" Thus said the Poet : ' When Death comes to you
All ye whose life-sand through the hour-glass slips,
He lays two fingers on your ears, and two
Upon your eyes he lays, one on your lips,
Whispering : " Silence ! " ' "

ARNOLD BENNETT
1867-1932

By
ROBERT LYND

ARNOLD BENNETT

by ROBERT LYND

WHEN Arnold Bennett had finished correcting the proofs of *Clayhanger*, he wrote in his diary: " I notice the far too frequent use of the word ' extraordinary,' but I loathe altering a work once it is done—no mistake about that." It was a wise instinct that made him leave the word undeleted. His excessive use of the adjective " extraordinary " was an expression of his perpetual sense of the extraordinary. It was as natural for him to write " extraordinary "—and mean it—as it was for Dominie Sampson to say " Prodigious ! " Arnold Bennett brought into literature something of the capacity for amazement of a youth from the provinces up in London for the day of the Cup Final.

One sometimes hears Bennett spoken of as though he were a materialist who wrote not from any spiritual compulsion, but with the motives of a tradesman. Those who take this view are as a rule poets or writers with private means. Their theory of artistic inspiration is that the artist works for his own pleasure, uninfluenced by the tastes of his audience or by the desire for applause or the need of making money. The poet, they say, speaks in reverie, and the world merely overhears him. This may be true in regard to lyric poetry; but the history of English literature, from Shakespeare to Dickens, and from Dickens to Bennett, shows that in the drama or in fiction it is possible—and even usual—for a writer, while remaining faithful to his genius, to be fully conscious of the existence of his public and to combine material with artistic purposes. In such matters, one must judge by results; and, if we do so, I think we shall be forced to admit that the divine spark is not necessarily quenched in a writer because he is often driven to his desk by the necessity of paying his bills.

It may be replied to this that Bennett's case differs from

that of the great writers, and that it is inconceivable that any dramatist or novelist of enduring genius should have confessed, as Bennett confessed in *The Truth About an Author*: " I have never once produced any literary work without preliminary inspiration quite other than that of ebullient imagination. I have never ' wanted to write,' until the extrinsic advantages of writing had presented themselves to me! " It must be remembered, however, that this was written in 1903, when Bennett was thirty-six years old, and before any of the novels that were to make his reputation had even been begun. It is also worth remembering that in the same year he copied into his diary a passage from Casanova, part of which ran: " The artifice which I employed was to record the thing simply, and just as it was, without omitting even any circumstances which might be hurtful to me. . . . I have learned by experience that truth is a talisman of which the charm never fails, provided that one does not squander it on rascals." After quoting this, Bennett adds: "What a motto for my *Truth About an Author*!" The quotation and the comment throw even more light on the nature of Bennett's inspiration as a writer than the confession that he never " wanted to write " merely for writing's sake.

As a child, it must be admitted, he was brought up in surroundings unlikely to awaken literary longings. Born at Shelton, Hanley, in Staffordshire, on May 27, 1867, and educated at Newcastle Middle School, he passed his boyhood in an environment in which literature scarcely existed outside the school-books; and it was not particularly interesting as it was taught from these.

He seems to have read none of the great authors in his youth; and he tells us that the first thing that impelled him to write was the offer of a Five Towns paper to " buy approved short stories from local readers at a guinea apiece." Soon afterwards another paper advertised for a serial story of local interest; and Bennett, having read a translation of *L'Assommoir*, sat down and wrote " a sinister narrative to illustrate the evils of marrying a drunken woman." Few men of genius have had an odder first meeting with their destiny.

He was a lawyer's clerk by this time, and, on coming to London in his twenties, he continued for some years to work in a lawyer's office before deciding to devote himself entirely to journalism and literature. He then obtained an appointment on a now extinct paper, *Woman*, which he afterwards edited from 1896 to 1901. He had already begun to dream dreams of the finer kind of authorship, and had sat down to write his first novel " under the sweet influences of the de Goncourts, Turgeniev, Flaubert, and de Maupassant." During the last year of his editorship, apart from his editorial work, he wrote three plays (two in collaboration), a serial story of 70,000 words, the draft of another novel of 80,000 words, about half-a-dozen short stories, and 196 articles of various length, besides collecting a series of his articles into a book, *Fame and Fortune*. His income during the year—the largest he had yet made—he was then thirty-three—was £620. " This year . . ." he wrote on the following New Year's Day, " I hope to make much more."

It was while he was editing *Woman* that he decided very seriously, partly on the advice of Mr. Eden Phillpotts, " to take up fiction for a livelihood."

" Till the end of 1899 [he wrote in 1898] I propose to give myself up absolutely to writing the sort of fiction that sells itself. . . . To write popular fiction is offensive to me, but it is far more agreeable than being tied daily to an office and editing a lady's paper, and, perhaps, it is less ignoble and less of a strain on the conscience. . . . Moreover, I think that fiction will pay better, and, in order to be happy, I must have a fair supply of money."

The decision may seem as coolly commercial as the announcement of it is candid; but the fact remains that it was this coolly commercial decision that set Bennett free to write *The Old Wives' Tale* and *Clayhanger*.

No sensitive reader, however, could begin even one of the " pot-boiling " books of Arnold Bennett in those days without feeling that here was an original talent, fresh, fantastic, and observant, that might possibly blossom into genius. The man who could produce so good work as this, one felt sure (or almost sure), had it in him to produce work that was very much better. The truth is that, whatever may have been the motives that drove Bennett to write, he became a craftsman and an artist as he wrote. He was moved by the wonder and the mystery of life; he was excited by the contemporary scene; he had a profound love of courage and justice; and his conception of the ideal spirit of the art he practised may be gathered from a note jotted down in early life: " Essential characteristic of the really great novelist: a Christ-like all-embracing compassion." Qualities of heart and mind so clearly marked as his could not but be reflected to some extent in what he wrote. It is not only in the important novels that one is aware of the personality of Bennett. Turn even to a minor novel, *Whom God Hath Joined*, and you will find his imaginative attitude to life expressed in the opening sentence :

> " When I was young [he begins] the road leading out of the Five Towns up to Toft End was nothing to me save a steep path towards fresh air and open horizons; but now that I have lived a little it seems to me the very avenue to a loving comprehension of human nature, and I climb it with a strange, overpowering mystical sense of the wonder of existence."

It was this loving comprehension of human nature, and this sense of the wonder of existence—a sense which some critics have denied him—that enabled Bennett ultimately to rise above the level of ephemeral fiction and to write two of the most enduring novels of his time.

His books, even his minor books, are shaped, too, by his incessant and ingenuous curiosity—curiosity about ethics and people and literature and painting and music and hotels and the latest fashion and gadgets and almost every phase of contemporary life outside religion. He surveyed life as a man who was ambitious to be at once an expert, a connoisseur, and a reformer. He had a passion for discovering the " right thing," whether in conduct or in books, and letting the world know it and, more than that, know that he knew it. It was characteristic of him that he called an early series of articles he wrote " Savoir Faire Papers." For, indeed, he desired, not only wisdom, but worldly wisdom. He aimed at becoming a man of the world who could " tell the world " about this, that, and the other thing. Thus we feel, as we read his literary criticism, that he was immensely eager not only to spread a taste for the books he admired but to prove his individuality in admiring them. He wrote about books with the assurance of a napping tipster; and he gave tips about life as well as about books. All those books about the

by ROBERT LYND

conduct of life, such as *How to Live on Twenty-four Hours a Day*, *Self and Self-Management*, and *How to Make the Best of Life*, revealed a very real aspect of the personality of " the man who knew "—a being, in this case, at once cocksure and benevolent. He was so eager, indeed, to tell the world what it ought to know and do that on more than one occasion he contributed a regular causerie to a weekly paper for nothing, or almost nothing. He liked to have a finger in the pie, if the pie seemed to him meritorious. It was a profound enthusiasm for good work and a profound desire to be associated with it that led to his becoming a director on the board of a weekly paper and to his theatrical enterprises.

Everything that we know of him goes to show that he was a very exceptional human being—that, even when he was ordinary, he was superlatively ordinary—and that he was also a born artist. His very script gave him artistic pleasure, and he exhibited his manuscripts to new-comers to his house with an artist's pride. He liked to spend a holiday sketching in water-colours. He was devoted to music, and, indeed, was one of the most conspicuous figures in the London of his day both in the concert-hall and in the theatre. You might quarrel with some of his artistic tastes, and feel that in all the arts he was inclined to overestimate the latest moderns, but you could not doubt the genuineness of his artistic responses. Though he wrote verse, no one would call him a poet on that account; yet no one who was not essentially a poet could have made so moving a use of Poe's " Helen " in *The Pretty Lady*. Nor could he have written *Clayhanger*.

It was thus a man of exceptionally complex character who set out to make his way into literature through hackwork in fiction. At once a sensitive artist and an impudent " card," an idealist who aimed at a loving comprehension of human nature and a realist with an ostentatious appreciation of money and of all the things that money can buy, a reformer and a worldling—there has been no other novelist of genius quite like him, or nearly like him, in the records of English literature. One sometimes wonders whether, if he had not left England, a man of such mixed qualities would ever have escaped from the rut of brilliantly accomplished hack writing. Luckily, some months after abandoning journalism for novel-writing as a profession, he went to live in Paris. He had already steeped himself in the French fiction of the nineteenth century; but now, instead of reading the

French novelists through the eye of a Five-Townsman, he began to look at the Five Towns through the eyes of a French novelist. Whatever may have been the cause—whether a deeper emotion about the life of his own people remembered from a distance or the imaginative stimulus of a foreign capital—it is certain that his talent ripened as a result of transplantation. We also know that it was in Paris that the central idea of *The Old Wives' Tale* first occurred to him, and that he immediately settled in his own mind that the book must be an English equivalent of Maupassant's *Une Vie*.

Bennett has left a record of the birth of the idea of *The Old Wives' Tale* both in a preface and in his diary. He tells us how one evening he was dining in the Duval restaurant in the Rue de Clichy when he found a " fat, shapeless, ugly, and grotesque " woman sitting at his usual table. She was so repulsive and fussy that all the waitresses were laughing at her; and Bennett, pained by their heartlessness, reflected : " This woman was once young, slim, perhaps beautiful; certainly free from these ridiculous mannerisms. Very probably she is unconscious of her singularities. Her case is a tragedy. One ought to be able to make a heartrending novel out of the history of a woman such as she." He decided that this particular woman was too " unsympathetic " to be made the heroine of a novel, realised that he must " choose the sort of woman who would pass unnoticed in a crowd " as his heroine, and then determined to " go one better " than Maupassant's *Une Vie* by making his novel the story, not of one woman, but of two. Businesslike though Bennett was in his methods, however, he did not begin to write *The Old Wives' Tale* at once, but left the idea to mature in his mind till the autumn of 1907, when he set to work on the first of his masterpieces " in a village near Fontainebleau, where I had rented half a house from a retired railway-servant." " I wrote the first part of the novel," he declares, " in six weeks. It was fairly easy to me, because in the 'seventies, in the first decade of my life, I had lived in the actual draper's shop of the Baineses, and knew it as only a child could know it." In the following August the book was finished, and no sooner was it published than it was generally agreed that it was immeasurably in advance of any other novel that he had previously written. Bennett's note in his diary, after hearing that the publication of a fourth edition was possible, makes it clear to us that he was by no means the single-minded idolater of success, basking in worldly prosperity and asking for nothing more, that some have thought him. "I had not in the least hoped for this success," he writes. "It alters the value of all my future books. Yet I was depressed all afternoon because I could not make a sketch. Another proof that public success is no guarantee of happiness or even content. I think it makes no difference." In his novel *The Glimpse*, the central figure propounds the same philosophy.

> "I was forty-two years of age [the hero declares] and in possession of what I had all my life up to about forty, instinctively and without questioning, considered to be the essentials of happiness. . . . And I said to myself: 'Is this all? Is this all it is?' And bent myself to another work, as it were to a forlorn hope."

Meanwhile, he had written the most brilliant of his short stories, *The Matador of the Five Towns*, and begun *Denry the Audacious*, which under its altered title, *The Card*, was to take a place among his books comparable with that held by *Mr. Polly* among the books of Mr. Wells. This fantastic extravaganza of success impudently achieved introduced in "Denry" a new comic character into English fiction; yet, when he had finished writing it, the best that Bennett could say of it in the privacy of his diary was: "Stodgy, no real distinction of any sort, but well invented, and done up to the knocker, technically, right through." All through this period, which was his great period of imaginative fecundity, we find the same note of self-questioning and self-criticism recurring. He is neither sure of success nor sure that success will bring content. Even when *Clayhanger* gets a good reception in the Press on its appearance in 1910, he cannot believe that it will appeal to the public.

> "I began [he writes] to foresee a comparative failure for *Clayhanger*. . . . Useless for me to argue that it is absurd for me to *expect* even a good circulation for books like *Clayhanger*, which arouses enthusiasm in just a few beings! This in spite of the fact that I cannot make less than £1,500 next year, and may make £2,000 or over— and this by doing only the work that pleases me—my very best work. I was still gloomy this morning."

How different a portrait of Bennett—a man of forty-three, who had just published his greatest book—this suggests from the portrait that has so often been painted of him as a highly self-satisfied " best-seller "! The truth is, Bennett was not even a " best-seller " in the ordinary sense of the word. If he had not been a journalist and dramatist as well as a novelist, he would never have been suspected of the crime of making a fortune out of writing.

Everybody would, I suppose, agree that either *The Old Wives' Tale* or the *Clayhanger* trilogy—at least, the first volume of the trilogy—is Bennett's greatest book. The only considerable competitor is *Riceyman Steps*, and even *Riceyman Steps* is scarcely a competitor. To me it seems that *Clayhanger* is the greatest novel that he wrote. Here he was doing " only the work that pleased him," recording the lives of people " who would pass unnoticed in a crowd," and doing this with his imagination, his observation, and his understanding sympathy all at full stretch. This is his fullest record of the world he knew best. It is, in a sense, an extremely unattractive world. No one who did not live in it would wish to live in it. Bennett himself once got into trouble for saying " You cannot conceive the dullness of the Five Towns." He was speaking, however, as a man who could not live comfortably except in a free and lively intellectual atmosphere. He was perfectly well aware that to the inhabitants of the Five Towns the crises of joy and sorrow are as real as they ever were to the heroes and beautiful women who people the great epics. He realised that the full tide pours as beautifully into the muddiest estuaries as upon the most magnificent shores. Who that has lived on the coast of Essex has not delighted in the spectacle of the wide map of mud, intersected with dirty creeks, that at full tide takes on so astonishingly the glorious aspect of the blue ocean? In *Clayhanger* Bennett has marvellously suggested just such a scene—the drab swept over and transfigured by romance— ugliness that reflects the blue of heaven at the hour of full tide.

Miss Rebecca West has said of Bennett:

> " He is a prestidigitateur with the ordinary, the medium, the mediocre things of life: the shirts, the boots, the coats, the trams, the trains, the suburbs, the small houses, the people who live in them. That is the

> secret of his greatness, which is otherwise hard to explain. . . . He has not let custom blunt his vision of the astounding bizarrerie of daily life."

That is excellently said, but it seems to me to limit Bennett's genius too exclusively to the surface of things and to leave out of account his great moral and imaginative qualities —pity, sympathy, understanding, and delight in the triumph of the fullness of life even amid flatness.

I do not wish to claim for Bennett a place beside Dickens and the great novelists of Europe. He had neither the abundant vitality nor the abundant subject-matter of the great masters. At the same time, I doubt whether a greater novel than *Clayhanger* has appeared in England in the present century.

Yet how devoid of beauty is the setting in which young Edwin Clayhanger sets out to make a success of his life, a heroic young egotist of the provincial lower middle classes! We are not even spared the " eructations " of the elder Clayhanger when he has had enough to eat. Even in the most commonplace surroundings, however, man is not commonplace to the imagination in his sufferings and in his strivings; and the early description of the child Darius's life in the factory makes us from the outset see the people of the Five Towns against the background of the eternal pitifulness of human life. Edwin himself, after leaving school, ceases to be commonplace when he decides to give up trifling with life and to make himself a man.

> " ' I'll show 'em,' he muttered. And he meant that he would show the world. . . . He was honouring the world, paying the finest tribute to it. In that head of his a flame burned that was like an altar-fire, a miraculous and beautiful phenomenon than which there is nothing more miraculous nor more beautiful over the whole earth."

" The mysterious and holy flame of the desire for self-perfection blazing within the tousled head " transfigures Edwin at once as surely as if he were a knight setting out on a quest. His striving is no vulgar striving. He aims, as Bennett himself did, not merely at success, but at making a success of life. It is true that, though his life is a romance, it lacked a romantic vocabulary. What Chapman's *Homer* did for the imagination of Keats, a new house with a hot-water system did for the imagination of Edwin Clayhanger. " The new house inspired him. It was not a paradise, but it was a temple. . . . I say," declares Bennett, " that the hot-water system of the new house, simple and primitive as it was, affected and inspired Edwin like a poem." Again, on first hearing of the girl who is to be the love of his life, his response is strangely unlike that of Rudel on hearing of the Lady of Tripoli. " Bit of all right is she ? " asks Edwin with a would-be knowing air. Yet, when we have come to the end of the vicissitudes in the lives of Edwin and Hilda, we feel not so much that we have been following a commonplace and prosaic route as that we have been watching the full procession of life with its variety and its purpose passing along the route. " What a fine thing life is ! " reflects Edwin at the end of *Clayhanger*. " What a romance she has made of my life ! " he says to himself when Hilda kisses him at the end of *These Twain*. The " fineness," the " romance," of life even in the materialistic, everyday world—this is what Bennett proclaimed and proved to his own generation. It was because he believed in this so intensely that he was able, while writing realistic fiction, to give it the gleam of heroic literature.

It is the custom to regard Bennett's literary life as having come to an end with the publication of the *Clayhanger* series, and to deplore his failure ever again to produce a novel of a high order with the possible exception of *Riceyman Steps*. It seems to me unreasonable to expect an author to have an unlimited store of genius which he can draw upon at will as the widow drew upon her cruse of oil. Most writers have their great periods of imaginative fertility, and it is surely ungrateful to complain that, having given us so much, they do not give us more. Better to be content with the best of what Wordsworth and Browning, Thackeray and Hardy, Galsworthy and Mr. Wells, Bennett and Sir James Barrie have written, and not to demand still further miracles of them. That is why I differ from the gloomy opinion of Bennett's later years expressed in Mr. Geoffrey West's able little book, *The Problem of Arnold Bennett*. Mr. West seems to me to be overshadowed by the problem " Why Bennett failed," whereas I think the only problem that will interest posterity is " How Bennett succeeded." I do not

by ROBERT LYND

believe that the true explanation of the quality of his later work is that " the hardening, as it were, of his spiritual arteries caused him to succumb to his environment and material possessions as his characters to theirs." I am convinced, on the contrary, that the reason why he did not go on producing *Old Wives' Tales* and *Clayhangers* was that he had expressed himself fully in those novels, had worked out the richest vein of his genius, and was compelled to turn to subjects of which he had much less imaginative knowledge. *The Pretty Lady*, *Lord Raingo*, and *Mr. Prohack* were undoubtedly on a lower level than *Clayhanger*, but it was a better sign of spiritual vitality that he should write them than it would have been if he had attempted to write an imitation of *Clayhanger*. There was certainly no evidence of hardening of the spiritual arteries in *Riceyman Steps* where, in the story of the two misers and the servant-girl, he returned to a lower middle-class world which he knew both intimately and emotionally. In *Imperial Palace* he wrote of a world with which he had no such lifelong emotional associations, the grandiose world of the big hotel; but even here he put a good deal of his real, if more superficial, self into the book. Did he not once say: " What I love is organisation ? " He was fascinated by it even as a young man, and he cannot be said to have betrayed his genius by writing of things that interested him.

Apart from his work as a novelist and dramatist—his plays *Milestones* and *The Great Adventure* were excellent inventions—Bennett will be remembered as one of the most attractive figures in the literary England of his time. He had as many friends as it is possible for any man to have, and they all found him as amusing a character as he was lovable. His presence brightened any company into which he entered. The grey plume of hair above his forehead, the flamboyant dress-shirt, the fob, the onyx waistcoat buttons, the touch of swagger in the erect carriage of his body—everything about him suggested that he had got himself up to play the leading part in a comic social pageant. He had few natural graces, but he made up for the lack of these with his airs. He succeeded even in turning his disadvantages into advantages. His stammer, for example, gave an original tempo to his conversation; some words being pronounced very, very slowly and the end of the sentence with a quick jerk, and in the result even an ordinary sentence, uttered in his high-pitched jackdaw voice, was sometimes as effective as a witty epigram. He could say, " She's a fool! " about a woman he disliked in a way that made it seem an original and picturesque judgment. He was a good listener as well as a good talker, and so eager was he not to miss anything that was going on that he seemed to have ears and eyes for all the conversationalists in a room as well as for the person with whom he was talking. He never failed to give other people the impression that he was deeply interested in them and their opinions. And this was not mere flattery. There was nothing in him of the self-absorbed egotist. His very vanity was playful and essentially social. He enjoyed the fun of being a great man and played the part in a way that made it fun for others. All his friends describe him as shy and diffident, and it was the mixture of deeper human qualities with ingenuous cockiness that endeared him to so many people. Though sometimes sardonic in his speech, he was supremely good-natured. Though in revolt against some of the orthodox opinions of what constitutes goodness, he was as surely a good man as a good writer. His success in life was not merely that of a worldly and courageous adventurer, but that of a magnanimous, courteous, just, and high-principled man.

LORD BIRKENHEAD
1872-1930

By
SIR CLAUD SCHUSTER

LORD BIRKENHEAD

by SIR CLAUD SCHUSTER

FREDERICK EDWIN SMITH was born at Birkenhead on July 12, 1872, the eldest son of the marriage of one Frederick Smith and Elizabeth Taylor. He was educated at Birkenhead Grammar School and at Wadham College, Oxford. He gained a Second Class in Classical Moderations and a First in Law, was not far from getting his Blue at Rugby Football, and was President of the Union. He won the Vinerian Scholarship, was elected to a Fellowship at Merton, and for three years lived at Oxford teaching Law and doing the work of a University Extension Lecturer in History.

In 1899 he was called to the Bar by Gray's Inn, and then practised locally at Liverpool, having been a pupil of Mr. Leslie Scott (now the Right Hon. Sir Leslie Scott, K.C.). In 1906 he was elected to Parliament as Conservative Member for the Walton Division of Liverpool, and moved his chambers to London, and in 1908 he took Silk. In 1911 he received a Privy Councillorship upon the occasion of King George V's Coronation.

When the War broke out he held a Commission in the Queen's Own Oxfordshire Hussars. He remained in England for some little time as head of the Press Bureau; but he soon went to France, and was attached to the Indian Corps. Upon the formation of the First Coalition Government he became Solicitor-General, and in November 1915 he succeeded Sir Edward (now Lord) Carson as Attorney-General, with a seat in the Cabinet. He held this office until the reconstitution of Mr. Lloyd George's Government at the beginning of 1919, when he received the Great Seal as Lord Chancellor. He went out of office when Mr. Lloyd George's Government fell at the end of 1922, and remained out through the Conservative Governments of Mr. Bonar

Law and Mr. Baldwin and through Mr. MacDonald's first Labour Administration. The rift between him and his Conservative colleagues, consequent upon the events of 1922, was sufficiently healed by the time of the General Election of 1924 for him to take an active part in support of Mr. Baldwin's appeal to the country, and when Mr. Baldwin returned to power, in the autumn of 1924, Lord Birkenhead, as he then was, accepted office as Secretary of State for India. He resigned that office in October 1928, going into the City, and he died on September 30, 1930.

He married in 1901 Margaret, daughter of the Rev. H. Furneaux, Fellow of Corpus. He was created a Baronet in January 1918, Baron Birkenhead upon his appointment to the Lord Chancellorship, Viscount Birkenhead in June 1921, and Earl of Birkenhead and Viscount Furneaux in November 1922, taking his second title from his wife's family name. He was High Steward of the University of Oxford, and had been Rector of the Universities of Glasgow and Aberdeen. He was a Bencher of Gray's Inn, and twice served as Treasurer of that Society. He was a member of the Carlton Club and of the Royal Yacht Squadron. He received from the King of Belgium the Grand Cordon of the Order of Leopold, and was created Knight Grand Cross of the Star of India when he resigned his Secretaryship of State.

In person he was tall, with long legs and a powerful frame, both physically and constitutionally of exceptional toughness. His face was long and well-shaped, with a straight, well-cut nose, and a peculiarly beautiful and sensitive mouth and lips. The well-known caricature of him in *Vanity Fair* scarcely does him justice, for it exaggerates his " legginess," and imparts to his face a certain effeminacy which was very far from his characteristic, either in appearance or in fact. In truth, the bones of his face, like those of his limbs, were big, and suggested power, though the ordinary observer, even if familiar with his features, would not have ascribed to them the over-osseous development shown in the portrait by Mr. Glyn Philpot which hangs in Gray's Inn Hall. He could, when occasion demanded, bear himself with dignity, though his sloping shoulders and a peculiar way he had of carrying himself, sometimes degenerating into a slouch, produced an illusion of lassitude, which in no way corre-

by SIR CLAUD SCHUSTER

sponded to the reality either of his physical or his intellectual make up. Especially was this the case when he was sitting on the Woolsack or at some conference or committee. In the latter case, he would remain silent, his body somewhat hunched, his head dropped, his eyes cast down and eyelids drooping, one elbow resting on the table, and his hands only moving at intervals to remove a long cigar from his lips. He appeared to be utterly bored and to be taking no interest in the conversation. The time would arrive for him to speak; then he would immediately deliver a terse but complete summary of such of the arguments addressed to the meeting as had any relevance to the question under discussion, leaving no point unnoticed and holding the gathering. When he had finished, he had produced the impression that he had spoken, and the matter in debate was exhausted.

He paid to the world in which he moved the compliment of dressing himself with decorum and in reasonable pace with the fashion, though he greatly resented the discomfort of being dressed up. He liked bright colours and a bright flower in his buttonhole. His complexion was of a dark tan, partly by nature and partly through constant exposure to the sun and wind. And it was difficult to tell whether his hat slipped to the back of his head by reason of his cranial construction or because he thought a rollicking mien suitable to his appearance and character.

These bare facts, his birth, his early provincial upbringing, Oxford, Wadham, the Bar, Gray's Inn, the Northern Circuit, Liverpool, the House of Commons, the Law Officerships, the Lord Chancellorship, were, in a sense, the man. The appearance and the carriage displayed him, so far as a being so diverse and so subtle could offer himself for the estimate of the eye. Everyone lives and struggles, and succeeds or fails, subject to the conditions of his heredity, his birth, and his education, and handicapped or favoured by the hundred little chances which come in his way. Thus, we say of So-and-So that he was at Eton, or at Oxford, or was a Fellow of such and such a College, or a member of such and such a profession, meaning that, by reason of the peculiar experience there acquired in the situation of which we speak, we may expect to find some particular quality in him. But with F. E. Smith each one of these things was intermingled with him so as to form the fibre of his being. He took what everyone of them had to offer for an advantage with both hands greedily; on the other hand, he paid back to the utmost of his power, whether in money or in admiration or in love.

First, as to his birth: he grew from a stout, North-country root, from one of those families of manual labourers, which from time to time struggle upwards to enrich the stock of the governing classes, and to make their contribution to the history of England. In his father the family had made its way into the middle class. Frederick Smith, the elder, had begun life as a private soldier in a line regiment; then he became an estate agent in Birkenhead. There was in him a dash of fire inherited from his mother, who brought into the family a wildness and a power of imagination which have been—perhaps fancifully—attributed to gipsy blood. Frederick Smith, however, was not content with his estate agency. He got himself called to the Bar; he became Mayor of Birkenhead; he was well known on political platforms in his native city; and he died young. Mrs. Frederick Smith supplied a corrective, and probably furnished the tough fibre. She lived to a ripe old age, delighting in her son's success and repaid by him in affection and respect. Of both his parents F. E. spoke throughout his life with reverence and gratitude. He probably exaggerated the poverty which came upon the family on his father's death. But he believed, rightly or wrongly, that nothing but early death would have deprived his father of a great success in the profession.

Then came the next step; he never forgot that he had failed to please the examiners when he stood for a scholarship at Harrow. But he regarded that as a comment upon the intelligence rather of the examiners than of himself. His affection for Birkenhead School and for Canon Sloman, his Headmaster, endured to the end.

Until at least the end of his Undergraduate days he spoke with a marked South Lancashire accent; and people with sensitive ears professed to detect the same tone in his speech at a much later date.

Two other influences had in his own opinion a share in the formation of his character and of his view of life—Francis Bacon and Henry Erskine. His admiration for both was carried so near to idolatry that, in a man less completely devoid of affectation, it might have been suspected of insincerity. And it is not easy even now to determine the causes which laid him under these enchantments. As to Bacon: F. E. was a scholar in the eighteenth-century sense, an omnivorous reader and well versed in the classic authors, an artist in words, fond of a well-turned phrase, and at home equally with the letters of Cicero, the more cynical phrases of which he was fond of quoting, and with the Greek Anthology, the epigrams of which he sometimes passed his lighter moments in translating. But he had read Law not Greats, and he did not seem to have any special love of philosophy for its own sake. He was too much a traditional constitutionalist to feel any sympathy for Bacon's constitutional views, and, if he thought that any defence for Bacon's conduct was possible, he never attempted to advance it. Probably the association with Gray's Inn was the first bond. Then he liked the slightly cynical expression of thoughts which were often noble. Then, if any philosophical view was to commend itself to his empirical spirit, it was that of the Novum Organum. Look at the evidence. Do not waste yourself on idle speculation. Perhaps these were the lessons which he learned from " the greatest, wisest, meanest of mankind."

It is more difficult to explain his love for Erskine. F. E.'s political career, and particularly the high Tory doctrines which emerged when, as Attorney-General, it fell to him, under pressure of war, to enforce the prerogative rights of the Crown, were in marked contrast to Erskine's whole outlook. And it is astonishing that a man of speech so direct and of wit so trenchant should have fallen under the spell of Erskine's tawdry rhetoric. F. E. was himself a rhetorician; but beyond that he held the strongest view of the high calling of the advocate, and of the essential values of an independent bar to the liberty of the subject. As a young man he was an ardent champion of those privileges, perhaps too ardent, and he found in Erskine his prototype. Later he was too loyal to his earlier ideals to perceive that they were out of harmony with his practice. And it gave him satisfaction to think that he had at least rivalled his great model in the early age at which he had attained the object of many lawyers' ambitions.

He was loyal, not only to his early ideals, but to his early friends. To have once befriended him, still more to have once been befriended by him, constituted a tie which could not be broken by advancing years, by divergent habits of life, by changes in the political kaleidoscope. Here again, he took and received with avidity. He accepted anything which those who worked for him could offer, and in some curious manner he made it his own. He gave back unfaltering friendship and a constant belief in the character and capacity of anyone whom he had once tested and found faithful. When it came to his turn to be the distributor of patronage, he remembered those with or against whom his earlier struggles had been conducted. He remembered his opponents without rancour, and his assistants with gratitude. To stand against him in a political contest, or to fight him in a hard battle in the Courts, was to become his friend for life. Such a habit of mind may lead to mistakes and certainly attracts hostile criticism. He had a tendency to make swans of his geese. But he made very few mistakes, and he was incapable of a lasting enmity.

It is impossible here to omit some reference to his family life. The present Lord Birkenhead, in the admirable description of his father, has said all that need be said of F. E.'s relations with the wise and gracious lady who was the companion of his whole working life, who shared every sorrow and anxiety (among many anxieties of her own), and enhanced every triumph. But it would be to paint an incomplete picture if a word were not added of the freedom of intercourse and the charm of his life at Charlton. Wherever he was and whatever he was doing, his heart always had a homing turn. Essentially he was a simple-minded man, full of the life of simple pleasures. It was indeed his simpleness of mind which made him on occasion almost naïve and outrageous in his outward expression whether of word or deed. But through it all—

> " *endued as with a sense*
> *And faculty for storm and turbulence,*"

he was—

> " *yet a Soul whose master bias leans*
> *To home-felt pleasures and to gentle scenes.*"

There was even an essential simplicity in his taste in food. Having amazing digestive powers, he could eat anything.

And he once observed, while engaged on a summer's day upon a beefsteak pudding, " This is the kind of thing I like. I can't think why you can't get it at the ——," naming a favourite and highly fashionable restaurant, whose chef would have fainted at the thought.

To know the man therefore it was necessary to see him at Charlton, dwelling in ease with the quiet charm of his house, delighting in the wit and beauty of his daughters and in the promise of his son, fondling his Cairn terriers, with whom he exchanged a devoted attachment. All this, with his stud-groom, his gardener, his horses, his garden, and his flowers, like everything which he touched, existed as part of him, and a necessary part so that without them he would have been incomplete.

To such a man both friends and familiar places appeared in a kind of glamour. In prospect he had had visions of high success. In retrospect he looked back upon his earlier aspirations, and, to quote the Happy Warrior again, he was—

> " *the generous Spirit who, when brought*
> *Among the tasks of real life, hath wrought*
> *Upon the plan that pleased his boyish thought.*"

Thus Oxford was a sacred place, and in it there was a peculiar sanctity in Wadham, so that, many years after he had attained to fame, he could deliver a speech, as sincere as it was fervent, extolling the peculiar virtues of a small college as against a large.

Liverpool was *the* city. He was ever ready to discuss local politics and their effect on the next General Election. It mattered more that the brand of thought which was peculiar to Liverpool Conservative politics was stamped on him at his outset. To the end he remained the Orangeman, and his periods were punctuated with Kentish fire.

The Bar was *the* profession. The Northern Circuit was *the* Circuit. And for its members he always had a kindly feeling in his heart. When, in 1919, the first batch of Silks of his recommendation bowed to the Judge and took their seats within the Bar, a voice was heard to murmur, " Promotion cometh neither from the east, nor from the west, nor yet from the south." But his affection centred with a special intimacy on Gray's Inn. He delighted in the close society, in the beauty of the building, yet perhaps as much as anything else in the fact that it was a small society, which, when he joined it, was, it may be, of least account among the four Inns, and which, during the time of his membership, rose in wealth and power and in the consideration of men and became pre-eminent for the splendour of its hospitality.

For the two great offices which he held in succession—the Attorney-Generalship and the Lord Chancellorship—he entertained a deep reverence. He was at all times inclined to lay much stress on the dignity and privileges of the Bar and on the dignity and privileges of the Attorney-General, both as head of the profession, and in respect of the function which, as he would preach, the Attorney-General discharges in the working of the constitution. And it may be that some claims which he made in this regard do not abide the verdict of history, and will be found not to endure the test of time. Be that as it may, he had no doubt looked forward to appointment to the office of Attorney-General as the fulfilment in part of a worthy ambition. When he came to hold it, he claimed for it, rather than for its holder, the respect of the profession, and of the outside world. The Lord Chancellorship had been the prize to which his thoughts and his efforts had been directed probably from a time before his call. But when that prize was placed within his grasp he hesitated, and finally accepted only with reluctance. He had been in every sense of the word a House of Commons man. Before he reached forty he had already taken his seat on the Front Opposition Bench, and he was younger than any possible competitor for a great place among his political contemporaries. He had not unreasonably allowed the idea to cross his mind that in the fullness of time he might become Prime Minister of this country. Removal to the House of Lords meant his transfer to a less turbulent and a chillier atmosphere, in which, as he thought, his gift for riding the whirlwind and directing the storm would find less scope; and in modern conditions it meant the abandonment of the highest ambition. It involved the exchange of the large professional income earned by the Attorney-General, to be followed, if he left office, by the vastly larger income of the great leading Silk, with an almost indefinite capacity for increase, for the much smaller salary of the Lord Chancellor, to be still further diminished when he should retire. Furthermore, it was necessarily accompanied by a circumstance which would have been disagreeable to anyone, and which was especially disagreeable to him, in that it would mean the enforced retirement of his venerable and respected predecessor.

According to his own account, he thought over the matter during most of the night, walking about the streets, and feeling an unusual degree of uncertainty because he could not seek counsel of his wife. But when he had decided (and indeed, on reflection, no other course but acceptance appeared to him to be possible), he set himself to the task of making his Lord Chancellorship splendid and memorable.

Except among his most intimate friends the appointment was unpopular. The House of Lords prefers a more sedate style of orator. His colleagues, the Law Lords, did not credit him with sufficient learning; the Bar and the public scarcely credited him with sufficient dignity. There were those who whispered of an unworthy political intrigue. He chuckled, as he remembered that he was a Vinerian Scholar, who had taught law for three years at Oxford, and had then conducted for nineteen years a very heavy practice at the Bar. This would do for learning. It would rest with him to maintain the dignity. If there was any intrigue, he was no party to it, and it was not to his advantage. Within a few weeks the predictions of the critics had been falsified.

Such was the man who now sat in what Campbell used to call " the marble chair," as the successor to Erskine and to Brougham. His hostile critics saw in him a young man of doubtful antecedents who had succeeded too fast, and who had gone farther than he deserved, and, in the main, by the aid of qualities which they regarded as meretricious. He had chosen his friends, for the most part, outside the charmed circle of quiet, steady professional men. He was slightly over-dressed, and over-much inclined to put his trust in chariots and horses. His style was over-exuberant and sometimes brutal. To the rank and file of the Conservative Party he seemed flashy and frothy, more or less as Disraeli seemed during his long struggle to acquire ascendancy. They thought him nothing but a man of pleasure, raffish and self-seeking. His personal extravagances were notorious. He did not suffer fools gladly, and he was prone too hastily to attribute folly to those whose minds were slower than his own. He was incapable of understanding that his words sometimes bit more deeply than he intended. He might be received in the great houses, but he could never win the confidence of the plain country gentleman and of the serious man of business. To someone who enquired why so many of F. E.'s personal friends in the House were chosen from the Liberal Benches, an intimate replied that after all the Conservatives were mostly very stupid people. Englishmen distrust cleverness, but they very much dislike being thought stupid by other people. On the other hand, to the convinced Liberal, the political Nonconformist, the temperance man, the social worker, he was a " son of Belial, flown with insolence and wine." He rode in the Bar Point-to-Point. He galloped for " General Carson." He was the very type of the successful Tory adventurer who sought his good where he could find it. He delighted to gall them with his epigrams, to lash them with his invective. He did not ask for their affection. He did not even care to win their respect.

Were any counts of this indictment true? It would be ludicrous to convict F. E. of lightness of metal, of affectation, or of insincerity. He was flashy, as the kingfisher flashes in the sun. He liked noise, bright lights, pretty women, the clash of argument, the hazard of the die. But he really liked these things as a child likes things. He didn't merely pretend to like them. He took a childish delight in the pleasure of the moment, and had a childish vanity in the exercise of his own skill, in the applause both of his friends and of the multitude. He thought nothing and no one common or unclean, and so he sometimes touched things and people who defiled. He sometimes forced the note; and then his eloquence rang hollow. But he was dyed in the wool. Under all the boisterousness, what first struck those who served with or under him was his essential calmness and sanity of judgment. Nor was he without respect for the opinions of others, though he was the last man in the world to be ruled by other people's advice. He might reject it impatiently and even perversely, but, if it were tendered honestly, he would return to it. " I have been thinking over what you said yesterday; I still think you wrong." " I have thought over what you said, and consulted my wife, and she agrees with you. I now agree also." " You may be right from your point of view, but I can't do it." One or other of these announcements was frequently the result of a night's reflection. And whichever decision was reached, his confidant usually admitted to himself that in the circumstances it was right. F. E. had brought to it a measured deliberation; and he gave the impression that, though the occasion was new, the principle to be applied had long ago received careful thought.

Next came, almost as a surprise, the seriousness with which he treated serious things. People thought that because he spoke lightly—sometimes irreverently—and revelled in chance and adventure, that he took a light view, and would commit great destinies to a hazard. He was in truth the gravest of men when he dealt with high matters. He did not pull a long face over them. But he felt the full burden of responsibility incumbent on statesmen faced with the terrific problems which confronted the Cabinet of the Third Coalition. His vision of them was that of a statesman and not of a party manager, and he often compared them enviously with those which rested on the Ministers who governed England, say, from the first Reform Act until the Great War. No one was ever less self-complacent. But, when the decision had been reached, he showed no sign of wavering. He would fight on to the end, taking the consequences and the perils, both personal and national, as all in the day's work.

Thirdly, there were at times in him a shrewdness and a puckish humour, which supplied a dash of salt to his own high estimate of himself and of his task. It broke out, in public and in private, in epigram and anecdote. Analyse, for example, the famous quip uttered in the course of the divorce debate. "My Lords, I agree with St. Matthew." The impudence of it was intended to shock; but it also illuminated the position of one who was accused by earnest men of approaching his subject with levity, and who was conscious that in their eyes his title to be heard was infirm.

Or take the declaration on the question of the admission of women to the Upper House. "They say that this House is doomed to perish. I confess that, if I must die, I prefer to do so in the company of my own sex."

Again, in lighter vein, after his match with Milligan, he explained his confidence as follows. "I knew that I must win. I looked at his feet. He wore such shoes as a young man buys ready made for the evening. They had never really fitted him, and were now a little worn, so that, when he ran, he would slip about in them. Now I have always taken great care about my footwear; and I calculated that the difference between a well-shod man and an ill-shod was a handicap of many yards in my favour."

This combination of solid qualities with external brilliance was suspected by few. A very astute colleague said to him, "You dazzle the public so that they cannot believe in the profound depths which lie below." He now brought his real gifts into prominence.

He very quickly gained the confidence of his judicial colleagues. He was an admirable judge, dignified, firm, courteous, patient, and laborious. His manner and his matter conquered the profession. He was equally successful in the House of Lords sitting as a legislative assembly. He was most difficult to report because of a habit, unexpected in an orator, of dropping his voice at the end of a sentence. And it is hardly an exaggeration to say that he never put the question right, and no exaggeration to say that he never mastered the simple form in which the result of a division is announced. But that very tolerant assembly bore him no grudge. They took a pride in his wit and eloquence, and respected the zeal with which he applied himself, though they did not always vote with him. When the history of our legal system comes to be written, he will receive his due for much accomplished and more attempted work, which could not win him any applause from the lay public, was undertaken solely for the love of it, and which would have borne more ample fruit if his Chancellorship had not come to a premature end. He will always be remembered for his stalwart, though ineffectual, effort to remedy what he regarded as a social injustice by the reform of the law relating to marriage and divorce. And he certainly hoped for posthumous fame from the passage of the mass of legislation on the subject of the Law of Property. The history of these subjects illustrates his habit of thought. He always asserted that his speech on the Divorce Bill had been composed when he was out for a walk in the rain during an Oxford vacation. And he had certainly marked down the Statute of Uses and the lumber of the pseudo-science of conveyancing as fitting victims, when he first came into contact with them as a student or as a teacher.

But the crisis of his fate, and, in ultimate analysis, that of the Government to which he belonged, arose on a very different issue. The verdict of the historian will turn, as the judgment of his contemporaries turned, upon the view taken of his action on the Irish question. This is not the opportunity to pass a judgment upon the merits of the Irish Treaty; he who undertakes to sketch his character is not under an obligation to form, still less to express, any opinion whether the settlement reached was or was not wise or timely. We are concerned only briefly to examine his share in the transaction, the duty which rested upon him, his motives, and the result upon his fortunes.

He stood in a unique position among the English makers of the Treaty. Sir (then Mr.) Austen Chamberlain had begun political life as a Liberal Unionist. Sir Laming Worthington-Evans did not carry the same weight. The rest were Liberals. The Lord Chancellor was an authentic Tory, the risen hope of the stern and unbending section of the party. Mr. Bonar Law was, for the moment, out of the fight. If Lord Birkenhead—for so the height of the argument requires that we should now style him—had called for support from his followers, he could have broken up the Government and anticipated 1922, with himself in the leading rôle. There were many reasons, apart from political ambition, why he should do so. He was, in the eyes of the public, essentially a party man. He had indeed differed from his friends on two occasions before the War. He had argued in favour of the acceptance by the Lords of the Land Valuation Budget; and they had rejected it. He had counselled resistance to the Parliament Act, and the official leaders had given way. But the memory of his unyielding spirit on the latter question had wiped out his willingness to give way on the former. Early associations with the Orange Party of his home-town, more recent associations with Lord Carson and the Ulster Covenant, made him the appointed champion. To fail the party now was, as he well knew, to lose them, and perhaps for ever. Still more, to assent to a surrender meant the loss of friends, and friendship was as the breath of his nostrils.

Like most politicians, he was the prisoner of his convictions. And he believed sincerely that the rule of an unmixed Liberal Administration had been disastrous in the past and would be still more so in the future. He thought that a purely Labour Government would bring about the complete and irremediable ruin of the country in a very short space of time. His membership of the Coalition Cabinets had not altered those opinions. The danger of a

Liberal Government was remote. But the far worse peril of a Labour Government, either unmixed or depending on Liberal support, was, he thought, upon us. Any step consistent with honour and with the maintenance of his political creed was preferable to such a calamity. On the other hand, F. E.'s Conservatism had never been a policy of mere negation. He had found it easy to work with his Liberal and his Labour colleagues, and he was much attracted by the audacity, resource, and cheery good nature of Mr. Lloyd George. He had found it more difficult to work with certain elements of his own party. Lord Birkenhead's mind was setting, therefore, in the direction of a central party, uniting all moderate men in a policy of conciliation and appeasement.

Ireland constituted the first task and the most perplexing problem before such a combination. He saw there a country in anarchy. The old Conservative policy of resolute government was, he thought, sound. But it was now impossible of execution. The means of enforcing law and order had crumbled in the nerveless administration which began in 1905 and had culminated in ruin at the Easter rebellion. There was no hope that the British elector, absorbed in his own domestic troubles, would be stirred again to the enthusiasm for the Union which had won victory in 1895. The Irish question would remain insoluble, a permanent ulcer in our own home politics. Meanwhile, British soldiers were losing their lives, and British treasure was being poured out in an interminable nightmare struggle. What, then, remained? To disentangle Great Britain from the fray; to safeguard Protestant and loyal Ulster from any fear of religious or political domination from the South. If this could be done his pledges to the Ulster leaders and to Ulster herself would be fulfilled. The sore would be healed, and Southern Ireland could be left to work out her own destiny, and Great Britain to achieve her own salvation. Such was his vision.

When he came into contact with the Sinn Fein leaders he formed a hope that this dream might be realised. He acquired a regard, even an affection, for their personalities, particularly for Arthur Griffith and Michael Collins, and later for Kevin O'Higgins. Physically a brave man, he admired their courage. His power of sympathy made him forget the history of the last few months. He was persuaded

by SIR CLAUD SCHUSTER

by their promises and by their attitude that they meant to keep their word. He knew the risks which he was incurring, and especially, though he regarded it least, his personal risk of losing his authority with his own friends and allies. He deliberated long. Then he acted.

This was the great moment of his life. During his Secretaryship of State he had to meet dangers in India. The time has hardly come when his administration of that great office can be discussed with full knowledge and in a dry light. By the time that he joined Mr. Baldwin's Government he was already not the man he had been. The burdens and anxieties which he had borne, the strains to which he had subjected himself, had begun to tell even upon his superabundant vitality. Already during his Chancellorship he had suffered from violent headaches and impaired eyesight. He was becoming impatient, so that he could not endure the prospect of the discharge of the more tedious duties of the Woolsack. He hated the long sittings and the tight knee-breeches. Yet he looked forward to returning some day or other to the place where he belonged. It was not to be.

JOSEPH CHAMBERLAIN
1836-1914

By
SIR FABIAN WARE

JOSEPH CHAMBERLAIN

by SIR FABIAN WARE

IN the minds of the present generation the name of Joseph Chamberlain is associated with the Imperial policy which he formulated and advocated in the years immediately following the death of Queen Victoria, and at the moment his title to fame would seem to rest largely on the new orientation which he then gave to British politics. By those of his younger contemporaries who opposed and survive him he is to-day charged with having run counter to the trend of Victorian thought, with having betrayed many of the positions won after bitter struggles by the orthodox economists of that great period of our history, and of having departed from the legitimate and consistent rôle assigned to Radicals by the strict classification of Victorian political parties. The belated and posthumous acceptance of his Imperial policy at the Ottawa Conference of 1932 has further emphasised this point of view, and increased the danger, historically, that the Victorian age may be deprived of its claim to one of the greatest of English statesmen. For in fact none was a more typical product of that age; in it were firmly planted his roots and his early political growth, and much of his mature achievement ripened under its most characteristic influences.

Chamberlain was born in the year preceding Queen Victoria's accession, and when the Great Queen passed sixty-five years later, and we younger Englishmen were stirred as no Englishmen had been stirred since the Elizabethan era, it was to Chamberlain that many of us looked, more than to any other statesman, as the living, creative embodiment of ideals and aspirations which we read into the tradition Queen Victoria had left to us. It was a moment requiring achievement, and we were conscious of it; for the spirit of the time by which we were influenced was one in which the tide of progress was running at its strongest. We were in no mere venturesome mood, but soberly alive to the responsibilities which the rapid growth during the last reign of an Imperial realm, and of an internal national development unexampled in its complexity and speedy unfolding, had imposed upon us. It required no peculiar prescience to foresee the dangers or to measure the weakness inherent in a structure which had thus grown up. Had not Kipling already sounded the note of warning in " Lest we Forget." Very seriously we asked ourselves, who shall guide us, who are the statesmen who have done things, and on whom can we depend for the practical achievements by which future events can alone be controlled?

As we had filed past Gladstone's silent form lying in state in Westminster Hall a few years earlier, up through the dominating feelings of reverence for what we then regarded as his mighty intellect, his moral grandeur, and his divine rhetoric, forced itself the question—what did he *do?* And when we turned to those whom we most trusted among his supporters and admirers and asked this question, and they replied haltingly and gropingly, we were made to feel uncomfortable, as if we had been guilty of some profanity, verging on indecency. Among the older statesmen who now remained Chamberlain stood out pre-eminently, almost exclusively, as the man who did things. Furthermore, he would *not* do things in which he did not believe; he had been Gladstone's natural successor as leader of the Liberal Party, but he had sacrificed his claim to that great heritage, resisting even that glittering temptation to be false to his convictions on the Home Rule question. Many of us who were not bound by party ties put our trust in him.

The environment which had shaped and encouraged the natural genius of this man of action was entirely Victorian, and it is in its relation to that influence that his political career should be studied, both to throw light on the movements of that age which, for good or ill, bequeathed to us an Imperial destiny, and also to learn how a man of determination and clear vision was able to use, and some of us believe might still use, a democratic constitution, based on the ineradicable English tendency to compromise, for positive achievement. Mr. J. L. Garvin's masterly *Life of Joseph Chamberlain* now appearing has made that study easy and enthralling.

by SIR FABIAN WARE

In writing on the first volume of that *Life* I was drawn into a comparison, as regards outlook, motive, and expression, between Chamberlain and another great Victorian, whose stature grows with the passing of time—Charles Dickens. I find this comparison wears well in my thoughts. Both were pure English in blood and soul and brain, and were born into much the same stratum of the greatest of human families, Dickens twenty-four years the earlier. From the days of the author of *Piers Plowman* onwards the class which had given England the archers who with their longbows blazed her name in history at Crécy and Agincourt, and the London 'prentices who had furnished not the least dreaded opposition to tyranny and privilege, had always found an advocate among the makers of our literature to claim its right to political equality and to protest against its oppression by other classes. And in passing we may notice that Chamberlain inherited both the yeoman and 'prentice strain. His direct ancestor in the seventeenth century, Daniel Chamberlain, was of West Country peasant stock, and this Daniel's descendant moved to London to be apprenticed to a master shoemaker, and had become Master of the Cordwainers Company.

This was a class which, bent on political freedom, through five hundred years of struggle, by plotting and counter-plotting in Parliament, by recourse to most bloody battle-fields when the issue could not otherwise be solved, had at last by its efforts secured a form of Government which was theoretically purged of privilege, even its administrative services being open to talent. Dickens showed that the form only had been changed, that abuse still prevailed, and that a cloud of oppression still hung over the lower classes, its blackness intensified by the smoke from the chimneys of the new industrial system. His denunciations were terrific and world-famous. A French encyclopædist says of him: " Il a fait une guerre acharnée à l'hypocrisie et l'égoisme, et cinglé de ses railleries acérées la société britannique toute entière." That he was Chamberlain's literary master is evident. At the lowest Chamberlain uses homely Victorian illustrations, such as " the flies on the chandelier," which are pure Dickens; so, on a higher level, is his thrilling and poignant outburst of radicalism in the following passage taken from one of his first great Birmingham speeches:

"We bring up a population in the dank, dreary, filthy courts and alleys ... we surround them with noxious influences of every kind, and place them under conditions in which the observance of even ordinary decency is impossible; and what is the result? ... Their fault! Yes, it is legally their fault, and when they steal we send them to gaol, and when they commit murder we hang them. ... It is no more the fault of these people that they are vicious and intemperate than it is their fault that they are stunted, deformed, debilitated, and diseased."

Under earlier than Victorian influences Chamberlain might have found no means of redress for the evils that Dickens exposed other than those attempted in the days of Wat Tyler and Jack Cade. But since then the great middle class to which he belonged had become a power. It differed widely in outlook from that "bourgeoisie" which had developed through the industrial system abroad, and for which under alien teaching our Communist friends ask us to-day "to keep the hell-fires burning bright." Such men as Dickens had shaken and disturbed its want of sympathy with the oppressed from among whom it had sprung, it suffered itself from the social ostracism of a higher class, and was united to all in a common patriotism, washed clean of many adverse prejudices by the air and the soil, the winds and the rains of England enclosed within her sheltering seas. To give the oppressed the political freedom enjoyed by the middle class was the task which Chamberlain set himself, believing that through control of the democratic form of political machinery which the English had evolved lay the road to human freedom. This seemed to him no mere pious hope, for at his start in public life he learnt how he, the man of action, could use that machinery to accomplish the ends in which he believed—and use it he did, some say to its destruction.

But, here let it be said, that no appreciation of Chamberlain is complete which does not recognise that perhaps stronger than all the other elements of which he was compounded was his spiritual ancestry; for the Victorian age marked a climax in the challenge of religious authority, which two centuries of Protestantism had failed to adapt to the English instinct for compromise based on individual freedom of conscience.

by SIR FABIAN WARE

" I boast a descent [he said] of which I am as proud as any baron may be of the title which he owes to the smiles of a king, or to the favour of a king's mistress, for I can claim descent from one of the two thousand ejected ministers, who in the time of the Stuarts left home and work and profit rather than accept the State-made creed which it was sought to force upon them."

Chamberlain's public life began in Birmingham, which throughout his career stood, unconquered by any enemy, as his stronghold in political warfare. Thither he was sent by his father, in whose London business he had already been trained, having entered it directly after the completion of his secondary education at University College School. Little more than a lad, he went to represent his father's interests in Nettlefolds' new venture, the launching in this country of an American invention which had revolutionised the manufacture of screws. Not least among the early impressions which were to mould his political thought must have been the fervour of patriotism into which he was plunged on his arrival in the Midlands where, in the words of Mr. Garvin, " with the Crimean struggle at its height, Birmingham pounded and flamed with munition work and war feeling."

His business career during the next twenty years was a typical example of rapid development and progress, based on English commercial genius and daring. All over the land men of courage were working in the same way, building up by their individual efforts that supremacy in the world markets which the Victorian era bequeathed to us. But while with iron determination and powers of organisation, by amalgamating rival firms and eliminating wasteful competition, he earned for himself what was, in those days, a considerable fortune, he laid a far stronger foundation for his future achievements by personal attention to the welfare of his employees, establishing an inexhaustible fund of confidence in himself among the working class—this was the greatest asset which he carried with him into political life when he retired from business in 1874.

Throughout this active period his tireless mind had been obtaining for itself that education and culture, in the academic sense, which for others were provided by the Universities. There are many looking back on their own lives who realise that what is thus assimilated is of the highest value in the formation of character and the development of intellect, and ask themselves whether we are right in assuming that the provision of free access to all the temples of learning is a condition essential to the welfare and survival of democracy. But to Chamberlain, as to many others who have had the same experience, the sacrifices of leisure and lighter enjoyments which this pursuit of knowledge entailed gave to it an added value and inspired him with a determination to make education available, as widely as possible, to his less fortunate fellow countrymen. It is therefore not surprising that it was as Chairman of the Executive Council of the new National Educational League, in 1869, that he first firmly planted his feet on the political stage.

> " If this matter of education is taken up by the working class . . . if it is made part of their political programme . . . we may yet live to see the glorious time when, prizing knowledge as her noblest wealth and best production, this Imperial realm, while she exacts allegiance, will admit the obligation on her part to teach those who are born to serve her."

His mind and his sympathies were now swiftly and irresistibly urging him to the conclusion that it was only by striking at the roots of the existing order of things that national regeneration could be accomplished, and before long he had formulated his Radical objectives: Free Land, Free Schools, Free Church, Free Labour. For six years a member of the Birmingham School Board, in 1873, as the result of elections into which his organising ability introduced new methods, he became its Chairman; the same year saw him elected Mayor of Birmingham.

The two and a half years which followed witnessed achievement by one man without parellel in the municipal sphere. Had his career terminated then, those thirty months alone would have provided the history of a life which would have taken its place among those of the world's great men. Boldly stating that, " in twelve months, by God's help, the town shall not know itself " he took " sagacious audacity " as his guiding principle and transformed words and conferences, pious resolutions and aspirations, formulas of grievances and their obvious cures, all that seething impotence of stirred consciences seeking salvation in negations, he transformed them all into action. Starting with bold financial measures he persuaded the municipality to buy out the lighting and water monopolies, clear the slums, and change a sordid town into a model for future cities. In June 1876 he was able to say, " I think I have now almost completed my municipal programme . . . the town will be parked, paved, assized, marketed, gas-and-watered and *improved*—all as the result of three years' active work."

Meanwhile the hammer of life had been striking him hard, and to appreciate the steel-like temper of the intellect which now became a force in national politics, it is necessary to realise that Chamberlain had learnt during this first stage in his career that he was no favourite of Fortune. Twice had he married, and during two relatively brief periods he had learnt to rely on the reinforcement of Victorian domestic life. His first wife died in 1863, his second in 1875. Only those who saw him at work in the third and last stage, when, nearing seventy, he shouldered a young man's task, and know what he owed to the perfect companionship and support then given him, can understand what a background of married happiness meant to him and estimate fully the effects of the intervals of stark loneliness on his character. After these blows he faced Fortune bravely, but with none of the gentleness given to those who sometimes win her smiles; there was hereafter a sterner grimness in the way in which he wielded the weapons of offence and defence, laying himself open to the charge of mercilessness by his enemies. Self-dependent by nature, he was thus more than ever flung back on to his own internal resources, and from there onwards we find him relying not at all on chance, much less on favour, but conscious that every step forward must be accomplished by painful unaided effort.

The practical success which had crowned his efforts in Birmingham not only encouraged him to attempt a similar revolution in national affairs, but, to one so filled with zeal for righting wrongs, it must have seemed as if this very triumph over the first citadel of privilege placed on him the solemn responsibility for completing the conquest of a Promised Land. He knew, however, that it was owing to his own leadership that victory had been won. His personal control of the municipal machinery, above all of the organisation of the electorate which he had effected, making of it an irresistible political instrument, had been essential to success. He had already been at work building up the famous "Caucus" which was to effect a similar organisation of the parliamentary electorate, and he was far too clear-visioned not to foresee that only he, the creator, could use the terrific power thus introduced into politics for the ends for which he had conceived it; nay, that without his own strong leadership it might be degraded into an instrument for evil as great as that which he purposed to remove. (Here it may be noted that when, ten years later, the Caucus turned against him, he fought it and subdued it.) He would therefore have been less than human, he would have belied his consciousness of the mission with which fate had charged him, had he not now seen before him the goal of national leadership.

Did he ever dream, as his enemies asserted, of fulfilling that mission by other than constitutional means? He had in him much of the stuff that would have made a Cromwell; but in him was a native pride in the English Constitution and a love and understanding of the English genius which immediately responded to the words of the great Victorian Poet Laureate reminding Englishmen that what was to be enduring in their freedom could only be attained by "broadening down from precedent to precedent." Had he lived in these days, when dictatorships are replacing democratic machinery where it has ceased to function, what might he have done? Some fifty years later during the Great War, England set up a dictator. I remember after the War, Philippe Millet's questioning Milner as to how Mr. Lloyd George had played his part, and Milner saying, "I know of no other Englishman who could have done what was wanted at the moment." "Could Chamberlain have done it if he had been alive?" Millet interjected. Milner paused for an instant thinking, and then answered firmly: "Yes, Joe could have done it, he would have done it—but in quite a different way."

It was, however, by constitutional means that Chamberlain now set out to achieve his object. Much, very much, he did; that he failed to do for the nation what he had done for Birmingham, that some of the things that he planned, big things such as the settlement of the Irish Question, were never carried out, that others have only been effected at the cost of wasteful delay, and that some remain still to be accomplished—if not too late—is due principally to his failure to obtain the leadership of a party which could give effect to his policy.

That failure of his may, I think, be ascribed to two causes. In the Victorian age the governing class was still a close preserve, admission to which was dependent on qualifications of birth and social status, and from that class leaders, Whig and Tory alike, were drawn. But Chamberlain, as he frequently admitted in Victorian language, was not " born in the purple." It is difficult in these days to appreciate the strength of the prejudices against which men like Chamberlain had to contend, and the young may well rub their eyes when they read such observations as he addressed to his friend Dr. Dale when he had been admitted to the Cabinet: " There is no reason now why in the future men without connection or rank may not run on their own terms with the ' governing families.' It is a hard pill for the Whigs." And even in his later years, when barriers had begun to fall and younger Imperialists clamoured for his leadership, he still thought the prejudice insuperable. At one time he seems to have perceived a good substitute for himself in Dilke, who had all the social qualifications which he lacked. The close alliance between the two, if it had not been rendered ineffective by the disastrous downfall of Dilke, might have made of the Radical Party the perfect instrument which Chamberlain was endeavouring to forge. Secondly, Chamberlain cared nothing for tactics which merely served party purposes or scored a personal advantage. To such methods, his mind ever concentrated on getting things done, he did not pay the attention requisite to the success of a candidate for the leadership.

I remember in 1906, after the crushing defeat of his policy at the polls, watching him lead the reduced Unionist Party in the House of Commons against overwhelming odds during the brief period when Arthur Balfour was without a seat. Bravely, sure of ultimate success, he fought every step, always on the offensive, and slowly placing on record every position won. And then one day, in the middle of a debate on Tariff Reform, Balfour, who had just been re-elected, entered the House, took his seat, and assumed control of the Opposition. Quickly the atmosphere changed, and the debate descended to a dialectical level, to which Chamberlain adapted himself. Disappointed, I asked him afterwards what had gone wrong. " Well," he said, " I told Arthur Balfour that I wanted to hit them in the eye, but he said, ' No, the right thing to do is to turn their flank.' So nothing was left for me to do but to make Campbell-Bannerman angry—which I did. Good enough for a Scottish debating society, but not what I wanted! "

In Parliament Chamberlain soon made his mark as a forceful administrator at the Board of Trade. From then onwards, and more than any man of his time, he was responsible for the social revolution achieved by legislation in the closing years of Queen Victoria's reign. The Whigs, who then dominated the party to which his Radical group was attached, were bewildered. Hartington told the Queen in 1885 that Chamberlain's ideas " almost amounted to Socialism." He struck at the roots of existing privilege by insisting within the Cabinet, in the face of strenuous opposition, on such extension of the franchise as would place the working classes in a position to save themselves, and when in 1884, owing largely to his persistence, the electorate was increased from 3,000,000 to 5,000,000 voters, he was justified in saying, " A revolution more important and more far-reaching than any previously accomplished in English history has been effected." Here it is impossible even to recite the measures for which he was responsible; but it may be said without exaggeration that there is hardly a social reform which has been placed on the Statute Book during the last fifty years which is not due directly or indirectly to his initiative. Of his four " F's " three have for all practical purposes been attained; his proposals under the heading " Free Land " alone have proved barren, and it is now generally accepted that until the industrial interests of England can take as wide a view as he did of the claims of agriculture, the future prosperity of the country will not be assured.

Chamberlain brought to the Departments of which he had Ministerial charge a hitherto unexampled practical business experience and ability; concentrating on his own duties there, he had to concur in much that was done by the Governments to which he belonged for which he cannot be held responsible. But he was ready to sacrifice everything, without calculation or thought of his personal interests, rather than consent to the abandonment of any principle which in his view was vital to national interests. It was thus that, having exerted himself to the utmost to furnish a solution of the Irish question compatible with what he conceived to be national honour, he resigned from the Government when Mr. Gladstone persisted in his Home Rule policy. He knew that in doing so he threw up his last chance of leadership and politically " went out into the wilderness." Later, with his Radical and Liberal-Unionist following he joined Lord Salisbury's Government, always subsequently acknowledging his indebtedness to that statesman for the opportunity thus given him of continuing his policy of social reform within the new party then formed. To the end he remained a Radical.

His interest in Colonial and Imperial problems during the last phase of his career was a natural one. In 1885 Merriman, the South African statesman, said to him: " In the Colonies we have everything you are trying to get, and more besides. We have realised the Radical ideal, and there is not a man even among the most Conservative of us who does not hold opinions compared with which those of your extreme left are quite moderate." His visit to the United States and Canada in 1887–8 had brought him into personal intercourse with the descendants of those who, like the ancestor of whom he was so proud, had, in the endeavour to escape from the oppression of privilege, left their homes in this country to live in freedom overseas. In 1888 he married Miss Endicott, daughter of a family of Devonshire ancestry associated for two hundred and fifty years with the best New England traditions.

To the direct and constant contact he thus formed with the overseas democracies may be attributed much of the vitality, and above all the actuality, that henceforward distinguished his Imperial policy. At every moment of his political career he had ridden straight for his objective—to promote the greater happiness of the masses of the people, to increase their enjoyment of life. Without the leadership his chance of carrying through in England the complete policy by which he believed this end could be achieved had disappeared. But he still saw things as a whole; he had what Balfour in speaking of him defined as " vision." In the kindred democracies overseas he discovered a well of progressive thought, youthfully daring, from which inexhaustible reinforcements might be drawn to strengthen the forces of liberty in the march of progress and in the accomplishment of the destiny of the British race.

A united Empire, with such irresistible forces within itself, might do for the masses of its people what he had failed to do for the English alone. Simply as usual, and in no florid language, he expressed this hope when he explained his attitude as a Unionist:

> "I am and shall be proud to call myself a Unionist and be satisfied with that title alone . . . since it includes all men who are determined to maintain an undivided Empire, and who are ready to promote the welfare and the union—not of one class, but of all the classes of community."

When the Unionist Party came into power in 1895 Chamberlain chose from among the offices offered to him that of Colonial Secretary. What I have said earlier as to his part in promoting Social Reform may now be said with no more exaggeration in relation to Imperial policy: every advance which has been made since that time may be traced to his initiative. Not only did he make of the Colonial Office the wonderfully efficient machine for the development of the Crown Colonies, which it still remains, but he raised it during his time to a foremost position among Government Departments as the agent of a great Imperial policy. If it may be claimed that Statesmen control events, then he, more than any other one man, promoted union, and suppressed disruption, among the self-governing Dominions of the Empire, and has a right to the title of founder of the British Commonwealth of Nations.

At the height of his power, his figure overshadowed that of any other member of the Unionist Party. Titular leader he never was—or the Government would not have ventured, while he was away in South Africa in 1903, to dig up the seed of Imperial Fiscal Union which he had sown. There, as has been said earlier, was his weakness, and, judged by the standards applied to success in political adventure, there was his failure. On that failure now concentrates the criticism of those who opposed him in his lifetime, and believe that the greatness of England can only be maintained by means and ideals other than those which he advocated. But leader of the new thought he was and recognised as such wherever the British flag flew. He was the first English statesman who talked to British Statesmen overseas as equal to equal. Recognising no superiority in himself, claiming no privilege as spokesman of the Mother-Country, neither domineering nor placatory, he dealt with them as partners in pursuit of a common ideal, and they recognised in him the master mind.

His policy of Tariff Reform was rejected by the electorate at the first appeal, it was half-heartedly supported by his party leader, it was strenuously opposed by the Civil Service, but he remained confident of its ultimate adoption. At seventy years of age he flung himself, with an energy equal to that he had shown in reforming Birmingham, into its advocacy on public platforms, into organising his own service to work out those details of its administration which the Government offices considered unworthy of their attention; he went on fighting until his body broke. The last words I heard him utter when I had gone to consult him, stricken and feeble, on a course of action were, " I have never seen the good of giving in; if you don't give in something always happens."

A study of Chamberlain's oratory throws interesting light on the methods by which he obtained his ascendancy. He loved a well-turned phrase and his French studies had made him a master of style. But he revolutionised, more than any other man, the rhetorical method which had reached its height under a Gladstone and a Bright. Oratory to him was but an instrument, to be kept sharp and polished for use, not for display. He enjoyed debate, but his practical mind never lost sight of the purpose in view. Some of us remember speeches of his of real eloquence which left us moved and inspired. But the general impression on those who heard him most often was that of a realist with quick appreciation of the intelligence and feelings of his audience and with unique power of appealing to both. I once asked a very wise and experienced parliamentary journalist, who loved to talk of the great speeches he had heard in the House of Commons, for his view of Chamberlain as an orator and in debate. He placed him very high, and gave me examples of his power. Many could be quoted; but one story he told me is worth recording, for it explains much in the attitude of his enemies towards what they called his ruthless realism.

It was in the course of a debate in the House of Commons,

when Tim Healy (I think it was) was denouncing Irish absentee landlords. Pointing his finger dramatically at Hartington, he asked when the noble Marquis had last visited his Irish estates. Chamberlain, who was sitting beside Hartington, slightly turned his head, and, speaking little above a whisper, but heard throughout the House, said (referring to the murder of Lord Frederick Cavendish in Phœnix Park), "Not since you killed his brother." It was, my informant said, the most dreadful thing he had ever heard in the House; "Healy just fell back into his seat and never finished his speech."

To the end Chamberlain retained his youthful appearance. Spare and sinewy in figure, his face clean-shaven and weathered by stern purpose, his hair black and meticulously brushed; spick and span, almost dapper in his dress, an orchid from the Highbury conservatories always in his buttonhole, a monocle in his eye. In private intercourse he was very attentive, quiet, and dignified, courteous in somewhat of the grand manner—they still used to read Chesterfield in the Victorian age. In his own family he was affectionate and paternal, and maintained rather old-fashioned ceremony; his sons always called him "Sir." To the working classes, who knew him best of all, he was just "Joe."

JOSEPH CONRAD
1857-1924

By
F. TENNYSON JESSE

JOSEPH CONRAD

by F. TENNYSON JESSE

IF to pass one's life with no abiding place for the foot—though the mind may carry a mark as unchangeable as the pointing of the needle to the north—is to be fortunate, then Joseph Conrad, despite illness and poverty, was indeed amongst the beloved of the gods.

The outward facts of his life are too well known to need more than a slight recapitulation. His family name was Korzeniowski. When he was a child of about six his father, having become involved in one of the innumerable Polish insurrections, was banished, but returned to Cracow eventually, where Joseph learned to speak French as well as Polish, which was his natal tongue.

Personal rather than political revolt was the form that his Slav temperament took, and at nineteen he was already a seaman in the Mediterranean, which is to say, that he was qualified to be a seaman anywhere in the world. For that sea, the cradle of alleged civilisation, and undoubtedly the cradle of navigation, is so treacherous, so sudden in her moods, that he who can handle a vessel upon her waters can handle a vessel in the Roaring Forties, or anywhere else where the surface of the globe is covered by that unstable element, the sea.

Conrad rose to heights in his chosen profession. He was third mate of the Clyde-built *Loch Etive*, and first mate of the famous *Torrens*. He was a British Master Mariner, and he ranged the world in the pursuit of his calling.

He did not learn to speak English until 1878, but he was one of the rare instances of a man in whom the power to acquire languages is associated with the creative power.

George Moore used to refer to him contemptuously as "the emigrant," and the present writer remembers walking with Moore through the pine-woods of Oxshott—too young and humble to protest to one so old and so great an artist, and yet with blood stirring in indignant protest—while this master of ships and of story-telling was thus described. But then (perhaps the same afternoon) Moore launched into a long dissertation to prove that Newman had a puerile intellect and that the *Apologia* was badly written. While as to Hardy . . . Hardy simply couldn't write at all!

Hardy, still alive, remained wrapped in his inalienable dignity in the heart of his own Wessex. Newman lay quiet in the grave, the first resting-place that arduous being had known, and the younger man, Conrad, his self-imposed integrity as an artist as great as Moore's, paid no heed. He had known realities too stark for such things to trouble him.

Like Ulysses, Conrad knew men and cities, and like Ulysses he knew that the sword in the last resort is mightier than the pen. Not for Conrad, passionately as he loved and understood literature, was the chatter of art and the *mot juste* in cafés. His words had been the sharp commands issued from the quarter-deck when the life of a ship and the lives of men might depend on what he said. The profundity of that experience moulded his genius. His, as he wrote in *The Secret Sharer*, was " the weight of silent knowledge and mute affection, the perfect communion of a seaman with his first command."

Conversations in Ebury Street were not for him, but the ritual of departure and the thrill of landfall; and the relief, as of the act of love accomplished, that every seaman knows when the anchor chains rattle through the hawse-pipes.

Conrad's art was as important to him, and he dealt with it as faithfully as he dealt with ships: " Like all fine arts it must be based upon a broad, solid sincerity, which, like a law of nature, rules an infinity of different phenomena. Your endeavour must be single-minded."

He is writing of the handling of ships in this sentence, but he might equally well be writing of literature.

It is true that George Moore could never have written: " A knife and fork and a serviette," but French was so essentially a part of Conrad's consciousness that what would be a vulgar error in a purely English writer was of no moment in him—and even had this been so, a slip would have been of very small moment in a story so profound yet so delicately handled as *A Smile of Fortune*.

There are four essential things which make the art of Conrad differ both from that of Hardy and that of George Moore. The first is simple enough. It is that, though, like most writers, he used his own backgrounds in his works, his backgrounds were world-wide. The scenes of violence and of sudden death, of dull horrors in lonely outposts, that were a commonplace to Conrad, must have made his work seem unreal to George Moore. Hardy's backgrounds were his own Wessex.

The second is that, whereas Moore made events evolve from character and spent his time perfecting the fine and exquisite filaments which he drew from his central idea, and Hardy brought a pressure from without to bear upon his characters and accepted predestined pressure of the Fates, Conrad alone of the three accepted the intrusion of blind and stupid accident as a factor in life. While never violating character or forcing the action so that it became untrue, he always tacitly admitted this possibility, and sometimes the whole of his story, as in the greatest of his books, *Victory*, depends upon this acceptance of accident. Something coming from without, as distinct from anything imposed from within the souls of his characters, or imposed upon them by Fate. . . . Conrad knew that there have been mute inglorious Miltons because of a tree falling or a motor-bicycle skidding, quite apart from the grinding poverty and lack of opportunity originally meant by Gray. Heyst, that delicately drawn character, whose chief strength was the weakness of his almost too great scrupulosity, clothes with words this knowledge of his creator's:

" ' Hang it all, whatever truth people told you in the old days there is also this one—that sparrows do fall to the ground, that they are brought down to the ground. This is no vain assertion, but a fact. That's why '—again his tone changed, while he picked up a table knife and let it fall disdainfully ' that's why I wish these wretched round knives had some edge on them. Absolute rubbish —neither edge, point, nor substance. I believe one of these forks would make a better weapon at a pinch. But can I go about with a fork in my pocket? ' He gnashed his teeth with a rage very real, and yet comic."

A Chinese servant, meaning no harm towards his employer, but greedy and selfish, steals Heyst's revolver, and inevitably brings about the death of Heyst and Lena, for they are left helpless in the hands of three scoundrels—a pervert, a brigand, and a man hardly human—all of them armed. These creatures had set out for Heyst's island by the mere chance of being told some stupid gossip, which was not true, in an attempt to steal a treasure which did not exist, but which had only been invented by Schomberg, the hotel keeper, in a fit of thwarted lust, stupidity, and scandal-mongering.

Conrad, knowing without question that such things occurred, and that brute force can slay the highest and the greatest, was not afraid to let a plain, solid, stupid reality such as the theft of a revolver bring about the end of two such lives as those of Heyst and Lena. His artistic soul was not revolted by such a commonplace business, for his artistic soul knew that it was true. After all, in the tragedy of *Romeo and Juliet*, what wrings the heart so much in that incomparable play of young love is that the death of the lovers was unnecessary, stupid, brought about by misunderstandings; the tragedy is not inherent in the antagonism of the Capulets and Montagues; the tragedy hinges upon stupid, blind accident.

In the story of *Freya of the Seven Isles*, we find another reference to this acceptance of stupid happenings: " There are occasions when the irony of fate, which some people profess to discover in the working out of our lives, wears the aspect of cruel and savage jesting."

And was there ever a more horrible example of sudden brutality than the idiotic tragedy which occurs to Razumov in *Under Western Eyes*, when Nikita, with a violent and calculated blow on either side of his head, deliberately breaks both his ear drums, so that Razumov stumbles out into a world for ever silent?

Razumov was no police spy—it was Nikita who turned out to be the traitor—but little by little, as the varied colours of a kaleidoscope held in front of the eyes of a child fall into place, so everything that had happened to Razumov in that apparently harmless country of Switzerland had come together to make that appalling ending necessary, not through force of circumstances or of character, but through the force of malignant happenings.

by F. TENNYSON JESSE

Many people think carelessly that Conrad is entirely a writer of the sea; when they do so they forget this tremendous book, and that other equally great achievement *Nostromo*.

The third factor which makes Conrad as a writer stand apart from his great contemporaries, particularly pure masters of style, is that Conrad knew the whole of life " in the round," as the sculptors say, faced it, accepted it. He gave half his soul to living, and the other half to art, or, to be more accurate and precise, he did not look on life and art as incompatible, but as inextricably woven together. He did not have to go into a place apart to read but a few choice books; he did not think the domesticities beneath his notice, he took them in his stride. He had known danger, knew also hard poverty and cruel illnesses. He wrote as simply of the baby and his little ailments, the satisfactory and unsatisfactory maids-of-all-work, as any suburban householder. Protected as much as possible from these irritations by Mrs. Conrad, there still was an anxiety he could not avoid—the anxiety he felt during the lean years for his wife and children.

The fourth essential difference is that physical danger was to Conrad an accepted and unromantic fact, as it is to every seaman. That grimmer danger of the lean larder was his also.

But the taking of risks has a profound effect on the mind, and however much of a commonplace danger may become, it always has dignity. This dignity was in Conrad's self, and so was inherent in his writings.

These four things were bound to set him apart from his contemporaries: the world-wide range of his backgrounds; acceptance of stupid accident—part of a seaman's life—which he knew as a man and appreciated as an artist; his complete acceptance of ordinary daily life and the domesticities, such as neither Moore nor Henry James, in their fine-spun exquisiteness, could wish to accept; and fourthly, the commonplace of actual physical danger, which had grown up with him from youth to manhood as he knocked about the world.

Yet though Conrad's stories may superficially seem to be stories of violent action, they do not belong to that cosy gathering which has been termed " the literature of escape." Not in Conrad's pages will a man find peace, or even a temporary easing from the fretting of his own soul. Though Conrad's stories, owing to his simple, natural, and quite unconscious use of his own backgrounds, contain of necessity a certain violence and richness, the important adventure in them is the adventure that takes place in the soul. Perhaps only in that marvellous description of the tartane leading the British sloop *Amelia* on a wild-goose chase in the pages of *The Rover* can the reader lose himself in the simple excitement of pure action.

Of course, the sea was part of his soul. He knew it too well for this not to be so. It was as much part of him as the earth which he knew so well was part of Hardy, and as has been seen, when he wrote about the handling of ships he might have been laying down a rule for the art of writing. To him both were arts, and the knowledge of one taught him the knowledge of the other, because the genius for both was within him.

George Moore used to say that he read very little but criticised much. Conrad wrote much, yet suffered from the delusion that he could not criticise, whereas his judgments were as delicate and sensitive of approach as his approach towards human beings was to creative work.

To understand this one merely has to read the letters in which he appreciates so fully the art of Cunninghame Graham, of Henry James, of Turgeniev and de Maupassant, of Bennett. Realise also that he wrote to H. G. Wells hailing him as: " Oh, realist of the fantastic "—a phrase with the true ring of understanding in its pure coinage.

Of course Conrad was not always consistent. He was too subject to moods, too alive to all perceptions for that, but whatever he wrote of the work of others or of passing events in the world was wrung from him, and was the truth as he conceived it to be. It was always alive, burning, never caused by jealousy or spite. He held art too high and life too lightly for that.

About himself and his work he was very often in the depths of despair, and yet his artist's soul told him perpetually that the root of the matter was in him, that he had a " rightness "—call it what you will.

> " All I know is that, for twenty months, neglecting the common joys of life that fall to the lot of the humblest on this earth, I had, like the prophet of old, ' wrestled with the Lord ' for my creation, for the headlands of the coast, for the darkness of the Placid

Gulf, the light on the snows, the clouds on the sky, and for the breath of life that had to be blown into the shapes of men and women, of Latin and Saxon, of Jew and Gentile. These are, perhaps, strong words, but it is difficult to characterise otherwise the intimacy and the strain of a creative effort in which mind and will and conscience are engaged to the full, hour after hour, day after day, away from the world, and to the exclusion of all that makes life really lovable and gentle —something for which a material parallel can only be found in the everlasting sombre stress of the westward winter passage round Cape Horn. For that too is the wrestling of men with the might of their Creator, in a great isolation from the world, without the amenities and consolations of life, a lonely struggle, under a sense of overmatched littleness, for no reward that could be adequate, but for the mere winning of a longitude...."

Yet with all his agony, as of travail, he made things difficult for himself deliberately, and this is the greatest technical riddle of his work. In many of his books he deliberately uses the exacting method of oblique narration. Usually he sees through the eyes of the seaman Marlow, " with his face worn and clouded, but with quiet eyes that glance straight, interested and clear."

That is the Marlow of *Lord Jim*, as it is of *Chance*, and it is a legitimate criticism that it is hardly the same Marlow who gives the direct narrative in *Youth*, with his perpetual " Pass the bottle." But what matter? For after all, the blundering Tom Lingard of *Almayer's Folly* bears nothing but a superficial resemblance to that creature of simple emotions, but of the most exquisite sensibility which is the Tom Lingard of *The Rescue*. Indeed, the most serious criticism which can be levelled at Conrad is that so enwrapped is he in the entrancement of his themes, in the wider issues of the human soul, that his characters themselves, except perhaps for Heyst, do not live on in the imagination. No one will ever be able to say " a Lingard," or " a Captain Antony," or " a Flora," as one may at any moment say " a Micawber," or " a Pecksniff," for whereas Dickens gathered up certain characteristics of the human being and made of them a living microcosm for as long as the English language shall endure, Conrad's figures are subordinate to the vast waters upon which they move, or to the strange violences illustrative of some particular theme to which they are subject upon land.

But at least no one has ever used oblique narration more conscientiously than Conrad, never does an action take place or a thought brush across the mind which could not have been known to the narrator. In *Victory*—to the present writer the greatest of his books—he comes nearest to making a mistake in this matter. It is true that the " I " who tells the tale is not a well-known personality such as Marlow, but merely stands for a collective mass of white traders. Nevertheless, it must be allowed to the hypercritical that Conrad unnecessarily introduced this personage, and that technically it would have been better to have written this book " straight " as he wrote his first book, *Almayer's Folly*. *Victory* would have been saved from the tiresome consciousness which will assail the reader that this anonymous " I " could not have known what Heyst and Lena felt, what they thought, what they said to each other.

But in *Under Western Eyes*, an elderly English professor of languages is chosen to tell of the intimate lives of people with whom he has only casual contact, and yet the book suffers from no aloofness, nor yet from that slight flaw which is open to criticism in *Victory*, for Conrad, here a master craftsman, used what may be known as the "journal trick," that is to say, the elderly English professor has access to the damning diary kept by Razumov—and it is, by the way, psychologically more than probable that a man like Razumov would have kept such a diary. But the professor avoids the difficulty and boredom of the journal form of writing by merely stating the source of his knowledge and writing the book from an outsider's point of view. It is a technical trick, but an extremely difficult one, and Conrad uses it with complete mastery in a language to which he had not been born, and he had not even learned until manhood.

Of many other great books that are examples of oblique narration not so much can be said. Proust nodded several times in *Du Côté de Chez Swann* when the little boy recounts the thoughts of Swann and Odette, and describes scenes at which he was not present exactly as though an impersonal author were laying bare the souls of the protagonists. In two great examples in the English language of oblique narration, either the story or the integrity of the author has suffered. In Samuel Butler's *Way of all Flesh* it is obviously impossible that he could have known and described with such accuracy Ernest's thoughts and reactions, however much Ernest had talked to him afterwards—and one feels sure that Ernest was but too willing to talk about himself; in *Wuthering Heights* the narrative loses, as the story is in a great many of its chapters at double remove by Mr. Lockwood out of Nellie Dean, so to speak. The peculiar interest that the period gives Samuel Butler's work, besides its violence and truth, makes such criticism of small account and *Wuthering Heights* surmounts most criticism that feeble mortals can make. Nevertheless, it must be admitted that into the dangers of oblique narration Conrad did not fall, even in *Chance*, which is like a set of Chinese nest-boxes, where there is the entirely impersonal " I," Marlow and Powell, so that the story arrives at the reader at fourth remove—even in this Conrad never loses intimacy, while still preserving the integrity of his difficult method.

What was the secret of his love for this difficult method of writing, which involves a constant watchfulness on the part of the author lest his characters betray him? It certainly cannot have been any shrinking of difficulties, for there is no form of writing more difficult. It was, I think, that scrupulousness, that extraordinary delicacy with which Conrad approached every human being, even those whom he himself created. He felt perhaps that he was doing them less violence dragging them out into the open, as perforce he had to do, when some third person intervened between himself and them. This may be a fanciful notion, but I believe it to be true.

There is yet a fifth reason why Joseph Conrad differs from other great writers who were either contemporaneous, or whose day overlapped with his birth. Quite unconsciously he gives it himself in *The Mirror of the Sea*. He is writing of a steamer which has lost her propeller " of all ships disabled at sea . . . the most helpless."

This particular steamship, losing her propeller down South, drifted away from the track of ships—it must be remembered that this was before the days of wireless—and Conrad writes:

" She would have been posted really as ' overdue,' or maybe as ' missing,' had she not been sighted in a snowstorm, vaguely, like a strange rolling island, by a whaler going north from her Polar cruising ground. There was plenty of food on board, and I don't know whether the nerves of her passengers were at all affected by anything else than the sense of interminable boredom, or the vague fear of that unusual situation. Does a passenger ever feel the life of the ship in which he is being carried like a sort of honoured bale of highly sensitive goods? For a man who has never been a passenger it is impossible to say. But I know that there is no harder trial for a seaman than to feel a dead ship under his feet."

In that sentence, " For a man who has never been a passenger it is impossible to say," so simply written, so without thought of effect, the reader discovers what it is that makes Conrad so different from his contemporaries.

Conrad never was a passenger, and this applies not merely to his life in ships, but to his passage through the world. Not Hardy, humble as were his beginnings and profound as was his knowledge of the human beings moulded by the soil which seems their matrix; not Henry James, with his thin fine web of analysis; not Galsworthy, with his great and generous heart; not even George Moore, with his high and pure devotion to the absolute, to abstract beauty, could say as much. Never in his life was Conrad a passenger. He had no bread save that which he had earned. His genius did not disdain the fireside and the frank and open domesticities of marriage. He risked his life again and again in the ordinary commonplace way of those who follow the sea. And with the care and reverence equal to that possessed by any of those others, he quarried his works into the finest form he could attain, spending hour after hour perhaps on a few strokes with the chisel.

No, Conrad was never a passenger, and in that sentence lies his greatness as a man and as an artist.

LORD CURZON OF KEDLESTON
1859-1925

By
SIR IAN MALCOLM

LORD CURZON OF KEDLESTON

by SIR IAN MALCOLM

SUPREMACY in the conduct of public affairs is rarely the portion of those who set out at an early age to achieve it. To such a generalisation there are, of course, a few shining exceptions, as in the cases of Mr. Pitt and Lord Birkenhead; but it is not untrue, on the whole, to say that England demands of her political leaders not so much a long apprenticeship to the art of government as the sound application of an intensive experience of life to those problems of perpetual occurrence upon whose solution depends the welfare of the State. The brilliant young man, the rising politician, seldom stays the course; rightly or wrongly, whatever his talents may be (unless they are of very exceptional quality), such an one is almost suspect in the eyes of the nation and does not easily secure its confidence.

Lord Curzon, the subject of this chapter, almost came within the limits of the category that I have indicated in the preceding paragraph. He only escaped it by virtue of his untiring industry and of his determination to become an acknowledged expert in that branch of political administration which is familiarly known as "foreign affairs." But this is not to say that thereby, or indeed thereafter, he gained the confidence of the multitude or became what is called a popular figure in British politics. He rose high in national estimation; he earned regard and admiration both at home and abroad; but, to the end of his life, he was a statesman without a personal following among the people. Which leads us to pause and reflect on one curious trait that runs through the British character: islanders though we are, and vastly dependent upon the surrounding world, how little attention do we give to the study of foreign affairs; how small a place in our thoughts (except in moments of crisis or sensation) does our Foreign Minister occupy; how poorly equipped for political life do we consider the man who has made himself a specialist in our relations with foreign countries. As a nation, we are inclined to think of him as almost a foreigner himself; considering our home interests not at all and, like Lord Roehampton in Disraeli's *Endymion*, " Not caring whether the revenue goes up or down, but thinking only of foreign politics."

Yet, in truth, few of our Foreign Secretaries have merited so circumscribed a reputation; and this will be admitted by all who can recollect how leading a part in domestic politics has been played by men like Lords Salisbury, Balfour, Rosebery, and Grey of Fallodon. Of Curzon, however, it may be urged, and with accuracy, that he was the leader and the example of a small band of young men such as the late Lord Percy, Sir Mark Sykes, Aubrey Herbert, Lord Lloyd, and a few others, whose special knowledge and public performances were centred exclusively in foreign affairs. Their qualities were of high value to successive Governments, but they were " caviare to the general."

That Lord Curzon, from his boyhood, should have taken the outside world for his province and specialised upon our relations with foreign countries, and with India in particular, does not detract anything from the immense services which he was able to render to the Empire. We merely offer that circumstance as an explanation of the undoubted fact that he was one of those prophets whose honour was greater abroad than in his own country; for whose home concerns he cared little and had nothing to do until he returned from India, with a great reputation; but then only as a brilliant pro-consul and administrator from a distant land beyond the familiar ken of his fellow-countrymen who prefer, generally speaking, to pin their faith and their following to public men who have identified themselves with the everyday lives and fortunes of their neighbours. Did he miss that popular support so withheld from him? Did he, indeed, realise that he did not possess it? I do not think that he did—until it was too late. So firm was his faith in his " star "; so confident was he that, equipped with quite exceptional knowledge and an inexhaustible capacity for work, he could overcome all obstacles by himself, that he underrated the necessity for team-work and even the advantages that are to be gained from the backing of the people. But here let it be noted that this defect, if it was a defect, was also a quality. Over and over again, Curzon's *mens conscia recti* led him to do the unpopular thing, once he had convinced himself that he was in the right, quite regardless of consequences; and in not a few instances his courage was rewarded.

Let us examine rather more closely the complex character of this man who for close on forty years was a foremost servant of the Crown. He started life at Eton, with no advantages but those which he carried beneath his own tall hat. He was poor, he was not strong, he had few friends. But within five years he had risen to the top of the school, had carried off all its principal prizes, had proved himself intellectually capable of great things in the future. So he proceeded to Oxford; still poor, still without influence of any external kind. Here history repeated itself; university prizes fell to him, he became President of the Union, and, although he did not succeed in obtaining a First Class in Greats, he went down with the reputation of being the most brilliant man of his year, unafraid of his destiny and unashamed of his ambition, which was to become Viceroy of India before he reached the age of forty.

Unlike Lord Palmerston, whom he resembled in other ways, he was not diffident; although he used to say that he had only a middle-class mind. Unlike him, too, in the description given by Victor Hugo of that veteran English statesman: " *Un homme qui appartient un peu à l'histoire et beaucoup au roman.*" Curzon had nothing of the romantic about him; his successes and his proud preferments were due to nothing but his own indomitable determination and insatiable power of work. It was in no spirit of romance, but of deadly earnest, that he set out as a young man to travel Persia, India, and the Far East, and to make himself master of their problems; an education self-imposed but essential to the great task to which he had set his hand. It may be said with great justification that if Curzon, after being elected to Parliament in 1886, had spent laborious days at Westminster and in the constituencies of Great Britain instead of consecrating his life to distant exploration, he would have known more of domestic politics than, in fact, he did; he would have had closer intercourse with his fellow-countrymen and with their interests at home. But, as we have already said, that was not the political future nor were those the interests upon which his eyes were fixed. And this Lord Salisbury knew when he appointed him to be his Under-Secretary at the Foreign Office in 1895 and Viceroy of India three years later.

Then it was that Curzon began to reap the fruits of the rich harvest whose seeds he had so diligently sown during the past ten years. No previous Viceroy had ever landed at Bombay so fully adapted by temperament and knowledge to face the mysteries and the problems of our Oriental Empire. He may have been "*l'homme autoritaire*" (as Gambetta once described Gladstone), but he was also universally acknowledged as master of his subject and as a man of intensely practical views. He had not been long at Calcutta before he had adumbrated some sixteen or seventeen major reforms, covering the whole political and domestic life of the sub-continent, which he determined to carry out for the good of India. It is now a matter of common knowledge that, during his term of office, they were all fulfilled, and (with the exception of the partition of Bengal) they remain to-day as a monument to the memory of his long Administration.

And here a tribute should be most warmly paid to all of his colleagues and subordinates who co-operated with so much loyalty to bring such great things to pass. For Curzon's ways were not always their ways. It was his invariable dictum that " if you want a thing well done you must be able to do it yourself; in fact, you must do it yourself." He had no power of delegation in his administrative outfit. Wherefore, with infinite pains and at great cost to his health, he learned the detailed work of every department concerned with his reforms—criticising, improving, informing, encouraging—until he became himself the actual master of the machinery by which each reform was to be carried out. It is not to be wondered at that such tremendous driving force caused much commotion and even friction in the hitherto smooth but slow running of departmental life in India; nor is there any cause for surprise that, when the immediate results of Curzon's methods were observed, his work was appreciated with ready or reluctant admiration and regard. And there we may well leave his work as Viceroy to speak for itself to future generations, no matter how the new and perplexing problems of Indian self-government may resolve themselves. Compared with that work, *by* SIR IAN MALCOLM

the manner of his departure from India, after two or three serious differences with the Cabinet at home, seems to the present writer of minor importance and may be forgotten amid the glory of achievement that he left with his heart in India.

In 1905 the man of action, broken in health and in spirit, and rebelling against a sense of ill-treatment at the hands of his oldest friends and colleagues, returned to England after an absence of seven years. He had lived too long with affairs to be able to live without them; like Lord Palmerston again, he would confess, " I like power; I think power very pleasant "; and he expected, not unnaturally, that his services would in some way be employed by the Crown. But herein he was disappointed. For reasons connected with the unhappy conclusion of his Viceroyalty, reasons which are not wholly creditable either to Mr. Balfour's or to Sir Henry Campbell-Bannerman's Governments, neither of these Prime Ministers would recommend the Sovereign to make him a Peer of the Realm, an honour which had invariably been accorded hitherto to a retiring Viceroy; on the other hand, King Edward VII had expressed his clear wish that Curzon, an ex-Viceroy, should not present himself as a candidate for Parliament at the General Election of 1906. Thus the doors of both Houses were temporarily closed against him; and the man who had won, in Disraeli's picturesque phrase, the " Blue riband of the Empire," was not even rewarded by the bestowal of the blue ribbon of the Garter which all previous Viceroys had worn. A bitter disappointment to one who, for seven years in the prime of his life, had held the gorgeous East in fee. Sadly and silently he retired into a seclusion that was darkened and deepened by the loss of his beautiful wife at the very moment when his fortunes were at their lowest ebb.

The subsequent careers of the majority of British Envoys returning home from distant posts after years of exile are matters for our sympathetic consideration. Generally speaking, they retire from highly responsible work, from brilliant positions as representatives of the Crown, from the glory and the comfort of Government Houses and Embassies, to a modest life of pensioned security. In many instances their age has earned them the leisure which they thus obtain; but others return at the height of their intellectual vigour, unable to find a place in public life which is already fully staffed by men who have spent their lives at home. So it was with Curzon at the age of forty-six, whose whole ambition it was to devote the remainder of his strength to the service of his country. After two years of heart-rending solitude, caused by bereavement, antagonism in high places, and the estrangement of old friendships, the fever for employment attacked him with redoubled strength. He was now burning to work for his country at home as he had laboured for her abroad. But the outlet for his energies was difficult to find; Viceroys do not fit in " anywhere "; least of all a Viceroy who had quarrelled with the Cabinet, whose knowledge of home politics was negligible, and whose pro-consular character was erroneously supposed to be domineering. Time, however, the great healer, was on his side. He only had to wait; for it was inevitable that sooner or later he would be summoned from his retirement to begin a new life of public service. And so it turned out: the man who, in his crisis of depression, thought that his career was closed for good in 1905, lived to become an outstanding figure in the history of our country during the next twenty years.

In the meanwhile, as his vitality and normal spirits returned, he entertained splendidly: shooting parties, week-end parties galore; the house full of brilliant and joyous guests amongst whom he shone, not only as a perfect host, but as the bright particular star. For Curzon, when he chose, could outstrip young and old alike in the buoyancy of his fun, in sparkling repartee, in Rabelaisian anecdote, or in entrancing conversation. Old friends may perhaps have noticed that his gaiety was less exuberant than of yore in the days of the Crabbet Club; that his infectious vitality was not so robust as they had known it years ago at the eclectic dinners of the " Souls "; that his talk had become rather more spacious and perhaps more egotistical than in his pre-Indian past; yet even so they still rejoiced in his company, and gave the best of themselves to complete the delightful entertainment that he offered. Also, during those long months of enforced unemployment, he was busy writing and planning books, delivering important lectures to learned bodies, collecting money to raise statues to the memory of Lord Clive in London and Calcutta, and attending sales at Christie's to purchase either for his own private collection of Italian masters or to add some new treasure to his beloved

Victoria Memorial Hall in India. Such were but a tithe of his occupations, yet sufficient to bid us salute the fruitful and abounding energy of a man who had almost given up hope of further public service. It will be observed, however, that these were all solitary personal efforts, though strangely varied in their nature.

I have already hazarded the opinion that the great British public places no great confidence in a young specialist; I feel almost as certain that a personage of mature age possessing so much expert knowledge on an infinite number of subjects lies under the same ban of suspicion. Curzon had still to " make good " at home, not by " star-turns," but by solid team-work—such are our peculiar standards of judgment—and I do not think that even his greatest admirers could justify the assertion that he was ever an abiding strength to any Administration except his own.

His new life began in 1907, when he was elected Chancellor of the University of Oxford and filled that post with an efficiency and distinction which eclipsed the records of his most distinguished predecessors. He may not have been a popular Chancellor, but undoubtedly he was a great one; and it stands to his credit that the famous Red Book (or " Scarlet Letter ") on University reform, which he composed in South Africa and finally carried through Council at Oxford, not only staved off the danger of a parliamentary Commission to intervene in the management of Oxford and Cambridge, but was the basis of the findings of the Royal Commission which was ultimately appointed to satisfy the radical suspicions and tendencies of the day. In 1908 he was elected to fill a vacancy in the representative peerage of Ireland, and thus at last he found his way into politics once more. Not that he cared about politics at all as such. He never tired of inveighing against a political career, and, if the truth is to be told, he was himself a very bad politician. But he was swift to realise that, in order to recapture the ear of the public and to affect the direction of foreign and Imperial affairs, he must have a seat in the House of Lords; and this he achieved through the assistance of Lord Lansdowne, whose influence over the Irish Unionist Peers was sufficient to secure Curzon's election.

From this period we may date his full return to public life, with occupations enough to satisfy even the most ambitious of men. He added the Lord Rectorship of

Glasgow University to his academic laurels; he was made President of the Royal Geographical Society; an Earldom of the United Kingdom was conferred upon him, and he began to take a prominent part in political affairs. Then, from the outbreak of war onwards and until the end of his days, he was closely engaged in the service of the Crown. But those who knew him best, and who had worked with him in his earlier years, were quick to notice in him a change which could never have been predicted of so proud and definite a character. It was observed that he was now increasingly reluctant to come to any decision upon important political subjects and inclined to reverse that decision at a moment's notice: that his judgment, once so swift and sure, now faltered in council; that his opinions, though usually dogmatic, were no longer dynamic; that he would often surrender an important point rather than fight for it to a finish. And the strangest thing of all was that whilst, over a period of years, these weaknesses were constantly declaring themselves—notably in the cases of the Parliament Bill (1911), the Women's Suffrage clause of the Franchise Bill (1917), the Government of India Bill (1919)—Curzon's administrative abilities were never better displayed than when, during the last half of the same decade, he was President of the Shipping Control Board and afterwards the first Minister for Air. It was, I am convinced, mainly his greatly impaired state of health—scarcely a day without considerable and sometimes excruciating pain—that accounted for these unreliabilities, for his persistent incapacity to realise the political consistency that was due from him to those colleagues with whom he was working; but it was partly due also to that solitary self-training which ignored the obligations of corporate responsibility, being content (as Curzon invariably was) with the knowledge that if he was placed at the head of an Administration, be it India, Oxford University, the Royal Geographical Society, or the Shipping Board, the work would be done supremely well.

However that may be, the fact remains that during this long term of office Curzon found himself constantly out of touch both with his colleagues and his party until the conclusion of the Great War. Nor did his troubles end then; for his tenure of the Foreign Office was so distraught by interference from Downing Street (until the disappearance of the last Coalition Government) that no one could say for

by SIR IAN MALCOLM

certain whether Lord Curzon or Mr. Lloyd George was in fact our Minister for Foreign Affairs. It was indeed a perplexing and wholly unsatisfactory situation which, possibly, would never have arisen if Curzon had been a more forceful man in Cabinet, and if his moral and physical fibre had been of a quality tough enough to face up to a brilliant colleague whose knowledge of foreign affairs was incomparably inferior to his own. For when Curzon was left to do his own business in his own way—e.g. at Conferences in Paris or Lausanne or elsewhere—he reaped successes of high importance which may be said to have crowned his career as a Foreign Minister. It will always remain, therefore, a subject of vain conjecture why, on more than one occasion, he did not resign office when the reins were wrenched from his hands and he saw the team being driven in the wrong direction.

Are we now any nearer to a true understanding of the reasons why, at the last, the final crushing blow fell upon the head of this devoted public servant, and why his Sovereign, acting under advice, preferred Baldwin to Curzon for the post of Prime Minister? It has always seemed to me that the official reasons given were solid but secondary: that Curzon was a Peer and that, with a strong Labour opposition, it was essential to have the Prime Minister in the House of Commons. It might be respectfully argued that these reasons alone were insufficient; that Curzon as Leader of the House of Lords had for five or six years spoken in the name of Great Britain and of the Empire with an authority unequalled since the days when Lord Salisbury was Prime Minister; that, of all His Majesty's available advisers since the outbreak of war, Curzon (with the exception of Lloyd George perhaps) had the highest reputation as a statesman abroad and in the Dominions; that as an Administrator of long experience he had claims both in years and in talents superior to those of any of his colleagues; that as an orator and exponent of public policy, whether in Cabinet or in the Senate, he was unrivalled. And one cannot but believe that all the foregoing claims would have been admitted.

But they were not sufficient, and rightly so. For it was essential at the time the choice was made, as it always is, that the Prime Minister should have the full backing of the people and the whole confidence of his party in Parliament; that he should have the particular gifts which go to make the captain of a successful team—gifts which are usually denied to a " star "; that he should be at the zenith of his physical powers in order to bear the ever-increasing burden of national responsibility that is laid on the shoulders of every Prime Minister to-day; and, finally, that his moral courage should be of the quality that urges him to fight to the end for what he considers right, and to be ready to resign his high office rather than accept responsibility for a policy of which he cannot approve.

And if these are among the foremost qualifications for a Prime Minister of the twentieth century, which of us who counted ourselves among Curzon's warmest admirers can say sincerely that he possessed any of them or can blame those of his colleagues of like opinion who may have been consulted and gave advice to that effect? To Curzon, most naturally, it mattered tragically that he was passed over; he never recovered from the blow, cruel and humiliating as he conceived it to be. But I make bold to say that his great international reputation as a Viceroy, as a Foreign Minister, as Chancellor of Oxford University, and as a polished orator and writer, has not suffered, can never suffer, as he did in his own person. That reputation remains brilliant and unscarred, great among the greatest in our history, to illuminate the memory of one of England's most devoted sons.

RANDALL THOMAS DAVIDSON
1848-1930

By
SIDNEY DARK

RANDALL THOMAS DAVIDSON

by SIDNEY DARK

WHEN Queen Victoria lay dying, Randall Thomas Davidson, Lord Bishop of Winchester and Prelate of the Most Noble Order of the Garter, knelt and said prayers by the royal bedside. He and the Lord Chamberlain were the only persons, outside the royal family, present when the Queen breathed her last, and Davidson journeyed with the coffin across the Solent on that dead, grey January morning of the last royal crossing, and read the Committal Prayers at the graveside at Windsor. He had been Bishop of Winchester for six and a half years, and for nearly twenty years he had been the Queen's confidant and adviser, having had a greater influence with her than any other man since the death of Disraeli.

Davidson had his first audience immediately after the death of Archbishop Tait, whose daughter he married and whose chaplain and secretary he had been for five years. The Queen had a sincere admiration for Tait, " the dear, excellent Archbishop," and on that account she was prejudiced in favour of his son-in-law. Davidson went to Windsor on December 9, 1882. He was seen and he conquered. The Queen wrote in her diary: " We went over various topics and I feel that Mr. Davidson is a man who may be of great use to me." The most important of the various topics was the appointment of Tait's successor to the throne of St. Augustine. Davidson succeeded in securing the succession for Benson, who, without his friend's backing, would almost certainly have remained in the comparative obscurity of Truro, and Davidson's success is evidence of the remarkable astuteness of a young man of thirty-four, new to the Court and its mistress. There were three candidates for

Canterbury whose claims had to be considered. The first was Harold Browne, Bishop of Winchester, then a man of seventy-two. The second was Joseph Barber Lightfoot, Bishop of Durham, and the third, Edward Benson, Bishop of Truro. It is quite clear from his letters to the Queen that Davidson had made up his mind before his first visit to Windsor that Benson ought to have the preferment, but he was far too clever to push his man too obviously. He admitted the great claims of Browne and Lightfoot, but Gladstone, possibly at his suggestion, discovered that no man of Browne's age had been appointed Archbishop of Canterbury for over two hundred years, and noting " the very high opinion Mr. Davidson has of Bishop Benson," the Queen agreed to Benson's appointment.

After the Archbishop's enthronement, Davidson remained for a while in his old position at Lambeth. In his life of his father, A. C. Benson says:

> " His [Davidson's] knowledge of public men, of the world, of organising, of Church legislation, of ecclesiastical movements, was of inestimable value to my father; moreover, he was intimately acquainted with the personnel of the Church and had the whole of the intricate business of which the Primate is the centre at his fingers' ends."

But Davidson was not allowed to stop at Lambeth for long. A year later, on the insistence of the Queen and with the very half-hearted acquiescence of Gladstone, who had no great love for him, Davidson became Dean of Windsor. " Davidson has gone to Windsor," it was said at the time, " as a nuncio, but not of Peter." His new position brought him into constant and intimate relations with the Sovereign. He was her " clerical adviser and major domo." Until Benson's death, too, he was the Archbishop's closest friend, his adviser whenever matters of particular difficulty occurred, and the liaison officer between the Primate and the Sovereign. Benson's letters to him, which always began " My dearest Dean," and afterwards " My dearest Bishop," are all written in terms of the greatest possible affection.

The most important ecclesiastical event during the years that Davidson was at Windsor was the Lincoln Judgment, delivered by Archbishop Benson in 1890, in the case of the Church Association against Bishop King, to be confirmed two years later by the Judicial Committee of the Privy

Council. The Lincoln Judgment is a landmark in the story of the Catholic revival in the Church of England. Dean Church was dying when it was delivered, and " its character and contents brought the Dean the last flash of happiness before the end." It is interesting to note that Mr. Benson says that Dean Davidson was, in this matter, as in so many others, his father's " intimate friend and counsellor."

In September 1891 Davidson was consecrated Bishop of Rochester. Practically throughout the whole four years that he spent in the diocese, he was a very sick man. The present diocese of Southwark was not constituted until 1905, and, when Davidson was appointed, Rochester was an immense, sprawling district, stretching from Maidstone on the east to Kingston on the west, and containing the whole of South London. To oversee such a diocese was a heavy task for a strong man. For a semi-invalid, it was impossible. The Queen was vastly concerned about Davidson's health, and it was a relief to her, as well as for him, when, in 1895, the death of Anthony Thorold made it possible for her, on the advice of Lord Salisbury, to arrange his translation to Winchester.

Benson died in 1896, to be succeeded by Temple, " a gnarled old man " of seventy-five. During the short period of Temple's primacy, Davidson had less influence in ecclesiastical affairs than at any time during his life. Temple was a far stronger man than Benson, with no need for another man to lean on, and the relations between him and Davidson were formal and distant.

So the Queen died and was buried, and the history of the post-Victorians begins. In 1901, Davidson was a man of fifty-three, and he was to live for another thirty years. The death of the Queen definitely divided his career into two parts. While Queen Victoria lived, he was primarily the Courtier Prelate. When he was appointed to Rochester, Benson, possibly appreciating the danger of his position, wrote: " They won't suffer you to drop them, yet it is a wonderful mark that He should after all call you from those slippery associations to the poor of His people." " They," or rather she, did not allow him to drop out of the Court and the string-pulling of the courtier. From the time that he went to Lambeth in 1877, until the Queen's death, he was always behind the scenes. As Dean and as Bishop he had the ear of his royal mistress as no other ecclesiastic had it. He was the power behind the throne.

In his attitude to the contemporary ecclesiastical controversies, he was always the moderate man, devoted to the middle way, and there is no doubt that he succeeded in considerably modifying Victoria's violent Protestant asperity, which is expressed in the letters that she wrote to Disraeli, at the time of the introduction of the abortive Public Worship Act. While he was Tait's secretary, Davidson had discovered the futility of endeavouring to kill the Catholic revival by persecution. Indeed, one of his first jobs at Lambeth was to get " poor Mr. Green " out of gaol. Poor Mr. Green was the incumbent of Miles Platting in the diocese of Manchester, who was sent to prison for disobeying the Public Worship Act, and who remained there, absolutely refusing any compromise, until the Bishop of Manchester petitioned the Lord Chancellor to release him. As I have noted, Davidson was consulted by Benson before the Lincoln Judgment was delivered and was presumably in agreement with the findings. His own point of view was expressed in a speech to the Rochester Diocesan Conference in 1892, when he referred with obvious impatience to the *minutiæ* of ritual.

While he was at Rochester he was petitioned by certain of the parishioners of St. Catherine's, Hatcham, to admonish the Vicar for his Popish practices, one of which was the use of *Hymns Ancient and Modern*. Davidson showed his usual astuteness in dealing with the subject, afterwards suggesting that most questions of ritual were concerned with taste rather than doctrine. He indeed cared for none of these things, and he was extremely annoyed by people who did. Later on, in Winchester, he took, however, very high-handed action with the famous Fr. Dolling, of St. Agatha's, Portsmouth, one of the saints of the English Church. Fr. Stanton said of Dolling that " he lived in obscurity, caring nothing for money or position, never resting, labouring in the slums in complete unworldliness and intense sympathy." Dolling was, for those days, an extreme Catholic. Thorold, Davidson's immediate predecessor, was an equally extreme Evangelical, but he refused to interfere with Dolling, moved as he was to admiration by the priest's " self-denying and Christian activities." But Davidson was definitely unsympathetic. He refused to allow Dolling to say Mass for the Dead, or to celebrate Holy Communion without communicants, and, despite a petition signed by five thousand persons, he was practically compelled to leave Portsmouth. I have no sort of doubt that Davidson often bitterly regretted the Dolling incident, but it is of great importance in his life, and it is not to be forgotten if one is to understand the man as he was when he became a post-Victorian.

The Queen's death had been immediately preceded by the raging Protestant agitation inspired by Sir William Harcourt, who had at the moment nothing better to do. This agitation followed the attempt made by Lord Halifax and the Abbé Portal to secure from Rome the recognition of the validity of English Orders. There was a great weight of foreign ecclesiastical opinion in favour of such recognition, the pro-Anglicans, including such distinguished theologians as Monseigneur Battifol, Monseigneur Duchesne and Monseigneur, afterwards Cardinal, Gasparri. But Cardinal Vaughan's influence was sufficient to secure from the Pope the Bull in which Anglican Orders were condemned as entirely invalid. Benson, High-Churchman as he was, had a strongly developed anti-Roman complex, and was frankly bored by the negotiations in Rome, and his views were entirely shared by Davidson.

It should be noted, in considering Davidson's equipment in 1901, that he had already acquired that close acquaintance with the Church Overseas which was to enable him to become, in later years, a sort of Anglican Pope, and that, through his friendship with Benson, he had become deeply interested in possible reunion with the Eastern Orthodox.

In 1901, Davidson ceased to be a courtier. King Edward had little of the keen interest that his mother had in Church affairs, and the only important ecclesiastical appointment for which he was personally responsible was the selection of Arthur Foley Winnington Ingram as Bishop of London. Canon Scott Holland very shrewdly said of the Davidson of Edwardian days:

> "Bishop Davidson's point of danger is not the Court. He has survived its perils with a singular simplicity. Rather it is to be sought at the Athenæum. There dwell the sirens who are apt to beguile and bewitch him. They have ceased to be mermaids with harps, and have adopted the disguise of elderly and excellent gentlemen of reputation who lead you aside into corners and, in impressive whispers, inform you what will not do and what the British public will not stand."

Davidson stood by the side of Archbishop Temple at the coronation of King Edward on August 9, 1901, and saved the aged prelate, worn out by the protracted service, from tottering and falling before the end. At the end of the next year, Temple spoke in the House of Lords in support of the Conservative Government's Education Bill. He sank back exhausted in his seat, and died at Lambeth on December 23, Davidson being appointed his successor by Arthur Balfour, with the entire approval of the country. Davidson was known at the end of his life as an extremely tough and tireless old man. I have said that while he was in Rochester he was a very sick man, and his appointment to Winchester was denounced in the *Church Times* on the ground that his health would not enable him to fulfil the duties of his position. But by 1902 his health was entirely re-established, and there was no question of his physical qualifications for his high position. He was described as a broad Low-Churchman. He was recognised as a definite Erastian. He was applauded as a " layman's parson." From the beginning of his Primacy, he made his position perfectly clear. He had no sympathy with the Protestants who believed that the history of the Church of England began in the sixteenth century. He was equally impatient with the Catholics who regarded the Reformation as " a lamentable blunder in Church life." The first important happening of the primacy was the appointment by the Balfour Government of a Royal Commission " to enquire into the alleged prevalence of breaches or neglect of the law relating to the conduct of Divine Service in the Church of England." The Commission was presided over by Sir Michael Hicks Beach, afterwards Lord St. Aldwyn, and consisted of fourteen members. Sir Lewis Dibdin, the Dean of Arches, is now the only survivor. The Archbishop himself gave evidence at very great length, and this evidence, which it is to be hoped Dr. Bell will print without excision in the Life of the Archbishop that he is now writing, is intensely interesting in its revelation of Davidson's own point of view and of what was unquestionably the mind of the majority of Churchmen thirty years ago.

He began by summarising the history of the Church from the beginning of the Oxford Movement, emphasising the fact that the Tractarians themselves were not ritualists. He repeated with evident satisfaction, the decisions of the Court of Arches that condemned Catholic practice in the celebration of the Holy Eucharist. He gave the Church Association a handsome testimonial for its " bravery " in prosecuting the Bishop of Lincoln, and, most suggestive of all, he defended the ecclesiastical jurisdiction of the Judicial Committee of the Privy Council.

Whatever developments there were in Davidson's opinions, and whatever inconsistency may be found in his public acts, he was, from the beginning to the end of his long life, a convinced Erastian. He was indeed almost the last of the Erastians, for Dr. Hensley Henson deserted from the ship of State years ago. To Davidson it was a matter of immense importance, both for the State and the Church that their intimate connection should continue. In his Creed he would have put in the word "Established" with "Holy Catholic," and I am not quite sure that he did not think that it was much more important. In the latter part of his evidence before the Royal Commission, he suggested the comparative unimportance of " modes of vesture and music." He was tolerant of ritual so long as it had no particular meaning or significance, but only then. He explained at length what his own policy had been in the diocese of Winchester, where he had forbidden Reservation, the celebration of Holy Communion with no communicants, the use of incense and Prayers for the Dead, and, for some odd reason, had deprecated the habitual attendance of children at celebrations of Holy Communion.

The report of the Commission was published in the summer of 1906, the Archbishop agreeing to its conclusions, which flatly condemned practices that are to-day common in thousands of churches, and urged the summary punishment of recalcitrant clerks. Incidentally, the Commission recommended that letters of business should be issued to the Convocations with instruction for Prayer Book revision, and this was the beginning of the controversy with which the Archbishop was insistently concerned in the later years of his primacy. The Revised Prayer Book, as it emerged from the Convocations, was condemned and finally rejected by Parliament in 1927 and 1928, because of its alleged Catholic bias, but revision was first suggested to dish the Catholics.

There was comparatively little stirring in the world ruled from Lambeth during the brief Edwardian reign. The Lambeth Conference of 1908 showed Davidson a masterful chairman with an intimate knowledge of Anglican life all over the world. That was indeed one of his great possessions. The Overseas Bishop, home on furlough, who called at Lambeth, found that the Archbishop always had an intimate knowledge of the circumstances of his work and of its peculiar difficulties.

Just before the War, Davidson had his first contact with Frank Weston, Bishop of Zanzibar, and, after Charles Gore, the greatest personality of the English Church in this century. Weston was a saint, the only saint whom I have ever known, very headstrong, as saints often are, with strong and definite convictions and without the smallest capacity for compromise. The English Church in East Africa had, and still has, the bewildering contradictions that are the penalty of comprehensiveness. In the diocese of Zanzibar, under the tutelage of the Universities' Mission to Central Africa, the Catholic religion is taught without any kind of reservation. A native Christian is nearly always a Catholic, and when Frank Weston died, the native members of the Roman Church in his diocese, in a beautiful tribute to his memory, expressed their conviction that " because of his holy life we are sure, through our Mighty God and our Lord Jesus Christ, his Lordship's soul is at rest before the Holy Trinity in Heaven." The neighbouring dioceses of Mombasa and Uganda were established by the Church Missionary Society, and there extreme Protestantism is the faith taught to the people. To Weston's horror, at a conference of Protestant missionaries at Kikuyu, the Bishop of Mombasa celebrated Holy Communion in a Presbyterian chapel, and Weston, in hot indignation, demanded that their Lordships of Mombasa and Uganda should be prosecuted for propagating heresy and committing schism. Davidson was as usual very wary. He deprecated such common Communions, but he declined to be a party to the condemnation of the two Bishops.

He was equally wary in 1918 when Dr. Hensley Henson was nominated by the Crown to the bishopric of Hereford. Weston vehemently, and Charles Gore, then Bishop of Oxford, with greater reserve, denounced the preferment on the ground of Dr. Henson's alleged heresy, and implored the Archbishop to refuse to consecrate him. In a long letter to Gore, Davidson said that no power on earth can force the Archbishop to consecrate against his will, for once exalting spiritual above secular authority. He went on to admit that he found in some of Dr. Henson's books " a want of balance and a crudity of abrupt statement." None the less, the Bishop-elect was in his view "a brilliant and powerful teacher of the Christian faith," and he was duly consecrated.

Davidson shared the dislike, felt by both Queen Elizabeth and Queen Victoria, for extremism in religion, and for overmuch enthusiasm. He disliked the crudities of the Modernists, and had no patience with their assumption of intellectual superiority, just as he disliked and feared the zeal and the conviction of the Anglo-Catholics. One of the most interesting and important documents that he ever penned was the ironic chiding of Dr. Barnes in 1927. He had been familiar, he told the Bishop of Birmingham, with the Modernist position for over fifty years. There was nothing new in it, nothing disturbing, nothing really worth making a fuss about. Then he went on, in a few stern words, to condemn the Bishop's references to the Sacrament of Holy Communion.

Davidson was very fond of referring to the tradition inherited from Andrewes and Ken, but never permitted himself to consider the implications of the belief in the Real Presence that has always been held within the English Church. He hated working things out. He would not let himself admit that, granted that the doctrine of the Real Presence is true, the Catholic attitude to the sacraments is inevitable, while granted, as Dr. Barnes believes, that it is a delusion, his condemnation, though not necessarily the bad manners of its expression, is justified. Just as Davidson earnestly desired that the Church of England should remain established, so he earnestly desired that it should remain comprehensive. He was once described as a "very good man without any principles." That, of course, was unfair. But he hated other men waving their principles in his face. He resented any course of action that was calculated to prejudice the Church in the eyes of the non-churchgoer and the indifferent.

In the last years of his primacy, Davidson was concerned with two matters of outstanding importance. The first was the conversations at Malines in which, as a consequence of the close personal friendship between Cardinal Mercier and Lord Halifax, Anglican and Roman Catholic scholars, discussed their differences and attempted to arrive at such agreement as would make reunion possible. These conversations had from the first the warm approval of the Archbishop.

He was to an extent responsible for the selection of the English delegates; he was informed of the course of the discussions.

The reunion of Christendom was always a subject of the keenest interest to Davidson. He encouraged frequent conferences with the Nonconformist bodies, and was the author of the Lambeth Conference policy that the basis of Christian reunion must be the recognition of the authority of Holy Scripture and the acceptance of the Creeds and the historic episcopacy. He had watched, with the keenest interest, the approach of the Anglicans to the Orthodox, and had greatly rejoiced at the recognition of the validity of Anglican Orders by certain of the Orthodox Patriarchs. It had, however, been specifically recognised by the Lambeth Conferences that there could be no real and effective reunion of Christendom without the adherence to some scheme of "the great Church of the West." With this admission it would have been entirely impossible for the Archbishop to have forbidden the Malines conversations.

I do not suppose for one moment that he imagined that the conversations could have any practical result. He did not perhaps realise the suspicions they would arouse or all the consequences of that suspicion, for there is no sort of doubt that the Revised Prayer Book was killed at Malines. I do not think that Davidson had any particular anti-Roman prejudice. Benson, who was in a way an extreme High-Churchman, was fanatically anti-Roman, and very definitely deprecated the negotiations in Rome that took place during his primacy. But the dignity, the solidity, and what may have seemed to him the worldly wisdom of the Roman Church, appealed to Davidson. In definitely permitting the Conversations, as the Vatican definitely permitted them, he felt that he was negotiating with a brother pontiff.

He was no great theologian, but he was a very expert ecclesiastical politician with a very high estimate of the value of prestige. He was once described by a very eminent Roman Catholic as "a perfect type of Renaissance ecclesiastical statesman," and I think that the description is not inaccurate. And as an ecclesiastical statesman, from many points of view, the Conversations seemed to him to be worth while.

In December 1923, in the very first conversation that I had with His Grace, he took pains to emphasise to me his personal responsibility for meetings which had been severely criticised by a considerable section of Church opinion. This was eminently characteristic. Above all things, Davidson was a strong man, as strong a man as Temple had been before him. He stood on his own feet. He never dreamt of sheltering himself behind his brethren. One of the men who knew him best once told me that during Davidson's primacy a meeting of Bishops in the library at Lambeth Palace was much like the sixth form attending a conference in the headmaster's study. At Lambeth Conferences, in Convocation and, latterly, in the Church Assembly, he dominated the proceedings over which he presided, and few decisions were taken of which he did not approve.

There was something a little grim about this short, thickset, strong-willed man with the beetling eyebrows and piercing eyes, who retained vigour of mind to the last days of his long life. But there was humour, too, and uncommonly shrewd judgment. Just before the publication of the 1927 Revised Prayer Book he sent for me to give me valuable advance knowledge of some of the changes that were to be proposed. I ventured to say to him how widefelt was the appreciation of his long labours in a work of extreme difficulty. "You had better," he said, "wait and read the Book before you become too grateful."

Davidson regretted what he felt to be the necessity for the revision, which was, from the beginning to the end, intended to check the Catholic movement. Persecution and prosecution had both been tried and had both failed. The decisions of secular courts were largely ignored, and practices, condemned by authority, were becoming more and more popular. In certain matters, such as Prayers for the Dead, public opinion had been greatly changed by the events of the War, and the æsthetic attraction of Catholic Services was felt by many people with little religious conviction. Repression had failed, and authority decided to try what could be done by concession, to give a very little and to add to the gift the admonition, "thus far and no farther." The Catholic was to be permitted to have his Prayers for the Dead with certain changes in the Communion Office, but the Modernist was not forgotten. He was no longer to be compelled to recite the Athanasian Creed, and the extreme Protestant was to be permitted to drop into extemporary prayer. The consequence was that there was little enthusiasm in the Church for the new Book, while its publication at once aroused a roaring, whirling, ill-informed Protestant agitation, Protestant fears having been aroused immediately before by the Malines Conversations.

There was a certain pathos in the speech in which the Archbishop introduced the Prayer Book Measure in the House of Lords. Referring to the opposition to the Measure, he said, "The attack has been largely against myself. I am an old man, I have been a bishop nearly thirty-seven years, and an archbishop for nearly twenty-five years, and my life has not been lived in private or silently." He protested his fidelity to the Protestant faith and urged that there was nothing in the Book that traversed Reformation sentiment.

I watched the Archbishop closely as he sat in the gallery during the subsequent House of Commons debate. Thanks to the votes of Scottish and Welsh members, the Measure was defeated. After the decision had been announced, the Archbishop walked quietly out of the House, as I described him at the time, "a strong, stubborn, stern old man, temporarily defeated, but determined to fight on." Unfortunately for his reputation, his passion for compromise and his horror of a break with the State, led him into the greatest blunder of his life. In the attempt to propitiate his opponents, almost entirely owing to his pressure, certain changes were made in the Book which made it quite unacceptable to the Anglo-Catholics and did nothing to diminish Protestant fears.

Had Davidson stood to his guns, and had the Bishops ignored the decision of Parliament, and had then done what a great many of them have done since and authorised the use of the Book as it stood, the whole history of the Church of England would have been different. But Davidson compromised, and just after his eightieth birthday Parliament again blocked revision. And that was the end of Davidson's official life.

He was not either mentally or physically worn out. He had not resigned, he protested, on account of "disappointment at recent events in Parliament." But the 1930 Lambeth Conference was approaching, and he felt that it should be presided over by a younger man. So he crossed the river from Lambeth to Chelsea, still keenly interested in passing events, happy with his old friendships, undaunted by the difficulties of the time. "I am an old man," he said, "and we are told that old men dream dreams. My dreams for the world I shall soon be leaving are rich in hope."

LORD FISHER
1841-1920

By
HERBERT SIDEBOTHAM

LORD FISHER

by HERBERT SIDEBOTHAM

THE Navy that Fisher joined as a boy of thirteen was still the Navy of Nelson and Rodney. Fifty years later his Admiral's flag was hauled down and his service afloat was over. In those fifty years ships of war had changed more in material, mechanism, and tactics than they had changed in the previous two thousand years. Themistocles of Salamis might have commanded with credit most of the ships of the British Navy when Fisher was a midshipman, but Nelson would have been a helpless layman if he had suddenly been put in command of the *Inflexible*, or of Fisher's flagship in the Mediterranean. Ten years had still to run before the Great War, and the pace of change did not slacken. These were the years of Fisher's reforms as First Sea Lord, and our Navy, hitherto prepared for war with France and Russia, had to adapt itself to the vastly changed conditions of a war with Germany. Yet that great struggle was hardly over before the old man's imagination was again on the wing to the conditions of war fifty years ahead. No soldier's and certainly no other sailor's career ever spanned such changes in the technique of his profession, and Fisher had a mind that to the end not only kept pace with change but tended at times to outrun it.

He was, in fact, the first real Radical that ever came out of the sea. No other word expresses his place in naval history, but it is, of course, to be understood in a professional and temperamental not a political sense, for Fisher had no party politics, and any party that had tried to contain him must have blown up violently. The voice of the sea is said to be the chosen music of liberty, but its service commonly makes conservatives and sentimentalists. A Major-General is to many the type of professional conservatism, but his chief failing, after all, is that he thinks that all future wars will be like the last one, or the last but one. But a sailor's devotion to tradition goes back to the oldest of man's wars with the force of nature, a war which, until the middle of the last century, had hardly changed its character from unrecorded time, and in which the victory of man depended much on constancy, little on liberty of thought. Fisher joined the Navy when it was still dozing in the glorious traditions of Nelson. The age of mechanical invention was beginning, which was to change the whole face of England, and though our British blue-water aristocracy might resist the entry of the new spirit into its domain, it could not prevent it. Steamers were crossing the Atlantic thirty years before Fisher joined his first ship, the sailing-ship *Calcutta*. Steam power was just beginning in the Navy, but even under steam, all ships still carried sails. The last of the frigates was not struck off the Navy List until 1861, and as late as 1892, when Fisher was Controller of the Navy, he turned down a memorandum by a Member of the Board, proposing to build sixteen new sailing-ships. The Board of Admiralty, having resisted steam as fatal to British naval supremacy, went on to resist steel ships on the ground that wood floated and iron sank. The first armoured ship in the Navy was the *Warrior* commissioned in 1863, to which Fisher was appointed for gunnery duties and on which he entertained Garibaldi, but the *Warrior* owed its armour, not to naval initiative, but to a suggestion of that eminent landsman, Napoleon III.

There must have been progressive men in the Navy before Fisher, for change had begun while he was still a lieutenant. But not one of them had change in his bones from beginning to end of his career as Fisher had. Already in some of his early lectures in the *Excellent* gunnery school ship in the 'eighties we may recognise in germ the ideas that he carried out later in the *Dreadnought*. As ships grew larger and more powerful, science superseded the old basis of adventure; navies became completely mechanised, one had almost said industrialised; the changes from mediævalism to modernity, which on land had been accomplished gradually, though with increasing momentum through the centuries, were crammed into half a century in the Navy, and had to be forced on the most conservative of all professions. That was mainly Fisher's doing. Fisher, first and greatest Radical of the sea, in effect changed the Navy of Nelson to the Navy that fought in the Great War.

by HERBERT SIDEBOTHAM

But that, by itself, hardly explains the place that Fisher had in the esteem of the crowd, for the ship is more than its machinery and the Navy than its organisation. Fisher captured and held the popular imagination as no British sailor has done except Nelson, and when he died the public sense of bereavement was probably more general and more sincere than over any other military or naval figure in the War. Fisher, it is true, was always a good showman, and he understood the art of publicity. His keen sense of humour, his instinct for the dramatic, and the strength and vividness of his personality made him the easiest of subjects to present for popular hero-worship, and the writers in the newspapers did not fail to make use of their opportunity. But the widest publicity, though it might have earned him temporary popularity, could not have enabled him to keep it as he did. He died twenty months after the Armistice, and even then, as the streets bore witness when he was buried, Fisher to the crowd was the British Navy.

Yet the crowd had had time to forget him. In the last ten years of his life he had held office for a few months only. He had ceased to be First Sea Lord in 1910. He was recalled to the Admiralty in October 1914, and he left it again, never to return, in May 1915. Fisher always had plenty of enemies, and their hostile influence was paramount at the Admiralty for the last five years of his life. He died under a cloud, and the man who had made the Navy that did more than any other single Service to win the War, was never invited to witness the surrender of the German Fleet. Besides, Fisher never fought a Fleet action at sea. He commanded the newest and best ship in the Navy at the bombardment of Alexandria, but hers were the only ship's guns that he ever fired in anger. Of Nelson we may say with certainty that peerless as was his genius in action, he could no more have done St. Vincent's work at the Admiralty than St. Vincent could have won the Battle of the Nile. But to discuss whether this greater than St. Vincent at the Admiralty would have been a Nelsonian Admiral in a Fleet action is mere idle speculation. The victory of the Falkland Islands was a battle that Fisher was exceedingly proud of, but though he made the victory possible, Sturdee fought it. Fisher therefore lacked the prestige of victory in battle which appeals most to the masses. Moreover, the period of Fisher's popular eminence was short. He was not known to the people under Victoria, and his *floruit* was almost exclusively Edwardian. That the people should still have persisted, as late as 1920, in regarding him as the one great representative of the British Navy was by no means a matter of course. Did they think that he had been badly treated and, as is the way with mass opinion, let sentimental sympathy exaggerate their estimate of his greatness? Or were they themselves conscious that great as the achievement of the British Navy had been in the War, it had not been according to expectation, and did they identify their own sense of grievance that the rendering of " Rule Britannia " in the War had been so unlike the old renderings with Fisher's own grievance?

The record of Fisher's reforms at the Admiralty is, at this distance, rapidly becoming one of professional and even antiquarian interest, nor shall we recapture the secret of Fisher's greatness through the ana that were once so fashionable. His interest for our time is in the questions that have just been asked. Fisher made the modern British Navy and foresaw the War and its date. But the War, when it did come, was disastrously different from all other wars that had been fought. Let it be conceded that the work of the Navy did most to break down the German *moral*. Still, our naval power did not save us as it had done in the struggle with Napoleon, and in all previous wars, from throwing the whole of our man-power into the struggle. We had to adopt conscription as though we were a continental nation, not an island, and many, who ought to have known better, came to think of the Navy as though it were a mere bridge enabling our youth to cross to the decisive battle-front. The War, in fact, made a clean break with all our traditional strategy. In the past its inspiration had been naval, but in this war it was definitely military. The break cost us hundreds of thousands of our best lives, and inflicted injuries upon us from which we may never fully recover. Was it inevitable? Was it for this that Fisher made the modern Navy? Was Fisher in any sense to blame that the Navy lost its old distinction of enabling us, not merely to win wars, but to win them at the minimum of sacrifice of British lives? If it was not Fisher's, whose fault was it? On the answer to these and similar questions must depend history's estimate of Fisher. If they are answered one way, Fisher was another St. Vincent, a mechanician of genius, a vivid personality, but not in the apostolic succession of British genius at sea; answered in another way they vindicate him as the greatest of Edwardians and a worthy successor of Nelson, but they bring a note of bitter tragedy into his life.

The Navy that fought the War was the Navy of his making, but the War as it was fought was not the kind of war for which he had prepared the Navy. Bold innovator as he was in the mechanism of the Navy and its internal organisation, Fisher was a devotee of tradition in his views about the use of the Navy and its place in our polity. Short of supremacy over all possible enemies, he would have no limitation on its strength, and none in the use that should be made of it. He was the British Naval delegate at the first Peace Conference in 1899, which discussed, among other proposals for humanising war, a project favoured by the United States for exempting private property at sea from capture. Fisher scourged the idea as though it was a moral vice. The essence of war, he said, was violence; moderation in war was imbecility. W. T. Stead was with him at the time, and wrote an account of the way he was talking. He told Stead:

> "I am not for war, I am for peace. If you rub it in both at home and abroad that you are ready for instant war with every unit of your strength in the first line, and intend to be first in, and hit your enemy in the belly, and kick him when he is down, and boil your prisoners in oil if you take any, and torture his women and children, then people will keep clear of you."

This is a translation into naval English of the frightfulness of German militarism, but it is a good example of his controversial method. If he disagreed with a proposition, he had no idea of deflecting it or circumventing it. His way was to bludgeon it to a jelly by stating its logical antithesis in its most violent and brutal form, as he does here. Twelve years later, writing to Lord Esher, he admits comically that perhaps he went " a little too far, when I said I would boil the prisoners in oil, and murder the innocent in cold blood, but," he continues, "it's quite silly not to make war damnable to the whole mass of your enemy's population. When war does come, might is right, and the Admiralty will know what to do."

That was written in April 1912. No German ever went

farther, and indeed Fisher never had the slightest sympathy with the denunciations of German inhumanity in her conduct of the War at sea. He held that her submarine campaign was perfectly justified. But in the same letter to Lord Esher, in which he refers to the views he expressed in 1899, there is a passage in which he shows us the reverse side of his passionate advocacy of a supreme Navy. He writes:

> "I fully agree with you that the schemes of the British Army General Staff are grotesque. Their projects last August, during the Agadir crisis, were wild in the extreme. You will remember a famous interview we two had with King Edward in his cabin on board the Royal yacht; how we stamped on the idea that then enthused the War Office mind, of England once more engaged in a great continental war. Marlboroughs cheap to-day was the kettle of fish advertised by the Militarists."

Because he had such faith in the virtues of naval power, he was an anti-militarist.

The interview with the King on the Royal yacht must have been in 1909, and by the "continental war" on which the King stamped, Fisher meant not a war with a continental Power, but a war fought on the Continent, and under the influence of continental strategy. Fisher had already made up his mind that war with Germany was inevitable, but he wished to fight it in accordance with our insular tradition, relying upon a supreme Navy and using military force only as an adjunct to the Navy. He was fond of telling of a talk he once had with General von Schwartzhoff, a German soldier of very high distinction, who expatiated on the true rôle of the British Army:

> "How the absolute supremacy of the British Navy gave the Army inordinate power, far beyond its numerical strength, because 200,000 men embarked in transports and God only knowing where they might be put ashore, was a weapon of enormous influence, and capable of deadly blows," etc.

Fisher is always recurring to this conception of our proper strategy in war. The Regular Army was, for him, merely a projectile to be fired by the Navy. Unfortunately, military

ideas of our right strategy prevailed over naval, despite the
" stamping " by the King which Fisher reports. As early
as 1909 Fisher sees in certain observations of the General
Staff, " the thin end of the insidious wedge of continental
war." Continental war Fisher always sharply distinguished
from coastal military expeditions in concert with the Navy.
Admiral Bacon, the biographer of Fisher, gives an account
of a meeting of the Committee of Imperial Defence in 1909,
at which Fisher gave a summary of his own views about our
right strategy in the War.

" During the Morocco Crisis the French Government
was within an inch of war with Germany and insisted
upon 120,000 British troops being placed on the French
frontier. The Cabinet agreed. At a Meeting of the
Defence Committee, where the military plans were set
forth by General Nicholson, Fisher remained silent,
seated opposite to Mr. Asquith at the end of a long
table. The only question put to Fisher was, whether
the Navy could guarantee the transport, to which he
answered, ' Yes.' Mr. Asquith then asked him if he
had anything to say, and he replied that he had nothing
to say that anyone present would care to hear. Mr.
Asquith pressed him: then a scene took place. Fisher
told the Committee that if 120,000 English were sent
to France the Germans would put everything else aside
and make any sacrifice to surround and destroy the
British, and that they would succeed. Continental
armies being what they are, Fisher expressed the view
that the British Army should be absolutely restricted to
operations consisting of sudden descents on the coast,
the recovery of Heligoland and the " garrisoning " of
Antwerp.

" He pointed out that there was a stretch of ten miles
of hard sand on the Pomeranian coast which is only
ninety miles from Berlin. Were the British Army to
seize and entrench that strip a million Germans would
find occupation, but to despatch British troops to the
front in a continental war would be an act of suicidal
idiocy arising from the distorted view of War produced
by Mr. Haldane's speeches, and the childish arrangements for training Terriers after war broke out. Fisher
followed this up with an impassioned diatribe against

the War Office and all its ways, including conceit, waste of money, and ignorance of war. He claimed that the British Army should be administered as an annexe to the Navy. . . .

"At this point Mr. Asquith said, 'I think we had better adjourn.' [Fisher's biographer thinks that the diatribe stopped the ambitious plans of the War Office.[1] If it did, it was only for a time.]

Fisher ceased to be First Sea Lord in January 1910. In the next four years we were committed beyond the possibility of withdrawal to the continental strategy against which Fisher had protested so strongly. The Great War brought suffering and sacrifices on this country immeasurably greater than any previous war in our history, not merely or so much because the strength of the enemy was relatively more formidable than our own, but because we fought it in a different and in a wrong way. All our other wars were insular, or at most peninsular, wars. This was a continental war and fought on continental inspiration. The chief significance of Fisher in our history is that he stands for the idea that the Great War could have been fought and won by us as a naval war with assistance from the Regular Army, but without raising vast armies and without conscription. Had this idea been accepted, and had Fisher been able to carry it through to success, he would have been greater than Nelson or Wellington. It was not to be. But that he should have conceived it so strongly and held to it so tenaciously contradicts the idea of his detractors that he was a mere machinist of war and puts him among the original thinkers.

It may be said that we could never have won the war against Germany as we won the war against Napoleon, that without the assistance of our Army the French must have been overwhelmed, and that however supreme we might still be at sea, we should, without allies, have been driven to a disadvantageous peace. Undoubtedly had the French dispositions been as faulty as they actually were at the beginning of the War, nothing could have saved the French

---

[1] See in Lord Riddell's "War Diary" a passage in which Mr. McKenna says that he had to leave the Admiralty "because he had objected to the proposal to send an expeditionary force to France" (p. 13). Mr. McKenna understood Fisher better than any other politician.

by HERBERT SIDEBOTHAM

Armies from defeat, and Fisher's formula for winning the War by naval supremacy alone would certainly have been inadequate to save France, as for that matter, Trafalgar was inadequate to save Austria or Prussia against Napoleon. But two things must be remembered. First, Fisher never thought of any interest but that of England and, except in so far as it might make our own task more difficult, the fall of Paris would have left him quite unmoved. But—a second and more important consideration—is it not possible that a frank avowal of our intention to stick to our traditional policy might have saved France from some of the mistakes which she actually made at the beginning of the War? French military policy long wobbled between the policy of defence and of the offensive which was her undoing; and it may well have been her reliance on our support on her left wing that led her to the unfortunate offensive into Lorraine, the failure of which brought the Germans into the heart of France. Useful as the support of the British Army was as the left wing of the French Army, how much more useful it would have been if it had been an independent Army on the German flank in Belgium, as Fisher wanted it to be.

We realised our mistakes very soon. At the first Cabinet Council after the declaration of war Lord Roberts at once suggested Antwerp as the natural advanced base for the British Army, and Mr. Lloyd George tells us that Lord French favoured the same idea, and gives it as his opinion that if five British Divisions had been on the flank of the Germans, they could never have penetrated so deeply into France, and that the whole course of the War would have been different.

No sooner had the Battle of the Marne been fought and won, than Lord French was anxious to get on the flank of the Germans in Flanders, where we might have been from the start. The Battle of the Marne might just as well have been won in front of Lille as in front of Paris, and Fisher had always counted on our being in occupation of the coast of Flanders. Besides simplifying our task of dealing with German submarines and German air-raids, such a position would have given us the military advantage that we went vainly two years later through the long agony of Passchendaele to obtain. Churchill's own enterprise to save Antwerp was only another attempt to catch up with the opportunity that we had let slip. But Fisher's ideas were not confined merely to the holding of the Belgian coast. He persistently advocated his project for landing on the coast of Prussia, ninety miles from Berlin. Had this project been practicable, it would have been of far greater assistance to our French allies in relieving the pressure on France than any we were able to give, at any rate for the first two years of the War. The Marne was a victory, partly because the Russian invasion of East Prussia had drawn away two German Army Corps from France. How many Army Corps would a threat against Berlin itself have drawn off, even though it had not been able to do more than maintain itself for a time?

Fisher came back to the Admiralty from his retirement at a time of discouragement. The Battle of Coronel had been lost, and a powerful German squadron was on the high seas. Our blockade of Germany was by no means effective. Churchill's attempt to save Antwerp had failed, and the Battle of Ypres which was to continue to the very end of the War, had just been joined. The victory of the Falkland Islands, which atoned for Coronel, was no great feat in the winning, but was made remarkable by its completeness, by the courage shown by Fisher in detaching overwhelming forces to the other side of the world, by the fierce energy with which he prepared and timed the expedition, and succeeded in infecting everyone else. A new spirit of the offensive had come into the direction of the British Navy; the Captain of the *Defence*, who did not know that Fisher had returned to the Admiralty when he received his telegram of instructions from home, exclaimed at once, " That must have been written by Fisher."

Churchill tells us that when war broke out he was tempted to ask Fisher if he would come to the Admiralty as First Sea Lord, and had he done so, the opening passages of the War might have been gloriously different. For the two were on the friendliest terms at this time and Churchill had the greatest respect for his genius. Better still would it have been had Fisher been born four years later, so that he could have been at the Admiralty in the four years after 1910, instead of the four years before. The combination of Fisher's knowledge and vision with Churchill's persistence and argumentative force in council might have defeated the pernicious influence of the soldiers and laid the foundations of a more glorious and less costly war strategy.

The new spirit also showed itself in the measures taken for tightening the blockade and in an immense programme of new shipbuilding that Fisher put in hand. Fisher never allowed details to overlay the main ideas of his policy. His central idea was to recover for the Navy the initiative in offence. It was no longer to be merely expectant of the blows of others, but so to use its sea power as to transfer the war to the points most favourable to ourselves, and by the choice of objective to make comparatively small military forces do the work of many times their number. Naturally the recovery of the coast of Belgium was a chief object of his desire; and had his projected landing on the coast been carried out early enough in 1915, it might still have been possible to repair some of the early blunders. But the project was delayed by political reasons. The Belgians did not relish the prospect of having the hardest of the fighting carried into the interior of their country, and were content that the issue should be decided at the extremity. Moreover, the French were interested in keeping us as the left wing of their own Army, and disliked the idea of a separate British Army operating independently in Belgium. The Baltic project, too, languished, for the victories of Hindenburg in East Prussia enabled him to invade Poland, and the Russians had no superfluity of men to spare for an offensive on the coast of Pomerania. On the other hand, the campaign in France became ever greedier in its demands for the new troops that were training. One suspects too that the details of the Baltic project were never really worked out, and as time went on its attractiveness waned. War is most prolific in examples of the fable of the Sibylline books, increasing in price and diminishing in number with every chance missed. The best chance for the Baltic project would have been very early in the War, but to be tried then the project, demanding long elaboration of detail, would have had to be worked out in advance before the War. But those years were spent in military conversations with the French which led us away from the natural use of our Army as the projectile of the Navy.

Doubtless one or both of these projects would have matured into action. But both foundered in the desperate ill-luck of Gallipoli and in the quarrel between Fisher and Churchill to which it led. These two men had a genuine regard for each other. Fisher had treated him as a son in the interval between 1910 and his return to the Admiralty, and his advice on naval affairs to the new First Lord was liberally given and gratefully received, if not always followed. They had indeed many ideas in common about the War. Churchill, it is true, had been a soldier and could not be expected to forget that he was descended from Marlborough, the greatest strategist among English generals. In the critical years before the War he was badly bitten by the military bug, and showed no real appreciation of the great traditional principles of naval war. But his cure was rapid when once the War had begun, and he has since become the leading exponent of an alternative strategy, which would have given us a victory at a less ruinous cost in life and money. He has even been given the credit of being the only man who had an alternative to the frightful carnage of our premature offensives in France. Yet his general attitude towards British military policy in the War was not materially different from that which Fisher had expounded so fiercely to the Cabinet as long ago as 1909. His efforts to save Antwerp recall that early advice of Fisher's that we should " garrison " Antwerp and at all costs keep control of the Belgian coast. The strategic idea again of his Gallipoli enterprise is almost identical with that of Fisher's Baltic project, and indeed is a left-hand version of it. When Fisher was first presented with it he recognised it as a child of his own, though with a bar sinister. He began by supporting it. He ended by hating it with an intensity that overmastered both his own duty to the country and the country's need of him.

If the two men had not liked each other, and had no ideas in common, the partnership must have broken up earlier, with results less tragic for both of them. Fisher would have given no measure of encouragement to ideas which had no sort of affinity with his own; nor would Churchill have continued to take an ell of advantage for an inch of approval unless there had been both sympathy and partiality to begin with. Churchill's case in the quarrel was that Fisher withdrew his support of the Dardanelles enterprise when fortune turned against it and it was most in need of his support; Fisher's, that his support was conditional from the first on its not making too great demands on naval strength in the North Sea. Churchill complained that just the little more effort that would have been sufficient for victory was refused; Fisher that the forcing of the Dardanelles had become an obsession with Churchill; that he had stretched personal loyalty to a point at which the interests of the country were in jeopardy; Churchill particularly resented the withdrawal of the *Queen Elizabeth*; Fisher replied that if he had not withdrawn her she would have been torpedoed as her dummy was.

The case of both is painfully clear. But Fisher can neither be absolved from responsibility for failures and mistakes which he must be held to have condoned by continuing in office, nor can he be excused for his leaving office in circumstances which were almost like desertion in face of the enemy. The juster Fisher's criticisms were of Churchill's mistakes the less one can excuse him for not making them more effectual in restraint of the First Lord, or for the circumstances of his explosive resignation. He did not, in fact, run away to Scotland as he threatened, but obeyed the King's command through Mr. Asquith to remain at his post. When the Cabinet was reconstructed and Mr. Balfour succeeded Mr. Churchill, he might still have continued to be First Sea Lord, but the conditions that he then demanded were such as no Prime Minister could accept. He refused to serve under Mr. Balfour; he demanded the retirement of Sir A. Wilson and an entire new Board of Admiralty, complete professional charge of the war at sea, with sole disposition of the Fleet and the right of appointing all officers; and that the First Lord in future should be restricted to policy and Parliamentary procedure. This was almost a naval *pronunciamiento*. After that Fisher had to go, and for the rest of his life he was under the cloud that hangs over a man who has attempted a revolution and failed.

The people forgave him, and, old as he was, there was to the end no real failing of his powers. He bitterly attacked those who continued the work at the Admiralty after he had gone, but in his letters that appeared in *The Times* under the standing heading " Sack the Lot " are to be found some of the best things that he ever said about naval policy. It has been said of Gladstone that by the time he was eighty he was becoming quite a good Liberal. In the same vein of coupled admiration and sarcasm, one may express one's astonishment at the rebellious vitality which turned this great Radical of the sea into a fierce revolutionary at eighty.

But always underneath this ferocity there was a certain loyalty and even tenderness of sentiment. You see it in his final letter to Churchill.

"You are bent on forcing the Dardanelles, and nothing will turn you from it—nothing. I know you so well. I could give you no better proof of my desire to stand by you in this Dardanelles business up to the last moment against the strongest conviction of my life. You will remain and I shall go—it is better so."

The old man was conscious of his age. He admired Churchill's qualities of mind, all the more perhaps because he had quarrelled with his judgment. It was a choice between youth and age; let age retire from the contest even though it knows itself to be right rather than damp the ardour of youth; give youth its fair chance. If age (as expressed in the last impossible demands to Asquith) must be denied, let youth have its fling. Better both divorced than this unhappy marriage. Of all the phenomena of human nature, none is more moving than this craving of age for its liberty, this mingling of generosity and envy in the judgments of age on ebullient youth. How far we are removed now from the estimate of Fisher by his detractor as a mere mechanist of the Navy.

Yet in the story of these days there is revealed an intrinsic weakness which must be acknowledged. Here was a man of the highest character and of acknowledged genius who nevertheless when he was in power split the Navy into two rival factions, and who with his ideas, both big and sound, nevertheless somehow failed to force them on his age and who could only escape from the fascination of Churchill by rebellion that was at once insolent and generous. What was the weakness? It was not intrinsic to Fisher's own nature, but to his education and upbringing. The Navy takes its men too young; it forms them in traditions of the sea which are innocent of all knowledge of conditions of life and politics ashore. It is a miracle if they escape—as Fisher did —the dead hand of tradition and acquire an independent and realistic judgment of their own. But they are still handicapped—as Fisher was—by having to fight their battles on land with weapons to which they are not accustomed. The true inwardness of the quarrel over the Dardanelles was that Fisher was always beaten in the argument, while still knowing instinctively that he was right. Fisher never could argue. *J'ordonne ou je me tais*, was one of his favourite sayings. He could roar out orders or he could make epigrams and vivid phrases; but of the gentler finesses of reasoning he was innocent. And thus he had all the right ideas about the War and failed to get one of them adopted. And not understanding why, he took fright of argument. On the Dardanelles he ran away from Churchill, though he knew that he was right; he was afraid lest the convincing argument should betray him into acquiescence into what he knew to be wrong. And as with the Dardanelles, so with our whole war strategy. He had not merely sound but brilliant ideas that should have shortened the War and made victory in the War by comparison both easy and cheap; yet people with not one-tenth of his abilities forced their own inferior ideas on the country, to its lasting injury. Perhaps the reason for such defeat is that the Navy takes its men too young and fails to equip them with the qualities for success in a democratic world where the plausible is more potent than the real and rhetoric prevails over knowledge and fact.

And, therefore, opposite the great Edwardian name of Fisher one has still to place a note of interrogation. He is clearly more than the glorified mechanic and hustler of naval power as his enemies think. Even in the errors and misfeasances of his fall from power there is a grandeur, moral as well as intellectual. He had in him that which, if only it had been fully tested, might have prevented most of our injuries to-day, have shortened the War, saved hundreds of thousands of lives, made victory not a mere mockery of exhaustion, but a word of good repute and genuine comfort. Had it come through the test, Fisher would have been a greater name in our history than either Nelson or Wellington. Because it was never brought to the test, what might have been fame, documented and proved magnificent, remains a subject for argument. One can only record a personal belief that history will reckon Fisher as incomparably the greatest of the Edwardians.

JOHN GALSWORTHY
1867-1933

By
HUGH WALPOLE

JOHN GALSWORTHY

by HUGH WALPOLE

HAD John Galsworthy died in 1910, leaving behind him *The Man of Property* and *The Country House* as his principal novels, *The Silver Box* and *Strife* as his two important plays, it is probable that he would appear, to critics of every school to-day, as an artist of fine performance and yet greater promise, untimely cut off.

The savage article by D. H. Lawrence in the first volume of *Scrutinies*, the scorn and derision of the critics of the post-war generation, the half-hearted apologetic articles that appeared after his death, would certainly seem incredibly false and unjust to all the critical schools of 1910 could they encounter them.

It may be also that again in 1960 the literary critics who are interested in the history of the novel and the theatre from 1900 to 1930 (and it will offer many curious and opposite subjects for study) will regard Lawrence, in his critical moods, as hysterically unbalanced and the younger critics of 1930 as too self-conscious to be born. Galsworthy will then receive his just appreciation.

Had he died in 1910 he would seem to us now, I fancy, as possessing something near to genius in his appropriateness, a prophet, who created more wisely and more truly than he knew.

As artist it cannot be questioned that he lived too long, but of how many artists is that not true?—of Tolstoi, of Balzac, of Tennyson and Wordsworth, of Meredith and Anatole France. Nor in the final estimate is this of importance. An artist lives by his finest work—one single work, if it is grand enough, is sufficient. Time sweeps away the débris.

That Galsworthy wrote his best novel—*The Man of Property*—and his best play—*The Silver Box*—early in his career was perhaps his personal misfortune, for every artist wishes to feel that, as the years pass, he moves forward in his art. And it is true that the origin of all the adverse criticism encountered by him in his later years comes from this: that both as man and writer he deliberately shut himself off, as the years passed, from the general action of the outside world.

By this I do not of course mean any physical retirement. He was interested in many things, in the success of the Pen Club which he helped to found, in many public causes, in the adventures of his friends; he lectured in America and Germany and Austria; no writer in England felt more deeply than he the horrors of the War and the suffering that the War brought to the world. His isolation was a spiritual one. Any study of his work brings one to the certainty that, early in his career, he received an impression of injustice and intolerance so deep and moving that he was unable, after it, to step beyond it. It confined him inside its own experience, and everything that later happened to him, however various, received the same shape and colour.

But it was his destiny to live and work through the greatest changes that the world, within so short a space of time, has seen. To those who knew him only casually, to all who knew him only by his photograph or the written word, he appeared a man apart. His portrait with the austere, rather melancholy features, the meticulous neatness of dress, the anxious kindliness, as of a man who wished his fellow men well but feared for their future, had about it something almost inhuman, a reserved nobility.

To his intimates he was very different from this. I have heard his friends—Conrad and Hudson, for example—speak of him with passionate affection, as of someone rare amongst men for unswerving loyalty and integrity and fidelity. But his shyness, his innate modesty, his hatred of interfering in the privacy of others allowed him few intimacies, and it is certain that the real man was little known to the outside world. He scarcely ever replied to criticism, and was moved to protest only by injustice to others, never by injustice to himself. It followed therefore that his work was static. What he thought and felt in 1910 he thought and felt in 1930—the same injustice, the same intolerances moved him always.

The technique of his work also did not change. *The Man*

by HUGH WALPOLE

of Property represents him technically assured and accomplished as does the *Flowering Wilderness* of 1932. Behind him, around him, however, between 1910 and 1930 the world of men suffered a complete transformation, not, it may be, in its deeper, more spiritual characteristics—for the impulses of the human soul do not alter—but in all the material visible circumstances; and it is of these that the novelist and dramatist must constantly be aware.

This awareness is the more important in Galsworthy's case because his principal work is a social chronicle, and depends for its essential truth on exactly this perception of social differences, and by " social " I mean something more important than the changing sequence of external manners and customs.

As I have said, had he never published any other novel than *The Man of Property* (it was conceived as a single work, and, when writing it, he intended no sequel) the whole of his art might have been found there. It is a study of social and moral injustice brought about by the greed and possessiveness of man. It appeared at a time when England was at the end of a period of possessive and wealthy domination, when the Forsytes were at the very top of the world and must, themselves, believe that they were there for all time.

Their power was derived from their tenacious adhesiveness, and the melancholy brooding over every page of this book comes, it seems, from Galsworthy's own belief at that time—that this tenacity will never be broken; all rebels against it will be broken by it.

These are the opening paragraphs of *The Man of Property*:

> " Those privileged to be present at a family festival of the Forsytes have seen that charming and instructive sight—an upper middle-class family in full plumage. But whosoever of these favoured persons has possessed the gift of psychological analysis (a talent without monetary value and properly ignored by the Forsytes) has witnessed a spectacle, not only delightful in itself, but illustrative of an obscure, human problem. . . . He is like one who, having watched a tree grow from its planting—a paragon of tenacity, insulation, and success, amidst the deaths of a hundred other plants less fibrous, sappy, and persistent—one day will see it

flourishing with bland, full foliage, in an almost repugnant prosperity, at the summit of its efflorescence."

In these rather stilted sentences Galsworthy states his terms, not only for this book, but for every other book that he was ever afterwards to write—his scorn of the top-dog who is in possession, his tenderness and pity for the under-dog.

The danger of this theme is at once apparent—unfairness to the top-dog (for whom there is always something to be said) and disgust of the under-dog at being pitied. In *The Man of Property* itself the danger is not so apparent—although it does sufficiently appear—but suppose that time passes and the top-dog changes places with the under-dog—what then? Will the under-dog forgive that tenderness? He will not only deeply resent it but it will seem to him the falsest of sentimentalities.

Nevertheless, *The Man of Property*—whose period is the late 'eighties—is, in itself, true to its time. This is not to say that every man in the England of the 'eighties was a Forsyte—Galsworthy does not pretend that it was so; there *were* sufficient Forsytes, their power and self-confidence and authority were strong and important enough to justify the emphasis. But even there—even in those opening sentences—the emphasis does not seem quite fair. The author's dislike is too strong for justice, and from the very first page we feel that we would like to hear something on the other side. In this city was there not one just man? Yes—old Jolyon Forsyte—he and he alone.

I believe *The Man of Property* to be a very fine novel, an important one in the progress of English literature of the early twentieth century, but I must admit at once to a serious handicap in my estimate of it, namely, that I cannot abide its two suffering under-dogs, the architect Bosinney and Irene, wife of Soames Forsyte. Now this is in all probability a personal defect in myself, but is there not also an irony in the fact that in all the Galsworthy novels and in some of the plays (Mrs. Jones of *The Silver Box* is an under-dog who has all my affection and admiration if she will allow me to say so), it is the upper-dogs rather than the under-dogs who win our sympathy? If the under-dogs *do* win our sympathy it is not because they are ill-treated by the upper-dogs, but because they are ill-treated (in his tenderness and care of them) by Galsworthy.

Consider for a moment Bosinney and Irene Soames. In Galsworthy's behaviour to them are to be found, I think, all the grounds for the charges of falseness and sentimentality brought against him. It is not that Bosinney and Irene are themselves false. Very far from it. The charge that Galsworthy cannot create human beings (a charge brought against him by Lawrence, whose own weakness, as novelist, this especially was) is ludicrously false. He was always creating them, from Soames and Jolyon and Swithin and Bosinney to the heroine of *Flowering Wilderness*. No. The sentimentality comes in, of course, through his personal attitude to them.

Bosinney and Irene are, Galsworthy feels (and makes us feel that he feels), creatures monstrously ill-treated. They are the victims of the Forsyte possessiveness. But are they? Irene (for reasons never sufficiently clear to us) has married a man whom she hates and, in the pages of this novel at least, she never ceases to show that she hates him. Soames may not be the most endearing of men (in the later pages of the Saga, Galsworthy grows fonder and fonder of him), but at least he is ready to do all that he can, save give his wife her freedom. There lies his criminal fault in his creator's eyes. But does Irene, on her side, make the slightest attempt to keep *her* part of the bargain? She hates Soames, and that justifies her, it seems, in playing the part from first to last of a female cad. Her own callous selfishness is to one reader at least infinitely more appalling than Soames's possessiveness. As for Bosinney, he is surely one of the most unattractive men in all fiction! Galsworthy seems to feel that there is something delightful in Bosinney's boorish rudeness to all the Forsytes and something charming in his dishonourable breaking of his bargains in the matter of the House. He was, it appears, quite irresistible to Irene, but his gifts as a lover are concealed from us, for we are never permitted, in the course of the whole book, to be present at any encounter between the lovers, but, as though we were all Forsytes (which very probably we are), we are kept at a distance, and only with gigantic Swithin or vagabondish George are we allowed to overhear them as in a dream.

Irene's misery and Bosinney's snarling unhappiness are,

throughout the book, uninterrupted. Did Irene never know a happy moment? Did she never smile at some organ-grinder's monkey nor delight in a spring flower, nor enjoy, in a self-forgetful moment, a fragment of the excellent meals that Soames provided for her? Did a new dress never give her pleasure nor an evening at the theatre amuse her? If such things occurred (and we fancy that she was a far brighter creature than Galsworthy allows us to believe), we are not told of them.

Having, however, thrown the under-dogs (not only in this book but in all that followed it) to the Forsyte lions, how excellent a story this is!

The English novel in 1910 was struggling out of a morass of romanticism, was struggling hard to tell the truth about life, with Henry James acquiring new subtleties, with H. G. Wells and Arnold Bennett new backgrounds, with Conrad new nobilities. Galsworthy, with *The Man of Property*, gave it a new technique. It is a queer fact that the two novelists who influenced him most strongly were Turgenieff and Dickens, two men as opposite as God could make them. His aim was to give the English novel the meticulous self-conscious care of the author of *On the Eve*, and to create, within the beautiful form, a life as vigorous and various as the world of *Martin Chuzzlewit* and *Great Expectations*. An impossible ambition, but the first attempt at a struggle to reconcile self-conscious artistry with spontaneous unself-conscious creation—the principal struggle for the English novelist to-day and for many days to come.

He had, also, in these pre-war novels an advantage that in his post-war novels he, and all his contemporaries, were to lose, namely, a fixed and cohesive background.

The London of the late 'eighties hung behind them like a rich figured tapestry. The room where it was he had in his most sensitive years occupied. He knew every detail of it, the odd little figures slightly out of drawing, the houses and trees, the shadows of purple and rich brown, a wash of gold over it all. So we have it in this first of the famous series. On page 5 of *The Man of Property* there is Swithin:

> " Over against the piano a man of bulk and stature was wearing two waistcoats on his wide chest, two waistcoats and a ruby pin, instead of the single satin waistcoat and diamond pin of more usual occasions,

and his shaven, square, old face, the colour of pale leather, with pale eyes, had its most dignified look, above his satin stock."

"The colour of pale leather"—is that not this artist's sign, the butterfly in the corner of the page? We shall meet it often again.

And what do they have for dinner at Swithin's—" a Tewkesbury ham, together with the least touch of West India"—that "least touch," the touch of the connoisseur, how often we shall encounter it as the Forsytes go down the ages!

They live, not only the Forsytes, but all the characters in all the Galsworthy novels, in a world composed of Russian leather, emeralds, cherry-coloured moons, azaleas, spring buds, spanking horses, gold-mounted Malacca canes, watercolours, Tewkesbury hams "with the least touch of West India," dogs, and a number of delicate and almost imperceptible scents. The characters who do not share this world of the connoisseur are the under-dogs who spend very much of their time hanging about in the rain at street corners.

Every novelist of character has his idiosyncrasies and a world furnished over and over again with the same furniture, but with Galsworthy (as with Balzac in a greater instance) these details are so significant that it may be that the cut of an emerald or the scent of a cigar is of more importance than a human being. They are used, these details, with the utmost adroitness, to heighten the drama, to express the pathos, to rub in the contrast, and the only possible criticism of them is that sometimes we see Galsworthy arranging them as a stage-hand places the table, the vase, and the bookcase before the curtain rises. There is a striking example of this in the last chapter of *The Man of Property*, when Soames desperately walks the streets. "Along the garden rails a half-starved cat came rubbing her way towards him." And later: "Something soft touched his legs, the cat was rubbing herself against them." We are forced to ask ourselves—what would Galsworthy have done had the cat been plump and well fed!

Nevertheless, what technical triumphs this book contains. The chapter entitled "Drive with Swithin" is possibly the finest thing he ever wrote, and should be given, as an example of perfect technical and emotional mastery, to any young student of the novel.

As the novel develops you can feel the Forsytes pressing like a slowly invading wall upon the prisoners, June, Bosinney, and Irene. The hum of gossip from the old maids, the solemn despotism of Forsytes at a business meeting, Forsytes slumbering in their clubs, Forsytes driving " a pair of spanking bays," Forsytes puckering brows over the evaluation of a piece of silver or a Bonnington or a pearl necklace, Forsytes holding in mid-air a bottle of " crusted Port," Forsytes going to bed and rising again, Forsytes in the bath and at breakfast, making love to their wives or their mistresses, all these symbolic figures crowd the London air, scatter gold-dust, and eagerly bend to gather it again while the Oppressed, the Undervalued, the true citizens of Galsworthy's ultimate spiritual Battersea Dogs' Home, struggle to survive for Galsworthy's sake if not for their own!

But, in this first volume of the Forsyte Saga, it is the true, deep and experienced passion, behind every page, implicit in every line, that gives the book its especial power. Because the background is so firmly dated that it is dateless, because the emotion from which the book sprang is so real and true, because of the freshness and originality of the technique, because so many real people live in its pages, therefore *The Man of Property* is one of the important books in the history of the English novel.

The Saga follows it. It was not, as I have said, originally intended, and it has all the formlessness of a work that grows without knowing the reasons of its growth. There *were* no reasons except the one excellent one that " people wanted to hear some more about those Forsytes."

Now this is a reason at which every superior critic will scoff. So self-conscious has the Higher Criticism of the novel now become that all simple joys are denied it. A novel must not have readers, at most only a *very* few. Readers must not enjoy themselves. Novelists must be ashamed, rather than proud, if they are happy.

It is one of the finest things about Galsworthy that, self-conscious artist as he was, he never lost the simple but, for a novelist, profoundly important love of story-telling. He says that he always found writing very difficult, that he had to struggle and wrestle before he could achieve a good ordinary page of simple narrative. But when, forgetting himself as artist, he was carried away into the world of spontaneous creation he was, like Fielding and Thackeray and Dickens before him, lost in the company of his characters. It is this that gives its value to the Forsyte Saga, not its social commentary which is often forced, not the philosophy of Forsyte possessiveness which is often monotonous, not its tenderness which is often sentimental, but its sheer creative zest. The characters in the Saga must often have felt that they could give a better account of themselves than Galsworthy has given (have not the characters of a novelist always a just and reasonable complaint against their interpreter?), but on the whole they permit him his discoveries, and sometimes, as with Swithin, old Jolyon, Soames himself, and his French wife (a wonderful sketch this last), they take hold of him, carry him away with them and exist, as every great character in fiction does, independently of their author. It is notorious that Soames took charge of him in this way—he has himself acknowledged it—and in Soames he does what every true novelist longs to do—adds a universal figure to the small company of immortals. Soames Forsyte, although he may be small in stature and tight about the nose, belongs to the company that includes Uncle Toby, Sophia Western, Dandie Dinmont, Mr. Bennett, Mr. Micawber, Beatrix, John Silver, the Reddle Man, and Uncle Ponderovo.

Of the novels outside the Forsyte Saga two were successful —*The Country House* and *Fraternity*—and there were some unhappy failures. *The Country House* is Galsworthy's best novel after *The Man of Property*, and Mrs. Pendyce, after Soames and old Jolyon, his most successful creation.

These novels all reveal Galsworthy's virtues and failings— the charm and delicacy of detached scenes (Galsworthy paints always in water-colour), a narrative gift expended sometimes on incredible themes like the Moslem incident in *Flowering Wilderness*, unceasing pity for the oppressed who so often move restlessly under his tenderness, an Englishness that is sometimes fine poetry, sometimes sheer parochialism, irony but no humour (he is at his worst when he is playful— recall if you dare the old lady with the nostrums in *The Freelands*), a passion (almost as though he were a Forsyte collector) for furniture, jewellery, clothes, and food, and the eternally recurrent theme of unhappy and restless physical love. There is no spiritual life in any of his characters, no mysticism, no religious faith. When his people are dead they are *dead*.

One change there is in the later novels, both in the second half of the Saga and in the books that are un-Forsyte. He is no longer sure of his background. This uncertainty is revealed especially in the dialogue and, most notably of all, in the slangy talk of the younger and more sporting generation of Forsytes.

But who *can* be certain of this post-war background? It is one of the problems of the new novelist that he must disregard the changing tumult and hunt for the permanencies. The Vicar of Wakefield, Quixote, Prince Andrew are of no time nor country nor fashion, or rather they are of *all* times, countries, and fashions! It is just this imperviousness to fashion that, I think, Galsworthy lacks in his later novels.

He tries to catch the accents, the tone, the snarl of the current traffic. He is distressed by a world that seems to him vulgar, cruel, and selfish. But no period, no stage in man's history can be stated in terms as simple as that. Man at any time and seen in any light asks deeper questions than those that concern his immediate safety or unhappiness. It is not enough to say that he is unjustly treated, because so many men will always rise magnificently beyond their own personal misfortune. This is what Galsworthy has but rarely shown us, and then in the plays rather than the novels—Mrs. Jones of *The Silver Box*, the antagonists of *Strife*, the proletarian in *The Skin Game*, the Jew in *Loyalties*— these are almost heroic figures. Old Jolyon is the only hero in the whole of the Forsyte Saga, and as it grows, the figures in it, except Soames himself, dwindle and dwindle until at last they vanish in the smoke of Soames's conflagration.

So, looking back, we greet that austere, lonely, dignified figure, apart save for a few intimates, generous, unselfish, courageous, distressed by the distresses of others. Through all his life he never did a mean nor disloyal act. He lived, immaculately, up to his own severe set standards, and his heart was as warm as his acts of generosity were secret. As artist he suffered because it was his fate to live through two violently opposed states of society to only one of which he really belonged. But *that*—his own individual possession— he seized, and preserved. The new world—the world of Joyce and Lawrence, of Epstein and Schönberg, of Stalin and Hitler—was not his, and could never have been his. It seemed to him to break all his rules of order, restraint, and courtesy. But that other world, that other England of the spanking bays, the club windows set with faces politely interested (but not too eagerly) in the passing crowd, the polite but tyrannous Board Meetings, the tyranny of class, a world built up out of the past, shining with gold, aromatic with delicate odours, sanctified by caste, this, as he himself said, he embalmed in amber; he was too modest to add—for posterity.

No one will ever be born again who has known that world at first hand; it is gone never to return; and Galsworthy is, and will always be, the most authentic of its painters.

EARL HAIG
1861-1928

By
HENRY W. NEVINSON

EARL HAIG

by HENRY W. NEVINSON

FROM his earliest years all the typical characteristics of the British race seemed to be gathered up in Douglas Haig. Born in Edinburgh (1861) of an old Scottish family, he inherited and further increased the industrious habits and scrupulous accuracy of the Lowland Scot. His concentration upon the subject in hand was never relaxed, and without effort he could set aside the ordinary distractions of the world. His conversation was not illuminated by flashes of silence; it was silence hardly relieved, and few men of equal eminence have been so free from the temptations of eloquence. He never read novels, but if ever the " strong silent man," at one time extolled by our novelists, existed it was Douglas Haig, and up to his marriage, at the age of forty-four, he is said to have been entirely indifferent to women. One of the chief obstacles to industrious concentration was thus eliminated.

When he left Scotland for the English Public School at Clifton, he became distinguished there for his aloofness from the common English interests in games and athletic sports as well as for his lack of interest in scholastic pursuits, though that can hardly be called a distinction. He was the same aloof and lonely figure at Brasenose, Oxford, where he remained three years, and left without bothering about a degree. He seemed to have no special or natural aptitude for anything except polo, in which he played for the University when he was twenty-one. That high accomplishment was no special qualification for the Church, or even for the Bar or Medicine, but a great one for the Army, and perhaps it was polo rather than his sister's advice that decided him for the career leading to his future eminence.

Yet the Church may have had some passing attraction, for, as a Lowland Scot of those days, he had imbibed religion, and he retained a respect for it throughout life. Religion for him was a lingering reflection of Scottish Christianity. In Handel's church, near Edgware, the inscription upon the marble tomb of a Countess describes her as being "Religious without Enthusiasm," and the same praise would apply to Haig. But none the less he regarded himself in the Great War as the direct instrument of God, much as Oliver Cromwell did. And one may remember that Foch was a worshipping Catholic, and always attended the Catholic services when possible, feeling himself more assured in his military resolution when he came out, though he had spent the time in meditation upon his plans of campaign rather than upon the Divine ritual which he religiously followed. In estimating Haig's finest distinction as a soldier—his calm and imperturbable mind—one must take account of his belief in a Divine power acting through his own spirit.

It might have been thought that the community of social life at an English public school and a famous college in Oxford—to say nothing of Oxford's peculiar beauty, and even the elementary study of the finest literatures of the world—would have encouraged the powers of imagination and sympathy. It would take long to analyse that inspiring power of "personal magnetism" possessed by the greatest leaders in war, such as Xenophon, Hannibal, Marlborough, Napoleon, and Roberts, but imagination and a sympathetic understanding of human nature were parts of it, and in those great qualities Haig was either lacking or, by his habitual aloofness, he veiled them from sight. Perhaps their apparent absence came chiefly from a Briton's horror of public emotion, for, like all our race, Haig was shy of nature. All the more impressive were his outbursts of rage when General Gough was made the scapegoat of misguided politicians after the German advance in March 1918; his memorable despatch to his troops on April 11, 1918; and his generous visit to Lord Haldane on the very day of the Peace Procession through London in 1919, when he presented him with a copy of his own War Despatches, and added an inscription calling him the "greatest Secretary for War that England ever had." The tribute was just, for if victory in the War was due to any one man more than another, it was to Haldane. And it was generous, for Haldane had been dismissed from the Government by Mr. Asquith under pressure of popular clamour, led by an ignorant or spiteful Press, and

Haldane's splendid service was still obscured by a cloud of foolish suspicion. Haig's paternal care for the survivors of his men after the War, and his foundation of the British Legion, are other proofs of an imaginative kindliness seldom displayed.

Such were the obvious or hidden characteristics of the man who was to direct our military forces during the greater part of the War. As always happens, his face and figure were the visible expression of those characteristics. He was rather tall, his figure powerful and capable of great endurance, kept trim and supple by daily exercises and a careful diet dictated by a haunting fear of old age and incapacity. The forehead was broad rather than high, the chin and jaws resolutely strong, the colour-blind eyes calm and unilluminated by passion, the dress always scrupulously exact even in extreme crises, as became a cavalry officer, whether of " the Shining Tenth " or of the 7th Hussars in which he held his first commission, being afterwards transferred to the 17th Lancers. It was at Sandhurst that he discovered his true vocation, and there he worked at the history and science of warfare with all the enthusiasm of a man who, after long uncertainty, feels assured of his true powers. He spent his leave in visiting the north-west frontiers of India, studying the Army-system in Germany, trying to learn French and German, without much result, and in 1896 he entered the Staff College.

While there he had the great advantage of instruction from Colonel G. F. R. Henderson, who wrote the military biography of Stonewall Jackson, and a story of Henderson's judgment of him appears to be true. "There is a fellow in your batch," he said to the students, "who one of these days will be Commander-in-Chief." A proof of Haig's industrious concentration, it was also one of the prophecies that have been fulfilled.

Haig's brief service in Egypt (1898) attracted Kitchener's attention to him, and in the following year he went to South Africa under Sir John French, with whom he served during the early part of the war, being present at Elandslaagte, about twelve miles from Ladysmith. It was the last of the old-fashioned battles as I saw it—Devons holding the front and slowly advancing up the rocky hill held by the Boers, while the Gordons and Manchesters swept round the Boers' left flank, and the 5th Lancers waited for the terrible pursuit on their right. Service under French in the clever Colesberg manœuvres for the protection of Cape Colony came next; then command of the 17th Lancers in Edinburgh, work as Inspector-General of Cavalry in India (where he had the brilliant Philip Howell as his personal staff officer), and then four years at the War Office under Haldane, with whom he was strenuously occupied in the entire reorganisation of the Army, consciously in anticipation of the approaching war with Germany.

Whether the Boer War was justifiable or not, it proved to Haig as to Haldane that the whole of our Army-system must be recast, and fourteen Territorial Divisions with an Imperial General Staff were formed. In 1912 he was given the Command at Aldershot, and the training for war became still more intensive. He is said to have been the only one among the great officers to prophesy that the war would be a matter of years. But Kitchener put it at three years, and on the staff of the *Nation* at the very beginning we called it " The Five Years War."

When the actual war began and the Germans made their fatal mistake in not dashing for the Channel ports at once, Haig's first duty in command of the First Corps was to superintend the Corps' retreat from Mons over 200 miles of country in exhausting weather. They reached a position well across the Marne in thirteen days, Haig seeking all the time to disengage from the enemy, but losing connection with the Second Corps, which was compelled to stop and fight at Le Cateau. Retreat is always the most trying movement to which an army can be exposed, and Haig's men were almost completely worn out before the turning point of the War came and the pursuing Germans were compelled to withdraw north-east to the Aisne. Haig then retraced his course, and brought up the First Corps so rapidly that he found himself in advance of the Second Corps on his left and the French on his right. After some sharp but successful fighting by the Aisne, he perceived the Germans were beginning the prolonged method of trench war, and Joffre allowed the British forces to return to their old northern position in Flanders for the protection of the Channel ports. In mid-October Haig found himself with his Corps in defence of the Ypres Salient.

There it fell to the Corps to hold the position before the city against the mass attack of two German Corps along the

Menin Road (October 30-31). It was one of the most dangerous crises of the War. We in Ypres got rumours from refugee peasants that the Kaiser was present at the German headquarters, and had given orders that the place must be captured at all costs. When the news came that Gheluvelt had been taken, the situation seemed almost hopeless. But it was then that Haig performed one of those actions which proved that, after all, he recognised the power of imaginative and personal leadership. Up the Menin Road towards Hooge, he was seen riding forward at a slow trot with part of his staff behind him as at an inspection. The very sight of their imperturbable Commander renewed the spirits and confidence of his troops. Gheluvelt was retaken, and that German assault was held in check, though two days later I saw great German shells crashing into the beautiful city of Ypres and beginning the destruction of the Cathedral and the famous Cloth Hall.

In spite of a renewed and formidable attack upon the British lines (November 11), the Salient was still held, but during the winter changes occurred, chiefly owing to differences of opinion among the strategists in the Cabinet at home. The main controversy lay between the "Easterners" and "Westerners"—whether it is wiser to strike an enemy at his strongest or his weakest point. Haig remained throughout an unwavering Westerner, never giving a thought to anything but the vast German armies along the frontiers of France and Belgium. If the Allies secured victory there, the rest would be a walk over, but so long as the main German forces were undefeated, the submission of Turkey, Austria, and the Balkan States would be of no vital importance. It may be noticed that in the end our victories in Mesopotamia, Palestine, and Bulgaria immediately preceded the final collapse of the Central Powers, but Haig's judgment could not be shaken. At the time the usual British form of compromise was adopted, and some of our finest Divisions were diverted, first to the heroic but tragical attempt to seize Constantinople through the Dardanelles, and then to "save Serbia" by the landings at Salonika, when it was already too late. Lord Fisher's proposal to attack the north of Germany through the Baltic was never developed. Sir Henry Wilson called the Home authorities "a Cabinet of all the indecisions."

But while these acrimonious controversies were proceeding

in London, Haig was appointed to the command of the First Army in France, consisting of Corps I, III, and IV. After careful training and superintendence during the winter, he first put his army on trial in the battle of Neuve Chapelle (March 10–13, 1915). A barrage bombardment was used to crush the German trenches before the British advance, and again, at longer range, to check the advance of German reliefs. But the British never reached their objective of the Aubers Ridge beyond the village, and the only advantage after heavy losses was an advance of less than three-quarters of a mile upon a narrow front. Ammunition was running short, and the reliefs came up slowly. The shortage of shells was still more felt in the similar battle of Festubert to assist the French flank only a little farther south, by the La Bassée Canal. Another vain hope of penetrating the German lines was attempted at Loos (September 24–25) over that crowded and desolate mining region, but the first success was checked by barbed wire and machine guns—the two almost unconquerable defences in the War—and final withdrawal was compelled by Sir John French's refusal to supply reliefs in anything like sufficient quantity or in time.

This failure led to a sharp interchange of recriminations between the Commander-in-Chief and the Commander of the First Army, with the result that in December French was called upon to resign, and Haig was given full command of the whole British forces in France, with Sir William Robertson as Chief of the Imperial Staff in London. Haig, who had always worked hand in hand with Robertson, could depend upon him to exercise some check upon the amateur strategists, such as that most brilliant improviser of warlike devices, Mr. Lloyd George, between whom and Haig an invincible distrust was mutual. Haig also felt distrust of the far more brilliant but devious mind of Sir Henry Wilson, and though he retained the highest respect for Kitchener, he was dubious about that famous " instinct " by which Kitchener arrived at his wisest resolutions, apparently apart from the accurate knowledge and close reasoning to which alone Haig trusted for action.

But further estimation of Kitchener's nature was tragically frustrated by the sinking of the *Hampshire* in January 1916, and Haig knew that difficulties with the Home Government would probably then increase.

That year was marked on the front in France by the

attempt to split the German line by a joint attack of British and French north and south of the Somme. Haig prepared for an attack on a ten to fifteen miles' front with nineteen Divisions, and he expected the French to attack south of the river with thirty-nine. But the German onslaught upon Verdun and its heroic defence under Pétain reduced the French Divisions to five on a six-mile front. Yet Haig's determination held. Trusting mainly to Sir Henry Rawlinson's Fourth Army, he struck blow on blow against the German line between July 1 and the end of September. It was in the last of these blows that tanks were employed for the first time, but in scanty numbers, their use as the cavalry of the future not being fully understood. A considerable amount of ground upon the low hills which the Germans had occupied, was gained, and, above all, the vital fortress of Verdun was relieved by the necessity imposed upon the Germans of bringing reinforcements round to oppose Haig's threatening onset. But if the Somme was " a kind of victory " its cost was very heavy. Our loss was estimated at 60,000 men on the very first day (our total loss was 412,000), and nearly all our losses fell upon the New Armies, which had proved themselves fighting troops almost beyond expectation. Heavy early rain put an end to the gallant but terrible experiment, and both in London and Paris the word went round, " No more Sommes."

The disastrous year, 1917, opened with extreme personal difficulty for Haig. Perhaps on account of the comparative failures at Neuve Chapelle, Loos, and the Somme, intrigues were on foot to remove him from command. Mr. Lloyd George was now Prime Minister, and both he and Sir Henry Wilson, who represented the British at the French General Headquarters, advocated the proposed change. Always with memories fixed on Napoleonic victories, the French could never realise that any but a Frenchman might be capable of command in war. So when " poor old Joffre " (his own title for himself at the time) was removed, it was agreed at a Calais Conference (February 1917) that the new French Commander-in-Chief, General Nivelle, should take command over the British and French Armies combined. Haig utterly distrusted Nivelle, and was tempted to resign rather than submit a British army to foreign and untrusted command. But he knew that he held the confidence of his army in the field as against the intriguers in London and

Paris, and, under an impracticable form of compromise, he resolved to remain at his post.

He even agreed to the general scheme laid out for the campaign of 1917: Nivelle was to strike with his French army in Champagne on the south, while Haig struck from the Arras region and farther north. Though the advance from Arras was fairly successful, the advantage was frustrated by Nivelle's complete failure on the Aisne, and the consequent mutiny of a large part of his wearied army. Indeed, the main object of the scheme was already frustrated by the strategic withdrawal of the Germans from the Somme Salient to the Hindenburg Line, thus shortening their defensive front, and leaving a desert behind them for the Allied troops to cross.

Disasters fell thicker than ever in that year of gloom. The submarine blockade reduced our food supply to narrow limits, and the best part of it had to be sent to the armies abroad. And the Russian revolution of March foreboded the Russian surrender which would allow the transference of many German Divisions to the front in France. There were only two rays of light: first, the possibility that large reinforcements might arrive from the United States, and secondly, that Pétain, who was appointed to supplant Nivelle in command, was a man after Haig's heart, in cautious persistence. He repeatedly urged Haig to continue his original design of advancing on the north with a view to clearing the Ypres Salient and even the Channel ports, including Ostend. By the well-organised battle of Messines in early June, Haig succeeded in strengthening the right or southern side of the Salient, but at the end of July began the long and heartbreaking attempt to advance from the north and centre.

The design in ordinary conditions might have been excellent, but the prolonged bombardment had already broken down the banks and dams of the canal drainage. Rain continued with unusual violence during August, and the whole region was soon converted into a sea of mud—such mud as Napoleon called " the fifth element," a more hopeless obstacle to advance even than a desert. Passchendaele was reached, a point about twelve miles from Ypres, and the Salient was pushed forward about five miles at the widest place, but by the end of September further advance became impossible, though Pétain still urged it, because Haig's movement pinned German Divisions to the northern section.

by HENRY W. NEVINSON

In October, after the utter defeat of the Italians at Caporetto, Haig was ordered to supply five of his Divisions to the shattered Italian front, and but for the brilliant but short-lived triumph at Cambrai at the end of November (obliterated by the German counter-attack ten days later), the ill fortunes of 1917 remained unrelieved.

The next spring opened with the crisis of the whole war. Both the British and French Armies were depleted of men and worn out by prolonged action. On March 21, Ludendorff, with the object of dividing their armies, attacked in strength at the weakest point, where General Gough's Fifth Army had been extended to hold twenty-one miles in relief of the French line. Our thin defences were driven back by the German onset almost within striking distance of Amiens. The situation was so critical that Pétain advised a general retirement to shelter Paris, and Haig sent for Lord Milner, War Minister in London. On the 26th ten of the ruling men in England and France met at Doullens, and upon Haig's own urgent representations Foch was appointed Commander-in-Chief of both Armies upon the French front. His proposal looked like an exact contradiction to his opposition to a similar proposal at Calais the year before. But he recognised three points of difference: Foch was a very different man from Nivelle; he was also a different man from the Pétain who was now recommending a retreat southwest to cover Paris, whereas Foch's rule was always "J'attaque!"; and thirdly, Haig perceived that if Amiens were lost the union between the Allies could never be recovered, and the War would be over. His reasons were sufficiently strong, but the action was, none the less, one of supreme self-sacrifice.

A violent German attack near Arras next day was held back by the British, though with difficulty, but a still more extended attack shattered a Portuguese Division into panic on April 9, and effected a breach in our line thirty miles in width and ten miles deep, bringing the Germans within five miles of Hazebrouck by the 12th. The promised French assistance was slow in coming, and in the extremity Haig issued his famous order proving that even a silent and undemonstrative nature may become roused to brief eloquence when needs must, just as stones may be driven to cry out. I may quote the last two paragraphs entire. After saying that words failed him to express the admiration which he felt for the splendid resistance offered by all ranks under the most trying circumstances, he continued :

> "Many amongst us now are tired. To those I would say that victory will belong to the side which holds out the longest. The French Army is moving rapidly and in great force to our support.
> "There is no other course open to us but to fight it out! Every position must be held to the last man: there must be no retirement. With our backs to the wall, and believing in the justice of our cause, each one of us must fight on to the end. The safety of our Homes and the Freedom of mankind alike depend upon the conduct of each one of us at this critical moment."

The arrival of the French was not helpful, for they were quickly driven off the important position of Kemmel, but at the end of the month they played a fine part side by side with the British in repulsing the last of Ludendorff's serious attempts to force his way through Flanders. After some bickering about the command, the last German offensive was driven back by the French armies under Pétain and Mangin in the second battle of the Marne (mid-July). It was a great movement, almost fulfilling the promise of the first battle of the Marne, but still Foch hoped to finish the War only in the following year. It was then that Haig displayed the resolute decision of genius to make an end at once. The German losses on their frequent attacks had been enormous. The men were sick of the repeated calls to attack at this point or at that; a deadly plague of influenza and the increasing hardship of our blockade were weakening the will to conquer among the people in Germany, and the Americans were at last being trained up to the point of action. Rawlinson's Fourth Army was prepared and redoubled for the crowning counterstroke to the German onset that had been so nearly successful.

At 4 a.m. on August 5, standing on the high ridge overlooking the Somme on the road to Bray, I heard the great bombardment begin, and then, through a thick white mist Rawlinson's army of British and Australian Divisions advanced. German prisoners soon began pouring down the road towards me, and, though thousands had been taken prisoner before, I had the feeling that this was at last the

by HENRY W. NEVINSON

beginning of the final stroke. Ludendorff himself called that his Black Day, and telegraphed to the Kaiser that he must make peace.

Pushing his four armies forward in turn (the Fifth was being reorganised under Birdwood), Haig pressed the German retirement up to the Hindenburg line, a strongly fortified position five to seven miles deep. In spite of the Government's advice, this too he assaulted in full force, and cleared on the last day of September. That triumph marked the end of the War. The flight of the Kaiser, the revolution in Germany, President Wilson's suggested terms of peace followed, and on November 11 I reached the market-place of Mons just in time to hear the trumpets blow for the Armistice.

On December 16 I saw Haig for the last time. He summoned us war-correspondents to meet him at the entrance of the great Kaiser Bridge over the Rhine at Cologne. We were a mere handful, and he was attended by a small personal staff. In his halting British manner—the same manner in which the Lord-Lieutenant of a county opens a local flower-show—he praised us for our services and loyalty, and having stammered out these few sentences, he added the significant words that the ensuing peace must on no account be a peace of vengeance. If only the Prime Ministers, Presidents, and Generals subsequently assembled at Versailles had laid those words to heart, how different the situation of Europe in the following years, and in this present year of 1933, would have been! After his attempt at making a kindly speech, he handed to each of us a little Union Jack nailed to a short stick of firewood, and we all marched off like good children at a school-treat. It was a symbol of his well-meaning simplicity.

If I attempt to sum up the personality of this distinguished man, I cannot do better than quote the judgment of that excellent military critic, Captain Liddell Hart, who is not unconscious of Haig's weak points: "He was the embodiment of the national character and the army tradition." [1] He was indeed imperturbable as Englishmen would always wish to appear, and at the worst crisis he gave no outward sign of apprehension. At an hour of extreme danger, as we have seen, he restored confidence by trotting slowly down the Menin Road; when all seemed lost he assured victory by

[1] *Reputations*, p. 123.

his Army Order of April 11, 1918. He never allowed the common diversions which are readily conceded to military men to distract him from his main purpose, and he thought no more of women than he thought of danger. His ambition was not personal, and he surrendered his chance of the highest distinction by his own proposal at Doullens, making Foch Commander-in-Chief of both Armies combined. All the same, he insisted, as against Foch, that the War must be finished in that year (1918) instead of being prolonged into 1919. A certain outwardly cold aloofness in his nature deprived him of that personal affection which has united some great commanders, like Lord Roberts, for instance, with their men. But he shared our Army's amazing power of quiet endurance, and we read that at any sign of undue excitement he would always say, "Don't fuss." To an eloquent officer he remarked, " Don't be a damned fool! " Borrowing from the New Testament, he liked the saying " It is the spirit that quickeneth," and borrowing from Mr. Asquith, the saying, " Don't mistake bustle for business." [1]

In his minute biography, General Charteris narrates an incident characteristic of Haig's self-restraint and kindliness. In 1912 he was appointed to the Command at Aldershot, and found the Army there afflicted by excessive cigarette smoking. Exhortations and orders were issued, but appeared to have little effect. At an outpost a sentry—in what he believed to be safe seclusion—was indulging in a cigarette, when suddenly there appeared Haig with his staff and escort. The man hastily threw his cigarette on the ground, where it lay emitting a thin column of smoke. Haig said nothing to the sentry, but stopped alongside the cigarette.

He sat motionless on his horse, his face set like a flint, and watched the smoke ascend, until the last trace of the cigarette was reduced to ashes. The sentry—equally immobile—stood stiffly to attention, but the perspiration of anxiety and despair streamed down his face. When the last vestige of smoke had disappeared, Haig rode off without a word. There were no more cases of smoking while on duty.[2]

In estimating his reputation as a great commander, one must remember that he had generals of high distinction to command the five armies under him—Horne, Plumer, Byng, Rawlinson, Gough (the scapegoat shamefully withdrawn to

---

[1] *Field-Marshal Earl Haig*, by Brigadier-General John Charteris, p. 212.
[2] *Ibid.*, p. 70.

by HENRY W. NEVINSON

shield politicians after the unavoidable failure of the Fifth Army in March 1918), and Birdwood, who was sent to take Gough's place. On a few occasions he allowed himself to be influenced by their suggestions, especially by the suggestions of Plumer (with Harington as Chief of Staff) and Rawlinson, commanding the Fourth Army. As to Haig himself, there is an ancient rule that a general should know by imagination what the enemy is doing the other side of the hill. Haig may have known that sometimes through report, but he seldom failed to let the enemy know what he was doing on his side of the hill. He seldom employed that " element of surprise " which has so often been the secret of victory. The heavy and ineffectual losses at Neuve Chapelle, Festubert, Loos, the Somme, and Passchendaele, to say nothing of the short-lived success at Cambrai, were enough to shake the confidence of any Government and any army. They did shake the confidence of politicians in London and of jealous enemies in Paris, but the confidence of the British Army remained unshaken.

Napoleon had a great saying: " War is like a woman : if you lose your opportunity with her, you need never expect to have the same again." Through want of imagination or undue caution, Haig may have lost opportunities during the first three years of the War, but the greatest opportunity came in 1918, and he took it to the full. He was a supreme organiser of men. I suppose no such perfect a body of men and horses has ever landed on any shore as the First Corps when I watched it landing at Boulogne at the beginning of the War; and at the end of the War, in the summer of 1918, Haig's armies were the only forces still capable of fighting. When by sheer courage and endurance his armies had checked the tremendous German onset of March and April, Haig saw that his opportunity had come, for the Germans had lost the " Will to conquer," " The spirit that quickeneth." Against the earlier advice of Foch, he hurled one after another of his armies upon the dispirited enemy. Against the advice of his Government, he continued the irresistible attack right up to the Hindenburg Line, and through that last obstacle till the Rhine was within reach. When in December, as I related, he met us correspondents upon the great bridge at Cologne, his terrible task of four years was accomplished, and I can imagine no greater honour due to any man, and no finer moment of happiness won.

LORD HALDANE
1856-1929

By
SHANE LESLIE

LORD HALDANE

by SHANE LESLIE

WHEN Lord Haldane died in 1929 he had not outlived his usefulness and he had seen his rehabilitation. He must therefore be considered amongst the fortunate of his generation. Life cannot have been dull or bitter in retrospect, for he penned his Memoirs, as he had passed through his period of persecution, with a sense both of dignity and serenity. He was a rare type in English politics, passing his years between heights of philosophical contemplation and the ordinary levels of party politics. As he wrote: " It has fallen to me to see much of philosophers and statesmen." He was more absorbed in studying the meaning of life than in sharing its occurrences. Occurrences in his life included a Peerage, the Woolsack twice, and the Great War. The meaning of life he sought from the sages of Germany, from Goethe and Schopenhauer. Their answer satisfied him.

He was a Gifford Lecturer by choice and only a Cabinet Minister by necessity. His desire was towards the metaphysical even when superintending National Defence or leading the languid and dignified indignations peculiar to Opposition in the House of Lords. In his Memoirs he wrote that he had not troubled as much as most people over the ups and downs of life. Most people would be content to have enjoyed his downs alone, for even under unpopularity and dislike he could transact Law and enjoy Philosophy. He could work his brain enjoyably hard and found long hours stimulating. He had the gifts enabling him to tread the depressions which lay between the peaks on which he attained power. Much as he enjoyed life, he was terribly short of pleasures. Good talk could attract him and good cigars tempt him. He was willing to surrender time to listening to Beethoven. It was his foible, for he never knew one note from another. Social adventures or romance he eschewed, not caring much that he was "gifted with a poor voice and only a dubiously attractive personality." Wise he was, but not always prudent; learned, but rather heavy; magnanimous of soul, but careless if he seemed a prig. Theatre-going he detested. Browning he read, and Emily Brontë he quoted without stopping.

He was born in Edinburgh in 1856. By his mother a Burdon he was related to the mighty legal brethren Lords Eldon and Scott. At Edinburgh University, Professor Sellar took charge of his open mind, introducing him to Jowett, Matthew Arnold, and Lucretius, and taught him what that poet "ought to be to those who knew his Poem." Out of the rugged magnificences of the Second Book Haldane drew his youthful creed.

He was brought up with his brothers on the Bible and hard walking. A mixture of the Major Prophets and hiking is solid and inspiring fare. The Haldanes used to tramp from their home to the top of Ben Lawers and back—seventy-three miles in twenty-three hours—or from Ballater to Cloan, taking the Grampians in their stride and completing over a hundred miles in thirty-one hours. When he became a London barrister, Haldane found the thirteen hours' walk to Brighton an easy stroll. Meantime he was sent to Göttingen at a period in his life when it was still hoped that the Philosophers could save a faith, which had been riddled by reading Renan and Strauss.

Well he remembered sailing from Leith to Hamburg in an old iron-carrier. Göttingen was reached in early dawn, and he was truly distressed to observe as his first glimpse of the Continent, "A woman and a dog drawing a cart containing a man and a calf." At Göttingen he studied Fichte and Goethe, and forgot there was such a game as golf. When he returned to Scotland, any love of sport had been destroyed and "a passion for Philosophy" substituted. He had received a great impulsion towards Hegel and Idealism at a time when most young men are thinking of propelling leather balls: solid in summer and aerated in winter. He had picked up the German habit of making close study. His old University never forgot him and, after he had written his first books, they were anxious to confer a doctorate of Theology; but the Faculty of Arts insisted on raising him in the sphere of Philosophy. He acquired this degree in company with a fellow-student named Tirpitz.

by SHANE LESLIE

He had heard great teachers and studied Philosophers, of whom few of his contemporaries had ever heard. Henceforth a certain intellectual pride entered into his armoury, which was to grate on those with whom he discussed his foreign achievements. He boasted of the new Masters he met at Göttingen, but even to-day it leaves little impression to be told that: " Wohler, the discoverer of synthetic urea, was a familiar figure in the streets. Ritschl was there and von Jhering." Nobody in England ever cared a damn for one of them.

One question had to be settled by the young philosopher immediately, and that was the baptism which his parents wished him to receive. He only consented on condition it was kept private. When he perceived an ominous crowd of Deacons at the ceremony, he " rose dripping from the font," and renounced the teaching of all the Churches. Symbolically he changed his clothes and walked away. The result he recorded, " was much consternation, but nothing was said, probably because there was nothing to say." For some reason his relative, the late Bishop of Argyll, was present, and for some more mysterious reason " was very kind and sympathetic."

In 1877 he went to the Bar, and followed the example of so many Scots in settling down unknown, uninvited, and unpaid in London. Tenacious of memory and confident in his powers, he translated Schopenhauer while he waited for briefs. He was willing to devil for others. After his work sifting German metaphysicians he found his tasks in Lincoln's Inn child's play. Difficult cases were referred to him and he was treated as the industrious apprentice. He worked, studied, and memorised by day and by night. His social bent was slight, but he has recorded that he was tempted to take lessons in dancing " in the company of a grave and distinguished member of the medical profession, Mrs. Elizabeth Anderson." But later even Terpsichore was banished from the garret which he took in Lincoln's Inn.

In his first year he edited Dart's *Vendors and Purchasers*, and made thirty guineas. Five years later in 1884 he made a thousand, and began to be known as " an energetic and pretty ingenious Junior." His power of argument was said to cause " greater strain " upon Counsel than that of any of his fellows. He found a suitable master in Horace Davey, who had a mind like a razor. Even Russell of Killowen could not deal with Davey. Haldane had only to lend his mind to sharpen Davey's razor and his day was bound to come.... It came. The Government of Quebec asked leave to bring a case before the Privy Council. Davey happened to be engaged to appear before the Lords. The night previous he sent his clerk to summon Haldane to a consultation at the Privy Council the next morning. Haldane sat up most of the night and mastered the real point. The following morning a few minutes before the case opened, Davey assured an agitated Canadian Solicitor-General that though he had to attend the Lords he had fortunately brought a learned friend, to wit, Mr. Haldane. After an embittered protest from the firm of solicitors engaged, the young and unknown Mr. Haldane called off "idle lamentations," and proceeded to win the case. A few days later "the venerable representative of the great firm of Freshfields" climbed to his garret and deposited a brief marked 150 guineas.

In 1883 came the Scottish petroleum case. Davey, finding it hopeless at Appeal, wisely left it to Haldane, who had studied it very closely for weeks in the manner he had learnt at Göttingen. He appeared before the Master of the Rolls, and the rest must be told in his own words:

> "Jessel, when he had caught the point, began to play with me as a cat does with a mouse. But I had the authorities even more at my fingers' ends than he had, the consequence of portentous study. He could not break me down, for I would not yield an inch. He began to get excited and to throw the power of his personality into the struggle with me while his colleagues remained silent. Four o'clock came and he looked very ill. He was suffering from Bright's Disease, but such was his courage that he had gone on with his work. Next day the Court was empty, for the Master of the Rolls was ill. Next day we were told he was dead...."

Needless to say that henceforth Haldane was pointed out as the man whose argumentative powers had killed Jessel. Later he had to argue the case before the Court of Appeal, and when he apologised for the absence of Davey, Lord Justice Lindley observed: "Mr. Haldane, the Court of Appeal is of opinion that your clients have no need to regret the absence of your leader." His fame and his income were now secure.

For some twenty years between 1885 and 1905, Haldane argued before the Lords and the Privy Council. Solicitors found out that he had the confidence of the Supreme Tribunals, and briefs befell him from every corner of the Empire: " A case of Buddhist Law from Burmah, appeals connected with the Maori Law of New Zealand, the old French Law of Quebec, the Roman-Dutch system of South Africa, Mohammedan and Hindu Law from India, the custom of Normandy."

Political ambitions were not long in coming to the surface. In 1885 he won East Lothian, and held the seat successfully for a quarter of a century. Five years later Lord Halsbury as Chancellor gave him a silk gown and whispered: " I think this will be a great success." Halsbury would not have cared to extend his good wishes to his politics, which were as Liberal as Philosophy could make them. He became interminably engaged. He was working at Home Rule Bills and Death Duties. He was delivering the Gifford Lectures. He was offered a chair at St. Andrews, but declined when he remembered that " Philosophy is as jealous a mistress as the Law."

He won a difficult case for the Deutsche Bank, who had been entangled by a City syndicate. He contested the claim of the Island of Jersey to sentence to death a fair Parisienne for immorality. As the Jersey authorities continued to refuse a reprieve, it was necessary to rescue the lady with the help of a British gunboat. But the case which absorbed him most dealt with the Free Church of Scotland. It was a battle between principles and principal: between funds and doctrines. The seceding Wee Frees claimed the funds on the ground that they had kept the doctrines. Haldane withstood them with all his brain, but only the pen of Macaulay could have described the press of theologians and thinkers who were summoned to the Bar of the Lords. The air was darkened by their metaphysics or made lucid for a moment by a flash of Greek from the Woolsack. Early Fathers were cited and no less than St. Augustine and St. Thomas Aquinas found themselves engaged in the struggles of the Scotch Churches. No one enjoyed the case more than Haldane. He wallowed like a leviathan in a sea of Theology. There was a tense moment when Lord James of

Hereford asked him how God could enter into a covenant with the Predestined. Haldane simply replied that the Divine Power was not anthropomorphic, and there was no more to be said. He kept Lords James and Halsbury baffled all down the line. The gulf between Scotch Theologians and English Lawyers proved wider than that between English Bards and Scotch Reviewers. In the end, Lords James and Halsbury held that Predestination could not stand beside the new affirmation which had been made of Free Will, but Haldane showed that the two doctrines occurred side by side in the New Testament. Though he won his case on Predestination, the Wee Frees won the funds, which was the more important, and Parliament had to pass a Bill to clear up the mess.

Philosophy had not drowned his ambitions. His mind was such that he could not conceive the meaning of sport. Drama, the race-course, and cards he shunned as insufferable methods of employing the time. But neither Messiah nor Philosopher could do permanently without friendship. In 1882 he met Asquith, and their lives were henceforth intertwined apart from their kindred love of the Law. They were a couple of briefless barristers sauntering on a Hampstead lawn, but London lay before them and London is well used to being conquered by Scotch visitants.

Once in Parliament, Haldane never missed his Committee work. Incidentally he was on the Prisons' Committee and visited the incarcerated Oscar Wilde. It was at his suggestion that the poet was furnished with pen and ink and sent to Reading. But his main interest was always Education. It was his ambition to inspire English Universities to meet their German rivals. He was at the back of every scheme for raising up Provincial Universities like Liverpool or Bristol. He had not been to Oxford or Cambridge, and imagined that one University was much the same as another. He did not realise how largely the national significance of the old Universities is based on sport. It would have made a vast difference to him had he been educated at either, for he would not have always remained an intellectual alien. There remained a certain fissure between him and the British mind which was yet to yawn periously. His Bill for extending London University was opposed by such as Sir John Lubbock and Dilke, but Haldane made one speech and carried it without a Division. Both Chamberlain and

by SHANE LESLIE

Asquith agreed that it was the only case they had known of a hostile House being converted by a single speech. This led to his preparing the plans for Universities in Dublin and Belfast. His Irish scheme was agreed to in both camps and pigeon-holed to emerge ten years later as Mr. Birrell's masterpiece. He found the old House of Commons " was of the old-fashioned sort and did not care much about Education." If the modern House has cared passionately for it, it is largely due to Haldane. Such was his abstract zeal that he even supported Balfour's Education Act, which to the sorrow of his Nonconformist supporters was intended to help and improve the Church schools.

He was the centre of a Liberal group which brought new ideas into the Commons. Rosebery wished to make him Speaker, but he knew that he had neither the voice nor the impartiality required. Metaphysics from the Chair would have puzzled and rattled most Englishmen. The Liberal group with whom he made his name lay betwixt and between the Fabians and the Eighty Club. He never marched with the Old Guard: with the uninspiring Campbell-Bannerman or the pompously dialectical Harcourt. Devotion to the dead Gladstone had left Morley the walking shadow of a shade. The thinking van of the Party consisted of Haldane, Grey, and Asquith. They were Liberal Imperialists and they supported the Boer War once launched. They had only to stand together, and whatever future lay with the Liberal Party was theirs. Their variety added greatly to their strength. But they were not all such undeterred workers as Haldane nor so austere in their lives. In England a political career is not necessarily connected with great elevations of thought. Haldane continued to allow himself less and less leisure. Grey's superfluous cogitations were given to the study of wild ducks, while Asquith took to pleasures that were less rural. Haldane noted that " London Society came to have a great attraction for him, and he grew by degrees diverted from the sterner outlook on life which he and I for long shared." This had its sequel under the drift of events.

Although the Commons was as unfit a bed for German ideas as a cathedral close for a crop of turnips, Haldane impregnated Asquith and Grey with Fabian thought which he absorbed in turn from the Sidney Webbs. Thereby he provided some fresh red blood for a Party which could not live for ever on the thin green ichor of the Irish Question. At heart he was more a Socialist than a Liberal, but needless to say a scientific Socialist, almost a Hegelian one. Certainly he was not a sentimental Liberal, and he was glad to cut loose from Rosebery. He had strong convictions, and he was certain that his own influence contained the redemption needed by the Liberal Party. As a man of thought he did not care what others thought. He once wrote that " the most ridiculous weakness is to be afraid of seeming ridiculous when you know you are in the main right."

This was the Haldane who arrived on the fields of victory which returned the Liberals to unequalled power in 1906. Balfour had already resigned and in this place Campbell-Bannerman had signalled an era of Gladstonianism. Home Rule was a certainty for Ireland. Augustine Birrell was then the flaming leader of the fanatical dissenters who intended to wipe out Church schools. A powerful Liberal Press was quartered in the Metropolis. Grey, Asquith, and Haldane, like the Three Musketeers, proceeded to choose the spoils of office in the name of high moral duty. Their entry was not too smooth. Campbell-Bannerman had refused to be made a Peer, which entailed only second place for Asquith in the Commons. Grey in loyalty refused the Foreign Office. Asquith urged the Chancellorship for Haldane, but in Haldane's words: " Had not been resolute about the solidity of our position. In the end it appeared that he had yielded, and was prepared in response to Campbell-Bannerman's appeal to enter his Ministry in any event." Haldane accepted the War Office, which Campbell-Bannerman said nobody would touch with a pole, on condition that Grey went to the Foreign Office. Haldane was certainly the choice of King Edward, who never ceased to support and help him. Haldane described this week of hesitation as the most miserable of his life. In the end he felt that the ethical should supersede the political, and that he was bound to consider the necessities of King and country. Campbell-Bannerman did not like his new lieutenant, and only observed: " We shall now see how Schopenhauer gets on in the kailyard." Haldane's opinion of Campbell-Bannerman was that he knew the War Office well, " though his studies of military problems had not been profound." Profundity was Haldane's foible. Before taking office he had sent a friend to buy up

by SHANE LESLIE

all books dealing with the subject of war. As his destination was still a secret, he did not wish to be seen making such unusual purchases himself. At any rate, the Liberal Party entered power to a sound of clamour and clarion. The high tide of the election was still behind them, and their standard-bearers seemed marked out for position and political power for a generation. Who could have imagined the disasters which were to engulf them all? Who could have foreseen the fates of the Three Musketeers: Grey sucked into the eddy of a European War; Asquith abandoned, betrayed, and broken; and Haldane, who alone was to accomplish work that was of historical and lasting effect, slinking like an outcast through the streets of London assailed as a traitor or worse!

December 11, 1905, was a memorable date in political history, for during a spell of thick fog a middle-aged gentleman wearing Court clothes might have been seen or not seen descending from a horse-drawn vehicle, which had lost its way in the neighbourhood of the War Office. A somewhat bedraggled figure entered the doors of Janus carrying a top-hat and a box which proved to contain the Seals of Office. From the outer fog he proceeded to examine the less temporary fogs which then obsessed the springs of British strategy.

The War Office had never known so queer a fish as Haldane in their midst before. They were too puzzled to protest, but they soon asked for an idea of his proposed reforms, and were told to their great amusement that " as a young and blushing virgin just united to a bronzed warrior it was not expected that any result of the union should appear until at least nine months had passed." What could they make of a War Minister whose only interest in shell-fire was that it had once been experienced by Goethe? Haldane did not keep them guessing long; for he instantly set to apply first principles. He invoked the guidance of Clausewitz, von Schellendorff, and von Der Goltz in strategy, names more often pigeon-holed than quoted in War Office circles. When the Army Council next enquired his notion of an army he replied: " A Hegelian army." Whereupon he noted that " conversation fell off." He had found comparative chaos at a War Office which had not recovered from the discomfitures of the Boer War. Lords Roberts and Midleton had endeavoured fruitlessly to organise " Six Phantom Army Corps." Haldane commented afterwards:

"The failure of their attempt was certain, for the first principles of organisation had not been agreed upon and much less realised." Mr. Arnold Forster had been substituted, "but unfortunately Mr. Forster was better as an author and critic than as an organiser, and his plans broke down."

Haldane took his time. He decided for efficiency not economy. He had discovered the curious peculiarity of the British Army, which may have accounted for a number of historical disasters in the past that: "The organisation in time of peace was different from that required for war, so different that there was hardly a unit capable of taking the field as it stood." He aimed at a scheme for mobilising six divisions, which could be sent out of the country in fifteen days. He conceived a British Expeditionary Force, and thought it out on German principles to the last button. This was very strange to the War Office and unpopular with the Cabinet.

Later he moulded Yeomanry, Militia, and Volunteers into a second line of defence. These were the far-famed Territorials. This was regarded as Haldane's folly, and the Generals, who had given him their best energy in reorganising the real Army, did not help him much here, for he recorded: "I employed my old devils at Lincoln's Inn to aid me in constructing a preliminary draft." *Cedant arma togæ!*

Already Germany was the shadow on the wall, and Haldane was best qualified of the Cabinet to enlighten both them and the country as to the shadow. The Cabinet being vastly ignorant of all German processes and purposes, left Haldane to himself. They were only susceptible to the general run of international suspicions. The only other philosopher in public life was Balfour, and Haldane thought he was anti-German in his conduct of foreign affairs. As for Grey he was obliged to note that he was

> "hampered by want of knowledge of the sources of German mentality. He knew little of the history or literature or of the spirit of that difficult mentality. This would have mattered less had the majority of the advisers on whom Grey had to rely known more. But they were mainly anti-German in their tendencies."

The Cabinet had the sense to send Haldane in 1906 to visit Germany. In some respects he was more German than the Germans. Germans appreciated his campaigns against British ignorance. His policy was to keep the anti-war party in power in Germany and to banish suspicion equally in England. It was a perfectly honest plan and the only possible one. He knew of the existence of the War Party, but he never believed it was dominant. He was indignant at the idea of suspecting Germany of war. It was not until the crisis that he sensed that Germany " had been born as a nation one hundred years too late."

The Kaiser received him as his guest and sent him in a State carriage to the Dorotheen Kirche, where he was grieved to find the graves of Hegel and Fichte sadly neglected. The Kaiser told him their names were no longer important to Germany. Haldane offered to add two statues to the Heroes Alley in Berlin at his own expense. " I know," said the Kaiser, " you want to put in the statue of Korner my great war poet." But it was not of Korner that Haldane was thinking.

The Kaiser invited him to witness the manœuvres, but it was the War Office Haldane wished to see. Grey had warned him that the French were nervous, and their Press had discovered that his visit coincided with the anniversary of Sedan. Punctiliously he visited the French Ambassador in Berlin, who courteously suggested that Haldane was only creating a *détente* as opposed to an *entente*. To the Germans he appeared harmless enough, and was allowed the run of the War Office. He particularly noticed the separation of the administration from the command, of tactics from brass-tacks. There was no doubt that he picked up important information. In return he told the Kaiser something about the business end of his own War Office. The Kaiser in a benevolent mood recalled certain suggestions of his own for the improvement of the English Militia, which he feared had never been sufficiently read! He found it odd that an English civilian should have read books known only to German or Japanese strategists. He authorised him to ask any questions he wished answered, and Haldane in a bold moment asked the Chief of the General Staff for permission to see his plans for the invasion of England. Von Moltke smilingly assured him that there were none in the building. But Haldane was well primed, and asked if the German Admiralty possessed any. Again Von Moltke smiled and said: " Very good ones, too! " If Haldane did not extract these, he at least obtained copies of documents on which he built up the British Territorials. While he was stealing a leaf from their book, he claimed that: " I did everything I could to give the Germans the sense that at least we understood them and were not wanting in the desire to let them live and to live along with them in the world."

In a short time the Kaiser repaid Haldane's call by visiting Haldane's royal master at Windsor. Haldane was called in as buffer between the Emperors. No Englishman knew the Kaiser better. He had found him " notwithstanding frank language, agreeable in manner." At the end he summarised him as " a very emotional and odd person, but with a touch of something like genius in his composition. He seemed to be ill-suited in his qualities for the Head of the State, but to be well-adapted for the rôle of a popular orator or organiser."

Negotiations were opened at Windsor. The Kaiser had not turned to the War Party, and he was amenable to Haldane's suggestions. Haldane suggested granting a Gate of British control on the lower section of the Baghdad Railway. Germany was otherwise welcome to her influence in the Near East. German Ministers were present, and a dramatic scene ensued:

> " The Ministers were divided, and the argument grew so hot that I interrupted it and said to the Emperor that it was not right that a foreigner, who was outside his Cabinet, should remain present. But the Emperor had a keen sense of humour, and besides, he wanted to have my support. Be a member of my Cabinet for to-night and I will appoint you—with all my heart, sir!—I remained, and the proposal was approved by a narrow majority."

Haldane caught the early train to London to consult with Grey, who insisted on bringing France and Russia into the agreement. Making this an excuse, the German Foreign Office later caused the Gate to break down. But for the moment Haldane appeared to have secured the greatest diplomatic triumph of the time. The Kaiser dined at his house in Queen Anne's Gate, and was enabled to meet such an odd kettleful as Kitchener, Edmund Gosse, and Ramsay MacDonald.

by SHANE LESLIE

From the moment of his own visit to Germany, Haldane had applied himself to strategy like a Carnot "organiser of victory" behind the scenes. French and German War Offices became aware of his efforts: the Germans with a feeling of faint alarm, which the Kaiser himself had communicated to Haldane. The French had sent Clemenceau to persuade the Cabinet to create a compulsory Field Army. Roberts and others had of course insisted on this early form of Conscription, which would probably have induced the German blow two years earlier. This Haldane realised, as well as the fact that a great Army was incompatible with a great Navy in any country. As he pointed out in reminiscence: "The Germans themselves in the end fell between the two stools in this matter."

As Secretary for War, Haldane determined that "our strength should be thrown into preservation of naval superiority." He always believed in the small professional army. He found the British Army small, and he left it small, but his bitterest critics could not deny that he had it taught its business. Previously it had no certain destination. In any case Clemenceau was sent back disappointed, and his crude scheme was dismissed. Haldane summarised the possible effects of Conscription: "We should have become weaker before we could have become stronger and the German General staff would have wished to strike early."

Haldane was steadily building up an efficient force which could strike without delay in any corner of the Continent. He saw that the problem of Home Defence had changed to one of offence. The soldiers at the War Office ceased to smile. They even wondered. He asked for unceasing work, and he gave toil unceasingly himself. He had had a revealing glimpse of the German War Office, and he set about achieving some of their shipshape organisation. In a sense he had stolen a feather from the German Eagle's wing in order to shaft the English arrow. He made the General Staff a power. He built up the Territorials, and noticing that squires' sons were going into business, he created the Officers' Training Corps in all the public schools and universities.

A great deal of idle criticism was maturing against him. Roberts's campaign for Conscription indirectly roused many enemies, since Haldane's better plans blocked the way. The followers of Roberts never explained how they hoped to impose a system which the nation only accepted after two years of disastrous war.

Kitchener was absent from England in those days, his ambitions being engaged in India. Morley was Secretary for India and had consulted Lords Midleton and Roberts, the wrong men in Haldane's opinion: " The result was that he drifted into the hands of Lord Kitchener, who made an army in India that was efficient in some respects but was lacking in all the modern equipment of transport. Results were disastrous when it had to take the field in Mesopotamia." The great militarists were out of date. Kitchener, with King Edward's sanction, was aspiring to be Indian Viceroy, and Morley, who had the appointment, was too nervous to battle with his Sovereign. Haldane cleverly asked for an audience ahead of the dreaded summons, and succeeded in postponing the subject by suggesting a dinner at which Kitchener and Morley could meet. The dinner took place with Lord Esher as referee. Kitchener tried to impress Morley that in Indian politics he was a Morleyite, which so disgusted Morley that as he went out he observed to Haldane: " That man shall never be Viceroy of India." Poor Kitchener never knew he had got on so badly—and, as the King died three weeks later, the issue never became difficult again. But so unforeseen are the plans of destiny that the time was approaching when Kitchener would supersede Haldane.

In 1912 came the Agadir crisis, and it was clear that the Kaiser was being pulled over by the War Party. Haldane used that year's drought as an excuse to stop manœuvres. The money saved was spent on mobilisation. This was a distinct preparation for war, and Haldane informed the German Military attaché before he found out for himself. The German General Staff consequently received word that six Divisions could be placed on the Belgian frontier with great speed, but the attaché was informed that they " attached no importance to his communication."

Meantime the sagacious Admiralty had made a ludicrous plan for scattering the Expeditionary Force along the Baltic coast, which was the surest way of causing their annihilation without affording the least military pressure. This Haldane attributed to the fact that Lord Fisher had not read farther in German history than the Seven Years' War. When the Admiralty were asked if they had a map of

by SHANE LESLIE

the German strategical railways, they replied that land-maps were not their business! The Admiralty needed overhauling, and Haldane was ready to take charge and give them the Naval General Staff, which Fisher opposed on the curious ground that it would cause secrets to leak! Both Haldane and Churchill pressed Asquith for the position: one offering imagination and physical youth, the other his experience and matured powers. To have sent Haldane to the Admiralty would have seemed to censure McKenna. So Churchill was sent as a compromise.

Meantime the German Fleet was growing to alarming size and Haldane was sent over to negotiate a holiday in shipbuilding and offer feelers. England still had the Portuguese Colonies, and an influence over the Near East to offer. It was the great moment in Haldane's life, but the decision of history had already taken unchangeable shape in the person of his old Göttingen contemporary Tirpitz. Haldane put his cards on the table and told them frankly that if France were invaded, Germany could not count on English neutrality. As for shipbuilding, England would put down two keels for one. The Kaiser courteously handed Haldane an advance copy of the new Fleet Bill, but " our Admiralty experts found in it much that was alarming, and we had no alternative but to go on with counter-preparations." The Fleet Bill proved little less than a declaration of war. At most the Kaiser was willing to delay the Bill when Haldane insisted that Germany must not inaugurate an English agreement by building a new ship. A programme of malevolent Navalism was to be slowed down in return for England's benevolent neutrality in the event of war. It was as much as Haldane could obtain to secure a little reduction in expenditure on both sides. The Kaiser afterwards claimed that he had guarded against " a foreign assault upon our right of self-determination."

The war was coming anyhow, and it came. Once the bolt fell, no one was more anxious than Haldane to see the Expeditionary Force despatched. It was Haldane's Divisions not Kitchener's Armies that held up the Germans in those first terrible days. Haldane immediately summoned Kitchener to the War Council, and gladly saw him given charge of the weapon which he had forged. The Expeditionary Force never deviated by a minute from their plan. Haldane's scheme had worked like clockwork. He did not think it was possible for his Territorial scheme to be put aside, but Kitchener, who had entered on the task of serving and saving England, instantly scrapped it, proceeding to raise troops by his own methods, whence "the confusion which arises from sudden departure from settled principles." It is now admitted for what it is worth that Haldane could have got his Territorials on to the field quicker than any of Kitchener's troops. Haldane's summary of Kitchener seems remarkably just:

> "He knew nothing of the modern science of military organisation which had been evolved in Europe. Consequently he was difficult to move. . . . Move his mind on to modern lines I could not. Nevertheless, he was a great man and a great moral asset to the nation."

Haldane had done his work and could conscientiously retire and watch its results. The simple fact remains. For the first time in history the British Army was ready for war. It is idle to try to estimate what would have been the course of events had a Haldane preceded the Crimean or Boer Wars.

When it was remarked that Haldane was doing no war work, the answer was that it was already done, and that it was an achievement which only the future could measure. But he was condemned to several years of seething and scathing unpopularity. Never had he been particularly popular. The only approach to popular acclamation he had ever received came by accident while he was driving in uniform through the streets of Birmingham, and was mistaken for a German Prince in search of the hand of Princess Victoria!

It will never make pleasant reading to recall how the English people treated Haldane when he was down. The strange thing was that the public turned far more bitterly against him than they had against those who really mismanaged the War Office before the Crimean and Boer campaigns. A period of frenzied misrepresentation followed. "I had a German wife. I was the illegitimate brother of the Kaiser. I had delayed mobilisation and despatch of the Expeditionary Force," were items he recalled in retrospective merriment.

by SHANE LESLIE

The general accusation was hysterical in the extreme. In particulars it was merely laughable. As Haldane wrote: "I was accused of having reduced the Horse and Field Artillery. This accusation was almost amusingly absurd." The truth was that in 1906 he found under 39,000 Artillerymen available, and left over 54,000 six years later. He bequeathed 81 instead of 42 Batteries to the Expeditionary Force. The Territorials were provided with 15 Batteries, with the result that "the Artillery of the British Army was increased about four times during my tenure of office." Against such figures there was nothing to be said. Rather than produce a mob of conscripts he had shaped his "Hegelian Army"—the so-called "Contemptibles," and for a reward he was made to appear in the patriotic Press as the greatest Contemptible himself.

The storm was discreditable to Press and country. But it was so fierce that even the toughest were compelled to yield. When Asquith asked his Cabinet to resign in order to build up a Coalition, he found to his own despair and to Grey's utter disgust that the Tory leaders insisted on omitting Haldane. As Asquith's biographers remark: "Let alone the meanness of it, how could men who claimed to be serious statesmen and who knew the facts surrender to this campaign of ignorance and malice?" But they did. It was found that any Coalition would be impossible with Haldane included. Asquith had to accept "the necessity of even seeming to desert an old friend." It was even more difficult to persuade Grey, who wrote later: "I have always felt that I ought to have left the Cabinet when Haldane went, and his continued exclusion will make the concession to ignorant and malignant clamour still more marked and injurious to the public service."

To omit a War Minister like Haldane from a War Cabinet was rather like leaving Hamlet out of his play. But as the Expeditionary Force by this time had perished on the heights, it was perhaps found appropriate to bury their achiever. As a result an opaque curtain surrounded Haldane during the War. At least he learnt who were his friends. There were few houses to which he was welcome, but it is noteworthy who opened him their doors: Sir John and Lady Horner, the Scarboroughs, the Curries, the Ian Hamiltons, and Edmund Gosse, who fought his battles from the vantage of Librarian to the Lords. Otherwise there was nothing but boycott, tirade, and hatred. His noble friendship with Asquith came to a close, although Mrs. Asquith stayed loyal to him. Haldane felt he had been jettisoned a little easily. Asquith had no idea even that he had caused scars. Haldane remained bewildered, and could not understand why he could not visit munition-makers or German prisoners of war. He was only remembered to have made " spiritual home " in Germany. It was forgotten how much he had done to abase her in temporals.

After the War he passed through a gradual rehabilitation. When politics were resumed, his gap with Asquith had swelled to a gulf. It was a pity Asquith had omitted to write to Haldane what he had said so emphatically to others about his exclusion from Office. Their friendship had limped wounded into the wilderness. Asquith himself was treated to a fair share of ingratitude and stupid abuse, from which he recovered on the wings of the Paisley Election in 1920. But Haldane's name appeared on the opposing Manifesto, for he had quickly seceded to the Labour Party, who were extremely pleased later to be able to appoint the most learned Statesman in Europe as their first Chancellor. He explained to Ramsay MacDonald, whom he had once introduced to the Kaiser, that he was not troubled by such a ripple as Capital Levy. He was satisfied with the great purpose underlying the Labour Movement. The Liberals he left gladly, for they had prejudices rather than principles about Education. He made his own terms with Labour, such as reducing his own salary by £4,000 a year. He took the Progressive leadership in the Lords to which Lord Beauchamp offered a phantom but pompous claim. Haldane demanded the Chairmanship of Home Affairs in the Cabinet and in Imperial Defence. In fact, he gently swayed England during the first Socialist Ministry, while the Premier developed an international mind. Haldane thought that both Whigs and Tories did not realise that with the advanced Franchise and Education the class-gaps showed increasingly unjust. In the end he was disappointed by Labour and especially with the vanity of MacDonald. Even Socialist Ministers were unappreciative of the Idealism he had learnt at Göttingen. He had yet to find a Hegelian Party.

And now that Time has cleared the arena, how stands the name of Haldane? The final reckoning must not be allowed to the Press which hounded him, nor to the Statesmen who relinquished him, nor with the foolish and excitable English people. The Philosopher knew that the militarists would one day do him justice. And so it was!

The British Army never had time to enter into civilian dog-fights or to appraise the utility of politicians at home. But they had begun to realise everything from the beginning. There was no monopoly in the claim to have served and saved England. The Army, who did the serving, kept a common-sense view as to who were the principal saviours in the field. Haldane had not expected any recognition until after his death. It was a surprise to him therefore, after the Army had come home and the streets were loud with the acclamation of various victory-mongers, for a tired gentleman wearing the uniform of a British Field-Marshal to call at the isolated residence in Queen Anne's Gate and leave a copy of his War Despatches with this remarkable inscription signed Douglas Haig:

> " To Viscount Haldane of Cloan, the greatest Secretary of State for War England has ever had. In grateful remembrance of his successful efforts in organising the military forces for a war on the Continent, notwithstanding much opposition from the War Council and the half-hearted support of his Parliamentary friends."

How curious! The Philosopher had given the War Office its purpose and destination. The Lawyer had moulded the British Army. The pro-German had saved England!

KEIR HARDIE

By
JAMES MAXTON

KEIR HARDIE

by JAMES MAXTON

IN the middle period of the nineteenth century the West of Scotland had little time or inclination for the finer and softer sides of life. The world was calling for products which the men of the Clyde area were ready and able to supply. Coal, iron, ships, steam engines, steel, and machinery were in demand from all quarters at home and abroad. The production of these commodities involved heavy, arduous toil, for the work of producing these necessities of a steam and machine age was aided little at that time by mechanical devices. The miner went to the coal face with his muscular strength, his skill, and his pickaxe, and by main strength wrested the coal from its hiding-place. The men produced in such conditions were stern, hard men, with little opportunity or surplus energy for cultural things.

From the midst of such circumstances emerged one man who stood out from his fellows, got below the surface of things, and made deep marks on the history of his time and ours. In 1856, in a tumble-down house in a dingy mining village of Lanarkshire called Legbrannock, Keir Hardie was born.

It is impossible to exaggerate the poverty of the housing conditions in mining communities in the West of Scotland at that date and for long after. Even now many houses survive with little addition to the amenities beyond what very tolerant Public Health Authorities have compelled. The house usually consisted of one apartment, and never more than two. There was seldom gas. Water had to be carried from an outside well. Sanitary conveniences, if provided at all, were of the crudest, and served several families in the miners' row. All the garbage, dirt, refuse—from human excreta to dead cats—was accommodated in a great open midden. The country-side, once beautiful open fields, was rendered smoky and black, with pitheads and great heaps of coal debris dotting the landscape. There was little to elevate, nothing to inspire. Yet inspiration came in these circumstances to Keir Hardie. Inspiration—not to paint beautiful pictures, nor to write wonderful poetry, nor to produce enchanting music—his inspiration was to spread the idea of a world cleared of poverty, crudity, cruelty, and tyranny.

His father was not himself a miner. He was a ship's joiner, who knew the shipyards of the Clyde and who had sailed the seas. His horizon was wider than that of most of his fellows of the purely mining community, but his poverty was as great. To be a worker was to be poor, and even in these days of rapid industrial development, insecure, and Keir Hardie's earliest impressions were those that come to poor men's children. While he was still in his early childhood the family moved into Glasgow, beside the shipyards. Poverty and insecurity dogged them there, and at the early age of eight years the boy had to set out in life as a wage-earner. His first efforts were in the position of errand boy, out early and late for a weekly wage which never exceeded half a crown. By the time he was ten years of age he was down in the pit performing one of the tasks which children were then expected to carry out. There he remained till manhood, going through the various grades which had to be traversed before the status of fully qualified miner was attained.

The Scottish miner out of the pit lived hard. His interests tended to run in one of three directions—sport, drink, or religion. These seldom mixed. Whichever interest the miner adopted, he did it with all his might. If he took up sport, he played strenuously; the mining community produced the finest pugilists, footballers, and athletes. It produced men who could consume alcohol of great potency and in great quantity. It produced men who took up religion with tremendous intensity, and the brands of religion most favoured were always, like the spirituous liquors, the fieriest and most intoxicating.

Keir Hardie was not seized by any of the three ruling passions. At an early age, although denied any formal education, he had learned to read, and to read was his greatest interest. He was not without interest in the sports and amusements of his workmates, but did not become absorbed to any degree. Drinking made no appeal to him whatever, and as a youth he took some part in temperance movements, and throughout his life used his influence towards the end of securing sobriety among the working class. Religion was not absent from his life, but his father was an avowed free-thinker, and Keir Hardie approached religion in a calm, rational way that differed in essence from the attitude of the religious enthusiasts among his fellows. The physical energy and the moral and spiritual force that might have been expended in sport or religion or dissipated in excesses, were expended first in developing his mind, and then, when he discovered his life's purpose, in furthering that purpose.

That purpose came to him with all the power and force with which a religious conversion affected men of his time. When he saw clearly what life called on him to do he went at it with every fibre of his being, and continued unflinchingly throughout his life. It was indeed a big enough task to absorb a man of the biggest stature. Hardie had read enough to be well informed about the history of mankind on this planet. He knew that it had been one long story of struggle and poverty for the millions. Always there had been a few chosen ones who lived lives of great ease and affluence, but these were the minority. This had been true all through the centuries. The working class in general accepted that state of affairs as being the right and natural state. It was the law of life laid down by an all-wise Providence. To them it was impious even to question its rightness. Keir Hardie questioned it, and from questioning came to deny it, and from that proceeded to assert that this type of society was not right, but fundamentally wrong. So far from being eternal, he regarded it as something to be ended, and speedily ended, and to be ended by the efforts of the poor themselves. Having conceived his work as being that of rousing the poor to that task, he girded up his loins and set about it. Others conceiving the same idea might have quailed before the immensity of the task, or if not afraid of it, might have spent a life-time wondering where to begin. Keir Hardie, with a simple directness which remained with him throughout as one of his greatest assets, hesitated not at all, but started right away to fight poverty where it was nearest, among the mining community of which he himself was a member.

It was there plain enough and pressing enough. Apart from the housing conditions already mentioned, the men had to work long hours underground; there was little provision for their safety or their health. There were inadequate safeguards to secure that the coal they were responsible for hewing and sending to the surface would be justly and fairly weighed and credited to them. For facing life under these conditions the money reward seldom reached an average the year round of a pound a week, and for many was considerably below that amount. There was no excuse that the industry was an unprofitable one either to the landowner who drew his royalties or to the mine-owner who exploited the minerals, or to the merchants who marketed the coal. For all of them there was a great and expanding market. Hardie threw himself into the task of removing these injustices, to make the work more safe, to reduce the hours of labour, to see that a man's output was fairly credited to him, to make the monetary reward more adequate. In addition, he directed the attention of his fellows to the great difference between the position of the owners, particularly the royalty owners, and the workers, the actual producers of coal. There were many ready to respond to his call. Many more were apathetic, and some were definitely hostile. Familiarity with the dangers of their task, its arduous nature and the poverty of reward had habituated them to passive acceptance. There were stories in circulation, as indeed there were in every branch of industry, of the working miner who, starting in poverty had, by hard work, sobriety, and thrift, raised himself to a position of affluence and had become a mine-owner. Everybody could do the same who was prepared to make the necessary sacrifices. If they were not so prepared it was their own fault and they must suffer the consequences.

Hardie's fellow-workers began to regard him as a representative man among them, and at the many meetings held to discuss grievances in the pits he was invariably appointed chairman and spokesman to make representations to those in authority. That type of workman, however efficient he might be, was not popular with employers and managers, and very soon he was informed that his services were no longer required. This dismissal extended to his brothers also, and he became a blacklisted man throughout the whole of Lanarkshire. He was determined not to be driven away from his task of rousing the miners and organising them for better conditions, and he opened a small shop for the sale of tobacco and stationery in the neighbourhood of Hamilton, the most important centre of the Lanarkshire mining area. He had acquired a reasonable expertness in the writing of shorthand, and in addition to his shopkeeping he made his first essays as journalist and local reporter for a Glasgow weekly paper.

Although there had been Trade Unionism among the miners previous to this period, the organisation had little stability, and at this date, 1879, when Hardie was a young man of twenty-four years, its resources in membership and finance were at a low ebb. Faced with a reduction of wages below the rate then ruling of about two shillings a day, the men were in the mood to offer resistance. Hardie threw himself into the work, and was appointed first, Corresponding Secretary, and then, by an overwhelming majority, Miners' Agent for the district. Shortly afterwards he was appointed Secretary for the miners' organisations for the whole of Scotland. Then followed a period of strikes, most of them resulting in the defeat of the miners so far as immediate objectives were concerned, but all under his inspiration and guidance tending to make the Miners' Union a real established organisation, and widening the outlook of the men on their economic problems.

His reputation as a Union organiser spread beyond the bounds of Lanarkshire, and he transferred to Ayrshire, where he took up house in Cumnock, now as a married man. Here he settled, and it remained his home till the end of his days, although his activities took him far afield and his visits to his home were rare pleasures which occurred all too seldom for a man who was a natural home lover.

The men in Ayrshire had never been organised in a Union like the miners of Lanarkshire. It was more truly pioneering work, but Hardie's personality, his obvious and undeniable sincerity, and his wide human sympathies soon had the minds of the Ayrshire men stirred, and within a year a demand was made on the mine-owners for an increase of wages of 10 per cent. It was of course refused. Hardie knew that the reputation of the Union was at stake. If the refusal was passively accepted, his year's work was gone. On the other hand, it was a big thing to expect such recent recruits to Trade Unionism to come out on strike with sufficient unanimity to impress the employers with their power. The men, however, did not hesitate for long: they stopped work, and right throughout Ayrshire the stoppage was almost complete. For ten weeks the pits lay idle, and this newly formed Union, without financial resources, was able to maintain a united front for that whole period. They returned to work, like the Lanarkshire men, defeated, but they went back as they came out, a united band, and within a few weeks the advance of wages was conceded.

The Union was not in a position to pay a salary to its secretary, and Hardie, with the responsibilities of a household on his own shoulders, had to use his initiative once more as in Lanarkshire to get a living. Here again his journalistic experience found him what he required, a small income, congenial occupation, and the opportunity to pursue his major task, the struggle for the abolition of poverty. He became acting editor of a local newspaper, the *Cumnock News*, which was strongly Liberal in its political tendency.

Here his thoughts first took a political turn. Up till this time he had seen the Trade Union with its strike weapon as the instrument by which he must carry out his mission. From 1882 onwards his mind more and more concerned itself with political thinking in the Parliamentary and Party sense. He became a member of the Liberal Association in Cumnock at a time when working men in general were looking to the Liberal Party, under the recently extended franchise, to become more and more concerned with working-class issues.

There remained a strong radical and republican feeling handed on from the Chartists; and the influence of Robert Owen, whose ideas had found their concrete expression in the Co-operative Societies, was generally to be found expressing itself among the working-men members of the Liberal Associations, although the general control of the party and its policy was far from being radical. Indeed, under the leadership of Mr. Gladstone, and with the Bright and Cobden Free Trade teaching, power in the party lay mostly in the hands of the successful new capitalists who had risen to affluence with the development of the machine age. Their influence was in the contrary direction to all Hardie's ideas. They were all supporters of freedom against State interference or State activity of any kind. In particular, they wanted complete freedom from that kind of restriction which would prevent them from exploiting their workers to the fullest. They wanted unrestricted liberty to employ children of tender years, to maintain long hours of labour, to keep wages at their lowest, and they objected to any legislation which compelled them to take reasonable precautions for the safety and the health of their employees. Some two or three miners' representatives were already in Parliament under the wing of the Liberal Party and through its electoral machinery, and most workers who were thinking in terms of working-class representation in Parliament looked to an extension of the number of working-men Liberal Members of Parliament as the road to effective working-class political power, which the Chartists had propagated and the Franchise Acts had made possible. Others who looked farther below the surface saw in the Liberal Party the party of the middle class and the new capitalists whose interests were antagonistic to those of the workers, and they believed that when miners like Thomas Burt and Abraham went to Parliament under Liberal auspices they lost the power to oppose the dominating political philosophy of that party. In 1887 the idea of creating a Labour Party had already taken hold of Hardie's mind, and as Secretary of the Ayrshire Miners' Union he was spreading the idea throughout Ayrshire.

The Ayrshire Union was now in a position to pay him a salary of £75 a year. His journalistic work was providing him with sufficient to meet his very modest wants, and he used the surplus that his Union salary gave him to start a newspaper called *The Miner*, which dealt with miners' problems, and gave him the opportunity to propound his social theories. His services were now in demand in every mining area in Scotland, and he travelled around enlarging his experience, getting to know the workers of Scotland, and, what was of as great importance, letting them get to know him. In the first issue of his paper he indicates its purpose as being to deal primarily with purely mining affairs, but to advocate reform in every direction which promised to bring relief to the toiling millions. This was also the teaching that he spread from the platform in his travels through the country, with insistence always on the fact that they themselves, the miners, the workers, must be responsible for the effort which would relieve them of their miseries. His message at first was a call to working people to believe that their poverty and toil were not things from which they would be relieved by the charity of some benevolent-minded great man. He taught the people that their poverty was a man-made thing, and that they themselves had it within them to remove that poverty.

In spite of his many activities Hardie found time at this period for much reading and thinking. He made acquaintance with the works of Carlyle, Ruskin, and Emerson; with Robert Burns, Shakespeare, and the Bible he was already on familiar terms. But the basic influence in his educational experience was not to be found in the books he studied, but in his intimate knowledge of the lives of working people, his capacity to see things with their eyes and to feel their difficulties as his own. His mind definitely reached the stage of deciding that better conditions for the workers could only be obtained when they consciously set out to achieve direct political influence through representation in Parliament by men drawn from their own class and pledged to a policy framed by themselves, with its object the direct improvement of their working conditions; but in addition, the Socialist conception was beginning to form itself in his mind. " Ours is no old-fashioned sixpence a day agitation; we aim at the complete emancipation of the worker from the thraldom of wagedom. Co-operative production under State management should be our goal, as never till this has been obtained can we hope for better times for working people." These words were written by him as Secretary in the first Annual Report of the Scottish Miners' Federation.

In the spring of 1888 a vacancy occurred in the Parliamentary representation of Mid-Lanark, and Keir Hardie was chosen as Labour candidate. He was defeated, securing 617 votes. The significance of the contest, however, lay in the break which was made by the working class with their traditional association with the Liberal Party. That party resented it keenly, endeavoured to buy Hardie off, and the Liberal Press and many of its spokesmen assiduously spread the story that Hardie was financed from Conservative sources. Almost immediately after the election steps were taken to form a Scottish Labour Party, with Keir Hardie as its first Secretary.

In the following year he widened his range of operations by attendance at a British Trade Union Congress, and shortly after, at an International Conference. In describing the International Conference in an article in *The Miner*, he declared quite definitely for Socialism. There were in existence at that date two Socialist organisations—the Social Democratic Federation, under the leadership of Mr. H. M. Hyndman, which included in its ranks in its first years William Morris and Eleanor Marx, daughter of Karl Marx; the other the Fabian Society, of which George Bernard Shaw and Sidney Webb have been the most distinguished figures, but neither of these organisations satisfied Hardie as a suitable instrument for working-class political struggle, although the Social Democratic Federation based its policy and tactics on the Marxist theory of the class struggle.

In 1892 came a General Election, and Keir Hardie was returned to Parliament for West Ham, while John Burns was elected in Battersea. The Liberal Party fully expected that Hardie in Parliament would join up with them, but that was far from his intention. He retained an independent position in the House, and proceeded outside to take the necessary steps for the formation of the Independent Labour Party. This was accomplished at Bradford in January 1893, from which date the party has had a continuous, though stormy, existence. Two or three weeks later, in February 1893, he moved an amendment to the King's Speech in the House of Commons in the following terms: "And further we humbly desire to express our regret that Your Majesty has not been advised, in dealing with the agricultural depression, to refer also to the industrial depression now prevailing, and the widespread misery due to large numbers of the working class being unable to find employment, and direct Parliament to legislate promptly and effectively in the interests of the unemployed." A Liberal Government was in power, and the Motion was seconded by a Conservative member: 109 members voted with Hardie, most of them Conservatives. Hardie had thus achieved for the first time a national platform from which to voice the wrongs of the workers.

That was forty years ago, and week by week in the Parliaments of the present time, the problem placed before Parliament by Hardie in 1893, now more pressing, more obstinate, and more extensive, comes up for consideration, but the solution seems still for the future. This represented the beginning of the political Labour Movement in Britain. Round Keir Hardie and the Independent Labour Party that he formed grew up the political power of Labour in Great Britain. He conceived of a great workers' political party which should be formed by a federation of the Socialist Parties then in existence, the Trade Unions, and the Co-operative Societies. It was not until the year 1900 that this organisation was actually brought into being, and in the interval much pioneering work was needed among the workers in general and Trade Unionists in particular, to wean them away from their allegiance to Liberalism and to get them to adopt independent political action. It was, however, accomplished, and although in later years the building up of the party in its organisation, and its rise to speedy electoral strength might be credited more to Mr. Ramsay MacDonald and Mr. Arthur Henderson, the initiating idea, the moral force, and the basis of organisation were the work of Keir Hardie's mind more than that of any other man. He had the power of standing alone for ideas that he believed right, and a great understanding of, and belief in, the working class to which he himself was proud to belong.

That quality of personal independence of thought and action was one that was very necessary for the man who was to try to place the working class politically on an equal footing with those who had traditionally been the political leaders of this country. On many occasions he had to stand quite alone in the House of Commons, putting a point of view that was far from being agreeable to the majority in that House. On several occasions, during the reigns both of Queen Victoria and of King Edward, he had occasion to make speeches with reference to Royalty and its privileges and making comparisons between the position of the Royal Family and that of the workers whom they ruled. On such occasions there were few to support him.

His opposition to war was a deep and fundamental part of his political faith, and the Boer War placed on him the duty of declaring his opposition in definite terms. He saw in it nothing but a greedy capitalism using the lives of men to extend its power and to increase its range of profit-making. He believed that the workers never desire war in any land, and that they could develop the power among themselves to prevent its taking place. At International Labour and Socialist Conferences he was ever urging the necessity of united action being planned by the working class and their

by JAMES MAXTON

organisations in the various countries, that could precipitate a great international strike of the workers in the event of war being declared. When the great European War of 1914 came, the fact that the European Socialists failed to make even an attempt in this direction, but instead lined up with their rulers for the prosecution of the war, and the fact that the workers of Great Britain and of his own constituency of Merthyr seemed to be carried away by the war spirit, had a most depressing effect on his mind, and may well be counted an important contributory cause in bringing about his death while the War was still in progress and before the International Socialist forces began to rally again and the working class of Great Britain began to see war as it really was.

From the date of his arrival in the House of Commons, the next quarter-century showed a steady increase in the return of Labour and Socialist members to Parliament in this country, in France, in Germany, in Belgium, in Austria, and in Australia, and a steady increase in the hold that Socialist principles were obtaining over the minds of working people. This development proceeded alongside a very rapid development of productive power through the increasing use of machinery and the substitution of large-scale production and big aggregations of capital for the small factories with limited capital of the earlier part of the century. The hold of the old Liberalism tended to lose its grip on the minds of the mass of the workers. Individualist theories became less and less real in face of the new forms of production, but the Liberal Party was still a big power in the land, and during this period, when the minds of the workers were just beginning to leave it in favour of the Labour Party, it produced socially ameliorative legislation in a quantity and at a speed never exceeded or even equalled in any other period. The need for such legislation was apparent. Already it was seen that increased productive power did not remove poverty. *Laissez-faire* theories did not work out in practice as anticipated. The factory manufactured unemployment almost as certainly as it produced cloth. Ill-health was a natural consequence of spending days in factories and nights in overcrowded and insanitary houses. There were plenty of evils to which Keir Hardie and his associates could call attention and for which they could demand redress. There was ample opportunity for questioning the soundness of the social foundations. Keir Hardie did this by speech and by pen, in Parliament, on the platform, and in the weekly journal of his party.

The Continental Socialist Parties, particularly that of Germany, took their Socialist teaching from the work of Karl Marx, and endeavoured to found their party policies and tactics on the basis of that teaching. Keir Hardie did not accept the theoretical teaching of Karl Marx in some of its most important aspects; indeed, he wrote critically of the conception of the class struggle as a motive force in social change, but in practice his own activities, his insistence on the working-class basis for the political party, his denunciations of the capitalist system and the capitalist class, his recognition of the rise and fall of classes as shown in his book, *From Serfdom to Socialism,* all go to show that he was probably more Marxist in practice than those who paid greater deference to Marxist theories.

A breakdown in his health in 1907 made necessary and provided the opportunity for a tour round the world, during which he visited Canada, the U.S.A., Australia, New Zealand, India, Ceylon, and South Africa. In one or two of these places, notably India and South Africa, his trip was scarcely of the kind best calculated to restore an invalid to health, but he returned to Britain with renewed vigour, and was accorded a great welcome by his supporters at a meeting in the Albert Hall in London. It was the first occasion on which that premier hall of England had been hired for any Labour gathering, and it had significance as marking the distance that had been travelled by the working-class movement from its feeble beginnings on the pitheads of Lanarkshire, with its meetings of forty or fifty men gathered in the open air. At this meeting Keir Hardie described himself in these terms: " I am an agitator. My work has consisted of trying to stir up a divine discontent with wrong. With what remains of my life I intend to follow the same course." That description was true, but it was not the whole truth. He was not merely agitator, but prophet and pioneer as well. He made vocal the desires and aspirations of the men and women of the working class of his time, and taught them how to express them collectively for themselves.

The movement that he set going for working-class emancipation has never since ceased to carry on the struggle towards that end. Sometimes the struggle has found its maximum expression in a great industrial struggle like the General

by JAMES MAXTON

Strike of 1926, sometimes in a very rapid development of the Co-operative movement, and sometimes electorally in municipal elections, or as in the Parliamentary Election of 1929. It has suffered severe set-backs and has made many mistakes, both as to its methods and its choice of men to direct its activities, but from the period of the original impetus given by Hardie the working class in Britain has maintained a voice and an influence in the affairs of this country, and through its experiences has gained in consciousness as to its ends and clarity as to its methods.

Hardie was the British expression of a world-wide movement. France had her Jaures, Germany her Bebel and Liebknecht, Austria her Victor Adler, Russia her Lenin. Britain produced, and continues to produce, men to carry on this struggle of the poor, but no one who more truly personifies the spirit of that struggle than the miner from the coalfield of Lanarkshire.

OLIVER HEAVISIDE
1850-1925

By
RICHARD WHIDDINGTON

OLIVER HEAVISIDE

by RICHARD WHIDDINGTON

TO the majority of people the unusual and arresting name of Oliver Heaviside conveys nothing.
This is hardly surprising, for to his own generation the man's work was, in the main, as enigmatic and difficult as the man himself.

Springing from a northern English farming family, Heaviside was born on May 13, 1850, in London, where his father, Thomas Heaviside, was an engraver and draughtsman of no small ability. As the child of an artist, the young Oliver was bound to be influenced by his environment, and there exist, in proof of this influence, very competent sketches of animal life purporting to have been executed by him at quite a tender age. Of other influences on his early life there is no very definite record—but it is natural to infer that his genius may have been biased in the direction of what proved to be his life-work by the fact that one of his uncles was Sir Charles Wheatstone, the inventor of telegraphy, and that one of his brothers—Arthur—six years his senior, was a telegraph engineer in the General Post Office at Newcastle.

After leaving school, Oliver appears to have obtained a post with the Great Northern Telegraph Company at Newcastle, which position, however, on account of increasing deafness, he was obliged to relinquish in 1874. This period of his early life is marked by the appearance of his first papers from 1872 onwards in which he dealt with problems in telegraphy.

His first published experiments, performed with his brother in 1873, led to a paper in the *Philosophical Magazine*, entitled " On Duplex Telegraphy," in which it was clearly shown that it was possible to send, simultaneously, messages between two connected stations as fast as the operating keys could be worked. This discovery led Heaviside to the suggestion that multiplex telegraphy would come eventually into everyday use—a prediction which has since been abundantly fulfilled in practice.

After retiring from his Newcastle post, he went first of all to live in London, and then, some fifteen years later, he moved to Devonshire, in which county he remained until the end of his life.

His early severance from those whose daily business it was to further the practical side of telegraphy—the " practicians " as he was later in life to call them—may have had the effect of stressing in his mind the importance of the more theoretical aspect of the subject. It was in all probability Mathematics and Physics to which Heaviside next devoted his close attention.

During this phase of his life he is said to have formed the habit of shutting himself up in his room so as to be quite free from that external interruption which would have disturbed the course of his studies. Food was taken at such intervals as were permitted by his work—he would allow no routine in this connection to interfere with him.

Thus at one and the same time he not only laid the foundations of that mathematical and physical knowledge on which his great contributions were based, but also encouraged within himself those eccentric qualities which were later to make contact with his fellows so difficult. His eccentricities made many people rather afraid of him—that must have been partly their fault—for the few friends he had were certainly real ones.

His work being the mainspring of his life, it was naturally enough one of his highest hopes to see his work published as soon as possible after its completion, but in view of the novelty of his methods and the abstruseness of the ideas—even though presented with typical clarity and unusual force—it was difficult for publishing authorities to offer the continuous facilities which Heaviside ardently desired.

The rejection of some of his pioneer work submitted to the Society of Telegraph Engineers was, to him, an especial source of deep pain not eased for many years—but it was fortunate for all concerned that his main contributions were made readily accessible to the world by the publication of his collected works in 1892 under the title of *Electrical Papers*, and later from 1893 to 1912 by the appearance of his three-volume work, *Electromagnetic Theory*.

by RICHARD WHIDDINGTON

These books give but a faint idea of the really considerable import and influence of Heaviside's work in the growing field of cable communication.

The effect of his work at the time was slight in comparison with the permanent nature of the mark it eventually made. His success was perhaps due to the fact that his flair for mathematical physics enabled him to become one of Clerk Maxwell's most penetrating interpreters.

It was this searchlight of specialised understanding which, brought to bear on the misunderstood questions of telephony, showed up the facts clearly in Heaviside's eyes.

His unique position in the early 'eighties is perhaps a little difficult to appreciate to-day, when almost every school-boy knows about electromagnetic waves—their mode of propagation and their electric and magnetic character. Then, although the existence of the waves had been predicted and their properties had been foretold, the experimental vindication of Maxwell's theory by Hertz and Lodge was yet to come.

When Heaviside entered upon the most important phase of his researches into telegraph and telephone transmission problems, the telephone itself had been invented about ten years. Clerk Maxwell's theoretical prediction of the possibility of electric waves in space had been experimentally verified by Hertz in Germany, and Lodge in England had just demonstrated the production of electric waves on wires.

Heaviside's genius led him to a novel interpretation and restatement of the theory of his great forerunner Clerk Maxwell, in whose honour the German physicist Boltzmann had aptly quoted from Goethe's *Faust:*

> "Ah! At this spectacle through every sense,
> What sudden ecstasy of joy is flowing!
> I feel new rapture, hallowed and intense,
> Through every nerve and vein with ardour glowing.
> Was it a god who character'd this scroll,
> The tumult in my spirit healing,
> O'er my sad heart with rapture stealing,
> And by a mystic impulse to my soul,
> The powers of nature all around revealing!"

Heaviside, as Clerk Maxwell's great interpreter, surely deserves a share of this eulogy.

To understand in its entirety the reasoning which led

Heaviside to the final conclusions that made possible modern long-distance telephony along wires, would require, a very considerable mathematical treatment, and it may be of interest to quote his own words in this connection before attempting to give a general picture.

> " Everyone knows that electric currents give rise to magnetic force, and has a general notion of the nature of distribution of force in certain cases, as within a galvanometer coil, for example. Further than this few go. The subject is eminently a mathematical one, and few are mathematicians. There are, however, certain higher conceptions, created mainly by the labours of eminent mathematical scientists, from Ampère down to Maxwell, which are usually supposed to be within the reach of none but mathematicians, but which I have thought could be to a great extent stripped of their usual symbolical dress, and in their naked simplicity made to appeal to the sympathies of the many. Let not, however, the reader (if he belong to the many) imagine that thinking can be dispensed with; there is no royal road to knowledge, and hard thinking and rigid fixation of ideas are required.
>
> " Even the machinery of the mathematician, so great an assistance when made to work, requires severe training on the part of the operator to make it work. But earnest students, if they will not or cannot learn the mathematical methods, need not therefore be discouraged, for the name of Faraday will shine forth to the end of time as a beacon of hope and encouragement to them. He was no mathematician, yet achieved results apparently only attainable by such methods."

Heaviside, in accordance with the views expressed in this quotation, having obtained results from his own special methods of mathematical reasoning, frequently attempted to explain himself in simple terms to the telegraph engineers of the time.

His books on this account, although in the main highly mathematical, contain many pages devoted to general expositions in lucid style, of the problem which dominated his whole life and thought.

Unlike that of the majority of scientific writers, Heavi-

by RICHARD WHIDDINGTON

side's style, whenever opportunity allowed, was light and humorous and singularly free from ponderous phrase and " laboured lucubration."

Could a reviewer say of any other scientific writer of the time that " his style is that of Whitman, except that Mr. Heaviside is not affected and has something to say . . . every line of the book is important, and it is full of interesting digressions on all sorts of subjects. . . . Mr. Heaviside's work bristles with humour of a type he has invented " ?

The humour was always to the point, though sometimes bitter and often aimed at official non-recognition of his work —an attitude fortunately changed to-day. He said, for example, in reference to a discussion in which he took part regarding the ether: " Lord Kelvin used to call me a Nihilist. That was a great mistake (though I did throw a bomb occasionally, to stimulate an official humbug to learn something about electricity and how to apply it)."

On another occasion he wrote: " If you have got anything new in substance or in method to propagate rapidly you need not expect anything but hindrance from the old practitioner, even if he sat at the feet of Faraday. Beetles could do that."

And now to present the problem as it appeared in 1885.

In telegraphy, as everyone knows, messages are sent along overhead wires or buried insulated cables in the form of electric currents of short or long duration, which produce dots and dashes at the receiving end, such dots and dashes being interpreted according to the familiar Morse code. The precise mechanical devices employed at the transmitting and receiving ends need not be considered, but in one arrangement the electric current is turned on, as it were by a tap—the Morse key—at the transmitting end, and an instant later, at the receiving end, the current so released deflects the needle of a Wheatstone galvanometer.

In telephony the principle is the same, but instead of a key mechanically turning on and off the current at the transmitting end, from full-on to nothing at all, a more subtle and sensitive device is used. This is the microphone transmitter, into which the sender speaks when using the telephone. This device controls the electric current flowing along the wire or cable, in exact sympathy with the sound of the speaker's voice. This fluctuating current, when it reaches the receiving end, is reconverted into sound by vibrations of the telephone receiver.

The problem to which Heaviside addressed himself with such conspicuous success was to find out why it was difficult to signal rapidly much more than fifty miles and impossible to telegraph rapidly, or to telephone successfully, over great distances.

Practical engineers had found that, with subterranean and submarine cables, there were two main troubles in long-distance telegraphy. In the first place, the signals became faint—a result which can be understood generally, since the cable will offer resistance to the current in much the same way as a water-pipe to the flow of water through it. In the second place, the signals seem to tail out—a dot becomes rather like a dash and a short dash becomes a long one—just as in a race the horses may all get off together, but will soon lengthen out into a long string.

The first of these effects in telegraphy—the fading away of the signal—is technically termed attenuation, while the second is termed distortion, because the shape of the signal is changed during its passage along the cable.

It is not difficult to see that, in telephony, attenuation corresponds to the words in the receiver being faint and that distortion corresponds to their being unrecognisable.

In searching for an explanation of these important facts, Heaviside, so early as 1887, was inspired to realise that electric currents of varying strengths, such as are used in telegraphy and telephony, must be regarded as being accompanied by electric waves in the space surrounding the wire, both currents and waves travelling at a velocity about equal to that of light—186,000 miles in a second of time.

This view proved to be epoch-making in the history of the theory and practice of telegraphy and telephony; Heaviside, it has been truly said, was the first practical radio-telegraphist.

He saw at once that in the sending of electric signals along wires the important thing was the space surrounding the wires rather than the wire itself—which acts merely as the guide to these waves.

Now, in telephony over considerable distances, it has been seen that two things may happen to the electrical impulses conveying the message by the time they reach the receiver. They may have become less intense—or be attenuated; they

by RICHARD WHIDDINGTON

may have lost their correct shape or be distorted. The effect of this attenuation may perhaps further be illustrated in rather more familiar terms. A listener to an orchestra—playing shall we say in the open air—is not surprised to find that as he moves away the music becomes fainter—there is, in fact, attenuation. The music, however, retains, in general, its full character—there is no distortion. This is because the sound of the first violin travels through the air to our listener at the same speed as the accompanying 'cello with its lower note, or put in another way, the shorter air waves emitted by the violin travel at the same speed as the longer waves from the 'cello. The high and low notes therefore reach the observer in the same relation to each other as when originally evoked a few moments before by the conductor. The analogy, so far, fits the case of wireless waves spreading out into free space—attenuation exists, but no distortion.

But now suppose the listener hears the band at the end of an avenue of trees. It can be seen in a general way that each sound sent out by the orchestra will, during its passage down the avenue, be reflected from the trees and from the ends of the avenue. Thus a single note in travelling to the observer will arrive in a drawn-out condition—it will possess a " tail." This is distortion, and it can readily be imagined that the music itself would on this account become unrecognisable or a voice unintelligible.

The analogy now fits—more or less imperfectly—the case of electromagnetic waves guided along wires.

In the telephone transmission problem, attenuation is quite unavoidable, and distortion may also exist owing, broadly speaking, to the electrical currents in their passage along the wire developing " tails," and therefore not arriving at the receiving end in the same state as when they were originally produced by the transmitter.

In actual practice along a simple telephone cable, speech cannot be sent for more than about fifty miles without becoming very considerably distorted. The problem in the 'eighties was how to extend this distance.

Heaviside pointed out that, since telephone currents were always linked with waves, which travel in the space surrounding the cable, the physical properties of both space and cable must be taken into account in the theory, and he distinguished four relevant properties, namely, the resistance of the cable, the resistance of the medium surrounding the cable, the self-induction and the capacity of the cable. These four properties affect in their several ways the propagation of the waves, and since, on Clerk Maxwell's view, the waves were composite in having electric and magnetic parts, the key to the situation was available, when it was realised that an exact balance between these four properties was necessary in order that there should be no "tail" produced in a wave while being guided down the cable. Heaviside completely solved this problem and expressed the result in a neat and simple mathematical form which is used in practice to-day.

In regard to the practical importance of self-induction in distortionless signalling, Heaviside once quaintly wrote: "If it is love that makes the world go round, it is self-induction that makes electromagnetic waves go round the world."

His practical solution at the time was to insert at frequent intervals in the cable "loading coils" to increase the inductance and "leaking coils" to reduce the resistance of the medium surrounding the cable—suggestions which were first put to the test in 1900 by Pupin in America, with triumphant success. What Heaviside termed in fun his "ironic circuit" was not found practicable as an improvement on the loading coils until quite recently. Advances in metallurgy have now made it possible to surround cables with suitable magnetic metal sheathing as he originally envisaged.

It is perhaps of interest to mention that it is only in the case of waves guided along wires that distortion is of any concern to the engineer—the free wireless waves in space are not distorted during their passage, although naturally an ill-adjusted receiver may itself mar perfection at the receiving end.

It is hardly a matter of surprise that a worker of Heaviside's outstanding ability, unusual energy, and fortunate freedom from outside interference should have wide interests within his chosen sphere of activity.

His numerous contributions to the art and theory of telephony loom less large in many minds to-day than the fact that a certain layer of the upper atmosphere has been called the Heaviside layer. The way in which the conception of a peculiar layer in the upper air originally came into being and the present deep significance of this layer is so particularly interesting as to claim special attention.

One possibility, which emerged from a consideration of current signals as waves along lines, was that of reflection of the waves at any obstacles in their path. Such obstacles might well—in the absence of suitable precautions—be the very loading coils or leakage coils necessary for the distortionless circuit. The effect of such reflections would be the production of a kind of echo, or series of echoes, in the receiving end, rather akin to the sound echoes observed when a speaker addresses a meeting in a badly designed hall. The electric echoes would have much the same effect in a badly designed telephone line—the speech would be indistinct owing to the echoing " background." Heaviside had clearly shown how to eliminate the possibility of this trouble in telephone lines.

The fundamental point of difference between the propagation of Hertzian waves and those used in line transmission was at first thought to be that the former spread out in all directions of space while the latter were guided along the transmission line. It was therefore only to be expected that much more power would be required to send signals by wireless than by wire. When the matter came to be examined closely, it was found that the power was very much less than was expected, which is in accord with the suggestion that the waves must be guided over the surface of the earth in much the same way as in ordinary wire telegraphy the waves are guided along the line. But still the wireless signals went curiously far for the power used. This led to the next suggestion that the waves were guided not only at the bottom but also at the top. At the bottom by the earth or sea—at the top by a conducting or reflecting layer in the upper atmosphere.

To quote Heaviside's own words:

> " Using wires we can send radiation anywhere we like in small quantities without loss. . . . But in ' wireless telegraphy,' though no expensive conducting wires are required, which gives a remarkable freedom in certain ways, there is enormous loss, and enormous power is required to send workable signals across the Atlantic, since they are being sent simultaneously everywhere. But for this loss . . . there is no reason to

limit the distance. . . . Sea water, though transparent to light, has quite enough conductivity to make it behave as a conductor to Hertzian waves, and the same is true in a more imperfect manner of the earth. Hence the waves accommodate themselves to the surface of the sea in the same way as waves follow wires. The irregularities make confusion, no doubt, but the main waves are pulled round by the curvature of the earth, and do not jump off. There is another consideration. There may possibly be a sufficiently conducting layer in the upper air. If so, the waves will, so to speak, catch on to it more or less. Then the guidance will be by the sea on one side and the upper layer on the other."

This prediction of Heaviside was made almost simultaneously with, though a little later than, a similar suggestion by Professor Kennelly.

In the last few years several investigators have directed their attention to the very interesting region of the upper atmosphere which contains the Kennelly-Heaviside layer, and the evidence for its existence is now definitely established as a result of the experimental researches of these experimenters, notably Appleton in England and Quäck in Germany.

One of the methods of experiment is delightfully simple and straightforward in essence. If anyone makes a sudden sharp noise near a reflecting wall or cliff, an echo will be heard by him at a time interval which will depend on his distance from the reflector. From this time interval it is easy to calculate the distance of the reflector from the origin of the sound. The wireless method is exactly analogous. A sudden sharply defined wireless telegraphy signal is sent out and a reflected echo is duly observed by a special recording receiver close by. When the signal sent out is not too strong, there is just one echo observable a minute fraction of a second later, corresponding to what has been termed the shortest possible delay. This echo corresponds to a wave going almost vertically upwards and returning almost vertically downwards, and from measurements on the exact time interval, it has been shown that the height of the Kennelly-Heaviside layer is about 100 kilometres in daylight; at night it is found to be higher.

Further researches have shown that very short waves are able to penetrate the Heaviside layer, but are later reflected from a second layer higher in the atmosphere. It is this second layer which makes long-range, short-wave, wireless transmission possible with extremely small amounts of transmitting energy. The great effect of this reflection may be gathered from the fact that with a transmitting power no greater than that used in a 200 candle-power electric lamp, signals have been sent from New Zealand to England. Had it not been for the reflecting layer the signals would have been inaudible.

Another phenomenon, often observed in transatlantic wireless signalling, and due to the reflecting action of these layers, is the reception in Europe of two signals for every signal sent out from America. This is because the waves can travel round the earth by two alternative routes—the shorter distance by the Atlantic, the longer by the Pacific—routes which are possible under existing conditions in virtue of the Heaviside layer.

Before leaving this topic, it should be said that the nature of these reflecting layers is indicated by the term which has been proposed to cover them—the " ionosphere." It has been discovered that these layers are rich in electrons and gaseous ions, or electrically charged gaseous molecules, and it is to this electrical sphere surrounding the earth that the wave reflections can be properly ascribed.

These are truly remarkable developments of the original suggestion of thirty years ago.

Many other problems attracted Heaviside's attention from time to time—problems in particular which responded readily to the unconventional type of mathematics in which his soul delighted.

One of them—the age of the earth—was of importance to the evolutionists who had been much disturbed by Lord Kelvin's outside estimate of 50 million years. Kelvin's calculation was as rigorous as could be expected, having regard to the nature of his assumptions—Heaviside was able to show that on certain other likely assumptions the age of the earth might well be 1,000 million years—a result which brought comfort and greater assurance to the geologists and biologists in their theories of evolution. Later this time was further extended, in the light of the discovery of radioactive elements in the earth's crust.

The discovery by J. J. Thomson in 1897 of the electron led Heaviside to further mathematical investigations into its properties when in motion, and he was led to the development of the equations which represent the variation of the electronic mass with its velocity—a result which is in conformity with and expressed in the theory of relativity.

Heaviside's life-work has had a very considerable direct influence on telegraphy and telephony; it has affected rather less directly the treatment of problems in electric power transmission and has undoubtedly left a mark on Physics.

Far from wealthy, he lived out his last years with the help of a Civil List pension which just met his simple needs. He lived alone towards the end and died in a nursing-home to which friends had removed him a few days before.

Much misunderstood, if indeed understood at all, by many of his contemporaries, Heaviside lived to enjoy the great satisfaction of seeing his views generally accepted and translated into practice the world over.

W. H. HUDSON
1841-1922

By
H. J. MASSINGHAM

W. H. HUDSON

by H. J. MASSINGHAM

IN re-reading Hudson for many days in succession, Hudson whom I once knew in the flesh and could even call my friend, and whose works were so familiar to me that now, as I re-read them, I can often anticipate the sense, almost the very words, of what is to come; in thus reviving old memories and attaching new threads to them I am governed by that quality of strangeness, of mystery, of a being apart which his writings and the unique personality that informed them convey to us. I did not gather that impression so strongly in the past as I do now, but I am convinced that it is distance from these old recollections which has given me the truer perspective.

On a purely objective view, Hudson will appear, not only a child of his own age, but one who blossomed at the close of an evolutionary series like a polychromatic sunset which composes forms and paints dyes unsuspected in the day that preceded it. Though both shared the same passion and brought to it the same craft of intent and patient observation, it is plain that Hudson is more remote than a century of time from Gilbert White, the first of our English school of true naturalists. Hudson has himself explained that difference in the essay called "Selborne," written at the end of *Birds and Man*. He muses in company with the genial and curious old naturalist in the small churchyard with its great yew and thus thinks aloud:

> "We are not like children gathering painted shells and pebbles on a beach; but, whether we know it or not, are seeking after something beyond and above knowledge. The wilderness in which we sojourn is not our home; intellectual curiosity, with the gratification of the individual for sole purpose, has no place in this scheme

of things as we conceive it. Heart and soul are with the brain in all investigation—a truth which some know in rare beautiful intervals, but others never. We are more conscious of many things, both within and without—of the length and breadth and depth of nature, of a unity hardly dreamed of in past ages, a commensalism on earth from which the meanest organism is not excluded . . . and if the mystery of life daily deepens, it is because we view it more closely and with clearer vision."

Gilbert White could never have written such words nor even dreamed the intangible thought that lies behind them. Hudson was indeed the first of our writers to fuse knowledge and experience of nature—and how wide and deep they were the close reader will be continually marvelling—with a highly sensitive and sympathetic awareness of her life and beauty which is the province of the poet. Both his poetry and his natural history converged like the barbs of an arrow-head to drive him into his many fiery crusades against the plumage trade, against bird-catching, against the slaughter and extermination of wild creatures which have inspired others to follow in his exalted wake. But though Hudson's harmonious blending of modern feeling with his own primitive instincts, the artist with the naturalist, the scholar with the gipsy, the elemental with the evolutionist, and the observer with the visionary was an achievement only possible to genius, yet contemporary feeling for nature is a sentiment so widespread and allied to a fair if rudimentary knowledge of natural sights and sounds that Hudson's readers will comprehend him in this respect as a familiar spirit, wiser, more aerial, and far more deeply instructed than themselves, but still of their fellowship. He will differ from them only in his power of expressing emotions which, if feebler and inarticulate, are yet their own as in greater measure they were his.

But Hudson's quality as a writer went much farther than his capacity for unifying the precise and speculative habit of the field naturalist with poetic sensibility, a passion for the many-coloured pageant of life and a melancholy-mystical apprehension of its fantasy. That mystery in life which so preoccupied his reveries was likewise in him.

by H. J. MASSINGHAM

"I feel the strangeness [he writes in *Hampshire Days*] only with regard to my fellow-men, especially in towns. The blue sky, the brown soil beneath, the grass, the trees, the animals, the wind and rain, and sun and stars are never strange to me; for I am in and of and am one with them; and my flesh and the soil are one, and the heat in my blood and in the sunshine are one, and the winds and tempests and my passions are one."

You may object that this is the common language of mysticism, and when a common pen expresses it is only too common. But Hudson means a great deal more than is to be found in the works of Ralph Waldo Trine, and articulates that meaning very much more lucidly and realistically than do the literary blood-brethren of nature who domesticate the universe. He goes on:

"I look at them (his 'fellow-men, especially in towns'), their pale civilised faces, their clothes, and hear them eagerly talking about things that do not concern me. They are out of my world—the real world. All that they value, and seek and strain after all their lives long, their works and sports and pleasures, are the merest baubles and childish things; and their ideals are all false, and nothing but by-products, or growths, of the artificial life—little funguses cultivated in heated cellars."

"The society of indoor people," he says elsewhere, "is unutterably irksome to me." It is not altogether unjust to Hudson, any more than it is the whole truth about him, to place beside these reactions two sentences also cropping up in *Hampshire Days*. He sees the fleas jumping out of a dead shrew mouse, and quite naturally speaks of them as "pretty sherry-coloured little creatures." Then, in one of his ruminative discourses about insects, he remarks, "The proper study of mankind is—spiders," and tells us how "miserable" is his life in England, because he is separated by so great a width of ocean from South America, where spiders are much more varied in species, much larger, and more ferocious.

Now I am certain that this voluntary abdication from the social consciousness, the corporate adhesions and the conglomerations of civilised mankind into a more passionate life with nature (but is it altogether with nature?) is a transformation into something rich and strange which is unique in twentieth-century literature. That literature, especially in latter years, is almost entirely a social product, as it conspicuously was in the eighteenth century. Even its introspections and dabblings in the subconscious are imitative of contemporary psychology and are utterly remote from Hudson's meditative solitude. From this angle Hudson may be called the last of the individualists, though his particular brand of individualism offers no parallel with any of its prominent figures, from Diogenes to Henry Vaughan the Silurist and William Beckford.

It seems to me indisputable that Hudson, whether we examine his personal style and idiom or peer into the recesses of his intricate mind whose expression was as lucid and limpid as running water, had no relations at all with the literature of his own time. Mr. Edward Garnett makes the mistake, I think, of stressing the literary and critical element of Hudson's genius in his Nonesuch edition of the *Letters*, published in 1923. Those letters reveal him an omnivorous reader of all kinds of contemporary books with any thought in them, while his own works contain innumerable references to the English classics, great and small. But his taste in literature was very uncertain, and the nourishment he extracted from it was only such as he wished to assimilate into his individual bent of mind. He would describe the song of the skylark as nobody has ever described it, even the poets, and run on to quote in perfect good faith a wretched jig or jingle like

" *Oh, the sky, the sky, the open sky,
For the home of a song-bird's heart,*" *etc., etc.*

In *Birds in a Village*, he says that the contents of books are " like Japanese flowers made of coloured bits of tissue paper," " a pale phantasmagoric world, peopled with bloodless men and women "—which is exactly the reverse of Shelley's
" *And from these create he can
Forms more real than living man.*"

Chance pickings from as many as twenty books written by a man of such dynamic force and so often crotchety views must not be taken too literally. Nevertheless, Hudson's most dominant feeling was that books were the issue of a civilised mentality, and that he hated as inimical both to his passion for nature and his absorbed interest in men and women and children as (whether they liked it or not) part of nature. In spite of his many friends and his durable devotions to them—" It seems to me," he writes in a letter, " that if I had preserved all the letters worth keeping I have received since I came to England, they would now number not less than 20,000 "—he was the happier the farther he was from men, or rather from men corporate and congregational. Perhaps he was happiest of all when drifting without even the intrusion of thought over the illimitable grey sea of the Patagonian plain, trackless, manless, almost colourless. His upbringing among the wide pampas of the Argentine before progress and the Italian immigration had torn away its primitive and cloistral veil and where the gaucho still lived in impulsive savagery and uncontaminated wildness was no doubt responsible not for creating but for bringing to flower this instinctive love for a primitive freedom, for a multiform uncircumscribed nature and for great solitudes. The desolation of Patagonia was his peace. Nothing in human art or man-created beauty could compensate him for the loss of these—and what a loss to have become a resident in St. Luke's Road, Bayswater!—so that he could roundly declare that " the life of even a single species is of incalculably greater value to mankind . . . than all the chiselled marbles and painted canvases the world contains."

Hudson's crotchets, oddities, whimsies, prejudices, and extravagances were nearly all a reflection from his overmastering desire to identify himself with and become absorbed into the life of nature. His dislike of gardens, of " mawkish dog-sentiment " (the " jackal taint " in the dog, he said " remains. It is unclean, let it remain unclean "), and other little eccentricities of a vital personality spilled over must be derived from the same source, his suspicion of what had been tamed and domesticated. How different indeed was Hudson's passion for the natural, elemental, and unconscious elements in human and all forms of life from that of D. H. Lawrence! Hudson's faith in them, his solace in their exercise and rapt contemplation of their energies, wherever manifested, never came into conflict with a civilised fear of and revulsion from them, as happened to Lawrence. Lawrence's traffickings with the unconscious were partly literary, and he showed himself a good deal the tortured slave of psycho-analytic theory. Hudson's intuitive surrender to the primitive and the "incult," to the sources of being and memories of the long-past haunting childhood of the human race, richly intermingled with his own personal memories of his childhood in the South American wilds, was completely reconciled with the aspects of his modern feeling and with the metaphysical side of his nature. He would not have comprehended any division between them.

Thus we are impelled to the question, What was the nature of the inspiration that drove Hudson to eschew the varied interests of society, to disencumber himself of his social birthright? By no means did he avoid the ways of men. Not only, as I have said, were his friendships numerous and constant, but in his travels through the countryside of England he lived with cottagers and agricultural labourers in daily amity and on the level of their livelihood. The most superficial reading of his English books supplies countless examples of these human associations, and he loved to describe his meetings with rural folk and to relate the vicissitudes and qualities and tragedies of their lives. Without a profound and delighted perception of human nature he could never have acquitted himself so masterfully of his extraordinary feat of memorising the appearances, habits, and characteristics of the Argentine people of his home. In illness and old age he wrote *Far Away and Long Ago*, whose reminiscences of his early life and its human contacts are so supernaturally vivid as to appear a manuscript contemporary with them and retouched in his later maturity rather than, as it was, an entirely new book written without notes from his sick bed. Naturalists might even object that he was over-prone to humanise and introduce human faculties into his natural-history observations of birds, animals, and flowers. A notable example of this tendency is seen in his perverse attempt to explain our emotional reactions to flowers by virtue of "the human associations of their colouring." We delight in the "azured harebell" only because it is like our veins, and flowers pigmented after our hair or eyes or skin are alone attractive to us. So the birds' songs which he most preferred were those, for example the willow-warbler's dying cadence, and the toll of the campanero in South America, which contained in them a suggestion of the spiritualised human voice.

But Hudson's approach to humanity was dissimilar from that of all other men, whether hermit or exile or prisoner or misanthrope or one bowed down by grief or misfortune. He regarded it as the principal branch, but still only a branch, of the mighty Tree of Life to seat himself beneath whose shade was at once the glory and the repose of his whole life. If his love of animal life was humanised, so was his attitude to mankind naturalised. Hudson took all sentient life for his province, and man was but one of the countries, if the most important, figured upon the map of his mind. He will not allow that men possess any attributes or faculties absent from the rest of the animal kingdom. Many of the senses bright and serviceable in the animal are nearly atrophied in ourselves, while our loftiest endowments exist in a rudimentary degree among our humbler brethren of the field. In this respect Hudson is at one with Darwin, but he carried this conviction much further than Darwin did until it was interwoven with his essential being and part and parcel of his mentality. Thus he speaks of the impulse of art at the close of the *Hind in Richmond Park*, the most purely reflective of all his books, that " it has its roots very deep in the world and is in all sentient life. It is inherent in the granite itself and pervades it like a subtle fire." " Beauty," he adds some pages later, " is in us all from birth to death—from the ant to the race of men: in the lowest and meanest of us." How close in metaphysical meaning is the former passage to Vaughan's vision of stones " that in the darkest night point to their homes." Some readers find Hudson's detachment from humanity oppressive. But it is the inevitable consequence of his attitude of life itself, the whole of life, to the religious contemplation of which he devoted all his days. If Hudson looked at Homo in precisely the same way as a naturalist looks at the shark or the nightingale, it has also to be remembered that his natural history was not as that of other men of science, but impregnated with a visionary quality diffused into all his descriptions, alike of the hoverfly in the New Forest as of the shepherd on the South Downs.

In reverting to the question as to the nature of the dæmon which diverted Hudson's mind from civilised ways and interests and brought it into unity with his primitive instincts, it is clear that this possession was much more powerful than a mere negative revulsion from the follies, crimes, and over-elaborated mechanisms of civilisation. Except in his loathing for the exploitation of animal life and the savagery of civilised man towards it, there was no conscious reformist nor rebellious aspect in Hudson's mind, temperament, nor writings. He was not sufficiently interested either in society or sociology to form constructive theories about them, nor to devote his energies to human betterment. He was a naturalist, and impartial observation is the naturalist's trade. Yet it is equally plain that Hudson was something more than a naturalist. He was more than a naturalist who spoke of " the dull myopic vision of those who are not naturalists." Referring to De Quincey's " gluttonism " or mental craving to know and enjoy all good literature, art and music, and the lives of all men, he would, he says, if he had that gift, " give it all for the power to transform myself for the space of a summer's day into one of these little creatures (flies) on the South Downs." Could a man devoured by such an aspiration find his heaven and home altogether in nature?

Certainly his style, his particular and Hudsonian method of self-expression, lends colour to the idea that he did find his ultimate satisfaction in nature. Conrad said of him as a writer, " One can't tell how this fellow gets his effects: he writes as the grass grows." At a meeting of the Hudson Memorial Committee I overheard one of the devotees remarking, " I can't understand why everybody doesn't read Hudson. He is so simple." It was, of course, his very simplicity, a clarity at once crystalline and perfectly reflecting the desultory processes of his enquiring mind, which alienated the average reader. No popular books are simple: they are written to a strict convention, and that convention would be destroyed if there was no barrier between what their writers thought and what they wrote. But Hudson wrote like nature because his thought welled up from his being into words, and the words flowed stream-like on their leisurely meandering course, anon torrential but never muddy, anon coiling and gliding serpent-wise through water-meadows rich and green. No writer is superficially more artless, and yet we know that Hudson's writing was a travail to him, even as (so Blake said) " a little flower is the labour of ages." If his language be analysed, it will be seen that it is very rare for him to use uncommon words or metaphors or similes. His is the language of every day, and the triumph of his art is that it seems instinctively and spontaneously to avoid the commonplace. It is a style like the old grassy trackways over the downs of Wiltshire, Dorset, and Sussex, following the contours of the rounded hills, always taking the line of least resistance, but occasionally and boldly traversing the summits, and crowded here and there with daisies in more profusion than throughout the whole of the surrounding country. Hudson's expression is in no sense an imitation of nature like Burne-Jones's painting: it is in and of nature, a natural growth whose ultimate form and blossom conceal the intricate workmanship which fashions them.

But just as the trackways have their destination at some archaic sepulchre or solar temple and the streams wind somewhere to the sea, so the flowers of Hudson's speech were seeking after some " sweet golden clime where the traveller's journey is done." In an obituary paper on Hudson, the late Clutton Brock made this revealing suggestion, which comes, I think, nearer to the heart of this strange man than anything else written about him:

> " Nature was to him something which offered always what she could not give . . . and all people and things shared the beauty and the want in Nature. . . . Most readers like a sadness which is resolved by a happy ending, a question put and answered, however foolishly; but Hudson's sadness could not be resolved, and his question was never put. Rather it was implied in the very cast of his mind, and gave both beauty and sadness to all he wrote."

Hudson's sadness can be in part traced to a much more definite origin than this. He felt that the spirit of earth was mortally wounded at the hands of a predatory civilisation, and that the doom of the finer and more lovely creations of her myriads was irrevocably sealed. To one who wrote, " My chief interest and delight is in life—life in all its forms, from man who walks erect and smiling looks on heaven to the minutest organic atoms " and of " the mystery and glory of life overcoming the soul with wonder and desire," the dislocation of the rainbow-dyed fabric of wild life and the impoverishment and desecration of the world of nature was a grief that struck to the roots, nor could his soul find appeasement from the contemplation of a tragedy which seemed to set at naught the slow flowering of the evolutionary purpose. That was one reason why his mind tended to dwell elegiacally in the past, before an organised barbarism had had the time to empty earth of her fairer children that he loved:

> " And when I recall those vanished scenes [he wrote in *Far Away and Long Ago*], those rushy and flowery meres, with their varied and multitudinous wild life—the cloud of shining wings, the heart-enlivening wild cries, the joy unspeakable it was to me in those early years— I am glad to think I shall never revisit them, that I shall finish my life thousands of miles removed from them, cherishing to the end in my heart the image of a beauty which has vanished from earth."

Nevertheless, that sadness and the ruminative music which emanated from it were likewise derived from less tangible sources. No continuous reader of Hudson can fail to be struck by the omnipresence of the mythopœic faculty in his work, in all his work, whether concerned with tales, romances, and fantasies, or direct natural history. He could not see the wryneck in an April wood but it must set him off telling some self-invented fable about it, half fanciful and half spiritual. His writings so abound with this element, passing like diffused sunlight through a canopy of leaves, that it is an important clue to the character of his genius. We see it perhaps at its brightest in a moving passage, falling upon the sense like a distant impalpable mysterious chant, of *The Land's End*. He is speaking of the pilgrims assembled at the headland of ancient Bolerium, among whom were six or seven aged men sitting dejectedly among the rocks and gazing out to sea. He singles one out:

> " He does not see before him a beautiful blessed land bright with fadeless flowers, nor a great multitude of people in shining garments and garlands who will come down to the shore to welcome him with sounds of shouting and singing and playing on instruments of divers forms, and who will lead him in triumph to the gardens of everlasting delight and to mansions of crystal

by H. J. MASSINGHAM

with emerald and amethyst colonnades and opal domes and turrets and pinnacles. . . . He sees only what his heart desires—a silent land of rest. No person will greet him there; he will land and go up alone into that empty and solitary place, a still grey wilderness extending inland and upward hundreds of leagues, an immeasurable distance, into infinity. . . . The sky in that still land is always pale grey-blue in colour, and the earth too is grey like the rocks, and the trees have a grey-green foliage—trees more ancient in appearance than the worn granite hills. . . . There he will remain motionless and contented for ever in that remote desert land where is no sound of singing bird nor of running water nor of rain or wind in the grey ancient trees: waking and sleeping he will rest there, dreaming little and thinking less, while year by year and age by age the memory of the world of passion and striving of which he was so unutterably tired grows fainter and fainter in the mind. And he will have neither joy nor sorrow, nor love nor hate, nor wish to know them any more; and when he remembers his fellow-men it will comfort him to think that his peace will never be broken by the sight of human face or the sound of human speech, since never by any chance will any wanderer from the world discover him in that illimitable wilderness."

That aged man is Hudson himself and the grey solitary illimitable wilderness his own Patagonia. But also it is something more than Patagonia, just as Rima in *Green Mansions* is more than a wild free Ruth and familiar of the virgin forest and Hudson himself more than the naturalist he claimed to be. The myths that Hudson wove into nature's green dress, at once personal, symbolic, and mystical, were a confession that he was seeking after something beyond nature, but only to be reached through nature and the unity with her of the human soul. From this aspect, Hudson's mysticism was identical with that of Vaughan and Traherne. But there is this very large and significant difference, not merely that the cast of Hudson's mind was more melancholy than theirs, but that he was a man of science whose knowledge of nature immeasurably surpassed theirs. Hudson's actual discoveries in natural history entitled him to the highest honours zoology and ornithology can bestow, and if he did not receive them it was because his hatred of the mortuary habit and the heavy cost in wild life it entailed excited the animosity of the pundits of those sciences against him. The uniqueness of Hudson as a writer consists, firstly, in the fact that he was the earliest writer in our literature to unify an exact knowledge of the processes, sequences, and mechanisms of the natural world with an emotional vision of its life and beauty, and, secondly, in the fact that he used his immense experience of natural life as an expression of " the passion and the life whose fountains are within."

In this respect, his romance, *Green Mansions*, which few of Hudson's more intimate readers regard as among the best of his works, offers a clearer revelation of his baffling and elusive mind than do his other volumes. In no other, not even in *Far Away and Long Ago*, does he bring together so compactly his feeling both for nature and humanity and cast over them both that veil of the supernatural which haunted all his reveries:

> " Doubtless into the turbid tarn of my heart some sacred drops had fallen—from the passing birds, from that crimson disc which had now dropped below the horizon, the darkening hills, the rose and blue of infinite heaven, from the whole visible circle; and I felt purified and had a strange sense and apprehension of a secret innocence and spirituality in nature—a prescience of some bourn, incalculably distant perhaps, to which we are all moving; of a time when the heavenly rain shall have washed us clean from all spot and blemish."

Rima, the guardian of the sanctuary whose sprite-like flittings through the chequered shadows of the woodland carry us to Wordsworth's

> " *The stars of midnight shall be dear to her*
> *And she shall lean her ear in many a secret place*
> *Where rivulets dance their wayward round,*
> *And beauty born of murmuring sound*
> *Shall pass into her face* ";

she is the embodiment of the " secret innocence and spirituality in Nature " which at the last is defiled by the savages.

by H. J. MASSINGHAM

She is at once human and natural and neither human nor natural, but the figure of a subtle dream that possessed her creator throughout his wandering and ruminative life. For that longing and " prescience of some bourn . . . to which we are all moving " was a possession in Hudson's life greater even than his passion for nature, and clothed that passion with a religious ecstasy. He was not one to sentimentalise over the ways of the hawk with its prey, but the violation of the natural order by man on the one hand and the impingement of an ultimate vision which transcended that order and filtered through it and yet was remote and uncapturable, these were what made him an alien, not only in the world of men, but of the nature in which he found his best solace and refreshment.

A brief estimate of Hudson as an historical figure or portent remains to be indicated. I doubt whether such tales as *El Ombu, An Old Thorn, Green Mansions, The Purple Land, A Little Boy Lost,* and others have had the smallest influence upon contemporary fiction. They were narratives in a traditional mould into which was poured the smelted ore of his rich personality. Since these stories have no dealings with psychological minutiæ, contain no representations of crazed, debased, or homicidal rustics, betray no Freudian discipleship, and avoid the neighbourhood of towns, contemporary fiction indulges no more relations with them than the county caste with the village grocer. His English books of natural history, on the other hand, have been the fountainhead of that appreciation of natural life and the countryside which has been one of the most powerful movements of our times. He was not able to arrest the mechanisation of the rural scene, nor stay, except in certain instances, the destruction of the grander, rarer, and finer types of bird-life by the vested interests, whether of science, commerce, or sport. But he did penetrate the national consciousness by delivering new values to it which stirred an imagination made sluggish by the severance from nature which the industrialism and morality of the nineteenth century went hand in hand to accomplish. He virtually gave the twentieth century new eyes that woke senses of reverence and delight long dormant in natural things. By closing the division between knowledge and sensibility in his own work, he opened up a new world from which the dwellers in cities had been so long exiled that it had lost all meaning for them. " All the most beautiful living things from insect to man," he wrote, " produce in us a sense of the supernatural," and, if he could hardly communicate so rare an experience to the generality of men, yet he enriched his age with the possibilities of a future in which the natural should no longer be estranged from the civilised. If he could not save the English land for Englishmen, he succeeded in implanting into many the longing and desire for that association between the external world and what stirred at the roots of their own beings but had been lost from their education, their livelihood, and recreations.

But to look at Hudson as one of the figures in an historical panorama is to miss both the man and the writer. He was too individualistic both in grain and by self-determination to commit himself to any streams of tendency. The specialisations of our age were repugnant to him, and the very rare type to which he belonged were " those whose reasoning and æsthetic faculties are balanced, whose interest is in the whole of life, and who have succeeded in preserving perfect independence of mind in a herd." His writings thus illustrate little more than himself, which most of his readers find a continent of sufficiently varied landscape.

But there is one other path he trod which stretches from the past into the present, and from the point of view of historical values is a highway. It was largely through Hudson's personal observations, combined with a delicacy of perception illuminated from within, that the demonisation of nature which was the gift of the nineteenth century to our own was exposed as a fallacy. As I have attempted to show elsewhere, the world owed its gloom and despair from contemplating nature, and so the universe, as an arena of cruel and predaceous forces insensible to the finer values and governed by a purposeless automatism to T. H. Huxley. Hudson went a long way towards weakening the foundations of this savage dogmatism, not only by finding in nature a congenial home for the exercise of a rarefied spirit, but by penetrating the lives, habits, and psychology of animals at first hand. Thus, he was not the man to write a commentary upon the ways of nature which obscured the actual text. He knew a great deal more about nature's methods of managing her own household than did Huxley and his Neo-Darwinian disciples. But the philosophy he gathered from the evidence of his intimate study of natural life differed radically from theirs. He demonstrated that pain in nature was a phenomenon almost as rare as the exercise of cruelty, that her life was spared all prefigurement of death, and that when that death arrived it was seldom other than instantaneous. He insisted upon the universal health of the animal kingdom and the enjoyment by each species of all its faculties and functions developed to the fullest capacity they could reach. He exorcised the spectre of fear which Huxley and his fellow theorists had despatched to stalk the earth by revealing that it was a natural device for enabling an animal to escape any danger that threatened it, and was dropped like a worn feather the moment that the occasion of that danger was overpassed. He testified again and again to the happiness of living creatures possessed by them as an inalienable right as familiar as running, flying, or rearing their young. And he found so many examples in the world of animals of mutual service, of affections and devotions and interests too commonly assumed to be human prerogatives and of the wide extension of the æsthetic impulse that the Darwinian implications of the unity of life were invested with a new and deeper significance.

The intuitions of the poet combined with the exact records of the man of science thus gathered their forces to defeat the most hideous legend that has ever dismayed the mind of man. If Hudson had done no more than to mitigate the curse of its distribution, he would be worthy of the " star-pointing pyramid " for his honoured bones that he himself would have scorned.

LORD KITCHENER
1850-1916

By
SIR IAN HAMILTON

LORD KITCHENER

by SIR IAN HAMILTON

AS I enter the lists with K.'s pennon fluttering from my lance, a voice from the crowd calls out, "You must not fight for him; he let us down over the Dardanelles!" That is as it may be. K. worked by incomprehensible laws; but, I fight for him on personal grounds. I owe his memory many a personal debt, the last and greatest of which, when on November 1, 1914, he travelled to Dunkirk to meet the French President, Joffre, and Foch [1] and tried to persuade them to let him replace Sir John French by me, has never yet even been acknowledged. So now, *laissez-aller!* and let me show all and sundry my hero working at the top of his form, and finally, as he falls.

There is no one between the era of the Congress of Vienna and the Treaty of Versailles whom Posterity is likely to decorate with the title of "Great" bar Bismarck and Victoria. The nominees of *The Great Victorians* will never be called "the Great"—not one of them. Try it! Gladstone? Gladstone was indeed a live magnet. To gaze into his eagle eyes (some day I will tell the story) conveyed the same mesmeric effect to me as when, in 1881, I stood with my arm in a sling face to face with Queen Victoria; or, as when one of K.'s china-blue eyes looked me straight in the face and the other squinted at me round the corner. All the same, the G.O.M. can obviously never now be changed into G.M.G.—Great Mr. Gladstone. Why do we still speak of King Alfred as "the Great"? He ought to have been forgotten a thousand years ago. He burnt the old woman's cakes. How about K.? K. would have gobbled up that old woman's cakes, and then, if she gave him any of her sauce, would have burnt—not the cakes, for they were eaten—but the cottage. There are forty-one names of great Victorians given in the Victorian book, and there is not one the golden

---

[1] See General Huguet's (Chief French Military Attaché to the British Army) *L' intervention militaire britannique en* 1914.

crown will fit. The Great Darwin perhaps we ought to say, or the Great Dizzy, or more plausibly—but yet it does not snap home with a click—the Great Rhodes. The world might say these things, but it won't.

Turning to the Post-Victorians, clearly we shall never say the Great Roberts, the Great Foch, or the Great Joffre, or the Great French, or the Great Haig? There are all sorts of reasons. Roberts is now once for all "Bobs"; Foch was too fantastic; Joffre too stupid; French has written himself down in his book "'14"; Haig will be found to have written himself down in his diary. They can all be grasped by the ordinary man. But K. has the prime qualification for canonisation; he appeared differently to everyone who met him. Almost at one time was the title within the grasp of Mr. Lloyd George. Just a tiny tincture of military common sense to reveal to him that he lacked mules (20,000) to carry out anything big from Salonika; that you cannot throw light railways across that accursed country; that the Salonika way may not have been as impracticable as Robertson made out, but that it had never been attempted by invading armies, even by the Ancients, and that the whole lay-out of the respective railway communications of the combatants was too much against him; whereas, on the other hand, he had Roger Keyes and the British Fleet on the spot, waiting, and only wanting the one word "go" to take our two Army Corps up the Danube. Had he backed Roger Keyes and the British Fleet instead of Joffre and Sarrail, and resigned at the end of the war, he would have become for ever the Great L. G.

Next, to weigh K. against a fixed star—Napoleon. What did Napoleon do for France? He all but did for her. Did he expand the imperium of Paris? Only for a few years; in the long run not an inch. But he took two inches off the average height of the French by keeping on flinging his tall Grenadiers into the mouths of all the cannon of Europe; and, when at last the smoke of Waterloo had melted into thin air, there stood a lot of short Frenchmen thinking how much nicer it would have been to be tall. Yet few grudge him his Great, not so much because of his Code and his roads or even Austerlitz, but because his figure is the most arresting in an era of glory and bloodshed.

That is exactly where the people of yesterday felt the greatness of K., and if it was not for the memoir-writing people of to-day his glory were better left at that. For how is an artist to paint a chameleon so that everyone who had ever seen a chameleon should recognise it! Take even K.'s actual features. The portrait by Charles Horsfall, frontispiece to *The Life of Lord Kitchener*, shows us a severely beautiful soldier type of the Victorian era. The picture conveys quite a look of K., and yet here is the exact impression he made upon a young girl as she sailed down the Red Sea together with him in 1889: "A tall, curiously ugly man with a waving red beard being run after by all the women, although, or perhaps because, they can make nothing of him." To delineate K. in all his aspects would fill a big book, but let me say this—where Napoleon took two inches off the height of the people of Paris, K. added one-eighth of an inch to the height of the population of London.

I presided a few weeks ago at Portsmouth over a big meeting of fine-looking men, average age fifty; broad chests, narrow flanks, keen eyes, not a pot belly amongst them; veterans of the South African War. The loudest cheer of the meeting was given in answer to a remark reminding these men how, thirty-three years ago, they—not the flower of the land like Napoleon's grenadiers, but weedy hobbledehoys—had just been starting life as factory hands, clerks, shop-assistants, when K. laid his mighty hand upon them. How he had marched them over veld and kopje until the soles came off their boots and their clothes would have disgusted a scarecrow. How they had starved on half-rations, shivered themselves to sleep under the stars, whilst danger, danger, danger hemmed them in on every side. And now, towards the end, there they sat, the fathers of finer, taller children than they could ever have bred had they stuck to the stay-at-home rut.

As to territory—Napoleon gained none. How about Cæsar? Did Cæsar himself gain for the bankers and bureaucrats of Rome as much as K. brought home for exploitation by the politicians and bankers of London? Did he gain as much for the Latin language, literature, commerce, as K. gained for our English language? K. gave us the Egyptian Soudan—a million square miles—none too bad! Cromer may have lent a hand, but K. did it. Not only that, but K., knowing what hopelessly hand-to-mouth, short-sighted people democracy's politicians are forced by their system to be, resolved to make assurance doubly sure by himself ear-marking the Egyptian Soudan for the language and ideals of Shakespeare. Alone he did it—quite alone. Alone (he has told me so) he conceived the idea of cashing his triumph in London so as to get the wherewithal to build and finance the Gordon College at Khartoum. If anyone wanted the African lion to roar at his or her supper they must pay. Any rich snob who tried to get roars for nothing must pay treble. How well I remember the roar that went up, not from the lion, but from the audience, when in a fit of nervousness, standing on the platform waiting for the arrival of K. and the last Duke of Rutland, I took up and balanced one of the bits of plate under which the table was groaning. The sharp-witted northern audience tumbled to the gesture in a flash. They understood about the loot, but they didn't understand who would benefit by it.

There were many instances, but the only two given so far to the public have been bowdlerised to death. Let me then repeat one of them more frankly. Briefly, the Crœsus of London, a domineering man accustomed to laying down the law, desired to make a record social splosh. In due course, the cream of the kingdom were bidden to come and sup with the super-lion. Once Crœsus was committed, K. slipped in his appeal for the Gordon College. The rich man dropped a crumb from his table, whereupon K. quite bluntly said he was d——d if he'd come under three times that amount.

The next bit of land K. pegged out for London was South Africa, from the Cape of Good Hope to the Zambezi—a piece as big as Europe. The organised forces of the Boers were defeated by Lord Roberts. "Bobs" was a marvel. Put him in the saddle with his own troops behind him and the enemy in front and Marlborough breathed again. But K. had a part to play, and played it all the same. His special contribution to our victory at that stage lay in his having a real grip of the arithmetical truism that if you want twenty to thirty trainfuls of supplies every day you must return twenty or thirty trains of empties to rail-head every night. K. also happened to be the only man with the Force who, by one glance of one of his eyes, could flatten out the Satraps, Consuls, Jacks-in-Office along the line and prevent them from barging in with their special trains or from holding up

by SIR IAN HAMILTON

the traffic to give themselves first pick of the rations. So K. reorganised the system, working fourteen hours a day. Later on it was the brave Lord Bobs, with his fine nerve and unerring military instinct, who led the legions northwards from Johannesburg—only one day's rations in hand and Christiaan de Wet busy attacking the one slenderly guarded line of communications! No other general would have risked it. No other general alive, and but few in history, would have dared carry a large army on half-rations through a wilderness against the fortified city of Pretoria. But it could not have been done without K.'s trucks.

Then came the departure of Lord Roberts; the guerrilla war, and, by March 1901, K. had won it. As far as he could see (which happened to be farther than anyone else) he had won it, and had ended it. Here I speak by the book, and the book in this case is the fifth volume of the *Times History of the War in South Africa*, chapter vii, headed " Middelburg Conference," which should be read by the student in conjunction with chapter xxi of the same volume, headed " Peace." No one who reads these chapters in the impartial spirit of 1933 can fail to realise that K., in the breadth, loftiness, and range of his outlook, saw farther into the psychology of the Dutch and the future of South Africa than Chamberlain, or his own civilian coadjutor, Milner. Further, I confidently put forward the claim for him that he showed himself a much more human, chivalrous being than President Wilson, Clemenceau, or Lloyd George showed themselves to be at Versailles. The choice lay between (1) an immediate peace, on terms, between the warring nations, made, man to man, each side being treated at the conference with equal personal honour and respect, each combatant still holding his rifle in his hand; or (2), unconditional surrender of the rifle first and then shut your eyes, open your mouth, and trust to the generosity of the conquerors. Compare the friendly handshakes given by K. to the armed Boer peace delegates with the surrender of their arms by the Germans on President Wilson's fourteen promises and the well-staged insolence of the reception accorded to their disarmed delegates at Versailles. These are the moments which bite into the souls of nations.

Many of us realise the truth to-day—but already in 1900 K. felt that way. To him Sir Alfred Milner and, in a lesser degree, the whole of the British Cabinet, were wicked to refuse to let him make an agreed peace in 1901. So long as that is clearly understood, there is no more to be said, except that the peace I myself saw being signed in Pretoria on May 31, 1902, was the identical peace K. had got the Boers to agree to sign at Middelburg in March 1901. Even at the very last gasp Milner (inadvertently) all but upset the apple-cart. When de la Rey, taking sudden umbrage at a polite but rather cynical remark of Sir Alfred's, sprang from his chair and made as if to leave the room, K. astonishingly made him sit down again by saying nine words, " Delegates cannot act so hastily, it is not civilised." To which, so overpowering was the force which emanated from K. when he was fully roused, the fiery and in many ways splendid de la Rey replied, quite mildly, " Your Excellency has been in many wars and in many countries; your Excellency knows best the manners and customs of the world." Half an hour later the Treaty was signed, but it was K. who sealed it with handshakes all round and the words, " We are good friends now."

That is why I say K. twice conquered South Africa. The Milner kindergarten form a strong, speech-making, middle-aged, ink-splashing clan to-day; they are indeed a bunch of fine feathers in the parental cap; a parent for whom I myself cherish the most respectful and indeed grateful memories. All the same, I hereby defy them, even putting their heads together, as they ofttimes do, to deny that the sort of peace Milner thought best for South Africa and the Empire in 1901 would actually have been swept clean off the map by the very first cannon shot of the Great War. K. was of one mind with his predecessor Alexander, who more than three hundred years before Christ said, " God is the common father of all men." He wanted Boers and British to be brothers; only he hoped they would do their love-making in English. Keen as K. was on the speedy reconciliation of the two races, it was almost more than he could bear to be the actual instrument by whose executive orders the constant dribble of blood was to go on for fourteen months longer than necessary. As he from the first foresaw, the wound thus grew so septic that only now, in this year of grace 1933—a whole generation of time wasted—at last the two races have come together and from the Cape of Good Hope to the Zambezi, yes, right up through the two Rhodesias, Africa will very soon know it.

by SIR IAN HAMILTON

From so much gained for the Empire there is something to be subtracted. K. might have saved us the Irish Free State, yet preferred to lose it. Big political personages may be surprised to hear this; or they may not; anyway, it is so. The full story will be found in a book called *Misfit*, by Captain J. White, pp. 327–36. I had approached Mr. Asquith, Lord Kitchener, and Lord Roberts in the hope of getting two Divisions of Irish Volunteers to join my three Armies of Territorials round London. Had I, as General Commanding-in-Chief of the Central Striking Force, been granted permission to equip these two Divisions with rifles; to give them good N.C.O. instructors, and to bring them over to train with the rest of our Territorials, there is no manner of doubt that, in due course, they would have volunteered to go overseas with the others to fight. Had one drop of their blood been shed for us overseas the romantic sentiment of Ireland would have whole-heartedly espoused our common cause. But it was not to be. Mr. Asquith turned down my scheme in three French words which, to his legal mind, spelt finality, "*Hors la loi*"; but it was K. who smashed it to bits by saying he would not trust John Redmond himself, not one yard, with a rifle in his hand. That was the end. So at least it may seem to us at the moment, but there is never " an end," and, personally, as a firm believer in the inspirations of K., I think time may yet prove him to have been right.

The *sine qua non* for any statesman or soldier whose generation wishes to claim for him that supreme title no monarch can bestow is vision. Take Sir John French or Harry Wilson and set the dream they dreamed in August 1914 of coming back in three months with their six Divisions against K.'s piercing gaze over unfought battlefields with its revelation of a three years' war and of seventy Divisions. But that well-known instance of the " sicht " was only a trifle compared with the following: In the *Life of Lord Rawlinson*, pp. 95, 96, we are given an extract from his diary relating to " a very interesting conversation with Lord Kitchener " which was held at Tokio in 1909.

" He told me confidentially that semi-official military conversations were going on between our General Staff and the French General Staff with a view to a combined plan of campaign if Germany attacked France. He said he did not like this, as we had no plan of our own, and it would mean inevitably that we should be tacked on to a French plan which might not suit us."

The foregoing transcript from Lord Rawlinson's actual, still existing diary reveals in one illuminating flash Joffre and his fatal Plan XVII; Festubert and Loos, those futile battles which paralysed the amphibious plan of the British; the deadly eel-trap of Salonika, for the sake of which the Dardanelles were wound up like a bankrupt concern; Joffre's words to me at the French Embassy, " You will deserve well of your country if you persuade Lord Kitchener who believes in you to send at once every man on the Dardanelles to Salonika," and my reply, "How can I as a soldier endeavour to weaken the forces of a successor to whom I have just wished that success which is well within his grasp?"; all these miseries shine out for one moment under that luminous remark of K.'s to Lord Rawlinson at Tokio in 1909, but—alas!—there was no one to interpret it. And so we were put under the heel of France, and these ghastly happenings were duly worked out because the Devil had put into the mind of a sincere man, almost a saint—Sir Edward Grey—the idea of letting French officers communicate their secrets to British officers, not grasping, it would seem, the apparently transparent truth that thereby the honour of the British Army became pledged, and that no British Government ever created since the days of King Harold could or would possibly repudiate that pledge whenever the day arrived.

Space is closing in upon me. Quickly then let me try to portray K. in full blast. In the summer of 1901 the campaign in South Africa had seemed to be dragging; by September we seemed to be losing ground. No sooner does a commander's reputation show signs of fatigue than the vultures drop in to have a bite. K. was ill. K. had no staff. K. had taken to drink. K. was sending home no news. Whilst K.'s reputation was tottering along in this parlous way, there came to pass the tragic defeat of Bakenlaagte. On November 1, cabling the news home, K. all but committed the happy despatch by saying he might have to demand "a large addition to our forces to carry on the war." This was the climax, and in much the same way as K. was asked in the Great War to accept Robertson as his Chief of the General Staff, so he was cabled by return to take me. But whereas Robertson's appointment broke the K. of 1916, the more elastic, less autocratic K. of 1901 gaily replied, " I am extremely grateful; there is nothing I should like better. He is just the man I want; Hamilton will be a great help to me." So from November 1901 to August 12, 1902, I lived in K.'s pocket. During those months I shared K.'s house, food, work, and play at Pretoria (work, twelve hours a day; play, half an hour's riding and half an hour's incredibly bad billiards); I sailed home next cabin to him on board the *Orotava* when his last South African despatch was written, and in England leave was given me for one month to help him to clean up the South African slate.

When I landed at Cape Town a cable and a telegram were put into my hands. The cable was from the Commander-in-Chief at home, and began with the words:

> " Cabinet most anxious that you should send very full telegram with your views x x x x x x. Never mind how long the telegram is. It is most important to know how the situation strikes you after your absence of nearly a year. State also what are your views as to Kitchener's health and general conditions."

The telegram was from K. himself: " Most welcome; hope you will leave to-night for the North." On my journey up country another telegram came in from Hubert Hamilton, K.'s Military Secretary, saying, " Chief hopes you will make his house your home and join our Mess of five persons."

These messages coming together struck me all of a heap. When I had sailed from England my intention had been that Victor Brooke, my A.D.C., and I should have commandeered a house and set up our own establishment. The idea that I might be going to chum with K.'s personal staff had never entered my head. In any case, the Cabinet cable had put me into an awkward relationship towards my Chief. But now the position seemed impossible. So the second day after my arrival, as K. was preparing to start for Cape Colony, I faced up to him with my reply cable for the Cabinet written out "in clear," and handed it to him with a few words of explanation. In this cable, the carbon of which now lies on my table, I reported K.'s health to be excellent.[1] Also I said, "He is in good spirits, but expresses regret he was not allowed to offer inducements to Botha to come to terms x x x he quite understands time for that has passed and that only alternative now very severe policy x x x." K. handed me back the cable, unread, with a smile.

A Gordian knot cut by a smile. I have never forgotten. So much so that, through all K.'s tenure in India (where I was present at his last friendly meeting with Curzon), and even through the political rumpus about who was to be the Duke of Connaught's successor as C.-in-C. of the Mediterranean, I have never once faltered in my feelings of personal affection for K.

Last but not least, though it may seem to be a case of dragging myself in again, it is essential that I should make it quite clear to numerous friends who think that because K. let the Dardanelles Expedition down very badly, I must on that account bear him a personal grudge. Nothing less true. When the grand official trial under Lord Cromer and the Royal Commission on the Dardanelles took place, Lord Birkenhead asked me to come and see him on very important business at his chambers. There he, and after a while another legal luminary of the first magnitude, advised me, nay pressed me, to be represented before that Royal Commission by Counsel. After debate it was agreed that Lord Birkenhead should approach Marshall Hall, and that the first dollop I should pay would be £700. All seemed settled, when, as I had already half-opened the door to depart, Lord Birkenhead said, "I think it only fair to let you know that when you attack Lord Kitchener I am going to defend him." Amazed, I ejaculated, "But—I am not going to attack Lord Kitchener!" "Oh yes, you are," he replied; "once the Commission gets to work you'll find you have no option." So I said, "Well, take no action till you hear from me"; went home, sent a wire, and saved my £700.

Now to describe K.'s methods: Lord Bobs's procedure was sometimes unorthodox; Lord K.'s was always extraordinary. K. was like one of those entertainers who plays six instruments at once. He gloried in his performances,

---

[1] K. was always a temperate man. One moderate whisky-and-soda instead of afternoon tea, otherwise hardly anything.

by SIR IAN HAMILTON

and when there were eighty instruments (columns), as in South Africa, enjoyed himself more and more; but he didn't play better! However, he did, by superhuman exertions, produce the effect of a band, and only once a week was there any discordance. That was when he had to write three letters to England, over two of which he sweated blood. He had to seem to tell the Government a lot and yet tell them nothing. Had he known the day would come when he must waste whole forenoons being cross-examined and worried, in the midst of playing all his beautiful instruments, by politicians gasping for secrets which he feared, no doubt erroneously, one or two of them would tell to their wives or non-wives within an hour of the break-up of the War Cabinet, I think he would have ordered out the *Hampshire* and sailed off in her right then.

The day's work started early in Pretoria. Any correct bureaucrat peeping into K.'s large office room at, say, 6 a.m. about Christmas, 1901, would have been shocked. Over the carpet was spread a huge map of South Africa. Crawling and sprawling over this in pyjamas were two human forms; one big and tall, the other less big and less tall. The first was K., the second was his Chief Staff Officer. Another figure correctly dressed in khaki stood by the office table with a basketful of telegrams. This was Hubert Hamilton, the Military Secretary. One by one he read out the telegrams, and as he did so either the big figure in pyjamas or the smaller would crawl and shift the position of a flag upon the map. Probably about forty flags would be shifted. There were about eighty commanders in South Africa at that time who had the right to address G.H.Q. In any normal G.H.Q. naturally these cables would have gone to the heads of the departments concerned—Remounts —Railways—Supply—Intelligence—etc., as the case might be. Here all came to K. He read them; got them into his head as I have indicated, and then Hubert Hamilton carefully laid them out—many of them with K.'s direct order or draft reply attached—in separate packets on the billiard-table in another room.

After breakfast, when we were shaved and clothed, the heads of departments—A.G., Q.M.G., Press, etc.—trooped into the billiard room to read their own telegrams. Then they went in to see K. or me, as the case might be. K. kept entirely in his own hands Railways, Intelligence, Finance, the Field Force Canteen, Supplies, but he hated the A.G. and all his works, as well as the Press, and handed them over to me, much to their disgust. That, however, was ungrateful of the Press. Most of the stuff I gave them was against K.'s explicit commands, and I had always to stand the racket when the mail came back from England. At 4 p.m. I might drag K. out for a nominal hour's ride; usually only half an hour; he was so eager to see "Intelligence" again. After dinner, barring bad news, K. and I played a very funny game of billiards, and then went to bed, praying for an undisturbed sleep. An occasional column commander was the only social excitement—that and the coming to dinner, or dropping in after dinner, of Sir Richard Solomon, who was very sympathetic to K.

Under K.'s system everything depended on the character, abilities, and experience of the small group who surrounded him and were the interpreters of his orders. Actually the South African group did contain three very useful men. They would surely have risen high had death only given them a miss. Hubert Hamilton ("Hammy"), the Military Secretary, and the two Aides, Marker of the Guards and Maxwell, V.C. ("the Brat"). Each of them possessed the supreme merit for any would-be servitor of K.'s—they were not afraid of him. When at our small table K. announced that he was going to issue some devastating *ukase*, "the Brat" would up and say, "All I can tell you, Sir, is that no one will pay the slightest attention to it!" "What the devil do you mean?" K. would thunder, knitting his brows into his most portentous frown, and Maxwell would rejoin, "Well, all the subalterns in the Army will laugh at you." And K. took notice. For a Commander to have on his staff someone frank enough and fond enough of him to enlighten him as to the true feelings of the lower strata of the military hierarchy, is like a dog to a blind man. As to Marker and "Hammy," they were serious soldiers, both possessing character, energy, and common sense. They were ready to take on responsibilities, and possessed a thorough knowledge of the working of G.H.Q. in all its ramifications. They were entirely unselfish and loyal. These excellent men owed their appointments to K.'s own perspicuity. Then why did he not get them back round him directly he entered the War Office? In any case, why did he not take steps to knock the

War Office itself into shape as soon as he had sized up its emptiness?

The War Office! If anyone wants to begin to understand why our War Office did not function, he must understand that a brick had been thrown into the works by the owner, Mr. Asquith, several months before the outbreak of war, and that, on the outbreak of war, just as K. entered by one door, so several essential parts of the machinery abstracted themselves and hurried off to France through another door. The reasons which had guided Mr. Asquith were excellent, and so was the brick, commonly known as General Sir Charles Douglas, Chief of the Imperial General Staff. Trouble verging on mutiny had taken place at the Curragh in Ireland. The war horizon was clear, and, politically, the moment seemed to demand that a soldier whose *forte* was discipline should be placed at the head of the Army —a soldier, if possible, in whose character and justice all ranks should have confidence. Sir Charles Douglas seemed to Mr. Asquith's powerful but ultra-civilian comprehension exactly to fit this special occasion and did indeed so fit it. He had begun his career as an Adjutant by drilling me as his first officer recruit. From this remarkable opening onwards he had managed to cling, practically without any break, to Adjutant-General's work for the whole of his career. When I got to Monte Video on my way home from inspections in New Zealand, I received a letter from him saying I would be as much surprised as he had been himself to know he had been appointed Chief of the Imperial General Staff. " One lives and learns," he added. Poor Douglas ! Unfortunately one dies sometimes in doing so.

Thus it came about that Kitchener, when he entered the War Office, found himself saddled with a so-called Chief of the General Staff whose mind was a complete blank on the subject of foreign armies.

The scandal of allowing the Empire to go to war under a dud Chief of the General Staff had been so far recognised by the organisers of the Expeditionary Force that they had meant to leave behind one real General Staff Officer to see Douglas through with the P.M. and with whoever might be made Secretary of State. Sir William Robertson was the Jonah chosen. Robertson, like Douglas, only in another sphere, was a specialist. He was through and through a General Staff Officer, and had the technique at his fingertips. With Robertson to bolster him up, Douglas might have been able to assert himself. But Kitchener had mightily changed since South African days, when he had strengthened and supported my position as his Chief of the Staff. Kitchener did not want the General Staff in the higher grades to be strengthened, and so he told Douglas he might let Robertson go. Thus, to Robertson's intense delight, and to the secret wonderment both of himself and the few outsiders who knew what had been intended, he was offered the post of Quarter-Master General on the Western Front (an office with the business of which he had no more acquaintance than Douglas had acquaintance with the business of the General Staff), and off he skipped!!!

Douglas was now doomed. Several times I have been in Lord K.'s superheated room when he sent for his C.I.G.S. and asked him a question. Speaking mildly K. liked a quick answer. "One moment, Sir," the highly alarmed Douglas would reply as he side-stepped towards the door ; "one moment, and I will let you know." "Wait," imperiously would cry K., and, to the messenger, "Colonel Callwell!"[1] In trotted Callwell; was asked the identical question just put to his own Chief, and at once answered it.

K. did not mean any harm, but Douglas, the rigid disciplinarian, went staggering out of the room. Very soon Douglas was taken ill with an ailment of old standing, and when he died Lord K. consulted me about a successor. Wolfe Murray's name coming up, I gave my idea of him: "An excellent officer; wide experiences; solid character; a great gentleman, but he has had an illness; he is no longer his old self; suffers from listlessness, and seems to have lost his energy and self-confidence." The reason these remarks have been remembered is because of my surprise when K. replied, with an air of finality and satisfaction, "I think he might do for me very well." Wolfe Murray may have helped to do for K., but certainly K. did for Wolfe Murray. The word "blank" might be sprawled across the record of his tenure of the greatest office in the Empire during its greatest war.

Then there was the Military Secretary. Into that post a man of strong character and perfect fairness had been placed—Sir Alfred Codrington. In the days when I was

[1] Colonel Callwell was a reserve officer filling Sir Henry Wilson's place as Director of Military Intelligence, a branch of the General Staff.

Adjutant-General, and was nominally responsible for the arrangements for King Edward's funeral, Sir Alfred had actually worked them out and carried them through. When it was over I brought up Sir Alfred to K. and said, " Here, Sir, is the officer responsible for this ceremony which has gone off without a hitch." " Humph, humph," snorted K., " all I know is, I've lost my taxi, and in it is my new Field-Marshal's cloak! " (Sir William Birdwood was present, so I have a living witness.) Now, whether it was the memory of the cloak or whether it was a certain firmness and orthodoxy pertaining to Codrington, he was straightway shot out of the War Office into the Eastern Command.

K.'s instinct had been right when for years it had warned him against the War Office, and his ambition had led him into a trap when he had tried for it. He did try, although Mr. Asquith has put down in his diary (*Memories and Reflections*, ii, p. 24): " K. was, to do him justice, not at all anxious to come in, but when it was presented to him as a duty he agreed." No doubt, the P.M. honestly believed this at the time. All the same, it was not so. I saw K. twice at Mr. Ralli's house, where he was holding a sort of running levee during the last two or three days of July 1914. He was quite open to me about his plans, until I happened to say Haldane had sent for me, from which moment he shut up with a snap. Later on Mr. Asquith resented the suggestion that pressure had been put upon him, and was at pains to explain that when he recalled K. from Dover on August 3 he did so, not in response to the insistence of outsiders, but merely to ensure his presence at the War Council of August 5. The P.M. had no need to seek excuses. A soldier Secretary of State may have proved awkward, but K. was worth the awkwardness—for, let who will claim to have " won the war," it is as sure as sure can be that without K. in a position to raise the armies we'd have lost it.

As to exactly what K. was pressing for at that time here it is: (1) public opinion must be mobilised to force Asquith to put him in as Secretary of State; (2) only second-rate, stop-gap appointments must be made in Egypt during his absence; (3) if any unexpected turn of the wheel should create a vacancy in the position of Viceroy in India whilst he was at the War Office, an acting man must be put in.

When K. had shed Robertson and Codrington, the War Office, already much debilitated by the loss of those who had left their office stools for France, would have fallen to pieces altogether had it not been for the sharp pin with a good head on it—Sir Reginald Brade, the P.U.S., who held the loose sheets precariously together. There was no one now left to stand up to K., not even Jack Cowans, although, as a matter of fact, K. rarely interfered with him. Sir Edward Bethune used to brace himself up with a nip when he was summoned to the presence. The same with all of them, except the dug-out Callwell and Braithwaite. Perhaps the most surprising case was that of Sclater, the Adjutant-General. Sclater knew K. well and had been A.G. to him in India. He liked K., and K. liked him, yet K., having determined to frighten him, frightened he became. I have seen Sclater lay a paper before K., and K. suddenly round on him about casualties—drafts—whatever it might be. " Why do you put down this figure? We've talked over the matter already. Write down so many." And Sclater would strike out something and write something, presumably what K. had just told him.

He had gained his first objective. Complete, unobstructed control of the Upper Chamber, but, alas, the small Star Chamber was unable to cope effectively with the mass of troubles which arose. To reconstitute the Pretoria group would not have been easy. How could they have chummed together in jolly isolation? Where was "Hammy"? where was Marker? where, above all, was " the Brat," who, like David playing on the harp to Saul, would have made him laugh at himself? And he wanted to be cheered up. " I had reckoned," he said, " on working with the King and two or three of the leading Statesman, but when half a dozen or so of the minor fry walk into the picture, and when I reflect that the Empire is at war, I tremble." All the same, any men K. really wanted might have been got back from France, but the vital fact was that K. did not want them. He could no longer have stomached that independence of spirit of theirs which used to be their chief value to him.

So Sir Herbert Creedy, now P.U.S. of the War Office, became Chief of his small Star Chamber for departmental work. There was no better man at his job, but he was no soldier and, except as K.'s mouthpiece, could not in those days carry weight. In place of " the Brat "—Fitzgerald. Everyone knew "Fitz"; I better than most, for he was

by SIR IAN HAMILTON

an old friend of my own A.D.C.'s, and used to visit us often on Salisbury Plain between 1905 and 1909 before the War. Good-looking, a brother officer (18th B.L.) of Clive Wigram, the King's Secretary, he was popular, and did his best. But in no wise could he replace "the Brat." His attitude towards his Chief was no real use, being one of deep, reverential loyalty. I am told that the members of the Royal Commission on the Dardanelles, to whom I handed over of my own free will all my private letters to Lord K., agreed privately that my own attitude was too much that of a schoolboy to a schoolmaster. That may be, but I could stick up to him too. When he ordered me to cut out the names of battalions from my despatches and call them "certain troops," I refused.[1] But Fitz was always afraid of K. Taken on his military merits the command of his regiment was his limit. He went about trying to help in the great Government offices and with high officials, but his brain had not the grip.

K.'s hope, then, of being able to revive the play as given at Pretoria fourteen years previously with a more pliant troupe of actors was a failure. Three-fourths of K.'s dynamic force ran to waste. Is it to be imagined "Hammy" would have allowed him—helpless, candid, childlike in such matters—to rush over to France just before the battle of the Marne, minus his magic wand, the Secretary, and the Flag, to sustain a rebuff from a meddlesome Ambassador as well as from French. As to the relations between Kitchener and French, "Hammy" would have soon got those on to the proper, i.e. the old South African, footing. Even the miserable Rump, all that was left of the Army Council, was pained by K.'s weakness towards French. They did not know that K. was prepared to stand anything sooner than say or do anything that would shake the confidence of the troops in their Commander in the field.

I have said nothing about the conduct of the Dardanelles operations, because I am too much involved. I have said nothing about India because, although I stayed there with K. and went through the Mhow manœuvres as his guest, "K. in India" is not my particular pigeon. But I will

---

[1] On New Year's Eve, 1916, Sir Reginald Brade returned my final despatch, writing me that K. "*personally insisted*" I should insert the words "on the Peninsula" after the sentence ending "these were all the forces available." I refused again, having already done so at a personal interview that morning. —IAN H.

say this much—there may be two opinions as to whether a little readjustment might not have eased the situation out there and saved the War Lord from being saddled with both executive work and administrative responsibility—there may be two opinions on that point; there is only one opinion as to the enormous increase of military power produced, without a penny of extra expense, by K.'s sweeping reorganisation of the Army in India which prepared it, for the first time, to work hand in glove with the other Brigades, Divisions, and Army Corps of the Empire.

To have written thousands of words about a man and to have said nothing about women seems almost irreligious, but here a fellow must watch his step. K. showed good taste in his friendships with the fair. Sometimes he sulked; sometimes he played pranks, yet, although there was not a vestige of " the lady's man " about him, he attracted them. Once or twice he thought of getting married, but the lady thought otherwise, and I am not allowed to tell about it. As to his tricks, they display a peculiar, elephantine turn of humour. There's only space for one or two simple examples. During the ball at " the Durbar " in India K. took Mrs. Lawrence Drummond round on his arm and introduced her right and left as Lady Kitchener. " Who is that person ? " enquired the wife of the Governor of Bengal of the Vicereine. " She is my cousin," replied Lady Minto, " and is staying with me! " Mrs. Lawrence Drummond is probably the tallest lady in Society, but hardly taller than the next trick K. played her. At his State ball in 1913 at Cairo he picked out one of the Egyptian Ministers who was only just short of being a dwarf, and told him off to take her down to supper. So they had to process together as best they might. In his friendships with women he showed always the best and nicest of himself. As to casual and trifling intrigues, I believe K. had a spotless sheet. I can only state my belief, and there it is. In Europe a bank clerk or even a banker may have the most hair-raising adventures or the most sordid misadventures with women, and no one, bar the women, any the wiser. In Asia or Africa a British officer flirts with a searchlight turned on to him. Pretoria, Simla, Cairo, Calcutta; whether with white, brown, or black; whether in the cantonment or the bazaar, his adventures, if he has any, are known. K.'s are unknown. There seemed to me to be something in him perhaps which shrank from intimacy beyond a certain point even with an angel.

K.'s nerves were his strong point and yet his weakest point. He was what is called "a bundle of nerves," but give him one moment, he could make them tense as ropes of steel wire and as unbreakable. Anything quite sudden and unexpected could, however, get under his guard and knock him clean out. A day or two after K.'s return from Fashoda my wife and I dined with Sir Harry and Lady Rawlinson, the fifth guest being K. We all then went to a theatre, or perhaps it was the opera, I can't remember. There we entered a big box, second tier on the stage left. The moment K. appeared the whole audience rose and cheered like mad. He was completely upset, and rushed to the back of the box, grinding out between his clenched teeth the words, " Fools! Fools!! Fools!!! "

There were several other like cases, mostly trifling, and one, at the very end of the South African War, which might have been most serious but for " Hammy." It has been very lightly touched upon in Sir George Arthur's excellent *Life*, vol. 2, p. 73. During the forty-eight hours of collapse no orders were issued by the real K., though many were issued by his impersonators. Ordinarily, however, K.'s nerves stood any racket, and at the blackest moments he was the bravest. The worst blow that ever befell him was when John Morley passed him over for the Viceroyalty in India. I could write another article about that alone, with sidelights from the late Countess Roberts and from Lord Haldane, who was at the fatal dinner of four where K. dished himself. However, my wife has just found this letter:

" Cloan,
" Auchterarder,
" Perthshire.
" 27 *Aug.* '16.

" Dear Lady Ian,

" Here are the documents back. I have read them with much interest.

" It was a dinner that Lord Esher described—substantially correctly. I was one of the four present. Esher (host) Ld. K. Ld. Morley were the others present. A private room at the Carlton was the place, and the dinner was given by the privately expressed desire of Ed. VII who hoped that M. would be impressed with K. as the proper man for the vacant Vice Royalty. But he was not.

"I shall be settled in London by the beginning of Oct. when I hope to see you often.

"Yours vy sincerely,
"(Sd.) HALDANE."

My wife was afterwards told by Lord Haldane that K. (the silent) had talked too much.

K.'s happiest hours were spent at Broome, alone with his friend and architect, Detmar Blow. There, amongst the beautiful art treasures he had collected, he would weave fantasies about them; talk quietly and be at peace, or work by himself, very cleverly, modelling in clay. Just as in the case of John Sargent, the artist, his lack of small talk was restful. In neither case did their shyness in society come from diffidence: it came from the want of atmosphere experienced by a very large fish amongst minnows.

In many ways he was a very lovable man.

* * * * * *

So now the time had come for the apotheosis of K. How should it be done? The Heavenly Powers must decide. He must not peter out in extreme old age. Now was the appointed hour; now, when he was on his way to carry out his greatest mission. Now, when he would have the *Hampshire* for his coffin; the *Hampshire*; his own battle-cruiser; beloved by him ever since he came out in her from Egypt to Malta. There—with his martial cloak around him. Do it now—So!!!

* * * * * *

On June 6, 1916, my wife and I were lunching with Mr. and Mrs. Winston Churchill in Cromwell Road. We were all in the dining-room except Winston, who lingered. Suddenly there was a confused sound as of people running and of shouts. We listened, and quite clearly we heard the words, "Kitchener drowned." Everyone turned to the window, and as we did so a strange figure in rags and with wild hair hanging over his face rushed past with a bundle of papers under his arm crying out, "Kitchener drowned! Kitchener drowned!!" Stunned, we sat down in complete silence. The door opened. Winston came in, walked to the head of the table, and said, "Happy is he in the manner of his death."

ANDREW BONAR LAW
1858-1923

By
QUINTIN HOGG

ANDREW BONAR LAW

by QUINTIN HOGG

"HOW fitting that he should lie beside the Unknown Warrior, the Unknown Prime Minister of England."[1] It was prophetic. Ten years have passed since this remark was made, and Bonar Law is almost forgotten.

It is not a little difficult to recapture a living picture of Bonar Law in his prime. So much has happened since those days in 1911 when he first took upon himself the leadership of his party that one is apt to think of him as a melancholy, rather pathetic personality, "gentle and shrewd," as Mr. Asquith called him, but dull, painfully doing his duty in a world he did not much enjoy. Yet it is a great mistake to confuse the Bonar Law of 1923 with the Bonar Law of 1911.

Just listen to this. Bonar Law is speaking to an audience of ten thousand people. At the end of each sentence, at each pause for breath, they laugh or cheer. They cannot restrain themselves. They are like a crowd listening to a melodrama. He mentions the name of a political opponent. It is greeted with cries of "Traitor!" and loud boos. It is amusing to note that all references to Mr. Winston Churchill are the signal for groans. The speaker appears to flag. "You are magnificent," his hearers shout; "go on." It is not often that a political leader thus rouses even his own supporters. It may not be altogether dignified. But it is certainly not pathetic. It is certainly not dull. It may not resemble the correct Balliol manner of Mr. Asquith, the main object of his attacks. But there is a vigour and a bitter tang about it which stamps it as in the true Attic tradition of "that beast" Demosthenes. Yet Bonar was always more at home in Parliament than on the platform.

[1] This was Lord Oxford's comment. See Lord Beaverbrook, *Politicians and the War*, vol. ii, p.16.

He preferred lucidity to rhetoric, in his own words, thinking " fire " superior to mere " fireworks."

A second mistake which can be made only too easily lies in forgetting that Bonar was cheated of the reward for his best achievement. His outstanding success was his leadership of the Opposition from 1911 to 1914 and his compulsion of the Government to compromise upon the question of Home Rule. By all rights this would have led to a period of office during which Bonar Law's powers of statesmanship would have been put to the test. The War cheated Bonar of this period of office. When he ultimately reached the goal he was already a dying man who had lost two dearly loved children in the War, and his actual achievements in the pre-War years have been dwarfed by the greater events which followed.

This is the reason for what at first sight seems so paradoxical, that one whose career was pre-eminent and even spectacular should live so short a time in the memory of his fellow-countrymen.

And yet his career was spectacular. But a little twist to the wheel, and what a study for the biographer he would have made!

The beginning was unpretentious enough. He was born in New Brunswick in 1858. His father was a Presbyterian minister from Ulster. He never knew his mother, but was brought up by a cousin of hers, a Miss Kidston, who came out to Canada for the purpose. In his twelfth year his father married again, and Bonar left the family home for ever. Miss Kidston brought him to Glasgow, where she had rich relations, and these practically adopted the child and finished his education. His home was in Glasgow or the neighbouring Helensburgh for the next forty years of his life.

His education did not take long. At the age of sixteen he entered the Kidston business, a firm of merchant bankers, and here he worked for the greater part of the day as a junior clerk. Only in his leisure hours was he able to devote himself to other interests, and it is indeed a remarkable tribute to his character that one of these included a spare-time class in Glasgow University, which worked from eight to ten in the morning before the business day began.

For though Bonar Law was unassuming, he was by no means unambitious. An orphan in Glasgow of obscure colonial birth does not always study Gibbons's *Decline and Fall*. Bonar had read it three times before he was twenty-one, because, as he said in after life to Mr. H. A. L. Fisher, " He liked to read of common soldiers becoming Emperors." Carlyle's *Heroes* was another favourite of this period. The later view of Bonar as wholly indifferent to his career is a mistake.

Another story illustrates this trait. When he was just twenty-one Mr. Gladstone himself came down to address the students as Lord Rector of the University. Somewhere in the audience the ungainly figure of young Bonar sat enthralled. " I left that gathering," he afterwards said, " with the hope and indeed the intention of one day occupying the position which was then filled by Mr. Gladstone."[1]

In view of this story, it seems curious that from Mr. Gladstone's visit until, at the age of forty-two, he entered Parliament the only political experience Bonar seems to have had appears to have been in the Glasgow Parliamentary Debating Association, one of those bodies then so common which modelled their procedure meticulously upon that of the House of Commons. Here Bonar made a great impression, for he obtained " Cabinet Rank," and his speeches are fully reported in the journal of the Society, in which the curious may still read them. This, together with the visits of Conservative leaders to the Kidston home, appears to have been the only political training he ever received.

In 1885 came Bonar's big chance in business. He was taken in as junior partner by an iron merchant named William Jacks. From this moment until he left the sphere of commerce this was Bonar's main occupation, and by it he amassed a considerable fortune, which was afterwards increased by inheritance.

In 1891 he married. His private life is not the proper subject of this essay. But it would be a mistake if it were not made clear that, in spite of business interests and political ambitions, it was in this channel that the main current of his vitality flowed. When his wife died in 1909 it was the

[1] Cf. H. A. Taylor, *Strange Case of Andrew Bonar Law*, p. 27. Mr. G. was not at this date P.M., but I can hardly believe Bonar's ambition was simply the Lord Rectorship. In any case, this could only be attained by success in politics. Lord Beaverbrook has told me that at the age of twenty-three Bonar was heard to complain that while Pitt had been Prime Minister at his age, he himself was not even a Glasgow baillie.

opinion of at least one of his admirers[1] that ambition began to wither, and when we come to assess the part he played in politics from 1917 onwards we shall have to bear in mind that the death in battle of his two elder sons had left him a stricken, even a broken-hearted, man. Bonar Law was not a Mr. Churchill or a Mr. Lloyd George, who, despite the warmest family affections, have so imbued their politics with their personality that it is impossible to draw a distinction between their public and their private lives. Bonar Law was essentially a man who lived his life in compartments, like the separate accounts in a double-entry ledger, and when one of the accounts was closed that part of his nature which it represented could never find its outlet in another way.

And so we find him in 1900, an iron merchant of forty-two, entering upon a career in the House of Commons.

Lord Birkenhead described him at his death[2] as "one of the most remarkable Parliamentary debaters I ever knew." This was not the product of experience, unless the Glasgow debates of his nonage rank as such. It was a natural gift, based upon a phenomenal memory, a well-disciplined mind, and an extraordinary lucidity of expression.[3]

His ability showed itself from the first. In 1900 influence counted for more than it does to-day. Then, as now, middle-aged business men did not usually succeed in Parliament. Nevertheless, within two years Bonar was Parliamentary Secretary to the Board of Trade. Within ten years, without ever having held Cabinet office, he was the leader of his party.[4]

The circumstances which led up to his election can be quite briefly told.

It had been a bad six years for Conservatives. In 1906 the party, led by Mr. Balfour, had suffered a calamitous defeat, but by 1909 Conservatives had every reason to believe that the Liberal Party would be in difficulties before the next General Election.

At this point, however, the Conservatives themselves

[1] Mr. Stanley Baldwin. This is denied by Lord Beaverbrook.
[2] *The Times*, October 31, 1923.
[3] One of the Ministers in his 1922 Government described his style of speaking as "like a powerful searchlight illuminating in turn every aspect of a subject."
[4] In the country he had made his name by giving up a safe seat to contest North-west Manchester in the election of 1910.

provided their opponents with a welcome diversion and a useful cry. Whatever the Constitutional merits of the question, the rejection by the Peers of the "People's Budget" of 1909 proved the undoing of the Tories. As a result of the election which it occasioned, the Liberals returned with a smaller majority but a new mandate, and armed with this they passed the Budget and dissolved again, pledged to destroy the power of the House of Lords.

It is most important to appreciate what followed. Both sides hoped for a clear majority as a result of the second election, and with this object in view the Liberals studiously avoided in their election addresses any reference to what was then, they feared, the unpopular subject of Home Rule.

When the election was over, both sides were disappointed. With the Irish Nationalists either could control the House of Commons. Without, both were in a minority. In these circumstances the Liberals were willing, as the price of one Constitutional revolution in the Parliament Act, to concede another in the shape of Home Rule, for which, the Tories urged, there was no mandate whatever from the British electorate.

A bargain was therefore struck upon these lines, and as a result the Liberals carried the Parliament Act. Its passage was accompanied by acute Conservative dissension. Conservative leadership had rightly come in for a good deal of criticism during the past six years, and Mr. Balfour now found his position intolerable and resigned.[1]

The problem was to find a successor. Two candidates immediately appeared in the field—Mr. Austen Chamberlain and Mr. Walter Long. But neither of these proved acceptable. Each had too many opponents to secure election for himself. Each had too many supporters to render possible the success of the other. In these circumstances men cast about for an alternative; and the choice fell upon Mr. Bonar Law. To many it seemed, in Mr. Asquith's words,[2] " a bold experiment." To Mr. Asquith at least it seemed incredible that anyone should regard a change from Mr. Balfour to Mr. Bonar Law as a change for the better. Mr. Lloyd George took a different view. " The fools," was his comment, " have blundered upon their best man."

---

[1] November 8, 1911.   [2] *Fifty Years of Parliament*, ii, 117.

As for Bonar, he took it all quite calmly. "If I am a great man," he said to his friend Max Aitken, "then all great men are frauds."[1]

The problem which faced Bonar was twofold. He had to unite the Tory Party and he had to oust the Government. But, above all, it was his duty to prevent the passage of the measure of Home Rule which at the time of his election was the next item of the Liberal Programme.

To achieve this he was compelled to take a decision which was most distasteful, and relegate the subject of Tariff Reform, of which he had been an enthusiastic supporter from the earliest years, but which had proved a great cause of dissension, into the background of the party's policy. For the rest he adopted an almost entirely destructive attitude towards the Government.

He soon saw that the methods of Parliamentary dialectic which had been employed by Mr. Balfour were wholly inadequate to the purpose. As a result of his bargain with the Nationalists, Mr. Asquith had in effect been compelled to substitute a Cabinet Despotism for Parliamentary Government. The situation was well summed up by an intelligent Socialist, a certain Mr. Philip Snowden.

"The question of the degradation of the House of Commons," said this critic, "is the most important matter in British politics to-day. The country has not a system of representative government; it is living under the tyranny of Cabinet autocracy."

Bonar realised that nothing he could do in Parliament would induce the Government to vary their proposals by a jot. He therefore determined not to confine himself to Parliamentary agitation. This must have been a difficult decision to take. His was not naturally the disposition of a demagogue. Instinctively he was a respecter of law and order. But during the next two and a half years he deliberately inflamed popular emotion in this country by speeches against the Government of extraordinary bitterness, and in Ulster boldly stood forth with Sir Edward Carson as the open champion of armed rebellion.

To justify such a policy required a careful choice of ground, and here Bonar and Carson were miles ahead of their

---

[1] *Lord Beaverbrook: An Authentic Biography*, F. A. MacKenzie, p. 82; *Politicians and the War*. The two versions differ verbally. Lord Beaverbrook confirms the one I have given.

party.[1] The traditional Tory objections to Home Rule were twofold. In the first place, the kingdoms were economically and strategically a single unit. In the second place, Great Britain owed a duty to the Southern Loyalists. These were sound arguments enough. America had engaged in civil strife for less, and it would have been a good thing for the peace of the world if the framers of the Treaty of Versailles had borne such considerations in mind in describing the modern map of Europe. But Bonar and Carson realised almost from the first that it was impossible to resist Home Rule for what is now the Irish Free State. From almost the first it became clear that they would be content with the exclusion of Ulster.

Here they were on impregnable ground. In Bonar's own words, " Ireland is not a nation: it is two nations." Again, " There are two nations in Ireland arrayed against each other in hostile camps."

If it was not right to coerce one of these nations it was not right to coerce the other. The Liberals throughout made the mistake of regarding the Ulstermen simply as a recalcitrant minority. The " minority " soon showed that it had " the soul of a people." It was willing to fight the British Army for its rights, and it had the sympathy of that very army in this defiance.

Bonar gave unequivocal support to Ulster's resistance. At a great meeting of the Ulster Volunteers outside Belfast he publicly shook hands with Sir Edward Carson " over this business."[2] In England, in a long-remembered speech at Blenheim, he said, " I can imagine no length of resistance to which Ulster can go in which I shall not be ready to support them."

It must not be thought that Bonar really placed his faith in civil war. In the long run he knew that he held all the trump cards. In the debates in Parliament he said :

> " These people in Ulster are under no illusion. They know they cannot fight the British Army. But they are ready, in what they believe to be the cause of justice and liberty, to lay down their lives. How are you going

---

[1] This was shown by the uproar which was caused in 1916 when Bonar accepted Home Rule with the exclusion of the Six Counties. Cf. Beaverbrook, *op. cit.*, vol. ii, p. 65.
[2] *The Times*, April 9, 1912.

to overcome their resistance? Do honourable members really believe that any Prime Minister could give orders to shoot down men whose only crime it is that they refuse to be driven out of our community? . . . That is a rock, and on that rock this Bill will inevitably make shipwreck."

On another occasion Bonar stated the case more succinctly by saying that if Asquith ordered the troops to fire he would stand infinitely more chance of being lynched in the streets of London than any Ulsterman would stand of being shot in Northern Ireland.

Very soon the Government showed signs of cracking. In 1912 a Liberal back bencher named Mr. Agar-Robartes had proposed an amendment to exclude Ulster from the operation of the Bill. Carson and Bonar accepted the amendment, but the Government Whips were put on against it, and it was beaten. Yet by the summer recess in 1913 Lord Crewe was playing golf with Bonar at Balmoral, discussing the possibility of a solution along these very lines, and all through October Asquith, Bonar, Redmond, and Carson were carrying on negotiations. These negotiations broke down, as the Government would not go the whole length of excluding Ulster.

Nevertheless, in March 1914 the Government receded from its original position by introducing an amending Bill, in effect giving Ulster the right to vote itself out of the Bill for a period of six years. This was clearly unacceptable. Once the principle of plebiscite was admitted, to limit its scope to a period of years was obviously ridiculous. Carson denounced the proposal as " sentence of death with a stay of execution," and he was supported in his opposition by Bonar Law.

A further attempt at settlement, the Buckingham Palace Conference, failed in July; but Asquith's account of it is instructive. The discussions, he wrote, turned entirely upon the area to be excluded.[1] Clearly the Liberals were fighting a losing battle, and although the position on July 30, 1914, when the amending Bill was to come up for Second Reading, appeared to be hopeless, although Ulster was armed and the Liberals still threatening, it is at least doubtful if war would have come of it. Bonar really held all

[1] *Fifty Years of Parliament*, ii, 156.

the cards. No Englishman in the Army or out of it was prepared to fight simply to throw Ulster out of the United Kingdom.

But the issue never was decided. On July 30, Asquith was invited by telephone to Bonar's house; he went, and was received by Bonar and Carson, who proposed that the amending Bill should be postponed owing to "the grave European situation." On August 2 came a second message. Bonar wrote to Asquith that he and Lord Lansdowne offered their " unhesitating support " in any measures " that might be considered necessary in supporting France and Russia."

Apart from a temporary recrudescence in September, the storm in the teacup subsided, and the nation, miraculously reunited, stood to arms.

* * * * *

Bonar's policy throughout the War is one of deliberate self-subordination. It falls naturally into three periods: the periods of " patriotic opposition," of the first Coalition, and of the ascendancy of Mr. Lloyd George.

At the beginning of the War, Bonar had to decide an important question of principle. An election, although in it he might well have hoped for success, would have been hopelessly unpatriotic. He could not oppose the policy of war. And yet he had no share in the decisions actually pursued.

There were some who desired him to insist upon a Coalition. Mr. Churchill was among these. But Bonar wisely enough refused. He thought that though a protracted struggle would inevitably lead to this form of Administration, this should be the last step to take and not the first. " While such a national asset remained unexhausted, why draw on another? "[1] Bonar remained of this opinion throughout the first nine months of the War,[2] and supported the Government in all matters except the Irish question, where he maintained in September 1914 that Asquith had deliberately broken his pledge to respect a political truce.

By May 1915, however, Bonar decided that the time for drawing upon the " national asset " had come. The War

[1] Beaverbrook, *op. cit.*, vol. i, p. 21.
[2] He even resisted a further attempt by Mr. Churchill at coalition in March 1915.

was not taking the successful course which had been anticipated, and Bonar took the opportunity of Lord Fisher's resignation to communicate[1] to Asquith a formal demand by himself and his colleagues to be given some share in the responsibility for the Government they were being asked to support. The result of this communication was the First Coalition.

It is now generally agreed that the First Coalition was from the beginning an unsatisfactory Administration. Among its minor faults was the lamentable intrigue by which it was determined that Bonar should not hold high office.[2] In the middle of a European War the Prime Minister wrote in his diary that it was of course " impossible " that a Tariff Reformer should be Chancellor of the Exchequer[3]; and so Bonar had to be content with the Colonial Office until the Second Coalition, when he proved a most successful occupant of the very post to which Asquith had referred.

Actually Bonar was rather amused than otherwise by this manœuvre. When asked to accept the Colonial Office he appears to have remarked quite blandly, " You mustn't think I am doing this because I am compelled to. I know quite well that I can have what I want simply by lifting my little finger. But I won't fight. I am here to show you how to run a Coalition by forbearance and concession." Later, when Asquith and Lloyd George had fallen out, he said that he only wished they could agree as well as they had done when they had combined to do him out of the Exchequer.

One important decision, which probably saved thousands of lives, stands to Bonar's credit at the end of 1915. By August it was fairly clear that the Gallipoli campaign had failed. Bonar Law was among the first to see the necessity for evacuation. He had to fight against an immense body of expert and political opinion. It was not until October that General Munroe was sent out to report upon the situation. His report confirmed Bonar's judgment. Still the Cabinet hesitated to act, and on November 4 a decision was reached to send out Lord Kitchener to survey the ground all over again. But Bonar made up his mind that this

[1] *Life of Lord Oxford and Asquith*, by J. A. Spender and C. Asquith, ii, 165. It appears that this letter had been preceded by other and less formal negotiations between the Government and the Tories.
[2] Cf. Spender, *op. cit.*, ii, 171; Beaverbrook, *op. cit.*, vol. i, p. 136.
[3] Spender, *op. cit.*, loc. cit.

decision was not to stand. He told his colleagues that unless it was rescinded he would resign. Rescinded it was, in spite of expert warnings that withdrawal might mean the loss of fully a third of the troops. Withdrawal took place without the loss of life, and the nation may well be grateful to the statesman to whose courage and persistence this was due.[1]

By the beginning of 1916 the First Coalition had ceased to believe in itself. Carson had left the Government in October, and was soon to lead a formidable Conservative cave in opposition. Mr. Lloyd George, who still retained the Ministry of Munitions, was in almost open revolt, and in close communication with the dissentient elements. Lord Curzon was, it is said, designing to supplant Bonar Law as Conservative Leader. In March Mr. Redmond left a record of a very interesting interview he had with Bonar himself.[2] Bonar said that the present situation could not continue, and that although he thought Asquith the most suitable Premier, he foresaw that he would have to go. He said that Mr. Lloyd George would succeed him. Redmond asked him what he thought of this, to which he replied, "You know George as well as I do." Redmond concludes: "He seemed very depressed about the whole affair."

By the autumn Lord Lansdowne must have been preparing his famous memorandum in favour of peace by negotiation. By the end of the year the only thing upon which a number, at least of the Tory ministers, agreed was that "with Asquith as Chairman either of the Cabinet or the War Committee, we can never win the War."[3]

Meanwhile, Asquith, apparently unconscious that anything serious was amiss, continued to conduct a European War according to the best model of Balliol statesmanship.

Some time in November, Carson and Lloyd George began to plot together for the overthrow of the Government. Both were prepared, if necessary, to allow Asquith to remain in

[1] There is still a minority which holds that withdrawal was wrong, and enemy documents are quoted to prove that at the date of withdrawal the Turks were preparing to evacuate Constantinople. I think this argument pays too little attention to the result of the campaign in Serbia which freed enemy troops for Gallipoli.
[2] *Life of Lord Oxford and Asquith*, ii, 246.
[3] Letter of Lord Curzon to Lord Lansdowne, December 3, 1916—*Life of Lord Oxford and Asquith*, ii, p. 256. This letter contains a contemporary account of the Council meeting of December 3, and is of the utmost importance.

the position of Premier. Indeed, at the time it was difficult to see who else had the prestige to fill the post. Both, however, were convinced that Asquith must at all costs be ousted from the actual control of the War, and that for the existing Cabinet should be substituted a small and effective War Committee, of which Asquith, although Prime Minister, was not to be a member. At first sight their chances of success appeared to be remote. It was not to be expected that Asquith would approve of this arrangement, while official Conservatives were irritated with Sir Edward Carson, and did not trust Mr. Lloyd George.

By a stroke of luck the conspirators secured the ear of Sir Maxwell Aitken, who had the confidence of Bonar Law.

Bonar Law at first would have little to say to the plan. As we have seen, he was profoundly pessimistic about the War, and had no faith in the existing Administration. But even apart from his personal prejudices against Lloyd George and his estrangement from Carson (for at this time Bonar was wholly at one with his colleagues in this respect), he did not believe that the scheme was politically practicable. Eventually, however, he was persuaded, first to reconcile himself with Carson, next to believe in the sincerity of Mr. Lloyd George, and finally to endorse the plan.

It was typical of Bonar that, contrary to Mr. Lloyd George's desire, he immediately insisted on communicating the scheme to Asquith. He would not, he said, be drawn into any intrigue against him.[1] Asquith, of course, gave an unfavourable reply.[2] Bonar's Conservative colleagues did not learn about the scheme until later.[3]

When they did learn about the proposal they unanimously turned it down, and proposed an alternative which proved acceptable to Asquith, but to which the Triumvirate would not accede. As Asquith had behind him the solid bulk of Liberal opinion, it looked as if the only outcome of the adventure would be that the adventurers were left out in the cold.

On December 2, Bonar Law and Lloyd George agreed to stand or fall together. Carson was already in opposition.

---

[1] Beaverbrook, *op. cit.*, vol. ii, p. 138. This was November 20, 1916. Spender, *op. cit.*, ii, 250.
[2] Letter dated November 26, 1916; Beaverbrook, *ibid.*, p. 153. This was actually a reply to a more official communication.
[3] November 30, 1916; Beaverbrook, *ibid.*, p. 160.

by QUINTIN HOGG

In these circumstances Bonar met his colleagues on the 3rd. Their original attitude towards the plan had not been improved by a flamboyant article which had appeared that morning in *Reynolds' Illustrated Newspaper* and which they all believed to be inspired by Lloyd George himself. So far as the plan was concerned, Bonar Law found himself in a minority of one.

Nevertheless, there were certain points of agreement, and ultimately the Tory leaders decided to act together. Lloyd George's quarrels with Asquith were, they determined, no concern of theirs. The Liberal chiefs must fight it out between themselves. As for them, since the Prime Minister could not be a Tory, they were prepared to serve their country in its hour of need under whatever statesman could command the requisite support from the other parties.[1]

To put this plan into operation it was necessary that Asquith should resign, and a resolution to this effect was prepared by the Tory Ministers, and given to Bonar to show to him. It is fairly obvious that this paper was intended to conceal their differences from the Prime Minister, and Bonar was therefore justified in simply explaining the effect of the resolution and telling him that its object was not to supplant Asquith himself, but to reconstruct the Government.[2] This was the truth. There was nothing to prevent Asquith from

---

[1] I think this is the accurate account of what took place. It represents the unanimous testimony of those who were present at the meeting other than Bonar himself (see *Life of Lord Oxford and Asquith*, ii, 255-7). In addition to the written sources I have had the advantage of a conversation with Sir Austen Chamberlain, whose view substantially confirms what I have written. The matter to my mind is really clinched by the letter written the same day by Lord Curzon to Lord Lansdowne, also substantially confirming this account, and containing the reference to Asquith I have already quoted.

It would be idle to pretend, however, that this view is unchallenged. Lord Beaverbrook, who was not at the meeting, but was informed by Bonar immediately afterwards of what had taken place, is strong in his view that the meeting was not merely hostile to the plan, as I have agreed, but intended its resolution to be merely a weapon in Asquith's hands with which to defeat Mr. Lloyd George. This view has been adopted by the biographers of Lord Asquith, but can hardly stand in the face of the evidence I have quoted. It should be added that if it were accepted, the unfavourable view of Bonar's conduct taken by these authors would be difficult to resist.

[2] I do not share the view of Asquith's biographers that an actual sight of the written resolution would have made much difference. A more sensible criticism is that of Sir Austen Chamberlain, who thinks that Bonar unwittingly gave Asquith the impression that the Tory leaders were less friendly to him than was the fact. This must be so, but to impute to Bonar an intention to deceive is, of course, grossly unfair, and quite uncritical.

remaining Prime Minister had he complied with this request. It is almost incredible, but he did not do so.

Instead, on December 3, and again by letter on December 4, he actually accepted Mr. Lloyd George's plan. Later, on December 4, he withdrew his acceptance in a second letter.[1] This conduct was too much for the Tories. Again they asked for his resignation, and at last Asquith complied.

The King sent for Bonar, but Bonar refused to serve unless Asquith would serve with him as a colleague. Asquith refused, and so the choice fell on Lloyd George. Thus the Second Coalition came into being, with Bonar Law as its Chancellor of the Exchequer.

It is the general opinion that these complicated manœuvres won the War for Britain. If this be so, no small share of the praise belongs to Bonar. It was through his authority and position that the thing was done. To achieve it he faced political ruin and the opposition of all his colleagues, and when in the hour of success he was offered the Premiership he had the strength of mind to refuse it.

Nevertheless, the formation of the Second Coalition marks the end of Bonar's independent existence as a political leader until his re-emergence in 1922. Henceforward his position is well described by himself. At G.H.Q. in France he said to Brig.-General Charteris, " My job in this war is hanging on to that little man's coat tails and holding him back." It was a fruitful alliance. Bonar's cool judgment prevented Mr. Lloyd George from making many serious mistakes, notably from risking our whole military position upon a desperate Eastern adventure, and Bonar's irreproachable reputation gave the Government a moral prestige which it would otherwise have lacked.

It should be remembered, however, that as Chancellor of the Exchequer Bonar held an important departmental position in the Government, and he filled it well, even succeeding, so it is said, in winning the admiration of that difficult critic Mr. J. M. Keynes. The size of his budgets was colossal. In 1917 he introduced a Budget of over £2,000,000,000, and it is a wonderful example of his powers of memory that upon this occasion the only note he used

---

[1] The reason for this change, Lord Beaverbrook ascribes to his interview with "the 3 Cs.," Chamberlain, Cecil, and Curzon, which undeceived him as to their attitude.

during his budget speech was a single row of figures written on a half-sheet of notepaper. The following year the figures were even higher.

When all this has been said, however, it remains true that throughout these years Bonar never seems to have initiated policy. Perhaps it was the death of his children. Perhaps his health was already beginning to fail. Perhaps his departmental duties, as well they might, claimed too large a share of his energies. Whatever the reason, Bonar failed to initiate, and his failure to do so deprives him of the right to be placed in the front rank of statesmen.

If we blame him for his failure to initiate policy during the War, what are we to say of his acquiescence immediately after it? It is not fair to complain that he suffered the continuance of the Coalition. It can hardly be suggested that any other arrangement was politically practicable. But was he justified in signing the Joint Manifesto—the Election address of the Coalition Leaders—which virtually promised a new heaven and a new earth? Surely this was an opportunity for " holding that little man back."

The truth is that Bonar, like most others at the time, was completely under the Wizard's spell. The vision of a united and resurgent England leading the nations of the world upon new, peaceful, and prosperous courses, was one which it was difficult enough to resist in the hour of victory; but it does not lie in the mouth of a statesman to plead human frailty, and Bonar was at least an assenting party to the mistakes of this period.

It is only fair to add that after the election he took a diminishing part in public affairs. In 1918 he exchanged the Chancellorship for the Privy Seal. He took part in the Peace Conference, but appears to have taken a gloomy view about the treaty. " I am not at all easy about the treaty," he said. " Foch's language is most disquieting. I fear we have not satisfied the French." It is also stated that he considered the policy of reparations to be a mistake, but he does not appear to have put this opinion on record. He supported the Irish arrangements in 1920, and again, from his retirement in 1921, he at least acquiesced in the Irish Treaty.

In this latter year it seemed as if the end had come. Aging, tired, disillusioned, broken in health and heart, Bonar Law resigned from his position. He was suffering from a terrible and incurable complaint. Who would have believed that the culminating point in his career had not yet come?

Within a little more than a year he was Prime Minister of England.

Without the reassurance of Bonar's irreproachable character the Tory Party had grown restive under Mr. George. His foreign policy had proved disastrous, and there were ugly rumours on men's lips at home.

Finally, at the end of September the policy of the Government drove Great Britain to the brink of war in the Near East, and bloodshed was only avoided at the cost of a humiliating withdrawal. This, the last of a series of failures abroad, drove into open revolt a powerful section of the Tory Party which was already alienated by the Irish Settlement and the general condition of public life at home. But it was a section without a leader. The Tory chiefs remained outside the movement, and it must have failed had not Bonar Law been persuaded to place himself once more at the head of his party. Attention had been focused upon him as an alternative leader by a letter which he had written to *The Times* during the Chanak crisis, in which for the first time he seriously criticised the policy of the Government.

Had the movement failed it is difficult at this date to assess the consequences. Nevertheless, it appears to be at least arguable that its success, for a time at least, saved Parliamentary Government, prevented, or at least postponed, a revolution, and raised the whole standard of public morality at home, whilst abroad the change in our foreign policy which it involved quite possibly avoided another war.

But Bonar paid for his intervention with his life. " I knew I was signing my death-warrant," he said afterwards to Lord Hailsham. Rarely can an ambitious man's desire have been fulfilled in circumstances more strange.

The short period of his Government will never occupy much space in English histories. Bonar Law came in on a cry of " Tranquillity " at home and abroad. Whether this would ever have proved a feasible policy will never be known. Bonar was only Prime Minister for two hundred days, and within three months of his resignation a new and untried leader had deliberately reversed the helm.

During his Premiership only two events of major importance took place—the British Debt Settlement with America, and the French occupation of the Ruhr. About the first, the only really certain thing is that Bonar disapproved of it. About the second, he afterwards told Lord Hailsham that he spent sleepless hours every night worrying and wondering whether he could not have prevented it. Perhaps, after all, Mr. Asquith was not far wrong when he wrote in November 1922, " Bonar has a very weak team, except the Attorney-General, Douglas Hogg, who seems to be a capable man and a good debater." It certainly was not the team to support a dying man.

He resigned in the summer of 1923, and in the autumn died. He now lies in the South Aisle of the Nave of Westminster Abbey. There let him rest in peace. Even if we omit the chronicles of the earlier years, the withdrawal from Gallipoli in 1915, the support he gave to Mr. Lloyd George in 1916, the management of the nation's finances in 1917-18, and his intervention in national affairs at the cost of his own life in 1922, these are no small achievements for a modest man. Apart from one of them, they were all accomplished in the teeth of the opposition of his oldest friends. Had he had a like confidence in himself on all occasions, he might have become a statesman truly great.

It is difficult to write of his personal character. Except by the authors of Lord Oxford's biography, it is practically unassailed. The devotion of his friends is known and proved. At his death he had entirely won his country's love. It only remains to recite the opinion of one of his political opponents:

" One of the most extraordinary men our public life has produced was Bonar Law, the most remarkable personality it has been my good fortune to meet. He was the greatest gentleman I have ever met in Parliament or without. . . . I never knew any man that so readily and so courageously offered the soft answer that turneth away wrath. No Labour man ever questioned his veracity or his honesty."

So writes Ben Tillett,[1] of the Labour Party. If these words had been penned by a political admirer they would be set aside as the product of prejudice or exaggeration.

[1] *Memories and Reflections*, p. 273.

DAVID HERBERT LAWRENCE
1885–1930

By
R. L. MÉGROZ

DAVID HERBERT LAWRENCE

by R. L. MÉGROZ

ABOUT 1955, that is to say, about a quarter of a century after his death, it may be not only possible but easy to read D. H. Lawrence as other great poets and prose writers are read, primarily for the power and beauty of his communication. The spate of personal and of critical controversy inspired by him may have subsided by then; indeed, will almost certainly have subsided, since the motives which account for much of the Lawrence literature of recent years will fail for want of nourishment. It is not that nothing will be left to argue about. Shelley's character and his achievement are not yet dead subjects of controversy, and Lawrence is at least as powerful and controversial an influence as was Shelley; but the Lawrence that concerns other people will be in his writings in twenty or thirty years' time, and not in the disparaging or the eulogistic memoirs of those who have been attending less to the reality of Lawrence than to partisan and egotistical considerations. In so far as it will be not Lawrence the artist that occupies attention, it will be as with Walt Whitman, a question of his revolutionary influence in modern civilisation. Because he much exceeds Whitman as an artist, Lawrence's influence or " message " will never rival his art in relative importance as Whitman's does; but for this generation at least the educational purpose to which Lawrence devoted himself is almost as important as his literary achievement. We have a need to see it in perspective, if only to clear the air so that he can be more fully appreciated as a poet-novelist.

There are excuses for the exposures and the eulogies of Lawrence by people who were stirred to hatred or love by him, but there is no excuse for and no reason why we should any longer tolerate the specious snobisme of those who say that " what Lawrence offers us is not a philosophy or an œuvre—a body of literary art—but an experience." The foregoing are the actual words of a recent pronouncement by Mr. F. R. Leavis, who, like Mr. T. S. Eliot, has something of a genius for saying the wrong thing more neatly than anybody else. This attitude towards Lawrence is scarcely negligible, since it resembles also that of Mr. Eliot. Let us get quite clear then, to begin with, that what Lawrence " offers us " primarily and permanently is a body of literary art, and also a genuine though rough-hewn philosophy. He also offers an experience that is peculiarly significant to his own generation, of course, but this he would never have done if he had been minus literary art and philosophy. He was not a sort of Oscar Wilde, a criminal whose crime made " an example " of some disturbing aspect of organised society, but whose actual achievement and influence as an artist was unimportant.

Lawrence did not flout social laws, and was more apt to favour co-operation with the social organism than to fight it, especially in sexual practice. Lawrence's chief offence, in the sphere of conduct, against society, that of taking an already married woman as a lover, has no exceptional significance to-day, and really affected him morally less than the woman. She had to leave a husband and children. We know enough about Lawrence to see that the openness and thoroughness of the deed, like the subsequent re-marriage, expressed his serious attitude to sexual relationships. This marriage lasted nineteen years, until Lawrence's death. Before it Lawrence's sexual experiences may have been intense, but were very limited in range. There was an inconclusive affair with the girl friend who was responsible for the first publication of his verse and then with a married woman. It is the occurrence in his externally unadventurous career of another married woman before Frieda Weekley, Baroness Richtofen, whom he married, that alone seems of some personal significance. We do find indeed without much searching an explanation in his partially arrested erotic development as a young man. His emotional attachment to his mother complicated his feelings towards other women, so that the growth of erotic love was dogged by shyness and hatred ; but he was a very attractive and intelligent young man, with a " fascinating " personality. While he was compelled by his complex emotions to keep generally free of women, it needed only the extra

by R. L. MÉGROZ

courage and experience of an already married woman who would be prepared to wreck her marriage to meet the fiery young man half-way before he retreated again. The invidious aspect of Lawrence's situation was his strong temperamental belief in monogamy. It should be remembered here that the English girl and young man of to-day are probably freer mentally and emotionally than before the upheaval of the European War, when a D. H. Lawrence was looking in vain for the erotic companionship he needed. Lawrence himself is probably the greatest individual influence during this period of some twenty years that has made for a saner and franker attitude towards monogamous sexuality.

A curious sidelight upon our social mentality is afforded by the diversity of the attacks which have been made upon Lawrence, at one extreme being the people with minds still carefully blinkered to avoid a direct perception of censored realities, and at the other the shallow purveyors of mixed ideas of " free-love " and amoral pleasure, who resent his sacrilegious seriousness and pain. The cowardice which is in both of these attitudes fights shy of Lawrence's ruthless insistence upon certain truths that seem particularly applicable to his own age, truths which of course include the primary importance of the monogamous basis of marriage. Even one of our younger critics, whose sympathetic antagonism to Lawrence comes from sharing something of Lawrence's earthy, " working-class " background, Mr. Clifford Bower-Shore, has been tempted to attack Lawrence for not being something that he, Mr. Bower-Shore, could more readily have approved. His chief resentment is interesting; it seems to be against the sport which Lawrence afforded to the smut-hounds. But one might as well decry Shelley for so often attacking the stupid cruelties of a society which had virtually exiled him, as to join the Yahoos in shouting down Lawrence because of his moments of angry bitterness against a society which some other ideal Lawrence might conceivably have ignored.

The Lawrence who concerns us could not be so stoically superior to the malice and the insults of other people. He was, after all, a student and lover of his fellows, and a poet whose mental and emotional power has rarely been equalled. The extreme impecuniosity as well as ostracism during the War, which he suffered after his marriage to a German divorcée, must have complicated his personal erotic problem, and it must also have caused him great mental distress as an artist. We have only to appreciate the power and beauty that is in *The Rainbow*, the novel which was suppressed in 1915 as obscene, to sympathise with the flashing anger and the recurring strain of bitterness in his generally serene, wise, humorous, and modest correspondence. This was only the first, though the most serious, of a series of set-backs which were accompanied by increased difficulty in selling his work to periodicals and finally to acts of stupid official persecution. But all the time the tide of his fame was flowing, and about three years after the War, first by American journals and then British, his work began to be reasonably paid for. This material improvement gave him a greater freedom to move about the world on his double quest of health and of a less effete atmosphere than that which prevailed, or to Lawrence seemed to prevail, in Europe and the United States after the War. Here, as ever in Lawrence's response to the external world, may be read or guessed a large subjective element, which he anticipates us in recognising. In a letter to Mrs. Carswell, for example, after complaining that Italy now leaves a rancid taste in his mouth, he adds that perhaps it is only his mouth and not Italy, which is probably as good a country to live in as anywhere. In so far as he did effectively criticise our top-heavy and mechanised civilisation, he was moved to it mainly by his own exceptional need for health and deep contact with the primitive sources of vitality. Besides the social criticism, among the fruits of his pilgrimage are his numerous descriptive essays and sketches, as well as the wide geographical range of scenic description in his fiction—prose which lives by values independent of sociology or religion.

Just as there are moments of petulance in some of Lawrence's criticism of people and of civilisation, so also in the central theme of the individual's sexual fulfilment there are times when the mature reader of his novels feels a sort of " provincialism " in the monotonous insistence upon obvious things. Against this charge of over-emphasis, especially of the almost mystical experience of the true sexual union, there is the reasonable retort first, that even sexually mature people may be too prone to take for granted what ought to remain wonderful, and that if Lawrence's criticism of modern society is in the main justified, comparatively few adults ever attain the deep and illuminating relationship that is possible in sexual union. There are reasons for supposing that the failure in our time has been predominantly male, as once it was female, and that the commonest psychological situation of the young men of the post-Victorian age resembles that of Lawrence in essentials.

The collected edition of Lawrence's *Letters* should correct any exaggerated impression either of bitterness or of sensual naïveté which parts of his work in prose and verse might produce in minds predisposed to a distorted view of this powerful temperament and undeniably great genius. Lawrence's confident consistency, as revealed in the hastily written letters, cannot escape the most careless reader. Let anyone re-read the things he writes about his own books, notably that letter about *Sons and Lovers* to Edward Garnett, from Italy, on November 14, 1912. There are also the painstaking and serious letters to friends about erotic difficulties, such as the one to Murry in 1913 (p. 157 of *Letters*), and that to Katherine Mansfield (p. 458) in 1918, and again that extraordinary letter on July 7, 1914, to " T. D. D." These three alone, with that one about *Sons and Lovers*, are enough to show how intellectually stable and self-critical Lawrence was, even about the themes which most deeply concerned and " inspired " him. The inspirational or dionysiac force expressed in Lawrence's work as a literary artist is exceptional, but of course it is just this creative tension induced by the two mental opposites of the controlling, rationalising intellect, and the deep, savage fury of the poet's subconscious demon, which places Lawrence among the great ones of our literature.

Nothing true has been said by any critical commentator about the symbolism and psychology of Lawrence's work which has not been more adequately stated by Lawrence himself. Perhaps the most remarkable of all these deliberate summaries of his intuitive vision is the " Foreword to *Sons and Lovers* " which he sent to Edward Garnett. Let the reader add to this, by way of a footnote to his philosophy of sex, which is fully stated in *Fantasia of the Unconscious*, what Lawrence said in a letter to Lady Ottoline Morrell (December 28, 1928):

" About Lady Chatterley—you mustn't think I advocate perpetual sex. Far from it. Nothing nauseates me more than promiscuous sex in and out of season. But I want, with *Lady Chatterley*, to make an adjustment in consciousness to the basic physical realities. . . . It's a question of conscious acceptance and adjustment —only that. God forbid that I should be taken as urging loose sex activity. There is a brief time for sex, and a long time when sex is out of place. But when it is out of place as an activity there still should be the large and quiet space in the consciousness where it lives quiescent."

The background to Lawrence's general ideas about sex reaches to the sources of European civilisation. The savage and pagan idea of sexual community was supplanted in the Christian era by that of lovingkindness, and the seasonal orgies of the old quasi-religious rites, the love-feasts and the mysteries, were more diffused and translated into expressions of human brotherhood than ever before. In other words, man became a little less animal, and marched still farther away from that primitive paradise in which the individual was not conscious of separateness. In doing so he also began to lose his implicit knowledge of reality. Theory became a substitute for that primitive mysticism. Mediæval Europe slowly acquired the new sense of kindness which no longer signified primarily sexual kinship, it expressed an idea of a higher intellectual level and potentiality, the common bond of all mankind with God the Father and therefore with each other as members of a family. Christianity had provided a new symbolism for the primitive union of the individual with the world. The old subterranean forces in the human soul remained potent throughout this reconstruction of human consciousness. Ardour of temperament merely added now a spiritual energy to the individual's motives, and the history of early Christian society and iconography clearly shows how readily sexual imagery became the fabric of private revelation and public altruism. The subconscious personality of the early Christian would, when it revealed itself in dreams, have seemed to him angelic. But the Pauline school was soon to transform the atmosphere of the Church. The all-powerful instinct at the base of this spiritual blossoming of love was soon to be identified with a nasty, dirty Devil seeking the damnation of souls. The ministers of God were gradually forced to be celibates; and before long priests in all ranks in the Christian Church, when they were not emasculated, had concubines instead of wives.

The psychological effect of the cult of the Cross (a male symbol) can be followed through the history of the convents and monasteries of the Middle Ages, those pitiable failures of the mistaken application of an ideal, which were before the Reformation to become a byword for sexual excess and degradation. Preceding this consummation there was a widespread repression of the sexual impulse as something unclean, which had nothing to do with any recorded teachings of Jesus of Nazareth, a repression which resulted in the average mind becoming the home of " the flesh and the Devil." The incomplete sublimation of the old primitive sexual orgy is illustrated by the well-known instance of the typical Hebrew temple song of prostitutes, " The Song of Songs." This utterance of unchecked passion was eagerly seized upon by the love-hungry inmates of the monasteries and convents and sung with religious fervour. The " Song of Songs " was a holy hymn; it had undergone a mystical transformation; the popular image of the Christ as a beardless youth, bridegroom of the Church, was fused into that of the lordly lover whose Beloved was the Church (i.e. its members).

The recorded dreams of the nuns reveal the same compensatory activity of the unconscious. Christ the Bridegroom of the Church became a veritable bridegroom in the aspirant's dreams. The transformation of the fleshly Devil into the Lord offered the repressed sexual impulse a means of subconscious expression. Sister Mechthilde, of Magdeburg, who saw Christ as a beautiful youth inviting her to the couch of love where she might " cool herself with him," was not exceptional. To the present day Sister Mechthildes have not become rare among pious women and girls educated in religious houses. Insistence on the agonies of the " Passion," " the precious blood," and " the sacred heart," represent a further phase of this religious eroticism, but tinged with sadism. These sublimating processes delayed, although they could not avert, the moral downfall of organised celibacy in the Middle Ages, and greatly assisted the mediæval task of the Church, which was to keep alive the flame of collective idealism in a disintegrating society.

Behind and preceding the psychological readjustment

brought about by Christianity in Europe was the great change to the patriarchal organisation of society from the primitive matriarchy, vestiges of which persisted into historical times among the pre-Islamic Arabs. Goddesses of fertility, such as the Syrian Astaroth, were Mother Goddesses representing the psychological remnant of the matriarchal and frequently polyandrous primitive society. In the splendid poetry of the pagan Arabs is often a poignant utterance of the male's erotic suffering which in essentials has an evident affinity with much European love poetry right up to our own day, right up to Lawrence. Gradually, in the most highly organised and civilised societies of Greece and Rome, the male gained almost complete ascendancy, with what consequence to morals any reader of their history knows. This overweening patriarchy was invaded by Christianity, which restored to women much of their lost power. But the priesthood of the Church was male, and sexual repression speedily induced a great fear of woman. The consequence of this was a belated return to patriarchal principles, reflected in the final choice of the Cross, now recognised as a male emblem, as the symbol of Christianity. Islam soon afterwards reflected the stronger vestigial remains of matriarchal sentiment by adopting the Crescent, or Cup, a female symbol, for its sign.

Subsequently the Christian Church met the still unsatisfied needs of many of its members by the additional mythology of the Virgin Mother, who is merely a finer version of the primitive Mother-Goddess. She completed a symbolically potent trinity of Father, Son, and Mother which inspired Lawrence, as it cannot fail to inspire any temperament resembling his, like a revelation of human reality. The long and fruitful conflict between Paganism and Christianity ever since the Middle Ages has been marked by the flux and reflux of patriarchal and matriarchal feelings. In one period the father—the " Lord and Master "—is predominant, and the resentment of the oppressed female grows. The next generation turns against the father, the son cleaving to the mother, the daughter tending either to an aversion to men or a contempt mixed with desire for them. In the succeeding period the predominating tendency is for the men to be betrayed or denied by the women, and this, by contrast with the over-rigid " Puritan " morality of the Patriarchal epoch, tends to the dissolution of moral standards, women being always instinctively destroyers of the man-constructed civilised society.

This very rough sketch of the psychological relations of individuals, families, and the community is true to essentials only, and would have to be modified by other factors where any particular epoch, such as Lawrence's and ours is described, but anybody can see that such historical psychology does define the perspective by which we can appreciate Lawrence. There is no need to go through his fiction, which is exceptionally autobiographical, to establish the now well-recognised crux of Lawrence's emotional situation. It is enough to know that Paul and Mrs. Morel in *Sons and Lovers* are his mother and himself, and to confirm the validity of the picture by Lawrence's early poems. And for the apprehension of the moral dissolution resulting from the uprising of dissatisfied women, one can turn again to Lawrence for the enduring expression and find in one variation on the theme—the conclusion of the poem on " Figs "— the utterance of an epoch:

. . . What then, good Lord! cry the women.
We have kept our secret long enough.
We are a ripe fig.
Let us burst into affirmation.

They forget, ripe figs won't keep.
Ripe figs won't keep.
Honey-white figs of the north, black figs with scarlet inside, of the south,
Ripe figs won't keep, won't keep in any clime.
What then, when women the world over have all bursten into self-assertion?
And bursten figs won't keep?

His poetry of sex and nature is another and more religious phase of the new mental world glimpsed in Whitman's *Leaves of Grass* and Carpenter's *Towards Democracy*. It is noteworthy perhaps that both of these men were exceptional as sexual beings, Carpenter in the direction of homosexuality, and Whitman in the narcissism of a sexual impulse which was strongly inspired by the common mother-complex. And Lawrence, in his personality and his work, is much nearer to Whitman than to Carpenter, although Carpenter's adoption of the Oriental doctrine of the universal self as the basis of a new social philosophy helped to prepare the English soil for a mystical artist like Lawrence. The noteworthy factor in these instances is that the influence emanating from the writer owes its energy to some excess in him of an emotional and perceptive tendency which is liable to be shared to some degree by a majority of his contemporaries. Lawrence was to an abnormal degree the male destined to dependence upon the woman, and to erotic suffering. There is a cruel truth in the cynical saying that in every union one partner is loved and the other does the loving. Lawrence's great psychic energy increased both his capacity for suffering and his resistance of destiny, and from this strong self-assertion came an occasional violence that usually took on the character of sadistic impulses, not as wild and perverse as Swinburne's, but as clearly marked as, for example, they are in his poem entitled " Seven Seals." The abnormal sexual excitation which his tuberculous constitution would have caused may be regarded as an additional irritant, strengthening the dependence upon the other sex, and probably driving him towards the very type of partner that he could not live with on equal terms of give and take. This very probable complication of his problem, which is not to be confused with the assertion that Lawrence was impotent or even a weakling, would explain his unnecessary insistence upon the adequate virility of certain male characters in his fiction, which stand for himself, like Rupert Birkin in *Women in Love*. Add to his great erotic needs a superfine nervous organisation and his immense capacity for feeling, and it is no wonder that among his other achievements he became one of the great poets of love.

The poignant personal aspect of Lawrence's erotic experience is most effectively conveyed in verse, where the central impulse is free from the secondary elaboration of characters and scenes belonging to the prose. Through the mouth of a character in *Glad Ghosts*, one of his short stories, he says: " My spirit is like a naked nerve on the air," and that violent phrase is terribly confirmed in the fearful beauty of his poetry. The poignant erotic feeling belongs partly to his *Birds, Beasts, and Flowers*—a group of poems introducing something unprecedented into English "nature" poetry—but more especially to the section of the *Collected Poems* entitled " Look! We Have Come Through! " Here is the

by R. L. MÉGROZ

erotic confession of an intensely creative and gentle man who is on the rack of primitive hungers, fears, and jealousies of sexual love. Here is the central part of the erotic testament which extends over so many tales and novels, and it leaves us a little awed by the poet's power of tearing the truth from his quivering self. If this poetry is seen in perspective, the comparable expression by Keats of his love for Fanny Brawne appears to be slight and fragmentary. And yet the only English poets who have exceeded Keats here are Shakespeare, Donne, D. G. and Christina Rossetti, and Swinburne. Is it wildly improbable that Lawrence as an erotic poet will in the future be placed next to Shakespeare?

To many readers of Lawrence's poetry the idea of his comparative greatness is still strange, chiefly because he so freely used "free verse" and the speech idioms of the age. In a letter to Edward Marsh, November 19, 1913 (as early as that), Lawrence wrote things about "scanning" English verse which some people still need to understand. Certainly many a reader who has approached Lawrence's verse wrongly is liable to the charge, "You are a bit of a policeman in poetry" which he launched at his correspondent.

> "It doesn't depend on the ear, particularly, but on the sensitive soul [he says]. And the ear gets a habit, and becomes master, when the ebbing and lifting emotion should be master, and the ear the transmitter. If your ear has got stiff and a bit mechanical, *don't* blame my poetry. That's why you like *Golden Journey to Samarcand*—it fits your habituated ear, and your feeling crouches subservient and a bit pathetic. 'It satisfies my ear,' you say. Well, I don't write for your ear. This is the constant war, I reckon, between new expression and the habituated, mechanical transmitters and receivers of the human constitution."

No question but that Lawrence is right in principle, although it remains true that he might have written more carefully for his own ear sometimes. Often in his verse, and sometimes in his prose, especially the novels up to, say, *The Lost Girl*—the novels which include the study of a locality with an industrial background—what he wrote triumphantly to Edward Garnett about *Sons and Lovers* describes just what he has often failed to do: " I tell you it has got form—*form*: haven't I made it patiently out of sweat as well as blood? ..." The sweat is often lacking, but not the blood. Much of his writing has the happy brilliance of a wonderful improvisation, so that perhaps any effective policing either of his style or the spontaneous uprush of his ideas might merely suppress what he has to give without improving anything. His ideas, which have used the terms of a diabolical mysticism antagonistic to Christian idealism, must have a liberating effect upon faith and a revolutionary influence upon our mechanised society. When his courageous sacrilege has been absorbed in a later ideology, this son of an English miner, who became the most powerful prophet of his age, will keep two high places in English literature, one in prose fiction, one in poetry, not lower than the positions held by Meredith, Hardy, and de La Mare. The smut-hounds will have other quarry before then.

SIR THOMAS LIPTON
1850-1932

By
WILLIAM BLACKWOOD

SIR THOMAS LIPTON

by WILLIAM BLACKWOOD

I

UP till the summer of 1930 four Scotsmen were wont to meet very frequently in an old-fashioned but immensely "comfortable" house in New Southgate. This is not a pretentious district of North London; had it ever been "fashionable" I doubt whether Sir Thomas Lipton would have bought the property. He once told me that he took over the place because it was within an easy carriage-ride of his London offices and because he felt sure that the ground would some day increase in value! Yet he came to love Osidge with the sort of love a married man generally gives to his wife. No matter how frequently he was called away from it on business trips or sporting adventures in different parts of the world, he heaved a sigh of relief on returning to the somewhat stuffy rooms and the rather unkempt gardens of his pleasant but by no means palatial suburban residence. And the old man's joy over his home-comings was made complete if he knew that the three guests at an early dinner-party would be Lord Dewar, Lord Inverforth, and Sir Harry Lauder. These three famous Scots were his most intimate friends and cronies. Another Scot was often asked to join the jovial dinner-parties—and that is how I came to get much of the information for the writing of *Leaves from the Lipton Logs*! But when that volume was published Sir Thomas Lipton was still alive. So much alive, in fact, that his literary collaborator had to tread very warily indeed in his attempts to present an absolutely authentic picture of the great merchant prince, international sportsman, and friend of Royalty as he really was during the last twenty years of his amazing life.

I always recall with a smile one evening and one incident

over the coffee at Osidge. The conversation had drifted to a discussion of how much the element of luck had to do with any particular man's success in life. Tom Dewar, one of the greatest personalities in the world of commerce—in this respect out-rivalling Lipton himself—and a man of wit, learning, shrewdness, and tremendous native ability, admitted quite frankly that he had had the luck to introduce Scotch whisky to the English public at the correct psychological moment, and soon found himself a millionaire in consequence. Harry Lauder, never given throughout his phenomenally successful career to underrating his own abilities by one jot or tittle, was equally willing to concede that he was fortunate to be coming to the front just at the time the gramophone was perfected and helping to carry his voice to the uttermost ends of the earth. What had Lipton to say about Luck? What set of circumstances had combined to help him as a young business man? What was his first fortunate " break "? Sir Thomas's answer was characteristic. " I never got help, or assistance, or a pennypiece from anybody," he growled, " and every Royalty in the world has dined with me on my beautiful yacht the *Erin*! " There was no further discussion about luck or good fortune that evening!

The little story illustrates an aspect of Sir Thomas Lipton's mental make-up which never failed to interest and puzzle me throughout all the years I knew him. That he must, as a young man, have possessed marked ability, goes without saying. That his ambition, commercial talents, and driving force were quite out of the ordinary his entire career demonstrated beyond cavil. That sagacity of an outstanding nature and a spirit of enterprise little short of colossal were thrown into the building up of his world-wide concerns was admitted by successive generations of British business men. That he achieved unbounded triumphs and vast wealth while still a very young man, and later in life a personal popularity unique on both sides of the Atlantic because of his yachting challenges and failures—all this is simple history. But never once did I hear Lipton give the slightest meed of praise or credit for his success in life to any man or any circumstance apart from himself, his own determination, his own courage, his own keen wits, his own alert, scheming brain. He had one pet phrase which he trotted out on each and every occasion when asked to indicate the

inspiration behind his prodigious triumphs as a merchant—
" My mother was my guiding star! " he would say, and, to
be just to him, he spoke the words with every symptom of
affection and veneration. But seeing that his old Irish
mother was frequently perturbed when she saw him blossoming out too strongly, as she thought, in the egg, butter, and
bacon business in the early Glasgow days, it is difficult to see
exactly how she guided her famous son to the unexampled
prosperity he ultimately achieved.

This is not being unkind to the memory of a truly remarkable man. All great men have had their failings, and
Lipton's chief failing was that he could never bring himself
to admit that any other man, or any fortuitous fact, had
played even the slightest part in assisting him up the ladder of
success. He was the most thorough and complete egotist I
have come across in a journalistic experience of almost forty
years. Occasionally, for the sheer amusement of seeing his
certain reaction to a given suggestion, I have urged him to
admit that at different times in his business life he must have
had the assistance of many brilliant associates and employees.
" I did everything myself! " he would sternly remark, and
brook no further encroachment on what was to him a distasteful and ridiculous proposition. Even in the company
of men like Lord Dewar and Lord Inverforth, both immeasurably Lipton's superiors from an intellectual point of view,
he had always to be top-dog. If either of them tried to
monopolise the conversation too long he would break in upon
it without the slightest hesitation and begin some story or
recount some experience richly to his own credit. He had
to occupy the centre of the stage always ; otherwise he
wasn't even faintly interested. I recollect picking up a
photograph in his den at Osidge shortly before he died
and pointing out that the three men in the picture had
all attained deserved prominence in life—himself, Lord
Camrose, and the late Lord Birkenhead. Sir Thomas took
the picture, glanced at it for a second and pitched it aside.
" Aye," he remarked, " that's true enough. But Birkenhead
didn't leave any money, and I can beat Lord Camrose's
boat every time we meet! "

That was the Lipton I knew. It may not have been the
Lipton of the days when he was starting a new shop every
week, of the time when he was competing with the great
canning and bacon kings of America on level terms, of the

years when he was selling more tea than any other man in the provision business, of the early years of his many *Shamrocks* and his intimate friendships with King Edward, Queen Alexandra, the Kaiser, the Empress Eugenie, and all the titled gentry of Europe. But it is pretty safe to assume that all through his long and perfectly astonishing life he must have displayed many of the characteristics which became so pronounced in his later years. In any event a brief survey of his romantic rise from poverty to riches, of his fierce struggles as a boy and a very young man, of his electrical energies when he realised that the ball of success was at his foot, may be found well worth reading in an age when hard work, self-reliance, and initiative do not appear to be the cardinal virtues in British business that once they were.

II

Thomas Johnstone Lipton was born in a tenement house in Crown Street, Glasgow, in the year 1850. His father and mother were two of the many thousands of Irish emigrants who were compelled to leave the Emerald Isle at the time of the great potato famine a few years previously. They couldr.'t afford to pay the fares to America, so crossed over to Scotland instead. Thomas Lipton, the father, worked at different jobs, and was known as an honest, "douce," religiously-inclined citizen ; his wife, from all accounts, was the real " head o' the hoose," and was primarily responsible for saving the few pounds which the couple ultimately invested in a small provision shop in close proximity to the house in which they lived. Altogether the Liptons had a family of five, four sons and one daughter. But with the exception of Tom, the youngest, they all died in infancy or in very early life. At one time it seemed that Tom himself would go the way of his sister and brothers, being rather weak as a child and having to attend the Eye Hospital for an infection seriously threatening his sight. But he grew out of the trouble and developed into an extraordinarily hardy and vigorous lad.

He started work as an errand-boy before he was ten years of age. His first pay was half-a-crown, out of which he got a penny to himself every Saturday. The messages he liked best to " deliver " were those which took him to the region of the Broomielaw and the vicinity of the ships moored there. For the water-side, the steamers, the cobbles, the little tugs, the warehouses with their merchandise from all over the world, he developed a boyish passion which never left him throughout his long life. At twelve years of age he left home to become a cabin-boy on one of the Burns steamers sailing between Glasgow and Dublin. He loved every minute afloat, and would probably have risen to be a Chief Steward had he not forgotten to clean one of the cabin oil-lamps the day a shore supervisor of the company took it into his head to make an inspection of the state-rooms. The boy was sacked on the spot. Fifty years later he was entertaining the head of the Burns Line on his yacht the *Erin*, and recalled the fact to Lord Inverclyde that he was a dismissed employee! With the pound or two he had saved from wages and tips he bought a steerage ticket to New York. The old s.s. *Devonia* took so long to cross the Atlantic that many of the passengers in the steerage quarters were certain the captain had lost his way or that the continent of America had disappeared into the ocean.

The very first thing Lipton did on arriving at New York was to secure lodgings free of charge. This he managed by quickly jumping off the gangway and making a bargain with one of the many lodging-house keepers who were on the quay touting for " guests " among the passengers. " What will you give me," he asked the most raucous-voiced of the gang, " if I get a dozen of the passengers to patronise your house ? " " Free board and bed for a month, my lad! " was the reply. Tom took " tough Mike McCauligan " at his word, hurried back on the steamer, and collected thirteen passengers with whom he had been friendly on the voyage and prevailed upon them to follow Mike to his cheap house in Washington Street ! This was the boy's first experience of " big business."

He had no more such lucky breaks during the two years he remained in America. Filling a variety of jobs in different parts of the Eastern States—he started by working on the tobacco plantations in Virginia, tried his hand at tram-driving in New Orleans, and finished up by being a grocer's assistant in the suburbs of New York—he became homesick at last and re-crossed the ocean to Glasgow. But in order that he should not have to confess failure to his mother he took her back a handsome present—a rocking-chair. He also hired a cab to convey him from the docks to the wee shop in Crown Street ; as he had hoped, a few of his old comrades saw his return under palpably flourishing circumstances and quickly spread the news that Tommy Lipton had made a fortune in America! Actually he started work in the tiny butter-and-egg shop of his parents the following Monday morning. Trade had been very bad during the boy's absence abroad, but it improved after his return, and there can be no doubt that the alterations he made in the premises themselves, the smarter way in which the window was dressed, the spirit of friendship and geniality he infused into his relationships with the customers, all tended to increase the weekly drawings. In a few months the Lipton family had over £100 in the bank. The old folks could scarcely get over the fact; the money represented wealth beyond their dreams. Tom wanted to use it for the opening of a larger shop. His father and mother simply wouldn't hear of it! Save it for a rainy day, they said. Not at all, argued the boy; invest it in selling more butter, more hams, many more eggs! The happy family were openly at loggerheads over the matter. Tom said nothing further when he realised that his parents were adamant. So he started to save his own wages. He felt sure his chance would come. It did.

One day he saw an advertisement in one of the evening papers about a quantity of sea-damaged American hams being sold off at the docks for what they would bring. He drew all the money he possessed out of the bank—£18—attended the "roup," bought the hams, and afterwards sold them to small shopkeepers all over Glasgow. His profits were in the region of 100 per cent. *Now* he could argue with his father and mother! *Now* he could show them that they would never become rich by sticking solely to the wee shop in Crown Street! They were converted. All the Lipton money was thrown into a common pool, and Tom started his famous shop in Stobcross Street, Glasgow. It was a great success from the moment it opened its doors. White paint, scrupulously clean windows and counters, the goods attractively displayed on cool slabs of imitation marble, the proprietor himself arrayed in a starched overall and exuding humour and courtesy to the customers—the place stood out like a beacon amongst all the drab stores of a rather drab neighbourhood. During the first week of his occupancy of the Stobcross Street shop Lipton traded more stuff over his counters than his father and mother sold in a month at Crown Street. In three weeks he had a couple of young assistants. The more youthful of these was so ragged that Tom bought him a cheap suit to smarten him up. Next day the boy failed to put in an appearance, and Lipton went round to his house to find out what had happened. "Oh," said the boy's mother, "Johnnie looked so respectable in his new suit that he got a better job this morning!"

In order to be early at the markets Lipton often slept on the premises. Food never troubled him. He could always boil one of his own eggs or fry a slice of his own bacon! Later he started going over to Ireland every week to buy supplies direct from the farmers and pig-breeders. In this way he saved the middlemen's profits, and was always sure of getting the best of everything at the cheapest prices. Moreover, he paid for all he got on the spot—ready-money, buying or selling, was one of his life's watchwords. The first time he went to Ireland he bought £4 worth of supplies. A few years later his firm's weekly cheques to Irish producers amounted to many thousands of pounds.

III

Lipton was one of the first men in Britain to realise the immense potentialities of advertising. He had brought home with him from America the memory of a placard which occupied a prominent place in the New York store in which he had been an assistant. It ran:

"*He who on his trade relies
Must either bust or advertise!*"

His first newspaper advertisement cost him 7s. 6d. It set forth to the housewives of Glasgow and district the benefit of shopping at "Lipton's Market," where the goods were "of superb quality, direct from the producer to the consumer, and offered at prices which simply couldn't be equalled in any other shop!" This "ad." paid for itself a hundred times. Probably it was the only advertisement of its type which had ever appeared in connection with eggs and bacon in a Glasgow paper up till that time! A weekly cartoon, drawn by a comic artist, and each sketch having some application to the goods sold in the shop, began to appear in Lipton's principal window. There was nothing particularly brilliant either in the idea or execution of the drawings, but they created a lot of comment and amusement among the type of people they were meant to attract; housewives stopped to laugh and remained to buy!

He conceived the original idea of buying the largest pigs in the Glasgow market and parading them through the streets, their fat sides bearing the stencilled announcement that they were about to die so that Lipton's customers should have the best "cuts" of bacon and the juiciest hams. Later in his career this processional idea was developed to include elephants pulling gigantic cheeses and parades of Cingalese and Indian natives advertising the aroma and cheapness of Lipton's teas—again "direct from the tea-garden to the teapot!" He chartered special steamers to bring his products from the ends of the earth to his stores in every city. For by this time his energies had spread to such an extent that there was a "Lipton Market" in practically every large town and city in the United Kingdom. The originator of this tremendous and ever-increasing organisation kept fully-employed staffs of estate-agents, architects, joiners, plumbers, and other tradesmen—he had even his own firm of solicitors doing nothing else but Lipton business. One thing he insisted upon doing himself, and that was to serve the first customer in every new store he opened. On three successive days he made what film stars call a "personal appearance" in Dundee, Newcastle, and Belfast! For weeks on end he spent three or four nights a week in trains or on steamboats.

Ireland was unable, long before this, to supply him with all the material he required. So he had agents in Denmark, Holland, and other European countries, and he started making frequent trips to the United States. Actually he founded an immense Lipton canning business in Chicago and Omaha during one of these visits, and he was wont to boast —a thing Lipton never hesitated to do all his life, even if his boasting was very simple and ingenuous—that he brought off one of the biggest wholesale orders ever known in the trade when he collared the Yukon supplies for the miners rushing there in their tens of thousands against the opposition of the Swifts, the Cudahys, and the Armours of that time. His freight cars ran on every mile of American and Canadian railways. And all the time the British business was forging ahead with such strides that his headquarters in Glasgow became too small to cope with the demands made upon it.

by WILLIAM BLACKWOOD

Characteristic of the Lipton "hustle" was the complete transference of the entire headquarter staff from the Clyde to City Road, London, in one memorable week-end!

IV

It was in the early London years that Thomas Johnstone Lipton first came to the notice of the Princess of Wales (afterwards Queen Alexandra of blessed memory) by assisting in the organisation of the greatest national dinner-party ever held in the world's history. This was to celebrate the Diamond Jubilee of Queen Victoria, and 400,000 poor people were entertained all over the Kingdom to a sumptuous repast free of all charge. Lipton contributed the sum of £25,000 to the cost, and was promptly elected to the Committee of Management. The feast was a colossal success. After it was all over Lipton persuaded the Princess to give her name to the Alexandra Trust, an institution he started and endowed for all time, and which had, and has, for its object the serving of good meals to the poor people of London at less than cost price. The Princess herself opened the Trust buildings. For Lipton she formed a sincere and deserved regard, and was one of his greatest friends up till the day of her death. The Prince of Wales (afterwards King Edward) likewise became on the most friendly terms with the merchant-prince. Thus from being merely a most successful business man Lipton blossomed out into a personal friend of Royalty. He was received everywhere, from Buckingham Palace downwards, and was duly knighted and baroneted, much to the delight of the British public, which seldom fails to applaud honours so thoroughly earned.

The story of Sir Thomas's attempts to win the famous America Cup with his successive *Shamrocks* is much too long to tell here; whole books have been devoted to the theme on both sides of the Atlantic. But, in a few sentences, here is the genesis of an altogether fascinating and romantic tale. Always fond of ships and of the sea, Lipton resolved, about the year 1898, to become possessed of a steam yacht on which he could entertain his Royal, aristocratic, and business friends. So the original and world-famous *Erin* was purchased. No yacht that ever sailed the seas saw so much entertaining on a lavish scale as did the *Erin*. Kings and Queens, Emperors and Empresses, Princes and Princesses, peers and commoners, sportsmen and commercial magnates of every nation entered their names in the yacht's visitors' book; in home waters and abroad the beautiful ship earned a reputation and a popularity unapproached by any craft afloat.

One day a friend suggested to Lipton that he should build a yacht to challenge for the America Cup. He liked the idea; it appealed to him on more grounds than one. It would be a fine thing to win the greatest sea-trophy known to yachtsmen—and it would keep the business name of Lipton well to the fore on two continents! So the first *Shamrock* was built. And the second—and the third—and the fourth! They were all beaten, as all the world knows. But Sir Thomas achieved undying fame as the gamest loser in history. The American people " went crazy " about him; for thirty years he was incomparably the most acclaimed Briton setting foot upon American soil. It is safe to assume that there will never be another individual who will make four separate and distinct challenges for the elusive America Cup. To begin with, no other man could stand up to four successive disappointments; and, to finish with, who nowadays could afford to spend half a million sterling on a series of sporting challenges in which the scales were so loaded against the challenger?

In connection with Sir Thomas's repeated America Cup challenges and his position as one of the leading yachtsmen in this country, it should be recalled that in his early racing days he was blackballed for membership of the exclusive and aristocratic Royal Yacht Squadron. It was said that King Edward himself proposed Lipton and was mortified exceedingly at the action of the Committee. However, many years later Lipton's name " went through " unanimously. And it is to the credit of the old man that never once did he enter the Club premises as a member. He treated his belated election with the disdain it called for !

Up till a few weeks before his death the old man was actually toying with the idea of still another " Cup " challenge. It was in his blood. It kept him alive, eager, determined, when physical frailties and failing brain-power must otherwise have taken him to the grave several years earlier. The last time I saw him, a few weeks before his death, he was smilingly assertive that he would " win that bloomin' mug! " before he cast off his moorings!

by WILLIAM BLACKWOOD

V

I have already indicated that Lipton was an extraordinarily complex character. I think I knew him as intimately as most of his friends now living can have known him. But even Lord Dewar and Lord Inverforth, his two most faithful and constant companions, Mr. John Westwood, his tried and confidential secretary for many long years, and Colonel Duncan Neil, his close friend and yachting mentor over three decades, have often confessed to me that they never seemed to reach the innermost recesses of the old man's heart. There was a "something" which none of them could quite fathom. The truth is that Lipton was vain, domineering, and immensely self-centred. He not infrequently referred to himself as "the Great Lipton!" Yet he was kindly in disposition nine-tenths of the time, could be affable to a degree, was generous often, and he had a simple, unassuming manner which won the sympathies, if not the real affection, of most men and all women with whom he came in contact.

He had little or no learning as the word is generally understood. Science, the arts, politics, history, invention, interested him not at all. I never heard him discuss intelligently the daily events of the hemispheres as they were reported in the newspapers. Try to draw him into a conversation on any one of the thousand topics the usual man takes delight in discussing, be it never so superficially, and Lipton would listen for a few moments. Then suddenly he would veer right away and come out with some completely inconsequential remark about himself, his business acumen, his yacht, or one or other of the Royal personages he had had the high honour of entertaining! Any prolonged talk which did not embrace "Sir Thomas," his amazing career, and his position as the world's most gallant sportsman was so much wasted breath in his company. Had I known him for fifty years instead of twenty I might have written differently of him. I would like that to be perfectly understood. He was in many, many respects an astonishing and singular man. It is inconceivable to me that there can ever be quite such another. Tom Lipton made his own standards in everything. His defects were, to a great extent, his peculiar qualities; he was frigidly unique in all that he did, said, and thought.

MARIE LLOYD
1870-1922

By
JAMES AGATE

MARIE LLOYD

by JAMES AGATE

LUNCHING some years ago at Mrs. Aria's I espied among the contents of her beautiful drawing-room a ridiculous, even a preposterous, little table—a rickety little thing about two feet square and which yet contrived to " let down " on both sides. Both its design and the gilt scroll-work adorning the legs betokened the late 'seventies, though the top had obviously been painted and varnished at a later date and according to the Japanese whimsey of the 'nineties. Eliza told me that she had bought the table in the street from a man coming away from the sale at which the effects of Marie Lloyd were disposed of. We spent an hour talking about the One and Only, and making my adieux I left the room casting a longing, lingering look at what had become, despite the Irving relics, its most treasurable possession. Next day one of Carter Paterson's vans stopped outside my house and disgorged this exquisite *objet d'art* with Mrs. Aria's card attached to its soundest leg. It is in front of me as I write, though I write not upon it, since it would hardly bear the strain of composition.

In an essay on another incomparable artist Mr. Maurice Baring has said that what she was like will be among the permanent guesses of mankind, and this is also true of Marie Lloyd. So long, of course, as there are people living who saw her and can communicate their recollections to each other, so long will Marie Lloyd still live, because there will still be a corporate sense of her. But the time will come when she will be a thing of the past, old dear—the old words but with a tragic difference. What, then, will remain? A few faded photographs and a few records stored away in the libraries of the gramophone companies. Presumably the day is at hand when one will be able to buy records and even films of great players as easily as one can buy copies of

Tom Jones and *Adam Bede*. But that day is not yet come, and in any case the demand for such records and films must first exist. What the eye does not see the heart cannot rejoice at, and I am persuaded that the public would only have to hear the old records of Marie Lloyd to want to buy them. It is not thought that there would be any demand for Marie, and therefore the opportunity to know whether this demand exists is not provided. Yet that there is a demand for the essence of Marie Lloyd is proved by the rapturous reception recently accorded to her three sisters and one daughter who, in an entertainment largely composed of Marie's old songs, contributed here a sketch for a facial resemblance, and there the hint of an intonation or flick of a gesture, the whole amounting to less than the shadow of a shade.

What, then, were Marie Lloyd's characteristics? What was she like? Our grandchildren will doubtless be told that she was a vulgar singer of indecent songs, whereby she will be confounded in the general mind with the big-bosomed, broad-buttocked, butcher-thighed Principal Boys who could look as Harriet Vernon looked but lacked her magnificent voice. Now, though Marie filled every corner of the stage, she was a little woman poised upon tiny, elegant feet. She was chic in the way that Réjane was chic. If Sans-Gêne was the mirror of an Empire, Marie was the looking-glass of the Promenade. Whatever she wore took on the gleam of white satin, though that which dazzled most was her smile, to which front teeth like those of a jovial horse gave an air of luxury in the Elizabethan, riotous, and best sense of the word. Was Marie Lloyd vulgar, and were her songs indecent? I can best answer by quoting something I wrote in *The Saturday Review* for October 14, 1922 :

> " When in the Tottenham Court Road, I saw, tucked under the newsboy's arm, the sheet which announced that Marie Lloyd was dead, everything around me became still. The street lost its hubbub, and for a space I was alone with a personal sorrow. In moments of emotion one is apt to notice the little things, and at once I remarked that, on the poster, the artist's name was prefaced with the word ' Miss.' Death, it seemed, laying his hand upon her who was known over the whole English-speaking world as ' Marie,' must use more

ceremony. 'Marie'—pronounced with the broad vowel beloved of the Cockney—was in everybody's mouth that day, in club and barrack-room, in bar-parlour and in modest home. On the high seas 'Marie's dead' would be droned from ship to ship. Returning from Kempton a party of bookmakers fell to speaking of the dead artist. One said, with tears in his eyes, 'She had a heart, had Marie!' 'The size of Waterloo Station,' another rejoined. Her abounding generosity was a commonplace of the profession. She would go down to Hoxton, where she was born, and make lavish distribution to the street-urchins of boots and shoes which she fitted with her own hands. She had numberless pensioners dependent upon her charity. She earned some two hundred thousand pounds, and gave it all away. 'God rest her,' said the bookmaker who had first spoken, and bared his head. That night, at Blackfriars Ring, a bruiser with the marks of many fights declared: 'We shan't none of us see the likes o' Marie again. She wur a great artist.' . . .

"From any cold-blooded, reasoned immorality her songs were entirely free. Flaubert, you remember, makes one of his characters conjure up the red lamp of a brothel with the reflection that of all life's experiences this youthful one has been the most truly happy. Marie Lloyd's honest spirit would have utterly disdained so pitiful a philosophy. The sailor of whom she sang might, as the result of an encounter in Piccadilly, miss his ship, but a mere incident would not turn him, like Flaubert's sentimental fellow, eternally adrift. There was no decadent Latin taint about Marie; she was almost saltily British. Villadom accepted her in the way it accepts the gay dog who makes no secret of his gaiety. Villadom will have nothing to do with the sad fellow whose pleasure is furtive, and it recognised that there was nothing sad or secret about its idol. Marie knew that the great English public will open its arms to vice, provided it is presented as a frolic. She knew, though she could not have put her knowledge into words, th. her art was one with the tradition of English letters, which has always envisaged the seamy side of life with gusto rather than with deprecation. Yvette Guilbert harrowed the soul with the pathos of her streetwalkers; Marie Lloyd had intense delight in her draggle-tails. She showed them in their splendour, not in their misery; the mopishness and squalor of their end were not for her. And that is why, when she came to the portrayal of elderly baggages, she refrained from showing them as pendants to her courtesans. A French artist would have insisted upon the inevitable descent to the procuress; the English artist rejected even Mother Peachum. Instead she gave happy life to battered harridans ludicrous in the sight of man, if not of God; diving into their very entrails for the unstilled riot which made old Jenny steal from her husband's bed to dance at the ball. Again she proved herself an infinitely greater realist than others more highly esteemed. She depicted the delight of humble life, the infinite joy of mean streets. When some jovial crone, emerging from the wings, flung at an unseen, routed foe a Parthian, ' And it wouldn't take me long, neither! ' you settled in your stall to listen to a reading from the Book of Low Life. There was unction here, and a smack of the lips over a Vulgate the accuracy of which, divined by the boxes, was eagerly confirmed by the gallery. Was Marie Lloyd vulgar? Undoubtedly. Vulgarity was her darling glory; she relished and expounded those things which she knew to be dear to the common heart.

" Marie's ' dial,' as the Cockney would put it, was the most expressive on the halls. She had beautiful hands and feet. She knew every board on the stage and every inch of every board. In short, she knew her business. But it is not my purpose to write now of technical excellence. Rather would I dwell on the fact that she was adored by the lowest classes, by the middle people, and by the swells. ' I hope,' she said in a little speech before the curtain at her last appearance at the Alhambra, ' I hope I may, *without bigotry*, allude to my past triumphs.' Poor soul, it is we who should ask to be delivered from that vice. Marie broadened life and showed it, not as a mean affair of refusal and restraint, but as a boon to be lustily enjoyed. She redeemed us from virtue too strait-laced, and her great heart cracked too soon."

Daughter of John and Matilda Wood, Marie was born at

by JAMES AGATE

Hackney on February 12, 1870, and had conferred upon her the names of Matilda Alice Victoria. Her father was a waiter at the Old Greek, and was commonly known as " Brushwood," from his habit of continually brushing his clothes. She used to declare that she had a narrow escape from becoming a school-teacher, and the mind boggles at what she might have taught! While still at school she produced with the aid of friends an entertainment of her own in the shape of " The Fairy Bell Minstrels." Marie's first professional appearance was on May 9, 1885, at the Eagle Music-hall, City Road, run by Mr. Thomas Broom, formerly mine host of a public house off Drury Lane. Here she appeared under the name of Bella Delmere, and sang two songs entitled " My Soldier Laddie " and " Time is Flying." She went sufficiently well to secure a return engagement, and when she reappeared at the same house on June 22, 1885, she was billed as Marie Lloyd. At the old Falstaff Music-hall, Old Street, E., she was spotted by George Belmont, who did so much to popularise the twice-nightly system at " Sunny Old Sads," as he used to call old Sadler's Wells, and the Sebright Music-hall, Hackney. " Barnum's Beauty," as Belmont christened himself, stated afterwards that he gave Marie Lloyd no fewer than eight engagements at salaries ranging from 50s. to £50 per week. It was at the Sebright that Marie appeared in February 1886. Shortly afterwards she was entertaining at the old Star, Bermondsey, which recently, after a period of picture shows, went back to variety. Her songs in these early days were " And the Leaves began to Fall," " Sure to Fetch Them," " Harry's a Soldier," and " She has a Sailor for a Lover."

Her work and success with the outlying London halls soon became known, and after an engagement at the Bedford Music-hall in Camden Town, she came nearer the West End, and appeared at the Middlesex in Drury Lane. It was at this hall that Marie Lloyd first became famous, and the town talked so much about her song, " The Boy that I Love sits up in the Gallery," that an engagement at the Oxford Music-hall followed, where she appeared for twelve months together. She was described on the bills as a serio-comic, and on August 6, 1887, a critic wrote of her : " She saucily told us that the good young men are not built that way now, and she found no one to dispute that dictum. Who, indeed, would have thought of contradicting so pleasant and vivacious a lady?" Of her dancing, the same critic said: "She gave a welcome specimen of her saltatory skill, for she is decidedly one of the cleverest step dancers on the stage. She was enthusiastically applauded."

Marie Lloyd had often appeared at the Middlesex in Drury Lane, and the story is told how, when Augustus Harris offered her the job of principal girl, she asked him, "Which theatre?" "The Lane," he replied, whereat she retorted that she had already played in the Lane. She pretended not to be thrilled at the prospect, but actually this was one of the proudest moments in her life. She played " The Princess All Fair " in " Humpty-Dumpty," produced on Boxing Day, 1891, and scored heavily with the number " Whacky Whacky Whack." In the same cast were Dan Leno, Herbert Campbell, and Little Tich. The following year she again appeared at Drury Lane, this time as Little Red Riding Hood in " Little Bo-Peep, Little Red Riding Hood, and Hop 'o My Thumb." Her quaint fun in this production was specially mentioned by the critics. Dan Leno, Little Tich, Herbert Campbell, and Ada Blanche were also in the cast. On Boxing Day, 1893, Marie Lloyd once more appeared at the Lane, in pantomime, this time as Polly Perkins in " Robinson Crusoe." A chronicler of the period refers to her as " dainty, arch, and exquisitely attractive in the pretty costumes, acting, dancing, singing— aye, and undressing too—without a word or an act which could bring the blush of shame to the cheek of consciousness, and yet piquant withal as the best pimento. Her songs are encored, and her Polly is adored." The principal artists were the same as in the previous years' pantomimes. Her salary at Drury Lane was now £100 a week. When Arthur Collins did " The Sins of Society " at the same theatre, he tried hard to persuade Marie Lloyd to play the music-hall heroine " opposite " Albert Chevalier, but she declined, as she had declined revue, declaring her conviction that variety was her job.

Marie Lloyd once appeared in revue; this was at the Tivoli, and was called " The Tivoli Revue." It was produced by Charles Raymond and Philip Yorke, the lyrics being by Roland Carse, and the music composed and arranged by Maurice Jacoby. Little Tich and George Gray were in the cast, and Marie appeared as Sarah Bernhardt and afterwards Marguerite Sappho, the prehistoric woman. Her very clever caricature of Sarah and excruciatingly funny performance as the Prehistoric Woman vastly amused George Robey, who elsewhere was depicting Prehistoric Man. Marie was promoted to the part of principal boy in 1898, when she played the title-rôle in " Dick Whittington " at the Crown, Peckham, one of the newly-built suburban theatres which have since gone over to the pictures. The pantomime ran for over two months. The following Christmas she also figured as principal boy at the Crown, playing Prince Heliotrope in " Cinderella," with her sister Alice as Cinders. That production also ran for two months. Marie appeared at other London and provincial theatres in pantomime, and in variety at every leading hall in the United Kingdom, America, South Africa, and Australia. In those old and palmy days, the three leading halls were the Oxford, London Pavilion, and Tivoli, known as the Syndicate Halls. Marie was booked there for months on end, her times being :

Oxford	9.40
Pavilion	10.10
Tivoli	10.35

Her admirers used to go from one hall to the other in order to enjoy over and over again a performance which was frequently identical. These houses were one-show-a-night-halls, and she used to fit in a suburban hall as well.

Marie Lloyd first appeared at the Palace, Shaftesbury Avenue, then under the management of the veteran Charles Morton, on December 26, 1897. Boxing Day was not a busy day with the ordinary Palace audience. For the most part this was made up of a fashionable after-dinner crowd, not found in the other halls in London, but on that night the building was probably more closely packed in every part than any other in town. The audience was largely composed of those who regarded Marie as the bright particular star in their amusement sky, all eager to welcome her back after her absence—and triumphs—in America, while others wanted to see the result of what they regarded as Mr. Morton's daring experiment. The wiseacres shook their heads ominously and prophesied failure. Marie, they declared, was not suited to a smart audience. She must tone down her songs, they declared, asking sagely what would then be left. But Marie was just as daring as ever, giving with redoubled gusto songs whose riskiness was accentuated by the spirit of gaiety and sophistication. Then came her imitators, and in shoals. So much so that prior to a provincial tour she delightedly published the following:

"Miss Lloyd, having no further use in town for her hats and sticks and sunshades, will be very pleased to give any original lady either or both of the above-mentioned articles (who are thinking of giving the public something new) on receipt of their addresses, as it will save them a lot of trouble and expense. Don't worry, girls. I am on tour, thinking out something fresh for you in my spare moments. It might be expensive, but it shall be original."

Eight years after her first stage appearance Marie went to Paris, and was received with greater acclamation than any English comédienne who had preceded her. When she returned to England she brought back a song entitled "The Naughty Continong." It was not often that Marie's sense of humour deserted her, but it did on the occasion of her French début. After she had sung her song there were ecstatic cries of "*Bis! Bis!*" "Take me back to England at once," she said. "Take me back to where they love me, away from these hateful people. I have done my best and they called me a beast!"

One of the proudest moments of her life was when she went to Germany and topped the bill over all the continental stars at the Winter Gardens, Berlin. She had the opportunity of studying the attitude of the Germans towards the English, and found that, while the ordinary people held the British in the highest regard, the Junkers were never tired of sneering at us. "I used to go about Friedrich Street," she said, "with my fists clenched at some of the remarks that were made. One day I overheard a burly officer with a scar on his cheek say something insulting about the British, and I promptly retaliated by giving him a blow in the face, accompanying the act with the remark 'There's one for the other side!' And then I went back home."

Marie's Australian trip at the beginning of 1901 was preceded by a banquet at the Tivoli Restaurant. Managerial and other admirers were present in great number, and glowing speeches were made in her honour. She was welcomed home the following November with a flourish of trumpets, special bills to announce her return being posted all over the town. At the Oxford Music-hall her reception was overpowering. She stood in the centre of the stage bowing and smiling, while the hall rang with tumultuous cheering. The reception was too much for the sensitive artist. Voice and memory both failed her, and in the middle of her song she broke down utterly. She tried again, and again broke down. " It's no good," she said, " I can't go on," and walked off the stage. Bouquets were handed up, and demands for a speech were made. Marie came on again with moist eyes, and was heard to say that she had come from a beautiful climate into the London fogs. " And if there is a cold going," she added, " your Marie is sure to catch it. I ought not to have come to-night, and I must get well before I appear again." Malicious people asserted that Marie was played out, but time proved them to be wrong, for she continued her triumphs shortly afterwards in a scene entitled " The Bond Street Tea-Walk," which became the rage.

When the Royal Performances in aid of the Variety Artists' Benevolent Fund were started at the Palace Theatre, the name of Marie Lloyd did not figure in the list, and she made no secret of her annoyance at the omission. The organisers were nervous as to whether a little of what you fancy does you good would be acceptable to the distinguished visitors.

Marie Lloyd took an active interest in the music-hall strike in 1907. Her house in King Henry's Road, N.W., was used as a meeting-place where the stars could air their grievances. But time was getting on, and so was Marie. She had always been fond of numbers about coster maids " coming over goosey " on the bridal morn and now the time was ripe for studies in later celebration. So we had the two songs by which she will probably be best remembered, the one entitled: " I'm One of the Ruins that Cromwell knocked abaht a Bit," and that one whose chorus ran:

> " *My old man*
> *Said ' Follow the van,*
> *Don't dilly-dally on the w'y! '*
> *Orf went the van*
> *With the old man in it;*

MARIE LLOYD

> *I walked behind*
> *With my old cock linnet.*
> *I dallied and dillied,*
> *Dillied and dallied,*
> *Lorst my w'y and don't know where to roam,*
> *'Cos you can't trust the speshuls like the old-time coppers,*
> *When you can't find your way home."*

Marie's fiftieth birthday was celebrated at the Bedford Music-hall, Camden Town, on February 12, 1920, and it was a night without parallel. Standing amidst great banks of flowers, she made a characteristic speech of thanks. She recalled that when she first appeared at the old Bedford her salary was the modest one of 15s. weekly. Though she had had her share of the hard knocks of life Providence had been good to her, and her earnest wish was that she might be spared a few years longer both to please the public and to do in private life what she could for the poor. Marie might well have claimed that if she had headed many a bill she had also footed many—a not inconsiderable number out of charity to her brother and sister artists who had fallen on hard times. To an interviewer she once said:

" I have no desire to brag—or, as the modern word is, swank—but I think I can justly say that no artist can claim more consistent popularity, and therefore I am very grateful to the public who have loyally supported me through all these years of strenuous starring. It is wonderful, by the way [she continued], how artists grow old by repute. People imagine that ' pros ' have a birthday every month. The other day an old man with long white whiskers tottered up to me and said— ' How well you wear! Why, my mother used to take me as a little boy to see you in pantomime at Drury Lane! ' ' Well,' I replied, ' then I must be wearing better than you do! ' On another occasion at a suburban hall an elderly man, with a grey beard down to his knees, asked, ' Do you remember me? ' ' No,' I replied. ' Oh,' he said, ' I used to be call-boy at the Bedford when you made your first appearance there.' Well [she went on], I have had a crowded hour of life—work and worry, sorrow and joy. People do not always get the credit for the good they do, and some get more than

by JAMES AGATE

they deserve. The wounded Tommies know what I do for them, and the gratitude which I know they feel is more to me than diadems and decorations. Personally, I feel as youthful as ever and can enjoy life with the best of them."

Marie Lloyd's house at Golders Green was the resort of celebrities of the profession, and many a merry gathering was held there. They called her house " The Flies," and its meaning was epitomised in an anthem set to the rhythm of " Where do Flies go in the Winter Time? " It ran thus:

" *They all go round to Marie Lloyd's*
 In the winter time,
And tickle a tune upon her tickolee.
 There's something nice
 Always on the ice,
And you never have to ask her twice
 For a drink of her kickolee.

" *Her front door is never known to lock,*
 It's always standing open, so you never have to knock.
Nobody knows what time it is, for the hands are off the clock
And we don't go home till morning
 At good old Marie Lloyd's."

Marie Lloyd figured occasionally on the films. Her last picture was for the Gaumont " Round the Town Weekly Budget," and the officials will never forget her visit to the studio. There was no lift, and she had to climb four flights of stairs to get to the scene of operations. Marie, who like Hamlet was then " fat and scant of breath," roundly abused everybody, declaring that it had " never taken her so long to reach the ' gods'." She invited all present to share a bottle of champagne which had providentially been provided for her, then dressed, sang her song " Round the Town " and gave a show as bright and amusing as if she had been facing her usual vast and admiring audience.

Marie Lloyd was three times married " with varying unhappiness." Her first marriage was with Percy Courtney, and was dissolved. She married Alec Hurley, the popular coster comedian, on October 27, 1906, and they went to America together the following year. Hurley died on November 30, 1913, at the age of forty-two. Marie was in

Chicago at the time, and expressed herself shocked at the news. Her third marriage was to Bernard Dillon, the jockey.

On October 7, 1922, the great comédienne passed away. She collapsed on the stage of the Edmonton Empire while singing her character song, "I'm One of the Ruins that Cromwell knocked abaht a Bit." When she swayed about on the stage in the song the audience thought she was realistically imitating a drunken woman; but actually she could have had little idea of what she was doing. She was buried at Fortune Green Cemetery, Hampstead, on October 12. The progress to her last resting-place was semi-royal. All the way from her home in Golders Green to the graveside the road was lined with a crowd so dense that police had to be summoned to keep the way clear, and so many crowded into the cemetery that the gates had to be closed an hour before the interment was timed to take place. The cortège was led by six large motor-cars heaped with floral tributes from leaders of the profession, jockeys, boxers, costermongers, stage hands, dressers, and all sorts of people high and low in the social scale. That morning Ellen Terry had herself taken to the house a laurel wreath of which the inscription ran: "In memory of a great artist. She gave lightness of heart to many a heart bowed down." Kate Carney, her contemporary, who is still with us, sent a wreath bearing the words, "A real white woman.—From her oldest friend." A floral horseshoe with whip, cap, and spurs inscribed "From her jockey pals" was signed by Steve Donoghue, B. Carslake, and other exponents of the "sport of kings." A spectacular touch was given to the cortège by Marie's own car following the hearse—empty except for the chauffeur, who had driven her to and from her engagements for so many years. The public filed past the open grave in their hundreds, showering flowers on one whose genius had so often taken them out of their drab and difficult lives.

J. P. Harrington, who had written so many of her songs, paid tribute to her in the following homely but sincere verses.

> "Marie, the final curtain's down, old friend,
> And in your ears has rung the last encore.
> Right in the limelight to the very end
> I see you standing. Now your part is o'er
> Eternity has claimed you evermore.

by JAMES AGATE

> "*Loyally will ten thousand lips attest*
> *The love and good deeds that cling round your name.*
> *Only your many pensioners know best*
> *Your generous heart. How, seeking no réclame,*
> *You gave by stealth and blushed to find it fame.*"

It was Marie Lloyd's boast that she was very, very lucky in the songs she got. She had not many failures, but she always said that there was a good deal of picking and choosing to be done. "You cannot say to yourself that you want a new song and just buy it." She spent a large amount every year on songs, and, of course, bought an immense number that she could not sing. "You may take it that one has to buy ten songs before one finds a really good one. A song," she said, "is often hit on by the merest accident." "Then you Wink the Other Eye" was said to have been suggested at a convivial gathering. George Le Brunn, sitting at the piano playing anything and everything, whispered to Marie about something that was going on. "Oh, wink the other eye, George," she said. He repeated the words to a kind of accompaniment—and thus was evolved one of Marie's biggest song successes. Marie was all in favour of keeping a song to herself and not publishing the number. Here are some of her successes.

"Oh! Jeremiah, don't you go to Sea."
"Never let a Chance go by."
"That was Before My Time."
"Don't Laugh!"
"How Dare you Come to London!"
"Poor Thing."
"What do you take Me for?"
"Actions Speak Louder than Words."
"Then you Wink the Other Eye."
"Oh! Mr. Porter."
"The Naughty Continong" ("You should go to France").
"Whacky, Whacky, Whack."
"Keep off the Grass."
"Twiggy Voo?"
"Among My Nick-Nacks."
"Johnny Jones."
"There They are, the Two of Them on Their Own."
"Salute My Bicycle."

"Hulloa! Hulloa!! Hulloa!!!"
"Everybody Wondered how He Knew."
"Clever, Ain't You?"
"The Coster's Christening."
"Everything in the Garden's Lovely."
"Folkestone for the Day."
"Garn Away."
"It's a Jolly Fine Game Played Slow."
"Rum-tiddley-um-tum-tay."
"Silly Fool."
"As if She Didn't Know."
"The Geisha Girl."
"Tiddley-om-pom."
"Tricky Little Trilby."
"The Wedding Bells were Ringing."
"You can't Stop a Girl."
"You're a Thing of the Past, Old Dear."
"Customs of the Country."
"Maid of London, Ere We Part."
"She'd Never had Her Ticket Punched Before."
"Millie."
"The Bond Street Tea-Walk."
"I'd Love to Live in Paris all the Time."
"A Little of What You Fancy does You Good."

Arthur Roberts was a great admirer of Marie Lloyd, and makes several references to her in his book *Thirty Years of Spoof*.

"As she was in her youth [he writes], so she was to the day of her death—the most improvidently generous woman I have ever met. She used to ask me to wait for her after the show to protect her from the sharks who were always hanging about the wings ready to seize her earnings. While she was on the stage—busily earning money for other people—she was the spirit of life and buoyancy. When she had thrown her last magic smile to the audience she would often totter to the wings. As an artist there is, of course, no limit by which one can gauge her répertoire. She could be everything and anything. She touched pitch, and it was immediately refined. If she sang about rags she made them into silk."

by JAMES AGATE

In his loyalty dear old Arthur is here talking nonsense. Marie never refined anything; what she did was to take a tiny segment of life, discover its true colour, and then raise it to its highest power of vividness. Where other artists in the same line needed an ell, Marie took only an inch. This, because she was a great enough actress to make an inch do an ell's job, and sufficient of an artist to know when the job had been done. Her powers of facial expression were extraordinary, and she had no need of words to tell you that she was a girl just up from the country whom all her dad's horses would never get back to the farm. Or that the streets were not what they used to be. Or that whatever the sport she would be game to the last. Through part of the 'eighties and all the 'nineties and nineteen-hundreds she was all that young men thought and Pitcher wrote.

To sum up, Marie within her range was one of the greatest artists who has ever stepped on the English stage, legitimate or otherwise, while on the boards of the music-hall she never had or ever could have any rival with the single exception of Vesta Tilley. Perhaps this is the place to dispel once and for all the popular notion that Sarah Bernhardt used to couple Marie Lloyd with Ellen Terry as the two greatest English actresses. This was another Marie Lloyd, a charming young actress who was awarded first prize for comedy at the Paris Conservatoire in the year in which Sarah was also a competitor. In her Memoirs, Sarah describes how, certain of the prize, she stood in the wings waiting to bound on to the stage when her name was called:

> " Premier prix de comédie. . . . Je fis un pas en avant, repoussant une grande jeune fille qui me dépassait de la tête. . . . Premier prix à l'unanimité: Mademoiselle Marie Lloyd! Et la grande jeune fille repoussée par moi s'élança, svelte et radieuse, sur la scène. Il y eut quelques protestations. Mais sa beauté, sa distinction, son charme timoré eurent raison de tout et de tous. Et Marie Lloyd fut acclamée. Elle passa près de moi et m'embrassa tendrement. Nous étions très liées. Et je l'aimais beaucoup; mais je la considérais comme une élève nulle. Je ne sais plus si elle avait eu une recompense l'année précédente, mais personne ne s'attendait à son prix. J'étais pétrifiée."

Not half so petrified as Marie would have been at the notion that " One of the Ruins Cromwell knocked abaht a Bit " could have meant anything to the Phèdre of all time.

How did Marie stand in relation, shall I say, to Yvette Guilbert? This is like asking whether Bernhardt or Duse stood higher?—a question said to be the authentic mark of futility in critics. " You cannot measure infinities against one another; any artist in whom genius rises as high as it has done in these two women partakes, in a sense, of infinity, for that genius admits you to states of feeling in which there is no less or more but only a sense of boundless release of heart and mind." If this be true, there is no need for comparison in any estimate of Marie Lloyd. She had genius, and it shall stand at that.

SIR EDWARD MARSHALL-HALL
1858-1927

By
RAGLAN SOMERSET

SIR EDWARD MARSHALL-HALL

by RAGLAN SOMERSET

IT is fair to describe Marshall-Hall as almost the last of the "bruisers" of the Bar. He and Sir Edward Carson were, so to speak, the storm before the calm. Just as Frank Benson and Henry Irving were to give way to men like George Alexander and Gerald du Maurier in the theatrical world, so the rough and tumble of the "bruisers" was to be superseded by the suaver but equally deadly methods of Sir Rufus Isaacs and Sir John Simon. On a famous occasion Sir Edward remarked that it was his "duty to be vehement." He was, in fact, the Cashel Byron of his profession, and like both that lovable if imaginary character and the modern Carpentier, he was a great deal more than a "bruiser." He was a "bruiser" with a brain. He had a high sense of the dignity and public utility of his profession. "Barristers are public servants, and may be called upon, just as a doctor may be called upon, to operate on a man suffering from a loathsome complaint." The metaphor is unfortunate, because the complaint of the prisoner is too often the overwhelming evidence of his guilt. Unlike that public executioner who described himself as "a weeder in God's garden," Marshall-Hall did not believe, and indeed cannot have believed, in the justice of every cause he espoused. He is on surer ground when he writes to Sir John Simon that "a prisoner is entitled to be defended by Counsel and Counsel are entitled to be paid reasonable fees." He would have been on surer ground still had he quoted the considered judgment which Dr. Johnson delivered on this point in 1773. "A lawyer," said the Doctor, "has no business with the justice or injustice of his cause unless his client asks his opinion, and then he is bound to give it honestly." Sir Edward's clients were not interested in his opinion. What they wanted, paid for, and quite frequently obtained, by his skill and eloquence, was the verdict of the Jury. But to compare his ministrations with those of the doctor to his patients, is to ignore certain essential differences. As his admiring biographer more frankly observes, he would "stick at nothing to defend a client." "If it hadn't been for dear old Marshall I should never have forgiven such a thing," said Sir Douglas Hogg after a more than usually flagrant disregard of the etiquette of the profession.

"Gentlemen, God never gave her a chance, won't you?" I have selected this passage from one of his perorations, because it is perhaps the best illustration of his contempt for the rule which forbids an advocate to identify his own opinions with the cause of his client. It is indeed difficult, apart from its implied blasphemy, to imagine a more irregular, improper, or irrelevant appeal. Juries are not torn from their businesses and penned in an uncomfortable box in order to give prisoners a chance. That may or may not be the function of the Judge or Home Secretary upon conviction. Juries are empanelled to decide whether the Crown has succeeded or failed in making out its case against the prisoner. Had any juror responded to this appeal, despite his honest belief in the guilt of the prisoner, he would have been false to the oath which he had sworn on entering the box.

In appraising the success, however striking or continuous, of a great criminal advocate, there is one other fact that must be borne in mind. The lay public seldom realise how difficult it is to convict anybody of anything in this country. The British criminal is treated with more than a little of the reverence which is quite naturally accorded to the British pheasant. Readers of Conan Doyle's fresh and admirable romance, will remember the exploit of Etienne Gerard with the roosting pheasants of his English host. The horror of the house-party when the dead birds were brought in, is but a faint replica of the horror felt by the whole legal hierarchy of Judge, Counsel, and Jury, when the zeal of a policeman in attempting to extract an admission from a prisoner, is shown to have outrun his discretion. It is right and just that this should be so, and, in all probability, the knowledge that the whole trial will be conducted in a spirit of meticulous fairness, adds enormously to the assistance available to the police from the ordinary public. In other words, it is recognised that, until he has topped the last line of firs and is alone in the sky above the guns, the depredations and immunity of the cock pheasant must continue. But the Crown has an uphill task. From the moment he steps into the dock the dice are loaded in favour of the prisoner. With few exceptions the Jury are allowed to know nothing but good of the real character of the man they are trying. Automatically the latter becomes an object of sympathy. The effect of even the greatest forensic eloquence is not merely ephemeral but largely overrated. Countless are the old "lags" who owe their liberty to the faltering incompetence of some young advocate, who has been allowed to try his 'prentice hand on a very poor prisoner. "My Lord, I ask you to consider the extreme youth of my Counsel," was probably the cry of an old offender who never realised how narrowly he had escaped acquittal.

There were, of course, as there always will be, borderline cases in which the eloquence of Marshall-Hall just turned the scale in favour of the prisoner, but many of his verdicts could have been obtained by lesser men. "All that a man hath, will he not give for his skin?" It was only natural to make assurance doubly sure by briefing Marshall-Hall. It was part of his art to lend to even the most squalid case the air of a crusade, in which the forces of light and darkness were so nicely balanced that the issue, up to the last moment, was all in doubt. The audience were pleased—and flattered. His handsome presence and admirable address did the rest.

Even casual contact with the great differentiates a man from his fellows. A juror who had been addressed by Sir Edward, felt a little the distinction of one who has passed through the consulting-room of Lord Dawson of Penn or survived an over (at village cricket) from Mr. J. C. Squire. If there was a loophole the prisoner squeezed through, and in most criminal cases the loopholes are numerous. The above reflections, however, explain rather than belittle his success, and that only in ordinary cases. In those where the chances of acquittal or conviction were about equal he was supreme. That supremacy was due to a combination of qualities in which his pugilistic eloquence was the spectacular but not the dominant partner. To it contributed his industry, sympathy, and above all his adaptability, and, in order to appreciate these, the reader must turn to his life.

Edward Marshall-Hall was born at Brighton on September

16, 1858. His father was a well-known physician and his mother was famed for a beauty which he inherited. To both of them he was devoted. Much has been written by a later generation, in whom filial piety is not the most conspicuous virtue, of the stern Victorian parent. Dr. Hall must have been an exception, for his son was allowed to choose his own public school, was sent to the University, and even permitted the equivalent of a Grand Tour at his father's expense. We learn from his biographer, that, in his choice of Rugby, he was influenced by reading *Tom Brown's School Days*, and it is not too fantastic a guess that it was the wonderful description of the fight that attracted him most. Nor is it surprising, in a boy who was later to rejoice in open conflict with more than one of His Majesty's Judges, that his time at Rugby should have been marred and shortened by a feud with his house-master. Mr. Belloc has pertinently observed that in the armies of the Republic, with which he served, the lawyers suffered most. In them, as in a public school, good comradeship counts for much, but abstract justice tends to go to the wall. It needs but little imagination to picture the young Marshall-Hall smarting under some real or fancied grievance and reacting on the house as a whole. He was not the sort of boy to smart in silence. In addition, perhaps owing to the influence of an extremely devout mother, he had "got" religion. Those of us who had the privilege of reading Rupert Brooke's lost masterpiece on the *Soul of John Rump* will not forget that it was one amongst other duties of a house-master, to prepare the boys for Confirmation. Probably Mr. Lee Warner believed that Revivalism was all very well when not carried to excess, but that a Revivalist might be highly inconvenient if he had a temper impatient of lawful authority and was likely to be the next Captain of the House. At any rate, he persuaded Dr. Hall to remove his son on the score of indolence. Quite a number of famous men have found it possible to forgive their schoolmasters, but it must be more difficult when the decision of the latter has deprived them of the privilege of playing cricket for their school. In Mr. Lee Warner's favour it must be noted that Marshall-Hall, like many other men with original minds, found it difficult to learn other people's lines by heart, and was singularly inept at converting English poetry into that nice blend of plagiarism and doggerel which has been known to generations of future statesmen as Latin and Greek verse.

by RAGLAN SOMERSET

Leaving Rugby a year before his time Marshall-Hall definitely intended to take orders. He was then eighteen and, perhaps as a corrective, was sent by his father to a tea merchant's office in the City. He remained there a year and, still fully intending to enter the Church, was despatched to St. John's College, Cambridge, to study Law. While there he was crossed in love and left Cambridge for some years.

When the Benchers of the Inner Temple conferred the honour of membership upon the Archbishop of Canterbury, they were expressing a good deal more than the desire to be associated officially with another important department of national life. It was a recognition of the probable eminence the Primate would have won if he had been faithful to his first inclinations as a lawyer. Acting on similar lines, we can imagine either a Cathedral Chapter or the Royal College of Physicians co-opting Sir Edward as a sort of honorary member. For Marshall-Hall was for long within measurable distance of taking orders. His desire to do so survived both a trip to Australia and a year in the Quartier Latin. What it failed to survive was his engagement to the lady who had refused him two years before, and it was perhaps the greatest tragedy of his life that she relented. He became engaged and returned to Cambridge definitely pledged to the Law.

Now, this matter of his very real religious experience, combined with an emotional crisis, is one of the things which no biographer, however tender to the past, can omit. It goes a long way towards explaining his subsequent career. He was a man of strong family affection, witness his devotion to his parents and that charming letter to his month-old daughter who grew up, as many of us know, to be worthy of it. His first marriage was a failure, and during his early years of struggle that domestic background, which was the inspiration of so many rising men amongst his contemporaries, was wholly lacking. The triumphs of the day's work turned to ashes on his homeward way, and the first chapter in his married life, which closed in 1888, left him stricken and wounded. Professionally success had already arrived, but in that year we find him so out of love with it, that he is contemplating a colonial appointment, from which the advice of his friends alone dissuaded him. Perhaps even the happiness of his second marriage never quite made up for what he had suffered. The scars remained, and it was only his amazing strength of character and resilience which enabled him to make even a partial recovery.

Members of the Bar who have entered middle life and either failed or succeeded, are on one point unanimous. Their best memories are of those days when work began to come. "The docker" who has chosen not wisely but too well, from the row of wigs, which is all that a rigid etiquette vouchsafes to his gaze. The poor prisoner who has been assigned Counsel in order that justice may not merely be done but appear to be so. The white brief on the bare table that was not there the night before, the telegram from the unknown country client who has been impressed by some casual encounter in the police-court, and wants to know if Mr. X can take a case on Thursday for 3 and 1. All these are unforgettable, like the face of that solicitor whom a well-known Lord Chancellor met in the Strand and, from sheer force of habit, shook warmly by the hand on the strength of an isolated brief in very distant days.

In the beginning Marshall-Hall was favoured by his Brighton connection, but it did no more than give him a running start. The stall-fed junior is not an uncommon phenomenon to-day, but to attain the most modest measure of success, something more is necessary than the careful selection of near relatives on the more lucrative side of the profession.

Having got his start, he kept it by ability, industry, and force of character. In choosing Counsel solicitors are quite often obliged to pay some attention to the wishes of the lay client. He was the sort of man, it was recognised, who would fight a murder case from the swearing of the jury to the word "Amen."

Like that of many other members of the Bar, his first brief was in the Court of Chancery, which he seldom revisited. He appeared to consent to an application. With the exception of a brief "to watch on behalf of an interested party," whose interest extends to many days of vigilance and "refreshers," there are few more effortless and remunerative tasks. Soon afterwards he made the acquaintance of that great but very different advocate, Sir Charles Gill, for whom he "devilled" assiduously at Sessions. It is difficult to envisage two men more dissimilar in manner and method, but they had one gift in common, that of securing the admiration of their juniors. Amongst contemporaries there is a sort of Trade Union of hearts, we feel that we must all stand or fall together, but the good opinion of the young is harder to obtain.

His first important case was a charge of receiving stolen goods. It was "devilled" for Gill and resulted in an acquittal, which he modestly, and no doubt untruthfully, ascribed to a cricketing friend on the jury. Already he began to develop those qualities which later, though only for a time, clouded his career. He had his first breeze with the Judge, and was told to sit down. It was the first of many, and like all quarrels with one's schoolmaster, it did not pay.

At the end of his first year Sir Forrest Fulton invited him into his chambers, and a well-known jeweller, recognising his knowledge of precious stones, offered him the management of his shop. He accepted the invitation of Sir Forrest, and from that moment his lines were set; indeed, by 1885 his fee book contained the name of Lewis and Lewis. He was to practise for forty-three years, to know vicissitudes, due largely to his own faults of taste and temper, and to die in harness at the height of his powers. He was in Sir Forrest's chambers for two years, when he left for those of Mr. Bargrave Deane. Finally, at the age of thirty, he settled down in Temple Gardens. It was not, however, until 1894 that his name became universally celebrated by the defence of Marie Hermann, accused of murder, convicted of manslaughter, and sentenced, despite a strong recommendation to mercy, to six years' penal servitude. A leader in all but name, he was briefed on behalf of G. E. Brock, chief of staff to the notorious Jabez Balfour, and in 1898 he took silk.

It is a date important for other reasons. His criminal practice had hitherto enjoyed an advantage it was not to have again, for until then a prisoner, except in certain cases, was not a competent witness in his own defence. Strategically it was a position of great importance. If he had made a statement before the Magistrates after the statutory caution, it had long been, and still is, the custom of the fairest prosecutors to put it in as part of their case. The prisoner was thus enabled to get it before the jury, without being exposed to the buffets of cross-examination. Countless were the acquittals secured by an adroit, if not positively aggrieved, reference to the one witness whose lips were sealed. By the Criminal Evidence Act of 1898 they were unlocked in every case, and a new situation arose. In theory, of course, it was still for the prosecution to prove its case and the prisoner was entitled to hold his peace. Indeed, if he did so, the Crown was expressly prohibited from commenting on his silence, but this prohibition did not extend to the presiding Judge, who might very properly mention the fact that, where so much needed explanation, none had been afforded by the party principally concerned. The thirty-five years since the Act was passed have witnessed a great education in Juries. They are quick to appreciate a prisoner's preference for the greater freedom and less responsibility of the dock. Moreover, the Court of Criminal Appeal very reluctantly interferes with a conviction if the prisoner has not given evidence. On the whole, the change has made for the better administration of justice, and has not pressed too hardly on the defence. Even a poor witness is better than none at all, and where he is the only one and has been badly dinted in cross-examination, his advocate, unless a Law Officer is present in Court, has the privilege of the last word and an opportunity of rehabilitating his damaged client. Juries, also, are quick to resent the harrying of a stupid but well-meaning witness, even if he comes from the dock. In 1898, when Marshall-Hall took silk, the question of calling or not calling his client caused him considerable anxiety. In a matter of such importance he believed that the client should decide for himself, and it is safe to say that his views on this point have never been challenged. Except in rare cases of insanity or infanticide he would be a bold advocate who declined to allow his client to tell his own story to the Jury. But we are writing in 1933. In 1898 the employment of a client as a witness was an untried weapon to be used warily if at all, and in his first two capital cases as a Q.C. Marshall-Hall did not call the prisoner.

The retrospect of his life falls naturally into periods. We are dealing now with three years of what the Germans would call his "Blütezeit"—his flowering time. His domestic tragedy was over and his second marriage had begun. Those of us who had the privilege of knowing Lady Marshall-Hall can appreciate the devotion with which she endeavoured to make up for his unhappy past. His daughter had been born and he was a devoted father. He entered Parliament as Member for Southport, though like more than one Attorney-General, he discovered that his forensic gifts were ill appreciated by that assembly. It is rather pathetic to think of him returning to his wife, as she once told me, in the small hours of the morning and crying, " Somebody has got to hear this speech." Here if anywhere is the artist rebelling against frustration.

He encountered Horatio Bottomley, and established with him that formidable combination in which he was briefed for the publishers in a libel action while Bottomley conducted his own case as the defendant author, with all the latitude and much more than the skill of an ordinary lay client. He encountered Lord Birkenhead, himself one of the " bruiser " breed, and it is pleasing to read the great impression the two made on each other. And then quite suddenly out of a clear sky came the thunder-bolt. He was publicly rebuked by the Court of Appeal for his conduct of a case. Still worse, he was rebuked, though with less asperity, by *The Times*. Competent authorities, such as Lord Birkenhead and Lord Finlay, agree that the censure was far in excess of the merits of the case, but it was sufficient seriously to injure his practice. He lost his seat at Southport, and for nearly four years his high promise wilted in the frost of judicial disfavour. In no profession in the world is it harder to emerge from a cloud than at the Bar. He became known as the man " who always had a row with the Judge," and his income dropped from thousands to hundreds. Then very gradually he achieved the impossible. Cashel Byron had come back. It was not done in a day, but by 1908 the successful defence of Wood the artist, accused of the Camden Town murder, had done much to restore him to his former fame. It was the fashion at the time to disparage this victory as a foregone conclusion. It was nothing of the sort, and Wood himself, judging by the gratitude which he expressed, would have been the last person in the world so to regard it. And he certainly knew the difficulties of the case. From start to finish it was a ding-dong battle which went the whole twenty rounds, with Cashel Byron, at his boisterous best. Until almost the end of the summing up of Mr. Justice Grantham, the issue was still in doubt.

For Marshall-Hall himself it was the beginning of a new epoch. He had once again asserted his supremacy. The man who in 1888 had been ready to take a colonial appointment, had found himself again. From now on to the grave his merits in a certain class of case were to remain almost unchallenged. There were to be temporary set-backs, quarrels with Judges, great victories like the defence of Greenwood, splendid failures like the defence of Seddon, but in his own field and within his own limits there was no one to touch him. Gradually, with security and returning confidence, he began to soften.

From time to time there was more than a note of weariness. "I sincerely hope that this is the last capital trial I shall ever be engaged in," was his opening in the Seddon case. He was even, towards the close of his life, ready to renounce the joyous dust and comradeship of the arena for the loneliness of the Bench. But it was not to be, and he remained the man who could do one thing supremely well.

He had "specialised in the greatest gambles there are, life and death, freedom and imprisonment." "Facts not principles for me. I do not know much law, but I can learn what there is to be known about men and women."

In a portrait gallery like the present volume there is little space for any attempt to summarise his famous cases, as has been done elsewhere. Suffice it to say that throughout those last twenty years, he appeared in nearly every sensational criminal trial.

What he described as his greatest victory of all, the defence of Lawrence at Stafford, attracted little save local attention, but in the main he had a "good Press." Any case in which he appeared became almost automatically "news," whether it was that of Seddon the truculent murderer with his harsh North-country accent, or Greenwood, the faded, frightened little Welsh attorney, whom he successfully defended at Carmarthen. In the life of every man there comes a time when he begins to take up the winter quarters of the spirit. Through his later years Marshall-Hall remained as much an artist, in the defence of Madame Fahmy and the "Stella Maris" case, as he had been in his triumphs of forty years ago, before his temporary eclipse at the opening of the century. But he was a different Marshall-Hall, mellower, more certain of himself, and admired, not merely by his clients, but by his Judges. Only rarely did he bicker with his schoolmaster now, and when the end came, there were few finer tributes paid to his memory than that of his old friend and rival, Mr. Justice Avory.

It is a curious characteristic of the English that they like their specialist to be an all-round man. To this demand

Marshall-Hall conformed. He was an ardent cricketer and a first-rate shot, who from the very outset of his life had a passion for fire-arms. He knew, none better, the facets of precious stones, and was familiar with the sinister alchemy of poisons. Indeed, his medical knowledge, which was of the greatest assistance to him in his cases, was probably acquired early from his father. He spoke and wrote a fluent and very tolerable French, which in any Englishman is a rare accomplishment. He was the personal friend of Maître Labori, and it is interesting to speculate on his probable success had he been born on the other side of the Channel, where the trappings of emotional advocacy are better appreciated. There, as here, in a *crime passionel*, he would have had no equal. Above all, he loved and was loved by his friends, who included such interesting contrasts as Lord Reading, George Alexander, and Arthur Pinero.

At even this little distance from his death, his obvious faults of taste and temper are becoming blurred as non-essential, while the clear flame of the courage and kindness of the man shines brightly in the memory of those who knew him.

I remember one salient instance of the latter towards a friend of my own whom he was briefed to lead in the successful defence of a doctor accused of manslaughter. Sir Edward's brief was marked with a heavy fee, and as the two-thirds rule (which has since been modified) never did apply to criminal cases, my friend's remuneration was on a less splendid scale. Marshall-Hall insisted on the solicitor making a reduction in his own fee, by which the two-thirds proportion was maintained. He did so at a time when he was, unquestionably, the busiest criminal Leader of the Bar.

It is well that such things should not be forgotten.

To those who look back on his career it gives a little the impression of one of his own best speeches, polished and rounded off, ending, not merely stopping, when all the ground had been covered. One feels, as he often said, that the responsibility for the verdict must now rest on the great jury of his contemporaries; by these his errors will be condoned or forgotten, his lovable character and erratic brilliance remembered.

" *Thus men go,*
The dropped sword passes to another arm,
And different waters in the river flow."

The life of a barrister is, in its way, as someone has said, a continuation of his university. Term and vacation succeed each other with unnoticed speed and rhythm, and to those who know him, the time between a man's first " docker " at Quarter Sessions and his memorial Service in the Temple Church, seems short as a winter's day.

Marshall-Hall's practice waxed and waned and, achieving the impossible, waxed again, but all the time, whether in his professional life or in his eager leisure, he reminded his friends of an undergraduate, enjoying every minute of it, yet ready to " go down " and take his part elsewhere when it was over.

MARGARET McMILLAN
1860-1931

By
MARGARET G. BONDFIELD

MARGARET McMILLAN

by MARGARET G. BONDFIELD

MARGARET McMILLAN is in the line of succession to the great names of Robert Owen, Richard Oastler, and Lord Shaftesbury in pioneer work for children. It will be remembered that at the beginning of the Victorian era the children in the factories and mines were worked with a rigour which may well seem incredible. The first attempt at regulation was made by Dr. Percival, and embodied in "The Health and Morals of Apprentices Act," piloted through the House in 1802 by Sir Robert Peel; apprentices were not to work more than twelve hours a day; boys and girls to sleep apart and not more than two in a bed; apprentices to attend church once a month, and all factories to be whitewashed once a year ! This Act was a dead letter.

Robert Owen's Bill (1818) raised the age of employment of children to nine years, but as inspection was left to the Justices, this Act also was inoperative.

After a tremendous campaign by Richard Oastler, supported by Michael Sadler and Lord Shaftesbury, the Ten Hours Bill became the Factory Act of 1833—the first measure affecting children to be enforced, due to the fact that four Government inspectors were appointed with power to enter the mills. Even so, it had taken over twenty-five years to secure for the mill children a maximum working week of sixty-nine hours. The 1833 Act also decreed that the children should attend school. The employers attempted to dodge this provision by setting up schools within the works, with schoolmasters who could not read. Nevertheless, by 1840 the inspectors had been able to enforce a large measure of compliance.

In the next thirty years little was done to regulate half-time, until the passing of the Elementary Education Act of 1870, and the establishment of School Boards. In this brief outline of one hundred years of legislative effort to save the children, let Margaret McMillan's own words carry us up to date:

> "The Forster Bill [1870] decreed that, sooner or later, every child should learn the three Rs. Mr. Fisher's Bill [1918] decrees that every child shall, sooner or later, have nurture as well as teaching. Between the passage of these two Bills lie nearly fifty years of struggle and anguish, of brave effort—yes, and voiceless sacrifice. The movement that reached its climax in the Bill of 1918 quickened its pace in the nineties and passed its goal in 1907, when the medical inspection of school-children was made part of our school system. But the history of education is really the history of democracy, and as the people advanced slowly to social hope and faith, the level of their demands in education and nurture rose with the tide."[1]

Then comes a cry from the heart of one sorely tried. The clause in the 1918 Act empowering the Education Authorities to set up Nursery Schools was largely inoperative. Margaret shared the bitterness of Owen, Oastler, and Shaftesbury at the meagre result of these years of concentrated effort.

> "As for the movement, after meeting the blasts of the first after-war years, it was forgotten or brushed aside by more instant and urgent problems. After twenty years there are not two thousand children in British Nursery Schools."[2]

Margaret McMillan's work has shown us how to bridge the most costly gap of neglect in child nurture. Its place in our history is well set out by Albert Mansbridge, in his finely documented biography. The writer of this essay has discarded any attempt at a chronological account of her life and work, and has selected only such of her letters and writings as may serve to portray her vivid personality.

Margaret grew up in an environment of scholarship, culture, strong adventure, and great causes. Her birth coincided with the opening of the United States Civil War.

---

[1] *The Nursery School*, p. 5. [2] *Ibid.*, pp. vii, viii.

by MARGARET G. BONDFIELD

"It is a very happy life. Our parents are modern and American in their ideas of how we shall be brought up. They impose no needless restrictions on us, and do not overwhelm us with the Atlas of unreasoning and almighty authority—and yet we are not left to the mercy of impulse and riot of selfish instinct. It is managed, somehow, that we little ones, Elizabeth and I, believe that the world is a splendid place. There is war, of course. We know that. It only means that we sing: 'Tramp! Tramp! Tramp! The boys are marching!' and also 'John Brown's body,' and stamp with all our might. Rachel knows more, for she is a little older. She went to Port Schuyler once and saw wounded men. That made her wretched, so she was not allowed to go to Port Schuyler again."[1]

Margaret had the dramatic temperament and a fine appreciation of beauty in any form, and an immense power of concentration, in the sense of excluding everything which did not immediately bear upon her thought. To some extent she escaped the conventional restrictions of her age—not altogether, for she remembers the discomfort of "very uncomfortable clothes, tight bodies, whale-boned up the neck and squeezed in at the waist, long skirts, tight boots, pinned-on hats, and stiffly dressed hair."

Clothes became for Margaret a regrettable necessity, to be forgotten as soon as possible. So much so, that she was a constant anxiety to her friends. When her sister Rachel was with her, she would certainly emerge tidily fastened up, but in Rachel's absence, the duty of seeing that all her strings and buttons were fastened was distributed among her fellow-workers. Yet she had a fine perception of the garb most fitting for others, and concerning clothing for children, she was all enthusiasm tempered by common sense.

"We have to get things that will lift the children of the gods sheer out of the gutter. Soft greys stitched with mauves or red, hollands edged with blue or rose, hollands slashed with green and orange and scarlet, darker garments embroidered with blue for gala afternoons. No two garments are alike, and each appears to have something gay and brave about it. Yet the

[1] *Life of Rachel McMillan*, p. 10.

cut should be always smart; no suggestion of freakishness or dowdiness, and none of mere lapse into peasant forms all out of harmony with the New Spirit."[1]

Margaret McMillan's *mind* was never in tight clothes. She was well read in the literature of three languages, and before her crusade became clear even to herself, she had experienced the life of a roving adventurer. She started work as a finishing governess in 1879. She continued to teach and study until Rachel unexpectedly emerged, from the long apprenticeship of waiting upon a beloved invalid, into the world of affairs.

> "I was sitting in a garden at Les Grottes, Geneva, one September evening, when I got a letter from Rachel which puzzled me. It described an experience of which I had no understanding and which I had no power to interpret . . .—a swift realisation of life where she had thought there was vacancy. Watchful love, strange intelligence, a throbbing companionship near, invisible, with power to confer a joy beyond expression. Joy, great joy, an adventure such as love is, but a greater adventure, and a keener joy than human love confers."[2]

Rachel had become a Christian Socialist. She became friends with Dr. Glasse and John Gilray personally; with William Morris and Peter Kropotkin through their writings; and her spirit was eager to take her part in carrying the message of this new country of the mind and soul.

It seems clear that Rachel was the author and sustainer of the purpose to which Margaret gave form and life with such passionate energy and concentration.

In 1887 the sisters went to London, lived in a home for working girls, and made their first acquaintance with factory workers at a Club in Whitechapel. This attempt to strike a new trail failed utterly. The East End had apparently no use for Margaret at that time, so she became companion to Lady Meux, a post which she held for four years. In her *Life of Rachel McMillan*, Margaret gives a rollicking description of this experience—the mixture of the new life and the old—the astonishing Lady Meux, whom she calls

---

[1] *Nursery School*, pp. 46, 47.   [2] *Life of Rachel McMillan*, p. 25.

by MARGARET G. BONDFIELD

" Lady X "—with her erratic likes and dislikes—her attempt to train Margaret for the stage. One would like to quote extensively, but I must confine myself to her vivid portraits of two women—one who had forfeited her place in Society, and the other who had defied Society from the barricades. Louise Michel

> " had taken off her hat, and the shape of her head was anything but reassuring. Why, then, did her features, her eyes, her voice contradict its testimony? Her mild, dark eyes, full of pity and veiled fire, might have belonged to Francis d'Assisi, and she had the profile of Savonarola, but the head was alarmingly narrow at the top. Like that of another prominent anarchist, it had no arch, but ended like the unfinished roof of a building. The whole physiognomy, despite its expression of strange forms of pity, was unfinished. This profile made you dream, when you got over your first alarm, of the substructure of a new and fine humanity. All the same, it was not reassuring. The beholder felt himself exposed to all the storms and terrors of temperament by reason of the unfinished roof."

On the anniversary of the execution of Ferri, the anarchist, Margaret took Louise Michel to see Lady Meux, who was always hungry for new sensations.

> " Lady X came in almost at once. She was dressed in pinks and greys as in Whistler's picture, a dazzling vision. She carried an enormous bouquet of carnations. Louise was touched at once by the sight of these flowers. Lady X held it out to her. She accepted the bouquet with trembling lips. ' O Madame, je vous remercie de tout mon cœur,' she said, gazing at the flowers and then into Lady X's eyes. ' You have well known that it was the eighteenth of March and have given these to me in remembrance.' Lady X's emotion was also genuine but of another kind! "[1]

After Lady Meux came the Labour Church at Bradford. From Park Lane to Peckover Street was to Margaret a move

[1] *Life of Rachel McMillan*, pp. 62, 66.

from death into life. She found men and women wage-earners brimming with life, enthusiasm, hope, and good comradeship. And so began that work which has left an imperishable mark upon our social history.

Between 1838, when Lord Shaftesbury first visited Bradford, and 1873, when he again visited the town, conditions of child labour had greatly improved, but in 1894, when Margaret became a member of the Bradford School Board, she had found children suffering with adenoids, with curvature, and all kinds of illness due to neglect and dirt; half-timers who slept exhausted at their desks, in every stage of physical misery.

Her lectures at the Labour Church were on one theme with variations—child nurture; in season and out of season she stressed the importance of the social environment of the child. A young teacher of that time has told the writer of the profound impression made by Margaret upon her generation:

> "I can hear her now, saying, 'If you don't wash your hands before each meal the microbes will *fly* down your throat,' and see her with both her hands cupped to hold microbes going up to her mouth. 'Moses insisted on washing, not as a religious ceremony, but because he was a great social reformer. . . . At your public schools and universities the students eat together—*not charity*, but as part of their education. Why then should not the workers' children?' Deep breathing—attend to the children's tonsils—open windows. She attacked some of the Froebelian occupations (*lèse majesté* in the educational world of that day!)—*large* swinging movements for children in school, *not* small movements; *large* circles done with both hands—*big* writing—the importance of training in colour. 'A revolution need not be bloody. Every time a wheel turns round there has been a revolution, and if you will attend to these things, you'll find a revolution *has* taken place.'"

Over and over again she hammered upon this theme until her friends were both irritated and disturbed. She was a nuisance to the School Board and to all in authority. She worried her colleagues because she would not be interested in anything else; nevertheless, they loved her with a protective tenderness, and instinctively did homage to her genius though they could not understand it.

She was one of the early members of the Independent Labour Party and took part in the general lecturing work; but, whatever the object of the meeting, she would pass on to the theme of child nurture as alone worthy to absorb the energies of the Movement—the foundation to which all the properties of Nature, Science, Learning must give service as required for the raising of the house of the spirit of man. Never did she swerve from this. On Committees, when some important question concerning grown-up people——or States—or the world—was on the agenda, she would mutter, " But what a waste of time!" and she would straightway pour out her latest thoughts on child-nurture until called to order by the Chair.

Her absent-mindedness grew with her concentration, and at times it caused trouble. On visiting a prominent member of the Labour Church she was invited to admire the polished brass fender and candlesticks in the little house. Said Margaret dreamily, " Yes, but wouldn't it be better to spend the time polishing your mind? "

On one occasion she was due to speak at Doncaster. A week before the date a telegram arrived, " Lost train, wire if I must still come? " It was opened by the host, who knowing the date was wrong, thought no answer necessary. When the hostess returned, however, she prepared to go to the station. " But," said her husband, " I didn't wire, so she won't come." " Ah! " answered the wife, " you don't know Margaret as well as I do."

Margaret arrived, astonished to hear she was a week too soon. She spoke for ten minutes to a meeting of about thirty people, and she had to borrow to pay her fare back. The following week, when she was really due to come, the hall was crowded, and for an hour she carried them into a mystical heaven. She also insisted on returning the borrowed train fare!

Her nine years' work changed the whole attitude of the Bradford Education Authority. A group of Labour men and women were at first her only support, but in the end there was no section of political opinion that was not proud of the reform of its school-life.

Margaret's work was so poorly paid that after a few years at Bradford Rachel had gone back to London, in order to earn money for both. Then in 1902 came another imperative sign, and, as at Geneva, Rachel changed the venue of Margaret's life.

" For the first time I felt that she was going away from me, that she was not all mine any more. There are such withdrawals. They are not estrangements. They do not imply desertion, but are mysterious reminders that the soul does not belong to any of its earthly lovers, and has depths and powers that are never given to a friend. She was gathering up her powers to do her own work—a work in which she was to be no longer a mere helper—a power in the background. To others she might still appear to be only an ally, but to me henceforward she was no more an ally, but a leader." [1]

Although Margaret's life had been so deepened and enriched by the Bradford experience, this second emergence of Rachel was of such a compelling nature that Margaret unhesitatingly left her work in the north to join her sister.

" The break with Bradford could not be other than painful. . . . The wild adventure of 1893 had become, in 1902, no real adventure, but a very exhilarating and ever-renewed happiness. London had nothing to offer in exchange. A more chill atmosphere could not be encountered or imagined. . . . This did not explain or touch our isolation, complete subsidal into a *new* isolation, more chill than that of the years before we joined the Independent Labour Party. The great revolt of the women and the formation of the new Labour Party, not to mention the outbreak, later, of war —all these movements swung past us like storms. We did not know how absolute our isolation was to be in the long years to come, but we knew almost from the first that we were alone. We went on alone, and strange to say, never was our work so strenuous, never our path so straight and so clear as now, when the joy of comradeship was lost for ever." [2]

The first experiment under their own control was at Bow, and it was a failure. They moved over to Deptford. If

[1] *Life of Rachel McMillan*, p. 98. [2] *Ibid.*, p. 99.

by MARGARET G. BONDFIELD

they had had foreknowledge of the struggle that was to be theirs, probably even their great courage would have faltered, but by living a day at a time they surmounted every kind of obstacle. Money was given by Joseph Fels, whom Margaret describes as "small, like St. Paul; curious, like Nicodemus; impetuous, like St. Peter. Full of traits and eccentricities that estranged and bewildered, but consumed throughout all and above all by a burning thirst for righteousness."

After a desperate hunt, friends came to the rescue with the offer of a house—"Evelyn House." Then came the convincing experience of the clinic, convincing in the sense that it was not going down deep enough. At last came the Nursery School in the garden, declared by Dr. Kerr to be "the greatest single contribution to practical education in our time . . . the demonstration of the Nursery School as the requirement of every child of civilisation." That this demonstration had been made was due to the sacrificial devotion of Rachel McMillan and the brilliant genius of her sister Margaret.

Her book, *Labour and Childhood*, makes clear just exactly what is meant by Nursery School, and wherein it differs from the infant class of that day. It was written in 1907, while the country was still being thrilled by both joy and alarm at the rise of the Labour Party in Parliament. Margaret's experience of the workers' outlook in Bradford had filled her with hope that the rise of the new political party meant the quickening of concern for education of the right kind, and she is at great pains to explain what this education needs as its foundation. "Every difficulty that a teacher encounters begins and ends with the organism of the child. There is the power. There too is the defect or weakness."

Before the mind and spirit can have their chance the mechanism of the body must be perfectly adjusted. It is a power-instrument which must be self-controlled, and that control must be taught from the start of consciousness in the child. Any defect in the human organism must be corrected as the first step in education. Nature is to be handmaiden to this new order of life, especially in the form of a garden.

"Apparatus can be made by fools, but only God can make a tree. Trees offer, too, shelter in wet and in sultry weather. In spring and summer their stillness, their movement, their streaming beauty, have a strange kind of reassuring effect even on the youngest. In towns the plane-tree seems to be the best of all, its big leaves offering a real shade to temper the heat of summer days. Under them our toddlers and three-year-olds sleep safely on July afternoons."

From that opening she proceeds to examine all trees, the flowers, their perfume, the herb garden, the kitchen garden, the greenhouse, the effect of terraces—all these things are to be brought in and dedicated to the service of the child, to the strengthening of its little body, and to the ennobling of its mind.

Then follows a forecast of the effect upon all education of the new seven-year-old coming up from the Nursery School. This new seven-year-old is a kind of new coin of the realm. The elementary teacher's work will be changed by this sudden inrush of new life from below. A new order of child will have presented himself for education, and the "newness" will not leave intact or unchanged all the formulæ and methods of yesterday.

Her lecturing work had brought her into the circle of the Women's Co-operative Guild, an organisation of housewives who gave Margaret McMillan a welcome to their platform and Press. Under the superb leadership of Margaret Llewelyn Davies and Lilian Harris, this organisation campaigned for school clinics, maternity insurance, and for the establishment of maternity and child welfare centres under the local authority. To follow maternity centres, the Nursery School was accepted by this powerful organisation as the next rung of the educational ladder.

In the Guild and its leader Margaret McMillan found a movement of power which was encouraging and a gracious personality most comforting; letters to Margaret Llewelyn Davies, extending through a period of thirty years, which the writer has been privileged to see, reveal her gay, sad, tempestuous moods, her difficulties, and her developing vision.

" As for the praise you give me I can't allow you to misunderstand so. I have sacrificed little or nothing. What *had* I to sacrifice? To be a fuming, discontented governess, raging inwardly—or this. There wasn't much choice. Mine is a virtue-of-necessity life, and as I know little that I have not yet acted on, even this must soon come to an end." (November, 1898.)

Margaret Llewelyn Davies had dodged a Conference, and Margaret McMillan is very wroth:

" and as for deluges of talk—why no. The speeches, thank goodness, won't wind on in a stream. I heard only *one* speech at our Conference—and hardly anybody heard *my* paper—except a handful of School Board members. 'Did you hear the Poor Law Section?' said I to a comrade. 'No, thank God,' said he, 'I didn't.' Oh, well, you are very wrong. Besides, you are not well, so that I'm in a disagreeable frame of mind about you."

After the Conference, she writes again:

" On the whole, you haven't lost much in not coming —except of course the spectacle, which is very suggestive. Many women *are* doing good work in the world." (April, 1899.)
" I got the *Co-operator* and had the awful experience of reading my own words. . . . I don't know why I can't be honest in conversation. Still I am—*rather* honest, don't you think so? I'm going to Harrogate next week. It's very gay, and the Duchess of Devonshire and Ellen Terry are there, so I feel I really ought not to absent myself. I *did* admire your women. They are not at all like any working women I had ever met. They are full of intelligence and ready to receive the finest kind of teaching. I felt sorry I could not really carry them on." (August, 1899.)
" The Headmistress has had a *very* bad report from the H.M.I. I went to Sir R. Morant, and he sent down a very able young man of the new order who really said the opposite, and now the first report is to be withdrawn, but very silently, so I don't speak of the matter to anyone, as I want to make it easy for them to readjust their whole method of inspection in poor areas. . . . The Suffragettes say that if the Vote is

won all will be well with the children. But it doesn't follow *quite* so naturally, I think. . . . Twelve large clinics would do for London at present and save tens of thousands of children. If we were working every day we could treat two thousand children a year. One thing the new methods show, is that inspection was on quite wrong lines—the pace and seasons of development were ignored, so quite wrong conclusions were arrived at." (May, 1909.)

" As for the points against philanthropic treatment, in the first place it's just bungling. ' You too bungle! ' you may say. Quite so, but we know we have something to learn, and there isn't one of my staff that isn't studying, and watching all day, and *trying* to get a grip of a new situation. They have learnt something. One day both doctors were ill. I got in a highly qualified man—but it was chaos that day. The same with Nursie. *She* got ill, and we had four, I think—all helpless and highly qualified. . . . But the real point is, that we don't want to hand our children over body and soul to a profession—to let them out to people. If we appoint an Education Authority, we put it *in loco parentis*. They (the members) are not a profession, and that is why they are an authority. . . . O, and suffrage. Well, I hate militant action now. I never felt quite sure of it, but now I'm sure I'll never be a militant suffragette." (February, 1911.)

In common with all the progressive women of her time, she was in favour of extending the suffrage to women. It did not possess her mind, however, and even when, as a member of a deputation, she went to the House of Commons, while waiting in the Porch she was so absorbed in the picture made by an old lady whose beauty of dress and features she is able to describe in detail, that she is—surprisedly—knocked down and trampled upon!

On March 25, 1917, Rachel died. What that meant to Margaret, and how bravely she lived through the twelve years' separation, and how fire her victory over disappointment and desolation, no words other than her own could adequately convey. It seems more fitting to put the fragments together in a rough mosaic without the intrusion of comment.

by MARGARET G. BONDFIELD

"At present I am living in a kind of dream—not quite able to realise what has happened. My darling was failing for a year, but I didn't know there was anything serious the matter. She helped me and advised me to the end almost, and she died as she lived— a glorious, selfless woman; too full of ruth for others to have any fear for self. I find the future a terrible thing to face, the world empty, and all the things that sparkled with hope quite dead now." (May, 1917.)

"I sit alone here and feel that loneliness is not what it seems. The silence throbs with love and cheer expressed in new ways—that is all. Yet don't think it's all nothing to me. It was too dreadful—but I kept sane, because I was quite alone and *had* to. I think for two years I was nearly mad with remorse and sorrow— for I had left her alone so much and did not see or understand. O how *lovely* she was! How *tender*! Now I feel she wanted to serve and wants it *now*, but I *might* have taken more care of *her*! . . . The two Ministries—Health and Education—are meditating some change. The Local Authorities let the 1918 Bill lapse—Nursery School clause inoperative. I'd like to get the type of school that would help the young mother who is 'moithered' with young children."

Here follows a reference to the death of a friend, and the letter ends with:

"Soon I will go too—and nothing will there be *there* for tears. Eager I lived, and eager I'll die, and I'll lay me down with a will—but not yet. There's a noise yet—behind the ramparts. . . ." (December, 1927.)

"Still, in these ever-brightening days, those who had faith in and patience with us in the darkness, appear as gifts, mysterious, inexplicable, from some unknown power who gave them to us in the day of adversity. To live through such years is to win new faith and trust in a beneficence that outsoars the little dim circle of our sense perceptions. To live through them is to win faith in humanity too. Progress is not a triumphant riding on; it is a painful stumbling on. In all parties and classes there are some who are moving towards some great end. These transcend at critical moments all their more conscious and more personal strivings. They move as to some distant music, and obey some impulse from the Unseen. Only after many days or years can we divine whither they were tending, and what the goal is which others, following them, will attain. To be in that army is to succeed, even in failure and in death. For the purpose in its movement is Divine Will, and the rescue of all children seems to shine in its centre to-day like a new-found star."[1]

[1] *The Nursery School*, p. 139.

LORD MILNER
1854-1925

By
SIR EDWARD GRIGG

LORD MILNER

by SIR EDWARD GRIGG

NOT long ago, in a B.B.C. programme to which I was contributing, I found myself described as a representative of "the Milner school of Imperialism," and wondered what, in 1933, the words were intended to convey. During his lifetime the real Milner and the popular conception of Milner were irreconcilable things; and even to-day, eight years after his death, the same misunderstanding widely prevails.

Thucydides has said that the whole world is the tomb of famous men. Alfred Milner lies in Sussex, in the deep peace of the England which he loved more than self or any passing thing. But if high service gives those who render it a permanent resting-place in the minds of men, then Milner's tomb is the world of English law and speech; for no man ever served it with greater fervour or deeper faith. It was a reasoned faith. The wide expansion of English principles of government and ways of thought, he attributed to the creative force of race, and he saw in the strong cement of race the only power capable of holding the structure together and adapting it to new conditions without disrupture or collapse. His whole political philosophy was based on this conception of race, which was in his view the key to all progressive organisation in human life. To its instincts he traced the growth of the social and political fabric in its successive developments—the family, the village, the sept, the tribe, the nation, and finally the multi-national commonwealth into which the British Empire is being transformed. For the consolidation and maintenance of such an Empire, which seemed to him to transcend all merely national aims, the creative race must, he held, have faith in itself and loyalty to itself. Otherwise the lesser patriotisms must disrupt it, and the larger conception fail.

There was found among his papers when he died a fragment entitled "Key to my Position," which Lady Milner has printed with the popular edition of *Questions of the Hour*.[1] This forms his last contribution to the problems of his time. Many people in these days dismiss a belief in race as a crude and reactionary thing, savouring of ascendancy and vulgar thirst for power. It was not so to him. He believed in race because without its support he saw no hope of steady growth for the ideals of government which were, in his opinion, best for the world. Such a faith is not mere arrogance, any more than Christian belief is contempt and intolerance towards other creeds. It was to him far more spiritual than material both in origin and aim, touching the deepest chords from which human principles of association have grown.

> "It is not [he wrote] the soil of England, dear as it is to me, which is essential to arouse my patriotism, but the speech, the traditions, the spiritual heritage, the principles, the aspirations of the British race. They do not cease to be *mine* because they are transplanted—my horizon must widen, that is all. . . . It is only a question of time when the expansion of the race will compel a new juridical conception, that of a common citizenship of all the countries which that race inhabits or controls."

Here is his guiding principle of action—*follow the race.* "The British State must follow the race, must comprehend it, wherever it settles in appreciable numbers as an independent community."

The dangers of too narrow a partiotism are manifest enough in Europe at this hour. They are exclusiveness and intolerance—vices for which Milner had no patience. In his mind the mission of the race was not to itself alone ; it was to establish higher standards, wider opportunities, and a better life in everything that makes for character and happiness among all types and conditions of men. There was no Hitlerism in his political faith, no wish to exclude or exterminate the best in other strains. The mission of the Empire, as he saw it, was one of service rather than of dominance, though only through the strength of the creative race could that mission be performed. He realised,

---

[1] *Questions of the Hour*, by Viscount Milner, Nelson, price 2s.

none more clearly, that neither the French in Canada nor the Dutch in Africa could share an instinctive devotion to English speech, traditions, and ideas, and that their strain of nationalism must find expression within the Empire as well as ours, if the unity of the Empire is to be preserved. In this he was the heir of Durham, and for most of his life much ahead of normal thought in England on this aspect of Imperial growth. He knew, moreover, that in the Dominions even British nationalism is not English in sentiment, but Canadian, Australian, South African, and that each of these must pursue its own development—outside the Empire, if that development prove impossible within. He believed, however, that all these national strains would be the richer and the stronger in a single political system formed on British principles of government and cemented by its British elements, and that they would gradually develop a binding loyalty, not to Britain, but to the system as a whole.

" Il s'agit non de l'hégémonie anglaise dans le monde, mais de la fraternité anglaise dans le monde." [1] This passage from a French writer is quoted with approval in his diary near the end of his life. Thus partnership, not domination, was his dream; partnership embracing essential common interests, but knitted by spiritual as well as material ties; partnership cemented by the principles of law and government which had brought it into existence—cemented, above all, by the loyalty of its scattered British elements to each other and to certain fundamentally British ideals.

During his life the breadth of the faith which inspired him was little understood. This was due in part, no doubt, to his own characteristics, which always stood between him and the mass of the people which he devotedly served. But the main reason is to be found in one of those historical accidents which sometimes affect the whole course of a public career and make even a great man the plaything of forces beyond his control. Fortune ordained that the long struggle between Disraeli's half-formulated Imperialism and Gladstone's dogmatic Liberalism, with its insistence on the rights of little nations and its dread of expansionist policies as inimical to freedom and right, should culminate in the issue which, at the end of the century, brought the British

[1] *Trois Etudes de Littérature Anglaise*, by André Chevrillon.

Empire and the Boer Republics to war. The stage was South Africa, then the cynosure of all men's eyes; and on to that stage stepped Alfred Milner, the Liberal, as unknown to the general public as Cromer (another Liberal) had been when he began his great Egyptian career. Milner had played a strong though subordinate part in the Liberal-Unionist movement which brought a large section of Liberal opinion to the support of the Imperial idea; and he took the burden of an acknowledged crisis upon him as the choice of Salisbury and Chamberlain, supported by the Liberal Imperialists of the moment, Rosebery, Asquith, Haldane, and Grey, but profoundly suspect to the larger Gladstonian section of the Liberal Party which, in the early years of the twentieth century, secured its last great lease of political power. Thus it came about that in the critical years of the dying nineteenth century, followed so soon by a violent swing of English political opinion from right to left, he was taken by a large body of his countrymen to stand for an anti-liberal and reactionary interpretation of the mission of his race.

There is nothing harder to correct than a popular conception of any public figure, when once it has been formed; and Milner did not possess the public art of making himself understood. Mr. Lloyd George, who gathered his first impressions of Milner as a " pro-Boer " passionately opposed to the Milner policy in South Africa, has put on record somewhere his surprise on discovering the real Alfred Milner, who became his colleague in the darkest days of the European War. It is permissible to surmise that General Smuts, between whom and Milner as colleagues in the War Cabinet, a close friendship developed, felt the same astonishment on coming to know what Milner really was. He himself suffered, in the main, silently, though he was deeply wounded by the country's ingratitude for eight years of gruelling responsibility and unremitting toil, which he believed (and rightly) to have created a new and better South Africa, unattainable without the war. This is the lot which we almost invariably reserve for those who have done the highest constructive work for the Empire oversea. Milner was only one of a long line which have suffered in the same way, and he was content to leave a better judgment of his services to the care of history; for he had by then become a great public servant rather than a public man, and shunned public disputation over anything, but more particularly over anything personal to himself.

A widespread public instinct is never perhaps entirely wrong. It is true that Milner dwelt apart from the ways of ordinary men, and that he understood much better what it was desirable to do than how, in a democracy, to get it done. " Pitch your ideal sufficiently high from the outset; go for a big thing." These were his words to the people of Johannesburg at the end of the war. "Don't be content with shabby makeshifts or temporary expedients; don't be content with anything less than making this a model city—a city built for permanence, fully equipped with all the essentials of health, of comfort, and of culture, not only for the few, but for the great bulk of its inhabitants." He was nobly planned for dictatorship on these high lines; and a dictator he then was. This was the spirit of all his work; and the municipality of Johannesburg is only one of many achievements which have stood the test of time. He was for the end, and was often impatient about the means, as also of public opinion when he believed it wrong. A famous example may be found in the advice which he gave the House of Lords about throwing out the Budget of 1909. " If we believe a thing to be bad, and if we have a right to prevent it, it is our duty to try to prevent it and to damn the consequences." He seldom made phrases, but there was a ring in this challenge which startled its hearers and carried far.

Akin to this absolute way of thought was his strong indifference to atmosphere and his rooted abhorrence of pleasing at the cost of pretence. This quality had been strongly marked in his undergraduate days, and it never grew less marked for all his long experience of affairs. Oratory left him cold, and he regarded it in most of its political manifestations as the weapon of the demagogue. He himself preferred cold reason and a steady regard for the essential facts. Bernard Holland, in his biography[1] of the Duke of Devonshire, relates from personal memory an incident at Oxford in 1877 which brings out this trait. Gladstone, in the height of his glory, a giant refreshed with three years of at any rate simulated sleep, had come to address a dinner of the Palmerston Club. The grand old man, with the fervours of the Midlothian campaign aglow within him, had

[1] *Life of the Duke of Devonshire*, 1833–1908, by Bernard Holland, vol. i, p. 201.

thundered on the Eastern Question in that vein of exaltation which carried his oratory to its most solemn heights. A quiet young man rose to propose a vote of thanks, and observed, while the echoes of Gladstonian eloquence were still reverberating in the company's ears, that "there was another side to the Eastern Question which must not be forgotten—that of the interests of the British Empire." Struck by such boldness and lack of taste in a Liberal gathering, Mr. Holland enquired who the quiet young man might be. "Alfred Milner, of Balliol," he was told.

I owe to the present Warden of New College another typical incident of about the same time. Milner was sitting for the New College Fellowship examination, and found that the subject set for English essay was one of which he knew nothing. Other men might disguise their ignorance under a fine flow of words. Not Alfred Milner. He wrote on his paper the simple statement that since the subject was unfamiliar to him, his views upon it could not be of value to anyone; and walked out of the room. But he won the Fellowship, which he greatly needed, all the same.

This is no biography, but I must try at least to indicate the quality of this uncompromising young man's subsequent achievement from a thumbnail sketch of the turning-points in his career. How did he ever come to be appointed High Commissioner in South Africa, this crusader without influence or means? His father was a doctor of wide education and brilliant parts, who preferred sport to practice, and had ultimately to abandon medicine for a Readership in English Literature at Tübingen University. The affairs of this polished but rolling stone were always embarrassed, and Alfred had a broken education, first in Germany and then at King's College, London. His mother, Mary Ierne Ready, was a woman of great charm and character, but she died when he was fifteen. It was proof of signal ability that he won a Scholarship at Balliol with none of the long preparation which most such scholars receive. From that moment he went ahead. University distinctions fell to him in profusion. He spoke at the Union and became its President. His chief friend was Arnold Toynbee; his chief interest, like Toynbee's, the social and economic problems of the day. Another was George Parkin, a young Canadian from Nova Scotia, subsequently the first Secretary to the Rhodes Trust, then an undergraduate rather older than his English con-

by SIR EDWARD GRIGG

temporaries with the tradition of the United Empire Loyalists in his blood. Milner never had more than just enough money to live on, and kept a careful account of every penny that he spent. There was no place awaiting him in the world, no key to unlock the doors of opportunity and open a career but what he could forge for himself from his own character and brain.

In both these there was a powerful bent, which never changed. Wedded to an intense sincerity, there glowed through his whole being a passion for public service which burnt until his death with what Walter Pater calls " a hard, gem-like flame." It was public service as service that he pursued; for from the very outset no one was ever more indifferent to the trappings of place and power. In this he and his distinguished contemporary, Lord Curzon, a great public servant, too, were conspicuously different. Impelled by this passion for service, he began when Oxford was over by throwing himself into a combination of journalism and the law, hoping to make of both a stepping-stone towards the political and social work to which he ardently aspired. But at first he found it difficult to shape a definite course, and veered a good deal. Work at the *Pall Mall Gazette* under William Stead, work at the Bar, work with Arnold Toynbee in Whitechapel—so passed about two years. He lectures in Whitechapel on Socialism, and feels that he is dong no good. On December 2, 1881, his diary records his difficulties of mind. " Bar or no Bar? All that is best in me cries out for the second, and yet I have no courage to take the plunge." But on December 16 his mind is at last made up—poverty and public work, wherever they may lead. " Bar thrown overboard," he writes. " Off I go upon the wide ocean. . . . I have nothing to fear in a life the first condition of which is celibacy. I am a poor man, and must choose between public usefulness and private happiness. I choose the former, or rather I choose to strive for it." He never turned back.[1]

But he did not abandon the prospect of a House of Commons career as quickly as that of a legal one. In 1885 he stood as Liberal candidate for Harrow, and was defeated by a thousand votes. The experience seems to have convinced him that his road to service was not through the

---

[1] Most of these particulars, and the quotations from Lord Milner's early diaries, are taken from the first volume of *The Milner Papers*, edited by Cecil Headlam, Cassell, 1931.

market-place. His speeches were above the heads of his audience, and he felt his first horror of that from which he later consistently recoiled—party politics, the party frame of mind, the party game. Long afterwards, for instance, he recorded with amusement the fact that in that election he never once mentioned the name of Gladstone, though a reference to the G.O.M. was more potent than any argument in evoking a meeting's cheers. Milner indeed was marked out for an administrative rather than a political life, and his talents were such that the opportunity which he needed to prove himself was not long denied.

At first, however, his pathway kept him in politics, though he was not himself to pursue a political career. In 1884, while continuing to write for the *Pall Mall*, he began to do secretarial work for Mr. Goschen, who had at that time refused to enter Mr. Gladstone's Cabinet, and was maintaining an attitude of independent criticism. It was not long before Milner was launched with his chief upon the foundation of the Liberal-Unionist movement, his services to which Goschen's biographer declares it would be "impossible to over-estimate."[1]

By the end of 1886, Mr. Goschen's detachment from official Liberalism was complete, for he entered the House of Commons as Liberal-Unionist member for St. George's, Hanover Square, and Lord Salisbury's Government as Chancellor of the Exchequer, Randolph Churchill having, as the story goes, "forgotten Goschen" when he resigned that post himself. Thenceforth Milner took on official harness, and never laid it down till he retired from the High Commissionership of South Africa, nineteen years later, in March 1905. A wonderful nineteen years for one who had no claim but capacity to higher opportunities for public work—but by all who could judge of it his capacity was soon realised. He was official Private Secretary to Goschen as Chancellor till 1889, and was then appointed Under-Secretary in the Egyptian Ministry of Finance. Three years he spent under Cromer in Egypt—an invaluable apprenticeship, during the last six months of which he wrote *England in Egypt*, a book which profoundly influenced opinion during a critical decade in Imperial affairs—and then, by the end of 1892, he was back once more in London as Chairman of the Board of Inland Revenue. A late-comer

[1] *Life of Lord Goschen*, by the Hon. Arthur Elliot, vol. ii, p. 82.

to the Civil Service at the age of thirty-two, and head of a great Department by the age of thirty-eight!

"There is no case of the selection of a young and comparatively untried man for high and responsible work which has reflected more honour upon the insight and foresight of a Minister, and been more fruitful of advantage to the public service itself."[1] So Lord Oxford, five years later, with his customary rotundity of phrase. But Milner, though he was concerned in shaping the first Death Duties (an impost which he afterwards declared to have been grossly abused), was not altogether happy under English official routine. His occupation, he said, was "hard, important and boring," and always his instinct was for service in the wider imperial field. Even in the Oxford and Whitechapel days his mind had steadily ranged the seven seas. Egypt had given him the taste of high constructive work, and the romance of Africa had caught him, as so many before and since. The Board of Inland Revenue is not a temple of high imperial thought. But Milner laboured there with increasing authority till a January morning in 1897, when he was sent for by Mr. Chamberlain to the Colonial Office. First, he was offered the post of Parliamentary Under-Secretary of State for the Colonies. His aversion from political life held good, and he declined. Then (in secrecy, because the existing High Commissioner Lord Rosmead, had not yet resigned) he was offered the great South African office which he filled for the next eight years. Private Secretary with no official experience in 1886—High Commissioner at the most critical post in the Empire in 1897. The ironic gods, withholding the price they meant to exact, had answered his prayer for opportunities of service with open hands.

The *Milner Papers*, admirably edited by Mr. Cecil Headlam, have given historians all relevant material by which to judge the first phase of Milner's High Commissionership, which ended, after two years of anxious diplomacy, in war. Could Milner have prevented that issue, and was the cause, as he saw it, just? The cause, for him, was a life-and-death conflict between Krugerism and British principles of government, a struggle against a local system with strong affiliations in Europe for the mission of the British race. As to the trial of that cause by war, it has again and again

[1] *Milner Papers*, vol. i. p. 26.

been said that either greater subtlety and suppleness, or else wider human sympathy, might have prevented it. If by that it is meant that Milner could have prevented war without sacrificing British to Boer principles throughout South Africa, I do not believe it. Rhodes was the only man, after the collapse of the Carnarvon scheme twenty years before, to whom a chance was ever given of reconciling the Transvaal and Free State Boers to a co-operative union of the four South African territories under some form of progressive government. Probably even Rhodes would have failed. The Jameson Raid took place against his orders, but the mere fact that he had organised it and held it in reserve seems to show that he despaired. In any case, from the day on which the Raid was launched, Rhodes's influence with the Dutch was broken for ever, and all hopes of an accommodation between the sea-board Colonies and the inland States was gone, at least until the Boers had tried their strength and failed. If British action was responsible for the war (as, in part, I think it was), that action had been taken and that responsibility incurred a full two years before Milner landed at Cape Town.

Whatever the feeling in England, Milner at least went heavy-hearted, with many forebodings, into actual hostilities. No one knew better than he that, in the words used later by Lord Salisbury in Parliament, " the South African Republics had been accumulating for many years past military stores on an enormous scale, which, by their character, could only have been intended for use against Great Britain." No one realised more poignantly the unprepared state of our own defences in the Coast Colonies. " We have a bad time before us, and the Empire is about to support the greatest strain put upon it since the Mutiny." Thus his private diary, on the first day of war. Certainly not the mood of England on that day, which has lately been so vividly recalled by Mr. Noel Coward's *Cavalcade*. But he still had with him then the support of his best Liberal as well as his Conservative friends. Haldane, writing immediately after the outbreak of war, declared himself satisfied that Milner's policy was " the only possible way of two that completely diverge." Grey, who was frankly critical of part of Milner's diplomacy, wrote in the same vein. " In my opinion," he said, " the end has justified the view you have taken of the South African question from the beginning. . . . I still think the criticisms made in my last letter hold good, but they do not touch the main issue of whether we are right or wrong in this war, and of whether it could have been avoided or not." These were detached observers, free from the bias of responsibility in any form and well qualified to penetrate to the truth of the situation through the dust of claim and counter-claim, charge and counter-charge, ultimatum and final reply. Impartial history, when it comes to be written, is unlikely to take a different view.

When at last the war was ended, there dawned for Milner an opportunity for which no living man was better qualified. A mangled site, littered with charred and broken remains, awaited the new builder's hands. The machinery of government, of production, of transport, and of every form of social and educational service, had to be created and nursed into efficiency. In the Transvaal and the Free State the Boer régime had established none of the normal services of a progressive State. The mines were in ruins, agriculture derelict. Politically, economicaly, and socially this was a formless chaos from which order and the means of livelihood were somehow to be evolved. Men were lacking no less than resources of every kind, and Milner's first care was to call them in great numbers to his side. Chamberlain wisely gave him a free hand, and he chose them mainly young—partly because he wished for willing and open-minded adjutants, partly because he had instinctive faith in the vision and energy of youth. Prospero waved his wand, Ariels sped in all directions, and with marvellous speed a new world began to take form out of the void.

The first necessity of a Prospero in this hard world is revenue, and revenue in the Transvaal depended entirely on the production of gold. Native labour proved deficient, and for eighteen months a steady attempt was made to use the labour of ex-service men in place of natives at a labourer's wage. But the attempt broke down. Milner felt responsible for doing everything he could at high speed to repair the ravages of the war. Steady production in the mines was the *sine qua non*, and Chinese labour offered the only means of securing it without long and ruinous delay. Milner adopted it for that reason, not knowing where else to turn. It was supplied to the mines on condition of their contributing in full measure to the reconstruction of the territories. Milner insisted on this, and obtained it in full measure. The later campaign against him, with its scurrilous imputation of motives from which no man was ever more free, was disfiguring to English public life.

He was often derided for the number of experts that he employed; but these imported advisers, who were certainly multitudinous, laid the foundations of a new agriculture and stock industry, from which South Africa as a whole has derived really incalculable benefit. He pursued large plans of settlement. Many of his settlers were broken and removed after he left; but some survived and are now one of the soundest elements in the population.

In education his achievement was equally remarkable. He found an absolute blank; he left an efficient system much in advance of that enjoyed by many much older countries at that time. But it was in the framework of administration that his greatest triumphs were won. A Civil Service was brought into existence second to none, municipalities established, official relations between the four Territories infused with a new spirit of reasonable compromise. His Customs arrangements were violently denounced, but they were little altered when self-government came in; and his Inter-Colonial Council laid the first foundations of the union which was afterwards achieved. High standards in everything, and on the whole remarkably high results—that was the keynote of the epic of reconstruction which stood to his credit when he retired, only three years after the war. And in finance it was the same. In spite of the ravages of war, he left the Colonies financially sound. Amazing that so much was crowded into so short a time.

To self-government in the Transvaal and Free State, when granted by the new Liberal Government in 1906, he was opposed. Much was made of his opposition, attributed by his opponents to a general dislike of free government and a bureaucratic cast of mind; but this was unjust, for Milner had already agreed to the introduction of representative government as a preliminary to the grant of complete responsibility. The Lyttelton constitution, which was representative in character, was planned before he left; and he hoped that it might satisfy popular feeling for a transitional period, while his great administrative work was taking root and British principles of government were being strengthened by the settlement of British families on the land. Who can say that he was wrong?

The immediate grant of self-government undoubtedly made a deep and permanent impression upon the best of the Boer leaders—on Botha, for instance, and Smuts; but it involved some costly sacrifice of British influence to Dutch at a formative period when temporary tendencies leave permanent marks. That tilting of the balance, largely caused by English party politics, has done South Africa no good, and it has never been repaired. In his farewell Milner had said to his friends: " If you believe in me, defend my works when I am gone. . . . I care for that much more than I do for eulogy, or, indeed, for any personal reward." Much of his best work was, in fact, endangered by partizan administration even before Union was achieved; and it is fair to remember that the spade-work of Union was done, in the spirit of his policy, by the band of young men, known familiarly as his Kindergarten, which he left behind. But even so, some lack of balance remained. In the constitution of the Union, a special weightage was, for instance, given to the back-veld constituencies to bring them in, and Dutch racial extremism has in consequence borne bitter fruit that might otherwise never have been.

To appreciate Milner's views and feelings on this score it is necessary to remember that the two white races in South Africa have not that country to themselves, but share it with a black and coloured population which outnumbers them by four to one. This fact was never out of his mind, and doubled his conviction that, for the welfare of all races in South Africa, British influence must be strong. In that Dominion the native question underlies all the main problems of government—a danger which no other Dominion shares; and it is on the native question that the cruder side of white racialism is most to be feared. In his opinion the feeling predominant in South Africa on that question was wrong, and he trusted that, in time and of her own accord, South Africa would change her mind. That was the note in which he spoke of the question in his greatest farewell speech, delivered at Johannesburg not long before he sailed:

" You know I am, in the opinion of the vast majority of men in this room, a heretic about that, and I am an impenitent heretic. I believe as strongly as ever that we got off the right lines when we threw over Mr Rhodes's principle of ' equal rights for every civilised man.' At the same time, I am prepared to rely, for a return to what I believe to be the true path, upon a gradual change in opinion in this country itself. It is a South African question, and nothing could be worse in principle or more unfortunate in its results, than to attempt to influence the solution of it, even in a right direction, by external pressure."

Africa is gradually coming to the forefront of men's minds as the touchstone of racial relationships in their most searching form. Milner certainly doubted whether the native question in Africa would ever be wisely handled under a system of electoral politics on the European model, and, however that might be, was convinced that only British influence would make for a policy on liberal lines. He knew, moreover, that British influence, to be effective on that question, must not be an alien influence, dependent on imperial authority and therefore doomed to wane. None understood better how a white population in daily contact with a black one reacts against the most tactful of lectures from those old bugbears of the Briton oversea, Downing Street and Exeter Hall. " The true Imperialist," he said, " is also the best South African " ; the mission of the Empire in South Africa must be part of the South African nationalism with roots in South African soil. He strove therefore to lay the foundations of a South African State which should give fair expression to Dutch independence of character and pride of race without sacrifice of the essential principles of which he believed the Empire to stand. This was the key to his policy of setting British families on the land. It was also the reason why, in the matter of constitutional development, he wished to gain time. Only a blind partisan could still maintain that this was mere British racialism, offspring of a reactionary mind. South African history has already justified many of his fears; and a new spirit must dawn in South African life, if the statesmanship of that Dominion is to prove that, in spite of all that has happened, his arrested policy was wrong.

The years immediately following his return from South Africa Milner spent in retirement, but his energies never flagged. He lived in great simplicity, devoting himself partly to Lord Roberts's campaign for national service, partly to the cause of Protection and Imperial Preference, partly also to the study of English agricultural welfare, which he had much at heart. He also paid a private visit to Canada, and spoke there with his usual quiet cogency on the things in which he believed. A volume of his speeches, published in 1913, went rapidly through three editions; the preface, contributed by himself, contains a statement of his position which will always be a *locus classicus* for students of imperial affairs.

And then there opened with the Great War the second phase of his official life. He joined the War Cabinet under Lloyd George in 1916, and served as Lloyd George's colleague till his final retirement in 1921. We shall learn more of that period when the relevant volume of the *Milner Papers* sees the light. At present little is known of it, except that Lloyd George and Milner, with Henry Wilson's aid, achieved by their several qualities combined the leadership which saved the Empire in the worst months of the War, and that Milner, with characteristic decision, was the man who brought into being the unified Allied command. This was done on a March morning of 1918 at Doullens, while the German guns thundered near to Amiens, and the whole world, except the British line itself, wondered whether the British line was being finally overborne.

The last phase of his life brought him a happiness which he had not hitherto known, for it gave him marriage, which he had thrust from himself in youth, and the sense which he had always lacked of having a genuine home. The story of those few years is a peaceful one—much quiet activity with friends (and friendship meant much to him); his book on *Questions of the Hour*; steady work for the Rhodes Trust (being now the only living Trustee of those appointed by Rhodes); and in 1924 a private visit, after twenty years, to the old South African scenes. His last decision was the building of Rhodes House at Oxford, but his ideas for that were never fully worked out. He was turning them over in his mind and had committed nothing to paper when darkness fell upon him out of a clear sky. He came back from South Africa in full possession of all his great powers. Within what seemed a moment of time he was gone.

Matthew Arnold said of the poet Gray that " he never

spoke out." Of Milner too it can be said that he never found full and continuous outlet for his powers of mind and soul. He could express himself in action—that was his natural language; all other expression was with him laboured and incomplete. After South Africa he always felt himself to be marking time. The European War, which, like South Africa, called out all his strength of character and mind for its special ends, was to him an interlude. We had to win it; we did. But thereafter the Imperial movement once more lost steering way, and the doldrums returned.

> "The work of British Imperialists during my lifetime [he wrote] has been to hold the fort, to keep alive the sentiments which made against disruption, which delayed it, against the time when its insanity became apparent. Their business has been, and still is, to get over the dangerous interval during which Imperialism, which for long appealed only to the far-seeing few, should become the accepted faith of the whole nation. . . . It will be the happier fate of those who come after us to create that State, which it has been our duty to preserve for them the possibility of creating. What makes this result possible, what makes it, thank God, I believe inevitable, is the shrinkage of the world."

These were his last words on the theme to which, throughout his career, his inner soul was given.

In private life he had a rare combination of reserve, simplicity, and charm. The tall, spare figure, the finely moulded head, the broad brows and firmly chiselled mouth, the clear and kindly eyes, the quiet and musical voice—all these suggested strength, a calm surface over hidden fires. For eager youth he was a listener without peer, who never seemed un-interested in the crudest of youth's arguments and ideas. No doubt he felt that the future was hidden there. To subordinates he was a charming and quixotically loyal chief, and he kept their devotion all his life. His courtesy was unfailing, a natural expression of his mind, and his sense of humour was keen.

But underneath the external calm, under features which always seemed perfectly controlled, under a constant readiness to hear other points of view, under a great capacity for amusement with what seemed to him absurd, there burned intense convictions and the decisive spirit of a born leader of men. His temper was not easily kindled. He was much more likely to laugh or shrug than gird at accident and the perversity of things. But he hated incompetence and opposition as all good craftsmen hate slovenliness and interrupted work; and against any real challenge to his faith or his resolve, he would collect his forces inwards like a strong place calling a garrison to arms. Heat against such challenges I never saw him display; his resolution froze rather than flared; and across his quiet face there would fall a vizor of transparent but impenetrable steel. One felt that intense sincerity and conviction, even to passion, inspired him in all important action and all deep beliefs. It may be that the days are coming when, with but a few of the unforgiving years in hand, he could have proved himself an even greater man. He was not made for normal pot-and-kettle politics, nor for the trimming compromises which they not seldom entail; for he was by nature an autocrat, impatient of half-measures and indecisive men. There is none among the leaders of his generation whose place it is so hard to fill to-day. There is none, amongst them all, who lived and thought and worked for what he believed to be the right with a soul at whiter heat, above everything mean or passing or small.

GEORGE MOORE
1852-1933

By
HUMBERT WOLFE

GEORGE MOORE

by HUMBERT WOLFE

ON the whole for literary appreciation the third person singular is both more sober and suitable than the first. The insidious " I " creeps between the subject and the audience, and only too often one is left with a bad portrait of the essayist rather than a good one of the object of the essay. Nevertheless, it is difficult to write of George Moore thus objectively, at any rate for me—and that for two reasons. I knew him individually, or so it seemed to me, both as a writer and a man. It would, therefore, be mere pretence to assume a cool and general attitude of impassive judgment. I shall leave that to later critics, who read him with the other classics at a distance, and to the biographers of the future who write of him and explore him with a purely literary curiosity. For me he was and is George Moore, the writer of all others whose cadences fitted into the crook of my mind, and the man whose friendship was exceedingly dear to me.

I would begin, therefore, by describing him as I saw him first in the ground-floor room at 121 Ebury Street in the evening of his days. It was early evening, because he had not then written *The Story-Teller's Holiday* or *Aphrodite in Aulis*, and his lingering illness had not yet laid its contracting hand upon him. How I had come to know him is not to the purpose. It may well have been that he had been courteous enough to feign an interest in some article of mine, or he may have heard (though this on reflection seems unlikely) of a poem of mine called " Requiem," that, published about that time, had made a little stir. However it happened, I found myself on an afternoon of late spring at the large family table so breathlessly that I not only found myself drinking tea but positively eating plum-cake—an experience which improving acquaintance enabled me to avoid repeating.

The occasion was for me so memorable that it involves no effort in fiction to recall either my first view of George Moore or my first conversation with him. He was sitting, as always, in the Victorian armchair with its back to the window, and underneath the French portrait of him made in the middle 'nineties. When he rose, as I entered, I noticed the extreme inconsistency between his light-blue eyes and the rest of his person. His face, like his clothes, was untidy and in a sense careless, while his eyes, for all their apparent shallowness, had in them the essence of order. They were not unkindly, but they were oddly, and (to me) beautifully impersonal. They were highly perfected instruments of observation and record, the unresting servants of one of the most acquisitive brains that was ever known. They were always searching, they searched me instantly, not so much for " copy " as for material. I do not mean by that phrase that George Moore was not the best of companions, but only that, as his time was short, he was chiefly concerned with what his visitors could attribute to his store, either by evidences of character or by knowledge or wisdom. He settled back into his chair and bade me take the one opposite. The afternoon sunlight lay round his back like a heavy frame. As I see the corner now there were, as in a picture of the period that he loved, the sideboard on his left, a table in the window, and just visible at the right the plate with the cake on it. The subject of the portrait sat with his body in shadow, but his full face was bright with reflected light from a mirror. " Well, Humbold Wolfe," he said, " I'm glad that you had the time to come to see me. It's less and less people I'm seeing now. It's a choice between writing and talking, and it's little I have to say. It's my time for listening."

This might well have seemed a discouraging opening to acquaintance, but in fact George Moore belied himself. In the course of the first two hours I spent with him he developed his theory of the novel and the business of the novelist, to which he was to recur again and again in subsequent conversation. I may, I think, without knowing his foible have praised Robert Louis Stevenson as a master of the art of story-telling. " But," said George Moore, outraged, " he wasn't a story-teller at all. He had a pretty talent for an essay, and his wander-books have charm. But in the story he was a Gil Blas, perverted by Sydney Colvin. To tell a story you mustn't invent the incidents. You must liberate the characters into their own incident. Now the reason why *Heloise* is a perfect story is that nothing was or could be imposed upon the people of the tale. It had the ' melodic line '—a natural and tuneful continuity." " But," I ventured, " isn't *Kidnapped* all Davy Balfour and Alan Breck? I mean, the adventures didn't happen to them, they happened to the adventures." He looked at me with disapproval. " Beware of epigrams, Humbold Wolfe, bad or good: they're generally only a quick way of telling an untruth. No, then, these adventures are nobody's at all, except Robert Louis Stevenson's, and no novelist is entitled to have adventures at the expense of his characters. How would it have been if I'd invented a struggle between Jesus and a lion at the Coliseum in *Brook Kerith*? That would have been an adventure, but not His." " You invented the meeting with Paul at the monastery of the Essenes." " I did not. Jesus's own character invented it. He wove Paul and the conflict between Paul and Himself out of His bowels. The story-teller only listens to His characters and clears the difficulties out of their way." " But if Robert Louis isn't a story-teller, who is of the English?" " Why would there be any of the English to be a story-teller? Fielding made a great noise, but it was his drum beating and not the blood in the veins of them that he was there to have fair play for. Jane Austen was better, but you can't tell a story that's stone cold. Ann Brontë, it's true, almost told a story in *The Tenant of Wildfell Hall*. For she had heat, but she bungled it with making it be told at second-hand. Meredith lost his story in a quick-set hedge of words, and never jumped out again to get the two eyes of him back." " And Hardy." " Hardy," said George Moore, flaming, " I'll read you a piece out of *Tess*—the seduction piece. Lumps of cold pudding—it will show you." And he read it with disastrous enjoyment. " Well then," said I, " are there no English story-tellers?" " The like of Balzac or Theophile Gautier or even poor Flaubert—no—not for me. I brought the philosophical novel into English." " That's an odd epithet." " 'Tis mine and has its meaning. The tale that flows from the philosophy of a man's nature—that's the only tale that has the right to the name."

I learned, of course, later that many of the things that George Moore said required considerable modification if they were to be truly interpreted. He could never resist the temptation of startling the shopkeepers (if—in order to humour his refusal ever to admit French into an English text—I so translate " épater les bourgeois "). But allowing for exaggeration at our first meeting, George Moore had disclosed his theory of the novelist's art with extreme clarity. Later, it's true, he elaborated the fundamental conception by insisting on the importance of style. " Let's have no buckets," he would say. "You must write like a vase—elegant and shaped." The substance must be in the characters. The author could only permit himself to make smooth their path by beautifully formalising it.

If this theory is examined in the light of George Moore's practice, it will be seen that he not only illustrated but justified it. For in what lies his supremacy? For me it is in his unflinching and universal appetite for humanity. So far from the current view of his detachment for life being a just one, it is so paradoxical as to suggest that it could only result from deliberate enmity felt for the man. George Moore was interested—and almost equally interested—in every manifestation of life. He was incapable of sentimentalism, because all sentiment was alike to him. The death of a favourite wolf did not tear his heart—as the separation of " Karm " from his owner was alleged to have torn that owner's heart. That is to say, that George Moore did not need to explain that it tore the heart. He recorded the fact and left his character to display—as he did display—the appropriate and (therefore) the heartrending emotion. Or in a major issue, when Jesus in *The Brook Kerith* carried the ram-lamb across the hills of Palestine, he left it to the reader to draw the parallel of the universal shepherd bearing in His arms the lamb of sacrifice.

As far as is possible to man—and it is never wholly possible—George Moore never let his people be affected or guided by his prejudices to a set goal. As an instance of this, it is interesting to remember his discussions with me on *Aphrodite in Aulis* while he was writing it. The tale as it first occurred to him was to centre round the statue of Aphrodite and particularly round one part of her person. For he wished to call it (to my undisguised horror) " The Fair Rump of Aphrodite." He had in his mind from the beginning that a Greek reciter of Homer was to have a son destined to achieve in marble the enduring shape of beauty that his father had failed to overtake. But, as the telling of the tale

by HUMBERT WOLFE

progressed, it became clear that George Moore's hero and his two sons had their own ideas of how the tale was to flow. His hero at the very outset of his career as a rhapsodist came upon love at Aulis—whence the long ships sailed. Inevitably the story became one of family life—the business of ship-merchants, the details of the farm, and the upbringing of children. Aphrodite only came in when the sculptor-son, in despair of making a fitting statue for his architect brother's temple, saw two naked girls swim out of the sea from an eastern island and measure their beauties one against the other. Here was the centre of the tale—in a mixture of passion by a Midland sea and of beauty recaptured from it. The father's unsatisfied desire was doubly fulfilled in the lives and in the makings of his two sons. And when the finished temple stood on its hill, there was as much of human tears in the marble as there was of the spirit of Pheidias in the cold and noble line.

What was true of George Moore's last book is in varying degree true of them all. What has been superficially analysed as inhuman indifference to life is really a white-hot passion for the truth about humanity in complete control. George Moore saw the world and the people in it as an infinite, and to him consummately interesting, series of subjects. He was like little Lord Fauntleroy when he found the table loaded with toys in his grandfather's house. He was spell-bound by the unbelievable wealth and variety that some august providence had vouchsafed to him. But, though all life was given him to play with, he played with it as it desired and not as he wished. He did not try to make a toy train behave like a camel, nor seek to bowl a top and spin a hoop. He never preached and he never short-circuited his characters' emotions. He had, for example, many definite views on the proper position of women in society, of the relations which subsist between the sexes, on education, religion, art, and even on horse-racing. It would be no more possible to find these views in his novels than it would be possible to discover from Shakespeare's plays whether he was a lover of Belphœbe or a sympathiser with Essex. The book was the thing with the one, as the play with the other. Nor did he, like Dickens or Thackeray, illustrate in the comedy or tragedy of his characters some general view of love, hate, happiness, or despair. Each figure—as he or she advances on to the page—carries a private destiny, like a field-marshal's baton in the knapsack. It is true that Abelard's tragedy was dictated to George Moore by fact or legend. It is equally true, however, that exactly that tragedy inevitably happened to George Moore's *Abelard*, not because it was an event of the Middle Age, but because he wove it out of his own being, as a spider spins its web.

If it be considered that, as compared with Balzac, George Moore's field of observation was limited, and if the contention is accepted, this does not necessarily or at all impair his universality. Given the right hunger for experience, you can concentrate a whole lifetime in the back of a bronze mirror, as was the habit of some of the great Chinese craftsmen. For supreme greatness it is not necessary to indulge in scene-painting. Masterpieces can be painted on a small canvas. And yet, even while that criticism is apparently accepted, one's mind goes back to *Esther Waters*, *Celibate Lives*, *The Untilled Field*, *The Brook Kerith*, and *Heloise and Abelard*, and the mere titles convict one of error. Is it possible to count George Moore's scope as limited when it embraces, not only the life and sorrows of a maidservant and of a whole generation of Irishmen, but also of the Middle Age of France and of the Jerusalem of the Saviour. What side of life, one may justly ask, did George Moore avoid, from what did he shrink as beyond his compass or outside his interest? If it be the little things of the world, he was urgently concerned with the way of suckling a lamb deprived of its ewe, or of the way that a tame wolf reared with his paws, or a bull-dog might hold you in a soft rubbery grip. If it were the great things, did George Moore not face the renunciation of His own Cross by the Saviour, and the death of a nation in *The Untilled Field*? He did not, it is true, like Mr. Bernard Shaw, explore the social anatomy of his own times, nor like Mr. Wells make the future his washpot. But he denied himself nothing of the ardours, the complications, and the simplicities of life as it is lived, enjoyed, and suffered by men and women.

I shall say something in a moment of the suggestion that he was such a self-centred egoist that the only face he could ever see was that of George Moore, and that the only thing that ever interested or concerned him was his own impact on life and that on him. It was wholly untrue, and its untruth has served to stultify criticism of the writer. What is regarded as cold-blooded head-hunting is in fact the exact

by HUMBERT WOLFE

opposite. George Moore could write with complete absence of passion, because all the passion was left to his characters. It was not his life but theirs that was in question. His first and compelling duty was to eliminate George Moore, and in that to the limit of possibility he succeeded. When, for example, Dickens was dealing with Joe in *Bleak House* he was in fact indulging in an orgy of transmuted self-pity (as well as, it must be admitted, in a savage and wholly admirable contribution to social reform). The sweeping of the stone outside the slum grave-yard as the only tribute that the waif could pay to his dead benefactor is nauseating, not because it was not a pitiful or possible action, but because Dickens was weeping for himself throughout. The sentimentalism insists in the transfer of the author's false emotion to the character who should have been allowed to exploit his own real feeling. But when George Moore describes Joseph of Arimathea riding away from his beloved Jesus, whom he could not save from Himself, there is no trace of George Moore's personal sympathy or despair. Jesus is enfolded in the hills and makes His way alone to the monastery. Joseph turns, without gesture or emphasis, and rides away from Jesus and out of the book. His sorrow remains his own— and in consequence is everybody's sorrow in irrevocable parting with the beloved. It is the classic quality, the hardness which concedes nothing to the maker but everything to the thing made. It is, in short, the melodic line.

I have said that the view that George Moore was incapable of true feeling was in part generated by the censure of his character as a man. All his life he was pursued by this attack—an attack in part justified by his own reckless artistic integrity. When he wrote his confessions, either in his youth in *Confessions of a Young Man*, or in his late middle years in *Hail and Farewell*, he regarded himself as being as little amenable to outside dictation as any other subject of his pen. "This George Moore now," he would reflect, "how would he be if this or that event came his way?" As dispassionately and as zealously as when he justified Abelard's castration in his own character, so he permitted the imaginary George Moore of his creation to mould himself to events that he neither softened nor explained. Little did it matter to the artist that the man might and would appear culpable. He could only palliate or remove the offence at the cost of deadening the character. Well, he would not.

So too when he dealt with his friends and acquaintance he brought the same magnificent neutrality to bear. He did not hold up Edward Martyn to ridicule because he hated or loved him. He was not swayed by a personal vendetta in his damaging account of Yeats's feet. Nor did some obscure Sadism lead him to expose real or fancied intimacies with women. " What do they mean by being angered? " he would say with his eyes blazing. " That was how it had to be. It was life."

Just that. It was life, and George Moore held death off while he permitted it to unfold in its vigour with the natural impulse of a great flower stretching its petals in the motion of a pagan dancer leaning back. But still it is argued that even great art is no defence of breach of intimacy, nor does it justify the man even though it may explain the author. Upon this I would record a conversation I had with George Moore some two or three years ago. He had always a schoolboy interest in salacity, which I ascribed to a reaction against late Victorian prudery, that had long outlived its need. For my part I did not wholly share this whim, and George Moore was led to express doubts upon my manhood, saying that for his part, since he was reputed to have invented his love-affairs, like Swinburne and myself it might in later years be gravely misunderstood in this particular. Upon which I observed mildly that I had been asked to write a booklet upon him, and that I was much puzzled as to how I could represent his character. " You have bade me call it," I said, " not ' Portrait of George Moore ' but ' Portrait of a Man.' I do not know where or who the man is." " And how should you before you write him down? You know a few facts, let your George Moore make them possible."

That at any rate was enough as the lesson on art, but it did not suffice to quiet my doubts on the perfectly ordinary side. I wanted, if I could, to be given material to dispel the legend of selfishness and inordinate vanity that surrounded him. It wasn't of course easy to put. I couldn't, for example, say, " Were you really after all a cad, dear George Moore, or did you just pretend—or, what's more likely, did they quite simply misunderstand and misrepresent? " What in fact I did was to enquire, " What did you think of Susan Mitchell's

by HUMBERT WOLFE

book?" "Humbert," he said (by this time after five or six years he had got my Christian name right), "you're after asking something different, but I'll answer the question you asked. It was a George Moore that she knew, a little light with a woman's weakness for side issues—but yet it was no bad book." "A George Moore she knew, but was there then a George Moore who deserved so to be known?" "You've read my confessions, haven't you?" "And the account of the Lovers of Orelay, and of the white cat upon which a boy—called George Moore—set a pack of dogs. But I thought——" I paused. He waited. "What did you think?" "I didn't think," I said slowly, "I hoped." "And why wouldn't you?" he said amiably. And that was all the satisfaction that I had.

But suppose, I said to myself as I walked away along Ebury Street, the things they say about him were true, how true is truth? He was plainly a bad poet at the outset. For his published books show it—and a bad painter, though I've never seen a painting of his to prove it. But if a bad painter and a worse poet could live to write *The Brook*, mightn't a bad friend and a doubtful lover become as strikingly a contrast to his old self? It's true, I thought, that he relentlessly exposed the weaknesses of his lifelong friends, and terribly he must have hurt the women that he loved if they survived to read his tale. And still he rejoices in his schoolboy bursts of low humour, and will recite that strutting poem in French of a king walking among his women with a feather pinned to his tail. But mayn't that mean at worst that he spoke aloud what many thought (and did) but never dared to express for fear of self-vilification? Yes, and not only that. If we can and do love Boswell, Pepys, and Benvenuto Cellini in spite, perhaps because, of their self-exposure, are we to refuse a similar acknowledgment to a greater than any of them? If we ask ourselves why we do not turn from them in anger, isn't it because we find in them a clutch on honesty that the eminent notably lacked? The world of monuments is full of façades—statesmen who, reputed to die murmuring, "My country how I love thee!" really are asking for a meat-pie, and saintly bishops who died of drink. When we meet a man who says "I was such a one—with all my imperfections on my head. Well?" we cannot but feel a secret warmth. "There, by the Grace of God," we mutter to our secret hearts, "go I. God-speed!"

Nor only that. For if we patiently consider the confessions, and most of all *Hail and Farewell*, I thought, we are conscious of that most moving of all figures of legend—the feaster who for ever provides his own skeleton. Isn't it abundantly true that George Moore, in spite of his dazzling achievement, failed momentously, and half knew that he failed, in all that he held most dear? He wished to be a lover, happy in his love. What came of all his lovemaking, even if his own tale be credited? Fleeting rags caught in thornbushes all along his path. He had dreams of settling in some corner of France with some chosen woman that might play him some of the formal music that he loved. Or again, there was his lady of *Hail and Farewell*. Where is the lady of dreams, where Stella? Gone on the wind to leave him alone by his fireside in Ebury Street.

Then there were friends, and what of them? He lost them one by one, through his own fault, they'll say. I mused. And what of that? Would he have missed Edward Martyn less because he had estranged him against his own will, because his relentless literary honesty would not let him do other than he did? If he came into the strange and whispering world of Dublin high of heart and of purpose, was he less lonely at the end because he rejected himself before ever they rejected him?

And in that matter of the Dublin adventure, did he set out in a very different spirit from that which sent Byron to Missolonghi? He had not the great good fortune to die splendidly under a Greek sky for a losing and lost cause. He had, on the contrary, the disaster of seeing tragedy in terms of farce. But there is laughter that is more difficult to sustain than tears. Ask any lover whether a knife or a careless smile hurts more? And ask George Moore's shadow if he would not have shared failure in Ireland rather than return to barren victory in England?

Nor let us judge him as having made the Irish pilgrimage for a whim or a jest, however he may have represented it. He had known Paris in the days of the heroes, and the London of his early middle years had its figures. He turned his back on all that to take his share in the Renaissance of a people. Some cursed spite dogged this jesting Hamlet that would not let him be born to set things right but only to see them wrong. He lost his friends, his hopes, and he came face to face with the Catholic religion as an enemy that was finally to divide him from his brother. So that if we read *Hail and Farewell* attentively we shall hear in it a small but desperate complaint against his own nature. No doubt he sacrificed his friends, but first of all it was his own secret and unexpressed hope that he laid in the memorable dust.

So then for me at least there emerges from all the tittle-tattle about him and his own testimony against himself a wholly different portrait of a man whose genius rode him on the snaffle. He could put up the defences of exaggeration, flippancy, and apparent callousness against everything but that. "Let you go, George [said his genius] and write yourself down not as you would be nor as you believed yourself to be but as I tell you." So with infinite patience and unflagging obedience he set himself down as that cruel and lively dictator commanded—and as such he bids fair to pass into history as the one man who wrote a million words and never one in his own defence.

In the long run, however, it is not the thing that a writer was but what he made that will prevail. This is his answer to misrepresentation, whether of his own seeking or imposed upon him. So when the body-snatchers grope among Shelley's ashes for some tiny proof of infamy, he is safe with "his profuse strains of unpremeditated art." So Byron refutes all calumny where he walks in beauty like the night. And so George Moore, pacing the little stone terrace in front of his Essene monastery of dream, need not abide our voices—or the voices yet to come. He is free.

LORD NORTHCLIFFE
1865-1922

By
R. D. BLUMENFELD

LORD NORTHCLIFFE

by R. D. BLUMENFELD

TEMPERATE phraseology in describing Viscount Northcliffe seems inadequate. The figure becomes merely flat; just like that of any other person in the crowd. You have to put it on, not with the brush, but with the palette knife, and then there comes forth the real Northcliffe, dynamic, volcanic, sulphuric, the composite of the mass-production era.

I am, however, disposed to study Northcliffe from an angle in which not only his good qualities will be clearly perceptible, but also his foibles and his weaknesses, so that it may be shown that this so-called superman, who is fast becoming a mythical, all-pervading giant, was really just a gifted, energetic person who was largely the product of an era; who had sense and courage and wit to grasp his opportunities and, above all, was endowed with a spirit of enthusiasm for the commonplaces of life coupled with the industry and powers of concentration to see things through.

The young reporter, coming open-eyed and wondering into Fleet Street, with his mind filled with shimmering pictures of the great journalistic princes of the pen who have reigned in the past in that street of mystery, has before him a vivid mental figure beckoning him to Fame and Posterity. That figure is Northcliffe, who, as I have said above, is rapidly becoming a great, alluring, mythical personage.

Well, it is granted that he was shining and glamorous. Otherwise we would not have given him an Abbey funeral; nor would he be written about in the many Lives that have been dedicated to his memory if he had been a mere, commonplace Fleet-streeter. It is just possible, perhaps more so, that a hundred years hence the name of Northcliffe will have assumed enormous proportions as representing the new era of British public articulation.

Actually he was born at a singularly opportune moment for the purpose of fulfilling his proper mission on earth. He believed that he had a mission. What exactly he believed the mission to be was never quite clear, certainly not to him, for he was a veritable cyclone of emotional contradictions. One policy neutralised the other, so that in the end he was always " all clear." But whatever his mission, whether to teach the former illiterates to read newspapers, to present news to a hitherto news-starved community, to foist standard bread and sweet peas, and new roses or agricultural small-holdings on a hitherto apathetic public, or to lead his countrymen *à outrance* against the Huns, the fact remains that if Alfred Harmsworth had been born in 1855 or 1875 instead of 1865—mark the ten years of difference—he would never have done any one of these things in the same way or with the same degree of success.

He was born in Dublin in July 1865, at a time when the majority of people one met either in town or country in all parts of the British Isles were untutored, uneducated, and un-informed. The Education Act of 1870 came into being at the psychological moment, for the first crop of this Act's sowing, the young men and young women compulsorily " educated," were just about ripe for light, easy, attractive reading material by the time that Harmsworth was old enough to project *Answers*, his first important venture in publishing. The young people, the first batch of Forster's Education Act specimens, came into what might be called " bearing " about fifteen or sixteen years after the measure had been introduced. They wanted something to read. Newnes and Harmsworth and Pearson gave it to them, and on this foundation were laid the fortunes of the three modern publishing dynasties, of which that of the Harmsworths was by far the most important.

I first met Alfred Harmsworth shortly after he had presented *Answers* with his epoch-making pound-a-week-for-life prize. He had already distinguished himself in a minor way at Coventry, where for a time he was Editor of the *Bicycling News*, a paper owned by the family of Iliffe, people of enterprise and courage. There he made such an impression on the Iliffes that, in spite of his youth, they offered him a partnership, which, owing to the consciousness of his mission, he declined. At the same time young Pearson, who had won himself a place on Newnes's staff out of Winchester

by R. D. BLUMENFELD

College, was asking Newnes to give him an increase of pay which was declined; whereupon Pearson left.

I wonder what would have happened if Harmsworth had remained in Coventry and Newnes had acceded to Pearson's request for an increase! Would there have been a *Daily Mail* or a *Daily Express*? Would there have been a Viscount Northcliffe, a Viscount Rothermere, or a Sir Hildebrand, or Sir Leicester? Would the *Daily Mail* have been burnt on the Stock Exchange? These two bright young men might have held on to their places, growing comfortably well off, even affluent. But I can hardly believe that Harmsworth would have been satisfied to remain in Coventry any more than Sir Edward Iliffe has chosen to do so. Harmsworth had a mission.

I first met him, as I say, when he was flushed with the success of his great *Answers* pound-a-week competition. He was a fascinating young man; buoyant, enthusiastic, clear-eyed, exceedingly good-looking; so good-looking, in fact, that he was almost the nearest thing to one's conception of a Greek god. His voice was fine and musical. He was endowed with a smile that lasted in the memory. He had even then begun to regard himself as a sort of reincarnation of Napoleon, and he cultivated a long light brown lock over his forehead. Also, he was beginning to collect Napoleona.

He was well dressed in loose tweeds. Always throughout the many years that I knew him, except towards the end when he became portly and careless, he was dressed with care, although even in the meticulous late 'eighties and 'nineties he preferred tweeds and rebelled against tail-coats and the conventional top-hat.

My first contacts with young Harmsworth gave me the impression of a forceful youth who would in good time become a successful publisher of books for the young. His whole outlook was cast in the direction of youth; the sort of youth that does things physically and is not too much concerned with the finer nuances of the mind. History interested him, particularly the history of the Napoleonic period. His outlook on foreign affairs was one of considerable indifference. He was Irish by birth and Liberal by inheritance, but when Joseph Chamberlain, one of his early heroes, broke with Gladstone over Home Rule, he cast in his lot with the Liberal-Unionists and deserted Gladstone. His adoration of Chamberlain was profound until his hero produced his

Tariff Reform scheme in 1903. " Stomach Tax! " cried Harmsworth in his daily press. Violent and impassioned anti-Chamberlain tirades followed for some days; not over-popular. Then the sudden and typical *volte-face*. Mr. Alfred once again became an ardent Chamberlainite.

But I am anticipating. Before then he was a most sedulous supporter of Lord Rosebery, and as he had been of Gladstone himself.

At this time I was London correspondent of the New York *Herald*, then one of the greatest English-language news-papers. It shared with *The Times* the undisputed first place on the world roster of newspapers. *The Times* had just emerged from its damaging Pigott-Parnell forgery case, but it was still the *Thunderer*. Our own paper was supreme in its sphere. We had only recently brought Henry M. Stanley safely across Africa in his Emin Pasha Relief Expedition when poor Emin, in spite of his vigorous protests, was forcibly " rescued " from the happy security of his Equatorial Empire in Central Africa.

It was in connection with this expedition that I met Alfred Harmsworth. I had gone to Richmond Terrace to see Stanley, who was a colleague of mine on the New York *Herald*, and found there this slim, handsome, alert-looking young proprietor of *Answers*. He wanted to engage Stanley to write the story of the Relief Expedition in a popular way. Stanley's book, *In Darkest Africa*, was already in print, but Harmsworth had an idea for something lighter; better adapted to the clientele which he desired to reach. In fact, I think here was the germ of the future highly successful serialisation of adventure stories. But Stanley was committed to other publishers and the young man started to go. I went out with him, and he offered me a lift in his brougham. His questions came with machine-gun fire. He told me that he envied me—being the correspondent of so great a paper—more than anyone he knew. I believed that, for it was ob-vious that he was afflicted with what we call the " paper bug." To him every reporter was a saint and every editor a deity.

It was at this time that this successful young man went on and on adding to his string of weekly fodder for the Forster-foster-children of 1870. One weekly followed the other, *Forget-me-Not, Funny Bits, Comic Cuts*, the *Girl's Own*, or what-ever they were called—all were poured down the greedy maw of the new public, and all brought golden grain to the Harmsworth mill.

I used now to see the young man from time to time. He had moved into a building of his own in Tudor Street, and it was said that *Answers* alone was making £80,000 a year. Brother Harold, a careful, painstaking, unpretentious clerk in Somerset House, had already thrown up his few pounds a week in the Civil Service to take over the business direction of the new enterprise, and George Sutton, the clever boy who had kept the petty-cash book (now Sir George Sutton, Baronet), was promoted to the trembling height of secretary to the man who was in future to be Mister Alfred.

More weeklies and more money. Meanwhile the Napoleon complex became an *idée fixe*. It *was* really Napoleon who guided the destinies of *Answers* and *Forget-me-Not*.

Then one fine morning K. J.—this being the future Kennedy Jones, M.P.—walked in and proposed an innovation. It was nothing less than the purchase of the derelict *Evening News*. Everybody knows this story; how they made a profit at once, and how K. J., making good his promise, got " Alf," as he loved to call his disgusted partner, a nomination as a candidate for Parliament; this time as a Conservative for Portsmouth, though Harmsworth was really a Liberal. It was here that " Alf " encountered the deep sense of bitterness in defeat. Portsmouth would have none of him. He was a bad speaker and he really knew nothing about politics as it was understood then. So he came home dejected and sullen, and started the *Daily Mail* with an expenditure of £10,000.

Here then begins the real story of Alfred Harmsworth. The *Evening News*, conducted by K. J., had brought the young Napoleon into a wider field. People were taking notice of him. He began to "think Imperially" with Joseph Chamberlain. The *Daily Mail* came down on the British Isles like a meteor, lighting up the dull, forgotten, sequestered villages where the only mental pabulum had been *Lloyds' Weekly News* and the *People*. The smug middle class began to sneer at the ha'penny upstart. It was something derogatory to publish a halfpenny journal, no matter how excellent its contents might be, but it was also something rather inexcusable to " take it in." So people read it surreptitiously. The halfpenny, even after the *Daily Mail* had reached a million, was not for years accepted as a respectable social affair.

The *Daily Mail*, in spite of its great and growing success, was a troublesome body. The reason for this was that the establishment was terribly amateurish. It was all very well to run prize-giving *Answers* and pretty-pretty *Forget-me-Not* and rapidly distributed racing news in the evening, but the new morning paper required the experience and skill of the professional journalist. Kennedy Jones was a first-class reporter, but certainly not an editor, while Harmsworth never was an editor even in his greatest days. He was a first-rate reporter, a personal journalist at all times dependent on mood and whim and predilection, but he had no mind for the co-ordinating qualities required of an editor. He could not suffer fools gladly. He could hypnotise himself at all times with any position of mind, wherefore he was sometimes a grave public danger. Having once made up his mind that there were sixteen inches to the foot and five and a half feet to the yard, he would proceed to force the British public to the same conclusion. If the British public, or rather his favourite " cabman's wife," declined to accept his ideas of measurement, he would still go on for a while and then suddenly sheer off with an impetuous sweep of the hand and cry, " Stupid, silly fools! They'll come to see it one day."

There was early in the day a trained journalist named Pryor. He had been employed on the New York *Sun*, and had once edited the Jamaica *Gleaner*. Harmsworth and K. J., in their inexperience of editors, thought he was a wonder. He was a good, sound sub-editor, but not a wonder at any time, but " Mr. Alfred " boomed him and eulogised him and loaded him with favours as " the greatest Editor ever." If Pryor had only left well enough alone he might have been able to carry on undiscovered for years, because technically he was quite a fair journalist. Besides, he was personally popular and amiable. Then ambition overweening, he went to South Africa personally to supervise the *Daily Mail's* Boer War correspondence. He had once been a telegraph clerk at Liverpool, and knew the intricacies of telegraphic correspondence. So off he went. In his place came Mr. Thomas Marlowe, a fine type of modern journalist, well-read, well-trained, firm, just, a man of the world; the right man for the place. The change was apparent at once in the improved aspect of the paper, and poor Pryor never got back his job.

Then, for the first time, it was noticeable that " Mr.

by R. D. BLUMENFELD

Alfred" could be bluffed, and that the strong, iron-nerved immovable giant was just as ordinary and evasive as most men who cannot make up their minds in a difficulty. Pryor came back from South Africa and wanted back his job as Editor. Harmsworth attempted to temporise, but Pryor, bull-dog-like, held on. "Where's my job?" was the burden of his cry. "Well, you see, etc., etc." He was never actually deposed. No one would tell him, and so he left of his own accord, justly incensed. In the end he rejoined his old chief on *The Times*, but I think it was largely due to the fact that "the Chief" hadn't the courage to say "No" to his insistent worrier. But Pryor never regained his place at the top; though he always hoped to do so.

When the Boer War broke out I was engaged in the profitable but uncongenial occupation of manufacturing type-setting machines. I hated the business like sin, and yearned to return to my own muttons of journalism. James Gordon Bennett, the proprietor of the New York *Herald*, professed to be incensed with me when I left him some years before. He said: "You will be crawling back one of these days wearing the buttons off your waistcoat." Sure enough I decided to crawl, and I wrote a telegram to Paris, where Bennett lived, announcing my proposed athletics. With this telegram in my pocket I went into Carter's hairdressing shop in Fleet Street. As I came out Alfred Harmsworth accosted me. "Come along to the *Daily Mail* and have some tea. When are you going to throw over your stupid machines and come back to your own affair?" I told him of the telegram I was about to send.

When we got to his room in the *Daily Mail*, Harmsworth said, "What's the matter with the *Daily Mail*?"

I replied, "It is like a garden that wants manuring."

"Right. Will you come in and be the manure?"

That was at about five in the afternoon. At six o'clock I was in the Editorial department as an executive.

I stayed there two years, and learned first to like and second never to understand Mr. Alfred Harmsworth. He was generous beyond words, unjust beyond human capacity to believe, impatient, suspicious, lovable, humorous, simple, and big-minded. He could be hopelessly brutal in his judgments and the next moment do or say the most angelic things. I found myself very soon in a difficult and equivocal position. Mr. Marlowe and I could have wrecked the paper between us owing to our separate instructions if he had not from the first played his part in the true style of a man of honour and discernment.

So far as intercourse with the great man was concerned—for by this time he had taken on the rôle and manner of a great personage—I had little difficulty. His attitude was ever friendly and courteous. We met constantly and dined together frequently. Only now and then would he overstep the bounds that separated the employer from one of his chief executives, and then I generally found that he was not inclined to quarrel in private and usually gave way. He was, however, impish and theatrical enough to stage a scene, say at the Editorial Council, when he could make a fine show of sham indignation and reprimand. He would almost certainly send for his victim afterwards and make things right.

In the meantime he grew both nationally and internationally. The *Daily Mail* was by now the chief topic of the music-hall patter, and there was hardly a play that did not contain a reference to this new public spot-light. It grieved Harmsworth inordinately to hear any other paper mentioned on the stage. He went systematically about the business of having the *Daily Mail* referred to at every public gathering.

"*Better be damned than mentioned not at all.*"

That was one of his favourite axioms. I chaffed him about this one day when we were being publicly trounced on account of the celebrated Peking atrocity hoax. I thought he would have a fit of apoplexy over this. No two things in the Northcliffe career gave him greater anxiety and cause for bitter feeling than the Peking massacre cable and the soap libel case. He was innocent, completely innocent of the first, and wholly guilty of the latter. There have been many versions of the Peking story, but as I was in the middle of it, I may contend that I knew the right one.

I was routed out of my study one Sunday afternoon during the Boxer trouble, and told that there was a most important cablegram from China. Would I join Mr. Harmsworth at the *Daily Mail* offices as early as possible?

I trundled down from the Chelsea Embankment in a hansom cab, and got to Tallis Street in due course. There was Harmsworth with a cablegram of some 1,200 words containing the ghastly details of the Legation massacres. The cable fairly ran with blood. It was authentic. It came from the highly paid mandarin whom we had sent north to

by R. D. BLUMENFELD

Peking to obtain direct and correct information. We sent a copy to the Foreign Office, but they had no intimation of such news.

Whatever else he may have been as a journalist, Alfred Harmsworth was a careful and conscientious purveyor of news. I never knew him wittingly to disseminate inaccurate information. On the contrary, he believed in the sound journalistic axiom which should be followed by every journalist, " When in doubt, delete."

The story was so terrible, so bloodcurdling that we were in two minds about publication. But the source, being so reliable, we felt that we would be taking a great risk if we withheld it. So we decided to cut out the most harrowing details and print the rest. That job, performed by Harmsworth, Marlowe, Mr. Watney (the Foreign Editor), and myself, left the cablegram still replete with horror-inspiring information. Then, in order to show that here was no attempt to obtain a great " scoop " over the other newspapers, the Chief decided that we should send the original cable, with emendations marked, to *The Times*, and copies to the others. They all printed it. A New York paper copied it as well, and embellished it with even more blood-curdling details than those which we had deleted. Such is the gratitude of beneficiaries that, when the inevitable disclosure of the hoax came along, and the whole world began to abuse the *Daily Mail*, this particular New York paper was loudest in its accusations of news faking!

As far as the soap libel, which cost the Harmsworth firm a quarter of a million, and did its chief proprietor not much credit, I am not in a position to say much about it, because I was then no longer on the staff. I had by this time become Editor of the *Daily Express*, the paper which was started by Arthur Pearson to rival the new giant; but I had, I think, perhaps an escape from the toils of that very libel suit. When Harmsworth, who had now become Sir Alfred, launched the attack on the soap magnates and tried to prevent their combination, he rang me up and said he would like to talk to me about this " new menace." Somehow, being an old hand, I scented lawyers' fees and went no farther.

Not only in accuracy of statement but in propriety of presentation was Harmsworth beyond criticism. If his rules of conduct were followed by many newspapers the Press would to-day be less eccentric in expression and certainly more devoid of slang. He objected to slang, and he had fixed ideas about what he called "sex appeal stuff." He was particular in insisting that the simple amenities of life should be imported into the columns of his papers. He objected, among other corruptions, to 'bus for omnibus, and every street cleaner was to be called Mr. That was due largely to the fact that, firstly, he was himself always polite even when he was unjust or wrong, and secondly, because such was his flair for what he called "window dressing" that he knew the street cleaner would be flattered and would perhaps become a *Daily Mail* reader.

Then, too, he had an inexplicable sixth sense of intelligent anticipation. I recall that in the middle of the Boer War he came into my room and said, " I think it is about time for those Germans to make fools of themselves. They are allowing their jealousy of England to run away with their sense of politeness. They will soon be sending up anti-British cheers in Berlin. Hadn't you better go over and have a look?

" My own view," he said—and here is where his sixth sense came in—" my own view is that the Germans are being led definitely and irrevocably to make war on the rest of Europe, and that we will have to take part in it. I don't see any escape; and if it does come we will go on the rack."

That was late in 1900. I made a Diary note of it at the time. A long time after, twenty years or so, I recalled this conversation at *The Times* office.

" Yes," he replied. " I remember that, and so far as the Germans are concerned, they will continue to make trouble for us in the future."

He was certainly a persistent anti-German. Nor have the Germans cause to love his memory, for Northcliffe propaganda in enemy countries was much more effective against the Germans than his propaganda against certain politicians at home. He had at his disposal all the best literary and newsvending brains; he had command of the Government's deep purse ; he made full use of both. Some of the propaganda was crude; some of it was really silly, as for instance the story of the German corpses tied together like bundles of asparagus to be converted into useful fats for military purposes. Few of us believed the story, even though it was iterated and reiterated in the most ingenious fashion and through all sorts of channels of dissemination. Few of us, I say, believed that particular yarn. There was one man who believed every word of it, and that man was Viscount Northcliffe. If he had disbelieved a single comma of it you may rest assured the story would have disappeared, such was his definite policy in the matter of false information.

I think this question of inaccurate news must have been impressed on him very early in his career; how, I do not know. I recall that it came up one evening when we were dining in his house in Berkeley Square in 1901. I had related to him an experience of mine at *The Times* office ten years earlier when we, the Editor and myself, as London correspondent of the New York *Herald*, had declined for our papers to put out some information calculated to give umbrage to a highly placed personage. It was not a matter of vital public importance. It was, however, extremely interesting. To-day it would be blazoned on any front page with a two-column heading. "The Chief" was properly impressed, and said that his one idea of the conduct of a newspaper was to have it run like *The Times*. I retorted that this would be turning any newspaper office into a Government office.

"Never you mind," he said; "one of these days I will surprise you all by showing how I can run *The Times*."

The next day he bounced into my room and recalled the conversation of the previous evening.

"Look here," he cried, his face all aglow with excitement; "there is nothing I would like better in all the world than to obtain control of *The Times*. I do not think they are getting on too well over there, and they might like to sell. If I went to them they would at once refuse me. Will you make them an offer instead? The Walters might care to deal with you. I've got a million pounds in Consols, and I authorise you to play up to that sum. It will be a great coup if you can get it."

I went to *The Times*, and after a short interval received the only answer to be expected—a polite but definite refusal. The young would-be purchaser was deeply disappointed.

In due course he achieved his ambition to control *The Times*. It was some six years later that the late Sir Arthur Pearson—always Northcliffe's friend and rival—managed to secure *The Times* for himself, or almost so. The trouble was that he talked too soon. I suppose it is part of the game, but

Northcliffe's action in this matter did not do him much credit. He went to France. From there he began publicly to acclaim Pearson as the great king of journalism, the all-pervading new personality in public life, the powerful man of affairs now at the head of the world's greatest newspaper, and so on, a great acreage of fulsome praise! Behind the scenes, however, he was working desperately to depose the usurper, and a few days later Moberly Bell, the manager of *The Times* whom Pearson did not want, secured a court order and gained control. Pearson was ousted. Northcliffe stepped in!

Well, as ye sow so shall ye reap. It was a bad stroke of business for the Napoleon of Journalism. He did not understand *The Times* and *The Times* did not understand him. He was unhappy there and he made a mess of the *Thunderer*. It was merely, as Lloyd George said, the *Daily Mail* for threepence.

Also Northcliffe became pontifical. He had now been Sir Oracle for so many years with no dog to bark when he ope'd his mouth that he really began to believe what he said, no matter how he said it. The War had brought him into closer touch with the great ones of the earth. As head of the War Mission in America, where he performed great and useful service, as head of propaganda in enemy countries, as a director of publicity in his own papers he had displayed energy, patriotism, and self-sacrifice, and he began to lay down the law.

He was obsessed by his old complex, the German danger, and in this he was as near right as anything. In the meantime he had first supported Kitchener and had thrown him over at a moment when it required great courage to attack the people's hero. His shell scandal secured for the *Daily Mail* the distinction of a Stock Exchange bonfire, which pleased Northcliffe a lot, for the *Daily Mail* had for some time failed to hold the limelight as of yore. But there is no doubt that Northcliffe's action in forcing the shell controversy proved to be a great national blessing.

The same with Asquith. Northcliffe had supported Asquith, and at the psychological moment he deserted him. He did likewise with Lloyd George, but now he caught a Tartar, for, strange to say, the little Welshman hit back at once and so hard that the Oracle of Tallis Street never uttered a sound.

by R. D. BLUMENFELD

Northcliffe certainly had a real grievance. He had been a thorn in Lloyd George's side for a long time, sparing no criticism and giving no change. Then about the middle of 1918 he went to see the Prime Minister, and said in words like these:

"Prime Minister, I am certain that the Germans are now beaten, and it is time that we organise a peace ministry. Here is where I come in. I did not join you before because I felt I would be of greater use outside, but now it is different. We will form the Northcliffe-George Peace Government."

That is in substance what he said, and in spite of his vast power he was incontinently snubbed; after which the Lloyd George Government was again violently assailed. Lloyd George said in Parliament on April 16, 1919, that Northcliffe was a man who was

> "here to-day, jumping there to-morrow. I would as soon trust a grasshopper. . . . I am prepared to make some allowances for even a great newspaper proprietor, and when a man is labouring under a keen sense of disappointment—however unjustified, however ridiculous his expectations—a man under these conditions is apt to think the world is badly run. At any rate, he is the only man who can make peace. Yet nobody comes near him to tell him so,"

and so on.

It was a crushing onslaught, and it marked the end of Northcliffe's power. He went on for a few more years in more or less indifferent health, and most of his time was spent in travelling abroad. It was already noticed that his mental grasp was no longer what it had been. He was more irritable and yet at times more placid. His despatches to his papers were eccentric; his telegraphic admonitions to the members of his staff so ludicrous that they were no longer looked upon with apprehension. Men were ordered to be moved from pillar to post. Sometimes they went, sometimes they just paid no attention. Two of his executives for whom he had done much in the past took umbrage and publicly sued him. It was a strange and tragic break-up, and it all ended in 1922 when he died in Carlton Gardens, his mind clouded and his work done.

His work done. What was it? Summed up, there stands to

the credit of Alfred Harmsworth a vast accumulation of public service. No one will say that he was ever actuated by other than the purest motives of patriotism; that is, so far as his war work was concerned. For the rest he was a founder of a new life and spirit in Great Britain. As I said at the beginning of this sketch, he was the instrument chosen for the purpose. He could not have done it if he had been born earlier or later. It was the psychological moment.

Motor-cars. Again prescience. His advocacy of the horseless carriage was due to a genuine desire to move faster. I remember driving with him and the late Mr. Hugh Spottiswoode from London to Calcot Park, Reading, in a six-horsepower Panhard car, at twelve miles an hour. His financial encouragement did much to start the early British motor industry. His £10,000 offer for an aeroplane flight from London to Manchester was not necessarily an advertising gesture. He could as easily have saved £9,000 by reducing the prize, and it would have proved just as attractive. No, this man had vision and the courage to back his vision.

He told me once that if we went on destroying the earth's natural resources in the way of timber cutting there would be no pulp for paper. The American newspapers in particular were using up paper in vast bulk. I was therefore not surprised when, shortly after, he embarked with his brother Rothermere on a great paper-making adventure in Newfoundland. They bought a whole province, built a town, a railway, docks; and Northcliffe's " hunch " was correct. It cost a great fortune to build the plant, but it has justified itself.

He could and did sway public opinion. The little Forster-foster-children of 1870 and their descendants have shown by their adherence to the Harmsworth Press how much they have appreciated the gift of contemporaneous reading which he gave to them. Not only that, but the fact that he led the way into the Elysian fields of lighter literature encouraged others to follow, with the result that there has been a great annual outcropping of cheap and excellent mental food with the consequent public benefit.

Northcliffe never sank his personality; not even at the beginning. He was ever a striking, almost theatrical figure. He was never vulgar in any form. He hated carelessness in dress as well as in work. He once came into my room at the *Daily Mail* office and suggested that I should put up an order in the reporters' room to the effect that in future all reporters should come on duty " properly dressed." I asked him how he defined " proper " dress. He replied, " Frock coat and top hat," and then he added, with a twinkle in his eye, " but not brown boots."

The next day, after I had issued the order, he came up and cried: " My God! I've just seen So-and-So ' properly dressed.' How can you send out this old Bohemian like that! He's the best reporter in England when he wears a tweed suit. In a frock coat he disgraces us."

So I took down the order.

That was the playful side which he retained even through the great days when he had become an international figure answering to what he firmly believed to be the Call of Destiny. It is a very strange thing this belief in one's Call. Northcliffe had it always. He often told me, in the early days of the *Daily Mail*, that he was right about certain things, " Because, you see, it is so ordained." His mother, for whom he had the greatest possible love, also believed in his Destiny, just as Madame Mère believed in the Destiny of her little Napoleon, her favourite among all the Buonaparte children. I recall once at a dinner saying to Mrs. Harmsworth, after her son had been created a baronet, " Well, you see, he has arrived at his destination. It has been a fine achievement," or words to that effect.

" Dear me," replied the adoring mother, " he has only begun. Alfred will rise to the greatest heights."

So there he is, the man who did so much to mould the form of the age, a human, vital personality, who caused the wheels to go round faster and more powerfully than before; who had great ambitions and achieved most of them; who lived his life like a cataract, and who proved in his own career how fleeting and how unfinished everything is that we attempt.

Above all, Northcliffe will be remembered as the supreme advertiser. Whether it be to advocate certain breads, to encourage aviation, to bring the Empire to the cottage door, to impress the Germans or to depress others, the fact remains that he was without a rival in the matter of making publicity. I can best display him in his own words.

" There is nothing new about publicity but the extension and development of publicity. Like agriculture, it is an old, old art in a process of intensification. When Rameses went through Egypt stamping his mark on the national monuments, he was a very early exemplar of one of the worst uses of publicity—the personal notoriety form of it, from which even to-day we do not appear to be free."

[Northcliffe at this time was not advertising himself as he did in his later years.]

"When William's Normans duplicated castles throughout England, they were publishing the fact of power. The church bell calling to the service within, the muezzin summoning the faithful at eventide to the mosque, the regimental march throughout a district, and the stationing of recruiting offices in the market places were all ancient forms of publicity. We English have been slower and staider than most peoples in developing advertising; we have avoided the pitfalls of the pioneers, and I am not sorry, therefore, for our lateness. . . ."

Northcliffe's new journalism and Northcliffe's personal influence thereon were the leading impulse of tons of thousands of humble British households. We can leave him at that.

I go almost daily past St. Dunstan's Church in Fleet Street. There, close to the pavement, is a fine bust of Viscount Northcliffe, with a proper inscription. It is a classical face, just a bit cynical, as if it were about to say: " No, that will not do. It will not convince even a child. What you must aim at is to convince your public. Write it again! "

SIR WILLIAM ORPEN
1878-1931

By
C. R. W. NEVINSON

SIR WILLIAM ORPEN

by C. R. W. NEVINSON

ORPEN closes an epoch of painting which dealt largely with the particular rather than the general. It stated æsthetically the visual world with an accuracy which was largely dependent upon facility of manipulation, sureness of draughtsmanship, and knowledge of craftsmanship, rather than the later development of his epoch, which was seeking the general or abstract expression of mental conception of emotions visually conceived from natural forms.

In considering Orpen it is impossible not to remember Millais, his Victorian predecessor. There is the same immediate recognition of his powers, the same precociousness, the same culmination peculiar in England, which forced portrait painting as one of the main outlets of pictorial expression and material advantage.

Paradoxically, as it is possible for an artist in modern times to get full recognition during his lifetime only as a portrait painter, portrait painting becomes a handicap to his survival. In the past, many a portrait painter survived because he painted a personality of historic or aristocratic importance. Old families and old houses have been the cause of much immortality. Quaintness of costume, and other decorative qualities forgive many pictures the lack of æsthetic standards or technical triumphs. In modern times, owing to the ugliness and drabness of modern costume, many portraits are doomed.

In the public auction-room, or knacker's yard as artists call it, where public opinion is expressed more forcibly than elsewhere, and subject counts most, it has been seen that pictures of other people's relatives merely dressed in Victorian or post-Victorian costume have no appeal, no matter how superb the draughtsmanship, the technique, or the characterisation. It is therefore inevitable that a proportion of

Orpen's output will suffer severely. He himself was conscious of this, and rightly considered it of no importance. It was inevitable, nevertheless, that portrait painting should play such an important part in Orpen's artistic life, as his dexterity, shrewdness, uncanny sympathy, and love of the particular were all part of his character, and no matter how often he complained of doing nothing but portraits in the latter years of his life, he never could resist doing yet another. This, I am sure, was the cause of the many self-portraits, not a *narcissus complex*, as so many have stated. With himself, he felt he could do an independent portrait, and therefore enjoyed it. He was so conscientious a man that he always felt handicapped by a commission.

It has been said that Orpen never painted a bad picture; actually this is not the case: he has told me himself that when out of sympathy with a sitter, he has abandoned the picture. He was always scrupulously careful to give his best in return for his price, and it was this reliability, springing from his sincerity, which made him the most sought-after post-Victorian portrait painter in the world.

Orpen was considered a successful man from the standard of worldly-minded people, and there can be no denying that he was. It would seem that fortune smiled upon him from his first scholarship, that struggle was unknown, and no technical difficulty too great for him to overcome, with an almost flippant insouciance. Men in clubs, with bated breath, discuss how much " he cut up for "; others are awed either by the prominence of the rulers and " swells " who patronised him, or by the wonderful historic record he has left of those who had charge of the destinies of nations. Never before in the history of art has an artist been able to leave such a record of public men, or of a nation's history. He has recorded the pre-War, student or Countess, the War, the private, the general, the statesman and the peace, the pressman, or the diplomat, the post-War, the scientist and the *nouveau riche*, and the still richer " New Poor." Yet in spite of this, Orpen always felt unfulfilled; within him there was always a conflict; to understand his work and his enormous industry, it is necessary to know of this secret battle, which was always raging within him. It was this battle which was the cause of much of his flippancy, and of a certain puckishness with which he is associated. As Sidney Dark rightly remarks, Orpen was always laughing

by C. R. W. NEVINSON

it off, and then, in my opinion, plunging back once more into superhuman industry as an escape from a certain disgust which steadily increased with post-War conditions; an emotion which no worldly success, no honour, no achievement, could stifle.

Orpen was not a superficial man, and towards the end of his life, the human tragedy of our modern civilisation and its seeming failure clouded his outlook in a way that must seem quite incomprehensible to many of our superior intellectuals, who, wrongly or rightly, are sufficiently egotistical to be interested only in fiddling while Rome burns.

I came across this secret place in his heart accidentally some few years ago, when he was dining with us, and suddenly, in the middle of a hilarious party, in which he was indulging in all sorts of light-hearted, puckish, and Orpen-esque quips and quirks, a Russian sculptress, after the manner of her race, said, " Why are you so un'appy, Sir Orps? " This question disconcerted him, and instead of going to bed early, as was his wont, he talked all night to us of his thoughts. He told me afterwards that it was a rare occasion, and that, like Landru, he never confessed, and that it certainly wasn't the business of Little Orps to hate anyone but himself.

It is in his independent work, and not in his portrait painting, that this conflict is most evident. It was inevitable that the work of Hogarth, Goya, Toulouse Lautrec, Degas, and sometimes the early work of Picasso, should influence him. The irony and incongruity, which is the theme of many of the illustrations by these men, roused him to paint, not only in a different technical manner, but often in a literary manner. Many of his War paintings show this love of incongruity: the splendid sunny day, polluted by the stink of a corpse; the picturesque villages, meant for peasants but inhabited by guns; the masquerade of love that went on in the billets behind the line; the farce of the Kaiser entering Paris enacted by British soldiers.

His series of so-called problem pictures consisted mainly in indulging his love of the incongruous; whether it was the virtuous and bedecked judge about to pass the sentence of death upon another man, or the naked girl sowing seed before a sterile English hypocrite in black clothing; wild beasts behind bars at Avignon, English artists in the Café Royal ambience of late Empire French *décor*; members of the New English Art Club paying homage to the Parisian

Manet; or the common soldier lying in state in the surroundings of the Pompadour, where etiquette and birth were of greater importance than valour and virtue. Socially, even, this conscious or unconscious love of the incongruous made his rebel mind enjoy the company of English clubmen. How often have I heard him laugh with genuine pleasure at the platitudinous and echoed opinions of some leader-writer on the staff of a respectable English newspaper, which upheld day after day the known opinions of official smuggery. He enjoyed the echoes of echoed opinion that resound down the stale corridors of brown lincrusta.

Orpen was an Irishman, and reverence for the English gods was impossible for him. It also accounted for his love of companionship, his secretiveness, his indifference to friendship, and his love of money. The innumerable stories, however, of his sending in bills to press lords for the use of his name in newspapers, and the solemn charges that he made to business men for lunches which he attended as a guest, were not due to any mercenary instincts, but to a puckish contempt for the pomposity with which publicity is treated, and the veneration that business men show for time and money. It is inevitable that a Celt should always feel an outlander in post-Victorian London; this psychological condition accounts for the success through sympathy of his portraits of beggars or common soldiers, ordinary airmen, and all those that English social conditions would consider outsiders. It accounts for his sympathy with intellectuals and scientists whom pukka sahibs place lower than outsiders, and who are the equivalent of outcasts in modern civilisation. It is worthy of comment that during the Peace Conference, when he was painting the rulers of the world, the *chef* at the Chatham Grill was his most outstanding portrait of that period. To account for the conflict and paradoxical qualities of Orpen's work, which often became tainted with bitterness and mockery, it is necessary to go back to the epoch before the War, when he was still at the Slade. It is this quality of irony which makes him differ from all other Victorian and post-Victorian painters; a quality which cannot be found in such portrait painters as Sargent or McEvoy, or poetic painters as John or Pryde, or such purely æsthetic painters as Matisse, Derain, or Picasso.

Looking back to pre-War days, it is very difficult for us to picture the conditions in which Slade students studied. It was an extremely exciting one, and yet the age was essentially dull; feelings and interest were abnormal in æsthetic, intellectual, and social matters; yet we were enveloped in a pall of stagnation; change was regarded with horror, yet all felt something was coming. Women had discovered their sex, yet it could not be realised that they were approximately half the population of the world. The internal-combustion engine had not yet changed the face of the earth, though it was apparent that it was about to shrink it. The Channel had been crossed by air, yet the sea still kept this country in a state of isolation, and Dreadnoughts were our only political thoughts; and in this silence before the storm could be heard the vague rumblings of guns. In this lull after so many summer days, the nerves of a placid people were really taut. This consciousness, vaguely felt by all, of an impending disaster, accounted for the abnormal opposition shown to any form of experiment, and accounted for the Slade students' adoption of a priggish attitude of superiority towards all affairs and all conditions that affected their lives.

I remember once at the late Arnold Bennett's, H. G. Wells describing one of his early short, fantastic stories, which was never published because it was considered to be in the worst possible taste, a story of a young Englishman who climbed up a ladder and looked over the wall of a Scottish castle, and there in the close were twenty or thirty dumpy old ladies being treated with the utmost courtesy by flunkies and courtiers, a supply of old ladies to be substituted for Queen Victoria, when in some distant future, she would eventually prove her mortality. Change was even more terrible than death. In the Edwardian period, after the disasters of the South African War, a flaccid wealth descended upon a portion of England; a certain pessimism, which combined the philosophies of " Let us eat and drink, for to-morrow we die," a certain optimism, " As long as we don't change we always muddle through," and a popular song, " There won't be no war so long as we've good King Edward." It must be remembered that music-halls in those days were not only the rendezvous of intellectuals and prostitutes, but supplied many of the " thoughts of the day." Humour, especially of the slap-stick variety, was an essential skeleton at all Edwardian feasts. Of works of art, every nerve was strained, not only by critics, but by the public in general, to make a *bon mot,* displaying not the wit of the 'nineties, but a blathering buffoonery.

The Slade students in those days had divorced themselves from all contemporary thought and fashion; largely through the leadership of John, they had adopted a form of Bohemianism, a pose which was at the same time a protection, and prevented diversion of thought from the study of drawing and painting, which was pursued with an earnestness and sincerity unknown in any of the other art schools of London and Paris. Draughtsmanship and craftsmanship were rightly placed by the students as the first essentials of good art. Post-Impressionism had not yet upset the ideals of representational painting, and the Impressionists had brought back the study of nature; the New English Art Club was stealing the prestige of the Royal Academy by painting pictures which were neither goody-goody illustrations, nor literary sentiments sickly enough to bring the blush to the cheeks of an Ethel M. Dell. The problem picture of the doggie with human expression in its eyes, saying its prayers with a little child beholding, was not considered a good picture by Slade students, even though it did express almost holy sentiments.

Orpen as a student had quite enough to do, and was completely untouched by everything that was going on outside the world of art, though his student work showed the contemporary habit, learned from Degas, Arthur Symonds, and Sickert, of visiting music-halls almost every evening; this had an influence on him, and his painting of Hamlet, for instance, was more a study of the Old Sadler's Wells than of Shakespeare's Hamlet, though it also showed an imagination of colour and design in the grand manner, which the portrait painting of his later life did much to cramp. Many of the modern young men, who so airily dismiss Orpen as no great painter, accept this particular picture. Actually, I see no reason why this should be put down as one of his greatest paintings; it merely happens to be more in tune with the immediate and fashionable æsthetic tastes, and as time has already played so many pranks with contemporary taste, not too much attention should be paid to these opinions.

Orpen had fame thrust upon him; always a loyal member of the New English Art Club, he probably had no particular intention as a youth of joining the Royal Academy of Arts; but painting, as he did at this period, intimate interior

by C. R. W. NEVINSON

portraits in the manner of the small Dutch Masters, he painted Wertheimer, the dealer, and this was sent to the Royal Academy, either with or without the consent of Orpen. The picture had such obvious merits of craftsmanship, colour, and representation, that even the Academicians of those days were compelled to give him recognition, and it cannot be too often stated that Orpen was grateful for the immediate recognition and generosity with which the Academicians treated his work from that time on. Orpen was never a disgruntled artist; the qualities he possessed had a universal appeal, whether academic or unacademic, and he was unaffected, because he was not in sympathy with that small section of the younger generation which did not appreciate his purely representational art, manual facility, and dexterous statement. Orpen was lucky in being just young enough to escape the influence of Post-Impressionism, and the reaction to photographic representation which in many ways was the cause of the later movement.

To-day, many a poor student at the Slade is worried to death at the choice which he knows he will have to make between photographic representation of the particular, and the concrete statement, or the unrepresentational stylistic formula of abstraction. It was this lack of conflict in his student days which made Orpen more vulnerable to confusion and complexity when public affairs of war and peace could no longer be despised and dismissed in the airy way of students in the Edwardian days, as things which had nothing to do with him. Most of us in life have become immune to the poison of distraction by slow degrees; Orpen received it in a gulp, and from the Somme onwards was never quite the same man as the diligent A.R.A. of pre-War days.

Actually the War roused in Orpen many enthusiasms, and it was also a release; he escaped from Society, and it is but necessary to quote his poem:

MYSELF, HATE, AND LOVE

I hate the modern simp'ring girls,
Their foolish walk, their stupid curls.
I hate all over-dressed young " earls,"
And ladies' bodies coiled with pearls
To flaunt in earth's poor hungry face.

SIR WILLIAM ORPEN

I hate Society's worst disgrace,
Old women, who do keep their place
By mothering young men of talent
Until they spoil them,
Sicken and soil them,
With all their useless nutriment.

I hate myself,
I hate them all,
All,
Except one man
Alone.
He I can admire
Truly
And with all my soul
Entire.

I mean the simple soldier man,
Who when the Great War first began,
Just died, stone dead,
From lumps of lead,
In mire.
Or lived through hell,
Words cannot tell,
For four long years
And more
Of misery
Until the war
Was ended.

No man did more
Before.
No love has been
By this world seen
Like his, since Christ
Ascended.

I am a coward—
And I hate
Myself
As much, or more,
Than others of my breed.

by C. R. W. NEVINSON

Likewise,
I hate the bully,
I hate the " swank,"
I hate the braggart,
I hate the " crank."

I hate all men who talk too loud,
Like those who glory when a crowd
Doth cheer them
On, to make long-winded words
About themselves,
And how the nations all do need them,
They, and their cursed breed, to lead them. . . .

This cry of the heart displays that sentimentality of the " Minstrel Boy to the War has gone " variety, so thoroughly Celtic, and the Irishman's hatred of the self-righteous ruling class, and the self-hatred and self-pity, peculiar to conquered races, such as the Celts, Armenians, Jews, and Negroes.

The War at first was for him an epic of heroism, which made many of his pictures almost light-hearted in colour, subject-matter, and technique, and caused many to say his War paintings were war without tears. It cannot be said of Orpen that the War caused that form of neurasthenia peculiar to those who did not have the luck to get killed in it. His disillusionment became more awful with the Peace. It was the Conference that gave him the horrors. It will be noted that, though Paris was full at the time of politicians, diplomats, publicists, eminent commentators, literary know-alls, and economists, Orpen, with an artist's intuition, was the only one to become profoundly suspicious of the Japanese. At this Conference, which was winding up the War that was to end war, he made the sinister figure a Japanese amongst puppets, a prophecy which we now see to be painfully true, not only at Geneva, but in Manchuria. The Irishman in him spotted at once the ruthless Empire-builder of the future.

Much about the same time, owing to his residence in Paris, another conflict was also taking place within him; this was purely an æsthetic one. Orpen, in much the same way as he had taken no interest in public affairs, had also taken little interest in the modern movements which had been shattering the standards of criticism and taste and execution since 1910; but in Paris he was forced to look at many manifestations which were around him of contemporary painting, and, as he said, though he could not believe that many of the painters who painted nothing with bits of string and newspaper meant very much, he was well aware that some meant a very great deal; and from that time onwards we occasionally see influences of his new surroundings in his painting, in which he abandoned accurate statement, and, in order to express more forcibly his emotions, used deformation and elongation of form; a method common amongst expressionists, who had based their theories upon El Greco, Daumier, Cézanne, Gaugin, Toulouse Lautrec, and Picasso's Blue Period. He also began to paint with a matt surface, that is to say, oil and varnish were banished from his palette; a problem which for Orpen must have been one of extreme difficulty, as the basis of his technique largely depended upon his painter qualities, and the juxtaposition of subtle tones and modellings, a method of painting that demands the use of oil as a vehicle. It is admitted that already in his War paintings he was tending towards the matt surface, but I think it can be safely asserted from the evidence of his brush work, that he was still using oil as a medium, but the canvas was very absorbent, and by this means the shiny patine of his average oil-painting was removed. It is interesting to note that he never used this matt method of painting in his more elaborate portraits; and how right he was, because retouching and repainting is usually futile on a matt texture, on account of the changes that take place as the colour dries.

His War portraits, by all appearances, were probably painted *au premier coup*, which accounts for the fresh brilliance and exquisite texture time is now putting on them; actually Orpen was so good a craftsman, so direct in his technique, owing to the sureness of his draughtsmanship, that his paintings will not deteriorate with time, but will slowly darken to the beautiful patine associated with the oil-painters of the Renaissance. It is to be hoped that they will not suffer as Sargent's paint is already suffering, owing to the stupidity and ignorance of some connoisseur, expert, or dealer, who has ruined them by applying a toned varnish, in order to give an Old Mastery effect.

As Orpen is bound to survive because of the history that he recorded of an age which certainly will not be forgotten until the next great war, it will be interesting to observe

by C. R. W. NEVINSON

the effect of time upon post-Victorian craftsmanship and chemistry. I am inclined to think that post-Victorian research and scientific chemical study have advanced the permanency of oil-painting, and that Professor Sir William Rothenstein is more or less right in his affirmation that little can harm a modern oil-painting. This could not be said of the Victorian epoch, when ignorance and commercial exploitation reached their limits. It is possible that on those grounds alone Orpen's work may survive all his immediate predecessors', and this survival will largely be due to the directness of his application of paint. As the Old Masters prove, oil-painting seldom survives alteration or glazing.

Orpen, as an official artist in the War, was most unofficial in his outlook; his independence of thought can only be gauged by a study of his War paintings at the Imperial War Museum, his gift to the nation. Here again, honour was thrust upon him; he neither wanted nor cared very much about his knighthood. According to his own account, he only received it because he was insulted by some brass hat, who accused him of making money out of the War, when he was actually losing it; so he presented all his pictures to the nation, and he was soothed by a knighthood—I quote his words.

It has often been said by artists that he took little interest in the work of others. Speaking personally, I found this to be very untrue. He was more then chivalrously gallant in the defence of other artists, as I well know; and he always sent visitors who wanted to see his War paintings, to go and look at mine in the same museum. This is a gesture that would be rare in the history of art, and particularly rare amongst post-Victorians. He also used his power in France to protect other official artists from the indignities and stupidities of old dugouts attached to G.H.Q. Intelligence and the Ministry of Information, though he was often out of sympathy with the paintings of some of the extremists. Again, on hanging committees I have known him fight against the rejection of a painting which was very far removed from his taste or genre. His generosity and impetuosity of mind often caused yet another conflict within him, which he hid by a desperate attempt to laugh it off, belittle himself, or to indulge in mawkish sentiment. This sentimentality his shrewd mind again thoroughly enjoyed, because of his love of incongruity.

After the Peace, Orpen painted nudes; one entitled " The Letter " is probably one of the finest and purest of his independent works. In spite of the title, there is no literature, no cynicism, and no comment, outside, or alien to, its pictorial values. This painting can be judged on the same plane as Goya, Boucher, Manet, or Renoir. It is a *tour de force* on a subject which has been painted a million times, and yet it is something new in outlook, perspective, and application of paint, simplification of form, and a masterly management of light and colour.

Orpen delighted in women's beauty and girls' prettiness. He was a defender of the post-Victorian girl, even though he did occasionally grumble at their wrinkled foreheads, which he put down to plucked eyebrows, mascara, and tiny hats; and again his love of incongruity made him paint clever women, especially those of the noblest and most intellectual calibre, and I think no one would deny his greatest portraits were often of these women. In the case of Dame Madge Kendal he achieved a work of art which will rank with the portrait of Mrs. Siddons. Here again his love of incongruity made a sympathy with his sitter; that a woman should have no terror of old age, but be an active, triumphant, laughing personality, whose mind showed no signs of senile rigidity, but was as elastic as ever, sensitive, and almost roguish.

The art of portrait painting is one which by its very nature must be impure, or rather a mixed one, as many of the modern examples prove. The mere mapping of a face is not enough; the mere creation of a pattern or decorative effect is not enough; the study of pure form or lighting is not enough; manual dexterity is not enough; the likeness is not enough; photographic representation is not enough; technical agility is not enough. To be a great work of art, a portrait must have a literary quality, which by means of physiognomy and expression achieves an abstract value equivalent to an essay upon the sitter. This demands a knowledge of life, and an appraising of human characteristics that amounts to a sixth sense, an intuition or an X-ray eye, and a knowledge of psychology that is usually found only amongst priests and some medical men. Even then we all know how women with angel faces can have the thoughts and characteristics of fiends or malicious imbeciles; often benevolent-looking old gentlemen are ruthless criminals, or sadistic egoists. Physiognomy is capable of endless disguises, and the story of the French criminologist who could see at Madame Tussaud's criminal tendencies plainly marked on the faces of revered statesmen, because he mistook the Chamber of Honour for the Chamber of Horrors, was not so far out as it appears.

Though a bird is known by its song, and a man by his language, it by no means follows that the face of either sex is an open book. It is the business of a portrait painter, among many other things, to explain the personality of the man, and to convey his character by his appearance, his pose, and expression, and at the same time, not to insult him too much. One of the greatest difficulties of portrait painting is to paint the subject as others see him, and not as he himself pictures himself. Men in particular of this post-Victorian age are inclined to consider themselves as Napoleons, strong and ruthless, with the charity of Christ, the respectability of a Victorian, combined with the dare-devilry of a Don Juan.

Sargent said that whenever he painted a good portrait he lost a friend. Orpen, possibly through his Irish blood, seemed to take a kinder view of the individual, in proportion to his disgust with humanity in the mass. Though it has been said that Orpen never had any need for friendship, few men have been more friendly disposed towards every individual.

His gift of sympathy and his attitude towards himself as "Poor little Orps" never roused antipathy, jealousy, and aggression in others. This gift was an immense help to him as a portrait painter, and helped him to understand others with an uncanny shrewdness. Few people troubled to disguise themselves before Orpen, and in any case they always felt that at least he only saw the best of them, though I regret to say he was often mocking at them, by means of an excess of sympathy. His lack of reverence, again, made it possible for him to tackle many a subject that would have overwhelmed a simpler artist.

Orpen always loved the masquerade, and he was fond of saying that an Englishman loved best of all wearing fancy dress. This love he was always grateful for, and he never missed the opportunity of painting the great ones in their robes of office. He painted these trappings with such joy largely because they were an escape from the drabness of modern costume. Even when he took a busman's holiday and painted himself, he almost invariably did so in some incongruous fancy dress. In years to come this costuming of his portraits will give a very wrong impression of the age in which we live. At his restrospective exhibition this was very obvious, and prevented many of the general public from looking at his pictures as works of art, as they were always being startled into criticising the clothes worn by the sitter. Even in his independent work of a serious, decorative description, his love of fancy dress, or fanciful dress, marred the seriousness of his intention. His Pilgrims at a Holy Well often had a quaintness and staginess which did not quite fit in with his dramatic intentions. Even his beggars and itinerants appeared rather to have dressed for the part, which gave them a picturesque quality not in keeping with a great art. His retrospective exhibition at the Academy proved his enormous industry, but it also betrayed a certain mental indolence. It has often been asked, if Orpen hated portrait painting so much, as he was wont to proclaim, why did he do it? He was obviously in a position to be able to refuse commissions if he wanted to. I think the solution can be found in that indolence peculiar to the Celt. To a man who had worked practically from the age of twelve in art schools, where subjects, tasks, or models were set for him, it was appallingly difficult, on leaving the routine, to set about doing independent work; it was far easier to get a commission and to apply his energy and industry and drown the voice of conscience by painting a portrait of a sitter who arrived and left at stated times.

To the thousands of English artists who paint, and paint pictures of rare beauty and genuine inspiration, which no one wants in these post-Victorian days, in an epoch where the educated classes respect nothing but the head-waiter and always have money for the Italian *restaurateur*, the attitude of Orpen towards his wanted pictures must seem ungrateful; but I think it accounts for his consciously or unconsciously continuing to accept more and more commissions; he, too, felt, in spite of his denials, a desire to do something that was wanted from his brush, rather than to spend thought on work that was unwanted; though his statement that no one ever bought his independent work must, I think, be dismissed as a Celtic exaggeration, often due to his Irish blarney, because he was fond of making this

by C. R. W. NEVINSON

statement to those artists who did manage to exist by the sale of their independent work.

It seems that he could have become the President of the Royal Academy, but that he refused on the grounds of his incapacity for public speaking and attending to those obligations, social and otherwise, that go with this rank. It is an irony that the man who took the post in his stead should have done so much to lessen the glamour of Orpen's retrospective show.

Good wine cannot be appreciated after eating (the most saccharine) sweets. The simultaneous exhibition of Dicksee's pictures stole a great deal of the thunder from Orpen, by mere *succès de scandale*. Except to those who remember those distant pre-War days, these pictures came as a frightful shock. They were too good to be true. The wildest extravagance of ridicule never even approached the achievement of these pictures. They became the talk of the town; they took the breath away from even the hardiest. To those who were scientifically minded, they displayed compensations and complexities, strange moral standards, which would have made Freud himself stand aghast. The false modesties and the incessant temptings of celibate monks by Glaxo girls of uncertain anatomy were really too much even for this generation. Much as in Paris, Fumists and Dadaists, by their monstrosities, have been able to distract an entire public from the serious work of modern artists, so Dicksee became the attraction of the Royal Academy, and Orpen's realism and sincerity suffered. As the stage cat can ruin the finest performance of Hamlet, so did the late President of the Royal Academy distract the public, and cause loud guffaws.

It has been previously stated that Orpen changed from a happy little man to a man with a dual personality, poisoned with secret melancholy and brooding. It is always difficult to say whether misery causes illness, or illness misery; it is almost impossible to put down mental condition to physical sepsis; one school of medical opinion is continually battling with the other.   Many a mental expert studies the kidneys, others the psychology of youth, and there can be little doubt that Orpen never really recovered from the illness that he had during the War; but I think there can be no doubt that the mental conflict within him that came from the War largely undermined his resistance, and that a calmer and less sensitive brain would have triumphed over physical condition, especially if his lifetime had been spent in more placid conditions than the aftermath of war. There was little to encourage a mind made pessimistic by toxins. But on the other hand, mere good health seldom has produced good work. The physically fit never express, never create, never criticise, but are absorbed with the placid existence of living well. Mental energy, as history proves, seems a compensation of the physically unfit. The energy necessary for introspection and meditation is conserved by inability for physical prowess; except for a few feats of adolescence, Orpen's work matured and became more profound from the time when his health broke down, though his tragedy must have been terrible at the very end, when he would escape to his studio, against doctor's orders, only to discover that his hand had lost its cunning, contrasting sharply with the tragedy of Renoir, who, though crippled with arthritis, and with hands which had become mere stumps with open sores, was still able to go on painting with brushes strapped to his wrist, and a week before he died was jubilant because he thought he was just on the track of discovering how to paint really well. The dramatic tragedy of Orpen's life was more secret, though no less poignant, than the ends of Greuze, Boucher, Morland, Manet, or Renoir.

Though Orpen's life was so similar to Millais', it differed from it entirely in its culmination. Orpen was never ruined by success; perhaps his ill-health caused him always to feel a failure; perhaps his Celtic humour prevented him from taking himself as seriously as Millais did; perhaps he had not that Victorian reverence for human honours. No "Bubbles" came from Orpen's brush; in fact, as his years increased, his work tended towards a greater severity, and his most facile period is associated more with his youth than with his middle age. In the case of his portraits it was apparent that his later work did not rely so much upon a formula of the lighted face, and the reflected light thrown upon the shadowed portion of the sitter. His brush work became more learned and did not rely so much on the flashy bravura of slick touches of filbert-shaped hog-hair brushes, contrasted against a smouched and woolly texture, in which the badger-hair softener or frayed brush played too large a part; a mannerism to which he nearly fell a victim. His conscious or unconscious love of incongruity was, once again, the cause of his weakness for this method of technique;

the slick, crisp touches, mingled with the indefinite, softened smudginess of his original painting in, worked together in a very liquid basis.

No painter of the last hundred years is so difficult to place as Orpen, for reasons that are essentially post-Victorian; the standards by which artists in the past have been judged, praised, or condemned have no meaning at the moment. Because Orpen had a wonderful facility, he was condemned by certain artists who prefer the naïveté of Rousseau, le Douanier. Because Orpen's draughtsmanship was accurate and visual, he was condemned by those who prefer the halting but expressive line of Gaugin, or the expressionist line mentally conceived by Picasso. Because his paintings were often of a literary character, sometimes amounting almost to illustrations, he was condemned by those followers of the æstheticism preached by Roger Fry, which lays down that art should be pure, and consist of nothing but form and colour and pattern. Because he was successful, he was automatically condemned by the "intelligentsia," of slightly Socialistic tendencies, who are convinced that public opinion is always wrong, and that democracy and art is impossible; minorities are always right so long as they are not members of the aristocratic class. Because Orpen painted all sorts of fashionable people, he was condemned by the Chelsea and Bloomsbury art circles, who specialise only in the patronage of a certain section of rank and fashion. Because Orpen painted the War, he was condemned by that section of aggressive pacifists, who at the time were so profoundly absorbed in their own sensibilities and precious selves, that they were insensible to the agony round them, and superior to the sufferings of others.

Because Orpen was shrewd, to the point of uncanny intuition, he was condemned by those who prefer to look upon an artist as a bungling dreamer with blunted senses. Because Orpen made money, and was conscientious in the making of it, he was condemned by that sentimental journalistic section which likes to picture art in a garret, scrounging and cadging, and eventually prostituting itself. Because Orpen developed his technique and personality upon a definite tradition of Western art, he was condemned by that section which prefers the exotic, or the Eastern formulæ that have been thrust upon us since Whistler. Because Orpen was sufficiently strong, as a painter, not to rely upon ugliness and distortion, he was condemned by those who mistake hideousness for strength. Because Orpen was never a victim of the latest art vogue, he was condemned by those who in recent years have confused miliinery with pictures, and the "latest" with the best. Because Orpen was a realist, and painted things as he saw them, and even as they saw them, he was condemned by those who think abstraction the only solution, and incomprehensibility a superior expression. Because Orpen was an artist, and used paint as his greatest means of expressing himself and his thoughts, he was condemned by those who now consider a picture an object never to be looked at and enjoyed, but to be written about, puzzled over, confused or embarrassed by, or startled at; a mixture of musical conundrum, making harmonies, cacophonies and rhythms, dramas, architectural constructions, significant forms, and mathematical casuistries.

In this chaos which now surrounds post-Victorian art, Orpen painted; and possibly because he ignored the opinion of all connoisseurs, experts, critics, artists, journalists, cranks, and æsthetic-mongers, time may prove him to be the most representative artist of the post-Victorian epoch; perhaps a master.

LORD OXFORD AND ASQUITH
1852-1928

By
ROSSLYN MITCHELL

LORD OXFORD AND ASQUITH

by ROSSLYN MITCHELL

IN the month of May of the year 1915 an eminent political observer wrote:

> " One of the most important features of this time is the remarkable confidence shown in the Government. At the end of nine months of unexampled trial, Mr. Asquith's administration seems as firmly seated as at any moment in its history. Pitt himself did not possess more authority over the public mind than Mr. Asquith and his colleagues exercise to-day."

Before the month of May had ended, the Government had fallen. In eighteen months its leader was a private member in opposition.

It was Mr. Asquith's unhappy fate to be Prime Minister at the outbreak of the World War in 1914. He had been Prime Minister continuously since April 1908, when he had succeeded Sir Henry Campbell-Bannerman. They had been years of constructive progress in every department of national life. There had been alarums and excursions, as has always been the custom of Parliament, particularly when a Liberal Government has been in office. But they were years in which the exercise of cool judgment, plain speech, deliberation, and determination had been the suitable and adequate mode of dealing with their problems. In the atmosphere of war such methods count for little, are indeed regarded not only as inadequate but as hindrances. There is then no value in modest stillness and humility, nor occasion fit for reason and deliberation. It is demanded of a leader of a people at war that he personify the sentiment of war, the emotions of war. Circumstances demand decisions of the hour, often irrational and sometimes contrary to the decisions of the previous day, and not unlikely to be overruled by the decisions of the next. When the teeth are set, the nostril stretched wide, the breath held hard, and every spirit bent up to its full height, to be rational is to be inadequate. A people in the fret and fever of war demand emotion to feed their emotions and rhetoric to express their feelings. They insist that their leader shall personify their own excitement and feed their fever. If he fails so to do, he appears to disapprove of their emotions. It is only by seeing and hearing their emotions expressed by their chief man that people are saved from being ashamed of themselves.

For such a situation Mr. Asquith was by tradition, training, and temperament the least suitable of all the leading politicians of his time. He was of Yorkshire breed. He was of Puritan stock and sympathy. He was of Balliol College.

To be of Yorkshire breed is recognised by all men except Lancastrians as a good start in life. To be of Puritan stock is recognised by all men, including Lancastrians, as an enduring advantage. To be a son of Balliol is recognised by all sons of Balliol as a superlative privilege. There are qualifications attached to the advantage in all cases. A Yorkshireman is expected to be a " true Yorkshireman," to play the part of the traditional Yorkshireman, to play it in the manner of the legendary Yorkshireman. He must appear dour, unemotional, reserved, and plain. Yorkshire pudding like Scotch haggis owes none of its popularity to external appearance. In the case of the Puritan the qualification is subjective. However firmly convinced he may afterwards become that the Puritan tradition and mode of life are heretical and restrictive of personality, the heir cannot discard either of them without feeling a loss of self-respect. He is the heir to an entailed estate, the leaving of which is personal humiliation. He knows he is a backslider. He knows he has fallen from grace.

"There, but for the grace of God, goes John Bradford," was the Puritan's cry of thanksgiving and pity on seeing criminals being taken to execution. There was in his heart equal thanksgiving if less pity as he himself went as a martyr to the faggots of Smithfield. To have refused to face the faggots would leave him an object of pity only.

Both of these traditions tend to emphasise the appreciation of realities and the scorn of trimmings. They extol the virtues and disregard the graces. They adhere to the rational and despise the emotional. They exalt argument and affect to contemn sentiment.

Those whose characters are framed in these twin moulds appear firm as a rock and just as hard. The tradition of Balliol emphasises this quality. The tradition of Balliol is Hellenic directness and Roman power, logic as unchallengeable as mathematics, factual exactness as irrefragable as Ben Lomond.

The nebulous, the dramatic, the imaginative, and the morally splendid are for the groundlings; for the sons of Balliol nothing is good but the clean-cut, the precise, the naked, and the irresistible.

These traditions were strong in Mr. Asquith. He had been trained in them. His temperament responded to them. Besides, he was by nature diffident and by deliberate choice truthful. Truthfulness was not an acquired virtue. It was inherent. He never had to consider if he should tell the truth, but only how he should express it so that there could be no ambiguity. Shyness and his direct mind led him to choose the simplest way of expression, and the simplest way of expressing a truth produces often the effect of gruffness.

When I was a young student my mind was obsessed by the horrible conditions in which the artizans and labourers of the City of Glasgow were doomed to spend their lives. I had had years of experience among these people. I knew their homes. I hated the houses in which they were forced to live. In my adolescent sensitiveness and Puritan temperament I felt called of God to rouse the people to fury against the housing evil of my city. Liverpool had undertaken a great experiment in slum clearance. I went to see it. A fortnight later I met Mr. Asquith at Dalmeny, and full of my passion I waited for a moment to speak alone to the great man. At last the opportunity came, and I said rather timorously: " Don't you think the people of Liverpool are doing a great work in their new housing venture? " Without turning his head he said: " Umph, never heard of it." It closed me up like an oyster, and as soon as courtesy permitted I left the frigid atmosphere for the glowing warmth of our host, Lord Rosebery. I was not yet of age. I did not know then as much of politicians as I know now. Almost without exception other politicians would have pretended to know all about it, or led me on to talk about it as a sort of encouragement to youth. Mr. Asquith was too truthful to do the first and too distant to do the second. He just bowled out the stark fact that he had never heard of it, and left the impression that he didn't care.

A few years later we met by accident in the golf-house at Dornoch. As I entered I passed Dr. Jameson of the famous Raid. Mr. Asquith and I smiled as we watched the famous raider leave the club-house. Mr. Asquith was standing at the golf-club counter and I said: " How do you do? " He nodded, and I reminded him of the day we spent at Dalmeny. He said: " I don't remember." I told him my name and he said: " Oh yes, I do remember." That was his style, direct, barren fact. " I don't remember." " Oh yes, I do remember." The next day he was to receive the Freedom of the Burgh of Dornoch. He had asked that only the Town Councillors should be present and that there should be no fuss. The militant suffragettes were on the war-path and had already attacked him on the golf-course. But the Provost was a friend, and knowing that I was an enthusiastic Liberal invited me and another friend to the Council Chamber to see the little ceremony. When Mr. Asquith came in and the Councillors had been presented, he looked at us and said: " Interlopers." This taciturnity and laconic speech led to the legend that he was superior, inaccessible, even scornful.

Many years later I listened in the House of Commons to three Prime Ministers and Mr. T. P. O'Connor, the Father of the House, express appreciations of him. They extolled his qualities of loyalty and veracity, his services to the State, and spoke of him in accordance with the legend that had grown up around him, his lucidity in speech, his stability, his imperturbability. They pictured him as a mythical Roman Senator, shunning rather than seeking the approval of the multitude, aloof, superior, stolid.

It was because of this accepted estimate of his character that he was able to achieve the mighty works of his Parliaments of 1906-14. It was because of this, also, that his career ended in August 1914. War is accompanied by a thousand incidents and theatricalities which his soul loathed. Emotion and passion, which are the dynamic of the war spirit, he distrusted completely. The origin of his power in times of peace unfitted him for power in time of war. The only phrase which he used that became popular was " Wait and see," the one phrase of all phrases to tantalise and alienate an anxious, nerve-wracked, and impatient people.

There remains one of the great " ifs " of history. If Mr. Asquith had represented Great Britain at Versailles, would the Treaty have been such a hotch-potch of international malignities? Would his granite stubbornness and his steam-hammer logic have been overborne by the acute and cynical Clemenceau? Who knows? Instead, he was, for the first time since 1886, without a seat in Parliament, a rejected leader, a defeated candidate, an object of ridicule to those who had been his colleagues more even than to those who had been his opponents.

I have begun at the end because the World War looms large in the lives of all who were prominent in the political life of the time. How came it that Mr. Asquith was Prime Minister in August 1914? In 1933 we are accustomed to see the exalted places of the nation occupied by men of lowly origin and meagre financial resources. In 1908 that was a phenomenon. But in 1908 Mr. Asquith was the inevitable successor to Sir Henry Campbell-Bannerman.

Mr. Asquith was the first Prime Minister who was not backed by money. The House thought it strange that Sir Henry Campbell-Bannerman, a merchant, should be Prime Minister. But he was rich. Mr. Asquith was always poor. When he entered the House in 1886 he was a lawyer in considerable but not peculiarly lucrative practice. He had been born of middle-class parents in Morley, Yorkshire, thirty-four years before. Morley is one of the small towns which are the vertebræ of Britain's backbone, the kind of town which sends its sons to high position in the wider world, and to which civil servants from the wider world go with regret tempered by hope that it is but a stepping-stone to higher things; the kind of town in which church is the resort of Society and chapel the social centre, where a professional man is recognised as a civic leader and his wife as a Lady Bountiful. At seventeen he had won a scholarship to Balliol College, the first won by a pupil of the City of London School. There he carried all before him, winning the Craven Scholarship by erudition, and becoming President of the Union by character. In 1876 he had been called to the Bar at Lincoln's Inn, intending to practise at the Common Law Bar. His early years were not encouraging, and he supplemented his fee-income by lecturing on Economics and

Commercial Law and writing for the *Spectator* and the *Economist*.

It was indirectly through politics and his membership of the Radical Eighty Club that he obtained his real start, for he was much employed as Counsel for the Liberal candidate in the many election petitions that followed the General Election of 1885.

In July 1886 he was elected M.P. for East Fife, and joined two other young members who had first entered the House in 1885, Sir Edward Grey and Mr. Richard Burdon Haldane. They were to become the great Trio of post-Gladstone Liberalism. But the Parliament of 1886 was a Gladstone Parliament, though Gladstone was in opposition, a Parliament of grey-beards in whose presence a man of thirty-four was a stripling. When, however, Mr. Asquith made his maiden speech, the House discovered that, though beardless, he had the mind and manner of a man of experience. Gladstone himself was attracted.

The years 1888-9 and the Parnell Commission were the foundation of his fame as a lawyer and added to his promise as a politician. By the gracious act of Sir Charles Russell, afterwards Lord Russell of Killowen, the greatest cross-examiner of his time, H. H. Asquith, his junior, was called upon to cross-examine MacDonald, the manager of *The Times*, as to how he came to get the letters from Pigott. Bit by bit MacDonald was squeezed into telling one of the most extraordinary newspaper stories in history, which revealed Pigott as an impecunious rogue who had hoodwinked the whole squad of the men of *The Times*. A new portent had appeared in the forensic sky. The man who had been regarded as a pedestrian of the *via trita via tuta* order was recognised as belonging to the order of successes.

In 1892 Gladstone, returned to power with a precarious majority of forty, including the Irish members, offered him the Secretaryship of Home Affairs. Here was a conflict and a deliberate choice to be made between law and politics. He chose politics, and accepted the invitation. With a mind constructive rather than creative, and a mode of speech crisp, clear, and concise in a party attuned to the rich splendour of Gladstone's oratory, his three years of office might have exhausted the stock of popularity which he declined to take steps to replenish. It was replenished by an accident. The accident was the Featherstone Colliery

Riot, where he sent a military detachment to support the police. In a volley two men were killed. The result was a vast publicity, an added respect from his party, and execration from thousands of the more advanced politicians among the people. The year 1895 brought the Liberal Government to an inglorious end, to be succeeded by eleven years of Unionist rule. The Home Secretary, having surrendered the seals of office, challenged tradition by returning to his practice at the Bar, and increased his Parliamentary prestige as the sledge-hammer of the Government. The South African War drew him away from many of his colleagues, and led to the formation of the Liberal League, in which he operated with Lord Rosebery, Sir Edward Grey, Mr. R. B. Haldane, and others of less eminence. It was a challenge to Sir Henry Campbell-Bannerman. The Liberal Leaguers did not understand Campbell-Bannerman. He had the appearance of moss, and his easy-going, rather soft manner, and the quiet, sly humour, known in Scotland as pawkiness, with which he viewed men and affairs led his colleagues to regard him, as the Cabinet of Abraham Lincoln regarded their President, as a quaint but fashionless person. But when it came to be a question of principle C.-B., like Abraham Lincoln, showed that the moss was growing on granite. Against the immovable firmness of C.-B., the rebel quartette—Rosebery, Grey, Haldane, and Asquith—could avail nothing. It was a futile struggle.

It might have split the Liberal Party in appearance as it did in fact but for the fortunate breakaway of Mr. Joseph Chamberlain. Only those who lived in Glasgow on October 6, 1903, can appreciate the excitement of that day. To a huge audience in the largest hall in the City Mr. Chamberlain, who had resigned from the Cabinet on September 17, announced his new Protectionist policy. The speech jolted the elements of the Liberal Party into each other's laps, and led to one of the most vigorous and extensive platform campaigns in history. On the subject of Free Trade all Liberals and Socialists were at one. The only rivalry was a rivalry in orthodoxy and excellence. It was a conflict of giants, in which Lloyd George charmed, Alexander Ure convinced, Winston Churchill surprised, Haldane instructed, and C.-B. bantered. But the acknowledged Chief among Chieftains was H. H. Asquith, who in massive eloquence and irrefutable logic followed the great Chamberlain round the country. No subject could have been more to the setting of his mind and the quality of his equipment. He had been called the sledge-hammer. He became an hydraulic press. Every "fact" that the Protectionist leader announced as the basis of his scheme Asquith blew into shreds, and every argument he crunched to powder. Those who agreed with him hailed him as the obvious leader, those who disagreed regarded him as their strongest opponent.

Three years later Free Trade was the main issue at the General Election which resulted in an overwhelming Liberal and Socialist victory. Sir Henry Campbell-Bannerman became Prime Minister and Mr. Asquith Chancellor of the Exchequer. His time had not yet come. His financial plans were orthodox and uninspiring. Only the provision of Old Age Pensions (5s. a week at seventy, subject to innumerable qualifications) had any platform value. But with the resignation of Campbell-Bannerman there emerged in the new Prime Minister a man of immovable tenacity, unshakable courage, and infinite Parliamentary skill. The period from 1907 to 1914 was a time of excitement and passion. Everyone in the nation was a politician. Health Insurance, Land Reform, conflicts with the House of Lords, Irish Home Rule, Disestablishment of the English Church in Wales, were a few of the great issues that divided the people. The Lords rejected the Budget of 1909 and the political timber-yard burst into flame. Two elections in 1910 were inadequate to reduce the fire. Then Mr. Asquith applied for and received authority to create peers sufficient in number to outvote the Conservatives and the fire subsided. The result of his courage and tenacity was the Parliament Act, which left the House of Lords defeated and disarmed. It was his hour of supreme triumph. Throughout the conflict, in the face of political and personal onslaughts, he had maintained an imperturbable calm. His lieutenants had provided and relished excitement enough. He remained cool and unmoved. Impervious to threats and cajolery alike, he had gone forward steadily to his goal.

No sooner was the contest ended than there broke out another, more serious and more sinister.

It was patience that had won the victory in the struggle with the House of Lords. It was patience that defeated him in the Ulster Rebellion which followed. His contempt

by ROSSLYN MITCHELL

for the gospel of anarchy, as he called it, was so complete and his faith in the sound sense of a democratic people so sincere, that he allowed the North and South of Ireland to form armies in defiance of Parliament, and accepted without action what was little short of mutiny in the British Army. His reply to the " Curragh Incident " was the assumption of the office of Secretary of State for War and a long and laborious process of trying to persuade two irreconcilable forces to reach a settlement by agreement.

On July 24, 1914, the Conference, invited by the King to discuss a possible settlement of the Home Rule problem, broke down. Mr. Asquith announced the failure to the House of Commons, and proceeded to a Cabinet Meeting, at which the condition of Ireland yielded place to the condition of Europe. Civil War was overshadowed by the advance of World War. How much the one influenced the other must be left for future historians to say. What concerns us is the effect of war upon Mr. Asquith.

In the opening weeks he hid his feelings of seriousness by an unusually humorous attitude towards details. His diary of this period reads more like a description of a group of amateur players preparing for a performance in aid of charity than that of a Cabinet engaged in war. But it would be inaccurate to assume that there was not serious work going on. Great Britain in the early days of the War fulfilled to the last button every obligation she undertook, and in ships, men, artillery, and medical services provided more than had ever been contemplated as likely to be necessary. Energy and expert management carried the country from a peace basis to a war basis with amazing smoothness. In the capital cities Mr. Asquith made speeches which, if not characterised by great moral fervour, were of superlatively fine eloquence. He was hailed as the Great Leader. Parliament voted as he invited it to. For nine months of war the Government retained in a remarkable degree the confidence of Parliament and People. Much as others loomed in the minds of the public as popular figures, it was Mr. Asquith who appeared to be the dominant personality of the country. So it was in May 1915. And in that month the Government collapsed.

What were the immediate reasons for the formation of the first Coalition Government is still uncertain. What is clear is that Mr. Asquith was unsuited to be Prime Minister in a time of war. He was a great leader of a party. He was never a leader of the People. He became the victim of his own rigid self-discipline. Caution appeared as hesitancy. Patience looked like inactivity and was even called indolence. Intellectual supremacy took on the aspect of indifference to sentiment and emotion. He had never been a popular figure in the full sense. He excited admiration, but aroused no feelings of affection. He seemed to lack sympathy, to be incarcerated in a dungeon of reserve. Constructive in mind, he was content to leave initiative to others, sometimes even to smile superiorly at their flashes of inventiveness. At a time when momentum was essential he seemed to be a brake on the machinery. He accepted situations rather than created them. He had none of the mystery of the seer, none of the flame of the pioneer. The confidence which flows from reverence or affection he had not known.

The Asquith Coalition Government lived through nineteen months of continuous military adversity. In December 1916 he was forced to resign. One by one his colleagues had turned against him. He was pursued by virulent attacks in the Press, which he treated with contemptuous silence. He was confronted with his first-mate leading a mutiny and surrendered. It would be unjust to those who succeeded him to suggest that the mutiny was the product of ambition and vanity. There was apparent to onlookers a marked change in the man himself. The rigid Puritanism of earlier years was gone. In its place there came a, for him, novel inclination towards the casual and careless form of life. It showed itself in his dress and bearing. The precision of mind and manners disappeared. From time to time the old form reappeared, but the occasions on which it showed itself were unworthy of it and gave the impression of querulousness and petulance.

On November 11, 1918, an Armistice was signed and the War ended. Immediately the Coalition Government of Mr. Lloyd George and Mr. Bonar Law went to the country on what was called the Coupon Election. Mr. Asquith did not receive the coupon, and was defeated in the constituency he had represented for thirty-two years. How far he had fallen in favour may be gauged by the kind of placard used against him: " Asquith nearly lost you the War. Are you going to let him spoil the Peace? " The Coupon Election meant the end of the Liberal Party. It did not mean the end of Mr. Asquith. After a year out of the House, during which he travelled and read Sir Walter Scott's novels, he was elected Member for Paisley at a by-election. The influence of the Coalition was still powerful. His selection by the Liberals was carried by a small majority. The election was watched with intense interest by the country, for his speeches, afterwards known as the Paisley policy, set out anew the basis of Liberalism. In the four years during which he represented Paisley he had a strange experience. In Parliament and among the public his influence steadily declined, but among the section of the Liberal Party which followed him there grew up a feeling of affection for him that approached reverence. At no period of his life had he known such devoted friendship and faith.

In 1924, when he faced his fourth election in Paisley, he was practically forgotten by the nation. He was no longer known as a Tribune of the People, but as a Senator. He was growing old, and in his speeches spoke always of the past. But it was in the future that the interests of the people lay, and he was defeated. On the day after the election the nation awoke to the fact that he was a great man. Newspapers, which a few years before had maligned and lampooned him, filled columns with praises of his parliamentary genius and his services to the nation. A few days later the King wrote to him: " It would be a matter of the greatest satisfaction to me to confer upon you a Peerage," which in January 1925 he accepted with the title: " Earl of Oxford and Asquith." In June 1925 he received the Order of the Garter.

In October 1926 he laid down the leadership of the Liberal Party. On February 15, 1928, he died.

So passed one of the few of the Victorians who remained. For forty-two years he had been more or less in the public eye.

He had lived through political triumph and adversity. Fortified by his own nature, the devotion of a distinguished wife whose brilliance had a daring quality, and of a family of unique intellectual attainments, he had administered the affairs of the public with the courage of a Cæsar, the modesty of a Cincinnatus, and the aloofness of a Coriolanus. He had stood by his colleagues in their day of anxiety, and lived to see himself driven from Parliament by them. He had held high office in the most critical years of British history.

Throughout he remained as he had begun, a Liberal. He was the last of the great Liberal statesmen, the last of the Gladstonian cohorts, the last of the political Victorians.

To the post-war generation he is little more than a name. To a considerable group of men, growing old, he is a legend. But much of the liberty they enjoy and the security they cherish they received as the fruits of his character and his activity. It is not necessarily a diminution of a man's stature to say that he was not suited to lead a people in the fret and fever of war. What he builded he builded well and it endures.

MRS. PANKHURST
1858-1928

By
REBECCA WEST

MRS. PANKHURST

by REBECCA WEST

THERE has been no other woman like Emmeline Pankhurst. She was beautiful; her pale face, with its delicate square jaw and rounded temples, recalled the pansy by its shape and a kind of velvety bloom on the expression. She dressed her taut little body with a cross between the elegance of a Frenchwoman and the neatness of a nun. She was courageous; small and fragile and no longer young, she put herself in the way of horses' hooves, she stood up on platforms under a rain of missiles, she sat in the darkness of underground jails and hunger-struck, and when they let her out because she had starved herself within touching distance of death, she rested for only a day or two and then clambered back on to the platforms, she staggered back under the horses' hooves. She did this against the grain. What she would have preferred, could her social conscience have been quieted, was to live in a pleasant suburban house, and give her cronies tea with very thin bread and butter, and sit about in the garden in a deck-chair.

Mrs. Pankhurst came to these cruel and prodigious events not as some who have attained fame in middle life. She had not lived in ease all her youth and dammed up her forces, so that there was a flood to rush forth when the dam was broken. She had borne five children, she had been distracted by the loss of a beloved husband, she had laboured long at earning a livelihood and at public work. Enough had happened to her to draw off all her natural forces. That she was not so depleted can be partly explained by the passion for the oppressed which burned in her as a form of genius; and she drew, no doubt, refreshment from the effect she had on her fellow creatures, the response they made to her peculiar quality, which was apart from her beauty, her courage, her pity. She was vibrant. One felt, as she lifted up her hoarse, sweet voice on the platform, that she was trembling like a reed. Only the reed was of steel, and it was tremendous.

On an Atlantic liner during a great storm passengers will feel in their bones the quiver that runs through the ship's backbone as her stern rests on a wave and her prow hangs in mid-air over the trough till she finds the next wave to carry her. Something of the same sort was the disturbance, the perturbation, the suspense at the core of Mrs. Pankhurst's being. She was not a particularly clever woman. One could name scores of women who were intellectually her superior. She was constitutionally naïve, she could swallow fairy stories, she had only an imperfect grasp of the map of the universe man has drawn with his thought. She was one of those people who appear now and then in history against whom it would be frivolous to lay a complaint on these grounds, since they are part of that map. She was the embodiment of an idea. Her personality was possessed by one of man's chief theories about life, which it put to the test, and which it worked out in terms of material fact. She went forward, precariously balanced on what there was of old certainty, hanging in mid-air till she could attain a new certainty, her strength vibrating as if it were going to shatter into pieces like glass, maintaining itself because it was steel.

She was born in Manchester on July 14, 1858, of North-country stock with character. Her grandfather, a master cotton-spinner, had in his youth been cruelly used by the State. One day he was carried off to sea by the Press Gang, and did not manage to make his return for many years, by which time his family had completely disappeared. Later he fled before the soldiers at the Battle of Peterloo, and with his wife, a fustian cutter of sturdy disposition, took part in the Cobdenite agitations of the Hungry Forties. His son, Robert Goulden, was brilliant and versatile. He began as an errand boy and ended as a manufacturer, he was an amateur actor who made a great impression in the heavier Shakespearean parts; he ran a theatre in Salford as a hobby, and he was a romantic Liberal. He took a leading part in that altruistic movement by which Lancashire, brought to beggary by the American Civil War and constrained by every economic reason to side with the South, solidly upheld Lincoln and the North. He had by that time married a Manxwoman, who bore him five sons and five daughters.

His eldest girl, little Emmeline, rattled a collecting box for the poor Negroes and learned to weep over *Uncle Tom's Cabin*, though, with an entirely characteristic refusal to restrict herself to logical categories, she gave the most fervent loyalty of her imagination to Charles the First.

When she was thirteen Robert Goulden took her to school in Paris. He left her at the Ecole Normale at Neuilly, a green and spacious suburb which must have been a pleasing contrast to Manchester. In any case, Emmeline's love of beauty would have made her a friend to France; but owing to an accident, Neuilly offered a seduction even more specially appealing to her temperament. Because Mr. Goulden had to make the expedition fit in with business engagements, he left her at the school during the holidays, when there was but one other pupil. This was a fascinating little girl called Noémie, who had no home to go to, because her mother was dead, and her father, Henri de Rochefort, was in prison in New Caledonia for the part he had played in the Commune. The two girls became instantly welded in a friendship that lasted till the end of their lives, and Emmeline learned to adore Henri de Rochefort in his daughter's talk, as later she was to adore him in his own person. He was something for a romantic little Radical to adore, a splendid, spitting cat of a man, who spoke his mind in the face of any danger, who, though Napoleon III sat on the throne, began his leader on the shooting of Victor Noir by Prince Pierre-Napoleon Bonaparte with the words, "*J'ai eu la faiblesse de croire qu'un Bonaparte pouvait être autre qu'un assassin. J'ai osé m'imaginer qu'un duel loyal était possible dans cette famille où le meutre et le guet-apenus sont de tradition et de l'usage . . .*"; who fought duel after duel, suffered arrest again and again, and endured exile and imprisonment with like fiery fortitude.

Emmeline was, owing to a real or maldiagnosed weakness of health, forbidden to take part seriously in the school work; she never then or later knew any form of study stricter than desultory reading, or appreciated its uses. But she was receiving, from Noémie and her absent father and her guardian, Edmond Adam, a thorough education in a certain department of French life, in the passionate and picturesque conduct of politics. There the prizes went to the daring. There it was no shame to act violently and fight one's enemies as if they were enemies. And in this atmosphere she spent those very formative years between thirteen and twenty; for she loved Paris so much that, when her own school-days were over, she coaxed her father to let her stay on as companion to a younger sister.

She tried her best to stay in France for ever; and that, alas, led to her smarting and tearful removal back to Lancashire. There was a curious event which, for the first time, revealed that Emmeline was an odd fish who was not going to take life as she found it. Noémie married, and thought it would be delightful if Emmeline found a French husband and settled down as her neighbour. Such a husband could be obtained, of course, only by a bride with a *dot*. But Emmeline knew that her father was well-to-do, and she found nothing abhorrent in the *dot* system. She had disliked the scenes that her father had made when her mother brought him bills, and had seen with her clear eyes that, in a masculinist and capitalist social system, where women have not economic freedom and wives are not paid, the dowry is the only way by which a woman can be given self-respecting security and independence. Romantic Liberalism could go and hang itself. She was a realist. But unfortunately her father was still a romantic Liberal. When Emmeline found a pleasing suitor and asked for her *dot*, Robert Goulden stormed the house down at the idea of buying a husband for his daughter, and immediately made her leave Paris and come home. She obeyed with the worst possible grace; and suddenly looked up through her sulks and saw someone as spectacular as Rochefort, Dr. Richard Marsden Pankhurst, and fell in love with him.

It was, on the surface, an astounding match. He was twice her age, a scholar with many academic honours, a distinguished jurist, whose studies filled all his leisure hours. He was dedicated to public work, of a laborious and unrewarded sort; he achieved great things in the promotion of popular education, he was a Republican, and an indefatigable enemy of Disraeli's Imperialism. He had a great position in the North. When he arrived at a meeting thousands waited cheering and waving their handkerchiefs. Though he had what would have been a crushing handicap for most politicians, an extremely unpleasant, shrill, edgy voice, the force of his mind and the transparent beauty of his nature was such that an audience never remained conscious of this defect for more than the first few minutes. He was a saint who had put all weaknesses behind him and wore himself out in acts of benevolence. Such works of art were these private good deeds that they had something of that immortality: a visitor to Manchester more than a decade after his death thought that he must have been dead only a month or so, so vividly had some whom he had helped spoken of him.

But Emmeline was just a wicked little thing, fond of pretty clothes and French novels. It happened, however, to be a perfectly right and wise marriage. Emmeline committed herself gravely and honestly to her love for him. Her mother was deeply shocked, and tried to inspire her to the proper female monkey-tricks by telling her of the coldness with which she herself had received her prospective husband's wooings, and was shocked still more when her daughter suggested to her betrothed as a protest against the then legal disabilities of married women, that they should form a free union. (Noémie's mother had married Henri de Rochefort only on her death-bed to give her children a legal protector.) Dr. Pankhurst would not consent, however, partly because he feared to expose her to disrespect, partly because he knew that those who challenged the marriage-laws were usually prevented from challenging any other abuses. So they married, and were happy ever after. Not the bitterest critic of Mrs. Pankhurst ever suggested that her husband did not find her, from beginning to end of the nineteen years of their marriage, a perfect wife.

They had five children: Christabel, who was born when her mother was twenty-two, Sylvia, born two years later, Frank, born two years later, Adela, born a year later, and Harry, born four years later. Theirs was not a home in which parents exerted themselves to keep their children's lives a thing apart, a pool of quietness in which they could develop until they were mature. Mrs. Pankhurst was a young woman, full of appetite for life, and wildly in love with her husband, so that she was delighted to stand by him in his public work. She did not neglect her children, but the stream of affairs flowed through her home, and the children bobbed like corks on the tide of adult life. One of them hated it. Sylvia Pankhurst's *The Suffragette Movement* stands beside Gordon Craig's *Memories of My Mother* as an expression of the burning resentment that the child of a brilliant mother may feel at having to share her brilliance with the world. But the other children liked it, and revelled in the dramas that followed one after another. First, there was the famous Manchester by-election, at which Dr. Pankhurst stood as an Independent candidate on a platform including Adult Suffrage, Republicanism, Secular Education, the payment of Members of Parliament, Disestablishment, Home Rule, Disarmament, and a kind of League of Nations. The year was 1883. He was not elected; but a quarter of the electorate supported him—an incredible proportion at that time—and his expenses were £500 as against his opponents' £5,000. It was a triumphant piece of propaganda work; but it ended in personal bitterness, in the first display by Mrs. Pankhurst of that ruthlessness which she shared with the armed prophets. Till then she and her family had lived in her father's home, a patriarchal dwelling where the Manx mistress of the house carried on all the domestic arts, even to bread-baking and butter-making. But though Robert Goulden had stood by Dr. Pankhurst during the by-election, he rebuked him afterwards for his Socialist extremism, and to mark a dissociation of political interests Dr. Pankhurst and his family left the Goulden home, accompanied by Mrs. Pankhurst's sister Mary. On this separation Mrs. Pankhurst reminded her father that he had promised her some property on her marriage. He denied ever having made such a promise. They never spoke to each other again.

This deep feeling over a matter of property was odd to find in a woman who all her life long regarded money chiefly as something to give away. But it was a consequence of the simple, surgical directness of her mind. If Robert Goulden wanted to accept the masculinist and capitalist world, then he ought to be logical about it, and protect her in the only way that a woman can be protected in a masculinist and capitalist world. The only reason he could have for failing to do so must be that he did not love her. But it must also be remembered that her childhood hero had been Charles I, the King who lost his crown and his head, and that she attached an importance to Henri de Rochefort's refusal to use his marquisate which was, since the renunciation had actually been made by a previous generation of the family, historically undue. The men she specially admired were those who had power and renounced it. It is an indication that in her there was an element of sex-antagonism, that neurosis which revolts against the difference of the sexes, which calls on the one to which the neurotic does not belong to sacrifice its special advantage so that the one to which the neurotic does belong may show superior. But neuroses often engender the dynamic power by which the sane part of the mind carries on its business. Mrs. Pankhurst sublimated her sex-antagonism. She was in no way a man-hater, loving her sons as deeply as her daughters, and she completely converted her desire to offend the other sex into a desire to defend her own.

Dr. Pankhurst stood for Parliament again at Rotherhithe, and was again defeated. There followed a painful libel action. A Conservative speaker had told a lying story which put into Dr. Pankhurst's mouth a coarse declaration of atheism. He was in fact an agnostic of the gentlest type, full of reverence and love for the person of Christ. He brought action, not so much for his own sake, as to bring a test case which would show how far Socialist candidates could find remedy in the new libel law for the flood of slanderous abuse that was turned on them at every election. There were aspects of this libel action which were calculated to remove certain comfortable illusions about human nature from the minds of the least critical. Dr. Pankhurst, never worldly-wise, appealed to Mr. A. J. Balfour as a brother agnostic, on the undisputable evidence of certain passages in *A Defence of Philosophic Doubt*. Mr. Balfour received the appeal without brotherly enthusiasm, and practised the arts of evasion to avoid associating himself with this crude imbroglio. The trial itself was conducted with what might have seemed shameless prejudice to those who did not know that British justice is above suspicion. Mrs. Pankhurst ran the risk of prosecution for contempt of court by sending a cutting letter to the judge who tried the case.

The Pankhursts went to live in London. There Mrs. Pankhurst was extremely happy. It is true that shortly after she settled there her son Frank died and her grief was terrible. But she had a gay time establishing herself as a political hostess with tea-urns in Russell Square for the Socialist London that was humbly proliferating in the Fabian Society, the Social Democratic Federation, the Independent Labour Party, and half a dozen other obscure organisations; a naïve and ludicrous parody it must have seemed to those who really knew the world, of the real social functions of power, where great ladies shining with diamonds received at the head of wide staircases under magnificent chandeliers. She worked hard for all feminist causes, for all issues which promised man more liberty, although always she regarded herself not as an independent worker, but as her husband's helpmate. She had much amusement, too, trying to support herself by running Emerson's, a kind of amateurish Liberty's. The French influence came back into her life at full strength, for Henri de Rochefort was an exile living in London, and he constantly visited her.

It had to come to an end soon. Both Mrs. Pankhurst and her husband were children about money. They spent it, not like drunken sailors, but like drunken saints. They gave it away with both hands. Emerson's, owing to bad costing, was an expensive toy. They had taken the Russell Square house on the fag-end of a lease without reflecting that at the end they would have to pay dilapidations. In bad order they retreated to Lancashire, first to Southport, and then to Manchester, where they got on a sounder financial footing, and Mrs. Pankhurst came to her proper form as a social worker. She helped to organise the unemployed in the slump of 1894, and did much to popularise her husband's views on productive public works as a means of relieving unemployment. She was elected to the Chorlton Board of Guardians, and blazed with rage because she found the little girls in the workhouse still wearing eighteenth-century dress, with low necks and no sleeves. For some obscure reason they had no nightdresses, and they had no drawers or knickers, even in winter time—a fact which infuriated her beyond bearing—because the matron and a couple of refined female guardians had been too modest to mention such garments to the male members of the Board. This was the kind of tomfoolery which Mrs. Pankhurst could not stand, and which her Movement did much to end. These, and many other abuses, she reformed.

There was a fight, too, against an attempt by the City Council to deny the I.L.P., now newly become formidable, the right of meeting in the public places of Manchester. Mrs. Pankhurst acted as chairman to the speakers at the test meeting, sticking the ferrule of her open umbrella in the ground so that the faithful could throw their pennies into it.

With eight others she was arrested, and stood calmly in the dock, dressed her prettiest, wearing a little pink straw bonnet. The case against her was dismissed, though she announced that she would repeat her offence so long as she was at liberty. This she did, although she was summoned again and again. She always wore her pink straw bonnet, and it became the signal round which the rebels gathered. This was a real fight, and it took a long time to win. She lived therefore for many months under the expectation of prison. She was willing then, had the need arisen, to prove the point she proved later.

There was an election, too, at Gorton, Lancashire, where Dr. Pankhurst stood as I.L.P. candidate. The I.L.P. had the scantiest funds, and had to use cheap methods of campaign, such as chalking announcements of meetings on the pavements. For £343 of election expenses against the Conservative candidate's £1,375, Dr. Pankhurst gained 4,261 votes against the Conservative's 5,865. The Pankhurst children helped in the campaign, and it was no minor part of their education, which was indeed unconventional.

Mrs. Pankhurst as a mother offers certain surprises to those who would expect her to have the same views as the kind of woman who has followed in her steps regarding feminism. She was thoroughly of her time. She believed in corporal punishment for children as mothers did in the 'eighties, and in making them finish their porridge even if their stomachs revolted against it. She had some of the prejudices of her Manx country-bred mother. She had no such great opinion of fresh air as a nursery remedy, and she strongly disapproved of spectacles, causing her younger son, who had weak eyes, great inconvenience thereby. And in one respect she was almost behind her times. She attached no importance to ordinary education for her daughters. They were often put in the care of governesses who gave them no lessons whatsoever, but trained them in such unusual subjects as the appreciation of Egyptian art; and when they did attend schools she connived shamelessly at their truancy. This was due in part, perhaps, to her knowledge that schools were so much part of the capitalist system that her family could have no comfortable welcome there, and it is true that at least one headmistress persecuted and humiliated the children because their father was a Socialist. In those days political rancours went deeper than we care to imagine to-day. When Mrs. Pankhurst was on the Manchester Education Committee she had to intervene to protect a woman teacher who had been dismissed by the owner of a school because it had leaked out that she was a daughter of Ernest Jones, the Chartist, who had been dead for over thirty years.

But there was also a deeper reason for Mrs. Pankhurst's unconcern about education. It is said that the only occasion on which she showed overwhelming grief about a personal matter other than over the death of her husband and her sons and her final alienation from one of her family, was when her daughter Christabel decided that she would not become a professional dancer. The child had shown great promise at her dancing classes, and it had been her mother's dream that she should become a great ballerina, who should practise her art all over the world. This anecdote has been repeated querulously, as if it were a proof of Mrs. Pankhurst's light-mindedness. But it surely gives a clue to the secret of her greatness as a leader. She knew that no culture can evolve values which wholly negate primitive ones. She would have understood that Sir Walter Scott's boy spoke better sense than the learned when, brought up in ignorance of "Waverley" and its fame, he accounted for the fuss people made of his father by saying, " It's commonly him that sees the hare sitting." She had not lost touch with primitive wisdom; she knew that man's first necessity is to be a good animal, that rhythm can prove as much as many arguments, that the mind is only one of the instruments of human power.

Dr. Pankhurst died. His widow was heartbroken. For a time she was too distracted to attend to any public work. But she could not be idle, for she was without means. Her husband had been splendidly careless about money. His last months had been spent in successfully organising opposition to a dirty and dangerous scheme by which the Manchester Corporation intended to pollute the Mersey with the town sewage by diverting it through a new culvert, designed to dump it in a part of the river outside the scope of sanitary jurisdiction. Had he not opposed the construction of the culvert he would have been instructed to act as Counsel for the scheme, and might have made over £8,000 by it. With poverty earned thus his family were well content, but Mrs. Pankhurst had to work. She became Registrar of Births and Deaths in Chorlton, and opened another Emerson's, which lingered on for some time and then had to be abandoned. She came back to public life for a little in 1900, in the Pro-Boer agitation. Then she began to feel a special interest in Woman Suffrage, perhaps because her daughter Christabel had suddenly, and for the first time, become keenly interested in feminism, and was studying for a law degree at Victoria University. It also happened that about this time she was stung to fury by an incident connected with a memorial to her dead husband. Though she had accepted some funds raised by his wealthier friends, she had refused to touch the subscriptions gathered from the predominantly working-class readers of Robert Blatchford's *The Clarion*, on the grounds that she did not wish them to give her children an education which they could not have afforded for their own; and she suggested that the money should be spent on building a Pankhurst Memorial Hall for the use of Socialist societies. When it was finished she found that the branch of the Independent Labour Party which was to use it as headquarters refused to admit women. This led her to review the attitude of the I.L.P. and the Socialist Movement generally towards feminism. She found that it was no more than lukewarm; and therefore on October 10, 1903, in her drawing-room at 62 Nelson Street, she held the inaugural meeting of a society called the Women's Social and Political Union.

For the first two years the proceedings of this society were limited to humdrum harrying of the Socialist societies. But the result of this routine was to force up to explosion point Mrs. Pankhurst's realisation of the wrongs inflicted on women by their status, and the indifference on this subject which was felt by even the most progressive societies dominated by men. It was becoming every day more clear, too, that a certain condition she found necessary if she was to act effectively was about to be abundantly fulfilled. Oddly enough, she never did anything important alone. She had to work with an ally. For that purpose Dr. Pankhurst had been perfect; but the development of her daughter Christabel made her see that he might not be irreplaceable. Though Christabel had never studied anything but dancing at all seriously until her middle teens, she was taking her law studies well, and when she went up to London to apply for admission to the Benchers of Lincoln's Inn she conducted the proceedings with a strange, cool, high-handed mastery that was remarkable in a girl in her early twenties.

In 1905 Mrs. Pankhurst came to London to find a private member who would give his place in the ballot to a measure giving votes for women. There was then, as for many years before, a majority of members in the House pledged to support Woman Suffrage, but this meant nothing more than a polite bow and smile to their more earnest female helpers in their constituencies. Hardly any of them meant to lift a little finger to make Woman Suffrage an accomplished fact.

Mrs. Pankhurst had the greatest difficulty in finding a sincere Suffragist among the small number of members who had been fortunate in the ballot that gave them the right to introduce a Bill on one or other of the Friday afternoons during the Session; but on May 12, Mr. Bamford Slack brought in a Suffrage Bill. Mrs. Pankhurst brought with her to the House of Commons an immense number of women, which was swelled by members of the more old-fashioned and conservative Suffrage societies, who had been excited by the agitation of the new movement. There were so many that they filled the Lobby, the passages, and the Terrace. When it became obvious that the Bill was, as usual, going to be obstructed and talked out, Mrs. Pankhurst looked round her at the great crowd of women. Much more than the future of the feminist movement was decided in that second. Then she scribbled a note to be taken in to the Prime Minister, in which, with the arrogance of a leader writing to a leader, she told him that unless he gave facilities for the further discussion of this Bill her Union would work against his Government. She was a little woman in her late forties, without a penny, without a powerful friend. The threat was comic. As soon as the Bill was talked out, there was an impromptu meeting outside the House which would have been stopped had not Keir Hardie intervened.

Mrs. Pankhurst went home. There were some new recruits in the North, a mill girl called Annie Kenney, an Irish school-teacher called Teresa Billington. All that summer Mrs. Pankhurst with these girls and Christabel and Sylvia went from wake to wake in the Lancashire and Yorkshire mill-towns, and stood on I.L.P. and Trade Union platforms. In the autumn Sir Edward Grey came to speak at Manchester, and failed to reply to a letter from the Women's Social and Political Union asking him to receive a deputation. They attended his meeting and asked questions regarding the attitude of the coming Liberal Government. But these were not answered, so they interrupted the subsequent proceedings, and were ejected. Outside the hall they addressed a meeting and were arrested on a charge of having assaulted the police, and were sent to prison for seven and three days in the third division. It is hardly necessary to say that the balance of the assaults committed on this occasion were committed by the stewards and policemen on the Suffragists; but the Suffragists would themselves hardly have troubled to raise that point. They candidly admitted they had meant to be arrested. For it was their intention to maintain that in a democratic State government rests on the consent of the governed, and that until they were granted the franchise on the same terms as men they were going to withhold that consent; and that they were going to mark the withholding of their consent by disturbing the peace, to the precise degree which the resistance of the Government made necessary; and that they would not take it that the Government had yielded unless whatever party was in power itself passed an Act for the enfranchisement of women.

For nine years this policy was carried into effect by innumerable women under the leadership of Mrs. Pankhurst. For nine years no politician of any importance could address a meeting without fear of interruption. There was never any lack of women volunteers for this purpose, even though the stewards nearly always ejected them with great physical violence, sometimes of a sort that led to grave internal injuries. One of the most brilliant Suffragists, or Suffragettes, as *The Daily Mail* started people calling them, May Gawthorpe, was an invalid for many years as a result of a blow received in this way. When the harried political organisers tried to solve the problem by excluding all women from the meetings, interruptions were made through windows and skylights, even if this involved perilous climbing over roofs and gutters, and evading police search by concealment in neighbouring attics for two or three days. There were also constant disturbances at the House of Commons. When a Private Member's Bill for Woman Suffrage was being talked out in 1906, Mrs. Pankhurst and some friends created a riot in the Ladies' Gallery. From that time repeated raids were made on the House of Commons by women seeking interviews with Cabinet Ministers, and these became in time vast riots which it taxed the power of Scotland Yard to keep within bounds. All the area round Whitehall and St. Stephen's Square was packed with people, watching while women threw themselves against a cordon of police, and withstood massed charges of mounted men. The spectators divided themselves as the night went on into supporters and opponents, and there would be dashes made to rescue individual women or to manhandle them. The police were ordered to make as few arrests as possible, so some of the women would find themselves thrown about like so many footballs.

Participation in these interruptions and in these riots meant imprisonment. Very soon the women were getting sentences of six weeks' imprisonment. They rose soon to three months, to nine months, to two years. To put the Government in an impossible position, they hunger-struck, abstaining from food, and sometimes even from water. At first they were released. Then the Government employed surgical methods of forcible feeding. The prisoners resisted that, but this meant that their gums were hacked to pieces with steel gags, and the tubes were apt to injure the internal organs, and the food was often vomited, so they frequently had to be released all the same. Then the Government passed the Cat-and-Mouse Act, which enabled them to release the hunger-striking prisoners when they were within touching distance of death, wait till they had recovered their health, and then arrest them again, and bring them back to death once more, and so on. It was one of the most unlovely expedients that the English legislature has ever invented, and it is ironical that it should have been the work of a Liberal Government. And it had the further disgrace of being ineffectual, for it entirely failed to quench the Movement. That spread like wild-fire over the country. It had hundreds of thousands of supporters, its income rose to nearly £38,000 a year, its weekly newspaper had a circulation of 40,000. It held enthusiastic meetings all over the country, though its militancy evoked attack, and Suffragist speakers were not protected as Cabinet Ministers. Many suffered grave physical injury. But for the most part these meetings were passionate acclamations of the rightness of the

by REBECCA WEST

Cause and its leaders. London saw long, long processions, longer than it had ever known follow any other than Mrs. Pankhurst.

The Press was overwhelmingly against them; which was one of the first proofs that the modern sensational newspaper has no real influence, that its readers buy it for its news and not for its opinions. There were, of course, certain noble supporters among journalists, such as Mr. Nevinson, Mr. Brailsford, and the late Mr. H. W. Massingham; but for the rest the Press loved to represent the Movement with contempt and derision. Mrs. Pankhurst and her daughters were crazy hooligans, their followers were shrieking hysterics, their policy was wild delirium. Nothing could be further from the truth. The Movement contained some of the *détraqués* who follow any drum that is beaten, but these were weeded out, for the Cat-and-Mouse Act was something of a test for the solider qualities.

But the Movement was neither crazy nor hysterical nor delirious. It was stone-cold in its realism. Mrs. Pankhurst was not a clever woman, but when she experienced something she incorporated it in her mind and used it as a basis for action. When she started the Women's Social and Political Union she was sure of two things: that the ideas of freedom and justice which had been slowly developing in England during the eighteenth and nineteenth centuries had grown to such maturity that there existed an army of women resentful of being handicapped by artificial disadvantages imposed simply on the grounds of their sex, and that sex-antagonism was so strong among men that it produced an attitude which, if it were provoked to candid expression, would make every self-respecting woman want to fight it. In both of these suppositions she was entirely correct. The real force that made the Suffrage Movement was the quality of the Opposition. Women, listening to Anti-Suffrage speeches, for the first time knew what many men really thought of them. One such speech that brought many into the Movement had for its climax a jocular description of a future female Lord Chancellor being seized with labour pains on the Woolsack; and left no doubt that the speaker considered labour pains as in themselves, apart from the setting, a funny subject. The allegation, constantly made, that all women became insane at the age of forty-five also roused much resentment. But apart from general principles, the wicked frivolity of the attitude adopted towards the women by the Liberal Government was the real recruiting serjeant for the Movement.

It must be remembered that the majority of the Liberal Members of Parliament, and indeed the majority of the Cabinet, were pledged to support Woman Suffrage. There was therefore every logical and every moral reason why they should have granted it; and they did not need to fear the ignominy of seeming to yield to force, for Christabel, with her fine political mind, frequently declared truces and gave them every opportunity to save their bacon. The explanation commonly accepted—and it is the only one that appears possible—was that the opposition to votes for women was insisted on by one important member of the Cabinet, influenced by the views of his wife who has since published book after book of almost incredible silliness. That the protection women can expect from men is highly limited and personal in its scope many Suffragists learned, as they noticed that the stewards of Liberal meetings not only ejected them, but thoroughly enjoyed inflicting as much physical injury on them as possible. They were to learn that even more poignantly in the next few years, as they hid in cellars from bombs dropped by the protective sex; but the previous lesson was even more disgusting, because it was completely gratuitous. The matter could have been settled in ten minutes. But it was not, and the Cabinet Ministers who might have settled it saw nothing to limit their stewards to the task of ejection and often even encouraged them to exceed it; and outside the halls they showed even less adherence to the standards to which, one had believed, our governors adhered.

Was justice, even British justice, blind? The case of Lady Constance Lytton suggested it was not. She, chivalrous soul, suspected that some of the Suffrage prisoners were roughly treated because they were persons of no social importance. She herself had been sentenced to six weeks' imprisonment, and had been instantly dismissed as medically unfit. She went to jail again, not as Lord Lytton's sister, but as Jane Warton, a seamstress, and although on the second occasion as on the first she had mitral disease of the heart, she was forcibly fed within an inch of her life.

Mrs. Pankhurst had said that she would go on applying pressure to the Government till it yielded. She continued to do so. She seemed made of steel, although she had suffered a most crushing bereavement in the death of her son Harry in distressing circumstances. He had contracted infantile paralysis, and to pay for his nursing-home expenses, which seemed likely to continue indefinitely, she had to leave him to go on a lecture tour in America, since for all the tens of thousands of pounds that were coming into the Union she drew no more than £200 a year. Shortly after her return he died, and this inflicted a blow from which she never recovered. But she went on inflexibly along the road she had planned. She thought of new ways of making the Government's existence intolerable every day. The plateglass windows of the West End of London went down one night in a few minutes to answer the challenge of a member of the Government who had reproached the Suffragists for having committed no act of violence comparable to the pulling up of Hyde Park Railings by the Reform rioters of 1867. Christabel fled to France so that the Movement could be sure of one leader to dictate the policy. Mrs. Pankhurst and the two other chief officials of the Union, Frederick and Emmeline Pethick Lawrence, were tried for conspiracy and sentenced to nine months' imprisonment, in spite of the jury's plea that they should be treated with the utmost leniency. They hunger-struck and were released.

But a new side of her implacability then showed itself. Her policy had meant a ruthless renunciation of old ties. She had cut herself off entirely from the Labour Party; she was even prepared, in these later years, to attack it as a component part of the Liberal Party's majority. She had silenced her youngest daughter, Adela, as a speaker because of her frank Socialist bias, and her second daughter Sylvia afterwards left the Union to form societies that were as much Labour as Suffragist in the East End. She had been merciless in her preservation of party discipline. There was no nonsense about democracy in the Women's Social and Political Union. Teresa Billington had long been driven out for raising the topic. Mrs. Pankhurst, Christabel, and the Lawrences exercised an absolute dictatorship. But now the Lawrences had to go. They opposed the further prosecution of militancy, and Christabel and Mrs. Pankhurst quietly told them to relinquish their positions in the Union. There was more than appears to be said for the Pankhursts' position from their point of view. They knew that the Government intended to strip the Pethick Lawrences of their fortune by recovering from them (as the only moneyed officials of the Union) the cost of all the damage done by the militants; and as they knew that in actual fact Christabel settled the policy of the Union, they saw no reason why the Pethick Lawrences should stay on to the embarrassment of all persons concerned. But the Pethick Lawrences were heartbroken. Not for a moment did the crisis appal Mrs. Pankhurst. Letters were burned in pillar-boxes; houses—but only empty ones—went up in flames; riot was everywhere. Mrs. Pankhurst was again tried for conspiracy, and this time received a sentence of three years' imprisonment, though again the jury fervently recommended her to mercy. She was then dragged in and out of prison under the Cat-and-Mouse Act, while militancy rose to a pitch that had never been imagined by its most fervent supporters, and acquired a strange, new character of ultimate desperation. Emily Wilding Davidson tried to stop the Derby by throwing herself under the horses' hooves, and, as she had anticipated, was killed. A vast silent cortège of women followed her coffin through the streets. Mrs. Pankhurst, rising from her bed in a nursing home to attend the funeral, was re-arrested. But they were careful never quite to break her body. Both the Government and the Suffragettes knew what was bound to happen if Mrs. Pankhurst should be killed.

Suddenly war came, and in the sight of the world her star darkened. Immediately the pacifism she had learned from Dr. Pankhurst vanished and left no trace. In an instant she stopped all militancy, all Suffrage work; with perfect discipline her army disbanded. She then declared herself a fierce Jingo, her paper *The Suffragette* became *Britannia*, and Christabel wrote leaders that grew into more crudely Chauvinist attacks on certain members of the Government, such as Lord Grey of Fallodon, for insufficiently vigorous prosecution of the War. But this did not represent nearly such a fundamental reversal as might be supposed. She had, after all, been brought up in France just after the Franco-Prussian War, and she had then conceived a lifelong hatred of Germany; and there was nothing surprising if *Britannia* translated it into French. " *J'ai eu la faiblesse de croire qu'un Bonaparte pouvait être autre chose qu'un assassin.* . . ." Rochefort would have thought himself failing in an obvious duty if he had let a day pass without announcing that somebody, somewhere, was betraying France. This astonishing trace of the influence of French politics on Mrs. Pankhurst, so little modified by time, makes us realise that the Suffrage Movement had been the copy of a French model executed with North-country persistence. We had been watching a female General Boulanger with *nous*.

Besides these patriotic successes and some propaganda for women's war service, Mrs. Pankhurst and her daughter did little, and they did not undertake any important administrative duties. They were both of them trained and temperamentally adapted for political organisation, for which there was now no place; and the older woman, who was now fifty-six, and had been leading a campaign life in and out of prison for eleven years, was too exhausted for any first-rate work. It is said that Christabel Pankhurst did much good work, much better than her writings would suggest, in an advisory capacity to a certain politician. But this was not ostentatiously done, and it must have seemed to many of their followers that Mrs. Pankhurst and her daughter had passed into obscurity. Yet it was then that she did perhaps the most decisive Suffrage work of her life. She persuaded a certain important politician that when peace came again she could reassemble her party and begin militancy where it had left off. There were many other causes which united to contribute to the triumph of the Suffrage cause at that time. Parallel to the militant movement had developed a non-militant movement, also immensely powerful, which had caused a dangerous discontent among the female members of the older political parties. But if the threat of Mrs. Pankhurst's existence had not been there women might not have been given the vote on the same terms as men in 1917, ostensibly as a reward for their war services.

After that victory, Mrs. Pankhurst wellnigh vanished from the eyes of her followers. The rebellious glory was departed. She repudiated utterly now everything she had fought for in her youth, besides her husband, and came out of the War a high Tory. She seemed a little puzzled what to do, for her ally had left her. Christabel, the quality of whose mind remains a profound mystery, had taken one look at the map of Europe, spread out in the sunshine of peace, and had grown pale with horror. Her gift for foreseeing political events had often amounted to clairvoyance, and there is reason to suppose that it did not desert her then. Her realisation had the effect, curious in Dr. Pankhurst's daughter, bred in agnosticism, of making her announce that here were the signs and portents that herald the Second Coming of the Lord Jesus Christ. She went to America and led a frugal life as an evangelist of a sober and unsensational kind, devoting her leisure to the care of an adopted daughter. For a time Mrs. Pankhurst lived in Canada, delivering lectures to women's societies on such subjects as the legal protection of women and children, public health, the blessings of the British Empire, and the contempt of liberty she had seen during a visit to Russia. But finally she returned to England and accepted the post of nursing the unpromising constituency of Whitechapel as a Tory candidate, a duty which she fulfilled conscientiously. She secured no financial advantage by this conservatism, for she was paid only a pittance and lived over a baker's shop; she could have attained a much higher standard of living by remaining an unattached feminist writer and lecturer. Now she enjoyed life in little, gentle, old-ladyish ways. She loved window-shopping, and sometimes bought a dress at the sales and remodelled it herself. She liked dropping in on her old friends, the Marshalls, where " she had her own chair," and talking about the old days in France, about her husband, about her dead boys. There were letters from Christabel and Adela, who, though long alienated from her mother by her Communist views, was ultimately reconciled to her. But Mrs. Pankhurst had never wanted to be old, and her body had been hideously maltreated. As a result of injuries received in forcible feedings, she still suffered from a recurrent form of jaundice. In 1928, shortly after women had received full adult suffrage, she went to church on Easter Monday in the country, was driven home to Whitechapel, took to her bed, and, for no particular medical reason, died. She left £72.

It is all forgotten. We forget everything now. We have forgotten what came before the War. We have forgotten the War. There are so many newspapers so full of so much news, so many motor-cars, so many films, that image is superimposed on image, and nothing is clearly seen. In an emptier age, which left more room for the essential, it would be remembered that Emmeline Pankhurst with all her limitations was glorious. Somehow, in her terse, austere way she was as physically glorious as Ellen Terry or Sarah Bernhardt. She was glorious in her physical courage, in her obstinacy, in her integrity. Her achievements have suffered in repute owing to the fashion of jeering at the Parliamentary system. Women novelists who want to strike out a line as being specially broadminded declare they think we are no better for the vote; if they spent half an hour turning over pre-War newspapers and looking out references to women's employment and legal and social status, they might come to a different opinion. Women who do not like working in offices and cannot get married write letters to the papers ascribing their plight to feminism. But even before women got the vote they had to work in offices, with the only difference that they received less money and worked under worse conditions; and then as now there existed no machinery to compel men to marry women they did not want. Few intelligent women in a position to compare the past with the present will deny that the vote brought with it substantial benefits of both a material and spiritual kind.

There were also incidental benefits arising out of the Movement. The Suffragettes' indignant denunciation of the insanitary conditions in the jails meant an immense advance of public opinion regarding penal reform. In 1913 it suddenly came into Christabel Pankhurst's head to write a series of articles regarding the prevalence of venereal disease. These were ill-informed and badly written, but they scattered like wind an age-long conspiracy of prudishness, and enabled society to own the existence of these diseases and set about exterminating them as had never been possible before. But Mrs. Pankhurst's most valuable indirect contribution to her time was made in May 1905; a dusty and obscure provincial, she sent in a threatening note to the Prime Minister, and spent the next years proving that that threat had thunder and lightning behind it. She thereby broke down the assumption of English politicians, which till then no legislative actions, no extensions of the franchise had been able to touch, that the only people who were politically important were those who were socially important; and all the democratic movements of her day shared in the benefits. It would be absurd to deny that the ultimate reason for the rise of the Labour Party was the devoted work of its adherents, but it would be equally absurd to deny that between 1905 and 1914 it found its path smoothed by an increasingly respectful attitude on the part of St. Stephen's, the Press, and the public.

But Mrs. Pankhurst's chief and most poignant value to the historian will be her demonstration of what happens to a great human being of action in a transition period. She was the last popular leader to act on inspiration derived from the principles of the French Revolution; she put her body and soul at the service of Liberty, Equality, and Fraternity, and earned a triumph for them. Then doubt seized her, as it was to seize a generation. In the midst of her battle for democracy she was obliged, lest that battle should be lost, to become a dictator. Later we were all to debate whether that sacrifice of principle could be justified in the case of Russia. She trembled under the strain of the conflict, and perhaps she trembled also because she foresaw that she was to gain a victory, and then confront a mystery. She had always said and felt she wanted the vote to feed the hungry. Enfranchised, she found herself aware that economic revolution was infinitely more difficult and drastic than the fiercest political revolution. With her childlike honesty, her hate of pretentiousness, she failed to put up a good show to cover her perplexity. She spoke the truth—she owned she saw it better to camp among the ruins of capitalism than push out into the uncharted desert. With her whole personality she enacted our perplexity, as earlier she had enacted our revolt, a priestess of the people.

This account is founded chiefly on my own recollections, and on the writings of Sylvia Pankhurst, in conversations with Mrs. Marshall, and from notes supplied by Mr. Arthur Marshall, to whom I would like to express my gratitude.

SIR CHARLES PARSONS
1854-1931

By
E. KITSON CLARK

SIR CHARLES PARSONS

by E. KITSON CLARK

IN 1877 Charles Algernon Parsons was placed 11th Wrangler in the Mathematical Tripos of Cambridge University; in 1927 he was admitted to the Order of Merit—fifty years distinguished by exercise of unusual ability, ennobled by undaunted perseverance. Through these qualities Parsons translated the individual visions that his imagination inspired into realities that have affected the general prosperity of the world.

As to his ability there is abundant evidence with which it is hoped to illustrate the later paragraphs of this short biography. As to his perseverance it was more than remarkable, a notable commentary on the advice of his great predecessor, George Stephenson, who preached to young, and indeed to old, engineers " perseverance " and again " perseverance " as the first essential in an engineer's profession.

By his work Parsons earned honour after honour,[1] received degrees from many universities, and medals from the highest scientific societies of his own country; he was awarded by Germany the greatest recognition which that nation's

---

[1] " As was to be expected, the achievements and the personality of Parsons brought a host of honours and rewards. He was made C.B. in 1904, K.C.B. in 1911, and was admitted to the Order of Merit in 1927. He was elected F.R.S. in 1898, was a vice-president ten years later, and was Bakerian Lecturer in 1918. He received the Rumford Medal in 1902 and the Copley Medal—the Society's highest award—in 1928. He was an honorary Doctor of many universities, including Cambridge, Oxford, Edinburgh, Glasgow, Dublin, Durham, Leeds, Liverpool, Toronto, and Pennsylvania. Other recognitions were the Albert Medal of the Royal Society of Arts, the Kelvin Medal, the Faraday Medal of the Institution of Electrical Engineers, the Franklin Medal of the Franklin Institute of Philadelphia, and the Bessemer Medal of the Iron and Steel Institute which was given him in acknowledgment of his services to metallurgy. He was President of the British Association in 1919. He served also as President of the Institute of Physics, and of the North-East Coast Institution of Engineers and Shipbuilders. In 1914 he received the freedom of the City of Newcastle."
—*Obituary Notice of Sir Charles Parsons, by Sir Alfred Ewing.*

engineering community could bestow, and he was the first whose career as a productive engineer employing labour gained for him enrolment on the Order of Merit. His admission to that high honour was happily complementary to that of Lord Kelvin, also a Cambridge Wrangler, a master of science and of the application of science.

Into his career the romance of technique has entered so largely that any account of him entails an attempt to set down in some way a description of his processes. This can only be done in the hope that the recital may be clear and not outlast the patience of those to whom such subjects have hitherto been, as Robert Stephenson once said of bridges, "mere mechanical matters of no literary interest."

In those fifty years a new method of making power came into the world and was brought almost to the human limit of perfection. The central fact of that period is known to the world as "Parsons's Turbine." It was the culmination of the story of steam, one of the great servants of mankind. And the story of steam is this—Hero of Alexandria, about 130 B.C., invented a steam engine which worked on a rotative principle and did nothing more. Nineteen centuries passed, and the use of steam came into being for the purpose of work, but not in a rotary machine. It began with the industry of mining. As pits were driven lower into the earth and water accumulated therein, the bucket pumps must needs reach deeper and deeper, and they became more laborious to work. The action of raising and lowering the bucket entailed reciprocating motion. The bucket was attached by long rods to a swinging beam, at the other end of which was a counterpoise of sufficient weight to balance the bucket and rods. It was necessary to apply power to raise this counterpoise and force the empty bucket down into the water. That force, by the invention of Newcomen, was derived from steam introduced under a piston connected with the counterpoise.

In the next process the steam pressure was destroyed by cooling water, and a vacuum was caused with the weight of the atmosphere upon it. Then the counterpoise went down, and the bucket came up. There was thus, in this the famous "atmospheric engine," a simple alliance of steam-power and gravity, and vertical reciprocating motion was obtained. By natural stages the device was elaborated. In vertical closed cylinders pistons were moved up and down by the alternate admission and removal of steam. And as, by the familiar example of the pedal and the spinning wheel, a reciprocating motion is translated to rotation, so the steam engine, firstly vertical, then horizontal, came into being, drove the machinery and ships and locomotives of the world, and became the accepted pattern of power production.

Literature illustrated it and Nature herself confirmed the practice. The heavens indeed declare the physical truth of rotary motion, and the earth takes it up with whirlpools and ripples of air and water. But she also transforms the motions of the celestial bodies into alternation—whether by making day and night or raising and lowering tides, and in her organic self, whether man walks, bird flies, fish swims, heart beats, or electrons batter, the initiation of effective effort seems to implement a reciprocating principle. So it was at first with steam. But there was waste and limitation in the process. As with the spinning wheel, so with the greatest steel rolling-mill, there is the difficulty of carrying the pin of the rotating member round the two extreme directional limits of its path. That reluctance and change in turning effort involves coercion of the engine by flywheel control, uneconomic weight in the foundations, and a robustness of detail disproportionate to output.

By contrast the act of the water-wheel had been for all nations a man-invented function of simple revolution, and as steam mechanism on reciprocating principles appeared to have reached its limit of efficiency, it was clear that a contrivance was needed in which steam could, like water, drive a shaft round by direct application. But steam had a quality which water had not: it was elastic, a valuable but hitherto intractable characteristic. Many men had worked at this subject, had made drawings, had acquired patents; yet very little came of much thought. It was Parsons who found his way through the difficulties by reason and courage and experiment—and " perseverance."

He recognised, as others had not, the essential complications of an equation composed of four variables—heat, volume, pressure, and speed. If steam is released from a container under pressure it gives up heat, it is increased in volume, it is reduced in pressure—and the expression of the changes of the three states may be manifested in motion. Parsons guarded against waste of heat by the course that he gave to the current; he provided for the increase in volume by the dimensions that he gave to his passages. In his treatment and use of the velocity he achieved his great success. The speed attained by steam emerging into free air may be as high as 4,000 feet per second, and while this speed may be used in very small machines, it is outside practical limits for ordinary services. Parsons, realising this fact, released his power charge by stages. As a civil engineer steps the fall of a reservoir overflow in order to absorb the destructive power of the head of water in successive reactions, so this mechanical engineer absorbed the force under his hand by using it in a series of successive impulses in order that it should do valuable work. As the water fell from step to step, so the steam passed from compartment to compartment at a velocity dictated by the relative pressures in each. In passing from compartment to compartment the steam thrust before it one of the containing walls. The walls took the form of a series of vanes fixed on a shaft in the manner of a multitude of windmill sails, and they moved at a determinable speed. Each vane was concave along its length, the steam poured in, imparting impulse by the velocity of its entrance and poured out again, assisting the movement by the reaction of its exit. Then by calculation as to areas, direction of flow, relative pressures, resultant speeds, and centrifugal forces, a rotary machine was born that became the driving mechanism that is honoured in all the world as the " Parsons Turbine."

It was now possible, by attaching the turbines directly to dynamos, to turn the rotors of the latter through the lines of magnetic force at speeds unattainable by reciprocating engines, and by such generation of current Parsons brought electricity into its own.

" The genius of Parsons, the most illustrious and the most revolutionary engineer of our time, opened up a new era in the production and application of power," are the words of Sir Alfred Ewing, a distinguished contemporary and friend. They are borrowed by his leave, like others in the pages that follow.

The admiration of the world is for the turbine, and for the electrical machinery developed *pari passu* with it by its great inventor, and duly so. And this central achievement is emphasised here as the essence of a special period of activity, but there were remarkable productions of his genius in other spheres: there were noteworthy years before and after that half-century.

The youngest of six sons of the third Earl of Rosse, Charles Parsons spent his boyhood at the family seat, Birr Castle. Lord Rosse was a scientist of great theoretical and practical ability. He was President of the Royal Society from 1848 to 1854. He had manufactured and set up the great telescope known by his name, and had executed work that was of notable service in the history of astronomy.

Charles was educated by resident tutors who took part in the astronomical investigations of his father. He lived in a home whose inspiration was science and whose expression was practical performance. His mother, a Yorkshire lady, an able photographer, a modeller in wax, and conversant with different handicrafts, was companion and teacher to this boy and his brothers in the occupations which were at once their delight and their study.

It had become by that time the custom for boys of such a family to spend three or four years at a public school, but a public school was not chosen in this case. The spirit of the public school was indeed at that time giving the mental spring to many of those who were to play great parts in and for Britain. But the range of subjects was limited, as the following witnesses. Arnold of Rugby had said, " Rather than have Physical Science the principal thing in my son's mind, I would gladly have him think that the sun went round the earth, and that the stars were merely spangles set in a bright blue firmament." Kennedy of Shrewsbury had refused a half-holiday which was the statutory recognition of a First Class in the Oxford schools, because he said that it was " only in Science." Great headmasters they were indeed, and standard teachers of wise and able men. But the scientist and Irishman, Lord Rosse, was not attracted by standards, and for his boys the schoolroom was at home, and like their playroom was a workshop. The toy cupboard, and with it the educational shelf, was a tool-chest. The exercises, as well as games, mechanical experiments.

Charles made models and inventions; he learnt the relation of observation to action in the navigation of his father's yacht when he was very young.

Of his brothers, the eldest became an astronomer, two died young, the fourth, Randal, was a clergyman, the next above him by three years, Richard Clere, became a civil engineer.

At the end of the list came Charles, born in 1854, the concluding year of his father's Presidency of the Royal Society.

Thirteen years afterwards, Lord Rosse died. The mother gave her life with all its sympathy and comradeship in making their home first at Birr, then at Dublin, and eventually in London. She took the three youngest boys each year for a tour abroad, and by her inspiration she bound their young lives closely together. When the three separated, and Randal went to the Church, Clare to engineering, Charles, after spending a year at Trinity College, Dublin, passed to St. John's College, Cambridge.

The shy boy of home training has sometimes in later years imagined that he had lost no little by the want of the experience of a public school, but though he always suffered a certain hesitancy in social contact, he learned a close relationship of friendship among the undergraduates at Cambridge. He played a keen part in the successes of the Lady Margaret boat. His physical strength, his "great long back"; the successful bump when their boat crashed into First Trinity with such violence as to throw the whole crew into a tumble of oars and timber in the water; the repair of the boat in a night, another bump of another Trinity boat in the next night's race, and the glorious supper-party that followed; the celebration by another dinner that he gave forty-three years later to those who survived—these are stories still told to-day. These are testimonies of the wide and kindly sociability that underlay the diffidence of the homebred youth.

Parsons was a mathematician, coached by the famous Dr. Routh. That stern father of Wranglers did not possess the whole of his mind. The table of his room in St. John's College was littered with models, contrivances reminiscent of the cardboard pins and sealing-wax that were the implements of his boyhood. Yet in spite of such diversions from the sacred curriculum, he was placed eleventh in the Mathematical Tripos; he might have been higher—though scarcely perhaps better educated for the purpose of his life. Sir Donald Macalister, Senior Wrangler in his year, said that he was better at problems than himself, " but less successful with book work." In spite of his high place in a Tripos list which contained as many as ninety-five names, Sir Alfred Ewing tells us that Parsons subsequently made little direct use of mathematical calculation in his professional life. He had gained indeed at Cambridge a sound knowledge of dynamics and an appreciation of the principles of mechanics which guided him through the ordered sequence of experiments to the unhesitating solutions of his problems, and he seemed to reach his results by some mental process which he did not attempt to formulate.

It is customary to talk of instinct in such a connection. There is an instinct in engineering matters that intuitively criticises a design—it is by no means rare, the perquisite of a skilled draughtsman. There is the instinct which permits our amateur novelists and essayists to make invention with easy fluency on their library table—this is not unknown, sometimes interesting, often dictatorial. But the instinct which imagines, sees encouragement through difficulties, converts ideas into facts, that is a rare thing and worthy of high honour. With such an endowment Charles Parsons entered the works of Armstrongs, in Newcastle, where he remained for four years after leaving Cambridge. He was picked out at that time as the most industrious apprentice that was ever known. He spent his leisure and some of his time in the works in designing a new type of steam motor. His work of achievement had begun.

He concluded his four years of apprenticeship at Newcastle, and entered upon two years' practical research in the shops of Kitsons, of Leeds, in which firm his brother Richard was a partner. As a boy he had experimented, at Cambridge he had conceived, at Newcastle he had devised, at Leeds he produced, a high-speed rotary machine. The object of this last design was the reduction of reciprocating motion. He was already moving away from tradition, taking the first steps towards his ultimate goal, the utilisation of the velocity of steam and the suppression of reciprocating motion altogether. The geometry of the schools, the observation of the works were united in the project of this " epicycloidal " engine. It was a clever construction, in which the cylinders swung round a crankshaft which revolved twice as fast as they, a combination whose flywheel was in itself; but it was by no means the final word. Many examples were made; their speed was great—900 revolutions per minute, and for this reason they were suitable for the generation of electricity. They were employed for the provision of lighting in halls and shops and sheds, and the writer can speak of them with the interest of one who undertook their supervision: excellent in mechanical contrivance, they were too generous in their appetite of steam, and their very speed, which was undoubtedly a source of valuable education to their author, was not unattended in their earliest form with a certain danger.

While Parsons was thus making modifications in the traditional means of employing steam, he was thinking out other applications of power. He turned his attention to the action of rockets. A rocket pushes its burden forward by reaction from explosion. He applied rockets to torpedoes, and by special leave was able to test them in the lake of Roundhay, close to Leeds. He attained a speed of 20 knots, and it may be surmised that he had already begun to envisage a partnership of the two distinctive agents for the transmission of force, namely, impulse and reaction, of which he made the marriage so successfully in his final work, the turbine.

While in Leeds he married, and wishing to settle down, he left Leeds and Kitsons for Gateshead, where an opening proved available for a Junior Partnership with Clarke, Chapman & Co. It was proposed at first that he should proceed with the rocket experiments, but the method was found to be uncertain, and as the firm was interested in electric light, the generation of electricity by a fast-running motor unit became the basis of his work. On April 23, 1884, he filed two consecutive patents, one for a high-speed dynamo, the other for a steam turbine to drive such a machine. His application in one case is worded as follows:

> "My invention is designed to produce an electrical generator which may be driven at a very high rate of speed, several or many times as fast as such machines are now driven, the object being to obtain a large current or a high electromotive force, or both, from a small machine, and also to obtain an increased efficiency."

For five years he worked with Clarke, Chapman & Co., his turbine being very suitable for electric lighting in ships, but the fruitful mind of the inventor was evidently a trial in that partnership. Parsons was dissatisfied with progress, was fertile in suggestions of experiments which would cost money and time, which depended for their eventual value on a future that was secure in his own mind but not in those associated with him. He left the partnership, but the patents taken out by him remained the property of the firm. For a second period of five years this arrangement held, and Parsons, who had by this time with the help of certain friends set up works at Heaton, near Newcastle, for the manufacture of turbines and dynamos, was compelled to develop the turbine on lines that differed from his original proposals.

According to his first designs he had caused steam to flow in a direction parallel to the shaft which he was causing to rotate, as the movement of air spins a windmill round by the motion of its sails. But by deprivation of his patents he was now constrained to adopt a different method, and the turbines that he made during the next years were actuated by steam that flowed out radially from the shaft.

It was not until the end of that period, when the early patents were recovered by him, that he was free to work out his original device; in other respects, too, it had not been plain sailing. Only small economy over the reciprocating engine was attained by his first compound turbine of 1884. But when he arranged to exhaust the steam after use into a condenser below atmospheric pressure, he developed the fullest use of steam heat that has yet been known. His inventions have alone made possible the enormous power stations of to-day, and conferred upon the world a cheap and abundant supply of electricity—whereas his earliest turbine developed hardly as much power as the engine of an ordinary touring motor-car, he lived to see his firm produce single machines that multiplied that power by six or seven thousand times.

After he had been working in this direction for two years an event took place, happy in its locale, happy in its scientific sequelæ, and at least as happy in its personal association. I quote the words of his friend, Sir Alfred Ewing, who tells this of the beginning of their friendship:

> "By chance it fell to me to make the earliest independent tests of a condensing turbine. In 1891, when Parsons had established his works at Newcastle, a scheme was under discussion for setting up an electric supply station in Cambridge. Somebody made the suggestion that it should be equipped with Parsons's tur-

bines. The turbine was a novel and little-tried appliance about which there was much scepticism; it was said to be a notorious steam-eater. A member of the Cambridge Corporation, who shared this scepticism, asked me to report on it, much as Balaam was asked to report on the Children of Israel. Parsons gave me every facility to make exhaustive trials; they convinced me that the turbine was the engine of the future, and, like Balaam, I came back blessing where I had been expected to condemn.

"That was the first of several such occasions. A few months later Parsons had me come again to test the effect of certain changes, one of which was the use of superheated steam. From time to time a new development gave opportunity for further trials. It was no small privilege to come in contact with the working of so exceptional a mind and to note some of the milestones in his astonishing career. The friendship thus begun continued without a break or cloud. If to some people Parsons seemed difficult, it is right to say that many others—I for one—found him wholly delightful."

To which quotation may be appropriately added a sentence from the correspondence of the great Swiss firm of Brown Boveri, international pioneers in electric generation, who in 1900 entered into close association with Newcastle with regard to the manufacture of Parsons's turbines: "The influence of the line of thought and achievement of the Hon. Sir Charles Parsons in our country and on the Continent has been profound."

In 1894 Parsons put a turbine into a ship. His small experimental boat, the *Turbinia*, was 100 feet long by 9 feet beam, and he connected the screw direct to the turbine-driven shaft, but the shaft turned too quickly. Screw propellers had given satisfactory service for many years, but here was a screw driven at a speed which was unknown to the more stately piston-driven engines of the day. The action of the water upon which a ship's screw acted had not been sufficiently well studied; its form had been determined by empirical methods. An attractive story, for instance, is told of an early experimental wooden screw. The thread was lengthened to two turns round the propeller shaft in order to make it twice as efficient; the second turn, however, imprisoned the water which had been thrust back and used by the first, and there was no success till by a happy flaw in the grain of the wood the screw broke in half, and the single turn performed the expected duty.

But with Parsons's screw the problem was of the opposite character; the water was not only released to freedom, it was thrown out with a speed so great as to produce "vacuous spaces" which were continuously collapsing so that the water rushed swiftly on to the propeller blades with so fierce a hammer-blow that it soon destroyed their surface. This action, known as cavitation, caused great loss of propeller thrust and consequently loss of speed to the ship. Therefore special consideration was given to the shape, diameter, and surface of the blades under scientific observation. The same accurate workmanship by which the correct shape was attained was applied to a degree unknown before to the formation of teeth in gears, and thus by a combination of gears and secondary shafting the speed was regulated to the desired rate, whether for slow merchant ships or fast warships and liners.

He had already made an advance beyond all existing practice in the use of steam for power, both on land and on sea. He then turned his attention to the quality of steam. The greater the pressure the greater the useful power. Arguing thus, he was an early and active advocate of very high steam pressures, and on this he laid noteworthy emphasis at the World Power Conference of 1924. He repeated it at other conferences, and pointed out a direction in which the most modern progress is now turning.

Later on, internal combustion came under his review, and here it might appear that there was a return to success of the reciprocating system. The production of power by the sudden combustion of vapour of oil naturally seemed to provide a counter-attack in favour of reciprocation. But it was a question of thermodynamics in the mind of Parsons. He pointed out that the heat was released at higher temperatures than in the case of the turbine, and that it meant waste. Further, he contended that internal-combustion engines could not be used in large units, and if the future held prospects for using gases as motive power in the labyrinth of a turbine, knowledge which was not available at present would be required as to special materials, temperatures, and capacity.

In twenty years from leaving Cambridge, Parsons had convinced the world of the new motive power on water, as the *Turbinia* demonstrated on British seas a speed and flexibility never known before. In twenty-three years he had, by a contract for Elberfeld, in Germany, established on land the efficacy of his revolutionary unit of power. Few years indeed for the birth and perfection of a new thing, but years do not measure the efforts, the checks, the advances, the fluctuations of hopes and disappointments.

A chapter of life that ended so well was preceded and followed by others really as remarkable. The boy, before going to Cambridge, had delighted to make cardboard clocks. His brother and he had designed and made a small steam-driven lorry that ran at a speed of 7 miles per hour. The man who had the vision had also the physical technique, the mind that conceived was served by a hand that could execute. There is a story how at one time a dispute had arisen as to the wage price of fixing blades in the turbine. The dinner-hour came; Parsons, with one of his staff, entered the workshop, locked the door, and when the men came back they found that the blading was done and in the time prescribed.

The keenness which carried him through all investigations might be seen in his chill morning hours of practice with torpedoes on Roundhay Lake, undaunted whether the rocket did good work, did bad work, or even exploded. It is said that one or more of the early epicycloidal engines of the Kitson period "went up," though when redesigned they proved constructionally sound and safe.

The resource with which he faced all difficulties was made manifest before the German specialists who had come to see the largest turbine that had ever been made run its preliminary trial. The blades had stripped in the preliminary trial, but before the visitors went away they enjoyed an excellent example of repair while you wait. The Germans indeed expressed an astonishment that a non-German could make so admirable an invention, and execute so satisfactory a performance.

In this personality there were many remarkable characteristics, and one was his notable physical as well as mental courage. His wife has described how, to join her in the hunting field, at one time he bought a horse and rode it, a happy and gallant tyro, to the surprise and pleasure of the company in the field. We have heard how he rowed. We know that he exceeded all official orders both when running the *Turbinia* up the Clyde and also round the ships in the 1897 Review, outpacing the patrol boats, to the indignation of the midshipmen in command and the admiration of the Fleet. We read of his addresses on motive power and cognate subjects in all our great engineering centres and elsewhere. We see him in his later years reverting to the early interests of his father's telescope and manufacturing parabolic reflectors for searchlights, and introducing new methods for grinding lenses. He endeavoured to compress carbon into diamonds, and disregarding caution if not reason, he attained the highest pressure which he could imagine by firing a bullet on his material placed in a hole in a steel block. He felt that the earth held heat in her depths which should be utilised, and proposed that a power should be drawn from the lower regions by deep bore-holes in volcanic districts. He made a vapour-driven flying machine, an auxetophone that would reinforce the sound of any musical instrument.

Such and the like arose from the fertility of this fascinating man, and the time and place into which he fell at a period of unequalled mechanical enterprise were of no less significance. There was rapid movement, not only in new processes, but also in new opinions as to the place of men and things.

He entered works at a time when the employers were masters, when as masters they knew and addressed their men by their Christian names; when the men were expected to give, and the master ready to exact, labour and attention in more difficult circumstances than would be accepted nowadays.

In another sphere, too, Parsons stood at a junction between methods. Trade Unions had been looked upon with disfavour by managers. Whether this was wise or not does not enter into the consideration of these lines, but there were difficulties on both sides. The Trade Unions found it impossible to understand how their interest depended on supplies of orders; the employers did not seem to see that their interests could not succeed without the ready alliance of the manual producer, and Parsons was working through the difficult period of the constitutional adjustment of their relations. He had experience also of two distinct types of men who were working side by side, the older craftsman with the craftsman's slow action that derived from experience; he made his object to suit the job. There was the modern mechanic who worked to a drawing, to whom a thousandth of an inch was as a sixteenth to his neighbour. Procedure was ceasing to be decided on practice, but based on calculation. The skill of both was playing its desirable part at that time, and there was stir in the air, for the new method of management, organisation, was coming.

In another sense he found himself at the meeting-point between views as to careers held by those who might be called, for want of a better term, the "professional" classes. It is not known if any man with a high degree had before Parsons taken up apprenticeship in manual labour as a basis for his future work. Men with University degrees had indeed found that beside the Church, the Bar, and the Services, there was a good life for mind and for purse in the commercial world, but it had been discovered in the office rather than in the shops. There was a radical change in the air. Technical instruction was being received in the realm of Higher Education, and the subject became admitted, though rather reluctantly, into literature and polite conversation. This was before the time of the juvenile interest in details of the motor world, which is an amusement.

And the time of Parsons's work was at the junction of two worlds. Two generations of men came and went. It was an age of expanding industry directed by individualism and organised under capitalism. In political stability precedent ceded to precedent, two Sovereigns passed away who had impressed their character upon events, two wars struck at the fabric of our economics, politicians varied the definitions of their aims, changing their lines of cleavage as they have done through all the course of time. Of these and other phenomena it cannot be said that there was novelty or permanency in their issue. But in these two generations a new power, the use of electricity, had arisen in the material world whose effect spreads far beyond that sphere and time. Just as man was placed at a meeting point of systems, so this achievement of available electric power came between two great developments. It was the central event of three epochs, each of which produced a profound influence on the lives, and it is believed the characters, of mankind. In the first period by steam locomotion on land and sea, men and materials were first transferred from place to place with a

by E. KITSON CLARK

rapidity that changed all relationships: community was brought near to community, nation to nation, and men prophesied peace on earth. In the third period, by the subjection of the ether, information, advice, consultation, exhortation, and sympathy are conveyed from one to another of all the individuals and communities of the world, and again there is talk of peace. In the second, by the turbine which manufactured electricity, power has been made available in any place for any man for the purposes of comfort, of safety, of production—a programme of simple utility.

Of the first and third periods it may sadly be said that they have brought their dangers, and there has not been peace. Locomotion has given power of action from a far range. Wireless has provided facilities for instruction from a distance, and both have concentrated in central authority a power that human beings have not yet learnt to be great enough to wield for the general good. But the function of the second was to help the individual, whether in groups or in isolation; by the second the personal mechanisms of life which encourage the conditions that civilise humanity, have brought to the general mass of the nations the amenities that had been the luxuries of the few, and in this benefaction there may be found in the end the true foundation of peace. This is the period and this the work that has been thus shortly under review.

Some indeed may call the setting of all these matters the cramping framework of capitalism, but however that may be, we may be glad indeed that in the frame is the picture of an inventor who, *felix opportunitate*, was endowed by birth with a home of considerable resources, with a privileged education, with finances that could bear and break partnerships, that could carry over periods of waiting and trial and change of policy. To that world of expansion which brought hope to industry, growth to trade, facilities to the individual, these fine powers were brought to bear, and there stands as a mark of those Post-Victorian days in the midst of the great things that were done *quorum pars magna fuit*, the undismayed engineer, Charles Parsons.

EARL ROBERTS
1832-1914

By
SIR JOHN FORTESCUE

EARL ROBERTS

by SIR JOHN FORTESCUE

THERE are few more curious military studies than that of the three Presidential armies—Bengal, Bombay, Madras—of the old East India Company. Beginning with a nucleus of a handful of European officers, a few hundred European soldiers, and as many native troops, they grew gradually to tens and hundreds of thousands without any essential change in their habits or their constitution. As in England, the unit was the regiment, self-contained and to a great degree independent. If the commanding officer were efficient, the regiment was efficient likewise. If he were inefficient, the regiment faithfully reflected his inefficiency, and the fact was accepted as possibly regrettable but certainly irremediable. Promotion went by seniority and, despite of the havoc wrought by the climate, was generally very slow. Subalterns frequently waited for fifteen years before they became captains. In the early days many most important operations were conducted, and brilliantly conducted, by captains. Any man of the grade of colonel was likely to be past his work, and a general was nearly sure to be too old and worn out for active service. One extreme case of a general's incompetence was seen in the Nepal War of 1814–16, when one poor, nerveless, ancient man actually deserted his army rather than bear longer the responsibility of commanding it. This delinquency was not accounted to him for a crime, hardly even for a reproach. After the return of peace he received a high and lucrative command and ended his days in prosperity.

The slowness of promotion rendered a regimental career unsatisfying to ambitious young men, who sought the earliest chance of exchanging it for another. Three courses were open to them: to seek employment on the staff of the Army itself, or in the Civil Service (such as the Revenue

Department), or in the " political," which signified more or less the diplomatic, branch. In all of these they received increased pay, while the passing years brought them automatically a slow though certain rise in military rank. It was in the " political " service that the most famous Indian administrators—such men as Henry Lawrence and James Outram—gained their great names. Others, having extraordinary linguistic powers, studied the histories of the peoples to whom they were accredited, and left behind them historical work of permanent value. The " politicals " were probably the ablest Britons in India, and they did not as a rule suffer from undue modesty. Living, as they often did, for years remote from their English fellows and absolutely alone among strange folks, they may be excused if they thought of little but themselves and their mission, and from want of any better channel poured out their souls into interminable despatches and reports. Whether they would have enjoyed so great a reputation at home, in the company of their peers, as they did in India, where signal ability was not too common, is an interesting question.

With their best men weeded out for other employment, the Indian regiments were inevitably relegated to the inferior and the idle. Most of them were good sportsmen, and not a few of them on most cordial terms with the high-born and high-bred Indian gentlemen with whom they were brought into contact. England was many months' distant. Leave to return thither, except on certificate of sickness, was not to be thought of except after a stay of ten years. So, like all of their countrymen in India, they settled down to make the country their home and the native troops their children. In time of peace they lived comfortably in cantonments, with a great host of servants. If ordered into the field, they fared forth in palanquins, taking all their servants with them, and did their campaigning likewise comfortably. In the Afghan war of 1839 one brigadier found that he needed sixty camels to carry all that would satisfy his requirements. The result was that an army on the plains of India was like a moving city, in which the combatants numbered from 10 to 20 per cent. only of the entire population. The army that marched to Seringapatam in 1799 moved in a hollow square with a front of three miles and a depth of seven, the intervening space containing 120,000 animals of all kinds from the elephant

by SIR JOHN FORTESCUE

to the ass. When it came to fighting, the officers could be trusted to show daring and reckless courage. They might not always lead intelligently, but they were above all things leaders.

The supreme military authorities in the three Presidencies were not as a rule of greater intellect than the regimental officers. They were extremely corrupt as well as imbecile, especially in the early days, and to the very last they were obstructive and unteachable. In spite of decades of remonstrance from commanders in the field they would never institute any organised service for transport and supply. " The greater portion of the carriage (transport)," wrote Sir Robert Napier in 1867, " has been hired carriage managed under a kind of social organisation peculiar to itself, which has existed from time immemorial and which goes on somehow, one hardly knows how." Such an institution fully satisfied supreme headquarters in India. It had gone on somehow from time immemorial, and that sufficed. The rest of the work of preparation for a campaign was carried on in the same casual fashion. Thousands of soldiers met their death storming batteries, because their august masters could not provide them with guns to silence the enemy's artillery.

As to staff, there was none worth the name within the length and breadth of India. There might be staff-officers, but there was no conception of staff-work in any quarter high or low. An officer on the line of communication in Baluchistan might receive his orders from the Commandant at the base, or the Political Officer of the district, or direct from the Governor-General, or from all three simultaneously —and no one seemed to think that such things mattered very much. If operations were carried on in rather a casual fashion, there was at least plenty of conquered territory to show for them.

It was into such an army in an India differing little from the India of Clive that Frederick Sleigh Roberts was born at Cawnpore on September 30, 1832. His father, Abraham Roberts, a good, sound officer of the Company's service, was then forty-six years of age, and had nearly as many more to live. The boy was sent home as an infant, educated at Eton and Addiscombe, and sent back in 1852 to join the Bengal Artillery. By that time his father had gone through the insane Afghan campaign of 1839–42, and two campaigns in the Punjab; but, except for decay of discipline among the native troops, there was little change in the Bengal Army. Young Roberts joined his father, now Major-General commanding the Lahore Division at Lahore, and there learned most of his regimental duty. After eighteen months he was transferred to a horse battery—about the smartest unit in the Company's service—and was intensely happy. Small and slightly built, though wiry, he had the ideal figure for a lightweight in the saddle, and became, as he remained to the end, a beautiful horseman.

After no more than four years of regimental service he was taken on the staff of the Quartermaster-General's department, and so gained the first step towards advancement. Possibly this appointment was a job, but, if so, it was nothing out of the way. In any case, he never again quitted the department until he finally took leave of it as Quartermaster-General. In May 1857 came the first outbreak of mutiny in the Bengal Army. Feebly handled by incompetent officers at the outset, the movement presently established its centre at Delhi. Thither, contrary to his better judgment, an unfortunate commander was hurried by a purblind Government with a totally inadequate force and a parody of a siege-train. However, the little column, about 3,000 strong, fought its way to Delhi, where it arrived on June 8, and luckily found the famous Ridge ready to its hand as a rampart of defence and a position for attack. The full blaze of the summer heat was upon it; cholera and other foul diseases dogged its steps; and an enemy outnumbering it by twenty to one harassed it almost daily by incessant attacks. It was all that the troops could do to hold their own, and the driblets of reinforcements which reached them from time to time just sufficed to make good casualties, leaving them no stronger than before.

Roberts himself arrived before Delhi just three weeks after the opening of the so-called siege, and took up his duties as D.A.Q.M.G. of Artillery. From his narrative it appears that there was little order or method on the Ridge until the chief command changed hands for the fourth time on July 17. The various regimental officers carried on their duties according to their own lights, never failing, however, to succour each other. From time to time at some moment of desperate peril some officer with or without a handful of men would dash into the midst of the enemy;

by SIR JOHN FORTESCUE

and, if he could not extricate himself, some other daredevil would plunge in and pluck him out. By such a feat of valour did young Roberts win one of the many Victoria Crosses granted to the brave men before Delhi. Once he was slightly wounded by a bullet which, but for the chance protection of a percussion-cap pouch, could hardly have failed to kill him. Sometimes he did duty as an artillery officer, sometimes as a staff-officer. To him, as indeed to many others, no service seems to have come amiss.

At last, on September 6, a fairly adequate force of 8,000 men with an efficient siege-train was assembled before Delhi. The operations, which had so far been mostly waste of energy, became serious; and on the 14th the city was assaulted and, after some vicissitudes, mastered at a cost of some 1,200 casualties. The total losses from beginning to end were 992 killed and 2,845 wounded, besides hundreds who died from disease and exposure.

On the 21st Roberts left Delhi as staff-officer to a column of about 3,000 men which, after a few small actions, reached Agra on the way to Cawnpore. Proceeding, according to the usual Indian fashion, without any precautions, it was there surprised by the enemy, but extricated itself with no great difficulty and went on its way. Eventually it joined the main force under Sir Colin Campbell—about 30,000 men—which was advancing on Lucknow. It was perfectly safe to transgress all the rules of war, and they were transgressed accordingly. But Campbell, who was not a great commander, missed his chance of striking the enemy a decisive blow, and the operations were prolonged for months. Before they were closed Roberts, worn out by ten months of arduous work, was fain to go home on sick leave, and in April 1858 he started for England. He missed nothing by his absence from the field. The campaign was carried on in such a careless and casual fashion as to furnish the worst possible schooling for a young officer.

He returned to India bringing with him a very comely young wife in July 1860, in which year the Sovereignty of India and the troops of the East India Company were taken over by Queen Victoria. His energies were for some time devoted to the arrangement of huge camps for a viceregal progress, a duty which had the advantage of introducing him to those in great places. In 1863 he was selected for a more serious duty. The Indian Government, against the advice of the Commander-in-Chief, had embarked upon an expedition to the Ambela Valley, reckoning that it was to be a mere military promenade of a few weeks. It proved to be a far more serious undertaking, lasting for four months and costing a thousand casualties; and, shortly before its close, there was a question whether it should not be abandoned altogether. Roberts and another officer were sent up to report on the situation. They decided that the enterprise should be carried through, and Roberts, after witnessing the final and decisive operation, went off with a small party of officers to superintend the destruction of the enemy's stronghold in the mountains. It was a most perilous mission, but the party returned in safety, and Roberts through these services gained the goodwill of the Commander-in-Chief, Sir Hugh Rose. Since Sir Hugh had been the only commander who had shown real energy and talent during the suppression of the mutiny, his approval was worth the earning.

Roberts's work next lay with the Abyssinian expedition of 1867, perhaps the most difficult and dangerous that we ever carried to a successful issue. The base was a waterless post on the Red Sea. The nearest water (not even then too abundant) lay at the foot of the mountains across twelve miles of desert; and the task of the force was to ascend these mountains by rocky paths to a height of 8,000 feet, and march 400 miles over more rocky paths to the Abyssinian capital, 10,000 feet above the sea. The great problem was how to feed the troops—the old problem of transport and supply—and the Bombay Government outdid itself in imbecility to impede its solution. Roberts who did not come upon the scene until late, found himself condemned to be chief staff-officer at the port of disembarkation, a most important but thankless duty which kept him for four months under a baking sun in an atmosphere poisoned by the corpses of thousands of transport animals. However, Sir Robert Napier (Lord Napier of Magdala) was his friend; and he was sent home with despatches, which gained him a brevet of Lieutenant-Colonel.

On his return to India he received a special appointment as A.Q.M.G. in his old department, and in 1871 found himself fitting out a small expedition against the Lushais on the north-eastern frontier—a quarter entirely strange to him. It was his first independent command in the field, and though a small one, was sufficiently exacting. The campaign was most trying, being conducted in trackless, airless, sunless forests, where the atmosphere by day was stifling, but, at a height of 6,000 to 8,000 feet, very chilly at night. The arrangements for transport were most defective—they would not have been true to the Indian type if they had been otherwise—but after four months of exhausting operations the offending tribes were brought to submission without great loss except through sickness. On his return Roberts found that on New Year's Day, 1872, Lord Napier, owing to an unexpected vacancy, had promoted him to be D.Q.M.G. Two years later he was further promoted to be Quartermaster-General, and so reached the top of his chosen department.

Soon afterwards the question of our relations with Afghanistan became pressing. There could be no question as to the steady advance of Russia eastward, and the Amir, Sher Ali, showed himself decidedly inclined to throw in his lot with her. His refusal to receive an English Mission left no doubt as to his intentions, and the Indian Government decided to invade Afghanistan in the autumn of 1878. The invasion was planned to be carried out by three columns, one through the Khyber Pass, a second through the Kuram Valley, a little south of it, and the third through the Bolan Pass upon Kandahar. The second of these, by the Kuram Valley, was entrusted to Roberts, who thereupon assumed the local rank of Major-General.

In November he began his advance with just over 5,000 men, and within a fortnight came up to the pass known as the Peiwar Kotal, where the enemy in a strong position barred his further progress. Feinting to make a frontal attack, Roberts turned the left flank of the Afghans who, taken by surprise, gave way after little resistance and retreated. The affair cost Roberts fewer than a hundred casualties. Moving forward twelve miles towards the Shutargardan Pass, he there established an advanced post, and then fell back to clear his communications in the lower Kuram Valley and in Khost. The pacification of the tribes occupied him until January 1879. Meanwhile, Amir Sher Ali had fled from Kabul, leaving his son Yakub Khan to reign in his stead, and after much negotiation Yakub was brought in May to sign a treaty with the British. Thereby he bound himself to yield up certain territory and to admit a

British Mission to Kabul. Thereupon the troops, excepting two brigades, were withdrawn from the Khyber Valley, and orders were sent to the Bolan column to retire from Kandahar. Roberts's column alone remained in position, since Kuram was a part of the territory to be ceded by Afghanistan to the British. Roberts himself repaired to Simla, where he learned that his services had been rewarded by the K.C.B.

In September came tidings that the British Mission in Kabul had been attacked, and that its members had been massacred to a man. By that time the Khyber column had been broken up, and nearly all the troops had retired from Kandahar. The Kuram column alone was in a position to move quickly upon Kabul, and Roberts was ordered to resume command of it without delay. From thenceforward "Bobs's luck" began to be proverbial in India. With a force increased to 7,500 men with 22 guns, but (as seemed to be inevitable in India) ill-equipped with transport, he pushed on over the Shutargardan Pass, and on October 6 came upon the Afghans in position at the gorge of Charasia, barring the way to Kabul, about twelve miles beyond it. From lack of transport Roberts could throw into action immediately no more than 4,000 men and 18 guns but, pursuing his usual tactics of a frontal feint and a turning attack, he dislodged the enemy with heavy loss, counting on his side fewer than ninety casualties. He followed up his success on the 7th, but a strenuous effort on the 8th to intercept the flying Afghans failed completely, and he was fain to be content with the occupation of Kabul. He was presently raised to the local rank of Lieutenant-General in command of all the troops in eastern Afghanistan. These numbered some 20,000 in all, of which 6,000 were actually with him in and about Kabul, and the remainder in the Khyber Valley.

By December there were signs that the tribes of Afghanistan were, as in 1841, disposed to lay aside their internal feuds for the moment and combine against the hated invader. Roberts, sending out three small columns, endeavoured to beat them in detail before they were assembled, but the operations miscarried, and there was one moment, on December 11, when his position was unpleasant if not critical. On the three following days he tried to restore the situation but, after a few local successes, was obliged to abandon the attempt, and to withdraw his whole force into an entrenched camp which he had already occupied at Shirpur, a short distance outside Kabul. The operation was not effected without difficulty, and Roberts confesses that the hours during which it was in progress were a time of intense anxiety to him. There appears to be no doubt that he took dangerous risks through excessive dispersion of his forces.

Once within the entrenchments he was safe, for he had gathered in plenty of provisions and of all other necessaries. For eight days, from December 14 to 22, the tribesmen swarmed about him, and at last, on the night of the 22nd, they delivered a great attack. Of course against steady troops armed with breach-loaders and well sheltered they had no chance, and were beaten off with heavy loss. By the morning of the 24th they had dispersed and Roberts was able to reoccupy Kabul. Having called up to him one of the brigades in the Khyber Valley, he was now stronger than ever, for his casualties had not been heavy. Then came up the question of the pacification of Afghanistan and the choice of a new Amir. But this was not to be left to Roberts. Sir Donald Stuart, who had again advanced to Kandahar, was now ordered to proceed with a part of his force to Kabul, and Roberts was his junior officer. It seems, unless report be more than usually mendacious, that the Calcutta Government was not too well pleased with Roberts's operations at Kabul, and if it did not recall him, at least contemplated recalling him.

However that may be, "Bobs's luck" intervened to set everything right. Ayub Khan, brother of the abdicated Yakub, had long been at Herat with a considerable force threatening to advance upon Kandahar, and on June 15 he actually advanced. A little force of 2,500 men, under General Barrows, was detached from Kandahar to stop him, with some thousands of Sher Ali's troops in support. These last deserted to Ayub Khan, who on the 27th engaged Barrow's column at Maiwand and practically destroyed it. The Afghan chief then beleaguered Kandahar, and it was obvious that troops must be sent to its relief. Sir Donald Stewart strongly recommended that this should be done from Kabul, and that the command should be entrusted to Roberts. This being approved, Roberts, after careful preparation, set out from Kabul on August 9 at the head of 10,000 men with 18 guns. His march was wholly unmolested by any enemy, though he had some difficulty over the provision of food and fuel, and on the 31st he reached Kandahar, having covered 313 miles in twenty-two days. On the following day, employing the usual tactics, he attacked and dispersed the levies of Ayub Khan. He had with him some 15,000 troops—the largest force that he had ever actually handled—whose casualties amounted to 250. Being seriously out of health, he was presently obliged to leave the Army, and before long to go to England, but not before he had received the G.C.B. for his services.

On his arrival at home he was amazed to find what a fuss was made about his march to Kandahar. Actually a special decoration was granted to every man who took part in it. Yet, as Roberts himself points out, there was no peculiar difficulty or danger about it, and it was not nearly so perilous as his first march to Kabul. But his little column had vanished into space for three weeks to re-emerge victorious, and these circumstances captivated the British public. In truth, Roberts's great military reputation rests chiefly on this march to Kandahar.

He returned to India in November 1880, as Commander-in-Chief at Madras, from which post he was promoted in July 1885 to be Commander-in-Chief in India. In these two places he did useful work in purging the native army of unwarlike recruits, establishing institutes for the British regiments, and forwarding the construction of strategic railways to the north-eastern frontier; while Lady Roberts did her part by organising a regular service of nurses for the military hospitals in India. So highly were his services appreciated that his tenure of the Command-in-Chief was prolonged for two years, at the close of which he was raised to the peerage with the title of Lord Roberts of Kandahar.

Thus, after forty-one years in India, he returned to England, and settled down near Ascot, with the prospect of ending his days in obscurity. The troops under his command had always been devoted to him, and Mr. Kipling had long made a hero of him; and there was no more popular figure in Queen Victoria's second Jubilee procession of 1897 than that of the little Indian warrior who rode along, looking straight to his front, his little figure swaying to every step of his beautiful Arab charger, on whose breast-plate dangled, by special grant of the Queen, the Afghan War Medal. The publication of his book, *Forty-one Years in*

India, in the previous year had laid his life before the public, and the public had welcomed it with joy.

Then unexpectedly in 1899 his military career was reopened. The Government, in spite of repeated warnings, had neglected military preparations in South Africa, and left the British Colonies open to invasion by the Boers. In two or three weeks there were three beleaguered garrisons—Kimberley and Mafeking on the side of Cape Colony, Ladysmith on the side of Natal, crying aloud for relief. Troops were hurried out, and an unfortunate General, with a wholly insufficient force, was expected somehow to set things right. Three reverses at three different points in a single week brought home to England the true state of affairs, and there was general dismay. Incidentally in one of the three actions Roberts's only son was killed, and the posthumous award of the Victoria Cross to the gallant boy could not console the father.

Apart from this melancholy misfortune, "Bobs's luck" still held good. Lord Lansdowne, who had been Viceroy in India during part of Roberts's tenure of the Command-in-Chief, was Secretary of State for War, and he secured the appointment of Roberts to the supreme command in South Africa. Reinforcements which quadrupled the original strength of the army there, were prepared and despatched, and Roberts set sail with Kitchener as his Chief of Staff. Neither of them, through no fault of their own, knew anything about the British Army. Their first act was to upset the organisation for transport and supply, which only needed expansion, from top to bottom, and to remodel it upon crude ideas of their own. Then the operations began. Roberts was concentrating on the westernmost of the three lines of railway which traverse South Africa from south to north. He planned to shift 30,000 men from the western to the central line, a distance of 100 miles, and to pursue his advance northward along that central line.

He started on February 11, 1900. On the 13th a convoy of 200 wagons with 2,500 oxen was captured by the enemy, through sheer mismanagement and bad staff work; and this mishap nearly wrecked the entire enterprise. However, the march was continued. On the 17th Roberts succeeded in surrounding a Boer force of 4,000 men at Paardeberg, and waited, with his troops on half-rations of biscuit, until the 27th for hunger to drive the enemy to surrender. Eventually the army occupied its objective, Bloemfontein, without resistance on March 6, and there sat down exhausted and paralysed. It had lost half of its transport animals, and there was much sickness among the men—the results of bad management.

For nearly two months the army remained stationary, and then at last it resumed its advance up the midland railway. Opinions differed as to whether the movement should be slow, so that every step forward might be consolidated, or whether it should be rapid, in the hope that the occupation of the capital at Pretoria might put an end to further resistance. Roberts preferred the latter course, which events proved to be wrong. His great superiority in numbers enabled him to brush aside the enemy with little difficulty or loss, but, except at Paardeberg, he never hit the Boers so much as a severe blow. He tried to do so more than once, but failed.

By November 1900 the struggle had changed from regular to guerilla warfare, and everything was in the utmost confusion. Roberts presently came home, leaving Kitchener to finish the war, but before his departure things were already in a wretched mess, while the waste and extravagance were appalling. The truth is, that Roberts had never got over the traditions of the casual and careless Indian Army. He knew not how to use a properly organised staff. He would give orders to this officer and that without troubling himself to approach the officer responsible for the department concerned. No doubt when he himself had been a junior member of the Quartermaster-General's department, he had been charged with a score of odd jobs, and had done them, though none of his business. The army of which he found himself in command was ten times larger than had ever before been entrusted to him, but he could not depart from his old ingrained habits. He did not increase his military reputation by his last campaign.

He came home to be raised to the title of Earl Roberts and to receive the Order of the Garter—the first soldier to receive an earldom and the first to wear the blue ribbon since Wellington. But Wellington, while still Sir Arthur Wellesley and before he had set foot on the Iberian Peninsula, had done greater and more important work in active service than had Roberts in his whole career. Lord Roberts was presently appointed Commander-in-Chief in England,

by SIR JOHN FORTESCUE

but can, no more than his predecessor, Lord Wolseley, have found himself comfortable in an office which was already doomed to abolition. When he finally retired he became a strong advocate of conscription for the Army, for, in common with all seeing men, he anticipated the struggle with Germany. His advocacy unfortunately was of small effect. If there had been conscription-lists of men, as there were of horses, in England in 1914, much confusion and waste would have been saved. When the War had fairly started and Indian troops had been brought over to Flanders, nothing could prevent the old man, though past eighty, from crossing the Channel to greet them. Thus he caught a chill, of which in a few days he died, doing duty to the last.

To call him a Victorian (whatever a Victorian may be) seems rather absurd, for he spent little more than seven years of his manhood in the England of the Queen's reign. He was rather a survival of very old days in India, and was fortunate in living at a time when India was considered—most wrongly—to be a good school for officers. He was not, in my judgment, the first British soldier of his day; but he was a fine type of the Indian product—temperate, clean living, a keen sportsman, a superb horseman, of daring courage, and always devoted to his men. There is one little picture of him which always comes back to me. When he held supreme command in India there were grand manœuvres at which many foreign officers were present. The last day was devoted to sports, and in due time came the moment for tent-pegging. Then a little man urging his horse to the top of its speed came tearing down, lance in hand, took the peg neatly, and returned with it transfixed. The foreign officers stared in amazement, for the little man was the Commander-in-Chief.

SCOTT OF THE ANTARCTIC
1868-1912

By
R. C. SHERRIFF

SCOTT OF THE ANTARCTIC

by R. C. SHERRIFF

TO be told that Scott was born near Devonport is to jump to the thought of one of those square-built, whitewashed houses on the slopes above the sea, with a flagstaff beside it, and a haze of tough rock flowers in borders of egg-shaped, whitewashed stones. The kind of house that cranes one corner window out to sea, a brass telescope lurking in its shadows—one of those houses that form a scattered ring round the coastline of southern England: looking from the air like the speckled tidal marks of some giant, solitary wave.

But the guess is wrong. It fails to apply to the birthplace of Scott. It must be recorded, almost with regret (for it would have seemed fitter otherwise), that the house of his birth lies somewhat inland from the sea; that Scott's great-grandfather, the first of the family to come to Devon, was not of seaman stock himself.

For although this great-grandfather was born in a fisherman's cottage on the bleak coastline of Midlothian, it was because his parents were in refuge, their home a charred ruin near the field of Prestonpans. The parents found exile with their son in France: they lived and died there, but the son, in middle age, returned and settled at Holberton, in Devon, and Devon, in due course, called four sons of his to the sea. Of these the eldest became the explorer's grandfather. He left the Navy in 1826, settled in a lovely house called Outlands, which remained for nearly seventy years the family home.

Here Scott the explorer was born in the June of 1868, a delicate, dreamy son of a father who had been prevented by his own delicate health from following the profession of the sea.

The pictures that remain with us of the boy's childhood are slight and shadowy: fair-haired, blue-eyed—so deeply blue that there were sometimes shades of violet in them. He emerges more clearly to us in his eighth year, riding proudly on his pony Beppo from his home to a day school at Stoke Dameral—through soft, quiet country fringed with the wild outskirts of the moors; country that drew from him his early delicateness and sent a sturdy little cadet to the *Britannia*.

Credit, we assume, goes equally to the Navy and to the boy's own will-power for everything that followed. Nature had given him very little armour to face the path he chose. He received neither brute strength nor an orderly mind. "Old Mooney" was the nickname his father gave him, but sometimes his spells of listless dreaming were broken by fierce bursts of temper; he was impatient of tidiness; his boyhood left a littered trail behind him. But if the Navy helped him, no one could have done more to give it opportunity.

"The faults of his youth," Sir James Barrie has written, "must have lived on in him as in all of us, but he got to know they were there and he took an iron grip of them and never let go his hold."

He became a Cadet-Captain, and at the age of fifteen went to the *Boadicea* as a midshipman. There is no hint in these early years that the fire of exploration smouldered in him: there is only the sure sign that the love for the service he had entered was passionately in his blood.

It was through a chance meeting with Sir Clements Markham that Scott became explorer. The great geographer was on a visit to his cousin, Sir Albert Hastings Markham, who then commanded the squadron to which Scott's ship belonged.

The lieutenants organised a service cutter race, the rules of which demanded proof of as many naval qualities as could be crowded in. Scott, then still a midshipman, won the race and dined with his commodore as reward. Sir Clements was present at the dinner—looking, even at that time, for the future leader of his *Discovery* expedition, and it seems that his mind was made up that night.

"My experience," he says, "taught me that it would be years before an expedition would be ready, and I believed that Scott was the destined man to command it."

by R. C. SHERRIFF

Actually, twelve years were to pass before the *Discovery* set sail upon her voyage to the Antarctic, and during those years Scott rose from midshipman to torpedo-lieutenant of the *Majestic*.

We are given one glimpse of him as a sub-lieutenant, on his way up the Pacific coast to join his ship in British Columbia.

He had to travel on a ramshackle old tramp steamer, filled to bursting point with Californians, with wives and children, hurrying off to a new mining camp in the North. They ran into a gale which lasted all the way to Victoria, and the ship became a shambles of sea-sick humanity and crying children. The few stewards on board were drunk or ill themselves—no meals were served, for the saloon (through lack of cabin accommodation) was filled with helpless, groaning women.

> "With a small body of volunteers, Scott dressed the mothers, washed the children, fed the babies, swabbed down the floors, nursed the sick, and performed every imaginable service for all hands. On deck he settled the quarrels and established order by his personality, or, if necessary, by his fists."

So Scott journeyed to join his first ship.

From then onward, for ten years, Scott lived the life of a normal officer of the Navy, and the next chapter of his life opens upon a June day in 1899. On leave from his ship, he met Sir Clements Markham by chance in London, and heard for the first time of the expedition. For all those years Sir Clements had been patiently preparing, and plans were now well advanced for laying down the keel of the ship.

Sir Clements records a remarkable coincidence upon the day that followed: he was just sitting down to write to the necessary authority to secure Scott's services when Scott himself was announced. He had come to volunteer his services as commander of the expedition. Coincidence is hardly, perhaps, the word: it rather shows the complete harmony of purpose between two men perfectly fitted for their respective tasks.

It is natural that the epic story of the last expedition should have thrown the voyage of the *Discovery* into comparative obscurity. The public has remembered Scott with constant faithfulness, but it remembers his death rather than his life. The name of Scott conjures in the public mind a picture of five men battling against solitude—of four men knowing that solitude had beaten them—of three men dying in a tiny green tent upon a white plain—of one man, lingering on alone to write a few final words of farewell.

Remembrance, to remain vivid, must always frame its picture. Of the rest the public know little: only perhaps that Scott " had been there before." But the voyage of the *Discovery* was magnificent in its conception and complete in its performance. It was upon this voyage that Scott first came to know Dr. Edward Wilson, who was to become so close a friend, and who was to go with him upon the journey to the Pole.

Two years went by in patient preparation, and the *Discovery* left the London Docks on the last day of July 1901. King Edward VII, with Queen Alexandra, paid a visit to the ship at Cowes, and showed the keenest interest both then and throughout the expedition.

Four months later the heavily laden, stolid little ship first sighted the ice pack a thousand miles to the south of New Zealand, and Scott has recorded his impressions of the sight that he came to know so well.

> " The wind had died away; what light remained was reflected in a ghostly glimmer from the white surface of the pack; now and again a white snow petrel flitted through the gloom. The grinding of the floes against the ship's side was mingled with the more subdued hush of their rise and fall on the long swell, and for the first time we felt something of the solemnity of these great southern solitudes."

Everything that Scott wrote was direct, simple, and effortless. We search in vain through his writings for a conscious literary style—a striving after effect. He did not enjoy writing for the sake of it: he wrote purely to describe what he had seen, and to make clear to his followers what he required them to do.

He stands with the minority of modern explorers in this respect, for recent exploration has too often been inspired by the book that will be written instead of the things that will be found.

by R. C. SHERRIFF

It is impossible, within the space of a few pages, to describe the expedition of the *Discovery*. Every word of Scott's own record must be read to gain a full appreciation of it. The weariness, the hardship, the aching patience of it all, are scarcely touched upon, but this and much more can be read between the lines. The expedition is fascinating enough to read about for the human side alone; scientifically it was one of the most valuable and productive endeavours ever made in the Polar regions. A long and continuous stretch of coastline of the Antarctic continent was added to the map. Sledge expeditions were made into the interior and valuable geological specimens collected; marine and bird life was studied; meteorology—magnetism; nothing was omitted from the plans laid by Sir Clements Markham, and Scott carried every instruction through to its end. We read every word of a staunch fight through a blizzard; we visualise every movement of the straining men, but sometimes we skip the lists of precious rock that the men have fought for and dragged behind them at the risk of their lives.

On September 10, 1904, the *Discovery* dropped anchor off Spithead; three years and two months since she left England.

The Press gave instant appreciation to the great adventure, and Scott became a popular hero. The glare of bright-lit drawing-rooms must have come strangely to Scott after three years of flickering lamps and uncertain, home-made electricity. The swift alternation of day and night must often have caught him unawares after the great darkless Antarctic summer and the long winter gloom.

For a little while he enjoyed the novelty of being chased by lion hunters and the deeper pleasure of coming into touch with celebrities whose paths would not normally have crossed his own. In this he was not attracted by the mere fact of distinction; for he had a genuine, artistic love of things in which his hard life never allowed him to indulge. It was at this time that Scott met Sir James Barrie, and the beginning of this great friendship has been charmingly recorded by Sir James in his introduction to *The Voyages of Captain Scott* :

> " On the night of my original meeting with Scott he was but lately home from his first adventure into the Antarctic, and my chief recollection of the occasion is that having found the entrancing man I was unable to

leave him. In vain he escorted me through the streets of London to my home, for when he said good night I then escorted him to his, and so it went on I know not for how long through the small hours."

The climax of those wonderful days is recorded in a letter that Scott wrote to his mother following his visit to Balmoral: of four crowded days beginning on a Tuesday evening, when, before dinner, King Edward VII sent for him and gave him the C.V.O., ending upon the Friday night, when Scott bade good-bye after lunching and dining almost every day beside the King; lecturing one evening and spending an hour of a wet afternoon showing the King photographs, sketches, and other souvenirs of the expedition. He left with his present of a stag's head and some venison which he sent on to his mother.

His days of relaxation were soon over. With six months' leave granted by the Admiralty he settled down to write his book, living quietly with his mother and sisters in London.

He was promoted captain, and for the first time in his career found a little relief from the financial worries that had haunted him since early manhood. For disaster had fallen upon the family fortunes soon after Scott had passed from his cadet days: the father, who in Scott's childhood had been so comfortably off, had suffered a grave loss of money, and had died leaving his family with no means to keep up the home in Devon. From that time onward the young naval officer took a large burden of the responsibility: the house was let, and Scott never ceased to watch and care for his mother and sisters through the difficult years that followed.

The book was finished in the summer of 1905, and immediately upon publication took rank amongst the best literature of travel. Before it was published, however, the author had returned to duty in the temporary capacity of Assistant-Director of Naval Intelligence at the Admiralty, and in August 1906 he went to sea once more with the *Victorious*. On New Year's Day, 1907, he was transferred to the *Albemarle*, and once again settled down to naval routine.

Scott was now thirty-nine. His busy life, and the cares of supporting his mother, had left him little thought for marriage. His pay, even with his new promotion, was not much over £700 a year; little enough even to support the calls of his rank. But marriage, nevertheless, was near at hand.

by R. C. SHERRIFF

During a short leave in London, early in 1907, he met Kathleen Bruce, a young artist, and from that time onwards his letters reveal how fiercely he fought the difficulties that lay before him.

A letter of touching unselfishness reached him from his mother:

> " . . . I want to say that *whatever* plans you make for the future will be suitable for me and you must never let me be a hindrance in any way to your making a home and a life of your own."

He could not have found stauncher allies to help him than in his mother and the girl whom he desired to marry. His struggle is expressed in a few words from a letter to Miss Bruce:

> " I am still young enough to believe we could win through, but in facing poverty we should be living and believing in a better future. The old can only live in the present. My mother is sixty-seven—only a strand of life remains. She has had a hard life in many respects. I set myself to make the last years free from anxiety. I can't light-heartedly think of events that may disturb my decision."

But happily the path grew smoother as the months drew on. Scott had proved himself in the higher rank that he now held; he had won golden opinions from his superiors, and a great future was assured. His letters show an increasing lightness of heart: in the summer of 1908 he received command of the *Bulwark*, a first-class battleship which carried with it a higher rate of pay and a separate command in the Channel Fleet. Scott cared little for money in the sense of intrinsic wealth: he only cared because of its vital need in lightening the dual responsibility that lay ahead.

The vigorous letters of this year are strange mixtures of light and shade: sometimes he is bursting with the joy of the future; sometimes there comes a hint of restlessness—from the *Bulwark* on a summer night he wrote:

> " Such a dull dinner-party to-night. Sometimes on such occasions I get depressed with the thought of an inevitable vista of such functions. Oh, dear me!—I am oppressed with a leaden feeling. I see full stomachs, —torpid brains."

And then the love of the sea drowns the dull dinner-parties under a foaming exultation:

" We left Plymouth early on Tuesday. That evening we were in a dense fog off the Land's End. It's always trying, creeping from fog signal to fog signal with the plaintive hoots of steamers drowning their shriller note. At ten we burst into the Irish Sea, and through the night plunged on through thinning banks of mist. In the morning we found the land half hidden in cloud, and at noon we were anchored at Berehaven. Wild signals from coastguard stations, trying to supply our wants. . . . In the afternoon we were off again up the long bay with steamboats puffing along beside us."

He goes on to describe a night storm—straining cables—surf thundering over villainous black rocks.

" How curious it all is," he ends, " to live on the verge of mischance."

His letters speak more and more of the marriage as the summer of that year wore on. A solicitor enters the correspondence, for they are negotiating for a house:

" I think it is a great point to have the house in our hands and furnished, so that we can marry and occupy as we think fit. What fun, our house."

And then the day arrived. Leave came in September, and Scott was married to Kathleen Bruce in the Chapel at Hampton Court.

It is recorded that bright sunshine filled the Chapel as the wedding party entered. As the service went on the sky darkened—and three great claps of thunder broke over the solemnity of the ritual. They went to Etretat for a short honeymoon, but in a few days Scott's leave was up, and he rejoined the *Bulwark*.

Scott's friends accepted his marriage as his leave-taking of the Polar regions: they assumed that his one great expedition had been the beginning and the end of his exploring days.

It is hard to say when Scott's plans for the new expedition first began to form: he probably brought them back with him from his first Antarctic voyage, for those desolate places are only silent while man is there. A whisper comes out from them when man gives back their solitude; a whisper that grows into a call, and weaves a spell that few can throw aside.

by R. C. SHERRIFF

It is clear that his plans to complete and extend the explorations of the *Discovery* voyage were already matured before his marriage. His life at sea gave little opportunity to work upon the intricate details of such an expedition, but a new appointment in the spring of 1909 gave much better opportunities to push ahead with his plans.

He became Naval Assistant to the Second Sea Lord—Admiral Bridgeman. His duties took him each morning to the Admiralty, but every evening found him busy at his desk in his new house in Buckingham Palace Road; working at the immense mass of detail to be completed before any public announcement could be made.

In September of that year, six months after his return from sea, the plans of the expedition were put before the public and an appeal made for financial support.

Scott's responsibilities upon the voyage of the *Discovery* were heavy enough, but they were nothing compared with the burden that he now took voluntarily upon himself. He had to a large extent been free of the financial and organising problems of the first expedition: he had been an appointed leader; lent by the Royal Navy to the Royal Geographical Society, under whom he directly worked. But now he proposed to accept all responsibility, from the first detail to the last. He no doubt felt that the deeper probing of the Antarctic continent that now lay ahead could best be carried out with complete freedom from outside control—that only by being able to act entirely upon his own initiative could justice be done to the enterprise.

Shortly after announcing the expedition Scott went on half-pay and began the thankless and unpleasant task of raising funds.

He toured the country—lecturing—seeking interviews with influential people—hating it—humiliating himself. We have all at some time or another undertaken the task of collecting money; we have all felt the humiliation of it—and the anger at being snubbed for trying to carry out a duty from which we are to receive no gain but from which most people suspect we shall.

For long, weary months Scott went upon his journey, occasionally heartened by an unexpectedly large donation —often depressed by wasted hours from which he came empty-handed.

The "dash for the Pole" has been given a far more prominent place in the aims of the expedition than Scott gave it in his own mind. Had the expedition been endowed in such a way as to relieve Scott of his public appeal, it is probable that he would not have included the "dash for the Pole" in his plans at all; in any case it would have been secondary to the main objects of scientific exploration.

But his difficulty is very easy to appreciate. A sum of £40,000 was required—and a great deal of it had to be raised in comparatively small personal subscriptions. The appeal had to be made not only to the generosity, but to the imagination of prospective subscribers. The lay mind is not easily excited about geographical specimens and degrees of latitude. Scott knew quite well that however attractively he displayed his scientific programme it would not draw one-quarter of the support that a "dash for the Pole" would inspire. Many a hand would go into a pocket to take even a tiny share of the honour of placing the British Flag at the South Pole.

This is not to suggest that Scott was insincere—or that he carried out his last epic journey to satisfy subscribers to the expedition. He appreciated its explorative opportunities, and, once convinced of its need, threw all his heart into it.

Funds came in slowly but steadily—£20 here, £30 there. Local Committees were formed, and by the spring of 1910 a sum of £10,000 had been collected—small enough, in those days of peace and plenty, when the work to raise it and Scott's great prestige are balanced against it.

The Government made a grant of £20,000. Scott was appointed on full pay to command the expedition. The *Terra Nova*, a tough old Scottish whaler, was chosen and purchased, the officers and crew were gradually and carefully selected, and the ship left England on June 1, 1910. Even then the full amount of financial support had not come in; to the very last moment Scott was at work: he travelled ahead of the *Terra Nova* to seek funds in South Africa. Again he had to spend valuable days upon the same quest in Australia.

The *Terra Nova* sailed from Cape Town on September 2. At Melbourne a telegram awaited him:

Madeira. Am going south. Amundsen.

by R. C. SHERRIFF

A whole year and more passed before the bitter confirmation came. Here are the last words in Scott's diary for January 15, 1912:

" Only 27 miles from the Pole. We *ought* to do it now."

And the next day:

" Half an hour later he (Bowes) detected a black speck ahead. Soon we knew that this could not be a natural snow feature. We marched on, found that it was a black flag tied to a sledge bearer; nearby the remains of a camp; sledge tracks and ski tracks going and coming, and the clear trace of dogs' paws—many dogs. . . . The Norwegians have forestalled us and are first at the Pole. . . ."

To quote passages from Scott's last diary is akin to hacking pieces from a perfect memorial. The diary must be read in its entirety: there is no more to say.

Word by word it bares the character of a great man whose death now stands back from us by more than twenty years. They have been years that Scott would have lived with all the passionate energy of his nature. But a blizzard kept him from them—and a few miles of snow-clad wilderness.

C. P. SCOTT
1846-1932

By
IVOR BROWN

C. P. SCOTT

by IVOR BROWN

THE name above this contribution may be unfamiliar, perhaps even unknown, to many readers of this volume. Yet its owner stood, for more than a generation, as high in his own profession as Sargent, Shaw, Hardy, or Asquith in theirs. That profession, journalism, is considered to be so powerful that it has been called the Fourth Estate. Of its strong effect, for good or evil, upon a modern community in which everybody has been taught to read and very few to think, there can be no question. Yet, by a curious accident of professional technique, the administrators of this Estate, the editors of newspapers, often remain unknown men. The drivers of the great engines of what is called " publicity " seek no publicity themselves. Could one reader of *The Times* in five hundred name its editor? Could one in fifty thousand readers of the *Daily Mail* do the same? It is true that the habit of printing signed articles has greatly increased in recent years, except in the case of *The Times*. But that only emphasises the paradox. The foreign correspondents and the critics of the arts have their identities blazoned to the world, but the man who selects them in the first place, watches and directs their activities, and opens their gateway to fame, is still an unknown quantity to the general public.

Great editors are " known to their own " in the profession. C. P. Scott was also known to his own city of Manchester as a fine citizen who worked for every cause of the humanities in his own place as well as in the larger spheres; his funeral service in Manchester Cathedral drew the tributes of the world, but it was also the voice of a city mourning, a city not easily articulate. Scott was known at least as much to the journalists and politicians of Europe and America as to those of England; he had, almost in boyhood, taken the editorial chair of a Northern paper locally esteemed, and had carried its name and its spirit to the far corners of the world. He was known, naturally, to the Liberal Party, and not always with agreement; that was inevitable, for that fissiparous party might have earned its name owing to its liberality in partition. He had sat ten years in Parliament, as the Liberal member for the Leigh Division of Lancashire, but his House of Commons career, a quiet one, ended in 1905, when he returned to concentrate upon the major function and pleasure of his life, the development and direction of a newspaper. Consequently the editorial anonymity, which is the custom of the profession, once more descended upon him. Of him, as of other great editors, it could be said that few citizens had more public influence with less public status. Such was the habit of his calling, not, in my own opinion, altogether a good one; but there it was, and he respected it. When he wrote, in 1921, for the Centenary Number of the paper which he had guided for fifty years, he did so " as a member of the working staff." There was no cant, no bogus humility, in that phrase. It exactly described his constant anonymous labour. In his later years he stayed closely by his paper, giving it of his own hand in writing as well as with all his strength and soul in supervision, a day-long, night-long journalist.

The *Manchester Guardian* has always been and still is a family newspaper in the sense of continuous ownership by members of one clan. It could many times have been sold for extremely large sums of money; the market-price of a newspaper does not depend upon its balance-sheet, but on the purchaser's assessment of its worth as a source of power and reputation. On this calculation the *Guardian* was, and is, valued far above its capacity for making profits. But the family have never wished to sell; it has never even considered the possibility of transmuting this trusteeship, exacting, laborious, and even dangerous as it has been, into an easy fortune. The younger members of the Scott family might to-day be, in John Tanner's phrase, members of the Idle Rich class. They are not; they are heirs to responsibility and not to riches; and it is unlikely that any of them regrets it. There was nothing unique in this loyalty; it was decent professional practice. It was the tradition of the Old Journalism, of a craft which had not become commercialised, and of men who regarded newspapers as personal creations and not as counters in the stock-market. Mr. G.

by IVOR BROWN

Binney Dibblee, in the volume which he wrote on *The Newspaper* for the Home University Library, stated:

"To my certain knowledge the late Mr. John Edward Taylor refused to consider an offer of a million sterling for the *Manchester Guardian*, at a time when such a sum would have very favourably represented the value of the paper. He wrote to me briefly, asking me *not to send on to him communications of that kind again*. I have known four or five other proprietors of great papers, who would have been capable of doing the same thing."

That was the spirit which Charles Prestwich Scott inherited in 1871, sustained until his death on the first day of 1932, and passed on to his successors.

He was the son of Russell Scott, a successful wine-merchant in the South of England, and of Isabella Prestwich, who came of an old Manchester family, once owners of Hulme Hall. Russell Scott retired from business rather young, and devoted himself to the care of his large family of nine children and to such public causes as drew his Liberal sympathies. The family were Unitarians; Russell Scott's father was a great pillar of this radical and active faith which has contributed to English public life out of all proportion to its numbers. Young C. P. Scott was a delicate boy, and did not attend a public school. Nonconformity made entrance to Oxford difficult, but the liberal-mindedness of Corpus Christi College did not impose the sectarian test which now seems unthinkable in a place of learning. Accordingly Scott entered Corpus, where, discovering the physical strength which his childhood lacked, he distinguished himself on the river as well as in the schools. He went down with a first in "Greats" and the intention to serve in the family craft. His cousin, the second John Edward Taylor, offered him work in Manchester, but he went first to Edinburgh and served a short apprenticeship on the *Scotsman* under its famous editor, Alexander Russell. In 1871 he went to the *Manchester Guardian*. In 1872 he was its editor, a post which he only resigned in 1929; to the end he remained its governing director.

In 1874 Scott married Miss Rachel Cook, one of the original students of the foundation now famous as Girton, and a woman of remarkable ability and force of character. She had taken the Classical Tripos at Cambridge with distinction at a time when such a feat was unheard of in a mere woman. When she came to Manchester she toiled strenuously and successfully for the cause of women's education, and lent all her wealth of cultural interests to the paper which her husband edited. It was one of Scott's great contributions to the *Guardian* and to journalism in general to develop the literary side of a newspaper, and in this task his wife was a wise counsellor. During his editorship they enrolled for the criticism of the arts a band of contributors which included the greatest of Victorian, Edwardian, and Georgian writers.

In this connection one may stop to ask whether there was anything especially "Edwardian" about C. P. Scott. There was not. Nor was he to be deemed Victorian or Fifth Georgian; he over-stepped epochs. Periods did not contain him. Consider a Gladstonian Liberal, attached to the supposedly glum and Philistine school of Manchester, who, at the age of eighty, chose to be sculptured by Epstein. His house in Fallowfield, with its William Morris wallpapers, had the beauty of the late Victorian "progressives"; but many of the pictures were by the rising Edwardian stars; he had picked them before their time. And then came the Epstein bust. Again, imagine a Gladstonian Liberal who, when his eightieth birthday was saluted by a dinner at the National Liberal Club, entirely neglected to feature himself as a veteran warrior of the old Liberal battles, and gave his somewhat astonished audience a stirring advice to keep in touch with Labour and create a really radical Union of the Left.

The miracle of Scott was his inability to age in anything but body, and even that decline came only at the very last. Well over seventy-five he was playing lawn-tennis, somewhat to the embarrassment of his fellow-players, so relentless was his pursuit of an evasive shot, so ready was he to risk a somersault in its capture. There are countless tales of his exploits on the push-bicycle which he refused to lay aside; on dark, greasy, or even snowy streets, treacherous with tram-lines and infested with modern traffic, he would obstinately pedal to the office and home again. But a great man should not become a legend because of strange tastes in locomotion. His genius lay in an elasticity of mind surpassing that of his muscles; it is commonly said that the mind, like the arteries, will harden at sixty, and that to be governed by old men is to be ruled by those who are incapable of new ideas. This judgment was not in the least true of Scott; the tastes of his younger writers and critics may sometimes have startled him, but he had an unfailing curiosity about the young idea, the next thing to happen. As an editor he pondered closely before engaging a man, but, having chosen, he was unshakably loyal to his choice. He trusted his young men in a way which gave them power and confidence to be themselves in any signed or initialled contribution. If they were wise they conformed to the temper of the paper, knowing that the presence of an initial at the bottom of the article does not entitle the writer to express views definitely offensive to its readers or to indulge a style of attack alien to the paper's traditions. He taught a code of manners; but he never imposed opinion except in his own sphere of political control, where, as editor, it was his duty to be firm in guidance.

He remained, then, of no period. There never was a man of affairs less addicted to the backward glance. Though much beset with requests to write his memoirs, he refused. It was my fortunate experience to stay alone with him in his house on several occasions for several weeks on end; he rarely talked of the past, even under suggestion. His mind was set upon the present and the future of the world, particularly on the contribution which the progressive parties could make to the delivery of man from the tyrannies of poverty, ignorance, and strife. Scott was no whit a Whig; he esteemed tradition in things of the mind and sense, but the domination of the past was, in politics, an ogre for Radicalism to slay. But more of his politics later.

With that swift darting mind of his he espied in the late 'eighties some essays in pastiche contributed to an Oxford paper. He judged them promising, brilliant even; a year or two later their author, C. E. Montague, was on his staff, where he remained, with an interval during the War, from 1890 to 1926. Montague followed the example of the good apprentice who marries his master's daughter. But it was not the family tie alone which bound Montague to Manchester; there was a marriage of true minds between the older and the younger man. The latter's gusty humanity was a perfect complement to the more philosophic Radicalism of the former. Montague was passionately a Liberal, intolerant only of intolerance. He had, perhaps, more understanding of the plain man than Scott; he hated a joyless, theoretic "uplift." "I broke out," he wrote in a letter of 1906, "as dithyrambically as I could on the happiness and reasonable moral satisfactoriness of the common un-self-pitying person and raged against the whole school of fastidious compassion with their negations and abstentions and refusals and their undervaluing of the common person's vitality and geniality." This outburst, it should be added, had nothing to do with his father-in-law. It was directed against a dry and donnish kind of reform which did not exist in Scott's vigorous passion for emancipation. But the extract shows one of the many virtues brought by Montague to his paper. It was, indeed, a solemn place when he arrived. The leader-writers went down to the office in top-hats; there was a cloistered calm about the rooms wherein they worked. The messengers had to be shod with felt and quiet as mice. Scott's chief assistant at the time was W. T. Arnold, grandson of Arnold of Rugby, and a profound classical historian, who combined his brilliant and nocturnal performances in Liberal journalism with mornings devoted to the Roman Empire. It was a fine workshop, but new windows could be opened with advantage. Montague, soaked in Swift and Goldsmith, an ardent Meredithian, and yet an enchanted observer of the Northern scene and all the moods and humours of its rough democracy, brought to this austere workshop of the Radical faith some new and challenging wind. Readers of his books need not strain their imagination to understand what the incursion of such a mind and temper meant to the *Guardian*. Scott, when he picked out that set of parodies in an Oxford magazine, had chosen even better than he knew. But the deed was typical of his divination.

Thus Montague's far-flung scholarship and his zest for savouring every vital sensation from spectatorship of a Cup Final to ardours and endurances upon the Cumbrian rocks and Alpine glaciers enabled Scott to broaden the range of a newspaper whose influence had hitherto been predominantly political. The Manchester stage was, in the 'nineties, an exciting place; in those days the greatest of European as well as of English players would go on tour to the great Northern cities, and there was also the Ibsenite movement, which was everywhere invading custom-ridden theatres, rousing new endeavour in a cloud of strife, and was at last to develop a Mancunian child of promise in Miss Horniman's Repertory,

by IVOR BROWN

where so many of our present theatrical leaders learned their business in a school of uncommonly hard work. The reputation of Manchester music stood high: the German colony saw to that. There was the increasing activity and prestige of Manchester University. There was plenty for a civilised newspaper to assess and encourage. Scott's intense political preoccupation never blinded his eye to the function of a newspaper as the critical stimulant of the general culture. To all such causes he gave his over-seeing eye and the services of a carefully recruited staff; to be enrolled on it was the ambition of mature scholars as well as of keen youngsters of the writing fancy. With Montague, Oliver Elton, Allan Monkhouse, Professor Herford, William Archer (at the London end) as regular contributors to the literary and dramatic sections of his paper, and later with Stanley Houghton and James Agate contributing, Scott may be said to have brought more brains and style to the service of the theatre than any editor before him. For the critical handling of books the reviewers called to service were equally numerous and notable; one day Saintsbury would be decanting his matured and aromatic wisdom, on another there would be the younger sparkle of a Dixon Scott, whose death in the War robbed English criticism of a wise judge and brilliant stylist.

This, however, by the way. Scott's passion was political, his paper, by tradition, political, and his place of residence a city where the strong brew of Victorian and Edwardian politics, particularly when laced with economic theory, was ever on the boil. The tradition into which the young editor stepped in 1872 was Whig. The paper had been founded shortly after the "Peterloo" rioting, amid the democratic fervour of the Northern cities in days when the populace were clamouring for votes and were being given dragoons instead. The *Guardian* had naturally demanded Reform; it had fought the Corn Laws; it had printed the speeches of Cobden and Bright in such fullness that the leading article, from the beginning a feature of the first importance, had to be omitted. In the early 'seventies it had outgrown the simple Victorian model of a provincial newspaper, broadened its technique, established a London office with a private telegraph wire to Manchester, and had so extensively and ingeniously reported the Franco-German War (balloon messages were sent by its correspondent from the beleaguered city of Metz) as to attract a wide national attention. The new editor was not its proprietor; John Edward Taylor, the second of that name, owned the paper until his death in 1905, when Scott, not without shouldering a considerable burden, undertook purchase from the heirs. Throughout these thirty-two years Scott kept up a continuous correspondence with his relative and proprietor; he had, however, great liberty, and there was a fortunate tendency of the two to think alike.

A great decision had to be made in 1886, when the paper, hitherto Whig, abandoned that wing of the party in order to support Gladstone and to demand Home Rule for Ireland. Henceforward Scott's Liberalism became increasingly Radical; the Irish Question, so long, so bitterly contended, became one of the major interests and passions of his life. The name of the *Manchester Guardian* became known and revered all over Nationalist Ireland as one of England's better voices; inevitably there were the mutterings of "Foreign Gold" when the baser type of Manchester reactionary contemptuously tore up a copy of the paper. The same muttering, with threats of violence to follow, was heard when the paper opposed the Boer War. The office had to have police protection, and so, though he never asked for it, did the home of the editor. Those who remember the "Khaki Election" and the hue-and-cry after "Pro-Boers," in which young Mr. Lloyd George was almost fatally submerged after his gallant resolve to speak for peace in Mr. Chamberlain's own city, will realise that the *Manchester Guardian* was taking a severe financial risk when it stood firm against the fury of the hour. Taylor and Scott were unshaken in that resolve, and they fortunately escaped commercial disaster while they retained their principles. Of course, there was much loss of support, even among old friends. The popular habit of "giving up the *Guardian*" has been wittily described by Mr. Haslam Mills in his history of the paper as "much practised in first-class carriages running into Manchester. It was often performed with great pomp and circumstance, newsagents, who were not responsible for the opinion of the paper, being addressed on the subject across their counters as though they were public meetings." It is a curious and praiseworthy habit of Manchester life to give up the *Guardian*—and then, rather more quietly, to renew subscription. Scott watched these waves of desertion without fear, and acknowledged the return of loyalty with a silent satisfaction. The practice continues. When his son, Edward Taylor Scott, who worthily succeeded him as editor in 1929, chose to be critical of the Liberal surrender to "National Unity" in 1931, he too could hear the old denunciations and wait for the calmer voice of Philip Sober.

The events of the 'nineties confirmed the anti-Imperialist in Scott. Against the new spirit of grab, with the new and rowdier journalism behind it, he patiently argued the Liberal faith. Against the Protectionist campaign, he fought unquenchably, with such brilliant supporters as L. T. Hobhouse and C. E. Montague behind him. (It must not be thought that Montague was exclusively a "literary" writer; his political and Free Trade advocacy was as trenchant with irony as it was informed with facts and figures.) Scott naturally welcomed the sweeping Liberal victory of 1906, but he remained steadily critical of the Liberal Imperialist section who were so strong in the Cabinet. The combination of naval expansion with a secretly Francophile diplomacy was resolutely criticised. So was the opposition of the Liberals to female suffrage, for which Scott's support was of a passionate intensity. To see this emancipation achieved was for long a burning desire, and, at last, a satisfaction hardly won. He criticised also the Liberal Government's slow motion towards Home Rule and its fatal vacillations in face of the Conservative appeal to armed revolt in 1914. Then came the War; until the last minute Scott was pleading for peace. The invasion of Belgium was as decisive for him as for the great majority of English Radicals. During the War he continued to be vigilant for civil liberties and to welcome every hope of a reasonable peace.

Like others who saw a world-leader in President Wilson, he was mistaken. Like others who had hoped that the wartime promises of a Europe appeased by a just settlement might be realised, he was disenchanted. But he was a man incapable of passivity or despair. To be sullen was not in his nature, and he continued to advocate a Liberal internationalism with an undimmed trust in the possibility of *homo sapiens* becoming, somehow and in some time, as good as that flattering name. He lived to see the Conservatives pass his beloved, his Radical measures. The House of Lords accepted its strict limitation of power. The great issue of Irish self-government was settled—or so it seemed. Women were not only politically enfranchised, but enjoyed educational, social, and professional rights hitherto dismissed as ridiculous and impossible. The League of Nations was potentially beneficial. Proportional Representation—a continual favourite in Scott's table of essential reforms—was gaining ground. Yes, but the party of his lifelong loyalty, the channel of his hope, the recipient of his unremitting labours, was split, diminished, a cluster of shepherds without a flock and possibly—as the cynics said—with more crooks than sheep. True, but Scott was interested in facts and ideas, not in names and in persons. The Radical tradition had passed over to the new Labour Party and, in so far as it was the genuine vehicle of Radicalism, he would give it his friendly support. To the straighter sect of party Liberals, this was painful. To Scott it was mere logic, the application of a principle instead of obeisance to a partisan vocabulary. Never mind the names of the men and the machine so long as they produce the measures!

So it need not be thought that, because his party was in ruin, this great man died unhappy. To brood was not in his character; he was nothing of a dreamer, yet his eye looked steadily forward. He had done his work, established his paper in power and good report. His son, Edward, after hard apprenticeship and a trial perhaps ungenerously long, was in command. The father could not foresee the desolating tragedy which occurred three and a half months after his death, when Edward Scott was drowned while sailing on Windermere. The new editor, inevitably subject to the handicap of being reared in the shadow of a mighty name, a difficult atmosphere for one naturally inclined to self-distrust, had matured rather late; he was not the scholarship, prize-winning, facile type; he lacked any kind of showmanship; he was nothing glib; but his early enthusiasm for economics had broadened into a wide, firm grip on national and international politics. His accession to the editorial chair in 1929 had not been a complete sovereignty, since his father was still, and actively, the Governing Director. He was just reaching to the fullness of his stature, a fine administrator, a shrewd economist, a resolute, hard-headed Radical, and a perfect companion, when the disaster happened. For the personal loss compensation was impossible; to fill the professional gap there was the presence of Mr. W. P. Crozier, a lifelong Manchester and *Guardian* man, reared in the tradition, of as much ability as industry, and now editing the paper with a courage and acumen which would have brought pride and gratitude both to father and son, who had died in such a sad succession, the one a patriarch, as full of honour as of years, the other a late inheritor, now striding to his ripening and suddenly destroyed in the bloom of this splendid self-discovery.

That C. P. Scott did not make a strong mark in the House of Commons was due, wrote Haslam Mills, to impatience with the waste of time and an inability to sit about "holding Roman principles in graceful attitudes." Certainly he was too active a man to be good at waiting for divisions; all the time he had his paper to over-see while Parliament was calling him to the tiresome, dilatory lobbies. Always he preferred quick decisions, and that, in part, accounted for his unbroken loyalty to Mr. Lloyd George, even when that name was detested by the Old Gang of Liberal orthodoxy. It was Lloyd George who had stood firm against the "the Lib. Imps." in the old days of the Boer War; it was Lloyd George who had pulled off the Irish Settlement. He put the measures through, and that was a primary factor in Scott's estimate of politicians.

As for "graceful attitudes," Scott had them in abundance. He showed them in all the traffic of his daily life, in conference, selection, decision, and in the actual task of writing for the paper. Indeed, his grace and courtesy grew with time. Some old men turn pettish and think age enough excuse for irascibility. Not so Scott. The senior members of his staff would talk in reminiscence of a brusque and even terrifying man, and his family paid him a veneration of a Victorian intensity. But his younger men found suavity in his strength; to be corrected by the editor was to feel almost as if a compliment had been bestowed on them. He paid, perhaps, rather too much regard to University distinction in his choice of recruits; it was harder to graduate from the reporters' room than from Oxford, and among his reporters and sub-editors he had immense reserves of talent. He could rarely bring himself to dismiss; a man once chosen had to behave with monstrous folly to achieve ejection. One remembers a piercing eye in that noble head; when most he looked the silvery senator, he had ever the fire of the young Radical within. The tongue was smooth, the manner diplomatic. Scott could make a hard bargain seem a light one. His less charitable and less discerning opponents called his prudence cunning; his self-esteem they magnified to vanity. He had done his work and he knew it; what humbug had he continually protested the failure of his editorial command, when he had made it a beacon to the profession! By enabling his men to write fully and freely, he had elicited the best and made his paper the premier training-ground of journalism. The pride of the exhibitionist was quite alien to his nature. He never paraded himself at public dinners with the prancings of the old warhorse; he was too busy with his paper, at which he worked from morn till midnight, with one brief interlude for air and exercise. He disdained secretarial aid, and wrote his own letters in a clear and lovely hand.

In the later years of his life he saw his craft altered to a commerce, its independence swamped in the tide of amalgamations, its standards of intelligence lowered, its purposes debased by those who made the Press perform, at considerable profit, in the world-circus of public entertainment. He had to modify the austere Victorian methods of newspaper production; as a Radical he had no objection to change. But the change had to be of detail, not of foundations. The basic belief in the function of a newspaper was in no way undermined. To give facts without colour and opinions without fear, that was the rule. To obtain the facts, far-flung facts, he built up a service of foreign correspondence on a scale that any other proprietor, with similar resources, would have considered grossly extravagant. To have first-rate emissaries abroad was his form of self-indulgence. To voice opinion was his own particular quality and task; he remained a writing editor, composing " leaders " and sub-editing the leaders of his staff, when other editors were acquiring the status of general managers of business concerns. Yet, with all his insistence on the old professional principle, he was determined to keep his columns clear of any tiresome solemnity and priggishness; he relished gay writing and particularly the supple wrist and gay ironic hand of C. E. Montague. He had a quick eye for good writing about sport; Neville Cardus was of his election. He outlived so many that he might have been pardoned a retrospective melancholy in his final years. But surely no man of eighty-six ever died so fresh in sympathy, so young in hope.

SIR HENRY SEGRAVE
1896-1930

By
J. WENTWORTH DAY

SIR HENRY SEGRAVE

by J. WENTWORTH DAY

WHEN Miss England II, the fastest boat in the world, leapt, like a white flying fish, suddenly into the air on Lake Windermere on that fatal Friday, June 13, 1930, England lost the man of a generation.

De Hane Segrave meant more to this country than a mere breaker of records. He was a man of science as well as a man of action. He contributed greatly to the sum of human knowledge. He explored the unknown at the imminent risk of death. He walked through the dark shadows to reveal new lights. This man, who stood to our youth as a hero in fact, was also an inspiration in verity. He dared greatly and died magnificently. One had only to meet him to fall under the spell of that quick brain, the swift tongue, the receptive mind and brilliant intellect which flitted from subject to subject and yet absorbed all it gathered. Here was a man out of the ordinary—no mere snapper-up of amusing superficialities, but a mind quick and bright as steel. It was that rare combination, the mind of a business man and a scientist allied to the courage and gaiety of a gentleman-adventurer. Such a restless, daring, dynamic personality was bound to succeed. He was the stuff of which conquerors are made. Drake was got from such stock.

Go back, for a moment of time, to that blue thirteenth day of sun and mountain winds on Windermere. That long and lovely lake, set amidst the everlasting hills of England's most majestic countryside, had been chosen by Segrave for his last and greatest challenge. The history of that challenge is short in the measure of time, but long in the momentous drama of its hourly incident and ending. Already he had smashed the world's speed records on land and water. He had been the first man to drive at two hundred miles an hour on land, the first to travel at a mile and a half a minute on water. The world's water-speed record, held then by Commodore Gar Wood, the "Grey Fox" of America, stood at 93.12 m.p.h. Britain had already spent more than a quarter of a million pounds in vain efforts to smash it. Segrave determined on a grand attack which would leave nothing to chance except the pilot's chance of living. So, backed by Lord Wakefield, whose firm sells Castrol Oil with a discerning eye, Miss England II was built. The boat was designed by Mr. Fred Cooper, a young British engineer. She was 38 feet over all, with a beam of 9 feet, into which was crammed no less than 4,000 h.p.—a terrifying output of power to be controlled by the hands of one man. It was like putting a bomb into an eggshell.

On June 11, in the red light of the afternoon sun, under a sky turning to apple green, Segrave climbed into the cockpit. With a sudden bellow of titanic sound, the boat shot like a white torpedo over the lake, throwing up a following mountain of water. Booming into the distance, a thunderous monotone of sound, it covered the measured mile, circled like a gull, poised on the wave of its own creation, and then came shooting back over the course. It was a trial run. No timekeepers were present. Yet both Segrave and those who watched were convinced that he had travelled at more than a hundred miles an hour—the first man to do so on water. Suddenly, as the watchers on shore strained their eyes, the boat, a far-away silvery dot on the twilit waters, swerved. A pillar of flame shot skyward. The roar of the engines ceased. The boat slowed down, stopped. There was silence. A speedboat leapt away from shore. Presently it returned, towing Miss England II. The crowd on shore pulsed, thickened, clustered at the slipway. A murmur ran through it like wind in grass. "What has happened?" Sir Henry, in a grey jersey, flannel trousers, and shoes stood on the foredeck, the sun gleaming on his bald head. He explained. A blade of the propeller had snapped. This had caused the engines to race. Hence the flames. None the less, although only under five-eighths of her normal power, he was convinced that she had done more than 100 m.p.h.

This was the third propeller that had failed. Each time either a blade had snapped or the metal had shown signs of weakness. Had either of those propellers fulfilled its task

Segrave would probably be alive to-day. The result was that he ordered two new propellers from another firm. They were rushed through at top speed and arrived just in time. The official timekeepers were due to leave for another engagement on the 13th. But for that fact I doubt if Segrave would have chosen such a fateful date. He was superstitious.

On the morning of Friday, the 13th, he climbed into the cockpit of Miss England II, a white-clad figure in an all-white boat. The gigantic engines started in a whirlwind of sound, and the boat roared away up the lake before the fascinated eyes of thousands of onlookers. She was going superbly, her 4,000-h.p. engines droning a titanic symphony. Once, twice she swept over the course, a white bellowing blur riding the wave of her own making like a seabird, a straight white furrow of flashing waters billowing in her wake. She swung round and came up the course for the third and last time. Her speed on the first run was 96.41 miles an hour, and 101.11 miles an hour on the second. Both were officially recorded. The third run was to give Segrave his dearest ambition—two miles a minute on water. The boat seemed to gather new, electric life. It leapt forward like a flying fish, half out of the water. The roar of its engines rose to a full-throated, deafening bellow. A wash like that of a liner winnowed out behind. Then came the end. Miss England II, white, pulsating, power incarnate, shot bows first into the air, turned over in a lightning twist—and sank. A sea of foam bubbled and seethed. Then silence. A second before she had been a thing of beauty, an epic of speed, grace, and power. A fraction of time and the beauty was tragedy. For a brief space her engines raced under water. Little blue whorls of smoke arose. The waters bubbled, white and frothy. The crowds, black, massed, stood frozen. Speech was stunned. Then the waters broke. A bald head appeared, gleamed in the sun. A white-overalled figure struggled feebly on the surface. The crowd stirred like a gust of autumn leaves. "Thank God—it's Segrave!" The whisper was the voice of a thousand throats. Mr. King, a Windermere man, dived in, fully clad, swam to the broken, pathetic figure and supported him until a launch took him aboard from the waters he had conquered—and by them been conquered. He was conscious. Twisted with pain, his blue eyes still lit with the old gay spirit, he gasped: "How are the lads?"—

his crew. It was his first thought. Then: "Did we do it?" The rescuers nodded. Not a man among them could trust his voice. The pain-stricken eyes closed, hooded like those of an eagle shot down in full flight. He knew that he was to die—but in the moment of victory. And he was content. A week before he had said to me: "When I go out, I hope it will be doing something, and while I am still young. God save me from old age and death in a bed." Segrave's thigh was broken in two places. Rib after rib was shattered. He was smashed, bruised, and broken. A few hours later he died.

"And thus this man died, leaving his death for an example of a noble courage, and a memorial of virtue, not only unto young men, but unto all his nation!"

De Hane Segrave, as he was known to all his friends, came of good, gentle stock. He was a son of one of those ancient landed families whose roots are the bone of history; whose present personal influence is half the life-blood of British character and leadership. Segrave was descended directly from those Sjo greves or Sea Lords who settled at Segrave in Leicestershire in the ninth century. Thomas de Segrave, Lord of Segrave in 1080, when Domesday Book was compiled, was a direct descendant of Harold, Prince of Denmark, who established the family in England. When the King, with his own hand, bestowed the accolade upon De Hane Segrave at Craigweil House, Bognor, in 1929, the old flower of knighthood bloomed again. A man of gentle blood had been knighted for truly knightly deeds.

Segrave's early interest in motoring began at his home at Belle Isle, on Lough Derg, Lord Avonmore's place, which his father had taken on a long lease. Belle Isle possessed a remarkably up-to-date garage for those days. Its electric-light plant was the wonder of the sleepy Tipperary countryside. At the age of eleven, he possessed a model railway of highly ambitious proportions. At his death he had just built a house to contain his newest model railway—a hobby which represented an enormous outlay, for everything was made to scale, and by the best makers. It was the dominant minor interest of his life. At twelve he could shoot well, sail a boat, swim with all his clothes on, pilot a motor-boat, and drive a car. His private school was Bilton Grange, Rugby, whence he went to Byrne's at Eton.

by J. WENTWORTH DAY

He was flying during the War, and went through the usual hair-raising adventures which befell those whose lot was to fly machines often 30 per cent. below the standard of safety and efficiency. Then came peace and the financial acrobatics of a false boom; Segrave lost £4,000 in nine months in a motor business.

With a thousand or two to call his own—and a fixed resolve not to call on his father's help—he went to Mr. Louis Coatalen, then the brilliant designer of the Sunbeam racing cars, and offered his services as a driver. Coatalen's reply, in effect, was: "Buy your own car, race it, and if you don't break either the car or your neck, we might look at you. Now run away!" He promptly spent £1,800 of his capital on buying the big white Opel, which had created a sensation at Brooklands on August Bank holiday, 1914, as one of the most modern cars of the day. Segrave acquired it in 1920, and drove it at Brooklands all that year, winning several races. He could not afford a mechanic, so he did the dirty work himself. He was constantly fiddling about with minor alterations and adjustments to fit his own ideas.

In 1921 Coatalen so far relaxed as to allow him to drive a Sunbeam in the French Grand Prix with the remark: "If you pay all your own expenses and pay for any damage you do, I will lend you the car."

Seven English cars were entered for the big race, four driven by men of the first rank. They were Lee Guinness, Count Zborowski, René Thomas, and André Boillot. The race was run at Le Mans on a circuit never before used for racing. The road surfaces were appalling. Segrave had to change no less than thirteen tyres during the race. A stone flung up by another car struck the wire-mesh guard in front of his face like a bullet, cut clean through it, through the moulded steel scoop, hit the steering wheel, and struck his mechanic Moriceau on the head, knocking him out. In spite of all these handicaps, Segrave finished seventh, just behind Lee Guinness. This began his true road-racing career. In the course of the next two years he fought his way, in a series of meteoric successes, to the first rank of the world's crack road-racing drivers.

A good road racer is the aristocrat of racing motorists. He must be able to drive at top speed, up hills, down valleys, over hairpin bridges, through villages and towns, over appalling roads, sometimes hugging the lips of precipices, all the time keeping up an average speed of 60 to 90 miles an hour. It is the most gruelling, nerve-racking form of contest in the whole world of motor racing. Only the fit and fearless survive. Brooklands and Daytona are picnics by comparison. Those years of racing at home and abroad were lit by the highlights of drama. Time and again Segrave looked death straight in the eye, winked, and passed on.

The old gay spirit that endeared him to his friends, that made him a dashing cavalier in the eyes of the public, was the secret of his success. He had all the *insouciance* of the Latin with none of the Latin's inconsistencies and irritabilities. He had all the Englishman's pluck and steely courage with little of the Englishman's phlegm and caution.

Throughout those years his business brain developed and sharpened. He was no hard bargainer, generous indeed to a fault, but he knew his own value and got it. From being a young and ill-paid racing driver he became, in the last year of his life, probably the most highly paid man in the motor-racing world, with an income running well into five figures.

His mind and activities ranged over the whole field of speed. Motor-cars, motor-boats, even aeroplanes, all were tools to his hand, weapons in his grasp. In the year of his death he had invented and almost perfected the finest stream-lined aeroplane then in existence, the Segrave Meteor, a thing of beauty, which, had he lived, would have become probably the fastest machine in the air.

Looking back over those years, during most of which I knew intimately from his lips the flirtations with death that were his almost daily digestive, there come to my mind, like a shutter of dreams, quick flashes of such gallant endeavour as have lit the lives of few men.

First, there was that momentous victory in 1923, when, for the first time in history, England won the Grand Prix of France, the greatest road race in the world, the Blue Riband of motoring. The course was over 500 miles at Tours. Segrave spent the whole of the fortnight before the race in constant practice, concentrating on high-speed cornering and quick repair work. He and Dutoit, his mechanic, spent hours each day practising wheel changes, repairs, filling up, and so on, timing each other with stop watches and constantly endeavouring to save a second here, a second there. An enormous crowd gathered on the morning of the race. The Grand Prix of France attracts as many spectators as the Derby. The long line of cars was drawn up, with the white-clad drivers and mechanics standing by the roadside, keyed up for the word to go. The signal was given, drivers and mechanics dashed to their cars and, in a bellowing volley of sound, like the rattle of field guns, the cars were off and away. Death took toll at the first lap. Vizcaya, driving a Bugatti which looked like a tank, took a corner in La Membrolle at a hundred miles an hour, skidded, cut a telegraph pole in half, smashed the barricade, and mowed a lane through the crowd, killing three and wounding eleven. It was a butcher-like and terrible scene. Yet, so excited were the watching Frenchmen, that some of them actually hurled abuse at the police for not clearing the dead and wounded away quick enough so that they could get back to their places to see the race.

Segrave began badly. His clutch slipped, and lap after lap the car lost speed. Half-way through the race he stopped and consulted with Dutoit whether it would not be wiser to retire. They decided to go on. A minute later the clutch slipped in with a bang and Segrave shot off at top speed, 70 miles to go, the Fiat team leading by so big a lead that he gave up all hope of winning. There was just a flicker of a chance that if he went all out he might finish second or third. He put his foot down. Three minutes later two of the Fiats dropped out, leaving Carlo Salamano in the lead, with Divo hot on his tail in a Sunbeam similar to that which Segrave was driving. Divo had to stop to fill up. Segrave was close behind. Divo lost his head. Instead of unscrewing the cap of his petrol tank he screwed it on more tightly. For thirty seconds he struggled with it like a madman. Then he realised his mistake. He tried to unscrew it. It had jammed. A minute later Segrave's car roared past him, hot-foot in pursuit of Salamano, who was flying miles ahead at a terrific speed.

The Fiat French pit staff lost their heads in a moment of crisis. Salamano had just enough petrol to finish the race and win at the speed at which he was travelling. But they signalled frantically for him to go all out. He did so. The result was that his petrol ran out, his car stopped—a mile short of the Grand Stand. The mechanic ran like a hare back to the pits for more petrol. Segrave, miles down the road, knew nothing of this. Suddenly he flashed over the hill at 116 miles an hour, roared past the stranded red car, wondered wildly for an instant if it could be Salamano, dismissed the thought as ridiculous—and, three minutes later, flashed over the finishing line, the first Englishman to win the Grand Prix of France.

There followed countless other races. Their tale is too long, too vivid, too packed with incident to be told in the space at my disposal. There was that awful moment in the Spanish Grand Prix at San Sebastian over a terribly dangerous course of 387 miles, when the car, driven by his bosom friend, Lee Guinness, skidded on a corner, ran up a hillside, rolled down again, turned over three times, flung Guinness and his mechanic clean across the road, and actually *over the telegraph wires on the other side* into a railway cutting. For four laps after that Segrave had to drive round the course, each time enduring the mental agony of seeing the body of his friend being carried by the roadside, sheeted, on a stretcher. That crash nearly cost Lee Guinness his life.

Probably the greatest feat which Segrave ever performed (he said himself it was the most dangerous) was at the Boulogne Grand Prix Meeting in August 1926.

The 26th was devoted to electrically timing the cars over six kilometres of a very dangerous road. It was narrow, heavily cambered, with a ditch on either side, lined with trees, and lay over three switchbacking hills. About the most dangerous course which could be chosen.

Among his opponents was the late Parry-Thomas, one of the most experienced and fearless drivers in the world.

Segrave accomplished the amazing speed of 140.6 miles per hour, the car touching the road in spots, at one time with two wheels in the gutter for fifty yards. This is the world's record which has never been beaten to this day. It was such a strain that, though it took less than three minutes, when he got out of the car he was physically sick.

Segrave's records over the measured mile at Southport and Daytona lack the spectacular risks of his road-racing career. But no account of his life is complete without the story of February 1929, when he arrived in Florida with two gigantic crates and a temperature of 102°. One crate contained the new mystery car, the Golden Arrow, and the other the mystery speedboat, Miss England. Segrave was pale, drawn, and ill. He lunched with me only two days before sailing, looking like a ghost, feeling like death. Yet he was determined to go out for the world's speed record on both land and water in a car and a boat, in neither of which had he even sat.

At dawn on March 11, 1929, 40,000 citizens of the United States lined the long miles of sandhills which overlook the great beach of Daytona. Thousands of cars were parked. Cinema cameras clicked like Maxim guns. A hundred flags drooped lazily from their masts. The black, dense crowds hummed like a million bees.

At zero hour, under a hard blue sky, a blazing sun, the great golden torpedo-shaped car, with a dull drone of engines, rolled up to a point four miles from the start of the measured mile. Suddenly, the roar of the engine rose to thunderous immensity. The car leapt forward. It sped over the sands, a thunderbolt of speed, scarcely visible to the watching crowds. As it swept over the first electric timing plate it was travelling at more than 231 miles an hour. It was impossible to see the man inside, impossible to see the wheels. All that one saw was an immense rushing blur, shooting with bullet-like directness for the great red bull's-eye lamp that swung between its poles at the end of the measured mile.

In a second, it seemed, the car had flashed over the mile and shot over the far timing strip. The roar of its engines droned into the distance. Field glasses followed it. It stopped. Segrave got out. He loaded blocks of ice into the immense cooling system. He changed the wheels. He took his seat again. Instantly the thunder of the engines rose dully in the distance. The car came swooping back again, a golden torpedo, skimming over the dazzling course, between the white line of the surge and the black line of the crowd-clad sandhills. It swept through shallow pools. White spray shot up like lace a hundred feet into the air. In a second it was on the Grand Stand. In a second it had passed. There was a swoop of sound, a tempest of thunder, a gale of noise that rose from a groan to a roar, from a roar to a bellow—and then droned away again into the blue distance. It was over.

The figures went up. The loud speaker announced to the sunlit air in a voice of brass, "Major Segrave has covered the mile at an average speed of 231.36246 miles an hour—an average of a mile in 15.56 seconds. He has beaten the United States record by no less than 23.81 miles an hour."

Wave upon wave of cheers rose from the packed thousands. Hats were flung into the air. Sirens screamed and shrieked. All Daytona went mad. Segrave was the hero of two continents.

A few days later he won the world's water speed championship from Commodore Gar Wood with a boat only 26 feet in length, with a beam of 7 feet. Yet she was fitted with a 12-cylinder Napier-Lion engine, the most powerful engine of her weight that had been built in England.

As one American newspaper said: " In a flaming streak of super-speed, Major Segrave has torpedoed our records with a contemptuous bravado which blows them to bits."

There followed, later, that magnificent race over the Templiner See, near Berlin, for the Motor-Boat Championship of Europe. On the starting-line, as the signal gun banged, the great 950-h.p. engine of Miss England I spluttered and stopped as her rival shot off the mark. Segrave almost decided to give up. He worked frantically at the engine. Ten minutes after his rival had started he was off—ten minutes too late. None the less, on the third lap, the driver of the German boat heard a sudden menacing drone coming up the long miles of the lake behind him. Looking over his shoulder, he saw the dreaded English driver shooting up on his tail, his boat half out of the water, a wash like a mountain billowing behind him. A sudden bellow of engines and Miss England I shot past and took the lead. Yard by yard she forged ahead. The German boat, straining every last pound of its energy, chased this amazing young man at the full output of its engines. Sir Henry passed the winning post a quarter of a lap ahead of his rival.

Here then, are a few, a very few, of the highlights in the life of this amazing young man, to whom death came so soon after in such heroic guise. De Hane Segrave lived only to explore the unknown, to achieve the impossible. He was no reckless gambler. His courage was not the courage of bravado. It was cold, deliberate, and calculating. He took risks because he wanted to find things out. He was a pioneer in the full sense of the word. He has bequeathed us a legacy of bravery and of true scientific research which will place his name among the immortals. He is dead and Britain has lost her modern Drake. We may console ourselves that we had, for too short a time, Henry O'Neal de Hane Segrave.

LYTTON STRACHEY
1880-1932

By
BONAMY DOBRÉE

LYTTON STRACHEY

by BONAMY DOBRÉE

THAT Lytton Strachey was born in 1880 was, though he might not have admitted it, a piece of great good luck for him. For at the time when his accumulating mind and his rejecting temperament had fused and matured he was the very man to say with maximum effectiveness just what the world was willing to hear. His first book, the admirable *Landmarks in French Literature*, attracted no great attention except among the few who could recognise in it, besides very able handling of material and a mind deeply sensitive to art, also a considerable craftsmanship in words; but when, in 1918, *Eminent Victorians* came out, the temper of men's minds was such that its effect was explosive. It was not so much the art of the thing, nor even its being intensely amusing to read, that assured its immediate popularity, but that it announced a man who, with beautiful precision, and the wit precision brings, could expose the rust beneath the gilded fudge and humbug which had brought the world to the dismal and terrifying pass in which it writhed. Men, hurt, disillusioned, bitter, were ready for image-breakers, and here was one able to destroy the most handsome and apparently indestructible bust with a delicate and gaily entrancing hammer. The mutterings of disapproval heard afterwards were then drowned in the plaudits: one weight at least was removed from the burden of moral existence; nobody need any longer admire the idols of his father.

It is, no doubt, a healthy thing to praise famous men, and in the Victorian age it was, besides, a very natural thing to do; for great men had produced a marvellously comfortable world to live in, and, it seemed, were going on doing so. But in 1918 matters did not look quite the same: great men had bungled their job, and it might be as well to look into their credentials, and test the assumptions on which their greatness had been so solidly pedestalled. Under a new eye of enquiry it seemed that a towering ecclesiastic had been only dubiously upright, and—it is the way with great ecclesiastics—to have been fonder of power than of God ; the venerated author of the Public School system was seen to have been the father of much that is odious in our education—priggishness, contempt of brains, snobbish and hypocritical complacency ; a ministering angel did indeed turn out to have been something very much worth while, not, however, a legendary figure of charity, but, rather, a great reformer, and an organiser of genius ; a Christian hero was revealed as an eccentric adventurer. Well, at any rate now, it was felt, men need no longer be duped by those who dominate over them : their quality of power must be admitted, it might even be admired, but it was essential to get things in the right perspective. And to-day it is a general feeling that though it is praiseworthy to laud famous men, it is wise to see first exactly what they were, an encouraging symptom, because it makes for clarity of thought, and leads us to make distinctions highly relevant in the new world which is being born. A reaction inevitably followed the first rapturous welcome, which was irritating in its excess, for Strachey was often praised for virtues which he did not possess ; but the swing of the pendulum, equal and opposite, proved just as provoking and even more excessive : he was blamed for not having qualities utterly incompatible with those he did possess, till " Stracheyism " became almost a term of abuse. The man, it is now asserted with all the glamour of moral rectitude, lacked reverence.

He did ; but he would have argued, in fact wrote to make plain, that the things for which he lacked reverence deserved none. His view of what was worshipful was not the common one, though it was not unique, for he belongs, one need hardly say, to the noble race of " cynics," and is blood-brother to Lucian, Montaigne, La Rochefoucauld, Mandeville ; a useful race, too, for they purge mankind of its occasional overweening conceit of itself. To lack reverence, therefore, is their salutary business, and the bigger the bubble they can prick, the more satisfied they will be. Strachey took his cue zestfully, and directed his sharpest attack on organised Christianity, which indeed, in its war-time inconsistency, did not imperiously demand exaggerated homage. Whether he reverenced Christ it is impossible to say; he certainly respected men who did not stop at professing Christ, but who followed Him, such as Newman. When, however, he examined great Christian figures—Manning, Arnold, Florence Nightingale, Gordon—he found, rightly or wrongly, very little real religion, but a great deal of self-deceit, and sometimes more general deceit; and since, like all "cynics," he hated cant and the coxcombry of piety, he did not temper his scorn of Christianity.

The Church, naturally, has not failed to protest, and the accusation of irreverence in this realm has been weightily expressed by the most bitter of his detractors, the Rev. Charles Smyth : " It is perfectly legitimate for the historian, upon due consideration, to defend the Christian revelation and all that it involves and has involved. It is equally legitimate for him, upon due consideration, to attack it. But it is not, and in the nature of things can never be, legitimate for him to dismiss it with a snigger." One can imagine Strachey lifting his eyebrows at this sweeping statement, and answering, " How extraordinary! " For it does not seem to have occurred to Mr. Smyth that though to dismiss something with a snigger may not be "legitimate" (whatever that may mean), that way may yet be the most swift and deadly of delivering a home thrust. For Strachey disliked Christianity, obviously. *Écrasez l'Infâme* was his battle-cry as surely as it was Voltaire's. And are not gay, laughter-feathered arrows far more effective than solemn denunciation? It was not for nothing that Strachey had read Pascal. And after all, his bias against Christianity implies its corresponding quality, tolerant humanism. He hated Christianity because in his view it destroyed, or smutched, a great deal that was lovely in humanity, and gave rise to muddled emotions, muddled thinking, and, abomination of abominations, hypocrisy and cruel dealing. He had no reverence for Christianity, certainly; but, on the other hand, he very much revered the things he believed it spoilt.

His attitude was somewhat distorted by some of his successors, who, seeing that biography could be made enthralling, so as actually to be read by a large number of people, very properly proceeded to imitate him; but, as nearly always happens in these circumstances, they imitated the wrong thing. They confused certain vices of his manner with the virtues of his matter; what was truth to himself in Strachey became flippancy in them, which is another illustration of the fact that style is inseparable from what a man thinks. They felt they were being deliciously naughty, whereas Strachey believed that he was telling a devastating truth in the most effective way. What he said he felt profoundly, but for him to have expressed it with the smoky ardour of a Carlyle would have been a falsity to his own sceptical nature. Some of his imitators fell into the error of supposing that Strachey was wholly destructive; he was not. In the same way some readers thought that because his feelings did not issue in outbursts or moral indignation, but in deadly ridicule, especially of pretension, he himself had no moral values, and that his exceedingly effective assumption of faint surprise at the follies of humanity was his only reaction towards life. He was, of course, destructive, in the way that Voltaire and Anatole France were so—" before a sanctuary can be built, a sanctuary must first be destroyed "—for he believed that many of the illusions by which mankind had lived were now harmful to mankind. He seems to have believed, in fact, that humanity in itself was so lovable, that it could exist fascinatingly without illusions; in fact, far from being too cynical, he was not cynical enough.

Thus it is false to accuse him, as is so often done, of having had no reverence for noble qualities in human beings, for he had a well-defined scale of humanistic values. He may have had no profound metaphysical convictions or emotions to quell his readers with (there is no unanswerable reason why he should have had), but he nurtured strong likes and dislikes which it is by no means dishonouring to own, any more than it is wrong to share his horror of exalting one's opinions to the dignity of dogmas. He loathed pomposity, intolerance, obstructionism, and loved the elusive light of reason; he was sympathetic towards people's ambitions, however much he might himself think those ambitions ridiculous, as, for instance, Madame de Lieven's: what he did detest was the love of power. It has been suggested that he found success the unpardonable crime in a man; but that was because triumph in the world of affairs is not to be obtained without a great deal of lying of one sort or another; success, in the world of art, such as Racine's, he bowed down to whole-heartedly. Above all, he admired two qualities: the first, a man's capacity for detachment from his immediate concerns, that detachment which distinguishes man from the animals, and which makes all artistic or scientific endeavour possible; the second was personal devotion, loyalty, a capacity for continued affection. These things come out again and again in his work. He despised shams, the reputations due to shams; and his unlimited regard for, not to say worship of, artistic greatness was perhaps due to the fact that there at least, in the end, there can be no shams. Naturally, being humanly fallible, he exhibited faults in this region. Sometimes his intelligence led him astray, away from the passionate centres of action to the mental ones, and he could not believe that others might hold firmly to ideas which he, in his own pet adjective, considered " preposterous." He was, no doubt, too sure of his point of view, and a little too complacently confident that it was the right one.

The chief clamour against him has been on the score of Gordon. Gordon, it is trumpeted, was a great and good man, a Christian hero who sacrificed his life for his God and his country. There are some people, it seems, who prefer this pasteboard figure to the palpitating, fascinating, and vivid individual that Strachey gives us; no one, surely, can dislike his Gordon: he is at least a human being. As for destroying the loyal public servant, Strachey is not half so damning as Cromer (if anything, it is to Cromer that he is not fair), and the somewhat hysterical and not always very honest attempts since made to prove that Gordon acted strictly according to orders have not been very convincing. But then, Strachey accused him of being a drunkard! This is not true: he said that in Equatoria Gordon resorted to the dangerous stimulant of B. and S.—most men in hot climates do—and that this, combined with the other dangerous stimulant of the Hebrew prophets, made him more than ever excitable and erratic. Surely it is absurd to deny all this. Gordon was unbalanced, a prey to nerves; he also had heroic qualities, but it does not derogate from the latter to realise the former; in fact, it makes him understandable. Strachey, thinking as he did, could not take Gordon's religion very seriously, if only for the reason that, in his analysis, it was not religion that was Gordon's motive power; and even those who defend Gordon are driven to plead that the form his religion took was common to all deeply religious Victorians. If so, it is strange that Cromer, his contemporary, should have found it as "preposterous" as Strachey did. But even given it was usual, that was no reason why Strachey should not laugh at it. Do any of us restrain our smiles at the American Fundamentalists? And at all events this was just the sort of thing Strachey itched to destroy: he did not think it did humanity any honour.

There is a third human attribute that Strachey did not reverence—the emotions of sex; and he could see no reason why he should. His view was, no doubt—and it is a tenable view—that a too exalted regard for sex has done mankind more harm, caused it more pain, misery, and cruel infliction, than almost any other human idiosyncrasy. But it must be freely admitted that Strachey was not happy in his treatment of sex. He might well laugh at it if he wished (after all, the first laughter recorded in history is that of Noah's sons on this very subject), but with him it was inseparable from a giggle. And, moreover, he cannot plead not guilty to the charge of having been obsessed by sex: a great many people are, but it is not a virtue, and in literature it becomes a crime. *Elizabeth and Essex*, his weakest book, is riddled with this obsession, which deforms the proportions, especially by reason of the undue space given to Gomez; it produces a feeling of discomfort in the reader, all the more so as in this book it often has a flaring sadistic flavour. We might adapt Mr. Smyth's strictures and say, You can laugh at sex, or you can exalt it; but you cannot both laugh at it and be ineluctably fascinated by it.

This double attitude was an error of art, and Strachey's work suffers from it. Sometimes the sly hint is well enough, and mildly amusing; but the obsession spoils the consistency of his attitude of detachment. For detachment was what Strachey aimed at. In his preface to *Eminent Victorians*, speaking of the lessons he had learnt from the biographies which seemed to be the last item of the undertaker's job, he wrote:

> "To preserve, for instance, a becoming brevity—a brevity which excludes everything that is redundant and nothing that is significant—that, surely, is the first duty of a biographer. The second, no less surely, is to maintain his own freedom of spirit. It is not his business to be complimentary; it is his business to lay

bare the facts of the case, as he understands them. That is what I have aimed at in this book—to lay bare the facts of some cases, as I understand them, dispassionately, impartially, and without ulterior intentions."

There, of course, the word "impartially" is qualified by "as I understand them," for no one can write without a point of view: he has to select such portions of the truth as seem significant and illuminating to him "as he understands" the truth.

But apart from all considerations of value and morality, or of the motive which dictated his subjects, Strachey was first and foremost an artist. History invited him most strongly, for he did not much care for philosophy. Of Voltaire he said, "' Il faut cultiver notre jardin ' is his final word—one of the very few pieces of practical wisdom ever uttered by a philosopher." The tortuous endeavours of men to extricate themselves from the tangles they made in their own minds filled him with impatient amusement, and he had, instead of philosophy, the Edwardian faith in science, the agnostic faith that came of having been intellectually begotten by Huxley. So being primarily an artist, and deeply attracted by history in so far as it exhibits human beings, his end was to make delightful objects of historical figures. His truth was to be the truth of art, which is superior to that of fact. To him, indeed, history, and biography as a department of history, was fundamentally an art, not a flat record. "That the question has ever been not only asked but seriously debated whether history was an art, is certainly one of the curiosities of human ineptitude. What else can it be ? . . ." and so on, in the essay on Gibbon. And he managed to discover that the best art in history was invariably to be found where the historian had disliked his subject: Gibbon on barbarism and superstition, or Michelet the romantic on the Classical ages. And again, how much better reading Macaulay was on James II, whom he loathed, than on William of Orange, whom he made "a lifeless image of waxwork perfection."

But it was in Saint-Simon, perhaps, that he found his clearest justification.

" He excels [he wrote in *Landmarks in French Literature*] in that most difficult art of presenting the outward characteristics of persons, calling up before the imagination not only the details of their physical appearance, but the more recondite effects of their manner and their bearing, so that, when he has finished, one almost feels that one has met the man. But his excellence does not stop there. It is upon the inward creature that he expends his most lavish care—upon the soul that sits behind the eyelids, upon the purpose and passion that linger in a gesture or betray themselves in a word. The joy that he takes in such descriptions soon infects the reader, who finds before long that he is being carried away by the ardour of the chase, and that at last he seizes upon the quivering quarry with all the excitement and all the fury of Saint-Simon himself. Though it would, indeed, be a mistake to suppose that Saint-Simon was always furious—the wonderful portraits of the Duchesse de Bourgogne and the Prince de Conti are themselves sufficient to disprove that—yet there can be no doubt that his hatred exceeded his loves, and that in his character drawing he was, as it were, more at home when he detested. Then the victim is dissected with a loving hand; then the details of incrimination pour out in a multitudinous stream; then the indefatigable brush of the master darkens the deepest shadows and throws the most glaring deformities into still bolder relief; then disgust, horror, pity and ridicule finish the work which scorn and indignation had begun. Nor, in spite of the virulence of his method, did his portraits ever sink to the level of caricatures. His most malevolent exaggerations are yet so realistic, that they carry conviction. When he had fashioned to his liking his terrific images—his Vendôme, his Noailles, his Pontchartrain, his Duchesse de Berry, and a hundred more—he never forgot, in the extremity of his ferocity, to commit the last insult, and to breathe into their nostrils the fatal breath of life."

Much of that might have been written of Strachey himself, in spite of his wish to be impartial, of his desire for his method, at any rate, to be detached rather than virulent. For he was, undoubtedly, more at home with his dislikes than with his admirations, but that the latter were not lacking is proved by his Newman and his Hume. We feel that his intensest

by BONAMY DOBRÉE

delight was in hunting a quarry down. It is not necessary to suppose that he began by disliking his victims; but as he pursued and dissected them he found that they stood for things which he abhorred, and so the general distaste became a personal one. Sometimes he merely made people ridiculous, but this did not necessarily imply dislike; rather the contrary indeed, so long as it was not the ridiculousness of dignity, " a mysterious carriage of the body," he would have agreed with Rochefoucauld, " intended to cover the defects of the mind." To him the weaknesses of humanity were touching and lovable; the people he could not abide were those who tried to impose upon others by their " virtue." His way then was clear to making his works of art: he would probe into the being of people whose motives he disliked, and state his selected facts in his own idiom, that is, coloured by his own point of view, fabricated into glittering figures; and he would not forget the final insult of breathing into their nostrils the breath of life.

That he succeeded in making works of art is incontestable; precisely how good they are time only will decide. It is easy to see that they are not perfect, distressingly easy to point out obvious flaws. His grammar is not impeccable, he indulged in platitudes (there is no need to repeat the wider charges against him), some of his jests are cheap, he was sometimes slipshod and fell into journalese. These charges are just, but it remains to be proved that his platitudes were not well placed, did not give point to what he was about to say; and after all, as Buffon remarked, we cannot endure a relentless corruscation of wit: Apollo knows that it does not do to keep one's bowstring perpetually taut. But at least he succeeded in the preliminary aim of all art, to give delight. He is never dull or pompous, turgid or insipid; he may infuriate you, but he will never leave you indifferent. His works have form, the pace is carefully controlled, both the play of prose and the play of ideas, as well as the succession of images, keep you continuously alert, and his transitions from one paragraph to another are perfect: he never jerks you from one thing to another. He is a master of comic irony, which need not necessarily be cheaper than the tragic sort, and at all events is never sentimental, though he does sometimes achieve his ironic effect too easily: that is where the danger of all irony lies. But as far as the artistic creation of figures is concerned, he is almost invariably wholly successful. His "characters" are brilliant, rich, exciting, and always alive—take his Gladstone or his Lord Hartington—while his narrative is lucid and swift. He brought much of the art of the novelist to his writing of biography, the most perfect of which is his *Queen Victoria*, for there the materials sifted themselves out by their natural importance, and the prose, having rid itself of the load of adjectives which in Strachey's earlier writing was excessive, had not yet weakened to the somewhat faltering accents of his last big book. It is often declared that he came to the throne to mock, and stayed, if not to pray, at least to kneel, but that, we may suggest, is splenetic criticism, first, because Strachey was too good an artist not to see the end of his work in the beginning, to see the thing as a whole; and secondly, because it is manifestly untrue. Whatever else you may say of his works, they are throughout consistent in tone except for his lapses in respect of sex. It is, of course, evident that he admired the Queen more when she was old than when she was young, but that, after all, is because the Queen was more admirable in age than in youth. Strachey liked the sapling, but it was the full-grown oak that captured his homage.

But though on the whole, especially in his more important works, Lytton Strachey achieved results which will always give him a place in literature, there are legitimate grounds for dissatisfaction against him: he did too much distort for the sake of art; for in a biography, just as in a novel, we want to have the sense that the thing is " true," and the checks in biography are more insistent than they are in novel-writing. It is not a question of his ascribing to Gordon an anecdote of his life at Woolwich which really belongs to Adam Lindsay Gordon; that slip does not affect the picture. Nor is it a question of his dramatising, contrary to evidence, the story of Newman's return to Littlemore; that distortion only serves to make Newman a still more sympathetic figure. It is rather in his shorter characters that the charge lies most heavily against him. Avowedly his attitude towards his characters was not that of a witness sworn to tell the truth, the whole truth, and nothing but the truth; it was rather that of a craftsman examining a piece of material to see whether it is suitable for him to make into a work of art; and sometimes, here was his error, he mistook his material, or found it less malleable than he supposed.

by BONAMY DOBRÉE

We know, of course, in picking up a volume of his shorter studies, that what we are to see is not so much portraits of men and women as a series of Stracheys (as we go, for instance, to look at an exhibition of Sargents), indeed, of Strachey caricatures, and his *Portraits in Miniature* are not inappropriately dedicated to Mr. Max Beerbohm. They are indeed light, crisp, well-flavoured, exquisite trifles to toy with; but even a caricature must be true to essentials, and with Stracheys we are not always sure that the smaller pieces are so. We do not know when he is distorting, not for the sake of making a fact vivid, but to make a differently delightful person. Thus in the end he makes Gibbon less interesting than he really was by blandly presenting us with a man so *insouciant* that he neglected his fatal disease; whereas the truth appears to be that Gibbon lived in terror of it. Strachey, then, is not the perfect biographer, because he did not always accurately assess the relation between life and art; and with him it was essential that he should do so, for his was not a markedly original, creative mind.

That it was not so is clear from his prose, which never, or very rarely, exhibits any original use of words, and he has quite properly been unfavourably compared with James Joyce in this respect. He was not, in fact, a creator through the word, though he used a wide vocabulary with an art which is at times consummate, even if he did not always maintain the same level. His later writings, indeed, show a distinct falling off; they suggest fatigue. But there are two considerations which should not be ignored in commenting on this unoriginality in the use of words. The first and most important is that his mind belonged to that class which is not profoundly original, but ranges with extraordinary lucidity over a wide range; it does not go deep; and this class of mind, while it has a great mastery over words, aims at its effects, the only effects it can get, by a persuasive clarity combined with a happy massing of images where it needs them. Such writers are Dryden and Macaulay (whose disregard for philosophy resembles Strachey's); it is the profounder but much narrower writers who are original in their use of words, because they want to make words express sensations and emotions which have never been expressed before, and it is in such writers as Sir Thomas Browne, Doughty, D. H. Lawrence, that we find this more poetic use of language. In a sense Strachey had a commonplace mind, as, notoriously,

Dryden and Macaulay had; on the other hand, his invariable limpidity, and honesty of self-examination, are not commonplace; they are, indeed, regrettably rare.

The second consideration is that to have chosen his words more craftily, to have refused the almost invariable *cliché* ("*palpably* absurd," "*gross* prejudice," and so on), might have been inimical to his art. Was it not, perhaps, part of his skill to subdue the reader's mind, not by the impact of surprising words, but by producing the strange effect out of ordinary materials? The striking adjective sets the mind off on its own adventures; he wanted to take the reader's mind on Stracheyan journeys. And after all, was it not the highest art he might have asked himself, to work within the most restricted limits? Think of Racine, he might have said, working with the smallest vocabulary any artist ever worked with, never using the rare word because there were no rare words for him to use, and hardly ever employing an unusual connection of words. That, surely, was the final, the enduring art.

Yet it is not as a stylist that Strachey will live, but for his services to the art of biography. What, in effect, he did for it was to rid it of its robes of ceremony, to clothe it in everyday wear, in easy, sometimes too easy, flannels. But not only the manner, the mental approach also was to be in undress. Why, he asked, pretend that the people we write about are really important to us if they are not, whatever they may once have been to people like us? And why suppose that their personalities are to be treated with greater respect than those of the people we meet? The dangers are obvious; he did not always evade them; but at least we see his people as human beings, and not as statues. He destroyed our belief in the value of the *O altitudo!* attitude; lives of men were to be written, not that we might pattern ourselves on them, but that we might understand them, and see the events of the past, not in a halo of glory, but in the garish light of the present. An enemy to cant and mugwumpery of all kinds, he begged us to rid ourselves of bugbears, of points of view that are dead, and to which we give only lip-service. He is not to be our model biographer because his sympathies were too restricted—the penalty he had to pay for having too assured a point of view; but at least a shelf labelled " Biography " need no longer fill one with the dreariest forebodings. He wrote imaginatively, and so once again raised biography from

by BONAMY DOBRÉE

the category of dull, improving, or informative reading to that of literature; for in this century, before his time, readable works were few and far between, though they did exist, as, for instance, Mr. F. S. Oliver's *Alexander Hamilton*.

But apart from being an artist he takes his place, and earns his niche in the history of our time, as the exponent of his age, or at least of a certain aspect of it. He stands for the belief that, however misguided, absurd, "preposterous," human beings may be, at least they are to be judged on their own merits, and not by arbitrary, probably deceptive, standards. He found men and women profoundly interesting, if not always admirable, and he made them so to us; and, it may be insisted once more, he did not like men or women the better for being admirable according to the standards people up to his time were supposed to accept. He voices, therefore, the modern deep suspicion of great men, proper to an age where values are being, if not altogether reversed, at least enquired into, and one may suggest that his popularity was as symptomatic as that of Tchekhov. In a sense, also, he brought great men close to ourselves, so that we could see them as flesh and blood, and that is no mean achievement. These things, however, may be temporary; what is permanent is the general attitude that he stands for, namely, for the freedom of the spirit, for the right to stand aside and be sceptical, for the bracing and clarifying east wind that blows through the Cambridge that had nursed his youth, and that he loved. That, one imagines, will be his most enduring influence, his contribution to that vague conception, the spirit of the age.

ELLEN TERRY
1848-1928

By
MARGUERITE STEEN

ELLEN TERRY

by MARGUERITE STEEN

WHEN George the Fifth came to the throne Ellen Terry had become a living legend. It is as a legend that we propose to deal with her, for it is as a legend that she became vitally important to the nation, as Gloriana is important, as Shakespeare was important, as all shreds and vapours of beauty blown about the history of a nation are important, and witness to the immortality of the sublime.

In one respect only it might be said that the Georgians were more capable of appraising Ellen Terry than their immediate forebears. They suffered, it is true, from not having seen her in her prime; but an immense volume of tradition was at their disposal, and theirs was the advantage of comparing the tradition with the living original, still blessedly in their midst, still contributing actively, if not in any public capacity, to the tradition itself. So long as breath was in her body Ellen Terry never ceased to add to the romanticism which had flourished for more than three-quarters of a century about her person.

Her latter-day influence upon the heart and mind of the nation was something more than the commonplace sentimentality with which the English like to surround their old idols: the compound of loyalty and indulgence which blinds them to intellectual and physical deterioration, and shows them only the idol as it was, not as it has come to be. In her case there was nothing to which to be blind; she retained to the end that quality of sweet and perilous illusion, of something altogether tenuous and legendary with which her art and her life were coloured.

Ellen Terry's significance did not end when she stepped for the last time with that so blithesome lilt from the stage of the old Lyceum, although it is to be admitted that by acting in the plays of Sir James Barrie and Mr. Bernard

Shaw she did not add one cubit to her stature as an actress. But that was not the fault of Ellen Terry; it was the fault of the people who were incapable of matching the wide-winged flight of her creative genius with a vehicle fitted to it. May heaven forgive them, for they tried to confine a Bird of Paradise in a canary cage; and how gracefully the Bird submitted!—of her love and simplicity doing her best to subdue that matchless spread of plumage to the mean accommodation provided for it.

In the opinion of some people the breaking up of the partnership with Irving was to spell Finis to Ellen Terry's career as an actress. The merry adventure at His Majesty's that followed it was probably regarded by these as a reverberation of Lyceum thunders. Nothing of the kind; it was Ellen herself, setting forth new bud and blossom, freed from the somewhat oppressive sobriety of latter-day Lyceum convention.

No intelligent person will deny that these two great artists—Irving and Ellen Terry—were each other's logical complement. But Irving was much older than Ellen Terry; at her period of fullest vigour he was already slipping a little downhill—not as an artist, but in physical power. Still unapproachable, the spirit of adventure had left him; whereas to the very last, as shown by her gallant venture into the films, Ellen Terry retained her adventurous heart.

His strong personal idiosyncrasy ironbound him to a particular type of production—for which, as he himself bitterly admitted to Toole, the demand was fast dying away. ("Ah, Johnny, they don't want *Coriolanus*—they want 'Kitty Rubbish'—dances and songs, you know.") "Little" plays could not contain him, heroics were necessary to him, splendour was the air he breathed. He clung by old standards, and the shifting tides of new dramatic development that followed Pinero and Wilde did no more than lap against the massive crag of his self-establishment, his devotion to old forms.

This was right and good, but it was unfortunate for the still young, still beautiful, for ever venturesome woman in artistic partnership with him: a woman with a son given over to the advanced theatre, with whose aims she was in perfect sympathy.

Ellen Terry knew that art, to survive, must not stand still; that there must be advancement, or ultimate extinction. She may, also, have recognised the supreme value, to new theatrical forms, of their appropriate recognition by the leaders of the old school.

She made her gesture with her old, infallible grace; she recognised the new forms in the most practical manner, by giving them a trial, and, in doing so, removed from herself for ever the stigma of any particular age or period. By this one triumphant gesture she carried herself above and beyond Victorian tradition, and, in doing so, demonstrated her personal greatness. She plunged headlong (and, if one must tell the truth, from a financial point of view, ruinously) into Ibsen; she launched the Armada of her charms on Shaw and Barrie, whose waters, incapable of sustaining her draught, left her high and dry—a stranded splendour, with an echo singing in her shrouds:

" *There are older seas*
That beat on vaster sands. . . ."

She ceased to act (save at isolated performances) ten years before she need have done so, literally because there was not one playwright capable of building a play to her measure. Sceptics may put this down to failing health; but it is reasonable to assume that had the suitable opportunity presented itself, hell would not have barred the way to Ellen's return to the stage. At the age of seventy-one did she not surge forward to play the Nurse in that disastrous Lyric production of *Romeo and Juliet*? Were there then any signs of the diminishing powers, the physical ills that her friends so fondly exaggerated? Her will to do the thing that none but she could do so well held all at bay; and there was plenty to hold at bay. There was a body racked with neuritis, a memory ever at odds with the text, the nervousness that wracked her before every performance—and there were seventy-one years packed with every painful and gay experience that living can bring to a woman. One may say that Ellen Terry took her experiences lightly; what a mercy if she did! For if this had not been so, her life would have ended in the middle forties. But it would be a fallacy to say that they had not left their marks on her.

Be that as it may, this *Romeo and Juliet*, of which *The Stage* wrote that it was "an unhappy example of the vaulting ambition that o'erleaps itself," ran for seventy-three nights, by virtue solely of Ellen Terry's presence in the cast. "No doubt," murmurs again the ever-present sceptic, "many people went in order to be able to say that they had seen Ellen Terry; these would hardly be in a critical frame of mind."

If one may pocket artistic scruple so far, one must be a little glad that Ellen Terry's last part gave her this opportunity of demonstrating her unassailable quality. She showed an irreverent generation the meaning of fine acting. Distressed, as she could not fail to be, by the knowledge that she was pulling the play out of gear, as, with her weight of experience and theatre-wisdom she could not fail to do, she simply could not help doing her best. And what a best! If one might pass an adverse criticism on Ellen Terry's swan-song, it would be that the Nurse which Shakespeare drew was never intended to be so beautiful.

It is not out of place here to compare Ellen Terry's Shakespearean record with that of Mrs. Siddons.

Of those earlier years of barnstorming, during which "the woman Siddons" learned her business, it is difficult to come by reliable information. Strolling players leave no such permanent records of their productions as those whose reputations are linked with some particular house of drama. But, round about the age of twenty, Mrs. Siddons had studied (in her somewhat cavalier fashion, which considered twenty-four hours ample time to devote to the character of Lady Macbeth) at least six recorded parts, among which was Rosalind—surely the strangest and saddest omission from Ellen Terry's repertory. It is impossible to doubt that she would have made the perfect Rosalind—distinguished, delicate, as Rosalind should be, yet full of brave masculine assumptions. With what inimitability she would have played Orlando's Rosalind in a more coming-on disposition! Unhappily, fate left it to the Siddons to play Rosalind "in a dress planned to conceal the person as much as possible."

In brief, the sum of Mrs. Siddons's Shakespearean parts is eighteen, against the royal list of Ellen Terry's on p. 597.

Sixteen plays, twenty-two Shakespearean parts—the majority of which are hung in the golden galaxy of English theatrical history, the shadows of whose splendours never forsook her, on or off the stage, throughout her life.

Admitted, then, that Ellen Terry's reputation is rooted in her Shakespearean experience, there is another influence, not

by MARGUERITE STEEN

Number of Plays	Date	Play	Parts	Number of Parts
1	1856	*A Winter's Tale*	Mamillius	1
2	1856	*A Midsummer Night's Dream*	Puck	2
3	1858	*Macbeth*	Fleance	3
4	1858	*King John*	Prince Arthur	4
5	1863	*Much Ado About Nothing*	Hero	5
	1863	*A Midsummer Night's Dream*	Titania	6
6	1863	*The Merchant of Venice*	Nerissa	7
7	1868	*Othello*	Desdemona	8
	1875	*The Merchant of Venice*	Portia	9
8	1878	*Hamlet*	Ophelia	10
	1880	*Much Ado About Nothing*	Beatrice	11
	1881	*Othello*	Desdemona	
9	1882	*Romeo and Juliet*	Juliet	12
10	1884	*Twelfth Night*	Viola	13
	1887	*Macbeth*	Lady Macbeth	14
11	1892	*Henry VIII*	Queen Katharine	15
12	1892	*King Lear*	Cordelia	16
13	1896	*Cymbeline*	Imogen	17
14	1901	*Coriolanus*	Volumnia	18
15	1902	*Merry Wives of Windsor*	Mrs. Page	19
	1903	*Much Ado About Nothing*	Beatrice	
16	1906	*Measure for Measure*	Francisca	20
	1906	*A Winter's Tale*	Hermione	21
	1921	*Romeo and Juliet*	The Nurse	22

to be ignored, which undoubtedly contributed to that spacious, that tireless art of hers.

Never from the start was she permitted to waste herself on colourless nonsense. One can as readily imagine Ellen sitting on a sofa, mumbling epigrams over a tea-cup, as one can imagine the Bird of Paradise aforesaid nurturing itself on canary-seed. Burlesque and melodrama were handmaids to her development—illiterate trash, no doubt, but trash with plenty of body in it; with " entrances " and " gags " and " laughs," on the getting of which the renewal of one's engagement depended—better training for the young actress than the tepid stuff which seems to be the lot of the beginner to-day. It was better for Ellen Terry to have to play, at the age of thirteen, a *fille de joie* in that rich old melodrama, *The Angel of Midnight*, than to make an entrance as a parlourmaid in a modern comedy by, let us say, Noel Coward or Somerset Maugham. It quickened her imagination, it kept her busy. In screaming her lungs out in *Atar Gull* with a property serpent round her neck, she was doing more for herself than if she had been voicing some tasteful and appropriate aphorism from the West-End stage, and being admonished, when she put more into it than was strictly necessary, to " take it easily, as though she were in her own drawing-room."

No one ever confused Ellen Terry's mind with these misleading comparisons between stage and drawing-room; no one prevented her recognising from the start that the theatre is the theatre, and that to mistake it for anything else is the most stupid and fatal of all errors. The playwrights of her period may not have produced literature (and, by the way, does anyone want literature on the stage?), but they produced actors, not the curious drawing-room hybrids which have passed for such in latter years.

Thus, when Ellen came to play Shaw and Barrie, there was a leakage of pure genius from the cracked sides of the vessel that was not fitted, by temper or capacity, to contain the rich wine of her art. One cannot wonder that, after seeing the failure of these two acknowledged masters of their particular schools of play-making, others were afraid to try the experiment of writing a play for Ellen Terry.

Her art was as difficult to analyse as Ellen Terry herself found it impossible to explain it. She was, in the best sense of the word, an intuitive actress; which is not to say that she did not know her business down to the flicker of an eyelash, but that she had sublimated it; had made it so much a part of herself that neither she nor anyone who knew her was positive of where it began or where it ended.

The Ellen Terry whom one beheld on the stage was precisely the Ellen Terry whom one met in the old house in the King's Road—seen through a magnifying glass. The only difference lay in the fact that the theatre prolonged her art, drew it out, enlarged it, rendered it more spacious. She must have learnt as a mere child that what appears natural in private life becomes not only insignificant, but false on the stage. She had all the art of delicate exaggeration at her fingertips; it sprang to her bidding without volition from the moment she quitted the shadow of the wings. But ask her to explain it, and in nine cases out of ten her explanation would resemble that of Nijinsky, who, when asked by what means he achieved his phenomenal elevation, replied in accents of surprise, " Oh, I just go up, and then I wait a little, and then I come down ! "

Just so; that waiting a little. That is the divine mystery

by MARGUERITE STEEN

that lies at the heart of genius; that is not to be revealed in a phrase to the curious, or even the sincere, enquirer; whose price is blood and tears—a child sobbing out the last lines of an epilogue, with a broken toe caught in a trapdoor, a woman swooning through a part with an arm on fire with pain.

What, then, can one write of this woman, who combined in herself one glorious trinity, of herself, of Shakespeare and of the art that linked the two?

"*Let's not say dull things about her.*"

So many dull things have, alas, been both said and written about her! She suffered from living in an age when dramatic criticism was as uninspired as a shopping list; when Mr. James Agate had not brought flavour into the most tasteless of all forms of writing, the most sterile, the most conventionalised, the most *bourgeois*—in fact, the most utterly unequipped to deal with that being of light and air that was Ellen Terry.

She picked up the mantle of Melpomene relinquished by Mrs. Siddons and wore it with an air, but it did not become her as the flying ribbons of Thalia. To her comedy parts she brought a divine levity, an absence of serious intent that melted her audiences to transports of worship. In a robuster vein—say, in *The Merry Wives of Windsor*—she was inspired by the very genius of merriment; she laughed richly, Elizabethanly; one could fancy that she "loved sack"; she inspired one to say to her "Go to!" Now and again one had glimpses of Mrs. Page pretending to be Ellen Terry; it was never the other way about.

And her fine ladies! What a bred-in-the-bone aristocracy they had! There was no aping of grandeur here; no gentilities to set one's teeth on edge. Her Portia, her Beatrice, her Imogen were fine, simply because she conferred her own fineness upon them. The Terrys as a family were born to the aristocracy of the stage, and Ellen Terry followed tradition.

Yet, when I am asked by people who never saw her what was so extraordinary about Ellen Terry, I fall back upon the baldest statement of fact, whose implications must be lost save on those who understand the theatre, and to whom the theatre is something more than a post-prandial relaxation.

She could speak, she could be silent; she could sit, she

could stand; she could move, she could be still; she could laugh, she could weep.

So simple! So much the business of every actress. Nine-tenths of it, so utterly beyond the average young actress of to-day.

For the benefit of those who may say on reading the foregoing, " How absurd; really, how ridiculous! "—one might elaborate: one might add that every word of Ellen Terry's fell like a drop of liquid gold into the ear of the farthest spectator, seated in the cheapest gallery; that her movements throughout a scene linked themselves into a lyric sequence, perfect as a classic frieze, haunting as a phrase of music, so that one had to exert compulsion on oneself, not to cry out, not to beg her to remain in that one attitude for eternity ; that in spite of the almost unearthly beauty which she brought into the performance of commonplace actions, not a note of her voice, not a movement of her body was false or forced. The rhythmic sense in her was so profoundly attuned to the cosmos she inhabited that she was incapable of performing an action at variance with it.

This that I have just written is, to my mind, far more ridiculous than my original statement that Ellen Terry could sit and stand and be still; but there may be some to whom, for their own reasons, it is more satisfying.

Ellen Terry was one of three bright torches burning in the Thespian temple of her day: Eleanora Duse, Sarah Bernhardt, and Ellen Terry were names that carried a worldwide significance, to which the latter contributed the least, because she confined her appearances to the English-speaking continents. She never, as Duse and Bernhardt did, challenged the great continental actresses on their own soil. In this she, or those responsible for the management of her career, showed their wisdom. Comedy is a delicate plant: it does not bear transplantation so well as tragedy does, and Ellen Terry was essentially a high comedienne. Such a line as Bernhardt's famous—

" *C'est Vénus toute entière à sa proie attachée* "

was beyond her range; Ellen Terry and Mrs. Alving are not compatible, although she once said that she would have liked to chance her hand on her. Tragedy, when she encountered it, never soared into those arid regions where

by MARGUERITE STEEN

tears are not. There was no grief under heaven which Ellen's tears did not water with their beneficent flood.

But her art was broader, less specialised than that of the Duse and the Bernhardt, because, in addition to her gift for tears, she possessed what they did not, a rich and ripe sense of humour, an inexhaustible technique for expressing the same.

Her egotism—that important part of the equipment of the artist—was of a different order from theirs; not only in the sense that the egotism of the comedienne must differ from that of the tragedienne. She lacked the barbarity of the Bernhardt, the tranced, spiritual aloofness of the Duse. She neither intimidated nor overawed her audiences, save in the sense that certain natures will always pay the tribute of awe to beauty, in whatsoever guise it may appear. But, using the key of her invincible romanticism, she entered their hearts and took possession of their troubles. She was capable of an exquisite and sincere sentimentality, which she used as her stepping-stone to higher things. And part of the secret of her hold on English audiences lay in her domesticity, which had a way of leaking over the footlights and submerging the audience in its warm tide.

Not that Ellen Terry's domesticity was of the humdrum, darn-the-stockings and sort-the-laundry variety! The shimmering veil of illusion lay across that, as across everything in connection with her private and public life. Her way with a potato in its jacket, with an egg poached in tomato soup, her love for unbleached linen, her housewifeliness somehow found its way into her acting, and became part of it, just as her acting found its way into her domestic life; and the result was something that baffles description, that can only be registered in terms of emotion.

There was something about her peculiarly British; for all her Paduan ladies, her exquisite assumptions of Gallic graces she never lost that island character, that breath as essentially English as Shakespeare himself.

It is easy to write of Ellen Terry as the public knew her; much more difficult to write intimately of that Well-Beloved who in fourscore years never quite lost touch with the little Nelly Terry who, clad in little more than her own beauty and a bunch of roses, capered into G. F. Watts's diningroom to scandalise him and his pompous guests; who walked along Kensington High Street, so proud of her wedding-ring that she wanted to stop and show it to everyone she met, saying, " Look, I'm married! "; of whom an old friend once told me that he met her on the very eve of her flight from that same marriage—" Looking divinely lovely— with holes in the tips of her cotton gloves! "

Her personal character was much more robust than that popularly attributed to her by Victorian sentimentalists; much finer, more exciting, more variant, more difficult in its manifestations. The popular conception of Ellen Terry was a smoked-glass vision, that the timorous or ophthalmic observer prefers to the direct rays of the sun. " Sweet " and " womanly " were the adjectives that she bore, with as much resentment as a nature as free from bitterness as hers was capable of feeling towards any misunderstanding, throughout her public career. " Sweet " Ellen Terry never was although she could act sweetness; she was an inebriating wine of incomparable bouquet, from whose effects those privileged to drink never recovered during the term of their lives. " Womanly," in the Victorian sense, she equally was not; for she possessed in overwhelming abundance every quality that had no place in Victorian womanliness— adventurism, the power of living for ever in advance of her period, sympathy to all new ideas and all new things.

The things that require courage in knowing are the most worthy of knowledge. A great deal of courage had to be brought to the " knowing " of Ellen Terry, save in a superficial fashion. A choice had definitely to be made between acceptance of the smoked-glass version, that is to say, the comfortable one, or the pure sunlight, which was often disconcerting, inconvenient, and fraught with dangers. No one, however, who made the latter choice could ever regret it; could ever fail to commiserate those others, groping in the twilight of their own *minauderies* and counterfeits, who never for one moment beheld the full glory of the image they affected to worship.

She had every inconsistency under the sun; she could be everything, and everything excessively, but only for a little while. No one has ever summed up her character more concisely than Charles Reade in his well-known description. He leaves almost nothing more to be said—and then concludes by speaking of her as " an enigma." She was an enigma—of a childish sort. One could not go far wrong with Ellen if one resisted the temptation to judge her probable sayings or actions by logic or precedent. In little things she was set; in great things her opinions were fluid. This is a common attribute of greatness.

It was, I think, Sir James Barrie—at any rate, the words have the Barrie-esque flavour—who said somewhere that in those days every man proposed to the girl he was in love with in some such terms as these: " As I can't have Miss Ellen Terry, please can I have you? " She was every man's romantic heroine, and every man, woman, or child across whom fell a ray of her sunlight became her devoted slave.

No great artist can ever have been so devoid of artistic vanity; she would accept a suggestion from any source, once she was convinced of its rightness. Her work was her work, not a thing to be rhapsodised or vapoured about; and work was her religion. She recommended it to those of her friends who were in trouble. " Work will cure all your wounds. I *know*." Never was the courage that lighted her earthly pilgrimage so called to account as in the lack-lustre days when the supreme consolation had deserted her; when there was no work, only a dead procession of uniform hours, a few people coming in and out, constant pain, memories. . . . And then a gust of gaiety, an expedition here or there, or the arrival of her son—who was also her *sun*—from the Continent, and life once again was bravely coloured.

In association with her, distinction separated itself for ever from outward show. Ellen Terry stumbling along a passage at the Farm, with a Shetland shawl about her lovely head, and a white dressing-gown clutched vaguely about the body that never lost its long, pre-Raphaelite line, was no less Ellen Terry than she who stood, in her finest panoply of stiff brocade, waiting in the wings for some tremendous entrance. Ophelia-Ellen, Portia-Ellen, Imogen-Ellen, Queen-Katharine-Ellen, Ellen herself; there is no separating the strands of that many-coloured splendour which is woven into the history of the nation.

Time cannot threaten the foundations of her immortality although laid in the most fleeting of the arts, the only one save that of the dancer which can leave no permanent record of itself. One cannot say of Ellen Terry—" In her day . . ." All days are hers. She is not of a single age: she is of all time, and timeless in herself.

SIR HERBERT BEERBOHM TREE
1853-1917

By
GEORGE BURNS

SIR HERBERT BEERBOHM TREE

by GEORGE BURNS

"HERBERT was for many reasons an enviable man," wrote his brother Max, " but I think what most of us most envied him was that incessant zest of his." No man ever enjoyed his life more. No man was ever more successful in his refusal to grow old. Sir James Barrie has made it fashionable to give the name of Peter Pan to all sorts of people, who do not know how to grow old with dignity and grace, and the term has become a considerable irritation. The man who strives to retain his first childhood, until his second childhood dawns, is a foolish man. Tree, who, when Queen Victoria died, was a man of nearly fifty, certainly never suggested callow youth, but he always suggested early and eager manhood. There was never anything about him of the undergraduate, but he remained, until his death, in that stage of life when men are forced to experiment and to adventure along new channels, the time which, for most of us, comes to a very definite end before we are forty. Bernard Shaw said that Tree always made him feel like a grandfather and, in my vivid recollections of him, he never made me feel that I was many years his junior.

Tree opened His Majesty's Theatre in 1897. For ten years before he had been the manager of the Haymarket, producing there, among other plays, *Hamlet*, *The Merry Wives of Windsor*, Haddon Chambers's *Captain Swift*, Henry Arthur Jones's *The Dancing Girl*, Wilde's *A Woman of No Importance*, and making more money out of *Trilby* than out of all the other plays put together. In the years before Queen Victoria died, he had produced at His Majesty's Gilbert Parker's *The Seats of the Mighty*, *Julius Cæsar*, *King*

John, *Twelfth Night*, and *A Midsummer Night's Dream*, and Stephen Phillips's *Herod*. His first production as a post-Victorian was *The Last of the Dandies*. His last production of any importance was Bernard Shaw's *Pygmalion*. The years between the death of the Queen and the breaking out of the War were the most important and the most interesting years of Tree's life. As an outstanding personality of the theatre, as, indeed, after the death of Irving in 1905, the unchallenged head of his profession, he is definitely a post-Victorian.

Tree was the last of the actor-managers, masters in their own house, whose first business it was to exploit their own personalities and for whom the dramatist was merely a collaborator of the scene painter in the provision of a frame and a setting for the actor's talent. The emissary sent to England by Sardou to watch Irving's production of his son Laurence's translation of the French dramatist's *Dante* complained bitterly that Irving was not acting the play as it was written, and he was told that Irving had never acted a play as it was written, and that he would not do so were it written by the Archangel Gabriel. Tree did not take the same wholesale liberties with the text as his predecessor, but he made the text and the dramatist's scheme subordinate to his own conception of the character for which he had cast himself. His productions were imaginative and often very beautiful, but they were Frederick Leighton and Alma Tadema. He carried into the Edwardian age the artistic ideals of the later Victorians.

A new era in English theatrical history began with the memorable Vedrenne-Barker seasons at the Court Theatre, which made Bernard Shaw a popular playwright, and was followed by the equally memorable brief season at the Savoy when, with the production of *Twelfth Night*, in which Henry Ainley played Malvolio, Granville Barker made the first successful English essay in the theories of stage production invented by Gordon Craig and brought to practical success in Berlin by Reinhardt. Tree was never too old to play experiments with himself. But it did not interest him to try to devise a new frame for himself. The elaborate and often beautiful scenery, and the conventional lighting in the Lyceum tradition, satisfied his æsthetic conscience, and enabled him to give a large public a " low-brow-high-brow " form of entertainment particularly suited to the times. Miss Viola Tree thinks that her father and Gordon Craig together would have been " gigantic." I think that, if they had ever attempted to work together, they would both have been corpses. " The subtleties of symbolism," says Miss Tree, " seemed to him mere mediocrity and cheating the public. ' These things will soon be Bakst numbers, dear,' was his comment to me on what was, I must say, one of the least beautiful of the marvellous Bakst ballets." If Tree were post-Victorian, he was definitely pre-War.

In my young days it was the fashion to denounce the actor-manager as the enemy of the theatre. It was said, and not without considerable truth, that he frequently cast himself for parts for which he was entirely unsuited, that he monopolised the centre of the stage, that he threw plays out of their perspective, and that at the best he was concerned with histrionic and not with dramatic art. I knew four of the pre-War actor-managers very well. Thanks to the fact that Laurence Irving was an intimate friend of mine, his father honoured me with much gracious kindness. I was actually in Charles Wyndham's employ for about a year. I knew George Alexander from my childhood till his death, and I was in and out of Tree's theatre almost daily for a dozen years.

These men were almost strangely dissimilar, although there was a certain affinity between Irving and Tree and between Wyndham and Alexander. Wyndham had most of the qualities of the successful doctor. Harley Street might have been his spiritual home. Alexander had many limitations of sympathy and understanding. He was, I think, essentially a good business man, and with all good business men he had the courage to make many experiments, and therefore did more for the development of drama than any of his contemporaries. It was an act of courage to produce *The Second Mrs. Tanqueray* in 1893. It was even a greater act of courage to produce a play by Henry James and to lose a great deal of money by so doing.

Irving was a great man, a man who must have succeeded in whatever profession he had adopted, a tremendous cynic, a man who shared his benefits left and right without any illusion at all as to the character of his protégés. Irving was a fantastic. A. B. Walkley wrote of him:

"Theophile Gautier and his generation divided mankind into the two great classes of *flamboyant* and *drab*. Don Quixote, Diderot, Shelley, the Devil (Milton's, of course), and Mr. Henry Irving, are all flamboyant. Sancho Panza, Voltaire, Wordsworth, the 'magnified Lord Shaftesbury' of Matthew Arnold, the British public, are all drab. It is the glory of Mr. Irving that he gives the world the spectacle, all too rare, of the two classes in their proper relationship; that is, the second subservient to the first. A flamboyant of the flamboyants, he has conquered the drab public. Don Quixote has brought Sancho to heel."

Even more than Irving, Tree was a fantastic flamboyant in appearance, in speech, in life, in a sense always acting and always certain of at least an appreciative audience of one. Tree lacked Irving's intellect, but he had a greater imagination. He shared Irving's disillusionment, but he had none of his cynicism. Like Irving he possessed carefully cultivated eccentricities, but those eccentricities were, in both cases, an essential part of the man himself. It is natural for some men to be unnatural. The average dull man who endeavours to attract attention by wearing an odd hat or acquiring an odd vocabulary is a nuisance and an affront. But some men are born odd, and their oddness is charming. One is delighted to meet the *poseur* of Pall Mall, but one would commonly run away from the *poseur* of the High Road, Tooting.

The world has changed and the theatre has changed with it. The built-up scenes of the Lyceum and His Majesty's have been transported to Hollywood, to be elaborated and vulgarised in the studios of the cinema princes. And in the theatre the scenery has been simplified and the scene painter put in his place as the definite inferior of the dramatist. This is an artistic advance. But now both in the world and the theatre the eccentric and the flamboyant are sadly hard to find. The actor has grown precise and genteel. He no longer shows off. Men do not stop in the Strand and gaze with half-amused admiration at Sir Nigel Playfair and Sir Gerald du Maurier as they used to gaze at Irving and at Tree.

Tree lived picturesquely and he lived very gallantly. Never was man less affected by failure, and he had his full share. All gallant men are not picturesque. All picturesque men are not gallant. But for the few D'Artagnans that have appeared within the orbit of our experience, fervent thanks are surely due to Almighty God.

To the pre-War actor-managers the theatre was necessarily something of a business, but to them all it was a good deal more than a business. Irving lost all the money that he ever made, and Tree not only cared nothing for monetary success, but when a play began to settle down into an accumulation of box-office profits, he was immediately bored, and was prevented with the greatest difficulty from taking it off. He would indeed have been a far greater actor if he had never had on his shoulders the cares of management, and if he had been obliged every month to play a variety of parts instead of playing the same part for many months.

In his essay on Tree as an actor which he contributed to the volume edited by Max Beerbohm—this essay is, by the way, one of the acutest pieces of dramatic criticism that I know—Mr. Desmond Macarthy contrasts the methods of Tree and Coquelin. Coquelin, as Mr. Macarthy says, " having once adjusted an intonation or a gesture to a hair's breadth, stereotyped it, so if one saw him in the same part years later, the impression was exactly the same." Tree was an improviser, and he never ceased to improvise. In other words, he never played the same part exactly in the same way, and since there was a good deal of the impish in his character, and since he was highly ingenious—the ingenuity was sometimes inspired and sometimes perverse— in the invention of stage " business," as the weeks went on, he added little tricks to his performance until he not infrequently approached the grotesque. As I write this I have in mind particularly his Malvolio, in my judgment one of the most completely successful of his Shakespearean performances. So long as he held himself in hand, he was almost beyond criticism. But when, not to put too fine a point on it, he began to play the fool, and no man more loved playing the fool, the performance, at times, was almost maddening.

I suppose it is roughly true to say that a character actor is the actor who can only play one type of character successfully, that character being more or less approximate to his own, while the supremely great actor can lose his own personality in his presentation of the conception of the dramatist. If this is a fair differentiation, it follows that the character actor must have a powerful, distinct, and attractive personality, while the great actor must possess a plastic personality and a larger measure of intelligence. He must say to himself not " How should I feel, how should I behave, and how should I look if fortune had made me Prince of Denmark, or the steward to Olivia? " but " What exactly did Shakespeare himself conceive to be the character of Hamlet and Malvolio? "

As one thinks of Tree, one recalls that in all his most successful impersonations the character, as conceived by the dramatist, had a considerable affinity with Tree's own personality. I entirely agree with Mr. Desmond Macarthy that one of his most successful performances, and certainly the most tragic, was his Richard II. From many points of view, the production of that play was the most beautiful and the most artistically satisfying of the achievements of His Majesty's Theatre. " The conscious courteousness of Richard II," writes Mr. Macarthy, " his flashy imperiousness, the delicacy of his untrustworthy nature, his exquisite gentleness, his spiteful arrogance, so inconsistent with it, his theatrical humility, and his rapid transitions of mood never found a better interpreter." Richard II was indeed one of the few artists who have ever worn a crown, and Tree, who was himself an artist, realised to the full how unhappy is the Tree who wears a crown, unless indeed it be of pasteboard and can be put aside when the curtain is rung down.

All real human beings have a certain innate dignity. It is the unreal and the imitation that are repulsive. Tree realised this in his performance of Malvolio, another of his outstanding successes. Malvolio is superficially a figure of fun to be jeered at by the drunken Sir Toby, the lightheaded and light-hearted Maria, and the singing clown. But Tree realised that there is real pathos in the stupid man who takes himself over-seriously, and, as I have said, there were both dignity and humanity—one thing can hardly exist without the other—in his impersonation.

I recall his D'Orsay in *The Last of the Dandies*. He shared his brother Max's admiration for dandies, and this was an admirable performance, as was his Beau Austin, years before, though it was, according to Mr. A. B. Walkley, marred by the superficial sentimentality that it sometimes amused him to assume. Writing in 1890, Walkley said:

"He had to recapture the fugitive graces of Brummell: and the dandy belongs to the category of the actor, the orator, the talker-types *qui parlent* (in Buffon's phrase) *au corps par le corps*, of all types the most difficult to reproduce. Mr. Tree nearly mastered the difficulty, and would have quite mastered it had he padded out his dandy with a little more regal magnificence and moderated his transports of lachrymose sentiment. Your dandy, to be sure, was born to invent new trimmings for his sleeves, but I do not think it would ever have occurred to him to wear his heart there."

I recall his Svengali, in the revival in which Phyllis Neilson Terry played Trilby—I did not see the original production; his Mark Antony, a really admirable performance, one of the few examples where Tree, as is pointed out in the criticism of the play in Mr. Shaw's volume of theatrical essays, descended to naturalism and discarded any attempt at the high falutin. Lady Tree has accurately described his King John as "strange, tragic, panther-like."

I recall half a dozen others of his outstanding successes, and many of his failures. And the failures are as illustrative of his personality as his successes. He was not good in Stephen Phillips's *Herod*, which I think a very fine play. He was much worse in the same author's *Ulysses*, which I am quite sure is a very bad play. His Caliban, bizarre and interesting as it was, was over-poetised. His Colonel Newcome, despite a beautiful wig "make up," was unsatisfactory, and I should think that his Shylock was the failure of his long career, if I were not able to recall his Macbeth. The truth was that one of the charms of his character was that he was always on the side of the beaten, whether their doings were good or evil. Consequently, again to quote Mr. Macarthy, "he was always better in representing weakness than strength, passivity than resolution, failure, whether of the faithful or ignoble kind, than victory." He never could have possibly conceived himself killing or deliberately hurting, therefore Macbeth was not within his horizon. He never could possibly have lived without laughing at himself and therefore how could he understand Shylock? It is true that his Fagin, with his heavy eyes and claw-like hands, was an amazing performance, but Fagin was never real. It is true that his Isadore Izard, in the English version of Mirbeau's *Les Affaires sont Les Affaires*, was vulgar and bitter, and never was man less bitter than Tree. But here the artist was having his fling as the man of business.

All art is of course the expression of personality. All that is worth knowing of a poet can be learned from his poetry. All that is worth knowing of a musician from his music. All that is worth knowing of a painter from his canvases. In their work they have told what their genius compelled them to tell, and to ask more is the mere impertinence of a generation that loves to peep through keyholes and to open closed drawers. In a very real sense, Tree the actor was Tree the man, and the qualities which made him an interesting and inspiring companion and endeared him to his intimates, and particularly to his dependents, are all to be deduced from his achievements behind the footlights. There was in the man a great gift for tenderness and sympathy. He revealed this in his Colonel Newcome, with all its shortcomings. There was self-revelation in his Malvolio, in his Richard II, in his D'Orsay. But there was much of Tree, much that his friends knew and loved, that was never revealed from the stage, not because he did not want to record it, but because of the limitation of his technique.

It is possible for an artist's technical equipment to be greater than his personality. In such a case his work will be at the best merely of academic interest, the smooth recitation of the comparatively meaningless. It is equally possible for an artist's personality to be greater than his technical equipment, and in this case his work brings with it a suggestion of disappointment, the conviction that much more might be said than is being said. This was true of Tree. None of us who vividly remember his acting and who were privileged to share his friendship can disagree with the late W. L. Courtney, who wrote: "Let us admit without reserve that Tree as a personality was greater than anything he accomplished." There were bits of him in all the characters he essayed, even in his failures; there was all of him in none of them. He would have been a greater actor if he had been a less vivid personality, less interested in life, less interested and amused by his own adventure of living.

by GEORGE BURNS

The theatre was his life, and certainly His Majesty's Theatre was his home; but it was the home of Tree the man more than it was the home of Tree the actor, and the best-loved part of the home was the wonderful Dome room where he entertained his friends, far more than the stage. Tree acted to live. Such great French players as Coquelin and Lucien Guitry, and I think our own Ellen Terry, lived to act, and it is interesting to note with this reflection that Tree had little or none of their technique. Courtney recalled that he once heard Tree say " technique is a dull thing, it enslaves the imagination," but obviously without technique, no actor can hope to get inside the skin of his part and to convey to his audience all that the author intended. And it was because of his lack of technique, of his riotous imagination, and of his immense enjoyment of himself that Tree often failed to convey the authors intention to the audience unless the author had conceived a character of close spiritual likeness to Herbert Tree himself.

It has been said of Tree that he was always acting. In a sense that is true. It is also true to say that he was never acting. Life to him was one long glorious charade. He loved pretending. One night, while he was playing Rip Van Winkle in a very elaborate make-up, a woman was taken into his room during one of the entr'actes. He looked at her with a little hesitation. " I am afraid you don't remember me, Sir Herbert," she said. And he apologetically answered, " I find it so difficult to recognise anyone in my make-up."

This implied identification of himself with his part may appear to contradict what I have already said. But that is not the case. Tree loved making up, and it was always tremendously interesting to sit and watch him in his dressing-room. He could change his face in almost a miraculous way, and he took infinite pains with detail, just as he took infinite pains that his characters should in their small manners be true to type. But it was the outward man who was changed; the inward man remained unaltered.

Tree had, as Desmond Macarthy has noted, the artistic temperament, if ever a man had it. He was puckish, resentful of discipline, original, indifferent to financial considerations, certainly not given to over-estimate the value of popularity. But for all this he was not a great artist, partly for the reasons that I have already stated, and partly because of his love of adventure and of his lack of any developed capacity for self-criticism. He was never arrogant, never pompous, never annoyingly self-satisfied, but I do not think that he realised that while his Malvolio was very good, his Macbeth was very bad. He prided himself on his versatility—no man ever succeeded in doing everything equally well—and he lived with an overmastering ache for experiment and new adventure. He wanted to dress up in different clothes every day. Having discovered, and incidentally having been immensely amused by the discovery of, how Tree looked and how Tree felt when Tree was pretending that he was Malvolio, he yearned to discover how Tree looked and how Tree felt if he pretended that he were Macbeth.

Never was man more alive. There was always with him the feeling that there was no time to be lost, that each day and each hour even must have its thrill. And the fascination of Tree as a companion—and he lives in my mind as the most fascinating companion whom it was ever my good fortune to know—lay in this spiritual restlessness reflected in his characteristic whimsical comments on men and affairs, and to an almost equal extent in his obvious and naïve enjoyment of the world and of his place in it.

I have heard it said of Tree that he was affected by what was sometimes a rather childish jealousy. I do not think that this was at all true, and he was certainly incapable of any protracted dislike. Now and again, as men will, who have the capacity for the epigram, he would summarise an acquaintance with caustic wit. " How does So-and-so live? " I once asked him. " Oh," replied Tree, " he draws royalties on plays that will never be written." And I would add the royalties were drawn for many a year afterwards, for Tree's generosity was unbounded. No borrower ever asked of him in vain, and the more undeserving the borrower the quicker was the response.

It has been also said of him that he was almost preposterously vain. But his vanity sat well on him. Vanity is indeed by no means unattractive so long as there is obvious justification for personal satisfaction with the part allotted to one in the drama of life. Why should not a pretty woman enjoy her good looks, and a witty man his wit! Tree was a man who laughed at his own jokes. And why not?

His exuberance, his naïveté, his abounding friendliness combined to make him a lovable man, and his courage and his eagerness were the qualities of his very real greatness. But the combination of gifts showered upon him by fate combined definitely to narrow the possibility of his artistic achievement. There must be a considerable element of austerity and hardness in the great artist. His eye must be keen, his judgment sane, his self-control complete. Tree was lucky enough to see life through rose-coloured glasses. His æsthetic judgments were adversely affected by the fact that his reading was limited. I have often wondered whether he might have had a greater success if he had been a painter or a poet and not an actor, for a little reflection justifies the assertion that while the qualities that I have enumerated are necessary for all artists, they are most necessary for the actor. On the stage the man must lose himself before the artist can find himself. Tree could never have lost himself, he valued himself too highly.

He dominated the theatre by the force of his personality, by the vividness of his imagination, by the charm of his character. And he was an actor! To-day the theatre is dominated by Charles Cochran, a showman of genius, and the best-known theatrical figure is Noel Coward. Is this progress or decadence? I am too old to try to answer.

The tragedy of the actor is that he leaves nothing behind. In a tribute to Tree, Lord Asquith said that he will be remembered as "a worthy and indeed an outstanding figure in the great procession of artists, the Burbages, the Bettertons, the Garricks, and the Keans, whose memory is the treasured inheritance of the English stage." But what do we know of the Bettertons, the Garricks, and the Keans? We know that in *The Duchess of Malfi* Betterton moved Mr. Pepys " to admiration "! We are familiar with Dr. Johnson's high opinion of Garrick. We know that Coleridge said of Kean that " seeing him act was like reading Shakespeare by flashes of lightning." But that is all. Mr. Desmond Macarthy told the whole hard truth when he wrote: " The triumphs of dead actors live for us only in pictures, in half-obliterated tradition, and in the pages of the few dramatic critics who happen to be still readable on account of their style."

Mr. Macarthy wrote in prose what long before Henley had written in verse in his " Ballade of Dead Actors " :

> *"The curtain falls, the play is played:*
>   *The Beggar packs beside the Beau;*
> *The Monarch troops, and troops the Maid;*
>   *The Thunder huddles with the Snow.*
>   *Where are the revellers high and low?*
>   *The clashing swords?   The lover's call?*
>   *The dancers gleaming row on row?—*
> *Into the night go one and all."*

And alas! neither Tree the actor nor Tree the man will be discovered " in the pages of the few dramatic critics who happen to be still readable on account of their style," for the critics of his time who were so gifted, were, for the most part, unattracted by his romantic exuberance. The pre-War world was in spiritual preparation for the War. Tree was always an alien post-Victorian.

Tree was a magnificent conversationalist and the most stimulating companion. If he loved the sound of his own voice, so did all his friends. "Silence," he once said, "is the wisdom of fools." His humour was spontaneous and often extremely ingenious. Perhaps most of his good things have been recorded somewhere or the other, but I vividly remember the incidents of one night in the Dome of His Majesty's Theatre which have not, I think, been printed. It was a supper that Tree gave to Signor Grasso, the tempestuous Sicilian tragedian. The party lasted till the early hours. The Sicilian was immensely pleased and excited, and when at last, at about three o'clock in the morning, we began to break up, he warmly expressed his appreciation, kissing every one of us, much to our embarrassment. We saw the guest of the evening into his cab, and were rather surprised to hear him tell the driver in his broken English to drive to the Garrick Theatre, where he was playing. "What on earth does he want to go to the theatre for at this hour?" asked someone. "I think," said Tree, "he has forgotten to kiss the fireman."

When Tree died, I wrote of him that he had advertised everything except his good deeds. And his good deeds were many. He lived and moved and had his being in the limelight, but with all other worthy men he had his secrets. And innumerable kindnesses, often done at great personal inconvenience, were the secrets that he hugged to his soul.

ARTHUR BINGHAM WALKLEY
1855-1926

By
HAROLD CHILD

ARTHUR BINGHAM WALKLEY

by HAROLD CHILD

IN a caricature by Max, Arthur Bingham Walkley, looking with contempt upon George Bernard Shaw, remarks that he " calls himself a non-smoker." Four offences are packed into the words, and of these the least is merely not smoking. Walkley enjoyed a good cigar, as he enjoyed, with "moderate self-indulgence " (to quote an old friend of his and mine), all the choicer pleasures of the palate; but a man with no taste for tobacco was rather to be pitied than blamed. A worse offence was to say " non-smoker "—a phrase to make one shudder. Worse still was, by calling himself a non-smoker, to declare himself one of a class, herd, or kind. Walkley was sociable, " clubbable," and in friendship eager, in his wary way, to give and receive affection. But nobody and nothing could lure him into any herd, or flock, or brotherhood. In calling himself, proudly, a critic, he seemed to draw near the gates. Adding "impressionist," he whisked away into the wild. And he would, I believe, have been indignant (or, as he would have written, " werry fierce ") with anyone who, calling him a post-Victorian, seemed thereby to try to " place " him in a " period." On principle, as the Civil Servant in *Pickwick* ate muffins (how those pet old tags of his crowd into the memory that entertains thought of him!), he would have protested that it was enough for him to " abound in his own sense." He would have admitted that he was born in 1855 and that he began to write when the Victorian era was beginning to turn " fag-end of the century " (he called it that just because everyone else said *fin de siècle*). He might even have agreed that, in his own wilful, fastidious way he hastened the change, and did a good deal to help forward a contemporary improvement in the English drama. But he would have denied that the accident of date had anything to do with the workings of his mind and with the manner in which he disclosed them.

Gravest of all was the fourth accusation made in the cartoon. It is one thing not to smoke. It is quite another thing to be a non-smoker. A non-smoker is an exception from the general run of men; he is tainted with superiority. The ordinary man is a smoker; the plain man is a smoker; *l'homme sensuel moyen* is a smoker. And Walkley feared nothing quite so much as not to be accepted for a plain man. A plain man with a delicate and well-trained taste, a very swift and merry sense of humour, a great deal of knowledge and a power of original and clear thinking—all that, certainly; but still a plain man, not a faddist, not a reformer, not an " intellectual," not an " educationist," not a busybody of any kind.

At Oxford he read mathematics and took two Firsts in them. Mathematics both pleased his precise and orderly mind and sharpened his sensitiveness to form and finish; he never dropped them, and declared in later life that he could study mathematics and " listen-in " to the wireless at the same time. But reading mathematics for his schools meant also that he learned for himself—for his own pleasure, as he would have insisted—a good deal that would otherwise have come to him through the curriculum. Perhaps that partly accounts for his freedom from conventional reverence and rules. He adventured for himself into his beloved Aristotle, his Origins of the Drama, and the rest of it. He came to them, and he came through them, fresh (*frais et dispos*) and independent. And when he began to write he maintained that independence.

In the 'eighties and 'nineties of the last century young men of letters were in danger from coteries and cliques. Walkley, a very respectable Civil Servant in the Post Office, and writing only in his leisure, kept out of all of them. Though he turned, like other minds of that time, to France for his patterns of form and finish, he never burbled about the *mot juste*, and he followed no fashions (though 'tis true, indeed, that here and there in his earlier works you shall find traces of his having written for *The National Observer*). From his lifelong friend, William Archer, he learned to take an interest in the drama (the nature of that interest may concern us later) ; and *The Speaker,* a Liberal and lively weekly, made him its dramatic critic. There every week he wrote side by side with another young author, who, with different tastes and wider sympathies, was at one with him in power of enjoyment, and in independence. To Walkley A. T. Quiller-Couch dedicated his book of *Adventures in Criticism*, reprinted from *The Speaker*. Then, in 1888, *The Star* was founded (and a shocking business that seemed to the Oxford which Walkley had not so very long left); and Walkley was its dramatic critic from the first, "cradled in the same new sheets" with Mr. Shaw as its musical critic. They had great fun. Walkley wrote not only on the drama. He wrote on books. He wrote on anything that took his fancy. He wrote always on life, and on the art of life. In articles about a certain Pettifer he wrote enchantingly about himself, very slightly disguised. He was mischievous, gay, witty. There were some very jolly quarrels, too—a brisk little dust-up with Mr. Shaw over split infinitives, and another much more serious engagement in which Walkley, his fastidiousness offended by George Moore's novel, *Sister Teresa*, shot barb after barb into an unhappy writer who tried to be facetious at his expense.[1]

Walkley was always a cool and dangerous fighter. Years later, in *Literature*, he laid low a much doughtier opponent on that same question of subjects which were or were not suitable for treatment in art—a question which Walkley always professed to settle by his own personal taste. In youth he was rather too much inclined to stone his enemy with whole quarryfuls of instances out of his much reading in five or six languages and his most obsequious memory; but he grew more artful as he grew older. The deadliest thing that he ever wrote was a very short letter to a popular playwright who had written, before the production of his new play, to ask Walkley to be kind to it. Walkley would not allow me to take a copy of that reply, and (worse luck!) kept no copy himself. I am sure the playwright did not long keep the original.

Adventures in Criticism—the title of Q's book—would have done better for Walkley's first book of reprints than his chosen *Playhouse Impressions*. That word "impressions" was an occasion for the scoffer, and it gives a clumsy and

---

[1] Walkley reprinted too few of his earlier writings. The collection of them made by Mr. George F. R. Anderson has given much help and (as A. B. W. would have liked much better to know) pleasure in the writing of this sketch.

misleading account of Walkley's art. Closely following the French stage and French dramatic criticism, he had been learning from Jules Lemaître ; but, however clearly he might explain what he meant, the word "impression" seemed to his English readers to rule out thought. There was some excuse for them. They knew that the word "impressionist" had been borrowed from the art of painting. An impressionist painter was one who painted what he saw, no matter whether it was there or not. An impressionist critic, therefore, was a critic who wrote about what he saw and felt, no matter what the author and the players and everyone else concerned in the production may have meant. And that was not dramatic criticism as the theatrical world understood it in the eighteen-eighties and a little later too. When Arthur Bourchier wanted to insult Walkley, he not only misspelt his name, which was silly, but also called him a "dramatic reporter," which was either sillier still or really rather clever. For your true impressionist is your dramatic reporter, your Clement Scott, who describes in as many and as noisy words, and with as few and as modest thoughts, as possible. And that was what another Clement, Clement Shorter, and all the theatrical managers, and most of his *chers confrères*, too, thought that Walkley ought to be. What he thought himself was that " in the general case description is only a subsidiary part of criticism, which is mainly concerned with analysis and æsthetic valuation." And very early in the day William Archer—affectionate admirer and stern critic—hit him with an inner, if not a bull's-eye. He called him ratiocinative. He told him that he was " not enough of an Impressionist and too much of a logician," that he was " apt to let some more or less relevant æsthetic or philosophical theory intrude between him and the actual work of art, and warp or obscure his perceptions." What Walkley really meant by " impressionist " was " individualist." He wanted to adventure into, to savour—as Arthur Clutton-Brock would have said, to " experience "—every work of art for himself, and then to think out his reasons for liking or disliking it. He believed, with Anatole France (whom he was one of the first to introduce to English readers), that the critic could never escape from himself, and that it was not only futile, but even in a sense self-deceiving, to come to any work of art with preconceived rules for judging it, as did the academic, or dogmatic, school, with

Brunetière for Headmaster, and William Archer (dear William, who "starts from wrong premisses and argues impeccably to wrong conclusions") for one of the ushers. The critic's business was to find out first of all whether the work of art pleased *him*. And Walkley was both logician and Paterian enough to go where his assumption led him. " The primary aim of all art . . . is to give pleasure. And this pleasure of art, it must be borne in mind, is in the first instance—whatever higher forms it may take in the long run—a pleasure of the senses," not a moral nor an intellectual pleasure. " We buy a novel for pleasure. We give Mr. Fisher Unwin 6s. for *Sister Teresa*, just as we give Messrs. Spiers & Pond 6s. for a pint of champagne "—he could even write like that under provocation; but a Paterian hedonism, austere and fastidious, was the true characteristic of the young man who had matriculated at Balliol in the year when *The Renaissance* was published.

He was not always clear in his mind about the difference between his own impressionistic approach and that of the dogmatics. In the very lecture to the Royal Institution on " Dramatic Criticism " from which I have just quoted, he said that for the critic there were two questions : first " Am I pleased ? " and next, " Am I right to be pleased ? " He has no business to be talking of " right " or of " wrong " any more than he is justified, when criticising *La Robe Rouge*, to say that " a study of manners and motives is more *important* than the exhibition of violent acts." All he meant was that he liked it better. The critic's second question is really, " Why am I pleased ? " " The business of criticism," he wrote elsewhere, " is to distinguish." And what gave Walkley his distinctive strength and quality as critic, what made him, in the theatre and out of it, as nearly as possible the " ideal consumer " of art, for whom in his Royal Institution lectures he was searching, was the nice adjustment (though not perfect adjustment, as Archer had noted) between his sensibility to impression and his power of analysis. He enjoyed intensely ; he was masterfully ingenious and acute in finding out why.

So much belongs to the ideal consumer. But the critic is himself an artist. Every critic worthy of the name must be an artist. Who can now, he would ask, read Dryden's plays? Yet Dryden's critical essays are as fresh to-day as ever—and nowhere, perhaps, did Walkley better show his power of bringing out the quality and the beauty of a piece of literature than in his comments on Dryden's essay *Of Dramatick Poesie*. The critic could never be a " dramatic reporter." He too must something make and joy in the making. And no other critic of his time—perhaps few in any time—had Walkley's power of communicating his impressions, of making the reader see and feel what he had seen and felt (and he could see and feel—witness his account of Réjane in *Zaza*—as quickly as Thomas Hardy himself), of interesting him in the reasons why (a good example is his two papers on *The Admirable Crichton*), and of making something new that was in itself a work of art. I asked him once whether, after all those years, he was not tired of the theatre. Never, he replied, of the theatre, of which he had the true playgoer's love. Few of the plays could interest him; but " I am always very much interested in what I am going to say about them." Not long after his appointment to *The Times*, he attended a great gala performance at Drury Lane, at which King Edward made one of his earliest public appearances after his illness. The enthusiasm was frantic. Walkley's notice never mentioned the King. And when a Great Power in the office remonstrated, he merely replied, " It did not come into my scheme." Perhaps two more *Times* memories of A. B. W. may be allowed to illustrate his concentration on his own work of artistic creation. One is of the little man behind the big cigar imperturbably writing in his tiny hand a dramatic criticism, while a German air-raid was making the fiend's own din overhead and every other soul in the office had stopped work and gone below. And the other (for which I will not vouch) is of three heads of departments or other great men outside the door of his room, each struggling not to be the one to go in and tell him that he really must finish off his " copy " at once. The situation was all the more acute because Walkley, artist and individualist to the marrow, was also one of the most considerate and accommodating of journalists.

His mistrust of " the rules " by no means left him without certain fixed principles, or (perhaps it would be safer to say) recurrent tests. One of them was that a play must be a conflict of wills; and that implied definition and symmetry in its form. Another was that a critic, being a man of literature, naturally preferred plays with " ideas " in them, because they made better material for his own art. These

grandiose in the City. So with his financial successors, except James White. The latter carried his ego and abundant vitality into a national arena, and in his case the public backed a character instead of a name. White, outside the City, loomed large as a national showman, through interests that had a double merit for him: they were in the limelight, which he loved, and they involved gambling, which was his ruling passion.

He saw chances quickly, and snatched them without hesitation. Otherwise, the messenger-boy from Board School would not have graduated, before his teens were over, from a bricklayer's labourer into a speculative builder. His own story was that, without capital, he built a small house, one room at a time, and as it arose, mortgaged each floor to buy more bricks; and that before long he bought the brickfield which had employed him. But one could believe only in part the tales of his youth: they seemed too racily good to be true.

Probably, this construction of a few houses for Rochdale workmen was his single venture in solid enterprise. He left it to promote local boxing; and it was on record that at nineteen he made a profit by selling, before he had bought it, three-quarters of the ownership of a tuppenny circus. He ran a theatre in Matlock; he brought his Northern wits to London, for further adventure in showmanship; he served in the Boer War as a mounted policeman; he returned to London, learned the technique of company promotion from E. T. Hooley, and dabbled in backers for vaudeville, land speculation, and boxing championships. And so to the enterprise which carried him into prominence.

Jack Johnson, the negro, won the world's heavyweight championship in Reno, and swaggered into England, trailing behind him notoriety from white entanglement in the United States. He fascinated and antagonised the followers of British sport. James White saw profit and excitement in finding a White Hope to match against the impossible negro. He picked on Bombardier Wells, then the favourite British boxer. His funds could not cover the guarantees needed, but for such opponents the public money would be certain. He hired his venue in Earl's Court Exhibition, and announced a symbolic battle between white and black. The response was louder than he had expected. In that

JAMES WHITE

by ALAN BOTT

IT was said of James White that he resembled the Card enough to have been Arnold Bennett's original. This was inexact: the Card conquered London with provincial gusto, but was an endearing grotesque who had tact and a peculiar sensibility. White, also, was a magnetic grotesque. But this millionaire from Rochdale rode roughshod over opposition, and his triumphs were those of the tremendous gambler.

He used £150,000,000 of public money during eight years. Yet he was never a real financier. He neither created, nor organised, nor promoted anything stable. All his dealings were in terms of speculation, even when their material endured. A few of his ventures survived himself, but did so because others with stabler vision adapted them. He left nothing notable except the eminence of men whose fortune he made by chance or impulse—that, and memories of a lavish, illiterate fantastic, who applied his wealth to antics bizarre as anything from a profiteer by Balzac or Petronius. Here is no greatness for thoughtful analysis. One can best explain James White, and the position he occupied, through a narrative of his fabulous doings, in which vast figures must have their place. It is for ironic relief, one assumes, that he is included in this gallery of eminent Georgians and Edwardians.

Personality separates him from other jerry-builders of quick fortune. Like Whittaker Wright and E. T. Hooley in the 'nineties, White could not have gathered his millions except in a roaring decade of prodigal values—his achievements, indeed, are a comment on the garish nineteen-twenties. Whittaker Wright kept to the rôle of company promoter, juggling in an office with figures and enticements. Beyond the circle of his associates, he was merely something

period (it was 1911) two minor Savonarolas formed part of the London scene. Father Bernard Vaughan, from his Farm Street Chapel, fulminated against the intimate sins of society; and the Reverend F. B. Meyer, from Regent's Park, launched Nonconformist thunder against whatever he regarded as unclean in life and art. Meyer represented many when he preached that it was unclean to stir up racial excitement over a conflict between white man and dubious negro. The Liberal press, with all Nonconformity behind it, backed him. Finally, a Liberal Home Secretary banned the fight.

Such were the strange, unsteady ladders climbed by White to the rarified heights of finance. The White Hope contest was absurd, even in terms of heavyweight boxing, for only a partisan imagination could have placed Bombardier Wells anywhere near equality with Jack Johnson. In terms of material failure, it left White with a desk-load of writs and a probable bankruptcy. Yet the collapse brought unforeseen advantage. If the man from Rochdale had not tried to match white skin against black, several big fortunes would not have grown as they did, large areas in London would have a different façade, and thousands of investors might not have lost their savings.

The fiasco gave White the familiar status of Jimmy to the camp followers of sport, and to the haphazard public. He was a champion against what were called the mugwumps. It also cemented his friendship with influential men, including Sir Joseph Beecham, who made Victorian and Edwardian millions from the purgative pills " worth a guinea a box." They had met in the National Sporting Club, and found plenty in common—Lancashire accents and certainties, Rabelaisian humour, quick eyes to the main chance, erratic generosity, a dislike of mugwumps, and a liking for the cruder forms of sport. Sir Joseph helped other sympathisers to side-track Jimmy White's writs ; and White, removed from the threshold of bankruptcy, sold Sir Joseph (as a salesman of ideas he was always brilliant) his plan for the Beecham Trust. This enterprise, beginning in the finance of pills, was to run like quicksilver across a dozen great industries and many acres of London land.

Beecham capital and Hooley methods made White, by 1914, into a financial agent of consequence. He had learned that rich men could be dazzled as easily as poor ones, and that it was easier to raise £200,000 for a glittering project than to borrow £2,000 on moderate security. Yet his outlook on national and international affairs was always naïve; he saw them only as factors for stock gambling. During the days when war shadows lengthened across Europe, the danger was explained to him. He suggested a big flotation, to be used for buying back Alsace-Lorraine from the Germans

The war expansion was just what his talents needed. The Government floated loan after loan, to finance expenditure that swelled like Alice in Wonderland. He had no direct concern with war material; but when war contracts depended upon a factory site, or the quick provision of plant, or adaptation to another man's process, Jimmy White was there with finance, introduction, useful acquaintance, and readiness to take commissions. It was easy money, and much of it he spent with easy generosity. Everybody within reach was entertained. Champagne spurted at the least provocation from old friends and new. He deluged military camps with sporting gear, and sent thousands of boxing gloves to the Navy's lower deck. He put American contingents under his bluff wing, wined them and dined them, took them to watch famous boxers perform at the National Sporting Club. His pink cheeks and genial profanity stayed prominent in the recollection of thousands of American soldiers, after they had gone home to shed their uniform.

Many comic knighthoods were delivered during and after the War; and nearly among them was one for James White. His friends suggested the honour, for munificence to Allied forces. They sounded him, but he preferred opportunities for a *chevalier d'industrie*. He asked instead for permission to float a company; for this was in 1918, when public issues were forbidden. He quickly had his permission, and was satisfied. He was among the few men who welcomed peace for the singular reason that it brought more excitement. His passion for gambling had fed on itself; and the race-horses he now owned did not satisfy a need for taking big chances.

Here, with the Armistice, was such a period as speculators may find, with luck, once in a lifetime. The land was flowing with ready money; owners of colossal war-fortunes had to invest somewhere. White imposed himself on the profi-

by ALAN BOTT

teers as a financial genius. He prepared flotations, propagated round London their dazzling virtues, and sent salesmen of his ideas to Cardiff, Manchester, Birmingham, or wherever profiteers could be shot sitting. The pupil of E. T. Hooley, pulling the wires from a holding company, worked underwriters, issue houses, nominee directors, propagandists, and price manipulators. And the gambler, sitting over a ticker-tape, thrilled to truncated symbols on a paper ribbon, that noted rises worth a million to his band of majority holders. A new thrill came when he chose the moment for withdrawal from a swollen market, leaving investors to continue without him their tumult and shouting over collapsed prices. In two years his personal fortune rose by £3,000,000; and the more he drenched with burst values a public eager to get rich quickly, the more anxious it seemed to follow him, whether in the City or on the Turf.

He operated through the Beecham Trust, now his own after the passing of Sir Joseph Beecham. Because of opposition from the Duke of Bedford's leaseholders, he had not fulfilled its earliest grand project—to buy the Covent Garden estate, rebuild the whole market, pull down scores of buildings to make room for warehouses, and connect with four railway stations through subterranean roads. The purchase had been negotiated for a trifle of £8,000,000, but this was profitably adjusted in less ambitious disposal, when rent and ground rent soared with everything else in the days of boom. Meanwhile, the alchemist of the Beecham Trust turned rubber into the equivalent of gold.

Jimmy White, looking at the new, gimcrack world through his cigar smoke, saw the millions waiting in motor transport. Everybody with a war fortune, large or shall, rushed to buy a motor-car, or several motor-cars. Every officer demobilised with a gratuity wanted a car. A bumptious brand of new youth, eager for speed and display, demanded cars, at any cost to parents. There was sudden petrol for all, after the war restrictions; and business firms had learned to change from horse-van to motor. Oil, metals, and rubber were the primary products for a hundred makes of petrol-driven vehicle; but manufactured rubber held the best chance for a British monopoly. Dunlop, in peace as in war, was supreme among the British tyres. White formed a pool, dominated by his Beecham Trust, to buy control of Dunlops. Through new issues he increased its nominal capital from

£7,500,000 to £20,000,000. Yet its share quotations more than trebled in value within eighteen months; after which the subscribers to White's pool began to unload their holdings upon a ready public. White boasted that at one moment the pool's profit could have been £7,000,000.

Any grandeur has a lure. The magnitude of White's adventure in Dunlop persuaded a horde of small investors to dance to his piping; and on this occasion the piping diverted his own cold judgment. He saw, for once, something more than a quick profit. He altered his custom, and did not use a tame representative in Dunlops, but elected himself to its Board, and himself planned the company's inflation. It was to be self-contained, to supply its own products all over the world, and to dominate the market in rubber products, from golf-balls to tyres for all cars and for a coming multitude of aircraft. It was using cotton worth £10,000,000 a year, but depended on four mills only. White therefore floated further paper millions, for a vast amalgamation in Lancashire cotton. He promoted motor issues for Dunlops' benefit, and issues to exploit the Dunlop concessions. Money from everywhere flowed round himself and the company.

It was his odd suite of offices in the Strand, rather than his town-house (in Park Lane, after the millionaire tradition), that best fitted his florid personality. He sat at an opulent desk, with gold and silver fittings. Round the room were massed flowers, and dozens of silver-framed photographs of the eminent. The main office connected with a dining-room, hung with sporting prints. A chef, part of the permanent staff, prepared a daily luncheon for twelve people, although in the end the guests might be two or three, or none at all.

All sorts of proposals were brought by callers—speculators, lesser company promoters, stockbrokers, provincial business men, sounding-brass advertisers, boxing promoters, "sports," charity canvassers, and platoons of touts and spongers, whom he alternately bullied and rewarded. A box of Corona cigars was open for all who entered; often two hundred went in a day. The more unusual a proposition, the better it was relished by the sleek, pink man behind the desk, who stared through prominent eyes that were something between violet and steel blue, and had a queer, luminous fixation (it was said, by some whom he persuaded against their own belief, that his eyes had a hypnotic quality). He was ruthless in buying and selling, but generous to any peddler of patents who could make him laugh, and sentimentally soft to all who could reach him with a pathetic tale. And his cheque-book often had a religious zeal—a Roman Catholic priest from Rochdale, kept waiting for five hours, went away with a contribution of £5,000, assessed by White at £1,000 an hour.

His speech, which came after sharp pauses, was a torrent of downright, almost Elizabethan English, interlarded with profanity, and uttered in a Lancashire accent that broadened with his wealth and his self-recognition as a " character." He was excessively fluent, except on matters outside the limited radius of his concern. At one of the hotels where he lavishly entertained notabilities by the hundred, the toast-master invited him to say grace. This was outside the radius, and he proclaimed: " Gra-ace? We doan't want Gra-ace. Let's eat! " Embarrassment was resolved by a guffaw from the first Lord Birkenhead, which the rest echoed and White accepted as a compliment. Birkenhead, with his taste for sprawling vitality and his extravagant zest for life, was an intimate of the Card from Rochdale. White made it a boast that he read no books except the Racing Calendar and an occasional Edgar Wallace (for Wallace, another connoisseur of zest, was also White's friend). Yet when Lord Birkenhead wrote a book on his American experiences, White bought hundreds of copies, and caused them to be distributed among callers in his office, with the Coronas.

For a time luck and an instinct for boom combined to enhance everything he touched. He bought in the West Country a small town and its surroundings, parcelled the area into lots, and sold them at a rich profit to the tenants of the former ducal landlord, who might himself have done the parcelling (real estate, however, was the single department of business in which White was a sound expert). His Beecham Trust purchased a famous brewery, floated it on an ocean of added capital, and retired at the profitable moment. A stockbroker waited hours to see him with an invitation to raise £2,000,000 for obtaining, from the then Lord Cowdray, control in an oil company. He was about to leave, and try another big speculator, when White arrived, listened, and quickly agreed. Control being established, White left for one of the seven short cruises which he made in his steam yacht, for which he paid £30,000. He intended to take his guests round the north of Scotland; but at Belfast he abruptly ordered the captain to make for Liverpool. " If I doan't get to London," he said, " I'll lose a million." The oil shares, bought at £5, were moving fast toward their record of £15, at which figure White's syndicate could benefit by £5,000,000.

His material success appeared boundless. It stirred his self-confidence into a form of megalomania. His inclination was to think in millions, or at least in hundreds of thousands. It was at this period that he took as a slogan: " Mista-akes? I doan't ma-ake 'em! "

His ventures on the Turf were as colossal in their different medium. He believed that for him it would not be difficult to win several Derbys. He spent £100,000 on an estate near Swindon, and on the training establishment included in its hundreds of acres. More tens of thousands went on yearlings, mares, and ready-trained runners: at one time he owned seventy mares, and a varied population of young stock. He won, in quick sequence, the Royal Hunt Cup, the Cesarewitch, the Manchester Cup, and the Lincoln. Jockeys often received £500 for each race they won for him. House parties were called out on Sunday morning to watch a long parade of horses, first the yearlings, then the two-year-olds, and then the three-year-olds, led by stable boys in spotlessly white coats. Did any of his variegated visitors wish to shoot, then a couple of guns, with beater and retriever, were ready for each. The others were invited to watch a spurred cock-fight, or a dog fighting a bear, or a fist-fight between stable lads.

The first tentative wave of post-War depression rocked White's balance, but did not upset his belief in his star. He clung to his Dunlop vision, did not foresee the coming fall in cotton, and had not cleared himself of perilous holdings. The Dunlop revenue, in one year, showed a drop of £8,000,000. White and his associates were later removed from the Board, and amid sane reconstruction the glittering £20,000,000 of capital was reduced to £9,000,000.

Enough was left for him still to rank as a millionaire : the oil episode alone had brought him more than a personal million, and since he was free of it, he could laugh when the shares descended to one-twelfth of the price he had imposed on buyers. Nor did the days of easy money vanish yet.

by ALAN BOTT

New deals and flotations restored his public reputation as a financier. He took care to joke about rumours of his insolvency, and instead of abating expenditure, he increased it. His horses won with fair frequency, his passion grew for gambling. His wagers on a runner were anything between £1,000 and £10,000 each way. On one day he received a cheque from his bookmaker for £50,000; although the bookmakers generally regarded him as manna from heaven. More often than not, he kept away from the racecourse, and watched for results over a tape-machine in his office, while savouring the risk.

He bought at Newmarket auction, for £35,000, a second great house and racing estate, but disposed of them a month later, in casual talk with another millionaire of those flamboyant years: a glossy personage who might have been model for the lines sung, in a revue of the period, by a group made up to represent a typical subject for Sargent's facile brush:

" *I like the way he's brought out the shine,*
Out the shine, out the shine
In this South African ring of mine—
We like smart shine."

The South African millionaire said he wished that he, instead of White, had purchased the Newmarket estate. " All right," remarked White, " it's yours." Fifty words decided the price, with a profit for the seller. The estate changed hands within four puffs of a cigar; the conversation turned elsewhere.

Another formidable wave of decline swept over trade returns and the stock quotations. His difficulties became graver than they had ever been. An enemy circulated the report that Jimmy White was in Queer Street. His reply was to assemble some bankers at one of the hotel dinners, and publicly ask what his credit with each of them represented. Under his pressure, they mentioned large figures; and the report was scotched. In the strange, dim-lit atmosphere of what is popularly known as high finance, your millionaire has banking opportunities denied to lesser mortals. Years are allotted to him for postponing a collapse that would overtake an ordinary merchant in as many months.

Again White pulled himself up with golden shoe-strings, tied to real-estate. The old General Post Office, in St.

Martin's-le-Grand, was to be abandoned. White flourished a Beecham Trust cheque, bought the site and the buildings, and disposed of them to his advantage. He continued, by the largeness of his ideas, to bluff bankers, investors, and much of the City.

The megalomania did not permit him to acknowledge mistakes, and demanded fresh outlets. He began another extravagance by buying control of a West-End theatre. He let the experts have their head for his first production, which ran in London for a year. On the night before its trial performance in Manchester, impulse made him hire, at a cost of £180, a special train which carried only himself and a friend from Euston, where he distributed at midnight five-pound notes to the station staff. The success again persuaded him that his genius was protean : that it was supreme in the theatre, as in finance, horse-breeding, and worldly wisdom. He boasted that the best actress was playing for him in the best play in the best London theatre; that his was the best jockey, riding the best horse; that he was patron to the best English boxer; that he had the best of everything. He gave high salaries to stage performers—so high that one production in his later sequence of failures could not have paid, even if the theatre were crowded to capacity for nine months.

His interference made rehearsal a lively bedlam; he was convinced that he knew more than the experts. In a musical play about Cleopatra, he introduced a skating scene, and partisan jokes on racing and the Stock Exchange. He changed the dresses, the lighting, the tempo of the music, made authors alter their script a dozen times a week. " 'Ere—stop that music! It's wrong—what we want is more alto! " Again : " 'Oo said pinks on this bloudy set? Turn on your purples. This is a night scene, not a fire. All this pink looks like an 'ouse of 'arlotry." He thrust aside an actor kneeling before Cleopatra's throne, and admonished: " Put some goots into it! It's noa use 'anding it out like a machine. Do it like this." The controller of Dunlops and the Beecham Trust knelt at the star's feet, and placed his grey bowler hat on the back of his bald head. He shifted a cigarette to the corner of his mouth, and suddenly roared: " 'Oosh! 'Oosh! Yer 'Ighness! I 'ear soomboddy coominger! " Stroking his incongruous, Chaplin moustache, he added, " That's the way—snappy-like, and lots of

two notions could not always lie down comfortably together. There is a sad little sentence in a paper called "Critical Disquietudes" in his last book, *Still More Prejudice*; he writes: "the drama 'of ideas,' as it used to be called—for it is mainly a thing of the past—often enough bad drama, of worse ideas." And time had been when he had such high hopes of this drama of ideas—had even gone to the length of deceiving himself a little about it. He was one of the very first to see the greatness of Ibsen. While the Clement Scotts were screaming and cursing, Walkley was quietly observing what a dramatist, what an artist, Ibsen was, and how stimulating were his ideas. Of *Rosmersholm* he wrote in 1891: "All this is very piquant, *bizarre*, fresh, of absorbing interest to the serious spectator, and to the more eclectic *dilettante* (say the Des Essarts of M. Huysmans), at least as fascinating as a Japanese curio or the rare edition (uncut) of the *Patissier Françoys.*" Nowhere is there a more impudently Walkleyish sentence; but to read these notices through is to realise that Walkley saw more clearly than most what there was in Ibsen, and also what there was not.

Years later, though he had lost his taste for Ibsen (to his great regret), he protested against the "Ibsenism" which, fastening only upon what was "parochial" (as he called it), had turned the great dramatic artist into a vestryman. But in Ibsen he could find harmony between the "idea-plot" and the "action-plot." Others could not achieve that harmony. Walkley had small patience with Brieux. He rated Hervieu for *La Course du Flambeau*. He was down on Pinero for surrendering to his public and rounding off his action-plot by the sacrifice of his idea-plot. Yet so eager was he for "ideas," for a development of the drama of Augier and of the younger Dumas, that he was ready to make swans out of geese. The capital instance is his praise of Hervieu's *Le Dédale*. The great idea of that play is that "a woman who abandons the father of her child under the law of man does so at her peril because she is infringing a higher law of Nature." And watching Hervieu laboriously adjusting his action to this precious idea, Walkley grows confused between the author's "reasoning" and his invention of a plot, and exalts as great drama a play which for dramatic power, artistic unity, and comment on life is not a whit better than some three or four of Pinero's supposed "idealess" pieces of first-rate story-telling. And, hovering between his desire for ideas as "copy" and his inherent love of a well-made play—not in the sense of Scribe or Sardou, but in a sense scarcely less exacting—he sometimes would not take ideas when they were offered. He mistrusted the "intellectual drama" because he found it too poor in emotion and too rich in ideas not expressed through emotion. Those who know "Mr. Trotter" in *Fanny's First Play* will have enjoyed their laugh at Mr. Shaw's mischievous little exaggeration of that foible. When he and Mr. Granville-Barker and others offered Walkley ideas in plenty, he turned away. They were not expressed in plays —in dialogues, entertainments, debates, but not in *plays*.

Another of these recurrent tests was the power and the duty of art to conform to the constant demand of pleasure for change and increase of stimulus. This chiefly affected his criticism of the classics and especially of Shakespeare. It happened that the very first notice which he wrote for *The Times* was of Tree's production of *King John* in September 1899. He did not much like Tree's productions: they were too bright and showy for his fastidiousness. But his conviction was that it was futile to restore the Elizabethan stage and the Elizabethan manner of performance without restoring the Elizabethan spirit, which was impossible. He insisted on the right of each age to get what it wanted out of the classics; and on this occasion, therefore, the jolly young waterman had to feather his oars with special neatness in rather treacherous waters. He responded with delight to Shakespeare's understanding of love—in *Twelfth Night*, for instance. But on the whole, Shakespeare was always a little too untidy for him. So sensitive was he to this untidiness that he was inclined to find it where it did not exist. He saw Shakespeare compelled to be untidy by the physical conditions of his stage, and was sometimes a little blind to the dramatic form and unity which Shakespeare had contrived in order to fit those conditions. And he was the more convinced of the right of every age to cut Shakespeare about, because, after all, a play, even by Shakespeare, was only a play, a work of art meant to give pleasure, not a sacred and inviolable scripture. No one, not even Shakespeare, had ever seen Shakespeare's Hamlet on the stage. Why should not, then, actors, as well as producers, give pleasure by treating Shakespeare and all other dramatists as they would? Duse's La Locandiera, for instance, and

by HAROLD CHILD

Duse's Paula Tanqueray were not much like what the authors meant, but how beautiful they were! (And, if anyone doubts Walkley's power to criticise acting, let him turn to these studies of Duse.) Moreover, a play being only a play, he had no patience with any attempt—on the part of Bradley or Raleigh, or another—to treat Hamlet or Macbeth or any *dramatis persona* as a " real " person, and to ask what he or she did or would have done outside the play. He forgot, perhaps, that, in creating a Hamlet or a Macbeth, a dramatist must have asked himself many a question of that sort, and must know a great deal more about the character than he could put into the play.

A third recurrent test there was which went deeper into the critic himself than either of the others. It was not by accident that Walkley took a great interest in the psychology of the crowd, and was so sure that a crowd is intellectually weaker and emotionally stronger than each of the persons composing it. The drama is an art addressed to the crowd—an art, no doubt, occasionally capable of giving choice pleasure to the ideal consumer, and exceptionally good at giving the critic opportunities to enjoy his own finest pleasure, that of expressing his feelings and his thoughts about it. But still, a popular art, and not one to be taken very seriously. He distrusted all talk of the drama as an educational force, a national institution and that kind of thing. His dislike of some of the plays of Henry Arthur Jones (he did not dislike them all; he gave, for instance, a warm welcome to *Judah*, and enjoyed some of the later and lighter comedies) was increased by the protest raised by both his nerves and his intellect against Jones's hearty, garrulous enthusiasm for the " Renascence of the Drama." The New Drama? There had been new dramas over and over again since Thespis, and there was nothing to make a fuss about. So, when he came before the Royal Commission on the Censorship of Plays in 1909 (feeling in the theatrical world running very high at the time), he blandly told it that " the importance of all art, and more especially the importance of the drama, is apt to be somewhat overrated nowadays, and we take these things a little too solemnly." On the whole, he was in favour of some sort of censorship, but it really did not matter much. One of the Commissioners, not pleased at this insinuation that the whole enquiry was a waste of time and money, pressed him hard, and got bitten for his pains. "There is a great deal of exaggerated talk about it," Walkley insisted, "inflated talk, a great deal of cant about art, and now more than ever before." "Do you," asked the Commissioner, "feel any sense of humiliation in concerning yourself as a critic with this unimportant art?" "No," replied Walkley; "one must live." Superb insolence! But the questioner had asked for it; and who was he that Walkley should lay bare before him his intense personal, private, all but secret devotion to his own art, the art of criticism?

In the dedicatory letter to *Man and Superman* Mr. Shaw tells his old friend and foe: "You must not expect me to adopt your inexplicable, fantastic, petulant, fastidious ways" (was that likely, or possible?); and later comes this sentence: "The only moral force you condescend to parade is the force of your wit: the only demand you make in public is the demand of your artistic temperament for symmetry, elegance, style, grace, refinement, and the cleanliness which comes next to godliness if not before it." It is very true; but it needs the addition of an earlier judgment by William Archer: "Mr. Walkley's individuality is . . . that of the scholar and the man of the world, disillusioned without cynicism, curious about all things human, deeply moved by few, and inclined, when he is moved, to smile at his own emotion . . . a typically and admirably English mind—not least English, in its affection and admiration for many things French."

When he was appointed to *The Times*, some thought that he would never do for *The Times* (it was, indeed, a bold stroke, and Mr. Shaw's "prophetic ear" might well catch "a rattle of twentieth-century tumbrils"); others thought that *The Times* would very soon do for him. Neither foreboding was realised. He had an absolutely free hand, and he used it. It was in *The Times* that he invented the phrase "janitorious drama" for the *théâtre du concierge*; that he called Tree's *The Tempest* "The Girl from Prospero's Island"; that he parodied Henry James talking to a lady after too good a lunch; discovered "the chocolate drama," and discoursed, like a scholar, a philosopher, and a man of the world about lipstick and about the armadillo. His wit was not blunted, nor his delicate naughtiness overawed; and his complete reliance on himself was not shaken. He quickly learned to keep the first person in and leave the first personal pronoun out; and in the very first number of the

Literary Supplement (January 17, 1902) he restated his conception of art as a means of pleasure. As years went on, his tastes naturally changed or widened—doubtless by that " inevitable process of time," which, as he remarked, had changed Sarah Bernhardt's hair from raven black to golden. He found in Croce a great help in his favourite game of analysing and reasoning about his impressions, and he found in Proust (revolted by his M. de Charlus, but rather oddly charitable to his want of neatness and definition) some subtlety of interpretation which even his once adored Anatole France could not give—which perhaps only his ever and devoutly (but not by any means blindly) adored Jane Austen could consistently give. As he grew older, his love of form did not cool (he more and more enjoyed a trim and witty comedy, by Maugham or another, because the drama " of ideas " had gone so drably " repertory " and formless); but his love of analysis and reasoning increased. How the thing was done (and in Proust you certainly can see the thing being done) came to interest him more than what, when done, the thing was.

In middle life Walkley became a keen pomologist—a grower of apples and pears. In pomology, as in all things else, including his personal appearance, he liked to be as French as possible. He went to France for his fruit-trees and for his manner of growing them. And as he pottered, secateur in hand, about the large garden round his small house at Pound Hill in Sussex, his companion's first " impression " would certainly be the tidiness and trimness of these extremely " well-made plays," these growths of a freshness, a grace, a symmetry like Walkley's own prose, these espaliers and other trees, greenly vigorous, yet formally and strictly trained along their wires. Every leaf was as if named and numbered; as Hialmar Werle might have put it, every hair of their heads seemed to be in place. But then another " impression " would follow. It was the process, not the result, that Walkley enjoyed. He told me once that he never cared to eat the fruit; he had lost interest by then. Again, it was getting Alpines to grow, rather than Alpines when grown, that drew him to his rock-garden; and, if he was to be believed, he only took to them at all because he liked their names. As in his gardening, so in his writing. The difference between the early miscellaneous papers in *The Star* and the " Walkley Wednesdays " in *The Times* is the difference between a young man abounding in his own sense of the fact as well as of the cause and an older man better pleased to ruminate on the process.

But the fundamental things in him remained constant. One was his common sense—the decency and moderation of the plain man which at bottom he really was. Another was his enthusiasm, the passionate love of his art which is just as clear when he is most frivolous as when he is most obviously serious; and a third was his fastidiousness. The negative face of that made him rather feared than loved in the professional theatre. It led, once, to an " incident," in which Walkley, holding a dignified and exasperating silence, let his attackers flounder deep into the wrong (but all the same it was lucky for him that Jones and Bourchier never hit upon his own printed definition of a *comédie rosse* as a play " deliberately and callously offensive "). Of the positive face of his fastidiousness, no more need be said than that there it lies, for the delectation of all who love wit, and grace, and finish, perception of beauty, and a penetrating but reverent curiosity about the mind, and, still more, the heart of men and of women. He may not in the future be read, perhaps, as much as he deserves, because the very short essay, the form in which he excelled, does not " collect " well; and he was too sound a critic of his own work to magnoperate, to try the *longue haleine*. Historians of the drama and of literature, therefore, may not do him justice in time to come. He would not greatly care. He deliberately wrote for the present, not for the future. Enough for him if to the more or less ideal consumers his work had given pleasure.

JAMES WHITE
1878-1927

By
ALAN BOTT

bloudy ginger." He declared that he could write better plays, and produce and act them better, than anybody concerned; but since his time was more valuable, he paid others to do it. The final argument was: " 'Oose money is it? I own every stone in this bloudy theatre." Yet he was well liked by his associates, in the theatre as elsewhere, because of his ready generosity and a virile, naïve charm.

It was revealed, after years of slapstick enterprise, that he did not own the theatre. Within a few months of taking possession he had mortgaged it to a bank. Much else, everything else, was to be mortgaged to the great joint-stock banks who were fairy-godmother to this financial Punchinello. Jimmy White, at last, was in Queer Street.

Many fortunes were affected by the constriction that followed the pound sterling's return to gold, half-way through the 'twenties. James White's was inevitably among them. He could manipulate a rising market, but temperament kept him from planning to profit from decline. Money grew dear, but commodities cheapened. His securities fell, investors dwindled in number, the ranks thinned among profiteers, who had been his horn of plenty. Also, his horses now won seldom, his dues to bookmakers rose; and the theatre, his absorbing toy, was a widening drain on capital, energy, and considered judgment.

Vanity would not let him cut his losses, nor reduce his display. He continued to face the world with flamboyant attitudes. Behind them he was like a fish caught in a tremendous net and floundering against every side of it. The struggle to be free continued for three years; it stayed unseen so long because White enmeshed himself in credit complications that spread through several banks and a dozen stockbroking houses.

A few more deals in real estate helped him to maintain the millionaire mien. There was one that secured the Tivoli site for a film theatre, concerning which, with allied production plans, a financial writer permitted himself the flowery comment: " Mr. Jimmy White, the popular millionaire and organising genius, is coming, like the financial Galahad, to the rescue of our fair Lady Cinema in Great Britain." There was the purchase, for £300,000, of the ground and remains of Wembley Exhibition (White had found profitable disposal for part of them, and talked of turning the rest into an English Hollywood). And there was a property deal for half a million, in Central London. Despite the legal experts whom White always had on tap in his office, this transaction later reached the law courts. The standard of commercial ethics revealed by the following extract, from a letter written by White to the South African millionaire already mentioned, astonished the lawyers in the case:

> "The purchase price to ——s to be the sum of £475,000, the deposit being £55,000. . . . It will be seen that the syndicate pay £75,000 more than we pay ——s for the property. ——s will receive the sum of £550,000 on completion, and they will then pay to me the sum of £75,000, such sum to be divided as to £37,500 to yourself and £37,500 to the writer."

The Stock Exchange gave him a last big profit, before it ended his career. He invented a scheme to amalgamate all the big stores in London, and launch the combine with £50,000,000 of capital and Mr. Gordon Selfridge as chairman. Mr. Selfridge was too level-headed to lend himself to the unwieldy enterprise, but permitted White to issue two successful flotations, on behalf of his London stores and others in the provinces.

Such transactions, which would give permanent ease to most men, could not extricate the floundering speculator. He made a heap of his remaining winnings, and risked them on a turn of pitch and toss. His gamble was, once more, in oil. His aim was to take, from a syndicate already in the market, control of an oilfield combine, and force the shares to an inflated price. He worked for two years toward that end, and persuaded other large holders of shares to join him. Then, when he thought himself strong enough, he played on a grand scale the stock-market game of bull against bear. This time, however, the opposing syndicate had at its head an operator harder, more ruthless, and cooler-headed than himself. White bought and bought, in the mistaken belief that he and the other bulls could corner hundreds of thousands more shares than the company had issued, thus forcing the other group (the bears, or speculative sellers) into a corner where they would pay anything for escape.

He was tilting against a flexible windmill. He had

miscalculated; for the bears did not exist—the other group could deliver all the shares it sold him. He asked for a meeting, to settle terms of armistice, but his chief opponent declined it. White continued to buy shares recklessly, and still hoped to find enough for control.

He was not normal during these last, harried weeks. The megalomania left its mask of heartiness, and was diverted into religious obsession. He kept his wondering camp-followers into the small hours, while discussing elementary theology and survival after death. He promised to start a periodical, which was to contain much about religion and the after-life. He joked about death and bankruptcy; and shortly before the settlement day for his huge purchases of shares, he posted to his friends a chocolate-coloured plaque on which was imposed, in embossed gold, a childish travesty of Nelsonian words. " B.C. Pref.—Victory or Westminster Abbey." The initials were those of the oil company that was breaking him.

He had to find three-quarters of a million pounds before the settlement day. The few rich individuals whom he asked for accommodation could not, or would not, give it (there were others, not so invited, who later said they would have helped him). Even the trustful banks would now do nothing. It seemed inevitable that he must face bankruptcy, at the least. He drove, on the afternoon of settlement, to his country house. He despatched his servants on long errands. He gave instructions that no telephone calls were to be connected. He wrote a rambling screed that compressed his past into the language of sensation, and that ended: " I bend my knees and look to God, for I have been guilty of gambling, and the price of folly has to be paid." He died from an overdose of chloroform, inhaled from a sponge that was found pressed into his mouth. A coroner's jury of publicans and stable lads used more than a convenient phrase when it recorded temporary insanity.

What remained? A crash, a nineteen days' wonder, many regrets, a multitude of individual losses, official estimates for £1,700,000 of unpaid income tax and super-tax, and a Beecham Trust dividend of a few pence in the pound, ranking against personal liabilities of nearly a million —owed to the great, oracular, joint-stock banks, which during a period of depression leave normal industry by the wayside.

JAMES WHITE

Among the possessions sold by order of a receiver in bankruptcy were four cleared cheques, framed in silver. Three of them, signed by James White, were for £3,160,000, £2,549,872, and £1,523,582. The fourth, made payable to himself in the Rochdale period, was for threepence-ha'penny. They were kept by one to whom he had been generous; one among many that knew him as a lusty adventurer who drank life in deep draughts, and staked everything for the sensation of risk. A special verse entered his litany for funeral: " Remember not, Lord, our offences, nor the offences of our forefathers."